Contents   W9-CDM-705

About the Authors

Nancy Webster Woodworth began her dining experiences in her native Montreal and as a waitress in summer resorts across Canada during her McGill University years. She worked in London and hitchhiked through Europe on $3 a day before her marriage to Richard Woodworth, an American newspaper editor, whom she met on a ski tow at Mont Tremblant in Quebec. In 1972 she started writing her "Roaming the Restaurants" column for the West Hartford (Conn.) News, which led to half of the book *Daytripping & Dining in Southern New England* (1978), since published in two other editions. She is co-author as well of *Weekending in New England, Inn Spots & Special Places in New England, Inn Spots & Special Places in the Mid-Atlantic, Waterside Escapes in the Northeast,* and *The Restaurants of New England.* She and her husband have two grown sons and live in West Hartford, where her ever-expanding collection of cookbooks and food and travel magazines threatens to take over the entire kitchen and den.

Richard Woodworth was raised on wholesome American food in suburban Syracuse, N.Y., and except for four years at Middlebury College, spent much of his early life in upstate New York. He was a reporter for daily newspapers in Syracuse, Jamestown, Geneva and Rochester before moving to Connecticut to become editor of the West Hartford News and executive editor of Imprint Newspapers. He is editor and publisher of Wood Pond Press and co-author of *Inn Spots & Special Places in New England, Inn Spots & Special Places in the Mid-Atlantic* and *The Restaurants of New England.* With his wife and sons, he has traveled to the four corners of this country, Canada, and portions of Europe, writing their findings — from a cross-country family expedition by station wagon to exchanging houses with a family in England — for newspapers and magazines. Between adventures and writing ventures, he tries to find time to weed the garden in summer and ski in the winter.

GETAWAYS
FOR
GOURMETS
In the Northeast

By Nancy and Richard Woodworth

A guide to the best dining and
lodging in 22 areas appealing
to the gourmet in all of us.

Wood Pond Press
West Hartford, Conn. 06107

Prices, menus, hours, and days closed in restaurants and inns change seasonally and with business conditions. Places in this book are assumed to be open year-round, unless otherwise noted. Readers are advised to call or write ahead to avoid disappointment. Prices quoted are for peak periods and were correct as this edition went to press. They are offered as a relative guide to what to expect and are, of course, subject to change.

Lodging rates are for double occupancy and include breakfast, unless specified to the contrary. EP (European Plan) means no meals. MAP (Modified American Plan) means breakfast and dinner.

The authors value their reputation for credibility and have personally visited the places recommended in this book. Unlike others, they do not ask the owners to fill out information forms or to approve the final copy. Nor do they rely on teams of young researchers or field inspectors with varying perspectives and loyalties to do their leg work. No fees are accepted or charged for inclusion. Theirs is an objective, specific and honest evaluation.

Readers' comments and suggestions are welcomed.

Cover Photo: The Audubon Room at The Inn by the Sea, Cape Elizabeth, Me.

Cover Design by Robert V. Smith.

Copyright © 1997, 1994, 1991, 1988 and 1984 by Nancy and Richard Woodworth.

Library of Congress Catalog No. 84-51593.

ISBN No. 0-934260-80-X.

Published in the United States of America.
Fifth Edition.

Introduction

Between the terrine and the truffles, dining out provides many an adventure. The best of these adventures is what this book is about.

It is written not by food critics who wax poetic or devastate with every precious bite. Rather it is written by travelers who like to eat and explore and who, as journalists and guidebook authors, are in a position to evaluate hundreds of restaurants and share their findings.

Ours is a highly personal guide to the best and most interesting places in 22 of the Northeast's most appealing destination areas for gourmets. They are the "best" as defined locally, by restaurateurs and chefs, and by our tastes.

We don't think haute cuisine should mean haughty cuisine. As journalists, we seek out the new and are skeptical of the old if it rides on pretension or reputation. As diners, we like to be comfortable in restaurants where the food is good and meals an adventure. We don't mind paying a lot if the experience is worth it, but we prefer for the unusual or distinctive place and we want our money's worth.

We also steer you to more than good restaurants. We point out the most choice places in which to stay. We highlight other attractions of interest to food-lovers, such as specialty-food shops, kitchen stores, bakeries, wineries, herb gardens and special museums – more than ever in this newly expanded edition.

Through our photographs as well as our reporting, we try to give you a feel for our destinations before you arrive. We want you to know what to expect, and what it will cost.

In the years we have spent researching five editions of this book, we have eaten in as many restaurants as time and budget have allowed. For most of those mentioned here in which we haven't dined, be assured that we'd like to, having visited and talked with the people involved.

In preparing earlier editions of this book, we were struck by how young some of the best restaurants and lodging facilities really are. With the easing of the recession of the early 1990s, many newcomers have emerged. And prices generally have risen to pre-recession levels, although many restaurants now offer less-expensive cafe and bistro menus or venues. Diners realize these days that good eating need not be beyond their aspirations or pocketbooks

For this edition in particular, we've noted a trend to more healthful eating. There's a lighter and often a vegetarian accent on many gourmet menus these days. Many restaurants offer light-fare menus and encourage so-called grazing.

The continuing evolution is the nature of the business – and the hazard for a guidebook that aims to keep up with the times rather than stick with the tried and true. We find the food and lodging scene so fluid in the late 1990s that we would rather risk a few non-survivors than not share news about promising newcomers.

So here we are, many meals and miles (and pounds) later, having traipsed across the Northeast in sun, rain, and snow, from early morn to midnight. Some places we loved; some we tolerated. Some we can't wait to get back to; some may never see us again.

But all had a certain something that earned them a place in this book.

Our hope is that you enjoy the partaking as much as we did the finding.

Nancy and Richard Woodworth

New Year's calling treats are on display for Yuletide at Winterthur.

Brandywine Valley
A Feast for All the Senses

Mention the Brandywine Valley and most people think of gardens, house museums and art, probably in that order. And with good reason, for the region is unsurpassed on the East Coast in its extraordinary combination of the three.

This is an area of unusual visual appeal, especially during spring when the gardens burst into bloom, and in summer, when the renowned mansions and art museums are at their crowded height.

But the area straddling the Delaware-Pennsylvania border from Wilmington to West Chester is more than a treat for the eyes and more than a seasonal tourist destination. It's a feast for all the senses – especially so during the holiday season, which arrives early and leaves late.

Experiencing a Brandywine Christmas is like coming upon an oasis of color and sensation in the midst of a stark Andrew Wyeth landscape. Simply incredible are the museum treasures within half a dozen miles of each other in this valley that the du Ponts and the Wyeths have made famous. All the museums put on their best holiday spread, and Yuletide at Winterthur is the year's highlight for food lovers, who get to see and smell the feasts recreated from yesteryear.

Strangely for such a touristy area, this region long lagged in providing country inns and good restaurants in which travelers could rest their weary bones and sate their appetites between expeditions to the valley's attractions. The situation is much improved lately, however.

Most visitors are aware of the valley's museums and gardens. But they may not know the treats they offer those with special interests in food (locally grown mushrooms are a specialty), wine (the area has two wineries), decorating and gardening. And they probably are not aware of the newer inns and fine dining opportunities away from the tourist attractions.

Dining

The Best of the Best

Krazy Kat's, Route 100 and Kirk Road, Montchanin, Del.

As distinctive as the Inn at Montchanin Village of which it is the centerpiece, this polished new restaurant occupies the former blacksmith shop in the restored village that once housed workers at the du Pont powder mills. Owner Missy Lickle chose the unlikely name for an eccentric old maid who once lived there "and was crazy as a cat," in the words of her grandmother. The theme turns up at the entry in a local artist's cartoon-like portrait of a gawky feline with a goofy grin, in cat sculptures clad in Japanese robes in each of the front windows, and on the brocade vests worn by the wait staff. The theme broadens in the low-slung chairs with zebra-print cushions at tables set with beige over zebra-print cloths and stunning china designed by a Connecticut artist in the colorful jaguar jungle pattern. The tables seating 55 in two rooms are large and well spaced, the walls radiate a warm salmon color, and a fire burns in one of the original forges up near the ceiling.

It's an enchanting setting for exceptional fare overseen by executive chef Scott Daniels, who had been chef at The Back Burner, the owner's other restaurant that's part of her huge gourmet emporium known as Everything But the Kitchen Sink in nearby Hockessin Corner. Here he tinkers with the contemporary American menu every few weeks.

A bowl of olives and a basket of breads arrive with the dinner menu. One of us started with the zesty bluepoint oyster gratin ($9) teamed with prosciutto, tri-color bell peppers, shallots and parmesan cheese, while the other sampled the salad of field greens ($4), a first-rate melange dressed with toasted pinenuts, blue cheese and a zippy roasted garlic vinaigrette. Main courses ranged from $20 for oven-roasted free-range poisson with curried onion and smoky bacon sauce to $26 for grilled veal chop with porcini mushrooms. The sautéed crab cakes were bound with a shrimp mousseline and served with honey-jalapeño tartar sauce and sweet potato fries. The sautéed Chesapeake rockfish was of the melt-in-the-mouth variety, sauced with bluepoint oysters in a tomato-fennel cream and accompanied by crisp haricots verts and flavorful dark wild rice. Our bottle of Sterling sauvignon blanc ($19, from a well chosen and affordable wine list), was poured in the largest wine glasses we've seen, surpassed in size only by the balloon-size globes used here for red wines.

From a dessert recitation that included a walnut-praline tart and crème de cassis crème brûlée, we settled for the intense raspberry and mango sorbets, architecturally presented with enormous blackberries and an edible orchid in an almond tuile.

Although a place for serious dining and undeniably elegant (jackets are requested for men), the feline motif and lack of pretension imparts a refreshing light-heartedness. The meal and the setting were among the happiest of our recent travels.

(302) 888-2133. Dinner nightly, 5:30 to 10; jackets requested.

Zebra-print cushions on chairs contribute to distinctive look at Krazy Kat's.

Dilworthtown Inn, Old Wilmington Pike at Brinton Bridge Road, Dilworthtown, Pa.

In the quaint hamlet of Dilworthtown, this old wood, stone and brick inn has a classic continental menu and what is considered to be the area's best wine list. Winner of the Wine Spectator award, its 800 selections start at $19 for Georges Duboeuf beaujolais and rise rapidly into the triple digits. We counted more than 110 cabernets from the Napa Valley alone.

The original 1758 inn and its late 18th-century wing were restored in the seventies into a warren of fifteen small dining rooms, a bar and a lobby complete with plate-glass windows and plantings in a mini-atrium. Eleven fireplaces, stenciling, oriental rugs, artworks by Andrew Wyeth, rich wood tables with woven mats, antique furnishings and candlelight combine for a romantic, historic atmosphere. Tuxedoed waiters lend sophistication and elegance.

The leather-bound, eight-page dinner menu starts with a dozen appetizers ($5.75 for the house pâté of duck liver, port wine and truffles to $8.25 for shrimp cocktail with rémoulade sauce). Applewood-smoked salmon with roasted sweet corn and poblano rémoulade, and boneless quail stuffed with smoked boar bacon and cornbread are good choices.

Among the entrées ($16.75 to $24.50) are three kinds of steaks, stuffed Australian lobster tail, roasted muscovy duck with black currant and balsamic glaze, and specialties like crab casserole, lobster thermidor and rack of lamb. Many consider the kitchen at its best with its lengthy list of nightly specials: perhaps ginger-crisp lobster drizzled with a Thai apricot sauce and grilled portobello mushrooms with herbed polenta and white truffle sauce for appetizers; grilled mahi-mahi with melon and pineapple salsa, medallions of New Zealand venison with juniper berries, and veal osso buco for entrées. Desserts range from chocolate mousse to crème caramel. They include wonderful homemade sorbets and ice creams of exotic flavors.

Except for the specials, the inn preserves the traditional, according to co-owners Robert Rafetto and James Barnes. That's fine with its steady clientele, who rate it their favorite all-around spot for consistency, charm and service.

(610) 399-1390. Dinner nightly, 5:30 to 10:30, Sunday 3 to 9.

Chadds Ford Inn, Routes 1 and 100, Chadds Ford, Pa.

Andrew Wyeth and his wife have been known to dine at this restaurant, which was founded in 1736 and looks it. And several of his works grace the dining rooms.

The place is also popular with tourists. People started beating down the doors for lunch at 11:30 on the Saturday we were there, and the two long dining rooms on either side of the center entry hall soon were filled. So were three upstairs dining rooms. Only the tavern had empty tables and they filled up later, no doubt. Service by a young staff is geared to handling the crowds, however.

One yellow rose in a slender vase adorned our table, nicely set in beige and brown. The candles were lit at noon, though they were scarcely needed with sunlight streaming through the alcove windows. The low beamed ceiling and wainscoting enhanced the Wyeths on the walls.

It was here we first learned that the area's popular snapper soup ($3.50) is not made with red snapper but with snapper turtle. Thick and spicy, it tastes like the turtle soup we've had in New Orleans. From a wide-ranging and inviting lunch menu ($5.95 to $11.75), we also enjoyed chicken crêpes garnished with carrots, coleslaw and a piece of melon. Cantaloupe stuffed with chicken and fruit salad was another good choice.

The dessert tray, considered a strong point, held old favorites like pecan and pumpkin pies, chocolate éclairs, blueberry shortcake and a sour-cream peach pie. The changing selection included chocolate mousse cake and a strawberry-kiwi tart at our latest visit. The bill came on a doily, with a dollop of M&Ms.

At night, the historic atmosphere is grand, the presentation stylish and the service leisurely, at least the midweek evening we dined. Almost everything on the short dinner menu ($14.50 to $24.95) appealed, from the rainbow trout with orange-mango coulis to the brace of quail with sausage and couscous stuffing. We especially liked the mustard-sauced Australian loin of lamb and the tender grilled venison steaks topped with port wine and plum sauce. These were accompanied by broccoli and roasted potatoes. A hot popover came first; a key-lime puff finished.

The lengthy wine list starts in the twenties.

(610) 388-7361. Lunch, Monday-Saturday 11:30 to 2; dinner, 5:30 to 10 or 10:30; Sunday, brunch 11:30 to 2, dinner 4 to 8.

The Farm House Restaurant, 514 McCue Road, Avondale, Pa.

This once rather ordinary-looking restaurant in the 18th-century farmhouse that doubles as the clubhouse at Loch Nairn Golf Course is on the way up in culinary circles. Owners Virginia and Hank Smedley have enhanced two small and atmospheric dining rooms off a spacious lounge with barnwood walls, country artifacts, baskets hanging from the beams, candlelight and fresh flowers. We particularly liked the looks of the canopied outdoor patio, glamorously set for dinner with white linens on large tables flanked by heavy wooden chairs.

The chefs also know what they are doing. The reputation of the crab cakes preceded our arrival recently for lunch. We were seated in rather formal surroundings and faced a rather daunting menu strong on dinner-type fare. Yes, there are salads and sandwiches, although caesar salad with pan-fried oysters and sautéed salmon on a warm croissant are not typical golf-club style. A basket of sundried tomato-basil bread and garlicky focaccia staved off hunger as we studied the three dozen possibilities, augmented by such specials as a sampler of smoked fish from the restaurant's smokehouse. But it was the crab cake we were after. It turned out to be

Table for two at Chadds Ford Inn.   **Hearthside dining at Dilworthtown Inn.**

an unpriced special, sautéed to lock in the flavor and then broiled and served over whole-grain mustard sauce. Thick with tender crabmeat, with no filling and absolutely luscious, it came with roasted peppers, snow peas and potatoes, and was well worth the $14 price tag that showed up on the bill. We also sampled the rich mushroom soup ($3.50) and an appetizer of chicken liver pâté ($6) with fresh figs, apple slices and crostini rounds. Service was so leisurely that we ran out of time for dessert. The choice included key lime pie, chocolate mousse torte, crème brûlée and cheesecake laced with grand marnier.

Dinner is a similarly elegant, leisurely affair. The menu pairs the luncheon appetizers with more substantial entrées, priced from $15 for sautéed chicken topped with hollandaise and mushrooms duxelle to $22.50 for surf and turf (petite filet with crab cake). The range is indicated by salmon florentine, sautéed shrimp in saffron cream sauce over linguini, steak au poivre and charbroiled venison flank steak with lingonberries and port wine sauce.

(610) 268-2235. Lunch daily, 11 to 3; dinner, 5 to 9.

Chadds Ford Cafe, Route 1 at Heyburn Road, Chadds Ford, Pa.

Some of the Brandywine area's more exciting cuisine is served up amidst simple, plain-Jane surroundings.

Don't let the nondescript facade or the neon cafe light in the window deceive. Gone is the deli that was originally the focus of the Chadds Ford Deli Cafe opened by sisters Barbara Cohen and Joan Winchester. Gone also is the earlier menu emphasis on breakfast and family dining, although you can still eat at small tables by the display counters in front. The straightforward rear dining room remains, with its Wyeth prints on the walls, Amish-made table tops, and a bench and a corner cupboard also made by Amish farmers. Now the sisters proclaim "casual elegance for the informal gourmand."

They brought on talented chef Frank Perko as a partner, and his menu gets more interesting with each writing. Consider some of his summer dinner offerings ($15.95

to $21.95): coriander salmon over spinach, sweet white corn, shiitake mushrooms and red bell peppers; grilled pork tenderloin with a bourbon-honey-mustard sauce, and cardamom-spiced veal steak with cabernet sauce. The grilled raspberry chicken and spicy Thai beef salads are hearty enough to serve as entrées. The "seafood pagoda" – shrimp, scallops and crabmeat sautéed with vegetables and layered between crisp wonton wafers with a mango-ginger-lime vinaigrette – has become a signature dish.

Starters ($3.95 to $8.95) are equally alluring, among them a duck napoleon and almond-coated brie served with raspberry coulis and grilled focaccia. We tried a couple for lunch: the signature split-bowl soups (half black bean and half cream of jalapeño with smoked pepper sauce, both wonderful and the latter half spicy enough to make the eyes water, which is the way we like it) and the fresh spinach and mozzarella fritters, served on a pool of herb-tomato coulis. Also good was the cobb salad, one of nine luncheon salads ($5.95 to $6.95). Other possibilities ranged from a crab and asparagus quiche to a smoked salmon and dill havarti sandwich on swirled rye bread.

The Sunday gourmet brunch packs in the crowds for frittatas, burritos and fancy egg dishes. Consider the tour de cafe, a sautéed veal medallion topped with tomato confit, poached eggs and green onion-hollandaise sauce ($9.95). The cafe serves no liquor, so bring along a bottle of wine for dinner.

(610) 558-3960. Open Monday-Saturday 11 to 9 or 9:30; Sunday, brunch 8 to 2, dinner 5 to 9. BYOB.

The Back Burner, Old Lancaster Pike, Hockessin Corner, Del.

Started as a cooking school, this quickly became a local favorite for interesting American cuisine in a country setting, and in a 1996 readers' choice poll was ranked the No. 2 restaurant in Delaware. The barn-style establishment, casual but sophisticated, is part of the fantastic Everything But the Kitchen Sink culinary complex. "This area was farmland when we opened," said owner Missy Lickle. "We began a cooking school and started serving lunch to get people out here." A full-fledged restaurant was the next step, followed by a thriving deli and takeout operation called The Back Burner to Go.

The dining-room menu here changes every week. For dinner ($15.95 to $23.95), you might find crab cakes mousseline, baked salmon served over "eggplant caviar," baked Chilean sea bass fillet topped with jícama salsa, grilled calves liver, filet en croûte with puff pastry and grilled rack of New Zealand lamb. Start with baked brie or crab-stuffed mushrooms, signature appetizers. Finish with chocolate-amaretto cake or tirami su.

Lunch time produces interesting salads (how about one of blackened chicken?), hefty sandwiches and half a dozen entrées ranging from $5.95 for quiche or omelet of the day to $12.95 for baked Atlantic salmon or shrimp and scallops chardonnay.

The wine and beer lists are as good as everything else about the place.

(302) 239-2314. Lunch, Monday-Saturday 11:15 to 2:15; dinner, Monday-Saturday 5 to 9.

Marshalton Inn, 1300 Strasburg Road (Route 162), Marshalton, Pa.

Lit by candles, the various dining rooms of this inn, built in 1793 in the Federal style and listed on the National Register, are dark and intimate at night, with oriental rugs on bare floors, candles in tin holders, fires in the hearth and fresh flowers on polished wood tables.

The fare has been upgraded under a partnership of four owners who also own Buckley's Tavern in Centreville, Del. Executive chef Joe Schafer, who worked at Philadelphia's famed Le Bec Fin, oversees an innovative, regional American menu. A new wood-burning grill brings out the flavors of salmon glazed with honey and mushrooms, chicken with roasted garlic sauce and filet of beef with grilled shiitakes. Other entrées ($14.95 to $19.95) could be crab galette with a smoked corn and tomato relish, Vietnamese tuna steak in a sweet and sour chile sauce, basque lamb stew and venison paillard in a juniper sauce laced with cinnamon and pear.

The chef dazzles with starters ($5.25 to $7.95) like black and white soup (a puree of white beans swirled with a puree of black beans), goat cheese bruschetta, seared sweetbreads with smoked tomato sauce and arugula, and duck confit with lentils and roasted peppers. Desserts ($5) include caramel flan with roasted fruits and almond pralines, cinnamon apple slump in a bing cherry sauce with vanilla ice cream, and banana bourbon cake with mocha rum cream and vanilla sabayon glaze.

The lunch menu ($5.95 to $10.95) entices with a spinach and crab salad, a chef's salad incorporating roasted peppers and goat cheese, and a turkey and brie sandwich with papaya-pear chutney on an herbed cheese roll.

Similar food is offered for dinner in more casual surroundings at the inn's sizable **Four Dogs Tavern** across the parking lot. There's a cozy lodge feeling to the open-hearth loft dining area in the front, as well as the skylit rear lounge, also with an open hearth. The outdoor dining terrace in back is the place to eat in summer. The tavern menu is a with-it compendium of temptations, from arugula salad, smoked duck tacos and oyster pan roast to a vegetable napoleon, grilled swordfish sandwich, scallops pappardelle and chile-crusted sirloin. Prices range from $6.25 for a meatless black bean burger to $17.95 for filet mignon with aged provolone.

(610) 692-4367. Lunch, Tuesday-Friday 11:30 to 2:30, Saturday to 3; dinner, Tuesday-Sunday 5 to 9 or 10. Tavern, dinner nightly 5 to 10 or 11; Sunday brunch, 11 to 3.

La Cocotte, 124 West Gay St., West Chester, Pa.

Chef Henri Noebes has sold the charming French restaurant he started in 1974 in downtown West Chester to Jeff Lonsdale, who worked with him for nine years. Very little has changed, according to satisfied patrons. Beamed walls, lace curtains and white linens convey an authentic country French atmosphere. The biggest pepper grinder we ever saw is utilitarian as well as a conversation piece.

Jeff has updated the menu a bit. "We never stray too far from the heart of the matter," he says, referring to the classic French staples like onion soup gratinée and pâté chasseur among hors d'oeuvres ($4 to $9.50). Yet he adds ginger and soy to a passionfruit puree accompanying a baked lobster tail appetizer and serves sautéed oysters on grilled ham atop seasoned foccacia croustades.

Main courses are priced from $16 for beef tips with exotic mushrooms over fettuccine to $23 for lobster newburg or steak au poivre (the latter was hailed by a traveling Connecticut restaurateur as the best he ever had). Besides the signature dover sole and duck flambéed with grand marnier, look for surprises like grilled pheasant with black bean sauce, roast poussin stuffed with andouille sausage, vegetable paella and braised lamb shanks with a Moroccan pepper sauce over couscous.

For dessert, how about crème brûlée with a raspberry tuile, hazelnut cheesecake, napoleons, chocolate mousse, gâteau St. Honoré or pear pernod? The wine list is priced mainly from $20 to $50.

(610) 436-6722. Dinner, Monday-Saturday 5 to 9:30, Sunday 4 to 8.

More Dining Choices

Buckley's Tavern, 5812 Kennett Pike (Route 52), Centreville, Del.

Immensely popular locally is this tavern built in the late 1700s, all spiffed up with a pretty, white-linened interior dining room and an airy garden-room addition. The singles head for the tavern, where snacks and light entrées are available all day, or the open-air bar on two upper levels outside.

Lately, the former tavern and dinner menus have been combined into one extensive, interesting menu appealing to a variety of tastes. We ate light at a recent visit. One enjoyed spring rolls and a half serving of an addictive pasta of farfalle with smoked salmon and roquefort. The other liked the caesar salad and porchetta (sliced pork roasted with garlic and rosemary, served on an onion roll with roasted peppers). With a $12.75 Round Hill chardonnay and a slice of key lime pie, the bill came to a modest $38 before tip.

You also could try, as we did on an earlier occasion, one of the handful of entrées, priced from $13.95 for Jamaican jerk chicken to $18.95 for filet of beef over linguini or lavender-marinated lamb steak. We liked the crab cakes, their flavor heightened by a dill mayonnaise laced with orange, and the linguini with smoked chicken and red peppers. Votive candles cast shadows on bare, rich wood tables flanked by comfortable, cushioned chairs as we lingered over a Hogue Cellars chardonnay from Washington State for $13.50.

With a wine store operated by Collier's of Wilmington in the front of the building, you would expect the tavern's selection to be excellent. It's also very reasonably priced, and many wines are available by the glass.

The special cappuccino-pecan-praline ice cream was a hit among desserts ($3 to $5). They included a light lemon-ginger cake and chocolate cups filled with raspberry mousse and served on a pool of crème anglaise. The cheesecake studded with black raspberries and strawberries is to die for.

(302) 656-9776. Lunch, Monday-Friday 11:30 to 2:30, Saturday to 3; dinner nightly, 5:30 to 9:30 or 10; Sunday brunch, 11 to 3.

Courtney's, 7288 Lancaster Pike, Hockessin, Del.

Dishes employing local mushrooms take top billing at this Italian restaurant owned by a Vietnamese man and named for his daughter. And based on their success, energetic Mark Chew planned in 1997 to open **Samantha's Cafe,** named for another daughter, at 110 East State St. in downtown Kennett Square, the heart of mushroom country. The cafe was to feature seafood, steak and his specialty, mushrooms and pasta.

Mark's mushroom cooking expertise has earned him quite a following at Courtney's, an otherwise unassuming but good basic Italian restaurant hidden in a strip shopping center. He's on friendly terms with Kennett Square growers, who deliver top-grade mushrooms every morning. He has named many of his creations for the growers, some of whom also are pictured in a mural along a dining-room wall portraying happy staff and customers.

A portion of the Courtney's extensive Italian menu is devoted to mushroom dishes, from basic spaghetti with mushrooms ($8.95) to portobello mushrooms stuffed with crabmeat and maitake mushrooms with crabmeat in a marinara sauce over cheese-filled ravioli (each $13.95). You can order wild mushrooms fra diavolo or sautéed mushrooms in a blush cream sauce on a bed of lobster ravioli. Mushrooms also figure prominently in many of the veal, poultry and steak entrées, priced from $12.95 to $15.95, as well as in an appetizer called grilled portobello au poivre ($5.95), a finalist in the National Mushroom Cook-off, and a salad of grilled portobellos.

One of the restaurant's waiters painted the stunning pictures of mushrooms on the walls before he left to pursue his calling as an artist. A lighted mushroom tank, which looks like an aquarium, serves as a divider between the dining room and the rear bar and cigar lounge.

(302) 239-9080. Open Monday-Friday 11 to 10, Saturday and Sunday 4 to 10.

Hartefeld National, 1 Sheehan Road, Avondale, Pa.

The name of this big new place is as confusing as its location, tucked away behind mushroom and mulch farms and with signs that steered us the wrong way. You will know you're there when you reach the showy fieldstone clubhouse and the valet tries to park your car. Golfers and other sporty types are much in evidence at this much-ballyhooed public golf course and apparent residential development.

Everyone in the area recommended the setting, especially that of the two-tiered **Rainbow Grille,** the main dining room with tall windows onto the rolling fairways. Paneled in rich wood with sports photos on the walls, it's contemporary, spacious and clubby. The principals also own the acclaimed Columbus Inn in Wilmington, so they bring a solid food background to the operation.

Lunch is popular with daytrippers as well as golfers. The vast menu ($6.50 to $12) has something for everyone, from quesadillas and cobb salad to grilled yellowfin tuna and crab marinara over linguini. Corned beef and cabbage, chicken pot pie with dumplings and veal meatloaf revive memories of earlier times.

At night, the chefs combine lunch appetizers and low-priced "country casual fun food" with more elaborate offerings, among them a salad of grilled portobellos stuffed with crabmeat and main courses ($16.95 to $22) like blackened salmon, shrimp and veal diablo, stuffed grilled veal chop, New York strip steak and rack of lamb.

The grill provides informal dining, according to the establishment's literature. The Walker Cup Room caters to golfers, and there's an Irish Pub.

(610) 268-8800. Open daily, 11 to 9.

Pizza by Elizabeths, 4019A Kennett Pike, Greenville, Del.

Two Elizabeths – Greenville residents Betty Snyder and Betsy Stoltz – own this high-style, gourmet pizza parlor in the heart of du Pont country. No ordinary pizza parlor, this. In the midst of a shopping plaza called One Greenville Crossing,, the place is a beauty in beige and green, with a Mediterranean terra-cotta tile floor, oversize dried-flower wreaths on the walls and half a dozen booths and tables. The pizza toppings are displayed in containers at the pizza bar. Baking in a wood-fired oven makes the crusts crisp and chewy. The beverage list includes not only Evian and cappuccino but Samuel Adams beer and a connoisseur's selection of wines, priced up to $42.

Pizzas come in regular and mini sizes. You can try some of the owners' favorite creations named after famous Elizabeths, from $8.50 for the basic Barrett Browning to $13 for the Taylor (with goat cheese, rosemary, sautéed onions, sundried tomatoes and black olives). Or you can create your own pizza from a selection of four sauces and about four dozen toppings. Breadstick appetizers, green salads and cookies and a few rich desserts make up the rest of the menu.

In 1997, the owners planned to open a second Elizabeths in Rehoboth Beach, Del. *(302) 654-4478. Open Monday-Saturday, 11 to 8:30 or 9.*

Dining and Lodging

The Inn at Montchanin Village, Route 100 at Kirk Road, Montchanin, Del. 19710.

The light-heartedness of its restaurant called Krazy Kats (see Dining above) extends to the deluxe accommodations in this charming complex on the site of a 19th-century workers' village. In 1996, local preservationists Missy and Daniel Lickle opened the first half of 37 planned bedrooms and suites in eleven buildings on a twenty-acre site formerly occupied by mill laborers who worked at the nearby du Pont powder mills and factories along the Brandywine River.

Guest accommodations were dictated by the idiosyncrasies of a row of turn-of-the-century duplexes, dependencies, a schoolhouse and a railroad station that made this a thriving workers' village in the midst of du Pont country. Most units are one- or two-bedroom suites with sitting areas and wet bars. Our quarters in Belin, which turned out to be fairly typical, contained a cozy downstairs sitting room with plump sofa and chair covered in chintz, a TV atop a gas fireplace and a kitchenette area in the corner with wet bar, microwave and mini-refrigerator, complete with automatic icemaker and stocked with soft drinks and mineral water. Coffee and end tables were charmingly painted with flowers and rabbits. Everything was jolly looking and colorfully decorated in mix-and-match patterns that flow together. Up steep stairs was a skylit bedroom with a king bed dressed in Frette linens, about the most comfortable we've had the pleasure of luxuriating in, and a stunning, huge, all-marble bathroom. The latter came with chandelier, a deep tub embedded in marble, a separate shower encased in thick clear glass and, if you turned on the right switch, heated towel racks. Wood-look venetian blinds covered the windows, padded hangers and ironing equipment were in the closet, and a country window had been painted whimsically on the wall beside a real window. The inn's distinctive cowbird logo – a bird perched on the back of a leaping cow – was everywhere (monogrammed on the terry robes, embedded in the marble above the bath). The bed was turned down with chocolates and a copy of the weather forecast, and a thermos of ice water was placed beside. The only downside was traffic noise from the busy intersection out front.

Breakfast the next morning beside the front windows in Krazy Kat's was a feast of fresh orange juice, muffins, and a choice including eggs benedict and an omelet with smoked bacon, brie and chives, tasty walnut-raisin toast, garlicky browned potatoes and garnishes of large blackberries.

Afterward, Missy Lickle led a tour of the six-acre site, a steeply sloping complex sandwiched between main road and train track (golf carts are lined up to transport luggage from parking areas as well as guests of limited mobility). All is artfully landscaped and full of surprises, from picket fences to gas lights to porches with wicker rockers. Room sizes and configurations differ, but each appeals in its own right. Some have poster beds and some kingsize. The Jefferson offers wicker porches front and back and a bathroom walled in travertine marble up to the vaulted ceiling. Missy, who decorated with goods from her huge gourmet emporium known as

Comfortable furnishings and fireplace are typical at the Inn at Montchanin Village.

Everything But the Kitchen Sink, incorporated fine period and reproduction furniture, Staffordshire figurines, colorful fabrics and a sense of whimsy.

Like the outbuildings of a plantation, the character of Montchanin derives from the visual harmony of the whole. The property is notable for 19th-century stone, frame and stucco construction and paths, gardens, carriage ways and such. It represents the core of the old village named in honor of Ann Alexandrine de Montchanin, mother of Pierre Samuel du Pont de Nemours.

Almost next door are Winterthur and the Hagley Museum, and not far away are the Brandywine River Museum and Longwood Gardens. "We're surrounded by treasures and have everything right here," says Dan Lickle. "How could we miss?"

(302) 888-2133 or (800) 269-2473. Fax (302) 888-0389. Doubles, $140 to $170; suites, $180 to $325.

Pace One, Thornton and Glen Mill Roads, Thornton, Pa. 19373.

For twenty years, innovative chef Ted Pace has been serving fine meals in the basement of a 250-year-old fieldstone barn in the hamlet of Thornton. Since 1985, in the restored upper levels, he has offered seven guest rooms as well.

Rooms are distinguished for the Lancaster oak beds made by the carpenter who built the inn, the original watercolors of Brandywine Valley scenes by a local artist, and the variety of striking wreaths created by the decorator. Though different in each room, all the sheets, pillowcases, comforters and shower curtains in the private baths match. All rooms have handsome tables and chairs, and you'll be struck by the beautiful carpentry throughout.

A continental breakfast of fresh fruit, juice and breakfast cake is set out in an upstairs sitting room for overnight guests.

Ted Pace, who hails from a Pittsburgh restaurant family, is the guiding light behind the downstairs restaurant, which is known for consistency and creativity.

Diners sit in a dimly lit interior room with stucco walls, bare pine floors and low ceilings or in a bright outer room enclosed like a porch. Inside, good artworks and vases of fresh flowers provide color; pierced lanterns create neat shadows.

Our lunch began with a cup of the locally ubiquitous snapper soup ($3.50, served with a small pitcher of sherry) and a terrific vegetable pâté that looked like a colorful mosaic. The generous seafood salad niçoise ($7.95) and the puff pastry filled with crabmeat, spinach and red peppers ($9.50) were excellent. We also remember fondly a Sunday brunch that included a lobster, crab and shrimp casserole. The pumpkin-brandy cheesecake was as delicious as the menu said it was.

Dinner entrées run from $16.75 for chicken stuffed with spinach and portobello mushrooms and topped with montrachet cream sauce to $26.95 for rack of lamb with a mushroom demi-glace. Other choices are baked flounder with a saffron-cream sauce and beluga caviar, roast stuffed pork tenderloin, grilled veal chop with a red-pepper vinaigrette, and a mixed grill of lamb, spare ribs and quail served with cranberry chutney. Lighter entrées are available, as are half a dozen appetizers. Most folks opt for the soup cart, which offers all you care to eat of, perhaps, squash-apple bisque, shrimp and corn chowder, and clear mushroom soup. Acclaimed are such desserts as lemon cheesecake, key lime pie and kiwi crêpes. The wine list contains good values, particularly among California whites, and there are numerous half bottles.

(610) 459-3702. Fax (610) 558-0825. Lunch, Monday-Friday 11:30 to 2; dinner, Monday-Saturday 5:30 to 10; Sunday, brunch 10:30 to 2:30, dinner 5 to 9. Doubles, $95.

Lodging

Fairville Inn, Route 52 (Kennett Pike), Box 219, Mendenhall, Pa. 19357.

Fortuitously situated in the heart of museum country, this luxurious B&B is lovingly tended by Swedish-born Ole Retlev and his wife Patti, transplanted Vermonters who ran the acclaimed Deerhill Inn in West Dover. If their latest pride and joy bears more than a faint resemblance to Deerhill, that's because it was designed by Patti's uncle, architect Rodney Williams, owner of Vermont's famed Inn at Sawmill Farm. And Patti, who did the decorating, seems to have inherited her design flair from her aunt, Ione Williams.

No expense has been spared in the conversion of the former private home. Ask Ole to tell you about the "Retlev Memorial Highway," which is what he calls Route 52 since he had to shell out $38,000 to lower the roadway for better sight lines in the long haul toward zoning approval.

The original 1826 house contains five guest rooms, a spacious living room with a stunning copper table, and a cozy breakfast room with pink and white linens and copper utensils hanging about.

Most choice accommodations are the ten out back in the Carriage House, built by an Amish family, and in the nearby Barn. Each is the epitome of elegant comfort. Accented with barnwood, beams and occasional cathedral ceilings, eight rooms have gas fireplaces, and all boast decks or balconies looking across three acres of fields toward a pond. Lamps with pierced shades made by Patti and her mother

Main 1826 house at Fairville Inn.

cast pleasant shadows. All possess spacious full baths (ours had two vanities and a separate dressing area; the towels were thick and matched the decor), king or queen beds, oversize closets, unobtrusive TVs, phones, elegant country furnishings, crisp and colorful chintzes, and flowers from Patti's prolific garden. Each of the spacious suites has a balcony with wrought-iron furniture, a sitting room with a loveseat, and a bedroom with a kingsize canopy bed and two wing chairs by the fire.

On fine linens and china in the main house, the inn serves a continental-plus breakfast. It included, when we were there, a generous fresh fruit cup of kiwi, melon, grapes and strawberries, as well as fresh orange juice, cereal, cinnamon-raisin muffins, sticky buns and Swedish coffee bread. Afternoon tea with at least ten kinds of homemade Swedish butter cookies is a culinary treat as well.

(610) 388-5900. Fax (610) 388-5902. Doubles, $125 to $175; suites, $185.

Whitewing Farm, RD 6, Valley Road, West Chester, Pa.

Overnight guests can partake of the good life in this stylish B&B fashioned from the former estate of the treasurer of the du Pont Company. Local contractor/architect Edward DeSeta and his wife Wanda moved in 1992 with their three children and no intention of running a B&B. An innkeeper/friend who had overbooked called breathlessly one day to ask the DeSetas to put up her guests in their pool house. "All you have to do is serve them breakfast," Wanda recalls being told. "And I've been serving breakfast ever since." Mighty good breakfasts, we might add, to go with comfortable accommodations and elaborate common facilities that would do many a larger establishment proud.

Consider: A sprawling fieldstone and clapboard mansion dating to 1796 and four outbuildings transformed into seven private guest rooms and a suite. Forty-three acres of rolling property backing up to Longwood Gardens. A swimming pool and a stocked, twelve-foot-deep fishing pond, ducks quacking around lily ponds and a waterfall, a ten-hole chip and putt golf course, a tennis court, a greenhouse and perennial gardens for the growing of flowers. The DeSetas use a golf cart to transport guests around the property.

The family quarters are upstairs in the mansion, but the lovely downstairs is shared with guests. A knockout country kitchen with french doors onto a terrace was created from five small rooms. From it come the cookies and pumpkin bars that greet arriving guests, as well as gourmet breakfasts served on the terrace or in the formal dining room. Unfolding one after another are a paneled reading room with fireplace and TV, a living room full of substantial antiques and some of the couple's diverse collections, a huge beamed game room with fireplace, pool table, TV and even a small kitchen for refreshments, and a large sun porch overlooking the grounds.

There's so much space in which to spread out that most guests spend little time in their rooms, which are comfortable indeed. Two are in the converted stables, and three in the carriage house. Renovated for the purpose, each has a queensize bed (one is kingsize), modern bathroom (shower only) with marble floor, TV, and a veritable library of books. They're decorated in a hunt theme with pale yellow walls, splashy fabrics and thick green carpeting. The gatehouse harbors a suite with a skylit living room, fireplace and sofabed. Two simpler rooms have been fashioned from the former men's and women's changing facilities in the pool house, where the decor is garden style, the bed headboard is a picket fence and a patio with wrought-iron lounge chairs faces the idyllic fish pond, with its frogs croaking and its fountain lit at night.

Wanda prepares and Ed serves a breakfast worthy of the site. Her specialty is sautéed apples on an English muffin. The main course could be pancakes with raspberry sauce, french toast made from french bread with blueberry sauce, or scrambled eggs with cheddar cheese and fried red-skin potatoes. Ed sometimes gets so involved in conversation he forgets to serve. "We have guests who come here and never leave the property," says he. We understand why.

(610) 388-2664. Fax (610) 388-3650. Doubles, $95 to $115; suite, $185.

Hamanassett, 725 Darlington Road, Box 129, Lima, Pa. 19037.

The 19th-century mansion and 48 hilltop acres that served as headquarters for the Lima Hunt is now a B&B run by a retired school teacher who has lived here since her marriage in 1949. Evelene Dohan, mistress of the manor and jack of all trades, offers huge common rooms and six comfortable upstairs guest rooms and a suite, all with private baths, sitting areas and television sets and most with oversize beds. All are quite spacious, nicely furnished in traditional, unshowy decor and impart a much-lived-in air. A two-bedroom suite comes with a formal living room. A two-room affair with two double beds and a living room would be a suite anywhere else, but because the rooms are "connected through an open archway, it is not a suite," Evelene insists with the precision of a school marm.

With the grace of an heiress, she goes about making her guests feel at home in this house in which she raised five children. There's plenty of home to enjoy: a formal living room/library with fireplace, where the shelves are stocked with more than 2,000 volumes; a cozier Green Room parlor with another fireplace outlined in Delft tiles; a huge, plant-filled solarium to end all solariums, and a majestic front loggia outfitted with lounge chairs overlooking the gardens. Guests stroll through the formal English boxwood gardens with statues of Psyche and Aphrodite and inspect the colorful flower gardens everywhere.

Elaborate breakfasts are taken at individual lace-covered tables in a chandeliered dining room open to the solarium. Evelene "studied at the Cordon Bleu, so cooking doesn't bother me." She prepares an extravagant buffet: juices, stewed fruit and

Daffodils brighten pond in front of Whitewing Farm.

melon, cereals, a couple of hot dishes such as tomato-mushroom omelets and pancakes with raspberries from the garden, Virginia ham, turkey sausage, Philadelphia scrapple, creamed mushrooms with basil sauce and assorted pastries from croissants to sticky buns, all homemade except for the English muffins.

Guests depart well-fed and restored, returning down the winding driveway pasts forests and gardens to Route 1, a half mile and another world away.

(610) 459-3000. Doubles, $90 to $100; suite, $120 to $170.

The Pennsbury Inn, 883 Baltimore Pike, Chadds Ford, Pa. 19317.

Everything is for sale at this B&B opened in 1996 by partners in a Hockessin Corner furniture and design company as a showcase for their wares. Frank (Chip) Allemann, store owner, and designer James Pine transformed a fieldstone and yellow brick house dating to 1714, close to Route 1 but screened from passing traffic by high, thick hedge. The result is a showplace of decorator-quality common rooms and six guest rooms furnished to the three periods in which the house was built.

The guest quarters vary widely, from the grand rear Winterthur Room with vaulted ceiling and queensize cherry bed, loveseat, armchair and little deacon's bench to the cozy front John Marshall Room with a double bed and built-in fireplace. Feather beds with down comforters are the rule, as are modernized baths with pewter or chrome fixtures and splashy but spare decor. Yet show sometimes comes at the expense of comfort: A solitary wing chair and three stiff wooden chairs placed strategically around the perimeter are the seats in the Lafayette Room, reached via an impossibly steep winder staircase. The large palladian window and side windows in the Winterthur Room have no shades or curtains for privacy or to darken early morning's light. Only one of the inn's six bathrooms includes a bathtub.

The main floor offers three comfortable common rooms. One is a library with TV and stereo and another a magnificent garden room off the kitchen with a couple of dining areas and a sofa and chairs facing a huge fireplace. A manager prepares a full breakfast of juice, muffins or scones, granola and perhaps croissant french toast infused with fresh fruit or scrambled eggs with cream cheese and chives.

The inn offers eight wooded acres in back. Nine more rooms are planned in smaller historic buildings that will be moved to the property to create the ambiance of an 18th-century Colonial manor.

(610) 388-1435. Fax (610) 388-1436. Doubles, $140 to $225.

Scarlett House Bed & Breakfast, 503 West State St., Kennett Square, Pa. 19348.

Victoriana reigns in this stone house with rust-colored shutters astride a hill at the edge of Kennett Square. Samuel and Jane Snyder, who ran a small B&B for eight years in Long Island, wanted a bigger place in which to entertain and display collections from their international travels. "We saw the woodwork and fell in love with the inside of this house," said ebullient Jane. They are only the third family to occupy the house purchased from the Scarlett family, to which the lady of the house had come as a bride in 1923.

The wide entry foyer is notable for chestnut woodwork, doors and stairs. Each of two window nooks on either side of the door contains facing benches that are replicas of originals in the old Quaker Meeting House in Kennett Square. Off the foyer are two fireplaced parlors, one sporting a collection of music boxes.

Upstairs is another sitting area, this one beside sunny windows full of plants on the landing, and a suite and three guest rooms (two of the rooms share a hall bath). Each comes with prized antiques, bathrobes, toiletries and a long-stemmed rose. The rear suite offers an ornate Jenny Lind walnut queensize bed with matching dresser and a side sitting room. The front Victorian Rose room has an Empire chest and lacy pillows on the high-back walnut queensize bed.

"I love china, silver, lace and flowers," Jane says, "so this a great outlet for me." She leads the way to two chandeliered dining rooms in the rear, where lace-covered tables bear lavish displays of roses and floral draperies dress the windows. The tables are set with Limoges service plates, and Jane has a different china pattern for every day of the week.

She and Sam both love to cook. Their three-course breakfast begins with a fruit and cereal course, perhaps fresh muesli with cantaloupe, honeydew and dried apricots. The main course could be "egg in the hole" garnished with crab, Kennett Square mushrooms, sour cream and caviar, accompanied by sweet-potato rounds spiced with cinnamon and nutmeg. Another day might yield a quiche of many vegetables and three cheeses, accompanied by cherry tomatoes stuffed with roasted garlic, basil and goat cheese. The dessert course could be a chocolate-macadamia coconut cake served with non-fat yogurt, bananas and star fruit.

In the afternoon, Jane offers complimentary refreshments in the second-floor sitting area, where a hidden mini-refrigerator is stocked with cold beverages, and sherry, fruit and cookies are at the ready.

Outside are a broad, wraparound porch and prolific gardens. The Snyders added a fish pond and were about to build a pergola.

(610) 444-9592 or (800) 820-9592. Doubles, $75 to $100; suite, $125.

Faunbrook, 699 West Rosedale Ave., West Chester, Pa. 19382.

Victoriana and fine art are in their element in this Italian Federal-style villa built about 1860, long the family home of Smedley Darlington, banker and congressman, who was known as the "autocrat of Chester County." Today, the awe-inspiring structure houses a seven-bedroom B&B operated by energetic Judi and John Cummings, who have furnished it with sweat equity and TLC.

The place was a wreck when the couple bought it in 1982. They undertook a gradual restoration and stocked it with items acquired from here and there. There's a lot of dramatic art, much of it the work of a lifelong friend, Harry Dunn, whose works are for sale here.

Monticello windows (patterned after Thomas Jefferson's invention) slide up to open the main floor onto the wraparound porches, full of decorative wrought iron and looking onto grounds dotted with fountains and statuary. Guests find plenty of room in which to spread out: the formal parlor with two facing loveseats and an antique grand piano, the comfortable library and a front sun room. The last, all paneled in fine wood (even the ceiling), contains a maroon velvet loveseat and two matching chairs.

The library opens onto a fancy dining room in which Judi serves an elaborate breakfast around 9. Typical fare would be juice, fruits, homemade breads and sticky buns, and perhaps orange-croissant french toast with bacon or frittata with sausage and peppers.

The second floor harbors a master suite with a full bath, working fireplace, feather bed, a chaise lounge, a mirrored dressing table and an armoire. Two smaller bedrooms, dark and intimate and each with fancy stenciling, share a second-floor bath. Four bedrooms on the third floor share one bath. Each is decorated imaginatively with a flair that earned Faunbrook a readers' choice award in 1996 as best B&B in Chester County.

(610) 436-5788. Doubles, $70 to $80; master suite, $110.

Brandywine River Hotel, Route 1 at Route 100, Box 1058, Chadds Ford, Pa. 19317.

Set back on a hill behind the rustic Chadds Ford Barn Shops and the historic Chadds Ford Inn restaurant is this newish brick and shingle hotel with 40 deluxe guest rooms, among them ten suites with fireplaces and jacuzzi baths.

One of the restaurant's owners bought the hotel in 1996 and upgraded the room appointments, which were designed to resemble a wealthy Colonial home: Queen Anne reproduction furnishings in cherry and classic English chintz, wing chairs, oriental rugs, brass sconces and paintings in the Brandywine tradition. Rooms come with telephones and remote-control TVs hidden in armoires. Five new executive suites offer one double bed and a sitting area with a sofabed.

A complimentary buffet continental breakfast of granola, corn or blueberry muffins, croissants and danish is served in the fireplaced hospitality room, decorated in the style of a Colonial meeting hall. It is also used for meetings and functions. Afternoon tea or hot spiced cider and cookies are set out by the fireplace in the lobby.

(610) 388-1200. Doubles, $125 to $135; suites, $149 and $169.

Museums and Gardens

Because of their restaurants and gastronomic appeal, the area's favorite attractions are of special interest.

Winterthur Museum and Gardens, Route 52, Winterthur, Del.

Four generations of du Ponts lovingly cared for this noted country estate that today combines art, history, beauty and learning. Henry Francis du Pont, collector and horticulturist, created an unrivaled collection of early American decorative arts, now on display in period settings in the vast mansion-museum, and a matchless 20th-century naturalistic garden. A research library and the new Galleries, with special exhibitions on two floors, also are open to the public.

For food lovers, it is at its best during the annual **Yuletide at Winterthur,** when the mansion- is decorated with Christmas trees, flowers and the appropriate foods of each era represented in the rooms. The tour theme is holiday dining and entertaining of the 18th and 19th centuries, as well as the ways the du Ponts entertained in the home they occupied until 1951. Interestingly, most of the food is so well preserved (some of it freeze-dried by the Smithsonian Institution) that it not only looks real but smells so, too.

Yuletide celebrations are recreated in more than twenty period rooms, from a parlor prepared for an evening musicale to a nursery ready for an infant's holiday christening. When we visited, the du Pont dining room was set up for Christmas meals as the family would have had them in the 1930s and 1940s. Other rooms are set for everything from a Maryland hunt breakfast to a tea party in the Baltimore drawing room. Several rooms are ready for the New Year's Day calling – an occasion when the ladies stayed home to entertain the gentlemen who made the rounds to call (the 300 or so du Ponts in the area continue the family custom to this day, our guide said).

If all this makes you hungry, stop after the tour in the Pavilion Cafeteria in the Visitor Pavilion, where breakfast and lunch are available in a large and handsome room, with floor-to-ceiling windows looking onto the gardens. A salad bar has just about everything you could imagine, and we enjoyed the Thursday Mexican fiesta bar where we made our own tacos and salads. Prepared sandwiches and salads and a few items like a hamburger and smoked salmon plate are in the $3 to $5 range. The restaurant devotes one section to a fancy garden setting where afternoon tea and Sunday brunch are served.

(302) 654-1548. Monday-Saturday 9 to 5, Sunday noon to 5. Prices vary, $8 to $21. Yuletide at Winterthur: Nov. 13 through Jan. 12, reservations required, adults $13.

Longwood Gardens, Route 1, Kennett Square, Pa.

For years the 350-acre private preserve of Pierre S. du Pont, the horticultural legacy he left is the area's single most popular showplace. The year-round focal points are the Crystal Palace-type conservatories in which spring begins in January and the spectacle changes monthly through Christmas. How appealing they were on the blustery December day we first visited, brightened by 3,000 perfect poinsettias in red, pink and cream, unusually large and grown singly and in clusters. Outdoors after dark, 200,000 lights glitter in Longwood's trees and colorful fountain displays are set to music. The indoor plants alone – from bonsai to cacti to impatiens to orchids – are so lush and spectacular as to boggle the mind as to what's outside the rest of the year, which, we discovered on later visits, is plenty.

Longwood's large shop is filled with items for the gardener – small pots of herbs, orchids, tiles, garden chimes, books, placemats and cookbooks, many with an herbal theme. Packets of Brandywine bayberries smell heavenly; tins of various sizes are decorated with flowers and horticultural notes.

Basement keeping room at Hagley Museum's Eleutherian Mills.

Meals are available at the Terrace Restaurant (garden admission required). A formal, sit-down restaurant plus a cafeteria that can accommodate 300 at a time, it is done in fine taste in shades of pink and brown, with walls of windows looking onto the gardens and black wrought-iron furniture on delightful dining terraces. The cafeteria does all its own baking and boasts mushroom specialties, chili, deli sandwiches and local wines and beers. A separate line leads to the desserts, among them a luscious hazelnut torte and, at one visit, a celestial cheesecake topped with almonds, whipped cream and all kinds of fruit, including kiwi, in a decorative pattern. Lunch and brunch (and dinner on the nights the gardens are open) are served in the plant-filled dining room. You could start with double mushroom soup with pernod and tarragon, go on to wild mushroom salad, and for your main course have sliced tenderloin of beef with zinfandel sauce ($12.95). Finish with a pastry or one of the Terrace sundaes.

(610) 388-1000. Daily, conservatories 10 to 5, outdoor gardens 9 to 6, to 5 in winter. Extended holiday hours in December. Adults, $10.

Hagley Museum, off Route 52, Wilmington, Del.

The aroma of fresh cookies emanates all year from the woodburning stove in a typical worker's house, part of this fascinating restoration of the early mill community where E.I. du Pont started the du Pont Company as a gunpowder manufacturer in 1802.

Eleutherian Mills, the first du Pont family home in Delaware, is furnished to reflect the tastes of five generations of du Ponts. We particularly liked the basement keeping room, left as it had been furnished by Louise du Pont Crowninshield, who died in 1958. The formal dining room is remarkable for its scenic American wallpaper, a curious hand-blocked print with Spanish moss adorning trees around Boston Harbor. At Yuletide, it's set for a Twelfth Night celebration. A children's tea set with silver spoons is a highlight of the master bedroom in this house, which impresses because it feels like a home rather than a museum. (The French garden outside has been restored with espaliered fruit trees and organic fruits and vegetables – in season, it's not only beautiful, but functional.)

In keeping with the period, the simple Belin House Coffee Shop on Blacksmith Hill offers sandwiches, beverages and homemade desserts daily from 11 to 4. With lemonade and a piece of pie, you can quite imagine yourself back nearly 200 years in time.

(302) 658-2400. Daily, 9:30 to 4:30, March 15 through December; same hours weekends and one tour at 1:30 on weekdays, January to March 14. Adults, $9.75.

Brandywine River Museum, Route 1, Chadds Ford, Pa.

This special place made famous by the Wyeth family is extra-special during the holiday season when you not only can gaze at paintings but watch an elaborate model-train layout, enjoy Ann Wyeth McCoy's fabulous collection of dolls, see a ram made of grapevines, magnolia leaves, cattails and goldenrod, and eat roasted chestnuts.

Inside a century-old gristmill with white plastered walls and curved glass windows are three floors of beamed galleries that make up a permanent repository of the works of artists inspired by the Brandywine Valley. The paintings of three generations of Wyeths – Andrew, who lives nearby, his father N.C. and his son Jamie – fill the second floor.

An attractive cafeteria-style restaurant has bentwood chairs and little round tables on a floor of old paving bricks in a glass tower that affords a great view of the Brandywine River. It's open from 11 to 3, serving main dishes, salads and wine or beer. Try the Brandywine melt, an open-face sandwich of roast beef, turkey, coleslaw and swiss cheese. The ploughman's lunch brings sausage pâté, cheese and breads.

Museum volunteers have put out a marvelous cookbook, named *For the POT* after the Jamie Wyeth painting of a chicken in a pot that graces the cover. It has unusual recipes, many calling for Chester County mushrooms, and several of the Wyeths have contributed their specialties. A raspberry meringue, called "Berried at Sea" from the Andrew Wyeth painting of almost the same name and sent by Betsy Wyeth, sounds out of this world.

(610) 388-2700. Daily, 9:30 to 4:30. Adults, $5.

Gourmet Treats

Brandywine Gourmet, 126 East Gay St., West Chester, Pa., is the area's best gourmet shop. Elizabeth J. Fisher specializes in fine cheeses, pâtés, coffees and gift baskets. She also has a back room full of hard-to-find ingredients, specialty foods, jam and more.

P.U.F.F., Rockland Road, Montchanin, Del., stands for Pick Up Fine Foods and means exactly that. Run by the sister of the owner of the Inn at Montchanin Village across the street, the delectable little food emporium occupies the restored du Pont Train Station. Expect anything from quiche and dill tuna salad to brie in phyllo, blueberry-lemon bread, oatmeal raisin cookies – all the makings for a picnic or a take-home supper.

The main street (Route 52) of Centreville, Del., has several nice shops. **The Troll of Scandinavia,** 5808 Kennett Pike, makes up good sandwiches for $3 (small) or $4.50 (large) – one of the most popular is London broil. At one visit, chef-owner Hebba Lund's soup of the day was pumpkin-mushroom and the chocolate-hazelnut torte with raspberry filling looked delectable. We sampled the famous confetti cheese spread with carrots and celery and found it worth the raves. Next door, **Communiques** is a great card and stationery store with a difference – an interesting selection of books and gifts, a coffee stand where you can sip a sample or something larger, and special events from art classes to poetry readings. Across the street is **Wild Thyme,** an exceptional garden and gift shop.

In tony Greenville, Del., you can pick up a sandwich or salad at the deli at **Janssen's,** a fine, family-owned market catering to the carriage trade at 4021 Kennett Pike. We liked the Brandywine chicken salad sandwich on a hard roll and another chicken version with almonds and grapes in pita.

Just a shopping complex away in 2 Greenville Crossing at 4001 Kennett Pike is **The Country Mouse,** with a selection of more than 100 cheeses and pâtés. The original emphasis on cheese has been expanded to embrace breakfast and lunch items, salads to go, smoked Virginia meats and more in a pleasant little cafe with seating inside and out.

Across road at Powder Mill Square are more treats: **Brew Ha Ha!** (the latest in a local coffee and newsstand chain, with great pastries as well as fancy coffees), **Einstein's Bagels** (countless bagels and more coffee), and **Kitchen Kapers,** part of a regional cookware chain.

Worth a side trip is the hamlet of Dilworthtown, Pa., northeast of Chadds Ford, and Audrey Julian's **Dilworthtown Country Store,** chock full of American country crafts and folk art. It's been a country store since 1758 but took on its sophisticated form a decade or so ago. The owner shops craft shows to find unusual things – we fell for a tin wreath of sassy spotted cows with "Welcome" in the center and treated ourselves to an anniversary present.

Another worthy side trip is to the hamlet of Glen Mills, Pa., where across the tracks from the train station lies a good-looking Victorian building known as **Pratt and Company.** Inside, Joy Juliano and Margaret DeMarco display collectibles, gifts and period home furnishings in several rooms. The store closes for the better part of a week in early November to prepare for its special Christmas extrava-ganza, featuring handmade gifts reflecting the spirit of Christmases past. Gorgeous Christmas items (especially the stockings), pretty linens and dried flower arrangements abound.

A Gourmet Mecca

For those with an interest in things culinary, the best side trip of all is to Hockessin Corner, Del., and the incredible **Everything But the Kitchen Sink** complex. It's located in a warren of old warehouse buildings beside the railroad track, just off Route 41 on Old Lancaster Pike. Here, Missy Lickle oversees The Back Burner Restaurant, a cooking school and room after room of kitchenware, a fabulous ar-ray of china, MacKenzie-Childs and Lynn Chase dinnerware, cookbooks, gad-gets, gourmet foods, paper goods, linens and even adorable baby clothes. We've never before seen such an interesting selection in one place.

Offbeat Gourmet

Phillips Place, 909 East Baltimore Pike (Route 1), Kennett Square, Pa.

This area is a center for the cultivation of mushrooms (about 80 mushroom growers are located within a 25-mile radius) and good place to find out about them is at Phillips Place, which has a deli (The Market Place) and a mushroom museum (the Mushroom Place), where you can see them growing at all stages. The museum has a new film, which it says justifies the admission charge, but unless you're really into mushrooms, you'll likely find it a letdown. The adjacent Cap and Stem Gift Shop offers gift items with a mushroom motif, from bumper stickers to neckties.

At **The Market Place** behind the museum, you can buy specialty items like mustards, vinegars and crackers as well as foods to go. The sit-down deli offers mushroom soup every day; adding a couple of others like a dandelion and bean soup at our latest visit. You'll also find a portobello mushroom sandwich ($6.95), a steakburger melt, mushroom quiche and a portobello mushroom stuffed with chicken salad, sautéed onions and topped with provolone cheese. You can have all this inside on ice-cream parlor chairs or outside on a pleasant brick patio. The deli is open daily 10 to 4, to 6 from Oct. 1 to Jan. 15.

You also can pick up recipes for mushrooms and pamphlets about them. Did you know that mushrooms are high in potassium? Did you know they are 99 percent fat-free? Maybe you don't want to know all these things, but the complex is fun, anyway.

(610) 388-6082. Museum daily, 10 to 6. Adults, $1.25.

A Boutique Winery

Chaddsford Winery, Route 1, Chadds Ford, Pa.

Eric Miller explains why he started his winery in this location and why he expends much effort making elegant chardonnays that are finished in French oak barrels and retail for $24 to $26 a bottle: "Well, this isn't Disneyland, you know. We've got a lot of traveling connoisseurs who know their wines."

The boutique-style winery, opened in a converted barn in 1983, imports most of its grapes from vineyards in Chester County and elsewhere.

Eric, who comes from a winemaking family (his father owns Benmarl Vineyards in New York's Hudson Valley), and his wife Lee, author of a book about wine, live next door in a house whose image is imprinted on some of the labels that mark their bottles. They have a private tasting room where they cater dinner parties. A cabernet sauvignon is offered for $21, and the winery bottles spiced apple wine ("good with ham," they say) and a sparkling blanc de blanc for $27. The Chaddsford white ($6.99) is great to accompany a picnic lunch on the winery's pleasant outdoor deck.

After hearing the Millers talk about their chardonnay ("it's a good dinner companion and keeps your mouth fresh for the food") and tasting it ("showing honey and vanilla in the nose"), we splurged and laid down a bottle for a special occasion.

(610) 388-6221. Monday-Saturday 10 to 5:30, Sunday noon to 5. Closed Mondays January-March. Guided tours offered on weekends.

Daffodils are sign of spring outside Black Bass Hotel in Lumberville.

Bucks County
Romance along the River

There's something very special about the Delaware River section of Bucks County, Pa., and neighboring New Jersey.

In both look and feel, from the sturdy stone houses to the profusion of daffodils marching down to the river in springtime, it's the closest thing this side of Great Britain to the Cotswolds we love so well. There's a welcome sense of isolation and romance along the River Road, a narrow and winding route that thwarts fast-moving vehicular traffic and invites visitors to take to their feet. There are real country inns, both chic and quaint, and more good dining places than one has a right to expect. And there's the great river with its historic canal and towpath, which shapes the area's character and raises the rationale to laze along, whether by foot, bicycle or canoe.

We're not alone in our love affair with Bucks County, a meandering mosaic of suburbia and seclusion stretching north from the Philadelphia exurbs almost to Easton and the edge of the Poconos. Places like New Hope, the artist colony, are wall-to-wall people on summer weekends. More to our liking is the scenic rivershed area stretching above New Hope to Upper Black Eddy, especially in spring or fall.

Consider Lumberville, Pa., for instance. It's so small that you can drive through in less than a minute and canoe past in a few, yet so interesting that a walk through with stops can take a couple of hours. From our base at Lumberville's 1740 House, we walked the towpath down to Stockton and Phillips Mill, checking out inns and restaurants along the way as we rekindled memories of the British countryside (after all, the area was settled by the English Quakers and names like Solebury, Chalfont and Wycombe persist).

This chapter generally focuses on the strips of Bucks County and New Jersey along the river north of New Hope – and places within walking distance of the river. Thus we stress several river towns in New Jersey's Hunterdon County like Lambertville, which is being revitalized to the point where "there's a restaurant for almost every family," according to one local foodie.

Because liquor licenses are limited, inns and restaurants without them – most of them in Hunterdon County – invite guests to bring their own wines. These can't make a profit on liquor, so they have to be extra good with their food, explained one restaurateur.

And good they are. New restaurants are emerging to compete with the old, and several inns have outstanding dining rooms. At peak periods, dinner reservations are hard to come by. Most inns require at least two-night minimum stays on weekends.

So book well ahead and prepare to relax. Here's a perfect place for a gourmet getaway, especially for anyone with an iota of British blood in his body and a bit of romance in his heart.

Dining

The Best of the Best

The Ferry House, 21 Ferry St., Lambertville, N.J.

The newest culinary gem in Lambertville – which has more than its share – occupies a restored 18th-century house built at the site where the original Coryell ferry crossed the Delaware River to New Hope. Chef-owner Bobby Trigg offers a formal dining room on the main floor, outdoor dining on a slate patio where tables are topped by Perrier umbrellas, and a more casual new bistro called simply **The Upstairs.**

The dining room, neatly divided into two by a half-wall divider, is a beauty in dark green and white. Upholstered chairs are at tables crisply dressed in double white cloths and topped with salmon-colored Villeroy & Boch faux-marble service plates.

This was a stylish, refined setting for a lunch of distinction. One of us enjoyed a sandwich of roasted red pepper, prosciutto, marinated goat cheese and arugula on toasted focaccia ($7). The other was amazed by a salmon BLT with ginger and cilantro ($8), an explosion of tastes lurking between slices of a man-size English muffin. Each was artistically presented on parsley-flecked plates with crispy sweet-potato fries and garnishes of fresh strawberries and raspberries. We would have

Chef Bobby Trigg with an array of desserts at The Ferry House.

liked one of the homemade ice creams (perhaps ginger or passionfruit) or the tequila-lime sorbet, but, alas, they weren't to be ready that day until dinner time.

Our lunch testified to what delights this talented young chef might whip up in the evening. The extensive press reviews (including an excellent rating from the New York Times) have applauded such entrées ($23 to $28) as poached salmon with shrimp wontons and saffron-basil broth, citrus-crusted swordfish set on a blue crab and wild rice sauté, and roast rack of lamb on a glazed shallot and pepper sauté with mint jus. Starters ($7.50 to $10) are equally arresting, perhaps smoked salmon and herbed cheese wrapped with greens and citrus in a green onion crêpe, warm duck salad with lentils and smoked bacon, and grilled quail with black currant sauce, couscous and wilted arugula. The dessert tray includes a signature crème brûlée, triple layer chocolate-espresso mousse cake, and a miniature bittersweet-chocolate canoe (patterned after the restaurant's logo) filled with small scoops of chocolate ice cream and laden with strawberries and raspberries.

The more casual upstairs, funky with small rooms and sloping floors, is open in the evening for what Bobby calls "black-tie food at blue-jeans prices." The sixteen treats here ($7.50 to $15.50) range from rock shrimp and corn fritters with chipotle-maple syrup glaze to an alsatian onion and white pizza to red chile seafood paella. Were not the downstairs fare so highly rated, the popularity and prices of the upstairs dinner operation could put the downstairs out of business.

Bobby, an area native, left his job as an investment banker with Salomon Brothers in 1987. He was flush with an early-retirement package that put him through a year's crash course at the Philadelphia Restaurant School and a two-year apprenticeship with award-winning chef Jean-Pierre Tardy in nearby Newtown, Pa. "I was 26 and the clock was ticking," he recalls. Four years later he had his own restaurant and a staff of young admirers.

He stages frequent special events, ranging from a chile-pepper fiesta (the dessert was soft banana taco with papaya and strawberry salsa and black pepper ice cream) to a shellfish and truffles dinner. One at our latest visit was a five-course mushroom dinner culminating in black truffle crème brûlée.

(609) 397-9222. Lunch daily, 11:30 to 3; dinner, 5:30 to 9 or 10; Sunday brunch, noon to 3. BYOB.

Anton's at the Swan, 43 South Main St., Lambertville, N.J.

Anton Dodel launched this fine establishment in 1990 in the Swan Hotel. The New York Times cited Anton's as one of the year's ten best in New Jersey, and it has earned high marks ever since.

Trained at La Bonne Auberge in New Hope and our late favorite Panache in Cambridge, Mass., Anton is, in his words, spontaneous and eclectic. His short menu changes monthly. The one we salivated over mentioned entrées ($22 to $29) like steamed salmon on a tamarind-peanut sauce, sautéed lobster with apples and braised fennel, roasted pork loin with persimmons and wild mushrooms, and grilled rack of lamb with pesto and garlic custard. Starters ($7.50 to $9) included wild mushroom napoleon with spinach cream, goat cheese on fried green tomatoes, oyster and sweet-potato pie, and grilled pork sausage with bacon and swiss chard. Polenta sticks fried in goose fat and sugar-snap peas might accompany the skillet-roasted beef tenderloin. "This restaurant is not for those who worry about butter and fat," says Anton. He makes his own butter and says it's fresher than the norm.

Dessert ($5) always includes something chocolate and always a flan, but you might find a poached pear in caramel sauce or a cornbread pudding.

All this good eating takes place in a subdued room with paneled wainscoting, a wall of mirrors, hurricane lamps atop white-linened tables and step-down windsor chairs.

Anton rebuilt the hotel's kitchen in order to produce a sophisticated menu and style, "one like a well-established restaurant in France." He cooks more casual fare for the Swan's popular bar, where some regulars eat four or five times a week. He was toying with the idea of offering excerpts of the restaurant's menu there at lower prices, mostly $10 and under.

Anton's choice wine list is priced from $15 to $140.

(609) 397-1960. Dinner, Wednesday-Saturday 6 to 10, Sunday 4:30 to 8.

The Frenchtown Inn, 7 Bridge St., Frenchtown, N.J.

The food is inventive and good, the service friendly yet flawless, and the setting comfortable in this acclaimed restaurant with a handsome new grill room on the side. Founding chef-owner Robert Long departed in 1996 after a ten-year stint, but left the establishment in good hands. New chef-owner Andrew Tomko, a culinary graduate of Johnson and Wales University, was executive chef at the Inn at Millrace Pond in upstate Hope for six years before he and his wife Colleen returned to their home area to buy this restaurant. They retained the staff, cooking

Wall of mirrors and paneling are backdrop for dining at Anton's at the Swan.

style and some of the menu favorites, and barely missed a beat. They live upstairs with their two infants, and hoped to fulfill their predecessor's plan to convert the third floor into a nine-room B&B within a few years.

Arriving for a Friday lunch without reservations, we found the front dining room with its planked ceiling, brick walls and carpeted floors full. So we were seated in the more austere columned dining room in the rear, outfitted with pink and green wallpaper, crisp white linens and Villeroy & Boch china, two sets of wine glasses and fresh flowers on luxuriously spaced tables. Although we could have been happy ordering anything on the menu, we can vouch for an unusual and airy black bean soup, the charcuterie plate of pâtés and terrines ($7.75 – small but very good), the corned beef sandwich on brown bread and a sensational salad of duck and smoked pheasant with a warm cider vinaigrette on mixed greens ($9.25). A layered pear-raspberry tart with whipped cream ($5.25) was a perfect ending.

A later visit produced a memorable (and reasonable) dinner in the white-linened Grill Room, where singles were eating at the bar and dinners are priced from $8.25 for a burger with coleslaw and steak fries to $14.95 for grilled hangar steak with béarnaise sauce. A special salad of baby lettuces and goat cheese, an appetizer of crispy rock shrimp with wasabi and mustard oils, and two small, exotic pastas ($6.95) were enough for two to share. With a raspberry sorbet for dessert and a $15 bottle of Preston fumé blanc, we were well satisfied for less than $50.

That was barely half what you'd expect to pay for one of the remarkable dinners in the more formal dining venues just across the hall, where main courses are priced from $19.75 for roasted pork tenderloin with mustard gnocchi to $26.75 for filet mignon with a port, rosemary and garlic marinade. Choices include sautéed sea bass over caramelized cabbage, grilled Maine salmon on jasmine rice with Maine mussels, and magret duck glazed with maple bourbon and served with cured foie gras and sweet onion jam. The food comes from the same expert kitchen, but the grill represents unusual value for the area.

(908) 996-3300. Lunch, Tuesday-Saturday noon to 2; dinner, Tuesday-Friday 6 to 9, Saturday 5:30 to 9:30 (no grill menu Saturday); Sunday, brunch noon to 2:45, dinner 5 to 8:30.

Hamilton's Grill Room, 8 Coryell St., Lambertville.

Former Broadway set designer Jim Hamilton and his daughter Melissa opened this gem, hidden at the end of an alley in the Porkyard complex beside the canal and towpath. Jim, an architect who designs restaurants, installed an open grill beside the entrance and built the wood-fired adobe pizza oven himself. Chef Melissa has turned over the Mediterranean grill concept to executive chef Marc BrownGold, who moved here from New York's Tavern on the Green.

Marc created the option of grazing portions to let weekday diners try "a little of everything." About half the items are available in standard and smaller portions (at about half the price). You might start with a watercress salad with fennel and radicchio or fettuccine with duck confit and lentils. Then it's on to an adobe-oven pizza, pissalidière or green risotto with mussels and ricotta salata ($6.75 to $7.75). Or graze with half portions ($8.25 to $15) of entrées like grilled swordfish with anchovy and caper tapenade, grilled pork tenderloin with pear chutney and garlic-crusted rack of lamb.

The menu is similar but pricier ($14.75 to $28) on weekends, when the open grill yields things like a mixed grill of lobster, sea scallops and fish of the day, and seared salmon on a bed of coarse salt with ginger, red pepper and leek marmalade.

Our meal began with grilled shrimp with anchovy butter and a crab cake on wilted greens and sweet red pepper sauce, chosen among appetizers priced from $4.75 to $8. Main courses were an exceptional grilled duck on bitter greens with pancetta and honey glaze and ribeye steak au poivre with leek aioli. The oversize plates were filled with fanned razor-thin sliced potatoes and grilled zucchini and green and red peppers. The signature grappa torta and the grand marnier cheese-cake were fine desserts, and two biscotti came with the bill.

Patrons dine at a lineup of faux-marble tables in the mirrored grill room, beneath angels and clouds surrounding a huge gilt mirror on the ceiling of the Bishop's Room, around a big ficus tree in the dining gallery and, in season, outdoors around the fountain in the courtyard.

Hamilton's is BYOB with a twist. It serves its regular menu weekends at the **Wine Bar** annex, a small house across the courtyard for folks who want liquor service. In the main grill, the white wine we toted was stashed in a pail full of ice, and red wines and even water are poured in large hand-blown globes made locally.

(609) 397-4343. Dinner nightly, 6 to 10, Sunday 5 to 9. BYOB.

La Bonne Auberge, Village 2, New Hope, Pa.

"Four-star everything," report people who have eaten here and consider it comparable to the best in New York or Philadelphia. Those doing the reporting happen to be from New York or Philadelphia, where they expect four-star dining and are willing to pay for it. Many of the people around New Hope aren't, nor were we when we saw the menu prices.

There's no denying the food. The restaurant "seems a strong contender for 'best in Bucks,'" wrote Bon Appétit magazine. "Chef Gerard Caronello, originally from

Skylit dining room is elegant at La Bonne Auberge.

Lyons, makes the kitchen sing. His gracious, soft-spoken wife, Rozanne, sees to things up front. It all translates into some very good French."

There's no denying the setting, either. The pretty stone house is surrounded by nicely landscaped grounds and formal gardens atop a hill at the edge of the Village 2 condominium complex (through which you must pass – and can easily get lost, coming or going). The contemporary, airy, skylit dining room at the rear is gorgeous, its large and well-spaced tables dressed in pink and flanked by upholstered armchairs. Wines are stacked in a corner cabinet, windows look out onto the gardens, fresh flowers are on the tables and salmon-colored napkins stand tall in twin peaks in the wine glasses.

Downstairs is a cozy hideaway bar that even some regular diners don't know about. Nestled in wing chairs in a candlelit corner, couples sipping after-dinner cognacs (at $12 and up a snifter) might think they've died and gone to heaven.

Count on spending $150 to $200 on dinner for two with a bottle of wine. The printed menu rarely changes. Except for melon glacé or avocado vinaigrette (both $10), appetizers start at $13 for escargots provençal. The three soups (tomato, cream of watercress, and leek and potato) are $10. So is the house salad. Big-spenders can go for beluga caviar ($55).

Entrées are $33 to $35, except for grilled chicken dijonnaise, which is $27. The French classics (grilled salmon armoricaine, dover sole with a truffle-champagne sauce, escalopes of veal with morels, rack of lamb provençal and entrecôte of beef) are prepared to perfection, we understand.

Desserts are in keeping, and the wine prices sting, starting in the $30 range.

In addition to the regular menu, on Wednesday and Thursday evenings the chef offers a four-course, table-d'hôte dinner with a limited choice for $45. It's considered quite a deal.

For more than twenty years, La Bonne Auberge has been doing very nicely with a loyal clientele that appreciates the best.

(215) 862-2462. Dinner, Wednesday-Saturday 6 to 9, Sunday 5:30 to 9. Jackets required.

The Forager Restaurant & Bar, 1600 River Road, New Hope, Pa.

Contemporary decor with track lighting, purple napkins on white cloths, well-spaced tables, good prints on the walls and a new wood-burning oven distinguish this restaurant south of town. So does the food, which tends to be in the vanguard. The Forager was the first to offer Spanish tapas to Bucks County. The different international dinners served Thursdays for $17.95 have become an off-season tradition, prompting three-course Mediterranean dinners for $16.95 to be launched on Mondays.

Given the out-of-the-way location, chef-owner Dick Barrows has to be innovative to attract patrons to the large and pleasant restaurant he has owned since 1983. Innkeepers often recommend it for consistently good food in chic surroundings. The three dining rooms and the new bar off the entry are not steeped in history, as are many in the area.

The bar menu features burgers, wood-oven pizzas and pastas in the $6 to $9 range. We sat in the dining room and picked our way through an interesting bistro dinner menu. Entrées are priced from $17.95 for pistachio-crusted chicken served with North African couscous or Thai chicken curry with basmati rice and pineapple chutney to $21.95 for sirloin steak and french fries. We supped quite nicely on starters ($5.95 to $8.25) of deep-fried calamari, wood-oven roasted wild mushrooms with herbed polenta, and a stellar white pizza with crabmeat and creamy ricotta, plus a caesar salad bearing roasted peppers for one and a spinach and roasted beet salad with goat cheese for the other. Wood-oven baked apple crisp, Viennese chocolate torte, pumpkin cheesecake and profiteroles were among the desserts ($4.95). A trio of raspberry, lemon and mango sorbets capped our meal.

The house wine is Trefethen; its chardonnay ($24) turned out to be the most expensive item on our bill. Some other excellent Californias (Groth sauvignon blanc and Mill Creek merlot) are in the $20 range.

(215) 862-9477. Dinner nightly except Tuesday, 5 to 9 or 10.

Manon, 19 North Union St., Lambertville, N.J.

Dining here is reminiscent of the south of France, which comes as no surprise when you learn that young chef-owner Jean-Michel Dumas grew up in Provence. He and his American wife Susan gave a provençal name to the 32-seat charmer they opened in 1990 in the tiny space vacated by The Cafe, which moved to Rosemont (see below).

The downtown storefront has tables rather close together, outfitted with white butcher paper over white cloths. Each has a basket of crayons and a candle in a tall

Chef-owner Dick Barrows grills food in wood-fired oven at Forager Restaurant.

hurricane lamp, leaving little room for the gutsy food served in robust portions. In back is a refrigerated case displaying desserts and, through an open door, one can see into the kitchen.

Jean-Michel, who was a chef at the Inn at Phillips Mill in New Hope, relies on fresh ingredients cooked simply. At dinner, you might start with the wild mushrooms au gratin, the house pâté or one of the three salads (mesclun, warm goat cheese, or watercress, endive, apples and walnuts with roquefort). Soup of the day could be garlicky mussel or pistou ($5).

Among entrées ($17.50 to $24) are red bouillabaisse, roasted monkfish with pernod and tomato fondue, grilled salmon with a caper and olive red wine sauce, calves liver, breast of chicken with wild mushrooms, and lamb chops with rosemary sauce on a bed of white beans. Desserts include a classic crème caramel, tarte tatin, chocolate mousse, marjolaine and nougat ice cream with raspberry sauce.

The best deal is a three-course, prix-fixe dinner available on Wednesday and Thursday for $22.

Similar fare is offered at wallet-pleasing prices for Sunday brunch. The $17.50 tab is all the more pleasant because you can bring your own wine.

(609) 397-2596. Dinner, Wednesday-Sunday 5:30 to 9 or 10; Sunday brunch, 11 to 2:30. No credit cards. BYOB.

The Landing, 22 North Main St., New Hope, Pa.

The only restaurant right in New Hope with a river view is tucked back off the main street in a small house with windows onto the water and a brick patio around back. Christopher and Leslie Bollenbacher, owners for twenty years, are known for having the best and most consistent food in town.

Inside on either side of a quite luxurious small bar are two dining areas. The front room, welcoming in barnwood, contains booths and two tables for two with wing chairs at each. The rear room has picture windows overlooking the river.

The spacious riverside patio is the place to be in season. It's brightened with colorful planters and umbrellas, dignified by tablecloths at night and made practical by an enclosed bar at one side. A gardener has obviously been at work around the exterior, and there's equal talent in the kitchen.

The changing menu (which arrived in a picture frame when we ate there) is creative. Entrées ($17.95 to $24.95) range from grilled tuna topped with a Mediterranean olive salad, rosemary-crusted salmon in a citrus-vodka sauce, and Caribbean crab and lobster cakes to New Orleans spiced chicken, pork chop glazed with plums and ginger, and grilled veal rib chop with brandy beurre blanc.

Typical starters ($4.50 to $9.95) are rock shrimp and mushroom soup, jumbo shrimp with garlic and cumin served on mesclun greens, and mesquite-grilled pork medallions with melted gorgonzola, apples and pears. Desserts are luscious: cranberry-walnut tartlet, chocolate-macadamia cake, truffle torte with grand marnier and a frozen mousse with tia maria. A good wine list with more than 100 choices is priced from $15 to $65.

The Landing also offers theme dinners on Tuesdays. French bistro, Tuscany, Belgian fare and a New England dinner were on tap the month we were there.

(215) 862-5711. Lunch daily, 11 to 4; dinner nightly, from 5. Closed Monday and Tuesday in winter.

Church Street Bistro, 11½ Church St., Lambertville, N.J.

This tiny space behind Mitchell's bar has proved a launching pad for restaurateurs who moved on to bigger and better things. Europe-trained chef David Kiser, an instructor at the French Culinary Institute in Manhattan, leased the quarters in 1996 to present what he called variously "new bistro cuisine" and "cuisine of the market." Whatever he called it, the fare was earning high marks.

In two areas separated by a divider, he fashioned a country bistro look with white-clothed tables, spaced nicely apart, and accents of copper pots. The setting is serene and the feeling authentic French. There's an outdoor courtyard for dining in summer.

The short dinner menu changes seasonally and offers some of the area's more interesting dishes, with an emphasis on low-fat preparation. Starters ($6 to $9) include warm smoked trout with celeriac rémoulade and horseradish crème fraîche; yukon gold potato and goat cheese pavé with black olive tapenade, and bouchée of forest mushrooms with braised greens and red pepper essence. Main courses run from $16 for mixed grilled of free-range chicken sausages with caramelized granny smith apples and roasted shallots to $23 for herb-grilled veal chop with forest mushrooms. Several come in small and regular sizes. Typical are organic chicken stew with fennel, tomato, pernod, saffron and yukon gold potatoes; pan-seared tilapia with carrot, wasabi crust and beet-ginger emulsion, and grilled sirloin of Australian lamb with a roasted garlic and tomato jam. Specials at our autumn visit were mahi-mahi marinated in herbs and pommery mustard, and wild boar and foie gras duck confit sausages with braised lentils and balsamic glaze.

Desserts might be warm apple tart with homemade vanilla ice cream, pumpkin cheesecake and ginger crème brûlée. The well-chosen wine list is affordably priced.

(609) 397-4383. Lunch, Friday and Saturday 11:30 to 2:30; dinner, Wednesday-Saturday, 5:30 to 10; Sunday, brunch 10:30 to 2:30, dinner 5 to 9.

More Dining Choices

Lambertville Station, 11 Bridge St., Lambertville, N.J.

An abandoned train station has been transformed into a stylish Victorian restaurant and lounge that fairly oozes atmosphere. Diners on several levels of the

Old railroad platform has been enclosed for dining at Lambertville Station.

glass-enclosed Platform Room can watch geese glide by on the Delaware Raritan Canal and see tiny lights reflecting off the water.

The casual ambiance gives little hint of the treats to come, whether they be a fine carpaccio of buffalo appetizer or the braised sweetbreads served with brandy cream, as good as any we've had and bearing a gentle $12.95 price tag. Also good at our latest visit were a robust venison special with smoked walnuts, brie and apple and the house spinach and tropical salads.

On another occasion, our party of four sampled what was then an unusual appetizer of alligator strips ($6.95), which you dip into a mustard and green peppercorn sauce – interesting, if not the kind of thing we'd want every day. But it proved so popular that alligator is now offered here as a main course as well, sautéed with lemon butter for $15.75. Among other entrées ($9.95 to $24.95), the jambalaya was spicy, the boneless roast duck was properly crispy and had a raspberry sauce, the seafood fettuccine was more than ample, and the veal medallions with jumbo shrimp in garlic butter were excellent. The honey-mustard dressing on the spinach salad was super and the coconut bread tasty. For dessert, we liked the lime-almond cheesecake even better than an old favorite, key lime mousse pie.

A recent appetizer for the adventurous is rattlesnake Arizona, served over kidney beans and corn with a flour tortilla. A new creation is lobster sweetbread salad – chilled lobster and sweetbreads with mushrooms and onions in a curry dressing, served over spinach.

The Sunset on the Delaware special, offered weekdays from 4 to 6:30, is considered one of the best bargains around: soup or salad, entrée and dessert for $9.95. A Victorian lounge is on the mezzanine, and a dance club on the lower level is open every night.

(609) 397-8300. Lunch, Monday-Saturday 11:30 to 3; dinner, Monday-Thursday and Sunday 4 to 10, Friday and Saturday 5 to 11; Sunday brunch, 11 to 3.

Atrio Cafe, 515 Bridge St., Stockton, N.J.

Chef-owner Ricky Franco, hostess Marley Franco and her childhood friend, Laurie Giddio, the pastry chef, reopened this location of many restaurant incarnations in 1995 and named it for their partnership, "a trio." Ricky, a native of Brazil, trained at the French Culinary Institute in New York, where he cooked for twelve years at the Plaza and the Waldorf. Here he's in a much smaller, more personal venue, and his contemporary cuisine with an Italian accent shines.

The decor is simple, with cafe-style tables dressed in burgundy cloths against hunter green wainscoting, votive candles and plants here and there. The fare is more sophisticated.

Every one of the half-dozen entrées ($15.25 to $19.25) at our visit appealed, among them pan-seared salmon with an oriental ginger dressing and garnished with a spinach and feta-stuffed wonton, roast pork medallions with a carrot-ginger sauce, and garlic-dusted rack of lamb with cilantro-mint sauce. The ravioli might be topped with a shrimp, tasso ham and chick pea sauce; the monkfish could be sprinkled with black pepper, splashed with mustard-curry and served over watercress drizzled with a roasted shallot dressing.

Starters ($5.95 to $9.50) entice as well, from garlic-rubbed bruschetta with a mound of hummus and grilled shrimp, garnished with warm goat cheese, to lump crab cakes with a pommery rémoulade. How about pepper-dipped fried sea scallops over watercress with orange and apple salsa? Dessert could be chocolate decadence, key lime pie or a tart of poached pear with ginger-mascarpone cream.

(609) 397-0042. Lunch, Tuesday-Saturday 11:30 to 3; dinner, Tuesday-Saturday from 5; Sunday, brunch 10:30 to 3, dinner 4 to 8. BYOB.

Siam, 61 North Main St., Lambertville, N.J.

This small and highly rated storefront Thai eatery is run by an American and her Thai husband, who cooks with his two brothers and a sister-in-law. Musical instruments from the hill tribes in northern Thailand and swaths of Thai fabrics on the high walls comprise the decor.

The food is true Thai, much loved by local foodies but vastly underrated in the opinion of one of the area's top chefs. Much of it is flavored with garlic, onion, lime juice, lemongrass, ginger and hot pepper, and garnished with peanut and cucumber sauces. Specials of stir-fried beef with oriental eggplant, bamboo shoots, curry paste and basil and a grilled whole baby red snapper with sweet chili sauce were offered the night we visited. Appetizers are in the $3.75 to $5.75 range; entrées, $8.50 to $13. The stir-fried pork with spicy peanut sauce on a bed of watercress appeals. So does the crispy fish with ground pork, shiitake mushrooms and a ginger-scallion sauce. Thai coconut custard, sticky rice, kiwis and mangos are among desserts.

(609) 397-8128. Lunch, Wednesday-Sunday 11 to 2; dinner, Tuesday-Saturday 6 to 9 or 10, Sunday 4 to 9. BYOB.

Short's Bistro, 6 Stockton Ave., New Hope, Pa.

This started as a gourmet takeout shop, but it seems that so many people came in to eat that they had to add tables and end the takeout. Or so Michael Short tells it. He, who has been cooking for 40 years in New Hope, New York and Europe and once owned the nearby Wycombe Inn, returned from London in 1995. He and his friend Louise obtained some ice-cream parlor chairs, covered a few booths and tables with white over burgundy cloths, hung lace fabric strips over the lamps, mirrored a wall to make the place look bigger and voila! They have a 24-seat bistro that was packed nightly after they ended the takeout operation.

The kitchen is small, so Michael keeps the handwritten menu simple. Expect starters ($3.75 to $7.75) like herring and pippin apple, crab strudel, baked stuffed artichoke and soup du jour. The dozen main courses range from $8.75 for grilled cajun chicken over caesar salad to $18.75 for roast duck bigarade. Cajun shrimp, coq au vin, beef bourguignonne, calves brains in black butter, Maryland crab cakes and New York strip steak illustrate the range.

Desserts follow suit, from fruit tarts to crème caramel.

(215) 862-9000. Dinner, Tuesday-Sunday, 6 to midnight. No credit cards. BYOB.

Bucks Bounty, 991 River Road, Erwinna, Pa.

The Adirondacks meet the Southwest in this casual American restaurant put together by a Dutch chef. Johan Van der Linden, who used to be at the old Wilson Inn in Lambertville, N.J., opened his own restaurant here. It's notable for a unique vaulted ceiling, extravagantly colorful in yellow, red, turquoise and black – the design taken from an Alaskan Indian blanket. Long, narrow mirrors atop the wood wainscoting that doubles as the back for banquettes are bordered by Adirondack scenes. Sturdy Adirondack chairs are at green-clothed tables covered by glass tops.

It's a trendy yet casual setting for American/continental fare that ranges widely from home-style country (sautéed calves liver) to sophisticated (sweetbreads in a wild mushroom-cognac sauce). The dinner menu ($9.95 to $20.95) offers basic pastas, trout amandine, chicken dijon, crisp roast Long Island duck and rack of lamb. A bistro menu is offered on weekdays in the off-season. In either case, you might start with sautéed brie, onion soup au gratin or wilted red leaf salad with feta cheese and sesame seeds. Favorite endings are peach cobbler, crème brûlée and shoofly pie.

The lunch menu ($4.75 to $8.95) is not as interesting, although the food is good. One of us had an excellent tuna salad sandwich, while the other got the soup and half-sandwich special. The onion soup was tasty and the half liverwurst sandwich with a big slice of raw onion more than substantial.

Ever-improving, Johan has converted the old section with a takeout window into a cozy little pub, and created a shady garden courtyard for outdoor dining on the side. At a recent visit, he had his eye on the house next door for a six-room B&B.

(610) 294-8106. Lunch, Tuesday-Friday 11:30 to 4; dinner, Tuesday-Sunday 5 to 10; weekend brunch, 8:30 to 3:30.

Meil's Restaurant, Bridge and Main Streets, Stockton, N.J.

Behind the facade of an old gasoline station housing a bakery and restaurant is one of the area's more versatile eateries. Meil's moved here in 1990 from Lambertville, where it started in the dining room behind Mitchell's bar. The prices are right, the menu extensive and the decor jaunty: colorful balloon curtains over the windows, quilts on the walls (one wall contains a montage of black muffin pans) and tables covered with mint-colored oilcloths.

We sampled a classic salade niçoise ($9.75) and a not-so-classic huevos rancheros ($9.95), the salsa lacking coriander and the eggs resting on a heap of chili (we prefer our eggs resting on the tortilla). Interesting salads (warm sesame-duck and poached-salmon platter), sandwiches and egg dishes are featured at lunch, along with comfort food like chicken pot pie, beef stew and chili with cornbread in the $9 range. Something called "Day after Thanksgiving" (you know what that means) may top off the menu at $9.95.

Night brings some of the daytime fare as well as hefty pastas and main courses from $12.95 for meatloaf with mashed potatoes and gravy to $19.95 for peanut shrimp or grilled filet mignon with roasted garlic sauce. Mustard chicken, pork chops and sautéed crab cakes are mainstays.

Exotic omelets are available at breakfast, served with seasoned red-skin potatoes and French bread.

(609) 397-8033. Breakfast daily, 9 to 3; lunch, 11 to 3; dinner, 4:30 to 9 or 10. No credit cards. BYOB.

The Cafe, Route 519 at Route 604, Rosemont, N.J.

Lola Wyckoff and Peg Peterson moved their little cafe from Lambertville to a general store dating from 1885 in Rosemont. They have a lot more room to offer "fresh food at its simple best," as their business card attests.

It's a casual, drop-in kind of place where the floors creek, the chairs tilt and the service, we found on more than one occasion, is somewhat laid-back. Shelves are filled with the cookbooks they use, plus items for sale like gourmet foods, Botanicus soaps and striking ceramics, some done by one of the waitresses. A case along one side displays cheeses, desserts and baked goods. Things get more formal for dinner when candles, cloth napkins and 1940s cloths are on the tables.

Stop in for a breakfast burrito or the Adirondack breakfast, muesli and a bran muffin, which "gives you the strength to climb mountains," says the menu. For a leisurely breakfast we found a couple of omelets – the Russian peasant (with caviar) and the cranberry and brie (both $7.50) –worth waiting for. The addictive "potatoes from heaven" were grilled with olive oil, rosemary, garlic, onion and cayenne.

For lunch, we've enjoyed an excellent ham and black-bean quesadilla ($7.50) and a hefty turkey sandwich on whole wheat ($5.75) from a menu that included eggplant and mozzarella boboli, pasta with wild mushroom sauce and roasted red pepper ravioli with olive oil and garlic, most in the $7 to $9 range.

At dinner time, when entrées run from $13 to $16.50, you can still find sandwiches and omelets for much less. Try broiled flounder with herbs, chicken brazilia or pasta Wilhemina, named for the resident ghost, with chicken, broccoli, mushrooms and garlic. Mocha pot de crème and cranberry flan are popular desserts, and Peg's cheesecakes (maybe rum-raisin or espresso) are also in demand.

The Wednesday night ethnic dinners are a steal, $15 for three courses. The foods of Burma, Cuba and Belgium were scheduled in weekly succession at a recent visit. How about the Burmese offerings: coconut-chicken soup or split-pea fritters, chicken curry with lemongrass or gingered pork stew, and mango mousse or semolina cake with coconut? Here's a kitchen with reach.

(609) 397-4097. Open weekdays at 8, weekends from 9; dinner, Wednesday-Sunday to 9. Closed Monday. No credit cards. BYOB.

The Bridge Cafe, 8 Bridge St., Frenchtown, N.J.

This small cafe and bakery with a large screened porch facing the river is a good bet for breakfast, lunch and occasional dinners. Sip a mochaccino while you try an omelet (the Greek has roast eggplant, feta and tomato) or "better than french toast bread pudding," which is served with orange butter.

At lunch, a turkey burger comes on a crusty roll with tomato, red onion and curried mayonnaise. Other sandwiches and salads (in the $5.50 to $8 range) include a vegetarian stuffed flat bread and a caesar salad with grilled chicken. Soup of the day might be scotch broth or twin potato. Coconut layer cake and frozen non-fat yogurt with fresh berries are a couple of the good desserts.

"Mainstay" dinners, including a basket of the cafe's bread and vegetables of the evening, are in the $10.50 to $14.95 range. Fire-grilled pork chops over mashed white beans, broiled sea scallops, and Ken's seafood combo (including a fish cake, scampi and broiled scallops) are some.

(908) 996-6040. Breakfast and lunch daily, 7 to 4. Dinner, Friday and Saturday, 6 to 9, April-November. BYOB.

Offbeat Gourmet

Loafers American Bistro, 10 Bridge St., Frenchtown, N.J.

A restaurant that specializes in all-American meatloaf normally would not be considered gourmet, but this one is. For Loafers gives new direction and dimension to meatloaf. Consider: salmon and clam loaf topped with creamy dill sauce, turkey and stuffing loaf with mushroom sherry sauce, Tex-Mex loaf topped with salsa and guacamole, Greek loaf (seasoned lamb layered with feta cheese and eggplant), jambalaya loaf (chicken, crawfish and sausage), Thai loaf (peanuts, walnuts, almonds and pecans with rice on sesame noodles), pecan and rice vegetarian loaf. You get the idea.

Rick Baxter started making different kinds of loaves for friends of various ethnic persuasions in New York, and the idea gradually evolved in 1996 into a basement bistro with a seemingly obscure name and theme. "People call us the meatloaf place and think we do just meatloaf," says Rick, who has a full-time chef. "But we do far more than that. Once people understand the concept, they realize how complex these loaves are and how much work and time they take."

We were intrigued enough by the concept, which extends to terrines and pâtés, to stop in for lunch. A cup of meatloaf chowder with an appetizer ($6) of country pâté (veal, calves liver and pork) with dijon and crostini was plenty for one. The other tried the Tex-Mex loaf ($8) served in a pita with salsa and a side of nut slaw with grapes, coconuts, walnuts and pineapple. They were so good that we ordered the jambalaya loaf and a sauerbraten loaf (marinated steak with a ring of mashed potatoes and stuffed with sweet and sour cabbage) to take home for dinner.

The loaves aren't inexpensive ($7 to $10 by day, $10 to $13 at night). Nor is that all you can get. There are little pizzas, pierogies and salads for starters; a couple of non-loaf entrées like Garden State veggie ring and rotisserie chicken, and addictive garlic-mashed potatoes, shoestring fries and sautéed squash with jícama for accompaniments. Desserts run to ambrosia crumbles, bread pudding, banana cheesecake, and blueberry and peach buckle. A dessert sampler of any three is $9.50 for two people.

Whether the concept will catch on, we don't know. Nor do we know how often we'd want to eat here, although the funky decor could keep one interested for days. The place is full of artifacts, from an old Coke machine to weigh scales laden with bananas to antique photos on the walls. Check out the men's room, stocked with old barber shop and shaving accessories, and the ladies' room, a millinery fantasy. Rick and crew take Tuesdays off to redecorate. As with the loaves, there seems to be no limit to the possibilities.

(908) 996-0900. Open daily except Tuesday, 11:30 to 9 or 9:30; weekend brunch 11 to 2. BYOB.

Wine Bars and Pubs

The Boat House, 8½ Coryell St. at the Porkyard, Lambertville, N.J.

In the old ice house for the porkyard is an elegant bar, where cocktails are served, fifteen wines are featured by the glass and the walls are paneled with old twelve-foot-high doors. Appetizers are no longer served, since there's full food service at Hamilton's Grill across the alley. Hamilton's and the Boat House team up to provide food and drinks at the adjacent Wine Bar on Saturdays. Here you can get a glass of Columbia Crest chardonnay for $3.50 or a Simi cabernet for $6. This is also is a good, albeit an expensive, place to pick up a bottle or two of wine for BYOB dinner in a Lambertville restaurant if the liquor stores are closed. Our Mouton Cadet white bordeaux and a Ridge zinfandel came to a cool $27.

(609) 397-2244. Open Monday-Saturday from 4, Sunday from 2.

The Swan, 43 South Main St., Lambertville, N.J.

This is another great place to have a drink and maybe a burger, a wood-grilled pizza, a cheese plate with apples or a few more elaborate dishes up to $15. The public rooms are filled with art and antiques collected by James Bulger, who also owns The Boat House and a B&B, the York Street House. The main bar contains comfortable leather chairs to sink into and a greenhouse wall looking out onto a garden with a fountain, which is spotlit at night. A pianist entertains on weekends.

You can't beat the prices: our two after-dinner stingers came to about $6. Wines are available by the glass, and there are some exotic imported beers and ales. The bar menu is fulfilled from 5 to 11 p.m. by Anton's at the Swan, the fine restaurant in the other side of the building.

(609) 397-3552. Open Tuesday-Saturday 4 to 1, Sunday 3 to 10.

Inn of the Hawke, 74 South Union St., Lambertville, N.J.

Two young sisters took over this oft-changing inn, formerly known as the Wilson Inn and later the Elephant and Castle, a short-lived English pub. Melissa and Doreen Masset made cosmetic changes to turn the huge first floor into what they call a country neighborhood pub, with a long horseshoe-shaped bar in the center room and a couple of dining rooms on either side, one looking onto an outdoor courtyard that's great for sipping some of the draught beers that are featured.

A short menu changes daily. It ranges from fish and chips and a ploughman's lunch to roasted pork loin and grilled strip steak ($5.75 to $17.95). Upstairs are seven redecorated Victorian guest rooms, four with private baths ($65 to $105).

(609) 397-9555. Lunch daily, noon to 5; dinner, 5:30 to 10 or 11; Sunday, brunch noon to 3, dinner 5 to 9:30.

Dining and Lodging

EverMay on the Delaware, River Road, Box 60, Erwinna, Pa. 18920.

The culinary tradition at this charming country inn was launched by Ron Strouse and Fred Cresson, who were first known for fine cuisine at the Sign of the Sorrel Horse in Quakertown. They sold in 1996 to antiques dealers William and Danielle Moffly, who live on the premises. Chef Jeff Lauble, who was Ron Strouse's sous chef, maintained the inn's reputation for contemporary American fare.

Dinner is served only on Friday, Saturday and Sunday nights at one 7:30 seating,

Victoriana and fine dining prevail at EverMay on the Delaware.

and is in such demand that usually you must book far in advance. The six-course meal costs $52, including champagne and hors d'oeuvres, with little choice except between two entrées and two desserts.

The main dining room has been enhanced by new draperies and matching upholstered chairs. Out back is a little porch-conservatory, its tables for two set with white over fabric cloths and little electric candles bearing lamp shades. The room is narrow (a bit too narrow, we thought, since you could overhear others' conversations and the waiter's recitation of every course to every table). Also, a chilly evening was made chillier by the stone floors and wide expanse of windows.

But not to quibble. The meal was one of the best we've had, nicely presented and paced. Hors d'oeuvres of smoked trout salad, sundried-tomato crostini and country pâté with green peppercorns were served first. After these came in order a suave chicken and leek soup, sautéed chanterelles on a saffron crouton, and a salad of boston and mache lettuces, garnished with violets and toasted walnuts and dressed with a fine balsamic vinaigrette.

Thank goodness all these courses were small, for we needed room for the main courses: tender lamb noisettes wrapped in bacon and topped with a green peppercorn butter, and Norwegian salmon poached in white wine, served with hollandaise sauce and garnished with shrimp. These came with thin, crisp asparagus from Chile, a mixture of white and wild rice, and sprigs of watercress.

A cheese course of perhaps St. André, montrachet and gorgonzola precedes dessert. Ours was a perfect poached pear, set atop vanilla ice cream, with butterscotch sauce, golden raisins and pecans. These days a choice is offered, perhaps chocolate cones filled with white-chocolate mousse and raspberries, chocolate-chestnut torte or coffee-kahlua-honey-almond ice cream.

About twenty chardonnays are on the well-chosen, primarily California wine list, which contains some not-often-seen vintages.

EverMay is more than a memorable dinner. It's an inn with sixteen rooms (one named for Pearl S. Buck, longtime resident of the area) on the second and third floors, a newer loft suite on the fourth floor, and in a carriage house and a cottage.

They are furnished in Victoriana, as befits the era when the structure became a hotel (the original house dates from the early 1700s). All have private baths and telephones, and many have queensize beds. Fresh flowers and a large bowl of fruit are in each room, and at bedtime you may find fruit, candy and a liqueur in a little glass with a doily on top.

A fire burns in the fireplace in the double parlor, and decanters of sherry are placed on tables in front of the Victorian sofas. Afternoon tea with watercress or cucumber sandwiches and cookies is served at 4 p.m.

Although continental, breakfast is quite special, with orange juice, flaky croissants and pastries, one with cream cheese in the center, and the pièce de résistance at our visit: a compote of strawberries, grapes, bananas and honeydew melon, garnished with a sprig of mint and dusted with confectioners' sugar – colorful and pretty.

EverMay also has one of the strangest bathtubs in which we've bathed. It's in the carriage house and is, we assume, a Victorian number, with oak trim around the rim. It's narrow, so long that a six-footer can stretch out and so deep that you can barely see out. We would not recommend it for anyone with a touch of arthritis – it could take a crane to get you in or out.

We would recommend EverMay's cooking to anyone, however. It's so good that it could practically cure what ails you.

(610) 294-9100. Fax (610) 294-8249. Dinner, Friday-Sunday at 7:30. Jackets requested. Doubles, $80 to $170; two-bedroom suite, $200.

The Inn at Phillips Mill, 2500 North River Road, New Hope, Pa. 18938.
Depending on the season, hanging pots overflowing with fuchsias or wooden casks filled with all colors of mums mark the entrance to this small and adorable yet sophisticated inn. When you see its facade of local gray stone, smack up against an S-turn bend in River Road, with its copper pig hanging over the entrance, you would almost swear you were in Britain's Cotswolds.

Inside, that impression is heightened, as you take in the low-ceilinged rooms with dark beams, pewter service plates and water goblets, and a gigantic leather couch in front of a massive fireplace, on which you can recline while waiting for your table. Candles augment the light from the fireplace, and arrangements of fresh and dried flowers are all around.

The classic French menu is short and to the point, and the prices reasonable. The house terrine, foie gras with raspberries and rosemary, and a salad of warm goat cheese and roasted peppers on watercress are among appetizers ($5.50 to $8.50). We started with a springtime special, Maryland crabmeat in half an avocado; it was indeed special, garnished with shredded carrots and black olives.

Main courses range from $15.50 for chicken breast with pernod sauce and braised vegetables to $21 for veal medallions with morel sauce. We have never tasted such a tender filet mignon with such a delectable béarnaise sauce (and artichoke heart) nor such perfect sweetbreads in a light brown sauce as on our first visit. At our second, the sautéed calves liver in a cider-vinegar sauce and the filet of veal with roasted garlic and scallions were excellent, too.

A basket of crusty French bread (with which you are tempted to sop up the wonderful sauces) and sweet butter comes before dinner. Save room for one of the super desserts ($5) – once a lemon-ice cream meringue pie, about six inches high and wonderfully refreshing, and later a vanilla mousse with big chips of chocolate and fudge sauce.

Sometimes it is hazardous to bring your own wine. The host at a table of four next to ours was wondering where his expensive bottle of Clos du Val had gone when we noticed the waitress on the verge of pouring it into our glasses. We caught her in time and reconciled ourselves to our modest bottle of California zinfandel.

Upstairs are four cozy guest rooms and a suite, cheerily decorated by innkeeper Joyce Kaufman (her husband Brooks is an architect who did the restoration of the 1750 structure). The rooms are usually booked for weekends far in advance. One has its own sitting room. Honeymooners ask for the third-floor hideaway suite, where fabric covers the ceiling. Most beds are four-posters or brass and iron and are covered with quilts. They don't advertise it, but sometimes the Kaufmans rent a cottage in back of the inn, and share their small swimming pool with house guests.

A continental breakfast (juice, flaky croissants and coffee) is delivered to your room in a basket for $3.50 a person.

(215) 862-9919 (dining) and 862-2984 (lodging). Dinner nightly, 5:30 to 9:30 or 10. BYOB. No credit cards. Doubles, $80; suite, $90; cottage, $125.

Golden Pheasant Inn, 763 River Road, Erwinna, Pa. 18920.

A more romantic spot than the solarium of the Golden Pheasant is hard to imagine. Beneath the stars is a rainbow of orange chairs, green cloths, hanging lamps, a large vat of colorful mums and tiny twinkling lights all around. The place is so dim that we had to ask for an extra candle to read the menu. The canal bank beyond is illuminated at night, and it's all rather magical.

Well-known local chef Michel Faure from Grenoble and his wife Barbara have refurbished the two inner dining rooms from dark Victorian to the inn's original 1850s period, brightened with accents of copper pots, oriental rugs and their extensive Quimper collection from Brittany. The bar is in the front of the wallpapered main dining room, which contains a working fireplace. The inner Blaise Room claims hardwood floors, a beamed ceiling, recessed windows and exposed stone walls. The family live upstairs, and they have renovated six guest rooms to offer "a taste of France on the banks of the Delaware," according to Barbara.

She has decorated the rooms with country touches, antiques and four-poster beds, one so high that you need a stool to climb up. We're partial to the main-floor suite with its private deck and a stereo set. Overnight guests enjoy a rear patio beside the canal.

The geese along the canal don't end up on the menu, though pheasant occasionally does, roasted and flambéed with calvados, shallots and apples. French-born Michel, who was formerly at the Carversville Inn and worked in a number of French restaurants, including Philadelphia's esteemed Le Bec Fin and New Hope's Odette's, presents classic French fare rich with sauces.

Start with the pheasant pâté ($8.95), snails sautéed with hazelnut-garlic butter, bay scallops sautéed with saffron sauce or Michel's acclaimed lobster bisque. Entrées run from $18.95 for cornish hen with a mushroom-tarragon sauce to $24.95 for grilled filet mignon with bordelaise sauce. A baked crab cake comes with a light mustard hollandaise, and roasted pork loin with a currant and cassis sauce. Cassoulet of seafood bears a lobster sauce. Roast boneless duck might be sauced with raspberry, ginger and rum.

Desserts include cappuccino cheesecake, pecan pie, crème caramel, homemade sorbets and a specialty, Belgian white chocolate mousse with a raspberry coulis.

A three-course Sunday brunch is available for $18.95. Michael offers periodic cooking classes, followed by a sampling of each dish.

(610) 294-9595. Dinner, Tuesday-Saturday from 5:30; Sunday, brunch 11 to 3, dinner 3 to 8. Doubles, $110 to $145.

Hotel du Village, 2535 North River Road, New Hope, Pa. 18938.

The French name is a bit misleading, since the chef-owner is Algerian and his hostelry is English Tudor in an early boarding-school setting. The dining room is in the former Lower Campus building of Solebury School and looks exactly like one in an English manor house, with a glowing fire at each end, a beamed ceiling, small-paned windows and a fine Persian carpet on the floor. Crisp linens, candles and fresh flowers add to the luxurious feeling.

Country French cuisine is the forte of Omar Arbani, who arrived in Bucks County from Algeria by way of culinary endeavors in France, Denmark, London and Washington, D.C. His menu seldom changes. Partial to fine sauces, he shuns nouvelle to provide "the kind of home-style country cuisine you'd find in the restaurants of Bordeaux or Burgundy on a Sunday afternoon," in the words of his wife Barbara, a former New Jersey teacher, who manages the dining room and inn.

Prices remain among the more reasonable in the area. Appetizers, including escargots, shrimp sautéed in garlic butter, clams casino and mushrooms rémoulade, are $5.50 to $5.95, except $6.50 for lamb sausage, one of the few additions to the menu since we first dined here ten years earlier. Main courses run from $13.95 for chicken tarragon to $18.95 for tournedos or steak au poivre.

Our entrée of tournedos Henry IV, with artichoke heart and béarnaise sauce, was heavenly. So were the sweetbreads financière, with green olives, mushrooms and madeira sauce. Potatoes sautéed with lots of rosemary, crisp beans and grilled tomato with a crumb topping were worthy accompaniments.

Bread was piping hot and crusty – grand when spread with the house pâté ($5.50 for a small crock as an appetizer). Moist black-forest cake, crammed with cherries, and café royale were sweet endings to a rich, romantic meal.

The pre-dinner drinks were huge and one of us, who shall be nameless, ordered a bottle of Mill Creek merlot, which was ever-so-smooth. The trouble was he had forgotten his glasses and thought the price to be $10 (this was years ago); when the bill came it was twice what he had expected. Moral: bring along your glasses.

Hotel du Village serves dinner by candlelight in the elegant main dining room, paneled in rare American chestnut pieced together from other sections of the building, in an adjacent room that was originally a sun porch, and in a cozy bar. A new addition across the back houses a larger bar and a huge banquet facility.

Accommodations in twenty rather spare rooms in a converted stable in the rear reflect their boarding-school heritage, although all have private baths, king or queensize beds and air-conditioning. Guests get continental breakfast and have access to a pool, two tennis courts and pleasant grounds.

(215) 862-9911. Dinner, Wednesday-Saturday from 5:30, Sunday 3 to 9. Restaurant closed mid-January to mid-February. Doubles, $85 to $100.

The Stockton Inn, 1 Main St., Stockton, N.J. 08559.

"There's a small hotel with a wishing well," Richard Rodgers and Lorenz Hart wrote for the 1936 Broadway show, "On Your Toes." This is that small hotel, and guests still make wishes at the wishing well.

Prolific plants enhance main dining room at The Stockton Inn.

Dating from 1710, the place oozes history. It was a mecca for artists and celebrities, band leader Paul Whiteman used to sign off his radio shows with the announcement that he was going there for dinner, and in 1935 it gained national fame as the press headquarters during the Lindbergh kidnapping trial. The Colligan family ran it for 55 years until 1983.

Major renovations to the guest accommodations followed, and since it was taken over in 1989 by former New York restaurant manager Andrew McDermott, the food has been upgraded as well. "I'm now proud of the cuisine," says Andy.

He and his chef were invited to prepare a meal for the James Beard Foundation recently in New York. The contemporary American menu mixes the traditional with the trendy but, they stress, "not too trendy" – shrimp cocktail, prime rib and Maine lobsters from the inn's own tank are featured along with the likes of grilled swordfish marinated in jalapeño-cilantro olive oil, served with mango salsa, and pork loin sautéed with ginger and soy and served with garlic-mashed potatoes.

For starters ($6.95 to $10.25), we found the trio of salmon – home-cured gravlax with rillettes and smoked salmon from the inn's smoker – a sensational presentation, thanks to an assortment of sauces, condiments and delicious homemade baguette toasts. We also enjoyed the special salad, an arrangement of arugula, goat cheese, roasted red peppers and sundried tomatoes with a complex, smoky taste.

Among entrées ($16.75 to $28), the boned and rolled chicken stuffed with mushroom duxelles and flanked by an array of green beans, carrots, braised red cabbage and layered potatoes was excellent. So was the veal sauté with sundried tomatoes and roasted garlic. Desserts include chocolate-truffle torte, crème caramel and deep-dish apple pie.

All this is offered in six historic dining rooms seating 175. Five have fireplaces and three are notable for murals of local scenes painted by artists during the Depression in exchange for room and board (one pictures Paul Whiteman fallen from his horse on his way home to nearby Rosemont after over-imbibing at dinner). In season, there's dining on five outside terraces amidst two waterfalls and a pond stocked with golden trout. The Old World Garden Bar on the upper terrace has a dance floor, and there's piano music here and in two inside bars on weekends.

The inn offers three guest rooms and eight suites, three of them upstairs and the rest in three restored buildings nearby. All come with private baths and color TV and most with queensize canopy beds. Seven have fireplaces and four have porches or balconies. We were impressed with all the amenities – from the selection of timely magazines and a mini-refrigerator to toiletries and a mending kit – in the comfortable upstairs suite in the Federal House. The next morning, there was quite a spread of fresh fruit (kiwi, strawberries, pineapple and cantaloupe), carafes of juices and an array of pastries from croissants to muffins to nut bread to savor for continental breakfast in the inn's main dining room.

(609) 397-1250. Lunch, Monday-Saturday 11:30 to 2:30; dinner, Monday-Thursday 4:30 to 9:30, weekends 5 to 10; Sunday, brunch 11 to 2:30, dinner 3:30 to 9. Doubles, $85 to $125; suites, $150 to $165.

The Black Bass Hotel, 3773 River Road (Route 32), Lumberville, Pa. 18933.
The food has been updated lately at the venerable Black Bass, an inn dating from the 1740s and every traveler's idea of what a French countryside inn should look like. The late Harry Nessler, founding innkeeper of the 1740 House just down the road, liked to recall how one of his guests, Pierre Matisse, told him that the Black Bass "looks just like the inns my father painted."

Lunch may be a better bet than dinner here because (1) you should take advantage of the fact the dining room with its long porch and a new ground-level dining terrace overlook the river, (2) the food can be inconsistent, although we've had both a good dinner and a good lunch here over the years, and (3) prices at dinner are relatively steep – entrées like the Charleston Meeting Street crabmeat, a fixture on the menu, going for $24.95 at our latest visit.

Wander around the dark and quaint old inn and look at all the British memorabilia collected by innkeeper Herbert Ward, as well as the pewter bar that came from Maxim's in Paris. We enjoyed our lunch of New Orleans onion soup and the house salad. The soup, thick with onions and cheese, came in a proper crock; the crisp greens in the salad were laden with homemade croutons and a nifty house dressing of homemade mayonnaise, horseradish, dijon mustard and spices. Famished after a lengthy hike along the towpath, one of us devoured seven of the nut and date mini-muffins that came in a basket. Lunch entrées range from $6.95 for omelet of the day to $12.95 for the crabmeat or grilled salmon with potato-horseradish galette.

Dinner prices run from $17.95 for pan-roasted chicken glazed with tea and grand marnier to $25.95 for seared beef napoleon layered with potato crisp, walnuts and gorgonzola. If you don't try the crabmeat specialty, which many do, consider rainbow trout breaded with macadamia nuts and served with curry sauce and pineapple relish, or baked salmon brushed with molasses and pistachio nuts, roasted banana and ancho sauce. Finish with homemade ice creams or sorbets, walnut pie with bourbon cream, pumpkin-almond cheesecake or orange crème caramel.

Lighted stamped-tin lanterns hang from thick beams in the various dining rooms,

Suella and Mike Wass pamper guests at Whitehall Inn.

which are filled with antiques, collections of old china in high cabinets, and fancy wrought iron around the windows. The wood chairs look as if they've been around since 1740; it's a wonder they don't fall apart.

Upstairs are seven rooms sharing two baths and three suites with antique furnishings. Some have ornate iron balconies, upon which continental breakfast is served overlooking the river.

(215) 297-5770 (dining) and 297-5815 (lodging). Fax (215) 297-0262. Lunch, Monday-Saturday noon to 3; dinner, 5:30 to 9; Sunday, brunch 11 to 2:30, dinner 4:30 to 8:30. Doubles, $80; suites, $150 and $175.

Lodging

Whitehall Inn, 1370 Pineville Road, RD 2, Box 250, New Hope, Pa. 18938.

In the rolling countryside about five miles from the hustle and bustle of New Hope, this 1794 manor house on twelve acres has been open as an inn since 1985. The hospitality of its owners, Oklahomans Mike and Suella Wass, who keep an electric candle always lit in one room as a symbol for peace, is such that some guests return as often as five times a year.

We can understand why, because Whitehall is a true retreat from the cares of the world. Seldom are you as coddled as here.

Four of the six antiques-filled bedrooms have working fireplaces (and the inn-keepers lay a fire for you on chilly nights), four have private baths and some have canopy beds. While you are out for dinner, your bed is turned down and wonderful handmade chocolate truffles inscribed with a W for Whitehall are left beside it. Sip wine or Poland Spring mineral water (a bottle is in your room) from crystal wine glasses as you contemplate the fire. Soak in a tub made fragrant by the inn-keepers' homemade bath salts before you snuggle into your flannel-sheeted bed. From large containers of shampoos and fancy soaps to extra-thick colored towels and velour robes, the Wasses have overlooked no detail.

A swimming pool and arrangements for horseback riding are other draws. We still haven't mentioned the best part – the leisurely, four- or five-course candlelight breakfasts and elegant afternoon teas. Served promptly at 9, breakfast is cooked by Suella, who arises at 6 to prepare it, and served with aplomb by Mike, surely the cheeriest morning person we have met. It usually starts with fresh juice (honey-tangerine at our last visit) and the inn's secret blend of coffee that we think has a touch of chocolate and cinnamon in it, or English and herbal teas. Next come two of Suella's breads or muffins. Once we sampled tiny carrot muffins and cinnamon ribbon bread. At a subsequent visit, the blueberry sour cream coffee cake was a big hit. The warm apple and sweet paprika soup was unusual and tasty, and we understand the apple bisque tastes like apple pie à la mode. A fruit course follows, perhaps a baked nectarine stuffed with almond crunch filling and served with a pool of real French vanilla custard, or sliced oranges with orange flower water and a dusting of powdered sugar. Then there might be an appetizer of cheddar cheese and corn spoonbread, after which (can you stand it?) comes holiday french toast souffléed with eggnog and rum or a delicate spinach tart with toasted pinenuts and parmesan cheese. Just in case you're still hungry, Bucks County sausage patties might also be on the plate. And just in case you are *still* hungry, a fudge cup with creamy brownie icing or a little dish of jarlsberg cheese and chocolate-toffee crunch could finish the repast with your last sip of coffee. (For those with dietary restrictions, Suella will quietly substitute healthful preparations with the same presentations so no one will know.)

All this takes about an hour and a half, and there is good camaraderie at the two formally set tables. Candles on the tables and in the wall sconces, sterling silver so pretty that it is turned over to show the scrolled backs, and Villeroy & Boch china in the Petites Fleurs pattern create a gracious atmosphere.

Three or four kinds of cookies, tea breads and cakes are served at tea time, along with perhaps open-face cucumber and blue cheese sandwiches or three-onion tarts. We especially enjoyed the currant-orange scones with devonshire cream and strawberry preserves. Daughter Sarah (who won prizes in several baking contests before going off to college) might have baked the chocolate cookies. Tea is properly brewed and poured, of course, from a silver pot.

The spacious double parlor, a fireplace blazing at one end, contains comfortable chairs and sofas, a piano and a pump organ, a stereo and lots of books, magazines and games. Guests have filled many diaries with remarks about their dining experiences, most relating that the best food and hospitality were at the Whitehall. A jigsaw puzzle is always in progress on a sun porch. A decanter of sherry is set out near the fire for returning guests in the evening. Homemade potpourri from Mike's roses is everywhere.

Is there anything these innkeepers have not thought of? They even write notes after you leave to thank you for choosing them, and send repeat guests off with gifts of coffee, bath salts or potpourri. If you are a returnee, their computer tells what you had to eat at breakfast, so you will be served something different from Suella's vast repertoire.

Could there be more? Yes. They offer chocolate and baroque tea concerts in May and a strawberry concert in June. On summer holiday weekends, they put together gourmet picnics – on the grounds or to go.

This special B&B appeals to the romantic, as well as to the gourmet, in all who visit. *(215) 598-7945 or (888) 379-4483. Doubles, $140 to $195.*

Television and radio personality Sally Jessy Raphael owns Isaac Stover House.

Lambertville House, 32 Bridge St., Box 349, Lambertville, N.J. 08530.

All Lambertville was happy that their landmark hotel, which had been closed for eleven years, was about to reopen in 1997. New Hope developer George Michael bought the four-story structure dating to 1812 and set about restoring it to its original luster.

The renovation presented the opportunity to blend the building's historic charm and warmth with modern conveniences. The 25 guest rooms on the top three floors have private baths with jetted tubs (six are double jacuzzis). Twenty-two have gas fireplaces, eight offer balconies and six are two-room suites. Touch pad telephones with data ports, remote-control TV, bathrobes and toiletries, make-up mirrors and hair dryers are among the amenities. Furnishings are period antiques and reproductions.

The complex includes a courtyard suite and a new building in back where a casual restaurant and bar were planned. The inn's main floor contains several upscale retail shops.

A continental-plus breakfast is complimentary for house guests.

(609) 397-0200. Fax (609) 397-0511. Doubles, $135 to $195; suites, $225.

Isaac Stover House, 845 River Road, Erwinna, Pa. 18920.

A showplace. That's the way to describe this 1837 Federal-Victorian mansion owned by radio-TV personality Sally Jessy Raphael on twelve acres facing the Delaware River. She opened it first as a frilly Victorian B&B, representative of the later third floor added to the original structure. She eventually closed the place, only to reopen it in 1995 after redoing the entire house to showcase the Federal period.

Gone are the Victorian clutter, theatrics and whimsy experienced here earlier. Now there are Persian carpets on the floors, crystal chandeliers on the ceilings, and formal Chippendale furnishings and French Provincial antiques all around. "We did some serious shopping at antique shops and auctions," said resident innkeeper Vincent Howe, a former New Haven restaurateur who joined his famous friend in the new venture.

The main floor is a designer's dream, from the deep formal parlor to the rear porch outfitted in wicker, from the new taproom paneled in pecan wood for lively happy hours and convivial breakfasts to the showplace kitchen with custom-designed "critter" tiles and a huge fireplace. From said kitchen, Vince dispenses wine and cheese in the afternoon and a full breakfast in the morning, taken at small round marble tables in the taproom. The sideboard holds juices, granola and muffins. The main dish could be omelets with homefries or, on Sundays, eggs benedict with mimosas.

Upstairs on the second and third floors, overnight guests are cosseted in seven light and airy rooms. Four have private baths and one has a queensize bed. Down comforters and bed covers are coordinated with fabrics and window treatments throughout. The third-floor garden room, dressed in white and green wicker, is the only exception to the Federal period.

Although you won't likely see the owner (she gets here only occasionally), you can see her photo on a side table in the living room.

(610) 294-8044. Fax (610) 294-8032. Doubles, $125 to $175.

Chimney Hill Farm Bed & Breakfast, 207 Goat Hill Road, Lambertville, N.J. 08530.

Three deer were grazing in the back yard the day we revisited this rural retreat. "There are lots more," said Terry Anderson, owner and innkeeper with her husband Rich. "They ate every chrysanthemum and daisy off our porch this fall. We also have a brood of wild turkeys, rabbits and big fat groundhogs."

The animals are appropriate at this opulent manor house, sequestered atop a wooded hill beyond a high-rent residential area on the southeast edge of Lambertville. It was once a working farm, and the restored gardens put in by former owner Edgar W. Hunt, an internationally known attorney, are quite spectacular in season.

The inside of the house borders on the spectacular as well. Vacant when it was acquired by two aspiring innkeepers in 1988, they first put it on display as a designer show house.

The Andersons inherited most of the furnishings for the eight guest rooms, all but one with king or queensize beds and private baths and four with fireplaces. Each is awash in splashy fabrics. The smallest room has space enough only for a double bed and one chair. The rear Terrace Room is bigger with tapestry fabrics, kingsize bed, a large bath with clawfoot tub and its own balcony. We liked the looks of the Hunt Room master suite, where the covers and canopy on the step-up queen bed match the gently swagged curtains, and the sofa and the oriental carpet pick up the theme.

We also liked the looks of the splashy, sunken sun porch off the attractive living room, with windows on three sides and floors, fireplace and walls of fieldstone. Warmth and color come from ficus trees and the floral chintz that covers four wicker loveseats angled around a huge glass cocktail table.

Breakfast is served by candlelight at six tables for two in the newly redecorated 1820 dining room that was the original room in the house. Terry offers fresh fruit, cereals and plenty of homemade pastries, from muffins with farm-made raspberry jam to croissants filled with fruit or cream cheese. Baked french toast may be an additional treat on Sunday morning. In the afternoon, port and cream sherry await in the butler's pantry, where tea, cider and snacks also are available. The Andersons have added bathroom toiletries, and guests find in each room a "gift snack pack" with candy, goldfish and peanuts.

The new owners planned to add four more deluxe guest rooms in a rear carriage house. They also hoped to convert the barn into a conference and entertainment center, and to add a tropical hot tub in the rear greenhouse.

(609) 397-1516. Doubles, $135 to $195.

The Woolverton Inn, 6 Woolverton Road, Stockton, N.J. 08559.

Built in 1792 as a manor house by pioneer industrialist John Prall Jr., whose mill is nearby, this is a B&B on six bucolic acres – where curious black-faced sheep and goats may mosey up nearly to your car from a field next to the parking area. Its location off a country road, atop a hill away from the river, assures a quiet night.

New owners Elizabeth and Michael Palmer have been reconfiguring and upgrading eight bedrooms in the main house, all now with private baths – the lack thereof had been a major shortcoming since we stayed here a decade ago. The Palmers redecorated all the rooms, adding mostly king and queensize beds. Plush towels, monogrammed terrycloth robes and extra pillows are the norm. The new Letitia's Repose suite, made from two rooms that shared a bath, now claims a jacuzzi tub, a king bed and fireplace. Guests seeking seclusion might opt for the Bodine's Farm suite or the small Willet's Garden room in the former barn that also contains the innkeepers' quarters.

Guests have the run of the grounds, plus an elegant large living room with a portrait of Michael's mother over the fireplace. Family heirlooms have been interspersed among the sofas, wing chairs and oriental rugs that testify to the Federal period and the traditional style of what Michael calls "a classic country home." The dining room is big enough for the banquets and wedding parties that the inn caters. Elizabeth and Michael, who works in New York City, offer a full breakfast daily rather than just on weekends as in the past. Fresh orange juice, baked apple, apple bread and zucchini muffins, and creamy eggs with mushrooms and chives were served at our latest visit. Fruit and cheese are put out in the afternoon.

(609) 397-0802. Fax (609) 397-4936. Doubles, $100 to $180.

1740 House, River Road, Lumberville, Pa. 18933.

This new, built-to-look-old motel-type inn was among the first of its genre in 1967, and continues relatively unchanged, although it naturally has lost some of the personality imparted by its founder, the inimitable Harry Nessler, who was a presence on site and manned the front desk up to his death in 1994 at age 92.

Robert John Vris, the innkeeper's grandson, has assumed ownership, but has discontinued the dinner service that helped make the 1740 House special for so long.

He continues to offer 24 spacious, individually decorated rooms on two floors overlooking the canal and, beyond the towpath, the Delaware River. And the place maintains its charms: Glass doors open onto your own brick patio or balcony. There are kingsize or twin beds, and real wooden coat hangers that detach from the rod. The chambermaid knocks on the door to turn down the bed and give you fresh towels. A complimentary breakfast is served in the garden room. You can laze in a tiny swimming pool or paddle the canal beneath your room in the inn's canoe.

Breakfast is served buffet-style from 8:30 to 10 in a cheery, flagstone-floored garden dining room, where if it's busy you'll share tables. Guests help themselves to juice, cereal, croissants and a hot dish like scrambled eggs or creamed chipped beef, and toast their own English muffins or homemade bread.

This is a place to savor the peace and quiet of the river from your balcony or porch, to read in your room (there's no television) or in a couple of small parlors, to meander up River Road to the center of Lumberville and walk the canal towpath or cross the footbridge to an island park in New Jersey.

(215) 297-5661. Fax (215) 297-5243. Doubles, $75 (weekdays) to $113 (weekends). No credit cards.

Bridgeton House, River Road, Box 167, Upper Black Eddy, Pa. 18972.

The Delaware River literally is the back yard of this comfortable B&B, just beyond a landscaped terrace and on view through french doors and the third-floor balconies. Although smack up against the road, the onetime wreck of an apartment house built in 1836 was transformed by Bea and Charles Briggs and reoriented to the rear to take advantage of the waterside location.

A parlor with a velvet sofa looks onto the canal. Fresh or dried flowers, a decanter of sherry and potpourri grace the dining room, where breakfast is served. Following a fruit course (perhaps baked pears in cream or a fresh fruit plate) comes a main dish: waffles with strawberry butter, eggs roxanne or mushroom and cheese omelets. Fresh lemon breads, muffins and apple cake accompany.

Upstairs are ten guest rooms and suites overlooking the river, each exceptionally fashioned by Charles, a master carpenter and renovator, and interestingly decorated by Bea. Some have four-posters and chaise lounges; all have private baths, country antiques, colorful sheets and fresh flowers. Our main-floor room included a private porch with rockers and lovely stenciling, a feature throughout the house, done by a cousin who also did the nude paintings scattered about.

What Bea calls Bucks County's ultimate room is a huge penthouse suite with a kingsize bed beneath a twelve-foot cathedral ceiling, a black and white marble fireplace, a marble bathtub, black leather chairs, a stereo-TV center, a backgammon table and a full-length deck looking down onto the river.

(610) 982-5856. Doubles, $89 to $149; suites, $149 and $199.

Gourmet Treats

River Road Farms, just up River Road from EverMay in Erwinna, Pa., is a complex of buildings centered by a picturesque red wood and fieldstone barn built in 1749. **Chachka,** an interesting gift shop in the barn, is chock full of crystal and porcelain, much of it from Portugal. The real draws here, though, are all the "food accents" and the wild and wonderful preserves and relishes made by Richard deGroot, the "Gentleman Farmer" who lives next door. From hot or sweet pepper relish to carrot relish to Colonial cranberry ketchup to pickled cocktail radishes (yes, radishes), the relishes cost $3.69 and up. Most of his preserves, plum-rhubarb with amaretto, pumpkin marmalade with rum, spicy blueberry with cointreau, banana strawberry with framboise – have you ever heard of such neat combinations? – are in the $4.89 range for ten ounces. All are topped with calico bonnets

Richard deGroot makes and sells Gentleman Farmer's preserves and relishes at Chachka.

so they make great hostess gifts. Pastas, sauces and condiments like a *very* hot Thai garlic sauce (opened for tasting – we nearly choked) are dotted around. Chachka hosts outdoor festivals with seasonal food and entertainment on special weekends.

Lumberville General Store, River Road, Lumberville, Pa., is a true country store run by genial proprietor Gerald Gordon. On jumbled shelves you can find anything from ketchup to chicken soup, with more upscale things like Perrier, Pennsylvania Dutch preserves, antiques and Crabtree & Evelyn goods. A post office is at the rear and upstairs is an art gallery. At the deli counter you can get good sandwiches, soups, chili, vegetarian lasagna and pasta salads.

In New Hope, the **New Hope Cheese Shop** at 18 North Main St. purveys all kinds of usual and unusual cheeses, Tuscany toast with sundried tomatoes and wild onions, and cornichons to go with its pâtés. The smoked-salmon mousse is layered with spinach and topped with grape leaves and a fresh mozzarella roll has pepperoni or pesto sauce. Wheels of candies that look like mosaics and cost a cool $25 each brightened the windows at one visit, and we fell for a hefty Bucks County cookie. **Gerenser's Exotic Ice Cream** at 22 South Main offers such flavors as English mincemeat, African violet, Hungarian tokay, Swedish ollalaberry, Polish plum brandy, Greek watermelon, Indian mango, Jewish malaga and ancient Roman ambrosia. **Taste of Honey** at 15 North Main St. stocks kitchen items, wine accessories, placemats and paper goods, cookie jars and whimsical gifts.

New at 39 North Main is **Nice & Spicy,** which lives up to its name. Mike and Jennie Barkala, a pair of ex-engineers with a passion for cooking, offer 90 kinds of spices and herbs, more than 40 varieties of loose teas, imported organic pastas, grinders and mills, herbal wreaths, cookbooks and quite an assortment of dried fruits and nuts.

At **Lambertville Trading Co.**, 43 Bridge St., Lambertville, N.J., "when we grind coffee, the whole street smells," says Dean Stephens, who ran the Black Bass Hotel for a time and started selling herbs and spices to the public and to many restaurants, whose chefs rave about them. Since then, he's added a cappuccino bar where you can sip mochaccino and sample a dessert (chocolate-cranberry tart, brandied apricot mousse, $3 to $4) amid an expanded selection of food baskets, cream cheese spreads for bagels, chocolates, preserves, cans of almonds and such.

New in Lambertville is the **River Horse Brewery** at 80 Lambert Lane, near the Porkyard complex. This small microbrewery produces some highly regarded hand-crafted lagers. It offers a walking tour of its kegging and bottling operation, a tasting room and a shop with items for beer lovers.

Two very well-stocked wine shops on the New Jersey side of the river help you handle the BYOB situation at area restaurants. **Welsh's** at 8 South Union St. in Lambertville and **Phillips'** on Bridge Street in Stockton offer shelf after shelf of rare French vintages plus wines from most California wineries (about 75 percent of Richard Philips's 20,000 bottles are from California, including those from every boutique winery we have ever visited or heard of and many we haven't). A good selection of whites is kept refrigerated in both establishments. Prices are fair and the staffs are well versed to help you choose. Welsh's also has an incredible selection of cognacs, armagnacs and single-malt whiskeys.

Of interest among the antique and shopping emporia centered around Lahaska are the **Cookery Ware Shop** at Peddler's Village, which claims the area's most extensive collection of cookware and accessories, and the **Buckingham Mountain Brewing Co. & Restaurant** at 5775 Route 202, Bucks County's first microbrewery. Brew tastings and tours are offered, and cafe fare is served daily for lunch and dinner.

Those in the know like to visit the **George Nakashima Studio,** 293 Aquetong Road, New Hope, where his colleagues carry on the tradition launched by the late Japanese master woodworker. If you have a thousand dollars and up to spare, you might order a custom-made table. Even if you don't, it's fun to see what the locals call "The Compound," an extension of Nakashima's Zen philosophy. It's open Saturday from 1 to 4 (or by appointment) and is closed occasionally even then. Call 862-2272 to confirm.

Bargain Gourmet

Rice's Sale and Country Market, 6326 Green Hill Road, Lahaska, Pa.
For the benefit of weekend visitors, this famed market is now open Saturdays as well as the traditional Tuesdays from 7 to 1. It's like no other open-air flea market we've seen, and provided a high point on one of our Bucks County expeditions. Amish specialties, fresh produce, seafood, meats, honeys, spices and kitchenware are available, but foods aren't the best part – the incredible bargains on quality merchandise are. We did all the Christmas shopping (Jantzen and Ralph Lauren sweaters, a set of knives, perfume, a watch and a pretty homemade wreath) that two hours and our checkbook would allow. Everything from fine luggage to Evan Picone apparel is offered. Many of the same purveyors and bargain-seekers come weekly to this great flea market, which has been going strong for more than a century.
Open Tuesday 7 to 1 and Saturday 8 to 1.

Lineup of front verandas, a Cape May trademark, is on view from Mainstay Inn.

Cape May, N.J.
Two for B&B, Tea and Dinner

Victoriana, bed and breakfast inns, and dining par excellence. That's the rare combination that makes Cape May a model of its genre and draws visitors in increasing numbers each year from March through Christmas.

Cape May has shed its mantle as a long-slumbering seaside city that time and Atlantic City had passed by. Its potential was recognized in 1976 when it was designated a National Historic Landmark city, one of five in the nation – an honor it had shunned only a few years earlier. Now its Victorian heritage is so revered that Cape May celebrates a ten-day Victorian Week in mid-October, plus a week-long Tulip Festival, a Dickens Christmas Extravaganza, a Cape May Music Festival, Victorian dinners, a Victorian fair, and various inn and house tours.

The B&B phenomenon started here in the late 1970s as preservationists Tom and Sue Carroll and Jay and Marianne Schatz restored their neighboring Victorian landmarks into museum-quality guest houses, setting a national standard and launching a trend that has inspired the opening of more than 60 B&Bs locally.

Besides enhancing the Victorian structures in which they are housed, some of Cape May's B&Bs elevate the level of breakfast and afternoon tea to new heights – in formal dining rooms and parlors, or on the ubiquitous front verandas that are occupied everywhere in Cape May from early morning to dusk or later. The sumptuous breakfast and afternoon-tea ritual draws many couples year after year, and has resulted in publication of a number of Cape May cookbooks.

Where upscale B&Bs open, restaurants are sure to follow. "Our businesses attracted a clientele that demanded good food," says Nan Hawkins of the Barnard-Good House, whose breakfast feasts are the most lavish in Cape May.

Adds Dane Wells of the Queen Victoria B&B: "When my guests arrive, I tell them I know why they're here – for the food. Seven or eight of the best restaurants in New Jersey are within a few blocks of our inn."

Since the late 1970s, more than two dozen restaurants have emerged and, remarkably for a resort town, most have survived. Besides stability, many offer creative food and convivial ambiance. Some are small (make that tiny) and, lacking liquor licenses, allow patrons to bring their own wine. Prices, in many cases, are pleasantly lower than in other resort areas.

The result is that thousands of visitors come to experience the ultimate in bed and breakfast, tea and dinner in this, the culinary capital of South Jersey.

Dining

At peak periods, many restaurants are booked far in advance. Some of the most popular do not take reservations, which may mean a long wait for a table. Some also require a minimum of one entrée per person. Be advised that parking at many Cape May restaurants is difficult to impossible. Parking meters on the street gobble up quarters every half hour until 10 p.m.; a few restaurants offer valet parking.

The Best of the Best

410 Bank Street, 410 Bank St.

A gumbo of New Orleans, Caribbean and French dishes, many grilled over mesquite wood, is the forte of this restaurant considered by many to be the best in town. (The owners' companion Italian restaurant, **Frescos,** is next door and some reviewers think it's even better.)

Dining is pleasant on the recently enclosed outdoor courtyard, surrounded by plants, tiny white lights and Victorian lamps. If you can't eat there, settle for one of the narrow screened porches or the small, intimate dining rooms done in Caribbean pastel colors inside the restored 1840 house. Owners Steve and Janet Miller are theater-set designers, so both inside and outside are quite dramatic.

For appetizers ($6.95 to $9.50), we passed up the menu's crawfish bisque, crab terrine and blackened sea scallops with rémoulade sauce for excellent specials of ceviche and mesquite-grilled quail, now a menu staple. After those, both our entrées of blackened red snapper with pecan sauce and yellowfin tuna in Barbadian black bean sauce with a hint of sesame and ginger, served with crisp vegetables and rice pilaf, were almost too much to eat. We had to save room for the key lime pie, which was the real thing.

Other choice entrées ($20.95 to $27.95) include blackened catfish fillet in a lime-jalapeño sauce with bananas and tomatoes, Chilean sea bass creole, sautéed

Patrons dine New Orleans-style on enclosed outdoor courtyard at 410 Bank Street.

soft-shell crabs grenobloise, mesquite-grilled lobster, grilled Jamaican filet mignon and blackened prime rib. A French-style roast is offered nightly.

For desserts there are chocolate-pecan pie with amaretto puree, triple-chocolate ganache with grand marnier sauce, hazelnut cheesecake with raspberry puree and a Louisiana bread pudding with hot bourbon sauce that's the best around.

Service is by knowledgeable waiters attired in tropical shirts and bow ties. With the Key West-like atmosphere and a menu like this, who'd guess that the chef, Henry Sing Cheng, is Chinese? Experts consider him the top chef in town.

(609) 884-2127. Dinner nightly, 5 to 10:30, May to mid-October. BYOB.

Water's Edge, Beach Drive and Pittsburgh Avenue.

A family restaurant and lounge in front of La Mer Motor Inn was transformed into a sleek, hotel-style dining room run by a husband-and-wife team with a background in nouvelle cuisine and a menu that prompted us, upon discovering it, to cancel our dinner reservations elsewhere that night. Since our first visit, chef Neil Elsohn and his hostess-wife, Karen Fullerton-Elsohn, have put their somewhat out-of-the-way restaurant on South Jersey's culinary map.

It has winning ingredients – a well-tailored aspect of banquettes and booths dressed in white cloths with rose-colored runners, cobalt blue glassware, flickering votive candles, a select and reasonably priced wine list, an inspired menu and an outdoor deck with the ocean beyond. We were impressed with our initial dinner: an appetizer of strudel with escargots, mushrooms, pinenuts and an ethereal garlic-cream sauce; the abundant house salads with romaine and red-leaf lettuce, yellow cherry tomatoes, julienned leeks and a zesty vinaigrette; the poached fillet of salmon with smoked salmon butter, lime and salmon caviar, and sautéed sea scallops with tomatillos, cilantro and grilled jícama, followed by key lime ice cream.

On our next visit, we grazed happily through appetizers and salads ($4.75 to $12), the staff graciously foregoing the one-main-course-per-person minimum with the awareness that our sampling would cost more than a single entrée each. The scallop chowder was wonderfully creamy, dotted with thyme and flecked with prosciutto, and full of scallops and potato. The spicy pork and scallion empanada with pineapple-ginger chutney, encased in a radicchio leaf, was a standout, as was the house green salad with three medallions of Coach Farm goat cheese and a suave balsamic dressing. We also relished the fusilli with grilled tuna, oriental vegetables and Szechuan vinaigrette, and grilled chicken salad with toasted pecans, grilled red onions, mixed greens and citrus vinaigrette. A Silverado sauvignon blanc ($17) poured in oversize wine globes helped make a delectable feast, capped by an icy grapefruit and champagne sorbet as a finale.

Main courses are priced from $18 for roasted half free-range chicken with a parmesan-pignoli crust to $26 for grilled filet mignon with classic béarnaise and madeira demi-glace – about the only classic dish we've encountered here. You're more apt to find exotica like seared shrimp with lime, cilantro and tequila, avocado relish and crispy tortillas, or roasted loin of veal with figs sautéed with port and lime, creamy polenta and a spinach-stilton tart.

Desserts could be profiteroles, chocolate molten cake with vanilla cream and berries, raspberry cheesecake with citrus anglaise, and bittersweet chocolate-walnut pâté with espresso and vanilla sauces.

(609) 884-1717. Dinner nightly, 5 to 9:30 or 10, May to Columbus Day, weekends in off-season. Closed in January.

The Ebbitt Room, 25 Jackson St.

The intimate, candlelit dining room in the restored Virginia Hotel is elegant in peach and gray. Swagged draperies, crisply linened tables, delicate wine glasses, art-deco wall sconces and birds of paradise standing tall in vases enhance the setting. Chef Christopher Hubert's progressive American menu changes seasonally, with recent entrées ($18 to $28) ranging from grilled Florida grouper with a habañero barbecue glaze and basil-cheese grits to pan-roasted veal filets with lobster mashed potatoes.

Excellent hot rolls with a crisp crust preceded our appetizers, one an eggplant and gorgonzola crostini served with red-onion pesto ($4.75) and the other a zesty caesar salad ($6), served on black octagonal plates. Main dishes were an exceptional roast cornish game hen on a bed of caramelized vegetables, and filet mignon with three-onion salad and spicy steak fries.

For dessert, we wished for something frozen, but settled for an upside-down fig cake and pecan-praline cheesecake. The Danfield Creek chardonnay ($17) had the oakey taste we like. And the live piano music emanating from the lobby lent a glamorous air to a welcome addition to the Cape May dining scene.

(609) 884-5700. Dinner nightly from 5.

Virginia Hotel offers dining in elegant Ebbitt Room.

Spiaggi, 429 Beach Drive.

"This started as a tavern and just grew," says Maureen Horn, who with her chef-husband Steve relocated to Cape May in 1982 after operating a restaurant in Philadelphia for five years. Restaurant Maureen quickly became the best fancy dining establishment in town. A warm welcome, consistently good food and flawless service were its hallmarks.

After twenty years, Maureen advised at our latest visit, "it was time for a change." So Maureen's reopened in 1997 as Spiaggi (Italian for beach), with "cucina nouveau, light and fresh, served in a light-hearted atmosphere."

The evolution was a natural for Steve, who trained in Florence with Tuscan chef and cookbook author Juliano Bugalli. Over the years he had dabbled in Italian fare at his Es-Ta-Ti trattoria on the floor below Maureen, and showed a deft touch with seafood and sauces on a contemporary international menu.

His Spiaggi menu was broadened to appeal to diners who wanted an affordable pasta and a glass of wine at the bar as well as those who craved the signature rack of lamb and a great vintage in dressier surroundings. Look for starters in the $3 to $8 range, perhaps a grilled portobello mushroom seasoned with pancetta and shallots, homemade ravioli stuffed with sonoma goat cheese, and caesar salad laced with lump crabmeat and gulf shrimp. Pastas and main dishes ($14 to $25) vary from shrimp and pancetta with penne and a classic Mediterranean bouillabaisse to hazelnut-crusted swordfish, sautéed chicken with artichoke hearts and fontina cheese, and filet mignon with portobello mushrooms in barolo wine sauce.

Desserts include walnut cheesecake with warm caramel sauce and a winning strawberry tart.

The Horns gave a sleek city look to their sophisticated establishment is on the second floor of a beachfront Victorian structure that was once a bathhouse and saloon. The enclosed front porch, pristinely white and with a great view of the ocean and boardwalk goings-on, remained untouched. The interior was redone in gray, cream and cobalt blue, with white butcher paper atop the white tablecloths. *(609) 884-3504. Dinner, Tuesday-Sunday from 5, fewer days in off-season. Closed November-March.*

Union Park, 727 Beach Drive.

The restaurant in the 85-year-old Hotel Macomber, about to be condemned and the residence of a couple of ghosts, was revived in 1996 by new owners and getting great reviews. The ghosts turn up now and then in the kitchen and brighten and dim the crystal chandeliers in the dining room after hours, the staff advised.

Not to worry. A new spirit has been infused by Crystal and Charles Czworkowski, she a hotel general manager and he an attorney in Boston, before they moved to the town where she had summered with her parents to buy and operate the 34-room beachfront hotel.

Although Crystal was manning the hotel's front desk at our visit, her heart is in the interior dining room, a high-ceilinged space evocative of the Cape May of the 1930s. The setting is elegant and summery with white-clothed tables and pink napkins, a white inlaid-tile ceiling, white crinoline covering the windows and cherrywood-backed chairs that innkeepers advised are the most comfortable in town. A smaller, enclosed room at the side is reserved for smokers and cigar dinners.

Chef Andrew Keller from the Rye Town Hilton in New York features contemporary fare and presentation that the initial restaurant review called "simply out of this world." Buried amid the complexities of the dinner menu are three signature dishes named for the owners' young children.

Follow their lead and order the tenderloin of veal Casimir with lobster and asparagus or the Caskia ratatouille tart served with grilled polenta, sautéed greens and roasted eggplant, among entrées priced from $18 to $32. Other early favorites were pan-seared sea scallops with a saffron-infused lobster and wild mushroom risotto cake, and roasted rack of Wyoming lamb with dijon herb crust, presented wigwam style with asparagus spears perched over garlic-mashed potatoes.

Specialty appetizers ($7 to $9) were steamed lobster dumplings with ginger-plum sauce, grilled seafood sausage on a julienne vegetable nest, and a stratified parfait of Scottish smoked salmon and chilled lump crabmeat with crème fraîche and bermuda onions, two chives rising like antenna with a dollop of black caviar between.

Daughter Cezanne's apple cloud is the featured dessert ($6). Crisp phyllo triangles hold apples sautéed in port and brown sugar, flanked by a scoop of vanilla ice cream and a pool of hot caramel sauce. Somewhat similar is a phyllo basket of bananas sautéed in dark rum. The triple chocolate terrine comes with a tangy raspberry-cranberry coulis.

(609) 884-8811. Dinner nightly from 5. Closed Tuesday and Wednesday in off-season and January-February. BYOB.

Frescos, 412 Bank St.

New Jersey Monthly magazine once sent two writers to cover what they said "may well be New Jersey's leading center of gourmet restaurants." What did they rate best? Frescos, with three and one-half stars of a possible four. That was one-half star more than their second-best rating, 410 Bank Street. Frescos has slipped a bit, in the estimation of locals, and was undergoing a change in chefs for 1997, but still ranks near the top.

Enclosed porch of Spiaggi overlooks the beach for which it is named.

Crayons are on the tables for doodling on the paper overlays that cover the white-clothed tables in the restored Victorian summer cottage run as an Italian restaurant by Steve and Janet Miller of 410 Bank Street next door. Faux-marble columns and unusual art involving three-dimensional fish accent the spare white dining rooms, where brown leather chairs flank tables that are rather close together. We prefer the narrow wraparound porch, its tables for two far enough apart for private conversations.

The pasta dishes ($15.50 to $22.95) are Cape May's most extensive, ranging from ricotta-cheese ravioli with marinara sauce to jumbo shrimp and scallops in champagne-lobster cream sauce over pappardelle. Friends who dined there rated at 9.5 on a scale of 10 both the linguini with white clam sauce and fresh littlenecks, and the fusilli with a sauce of tomatoes, anchovies, black olives, capers and garlic. Other entrée choices ($18.95 to $22.95) include grilled tuna with a smoked almond-basil pesto, pan-grilled T-bone of veal with portobello mushrooms, and osso buco served over linguini.

We hear the key lime-cream-filled cannoli is even better than the signature dessert: a layered, rum-soaked sponge cake with imported mascarpone cream and grated chocolate.

(609) 884-0366. Dinner nightly, 5 to 10:30, May to mid-October. BYOB.

Peaches at Sunset, 1 Sunset Blvd.

Arguably Cape May's prettiest restaurant is this establishment with an offbeat name, derived from chef-owner George Pechin's nickname and its location at the head of Sunset Boulevard in West Cape May. "Peach" Pechin and partner Craig Needles started in 1983 with a small sidewalk cafe in downtown Cape May. Their debut as a gourmet-to-go cafe quickly evolved into a serious small restaurant, one that finally gained the space it deserved with this location. The original Peaches Cafe stayed behind for awhile before giving way to Kuishimbo, an equally serious (and good) Japanese restaurant.

A nicely restored Victorian house, striking in peach with green trim, holds Peaches at Sunset. Two small dining rooms are divided by a walnut-trimmed aquarium full of tropical fish beneath a stained-glass panel and a tropical design on the ceiling. Peach-colored napkins stand tall in wine glasses at each candlelit table. Dining is al fresco on a raised rear deck leading to a gazebo with a few pint-size tables.

Peach calls his fusion cooking contemporary Pacific Rim cuisine. The dinner menu offers about eight entrées ($17.95 to $24.95), among them Caribbean-style shrimp with Puerto Rican rum and mint sauce, baked sesame-crusted salmon with a corn and sweet-pepper relish, Cuban-style chicken stuffed with plantains and prosciutto, and twin tournedos with artichoke and niçoise tapenades. For starters ($$5.95 to $8.50), consider the creamy clam chowder that we once savored during lunch at Peaches Cafe, an exotic Thai chicken salad, fried oysters with wasabi mayonnaise or the signature roasted garlic served with mascarpone cheese on grilled sourdough bread. Finish with bourbon-pecan pie or crème caramel.

(609) 898-0100. Dinner nightly from 4:30, April-October; weekends rest of year.

The Washington Inn, 801 Washington St.

The best of the large restaurants in town, this has become even better with the new dynamic lent by David and Michael Craig, sons of the owners.

The attractive white 1840 plantation house is surrounded by banks of impatiens, and inside all is pretty as a picture. The Craig brothers redecorated, picking up the colors from their striking, custom-designed floral china. They seat 130 in several areas, including a candlelit wicker-filled front veranda done up in pink, a Victorian conservatory filled with greenery, dark and elegant interior rooms, and a romantic, enclosed brick terrace centered by a fountain trickling over an array of plants. Off a Victorian cocktail lounge is another enclosed, L-shaped veranda with more wicker.

Executive chef Mimi Wood's menu blends the traditional with the creative, starting with baked oysters, mushroom strudel and sea scallops wrapped in bacon ($5.95 to $8.95). At a recent visit, we liked the sound of her specials, creamy mustard scallop bisque and grilled portobello mushroom stuffed with shiitakes, crabmeat and smoked gouda. Entrées are priced from $18.95 for herbed chicken topped with mozzarella and tomato chutney to $24.95 for veal chop au poivre with stilton cheese, except $42.95 for filet mignon and lobster tail. Among the possibilities: pan-seared salmon with passion-fruit sauce, Asian veal sautéed with rock shrimp and black-bean sake butter, and grilled Kansas steak topped with horseradish butter.

The menu ends with "romantic international coffees." Desserts could be frozen key lime pie, crème brûlée, pumpkin-pecan cheesecake and strawberry napoleons.

David Craig likes to show the 10,000-bottle basement wine cellar, which holds an inventory of 850 titles and won the Wine Spectator Grand Award. The wine list has a table of contents, includes a page of chardonnays, and offers a Virginia red and a Lebanese wine, with a number of offerings priced in the teens.

(609) 884-5697. Dinner nightly, 5 to 10. Closed Monday and Tuesday, November-April.

Budget Gourmet

Louisa's, 104 Jackson St.

Tops on everyone's list for value is this tiny storefront restaurant that packs in the cognoscenti, who covet its twenty seats despite the fact that for years no reservations were taken and long waits were the norm. In 1996, reservations for the week were accepted starting Tuesday at 4 p.m. and were usually gone within two hours.

From a postage-stamp-size kitchen, Louisa and Doug Dietsch – she does the managing and the desserts, he does the cooking – offer some of the most innovative and affordable dinners in town. Formerly with the National Geographic Society, he has a natural touch for cooking and a rare way with herbs.

Feeling as if they're sharing their meal and their conversation with everyone in the place, patrons crowd together on molded plastic chairs of vibrant colors at tables covered with assorted bright calico cloths. The changing menu, posted nightly at the door and deceptively simple in terminology, might offer curried carrot soup, smoked fish rillettes, and hot and spicy ginger sesame noodles to start ($3.75 to $5.50).

Entrées ($10.50 to $16) could be soft-shell crabs, scallops with tamari and scallions, grilled salmon, grilled polenta with savory greens and grilled chicken with rosemary.

For dessert ($3.25), how about plum cobbler, peach oatmeal crisp, chocolate-banana bread pudding or mango upside-down cake?

We understand that some people come for a week to Cape May and contentedly eat almost every night at Louisa's. It certainly makes it easier now that they can book their table in advance.

(609) 884-5882. Dinner, Tuesday-Saturday 5 to 9, March-October. No credit cards. BYOB.

More Dining Choices

Cucina Rosa, 301 Washington St. Mall.

David Clemans, who has a reputation as one of the best cooks in town, opened this authentic and popular Italian restaurant in 1993 after selling the John F. Craig House, his B&B of many years. Former lodging guests may have lamented his move, but locals applauded since they now get to share the fruits of his culinary prowess. "This is my last permitted insanity, according to my wife," says David, who named it for her late grandmother. Here he teams with his stepson, Guy Portewig, who's the chef.

"We take relatively standard southern Italian dishes and make them very carefully," says David. Everything is done from scratch, from the marinara and meat sauces to semolina bread.

Prices are gentle. Appetizers run from $3.95 for eggplant parmesan to $6.75 for mussels in white wine and herb sauce. Clams oreganata is a house favorite, as is sautéed calamari with a marinara sauce that's almost as spicy as fra diavolo. Main dishes are priced from $7.95 for basic pastas to $21.95 for lobster oreganata. Widely acclaimed is the chicken portofino, stuffed with mozzarella cheese and Italian sausage specially made for the restaurant, rolled and baked with tomato sauce and served with pasta ($16.95). Other treats include shrimp scampi and grilled lamb chops, marinated in olive oil and Italian spices and served with fried potatoes sautéed with peppers and onions or pasta with a choice of sauce.

Desserts are David's forte. He makes fruit pies that change daily, lemon cheesecake and a rich chocolate cake. He also offers tartuffo, cannoli and spumoni.

The 64-seat restaurant is at a corner location along the pedestrian mall, with tables spilling out onto a sidewalk patio in season. The interior decor is soft and romantic in rose and green tones, with candles flickering on white-clothed tables. *(609) 898-9800. Dinner nightly, 5 to 10, Sunday 4:30 to 9:30. Closed January to mid-February. BYOB.*

Tisha's, 714 Beach Drive.

This little winner in the Solarium Building juts out over the ocean beside Convention Hall. Pretty in pink and white to match the glorious sunsets beyond, it seems to be mostly big windows beneath a high ceiling, with close-together tables and a few art and floral accents on the walls.

It's a summery backdrop for interesting fare prepared by chef-owner Paul Negro, whose fisherman-father often provides the day's catch and whose mother, Tisha, persuaded him to open a restaurant in nearby Wildwood a few years back. He jumped at the chance to move into the thick of the Cape May scene in 1995. Terrific bread from the Village Bakery and excellent salads, one caesar and one tossed with balsamic vinegar, come with the entrées ($14.95 to $21.95). At one visit, we enjoyed pork tenderloin with a dijon-caper cream sauce and clams aglio over penne pasta. An autumn dinner produced grilled lamb chops with mint sauce and grilled duck with raspberry sauce, each teamed with sautéed yellow and green squash, carrots, onions and roasted potatoes. Tirami su and an apple crisp with ice cream proved worthy endings and, a nice touch at our first visit, the chef sent out complimentary cordials of frangelico.

Based on his first summer of serving breakfast (from $3.75 for an egg and cheese sandwich to $9.95 for a shrimp and crabmeat omelet), Paul added tables for outdoor dining and offered lunch as well.

(609) 884-9119. Breakfast from 7:30 and lunch from 11:30, Memorial Day to Labor Day. Dinner nightly, 5 to 10. Closed Tuesday and Wednesday in off-season and November-April. BYOB.

Freda's Cafe, 210 Ocean St.

Chef Steve Howard and his baker-wife Carol moved their gourmet shop and deli in West Cape May to a downtown location behind the former La Toque restaurant. The kitchen also serves their new cafe in the old La Toque quarters. Colorful artworks enliven the intimate space, where tables are dressed with white linens and fresh flowers.

The short dinner menu ($11.95 to $17.95) pairs a fancy item like filet mignon au poivre with valfraise cheese against earthy barbecued spare ribs, black-eyed peas and rice. Nightly specials could be paella, rack of lamb and mixed grill with whipped sweet potatoes. At our latest visit, the seafood sampler yielded arctic char, flounder and shrimp encrusted with pesto and served with pasta topped with a Jersey tomato and a hint of gin.

Among starters are focaccia, crabmeat remicks, and warm goat cheese rolled in pecans with poached pears and watercress. For dessert, Carol makes a dynamite key lime pie, chocolate-bourbon cake and mocha mousse cake.

For lunch ($5.75 to $6.75), consider the lobster cake sandwich, a Freda's creation loaded with lobster meat, lettuce and tomato.

(609) 884-7887. Lunch, 11:30 to 2:30; dinner from 5. Closed Thursday except in summer. BYOB.

Walls of windows yield ocean views at Tisha's.

Congress Hall Cafe, 251 Beach Drive.

Dating to 1816 and once one of the nation's largest summer hotels, Congress Hall is undergoing a multi-million-dollar renovation under young owner Curtis Bashaw, who showed what he could do with the renovation of the Virginia Hotel. Here in the National Historic Landmark structure, 100 hotel rooms were under construction and guided tours for "sneak previews" ($8) were attracting many takers.

We got a taste of what's in store in the new cafe in the hotel's ballroom. It's an interim operation until the hotel dining room is up and running in 1998 or later. Chef Chris Huber from the Virigina's Ebbitt Room designed the menu, a jaunty array of salads, sandwiches, light fare and desserts, to eat here or take out.

The high-ceilinged cafe is cute as can be in black and white with bubblegum-pink walls. Eight tiny tables encircle a round banquette in the center. There are more tables around the perimeter and, our choice, larger tables outside on the pillared veranda (alas, the great view of the ocean we saw upon arrival disappeared behind parked cars as we were seated). We lunched on the eggless caesar salad with garlic-rubbed croutons and lump crabmeat ($7 and a staple in the Ebbitt Room) and a thick clam chowder with a side of crisp vegetable chips ($3.50), served with blue-cheese dip and a corn and black-bean salsa. Dessert was lemon mousse with fresh berries.

The all-day fare varies from panini to entrées ($8.50 to $13) like grilled tuna over tart greens and barbecued sirloin with grilled yukon gold potatoes and portobello mushrooms. We could understand why local innkeepers were enthusiastic about the place for light dinners, especially outside on a summer's evening.

(609) 884-2353. Open daily, 11 to 10 in summer; Sunday-Wednesday 11 to 4 and Thursday-Saturday 11 to 9 in spring and fall. Closed January to Easter.

Lodging

Since bed and breakfast is so integral to the Cape May experience, we concentrate on a few of the more than 60 in town, particularly those with bountiful breakfasts. Most require minimum stays of two to four nights, do not allow smoking inside, and access is only via push-button combination locks installed in the doors. Breakfasts tend to be lighter in summer, more formal and filling the rest of the year. The Cape May ritual is for the innkeepers to serve – and often sit with – guests at breakfast, and later to help with dinner plans as they review the menus during afternoon tea or beverages. So integral is the food element that many inns keep a log in which guests write comments on local restaurants; some of the reports are scathingly at odds with previous entries.

The Mainstay Inn, 635 Columbia Ave., Cape May 08204.

Mainstay owners Tom and Sue Carroll began the B&B movement in Cape May at the Windward House, now under different ownership, and purchased this showy Italianate villa in 1975. It was built in 1872 for two gentlemen gamblers and, says Tom, is one of the few Victorians in town that went through 100 years with no transitions. It later became a guest house run by a Baptist minister who never got rid of anything, and the collection is there for all to view. Tours of the museum-quality inn are given Tuesday, Thursday, Saturday and Sunday at 4, and upwards of 20 people gladly pay $7.50 to visit and join inn guests for tea. Except in summer, when iced tea is served on the veranda, tea time is inside and formal. The tea is served from a copper container and accompanied by cucumber sandwiches, cheese straw daisies, toffee squares, chocolate-chip meringues and the like.

The twelve guest rooms in the main inn and the 1870 Cottage next door have private baths, some with copper tubs and marble shower stalls. They are handsomely and formally appointed with lace curtains, stenciling, brass and iron bedsteads, armoires and rockers. The Carrolls recently added four luxury, two-bedroom suites with double jacuzzis, fireplaced living rooms, TVs with VCRs, kitchenettes and private porches in what they call the Officers' Quarters, an old World War I officers' house they acquired across the street. Outfitted in more contemporary style, the suites are designed for couples traveling together and for those who seek privacy. Modest antiques, stenciling, bright colors and plants "give a whole different atmosphere here than in the inn," says Tom. Guests in the Officers' Quarters have continental breakfast delivered to their rooms, since the Carrolls already had their hands full serving elaborate breakfasts in the main inn.

In summer, breakfast is continental-plus, served buffet-style on the veranda; other seasons it is formal and sit-down at 8:30 and 9:30 seatings around the table for twelve in the dining room. Strawberry french toast, chicken-pecan quiche, ham and apple pie, California egg puff and macaroni mousse are some of the offerings. Lately Sue has been doing less with breakfast meats and more with fruits like banana-pineapple crisp, cranberry-apple compote, orange crunch and banana-cream coffee cake.

So sought-after are Sue Carroll's recipes for her breakfast and tea goodies that she has published six editions of a small cookbook called "Breakfast at Nine, Tea at Four." It has sold more than 18,000 copies.

(609) 884-8690. Doubles, $140 to $195; suites, $195 to $255 ($325 for four). Officers' Quarters open year-round; inn closed January to mid-March.

Barnard-Good House, 238 Perry St., Cape May 08204.
Breakfasts are *the* claim to fame of Nan and Tom Hawkins, whose morning feast was judged the best in the state by New Jersey Monthly magazine.
Nan never serves plain juice. "It's blended with maybe strawberry or lime juice, sometimes five different kinds." That's followed by a soup course: perhaps fresh peach, blueberry or, in fall, a hot cider soup topped with croutons and whipped cream. In lieu of soup she might serve fresh pears poached in kahlua with sour cream and chocolate curls, or hot apple crunch with applejack brandy. Breads could be brioche, butternut squash rolls, biscuits or "dogbone scones," shaped by a dogbone cutter that Nan uses to make dog biscuits for all the dogs in her family at Christmas.
The main course might be swiss enchilada crêpes filled with chili, chicken and tomato, with a side dish of corn pudding. Or you might have ratatouille in cheese puffs with a side of bulgar with mushrooms, chicken and apple strudel with pistachios, plum-chutney waffles, wild rice and walnut pancakes, or a Norwegian ham pie with sweet-potato pancakes.
For dessert – "why *not* for breakfast?" laughs Nan – there might be applesauce spice cake, sour-cream brownies or brandy crêpes with homemade ice cream. The question struck a chord, for she and her family recently published a cookbook of 200 recipes called *Why Not for Breakfast?*
"I create as I go," says Nan, for whom cooking is a passion. She spends hours preparing for the next breakfast after serving the last. Guests dine family-style at a lace-covered table in the formal dining room. "My ego trip is seeing the joy of my guests in the morning," she says.
In the late afternoon, she puts out more goodies like chocolate-banana cake and lemon mousse in a meringue shell to accompany tea or beverages in the parlor or outside on the veranda.
The Barnard-Good offers three guest rooms and two suites, all air-conditioned and with private baths.
(609) 884-5381. Doubles, $90 to $140. Closed November-March.

The Abbey, 34 Gurney St., Cape May 08204.
A steady stream of passersby gawks at this elegant Gothic villa with its 60-foot tower and incredible gingerbread trim, all painstakingly painted a soft green with deep red and ivory accents. Inside, guests and tour visitors alike admire the parlor, library (with the largest free-standing bookcase you'll ever see) and dining room on the main floor, plus seven guest rooms upstairs. They're filled with priceless items, and ceilings are ornately decorated with paint, gilt and wallpaper pieces. We stayed in the Savannah, a summery room with white enamel bedstead, oriental carpets, a white wicker sofa with purple cushions and a small refrigerator in the bathroom. Owners Jay and Marianne Schatz converted the cottage next door into seven more guest rooms, all with private baths, and a couple of parlors and verandas, where continental breakfast is served in the summer.
In spring and fall, guests gather in the dining room of the main villa, where fourteen people can sit around the banquet table beside a Teutonic sideboard. "We have the noisiest breakfasts in town," Marianne said, and we agree. Jay, a non-stop comic, keeps guests regaled both with his stories and his selection of hats from a closet that holds a choice of 350 – he might pull out an Australian bush hat or a "Hagar the Horrible" beauty. His act, and Marianne's repartee, nearly upstage

their fairly elaborate breakfasts: perhaps pink grapefruit juice, a dish of fresh peaches and whipped cream, an egg and ham casserole with garlic grits on the side, and English muffins. Marianne also makes a great quiche with a bisquick crust. Guests share opinions of restaurants they visited the night before.

(609) 884-4506. Fax (609) 884-2379. Doubles, $100 to $225. Closed January-April.

Manor House, 612 Hughes St., Cape May 08204.

This impressive, gambrel-roofed house with warm oak and chestnut foyer and striking furnishings seems almost contemporary in contrast to all the high-Victorian B&Bs in Cape May. Guests spread out for punch, cider or tea in a front room with a striking stained-glass-front player piano or a library with two plush loveseats in front of a fireplace.

Upstairs are nine guest rooms, seven with private bath. They are furnished in antiques, with brass and wood king or queensize beds, handmade quilts and light Victorian print wallpapers. One is a third-floor suite with a sitting area and a whirlpool tub by the window in the bathroom. The newest is a secluded lower-level room with kingsize bed and private entrance. There are handmade "napping" signs for each door knob and the cookie fairy stocks the cookie jar every night.

Innkeepers Nancy and Tom McDonald, who had stayed as guests here many times, considered the B&B a model and acquired it in 1995. They maintained the tradition of sumptuous breakfasts, employing many of the former innkeepers' recipes. Among favorites are "asparageggs" (poached eggs and asparagus on homemade English muffins with mornay sauce), a corn and egg pie with jalapeño cheese and tomato relish, vanilla whole-wheat waffles, a french toast sandwich with raisin bread stuffed with cream cheese, apple crêpes and corn quiche. Juice, fresh fruit and sticky buns, a house signature, round out the meal. Tea time brings cheese spreads, bean dip, salsa, coconut-macadamia bars and chocolate streusel bars.

(609) 884-4710. Fax (609) 898-0471. Doubles, $108 to $161; suite, $175. Closed in January.

The Virginia Hotel, 25 Jackson St., Box 557, Cape May 08204.

Its gingerbread restored and its interior pristine, the Virginia, built in 1879 as Cape May's first hotel, was reopened in 1989 as what general manager Curtis Bashaw, son of the owner, calls a deluxe "boutique" hotel. Newspapers hang from a rack outside the dining room, and a pianist plays in the pleasant front library during the dinner hour in the highly regarded Ebbitt Room.

Upstairs on the second and third floor are 24 guest rooms that vary widely in size and shape. Like the public rooms, they are furnished in a simple yet sophisticated manner, which we find refreshing after all the elaborate Victoriana one encounters in Cape May. On your way upstairs check the stained-glass window in the landing; a local craftsman spent a year looking for old glass with which to restore it.

Bedrooms are equipped with private baths with new fixtures, telephones, and remote-control TVs and VCRs hidden in built-in cabinets. The restful decor is mostly soft peaches and grays. Room service is available, and terry robes are provided. There are eleven standard-size rooms, eleven premium and two extra-premium at the front of the second floor with private balconies. Five have a sofa and two upholstered chairs each, though one premium room with a kingsize bed has room for only one chair. The wraparound balcony on the second floor gave our expansive room extra space and was a pleasant setting the next morning for a continental breakfast of fresh juice, fruit, danish pastries and croissants, delivered to the room at precisely the time specified.

(609) 884-5700 or (800) 732-4236. Fax (609) 884-1236. Doubles, $180 to $295.

The Queen Victoria, 102 Ocean St., Cape May 08204.

Dane and Joan Wells are among Cape May's original innkeepers and are among the few who still live on the premises. Over the years, they had much experience learning what their guests wanted in their lovely 1881 corner property that has twelve rooms with private baths.

They used that experience in 1989 to refurbish a Victorian house and a carriage house next door with eleven luxury suites offering the niceties that many today seek: queensize brass or iron canopy beds, sitting rooms or areas, mini-refrigerators, whirlpool baths, air-conditioning and television. They also are decorated in a simpler, more comfortable style than the Cape May norm, outfitted with Arts and Crafts-style furniture but still authentic, since Joan once was executive director of the Victorian Society of America. They're named after neighborhoods in London; Dane is partial to the Greenwich, which, "if all the good eating at the restaurants here gets you, has a gout stool."

Each house has a living room, one in the original building with a piano and a fireplace and the newer one with TV, games and jigsaw puzzles. Pantry areas are outfitted with the makings for tea, popcorn, sherry, wine glasses and such.

Breakfast is an event in two dining rooms, with either Dane or Joan presiding at each. Always available are a fresh fruit compote, homemade granola, mini shredded wheat, homemade muffins and a basket of toasting breads featuring Wolferman's English muffins. Other options might be baked stuffed french toast with sausage patties or baked eggs and cheese with curried fruit. Afternoon tea brings crackers and a dip, maybe blue cheese or salmon, plus cookies and brownies.

Eighty of the house favorites are compiled in "The Queen Victoria Cookbook," exceptionally good-looking and outstanding in its genre. The recipes, scaled to serve twelve, are geared to entertaining.

(609) 884-8702. Doubles, $165 to $210; suites, $230 to $250.

The John F. Craig House, 609 Columbia Ave., Cape May 08204.

This attractive Carpenter Gothic cottage has long been known for some of the best breakfasts in town, and owners Frank Felicetti, formerly a lawyer in Wilmington, Del., and his wife Connie continue the tradition. They live in the house, so are more involved than was former owner David Clemans, who was on hand to prepare breakfast but transferred day-to-day operations to a caring staff. David, who now runs the Cusina Rosa restaurant, left most of the furnishings for the new owners.

Blended coffees and teas are put out for early-risers at 7:30. Breakfast is served at 8:30 or 9:45 in the lovely dining room with its lace tablecloth and scallop-shell wallpaper. There are always seasonal fruits on the table as well as homemade muffins and buttermilk coffee cake. The entrée, which comes out on a piping-hot plate garnished with fruit, could be anything from blueberry-stuffed french toast with ricotta cheese and almond flavoring to a bacon and gruyère cheese casserole to eggs with scallions in a ramekin. Homemade sourdough or dark molasses herb breads accompany. Frank does the cooking, while Connie serves. She also bakes the pastries and goodies for afternoon tea, perhaps baked brie with almonds and brown sugar, oatmeal-preserve bars, almond-cake squares or molasses-spice cookies. The couple gathered the recipes from their families.

The house, which comes in two sections, contains eight air-conditioned guest rooms, all with private baths. They are done in typical Cape May style, with lots of wicker and oriental rugs, lace curtains and elaborate wallpaper. Guests have use of the parlor and the requisite Cape May porches.

(609) 884-0100. Doubles, $135 to $175. Closed January and February.

Rhythm of the Sea, 1123 Beach Drive, Cape May 08204.

The name of this beachfront B&B derives not only from the ocean surf but from the fall, winter and spring concert series of "symphonic getaways." The concerts are presented by visiting musicians in a huge living room in which a concert grand piano takes center stage. Innkeepers Carol and Richard Macaluso import professionals who stay at the B&B and entertain inn guests and invited friends at a reception afterward. A four-course dinner follows.

Food is a big deal here, especially the three-course breakfast. Carol, who studied at the Cordon Bleu in New York, is known for her french toast made with homemade bread, hot three-berry liqueur sauce and slabs of Canadian bacon on the side. Other specialties are Cape May crab muffins (lump crab on English muffins), breakfast burritos, cheese blintz soufflés with grand marnier/mandarin orange sauce and individual baked-apple pancakes. Fruits and pastries accompany, among them a banana split with fresh fruit and cream. Richard may cook up some potato pancakes. The meal is served in a large dining room with three round tables for four, each topped at our fall visit with a vase of long-stemmed roses. Cucumber sandwiches, Russian tea biscuits, biscotti and scones turn up at afternoon tea, served on the grand front porch facing the ocean.

In addition to food and music, this 1915 summer house appeals to those who tire of fussy Victoriana. It is furnished simply in the Arts and Crafts style with Stickley furniture and Mission-style lanterns, wooden blinds and table linens. The six large bedrooms come with queensize beds and private baths, and four have ocean views. A fireplace compensates in one room without a view.

(609) 884-7788 or (800) 498-6888. Doubles, $160 to $225.

The Southern Mansion, 720 Washington St., Cape May 08204.

Cape May's largest and most elaborate mansion, the 30,000 square-foot Italianate villa known locally as the George Allen estate is a showy small hotel in the making. Barbara Bray and Rick Wilde, newly wed and barely turned 30, poured sweat equity and millions of dollars into restoring the 100-room house built in the mid-19th century for a Philadelphia department store owner and occupying much of a two-acre square block in the heart of Cape May.

With 30 bathrooms, ten fireplaces, shiny Honduran mahogany floors, twelve-foot-high molded ceilings, cast-bronze chandeliers, 23 gold mirrors and 5,000 square feet of verandas and solariums, this was hardly your typical South Jersey beach house, as Barbara is quick to point out. Amazingly, the original furnishings, chandeliers and artworks were intact, many stored in the basement and ready to outfit ten more guest rooms under construction in a new wing.

Financing the restoration with house tours and the backing of her father, a Philadelphia physician, Barbara opened in 1995 with the first of fifteen ample guest

Italianate villa known as George Allen estate is centerpiece of Southern Mansion inn.

rooms on three floors of the main house. They vary widely but come with an assortment of ornate, step-up king and queen beds, televisions cosseted in armoires, gilt-edged mirrors and chairs, gold damask bedspreads and draperies, velvet recliners and settees, writing desks and telephones with modems. Some of the bathrooms are small with clawfoot tubs; others have huge walk-in tiled showers with seats. The sink in one room is installed right in the room between two halves of an armoire.

Ten larger, more deluxe rooms under construction in a wing recreating the Civil War era at the side were to have king beds, some with fireplaces, porches and double jacuzzis. Beside the wing is an Italianate pool with columns and a waterfall. The main floor has a catering kitchen, a solarium restaurant seating 160 for sit-down dinners, and a ballroom with six gold mirrors that "will look like Versailles," as Barbara envisioned it. We got a hint of what was in store in the bright aqua and butter-yellow ballroom of the main house, now a breakfast room with three tables bearing vases of long-stemmed roses and end walls of 23-carat gold-leaf mirrors reflecting into infinity. This is the setting for a full breakfast for house guests. Afternoon tea and wine and cheese with crudités are served here later in the day.

Eventually, Barbara planned a full-service restaurant for house guests in the solarium. "We'll offer the amenities of a hotel but retain the antiques and charm of a B&B," said she. Meanwhile, as part of a fanciful experience, guests could order romantic dinners for two to be served in the rooftop cupola atop the fifth floor with a view across town. The nearby Washington Inn, which catered the dinners, was averaging four a week at $215 a couple.

(609) 884-7171. Doubles, $185 to $295.

Gourmet Treats

Cape May always seemed to be somewhat lacking in specialty-food shops, and our informant at the Visitor Center said someone would make a killing by opening one. Happily, Rhona Craig of the Washington Inn satisfied some of the need, taking space in the new Shops at Congress Hall. The result is **Love the Cook,** an incredible gourmet store and cook shop, so chock full of 10,000 kitchen items that browsers can barely get by on a busy day. From gadgets to cookbooks to dishware to olive oils and a few specialty foods, you can find it here.

Also of interest among the growing array of shops at Congress Hall are **Heaven on Earth** candies, **A Different Twist** for gourmet pretzels, and **Planting Peas** (gifts for the gardener). Diverse tastes were served by **Grant's Regard** ("cigars and such") and **The Best Vest Co.** (appealing apparel).

For an extensive selection of wines to carry to the BYOB restaurants, most visitors head for **Collier's Liquor Store** on Jackson Street just north of the Washington Street Mall.

La Patisserie, 524 Washington Mall, is the place for lovely fruit tarts, many breads and all kinds of sweets from chocolate croissants to raspberry puffs and cranberry squares. **Our Daily Breads/Gourmet to Go** at 322 Washington Mall has super desserts like Kentucky derby pie, apple-crumb cheesecake and southern pecan tarts. A piece of raspberry cheesecake and a cappuccino might hit the spot in mid-afternoon.

Mon Frère Village Bakery, next to the Acme Market in the Victoria Village shopping plaza at Lafayette and Ocean streets, isn't much to look at, but the breads are baked on the premises. Everything from boules and baguettes to fruit tarts is first-rate.

What's a beach town without saltwater taffy? **Fralinger's,** the original taffy emporium from Atlantic City, has opened a Victorian candy store at 324 Washington St. Mall. Although we're not into fudge and taffy, we're certainly impressed by its elegant fixtures and wallpaper borders.

For the ultimate omelet, head for **McGlade's,** a small restaurant with a large deck practically over the ocean (from which on some days you can watch dolphins playing). If you can face lunch after a mammoth plate full of the Uncle Tuse's omelet (with about a pound of bacon, tomatoes and sharp cheddar) plus a load of delicious homefries ($7.50) or the shrimp and garlic omelet ($7.95), you have more of an appetite than we do (we can't even eat an omelet each here, so choose one to share). We know some Cape May innkeepers who love McGlade's for dinner (entrées $13 to $16.50 – BYOB). It's on the pier beside Convention Hall, just behind Morrow's Nut House.

For shopping, we always check out the **Whale's Tale,** a gift shop extraordinaire, purveying everything from gourmet cookware and nifty coffee mugs to shell magnets and an outstanding collection of cards and children's items.

Our last stop in town is always the **Lobster House Seafood Market** at Fishermen's Wharf. Among the largest enterprises around, this includes an enormous restaurant that does one of the highest volumes in the nation, an outdoor raw bar, a moored schooner for lunches and cocktails in season, a takeout counter and one of the best seafood markets we have ever seen. We drool over the exotic varieties of fresh fish, which can be packed in ice to travel. We like to take home items like snapper-turtle soup ($3.50 a quart), lump crabmeat, oysters rockefeller (75 cents each) or clam pies ($1.95) to remember Cape May by.

Culinary students nearing end of training serve breads to diners at American Bounty.

Hudson Valley
New Mecca for Gourmets

Barely an hour's drive north of New York City lies an area that represents a different world, one often overlooked by travelers destined for Manhattan's urban attractions.

The central Hudson Valley, including the Hudson Highlands, remains surprisingly rural, at times rustic. It is a mixed-bag area of steep mountains and rushing streams, noted mansions and historic houses, hip boutiques and hippie pursuits, winding country roads and a mighty river with seemingly unending, interesting traffic.

It also is an area of fine restaurants, one of which we would go so far as to say could give any restaurant in the country a run for its money. That is The American Bounty, one of four esteemed restaurants at the storied Culinary Institute of America in Hyde Park.

Chef-owner John Novi of the highly rated DePuy Canal House, a CIA graduate, attributes the array of restaurants to the arrival of the institute in 1972. The CIA created a demand for better food supplies in the area as well as a pool of teaching chefs and a ready entourage of culinary students who needed places to serve their required eighteen-week externships. For its 50th anniversary in 1996, the CIA listed 38 food-related places in the area owned by its alumni, running the gamut from gourmet restaurants to McDonald's and Dairy Freeze franchises.

Between meals, you will find plenty to do. The Hudson Valley is the nation's oldest wine-growing region, and more than twenty wineries offer tastings and/or tours. The valley is known for its great estates and house museums, from Boscobel to Hyde Park to Montgomery Place, the latest of the Sleepy Hollow Restorations. Rhinebeck, Red Hook and Millbrook are upscale villages particularly attractive to tourists.

Following your own pursuits will spur an appetite for things culinary.

Dining

The Culinary Institute of America

A former Jesuit seminary high above the Hudson River at Hyde Park became the home of the nation's oldest and foremost school for professional culinary training when The Culinary Institute of America moved in 1972 from New Haven, Conn. It has been a mecca for gourmands ever since, not only for chefs but also for visiting professionals and knowledgeable diners who sample the fare cooked by students in four leading-edge restaurants.

This is not a traditional college campus, you find upon arrival as you watch budding chefs in tall white hats scurry across the green, most clutching their knife kits. It couldn't be when you learn the rallying cry for the hockey team is "mirepoix, mirepoix, roux roux, roux; slice 'em up, dice 'em up, drop 'em in the stew!"

The main red brick classroom building has an institutional tinge, but the aromas wafting from The American Bounty or The Escoffier restaurants at either end of the long main hall are tantalizing, hinting at glories to come.

The restaurants are the final courses in 21 months of study for the institute's 2,000 candidates for associate degrees, who arrive and graduate in cycles every three weeks. They work in the kitchens and then serve in the dining rooms.

Visitors don't get to see much behind-the-scenes action, except through windows into the kitchens off both restaurants. Tours for the public (by reservation, Monday at 10 and 4) and bus groups afford a glimpse into the mysteries of a variety of specialty and experimental kitchens, the pantry and the former chapel, which is now the student dining room and used for large private banquets and graduation ceremonies. Visitors may catch glimpses of the General Foods Nutrition Center (first of its kind in the country), the Shunsuke Takaki School of Baking and Pastry, and the Conrad N. Hilton Library and Learning Resources Center. At a recent visit, a display in the main hall outlined the CIA's new Center for Continuing Education at Greystone, the former Christian Brothers winery in California's Napa Valley, where a 100-seat restaurant features the foods of the Mediterranean.

Open regularly to visitors here is an expanded gift shop and bookstore named after Craig Claiborne, stocking specialty-food items and 1,300 cookbooks on every culinary subject imaginable. They may inspire you to try at home some of the dishes cooked up in the CIA restaurants.

Meal reservations for American Bounty, the Escoffier Room and St. Andrew's Cafe are taken three months at a time, generally starting the beginning of March, June, September and December. Reservations for Caterina de Medici are taken three weeks ahead. Make reservations with the hospitality desk at (914) 471-6608, weekdays 8:30 to 5.

Arched opening frames view of cloister-style dining room at The American Bounty.

The American Bounty Restaurant, The Culinary Institute of America.

We've had lunch at Lutèce, the five-star restaurant in New York, and we've had lunch at the CIA's American Bounty, and we liked The American Bounty better. Not only did we find the food more interesting and more attractively presented, but the staff is pleasant and helpful, and the cost less than half.

Opened in 1982 for the presentation of American foods (before they became trendy) and wines, The American Bounty complements the noted, more formal Escoffier Restaurant at the other end of the building.

The high-ceilinged restaurant is the institute's largest. It is stunning, from its etched-glass doors to its cream and green draperies with a floral motif, gathered back from high arched windows. The seminary heritage is evident in the two cloister-style dining rooms, seating 110 people at tables spaced well apart.

A changing array of America's bounty is in front of the window onto the Julia Child Rotisserie Kitchen, through which you can see ducklings turning on the spit as white-clad students near the end of their training.

The menu changes slightly with every meal. Seldom have we had such a dilemma choosing as we did for a springtime lunch, confronting such appetizer choices as Southwestern-style stuffed chicken breast with ancho-coriander flavored coleslaw and New York State foie gras sautéed with concord-grape sauce and fried grapes.

We settled for tomato and celery mousse on cold tomato hash, a heavenly dish decorated with a floret of mayonnaise and a sprig of fresh dill, and a sampling of the day's three soups served in tiny cups: chilled strawberry, the clam chowder and New Orleans gumbo "Ya-Ya" (whatever that means). With these appetizers was passed a basket with at least nine kinds of bread and rolls (bran muffins, corn sticks, cloverleaf rolls and biscuits were some), served with a crock of sweet butter.

For main courses, because of the season we ordered fresh asparagus on sourdough toast with creamed salmon and sweetbreads, and "baked fresh seafood variety, new garden style." The former had perfectly crisp asparagus arranged like a fan on crisp sourdough; the sauce was suave and rich. The seafood was served in an iron skillet and was pretty as a picture, rimmed by tomato wedges. Crabmeat, clams, mussels, salmon and more were topped with butter and crumbs and baked. Vegetables, served family style, were stuffed cherry tomatoes, yellow squash and tiny red potatoes.

Desserts include chocolate-cheese timbales, Shaker lemon pie and, at one visit, sautéed Hudson Valley apples with praline ice cream in a walnut lace cup and pear-blueberry cobbler with Wild Turkey ice cream. We tried the popular Mississippi river boat, a shell of pastry filled with an intense chocolate mousse with kiwi fruit on top and, weird sounding but very good, fried strawberries – huge fat ones in a sort of beignet, served with a sour-cream and orange sauce.

Prices for all this are fairly reasonable. Two people having appetizers, entrées ($11.95 to $14.95) and desserts plus a bottle of wine can have a memorable lunch of dinner-size proportions for $50 to $60.

At night, when dining is by candlelight, entrées might range from $18.75 for pan-seared prawns wrapped in pancetta with cannellini beans to $22.75 for spicy grilled beef tenderloin with ancho-cumin crust and tomatillo-chipotle sauce.

Service, of course, is correct and cordial – after all, these students are *graded* for this. But, as you might expect, it can be a bit slow. Not to worry. The food is worth the wait.

(914) 471-6608. Open Tuesday-Saturday, lunch 11:30 to 1, dinner 6:30 to 8:30.

The Escoffier Restaurant, Culinary Institute of America.

The great French chef Auguste Escoffier would be pleased that some of his traditions are being carried on in the restaurant bearing his name.

The dining room is pretty in pale pinks and raspberry tones, with comfortable upholstered chairs and elaborate chandeliers and wall sconces. On spacious tables set with ten pieces of flatware at each place, the gigantic wine glasses – globe-shaped for red, hurricane-shaped for white and a flute for champagne – take an inordinate amount of room. With classical background music, it reminds one of a small, select and comfortable hotel dining room and seats about 90.

Menus change seasonally. Lunch prices are $4.50 for $7.50 for appetizers, $16.75 to $18.75 for entrées. Dinner prices are $8.50 to $11.95 for appetizers, $18.50 to $26 for entrées. If you come for lunch, expect to spend upwards of three hours and not have any appetite for dinner that night.

The classic French menu has acquired nouvelle touches since we first lunched here in 1978. Gone are the escargots bourguignonne and onion soup. In their place are things like snails with wild mushrooms in puff pastry, garlic soup with chives and croutons, warm vegetable tart with goat cheese, and a salad of seared scallops with endive and watercress. Main courses could be dover sole meunière, sautéed shrimp with artichokes, grilled breast of duck with ginger sauce and beef tenderloin with black truffle sauce. We remember fondly an entrée of sweetbreads topped with two large slices of truffle and a subtle sauce, and chicken in a spicy curry sauce, accompanied by a large tray of outstanding chutneys, the tray decorated with white napkins folded to point up at each corner, giving it the appearance of a temple roof.

Dining room of St. Andrew's Cafe is light and airy.

Overfull diners have been known to moan as the dessert cart laden with noble tortes, rich cakes and more rolls up. But how can one resist a taste of a silky coffee-kahlua mousse and an incredible many-layered pastry square, filled with whipped cream and raspberries?

After partaking of the meal, could anyone possibly have room for a full dessert? Our waiter, a former teacher whose wife was putting him through school, replied: "That's nothing. Some people have two or three."

(914) 471-6608. Open Tuesday-Saturday, lunch noon to 1, dinner 6:30 to 8:30.

St. Andrew's Cafe, The Culinary Institute of America.

The institute's best-kept secret had been this cafe, transformed in 1985 from the old Wechsler Coffeehouse and stressing low-fat nutritious food. Dropping in for what we expected might be a quick snack, we were astonished to partake of a memorable three-course lunch, all specially designed to be less than 1,000 calories.

It was a secret, that is, until it moved front and center into the CIA's new General Foods Nutrition Center, behind and to the side of the main building. All here is state of the art as the CIA seeks to change Americans' eating habits through greater awareness of nutrition and the availability of healthful and delicious meals. That's public-relations jargon for what this cafe really produces, "good food that's good for you."

The cafe has gone upscale in decor since its move. Ceramic vegetables on a breakfront in the foyer greet diners, who may see the tiled kitchen through windows behind the bar. Beyond is an expansive, 65-seat room with generally well-spaced tables set with white linens, heavy silver and, surprise, salt shakers that were notably missing in the old coffeehouse. A coffered ceiling, arched windows and upholstered rattan chairs contribute to a light, comfortable setting.

The remarkable appetizers and desserts in the $3 to $4 range are what we most remember from two lunches here. We started the first with a Mediterranean seafood terrine with the seafood in chunks, on a wonderful sauce, and a smoked duck salad with raspberry vinaigrette, a beautiful presentation including about six exotic lettuces topped with raspberries, ringed by sliced pears. A later visit produced a crabmeat quesadilla with a jícama and citrus salad and an extravagant plateful of carpaccio of fresh tuna and oriental mushroom salad.

Hearty breads like rye, sunflower seed and whole wheat along with butter curls were offered no less than four times – surely the fourth would have blown the calorie limit.

Among entrées ($9 to $13), barbecue-grilled chicken breast with black bean sauce and roast medallions of lamb with wild mushrooms and a potato pancake kind of affair, came with crisp young asparagus garnished with sesame seeds. These were preceded by salads of fancy greens, including endive, and tender peeled tomatoes. Garnishing the chicken dish was a peeled-back tomatillo filled with fresh salsa.

Desserts were, once, a pumpkin torte with cinnamon sauce and glazed pineapple madagascar, a concoction with rum, honey and peppercorns. The second visit yielded a remarkable warm apple sauté with graham-cracker crisps and apple pie glacé, so ample and eye-catching when we saw it at the next table that we thought it must have been prepared for a visiting dignitary (not so), and a Hudson Valley pear strudel with amaretto glacé.

All this, with a glass of wine and a beer, came with tip to about $40 for lunch for two. And, according to the computer printout that you can request for a technical but interesting diet analysis, only the cappuccino took our meal over the 1,000-calorie limit.

The dinner menu, which also changes every few days, offers similar prices except that appetizers and wood-fired pizzas are $4.25 to $7.25 and entrées, $10.50 to $15.25. We figured one couldn't spend more than about $20 for a dinner of pheasant consommé with wild-mushroom ravioli, pan-seared sturgeon fillet with Finnish potato salad and asparagus, and raspberry bavarian with a minted fruit salsa. Wines by the glass, beers and natural juices are available.

As well as eating delicious food cooked with a minimum of salt, sugar and fat, you are given solicitous service such as is rarely found nowadays. If we lived nearby, we'd be tempted to eat here every week.

(914) 471-6608. Open Monday-Friday, lunch 11:30 to 1, dinner 6 to 8.

The Caterina de Medici Dining Room, The Culinary Institute of America.
Offering a varied menu of regional Italian cuisine, this is the newest and smallest of the institute's public restaurants and has been closed to visitors whenever we've been there (as often is the case for lunch, we were told).

The room honors the Renaissance patron whose greatest contributions to European culture and culinary history were her gifts of Florentine cuisine and refinements – among them the use of the fork, the cultivation of the green bean, the creation of ice cream and the introduction of sauce-making to the French.

Today, CIA students serve up prix-fixe meals (lunch, $21; dinner, $27.95) that reflect a trend toward Italian cucina fresca. The antipasti might be grilled calamari with arugula, stuffed portobello mushroom or grilled polenta with asparagus. For main dishes, how about herb-roasted monkfish with lentils and stewed tomatoes, roasted quail with sausage stuffing or the day's whole roasted fish, carved tableside for two? Dessert could be hazelnut torte with ricotta and chocolate, or a selection of homemade gelatos and sorbets.

Italian wines are featured, of course, in this venture's stated attempt to prove to Americans that there's more to Italian cuisine than Pizza Huts. One recent grad advised that some of his peers consider it the CIA's best restaurant.

(914) 471-6608. Open Monday-Friday. Lunch seatings, 11:30 to noon, dinner, 6:30 to 7.

The Best of the Best

Xaviar's, Route 9D, Garrison.

This restaurant, launched in 1983 by Peter X. (for Xavier) Kelly when he was 23, did so well that he opened a second restaurant across the Hudson, **Xaviar's at Piermont** (506 Piermont Ave.), plus an adjacent and more casual **Freelance Cafe and Wine Bar.**

Both Xaviar's earned the highest ratings in the Zagat Restaurant Survey, near-perfect 29s, the first ever awarded in New York, Peter says proudly, and happily maintained since. (There are now six restaurants in the country with 29 ratings, and his are two.) In 1996, the two Xaviar's added an "extraordinary" rating (the first outside Manhattan) from the New York Times, which praised the kitchen's artistry and declared Xaviar's a destination for those "seeking something close to perfection in this life."

The Garrison restaurant is in the clubhouse overlooking the grounds at the Highlands Country Club. The long room with 25-foot-high ceilings holds a dozen or so well-spaced tables. It's a sight to behold, decked out in white china and linens, white fanned napkins, gleaming wine glasses, crystal candle-holders and white candles, with a glass stallion here and a silver pheasant there. Arrangements of exotic flowers in crystal vases on each table, on fireplace mantels, on sideboards and even in the rest rooms add color – the bill from the florist must be staggering. Light is provided by candles everywhere and blazing fireplaces at each end.

In a space like this, Peter says, "you couldn't do anything else but grand dining." So he canceled the weeknight dinners of long standing to concentrate on special-occasion dining on weekends only. Dinner is prix-fixe, $72 for six courses and a pairing of six wines, with a choice between two menus. The staff suggests that a party of two order both menus to best sample Peter's culinary prowess.

Part of the special-occasion dining at Garrison is the Sunday brunch buffet, $32 including champagne. The buffet, lavish as you'd expect, is supplemented by any number of foods passed from the kitchen.

Dinner in Piermont also is prix-fixe, $48 for appetizer, salad, sorbet, main course, dessert and coffee, and petits fours. Peter improvises with the best of the night there when patrons order his dégustation menu for $65.

Wine Spectator gave its Best of Award of Excellence to the Xaviar's wine cellars, which contain more than 700 selections priced from about $12 to $1,000.

Peter, very much a hands-on chef, tends to cook weekends in Garrison and during the week in Piermont.

We consider ourselves fortunate to have sampled a number of his dishes, each a triumph of taste, texture and presentation. Consider his lobster ravioli in saffron sauce, garnished with the ends of lobster tails (they look like butterflies so that's what Peter calls them) and bearing a mound of caviar in the middle and two long

Dramatic dining room at Xaviar's.   **Owner Harrald Boerger at Harralds.**

chives on top. Or the seared sea scallops, served with potato pancakes and raspberry vinaigrette with a few fresh raspberries for good measure. Or the New York
State foie gras, surrounded by sliced kiwi, strawberries and sliced pears and served
with a glass of sauternes. Best of all – in fact, one of the best dishes we've had
anywhere – is the seared Pacific tuna tartare with wasabi and soy sauce, resting on
an oversize plate, the rim garnished all the way around with dollops of red, gold
and black caviar.

Finger bowls were presented before our main courses: mignon of venison with
grand veneur sauce and the best spaetzle we've tasted, and saddle of veal with
wild mushrooms and pommes parisienne, garnished with a tomato carved to look
like a rose. Both came with tiny, barely cooked haricots verts.

Desserts here are exceptional as well. One of us had an ethereal hot raspberry
soufflé, light as air. The other tried the grand assortment, nine little samples including hazelnut dacquoise, chocolate-chestnut terrine, frozen caramel mousse,
raspberry sorbet and praline ice cream. A plate of petits fours, chocolate strawberries
and chocolate truffles finished a meal to remember.

The silverware that came and went with each course was as noticeable as all the
extra touches that went into food and presentation. "We try to give people a little
more than anyone else does," explains Peter. Indeed they do.

*Xaviar's at Garrison, (914) 424-4228: dinner, Friday and Saturday 5 to 9:30; Sunday
brunch, noon to 3. Xaviar's at Piermont, (914) 359-7007: lunch, Wednesday-Sunday
noon to 2; dinner, Wednesday-Sunday 6 to 9. Freelance Cafe & Wine Bar: lunch and
dinner, Tuesday-Sunday.*

Harrald's, 3110 Route 52, Stormville.

Reservations are essential at this unlikely-looking establishment, for eighteen
years rated one of the dozen or so five-star Mobil Guide restaurants in the country
and widely revered since its opening in 1971. We tried unsuccessfully two weeks

ahead to reserve for a Friday – "we only have thirteen tables," the host reminded. There are two seatings on Saturdays, and the meal takes three leisurely hours.

Yellow lanterns and meticulous landscaping give something of a Japanese look to the Swiss-Tudor house that reflects the tastes and work of proprietor Harrald Boerger. He proudly introduced his wife, Ava Durrschmidt, "the only woman chef-owner in the United States of a five-star restaurant," who explained in a Swiss-German accent her philosophy that "simplicity is elegance." Until recently, hers was a kitchen in which men were not allowed to cook.

Three-foot-high blackboard menus are wheeled to the table, outlining the night's variations on seasonal dishes. Dinner is prix-fixe ($60 for six courses, with a $35 option for three courses on Wednesdays and Thursdays). It's served in three small, intimate rooms by waiters who perhaps intimidate more than the outgoing and down-to-earth Harrald, who usually visits each table during the course of the evening. The experience is designed to make guests think they are dining in a home rather than a restaurant, he says.

The meal might start with a choice of home-smoked rainbow trout (the house specialty), crab cakes, a galantine of veal and diced tongue with cashews and green peppers, and a poached egg en cocotte with diced chicken, ham, mushrooms and truffles. The soup course involves a classic French onion with emmenthaler cheese and a choice of one hot and one cold each evening, perhaps a light toasted almond crème and a cold Russian-Polish specialty called okroshka.

A mixed green salad with the house vinaigrette or country herb dressing precedes the main course. Typical choices are poached or sautéed trout au bleu with dill sauce, veal roast with pan gravy and dumplings, steak au poivre, stuffed free-range poussin, canard au cassis and zuricher rahm schnitzel served with four kinds of mushrooms.

Prior to dessert and coffee, a cart brings a selection of fresh fruits, cheeses, nuts and a glass or two of good port. Dessert could be chocolate sabayon cake, chocolate mousse made with Swiss Lindt chocolate, linzertorte or fresh fruit topped with whipped or heavy cream.

Before dinner, you might have drinks on the terrace or stroll the park-like grounds. The trout come from an outdoor tank that looks like a wishing well and has water so fresh it's poured as drinking water – "people bring containers to take some home," says Harrald. Another special touch is a small 200-year-old farmhouse used as a wine cellar with an extensive, 250-vintage selection that is "cheaper than any place I know, because wines should be affordable." Outside the wine house is an old-fashioned swing. Harrald explains: "My wife said she'd like a swing for her birthday. So I built her one for $12."

Harrald does not advertise because it embarrasses him and he doesn't need to. "I put the money I save back into serving our guests," he says. "We're giving them the very best of the best."

Local reviewers variously praise individual items as the best they've had, but it is the entire experience – from soup to nuts, as it were – that earned Harrald's its five stars year after year. Even after the new producers of the Mobil Guide changed their criteria in 1996 and reduced his rating to four stars (he was surprised to learn of it in the newspapers), Harrald remained philosophical. "We've had our day," he said. "We're not going to change a thing."

(914) 878-6595. Dinner, Wednesday-Saturday 6 to 9 (two seatings Saturday at 6 and 9:15). Closed January to mid-February. Reservations and jackets required. No credit cards.

McKinney & Doyle Fine Foods Cafe, 10 Charles Colman Blvd., Pawling.
The highest accolades go to this cafe, a fortuitous outgrowth of the well-known
Corner Bakery. "Excellent," declared the New York Times critic. "An all-time
favorite," swooned the Poughkeepsie Journal reviewer. Young partners Shannon
McKinney and Brian Doyle moved in 1992 to expanded quarters in the center of
Pawling from a smaller bakery that had attracted national notice. Shannon continues to man the bakery, while Brian has turned his attention to the expanding
restaurant operation.

And a fine restaurant it is. Sophisticated, stunningly executed fare is served in a
comfortable, homespun atmosphere. The old-fashioned, high-ceilinged storefront
cafe is a mix of booths and tables that came from an old Pawling pub, bare floors
and exposed brick walls holding local memorabilia and art displays. Many and
changing are the touches of whimsy: words of dining wisdom here and there; a
shelf bearing bricks, shutters, a clothesline with pins and an old flag; a beehive in
a ficus tree, and a window display with an amusing picture of chefs exercising
amid an array of spring-form pans. Brian lends his decorating skills and laconic
wit to a space that exudes personality.

His kitchen talents are equally diverse. For dinner, you might start with grilled
shrimp with Thai peanut sauce over angel-hair pasta or cornmeal-encrusted oysters
spiked with a Tanqueray horseradish ketchup. The night's entrées ($17 to $22,
served with an exceptional green salad) could be pan-seared cayenne red snapper
with braised legumes and sweet corn broth, crispy lemon-pepper duck breast with
peach chutney and ginger rice cakes, grilled veal chop with sundried tomato-
rosemary cream and filet mignon with mushroom ragoût and ancho chile sauce.
Save room for one of the bakery's fabulous desserts, perhaps triple-decker sour
cream raspberry pound cake, white chocolate pistachio mousse or the house special,
"shattered chocolate panacotta."

Interesting fare also is offered at lunch ($5.75 to $9.50), perhaps a soup of shrimp
and scallops in a creamy sauternes-leek broth, a sampler of several salads, Shannon's
"hogbreath vegetarian chili" with grilled jalapeño cornbread or a sandwich of
roasted chicken and apricot salad served on a just-baked baguette. Brunch brings
a panoply of egg dishes, banana pancakes, smoked salmon on bagels, and corned-
beef hash served in its own cast-iron skillet with a shirred egg and bakery toast.

The wine list is good and affordable, with many available by the glass. Also
offered are interesting ales and lagers. The adjacent bakery dispenses all kinds of
baked goods as well as quite a variety of foods to take out under the logo of
McKinney & Doyle.

Oktoberfest beer-tasting dinners, wine tastings, a Christmas madrigal dinner,
art exhibitions, mail-order – it takes their Word of Mouth newsletter just to follow
all that these engaging guys are up to.

In 1994, they added a smaller **East Branch Cafe** along Route 22 in Brewster,
offering a similar menu and price range. With an open kitchen and landscaped
grounds overlooking the East Branch Reservoir, it's open Thursday-Sunday for
brunch from 7 to 3 and dinner from 6 to 10.

*(914) 855-3875. Lunch, Tuesday-Friday 11:30 to 3; dinner, Tuesday-Sunday 6 to 9:30;
weekend brunch, 9 to 2.*

Xe Sogni, Route 44, Amenia.
Here's the recipe for one remarkable little Italian osteria. Enter the CIA at age

Shannon McKinney and Brian Doyle run Fine Foods Cafe and Corner Bakery.

17, train at the Old Drovers Inn (see below), work for your father in a gelato manufacturing company and buy out the other partner. Turn the front of the building into a restaurant, tuck an open kitchen into a corner, and cook up "Italian soul food" that changes every few days.

The recipe spelled success for Jason Thomas. With his father Michael as partner ("he's the worrier; I'm the cook") and his expectant wife and his mother as waitresses, he started with eighteen seats in 1995 and added fourteen more a year later. He now offers a series of cooking classes here in the winter. The remarkable thing is that Jason was only 20 when he opened, and has never been to Italy. "That amazes all my customers," he concedes.

The obscure, hard-to-pronounce ("zay son-yay") name is Venetian dialect for "these dreams" and this, for Jason, is the fulfillment of a dream. The two snug dining rooms are enchanting. The new room looks rather like a Renaissance chapel with arched ceiling, sponged yellow walls and handmade mirrors and sconces. The convivial original is surrounded by a floor-to-ceiling mural of the Tuscan countryside, painted by a friend who lives in West Africa, which seems to expand the small space and draw the visitor into the scene. You feel as if you're dining on the terrace of an Italian vineyard, with the aromas from a wood-fired oven filling the air.

The open kitchen yields a succession of tasty treats. For starters ($3 to $6.50), how about the house-baked bruschetta, fried calamari with a smoked tomato sauce or a mixed grill of portobello, shiitake and crimini mushrooms? Three pasta dishes can be ordered as appetizers or main courses. The main event ($17.75 to $20) could be grilled swordfish on herbed orzo, grilled duck or organic quail, veal chops with wild mushroom and marsala sauce, or medallions of beef tenderloin with horseradish-yogurt sauce. Sides of vegetables ($3) include braised red cabbage with prosciutto and apples. A couple of exotic salads are recommended to follow the main course.

Desserts ($4 to $5), like everything else, are made here by this one-man show. Expect raspberry or blackberry crème brûlée, cranberry-blueberry-peach pie, or apple and spice ice cream.

(914) 373-7755. Dinner, Wednesday-Sunday from 6. BYOB.

DePuy Canal House, Route 213, High Falls.

This National Historic Landmark, built of stone in 1797 by Simeon DePuy to serve travelers along the Delaware and Hudson Canal, is everyone's dream of what a cozy tavern should be.

Snowshoes, baskets, lanterns and the like hang from dark beamed ceilings, the floors are wide planked and sloping, fires are lit in season in four big fireplaces, and antiques, dried berries, fresh flowers and chintz abound. The china is Staffordshire, the cutlery pewter, and placemats an unusual blue slate. Dining is in two small downstairs rooms (the main dining room, reminiscent of a Colonial keeping room, seats only eighteen) and three more upstairs. Although High Falls native John Novi has owned his restaurant since 1969, he's always improving, adding an arbor-covered bluestone patio for more casual outdoor dining, opening a weekend cabaret in the basement art gallery with a bar fashioned from a century-old bank teller's cage, offering take-out ice cream in summer and preparing a line of food products to be sold in the New York Store planned behind the restaurant.

Best of all, Novi is an imaginative cook, whom Time magazine called "the father of New American cooking" in a 1985 article. He likes guests to come into his elegant black and white tiled kitchen, where a table for four or six can be booked at no extra charge. You also can watch the kitchen goings-on from an upstairs balcony.

Dinner is served from a changing prix-fixe menu of three courses (soup or salad, entrée and dinner, $28, not available Saturdays or holidays), four courses ($36), seven courses ($49), or à la carte (soup and appetizers, $5 to $22; entrées, $17.50 to $30; desserts, $4 to $12, and variations thereof). The variations make for some confusion, as do some of the contents – "shrimp sashimi with kirfir leaf in hot!! chili red sauce served with frozen cilantro crushed ice," "portobello with stones ginger wine sauce" and "smoked salmon-wasabi tobiko caviar-lobster tomalley mayonnaise served with Hanz copper blue corn chip sculpture."

Meals begin with a freebie or two: a pissaladière (small pizza) with baby peas and fresh mozzarella, and a clam strip with lemon and parsley on belgian endive at one visit. Soups could be caramelized leek and shiitake mushroom with milk drops of Norwegian gjetost cheese on edible paper or pear custard in hot sake with crumbled feta cheese on the side.

Instead of soup, how about a Russian pâté zakuska – smoked ham-hock pâté served with mustard byrd sauce, Paris toast and a shot glass of Russian pepper vodka? Other appetizers might be "reel of pasta, a Canal House original" pairing carrot pasta and ricotta cheese on a diced-tomato sauce; dandelion and soft Catskill goat cheese and "hard bread spread with roasted garlic," and foie gras and grilled radicchio on duck glace. Expect garnishes of dried day lilies, raw rhubarb or scallops soaked in beet juice and rolled in parsley and sesame seeds to look like strawberries,

Jason Thomas takes break from cooking duties in Xe Sogni dining room.

as we encountered at a springtime dinner (our pre-dinner manhattan came with a slice of apple instead of a cherry).

A complimentary sorbet, perhaps fennel, precedes the entrée in the four- and seven-course dinners, and by this time the waiter may suggest a stroll through the house or a look at the kitchen. Your main course might be soft-shell crab and conch cutlet with spinach timbale, grilled lamb tenderloin served in a tortilla basket cooked in a black iron skillet, or loin of goat with hearts of palm and sausage stuffing. The salad, composed of four types of greens and a mild Italian dressing, may be garnished with popcorn.

If you order the whole meal, you get a fruit bowl and a platter of three cheeses before dessert. The last could be Mama Novi's chocolate cake, English custard on mocha sauce or a special chocolate soufflé with brandy cream sauce.

The extensive wine list includes a number of Hudson Valley offerings.

Ever the entrepreneur, John has opened a B&B called the **Locktender Cottage** across the street. It offers two bedrooms with private baths ($85) and a second-floor suite with kitchenette and jacuzzi ($110). Lately he has sponsored semi-annual "epicurean road rallies for food-loving motorists." They begin with breakfast, include pit stops with snacks and lunch at historic sites, and end with a champagne reception at the Canal House.

(914) 687-7700. Dinner, Thursday-Saturday 5 to 10; Sunday, brunch 11:30 to 2, dinner 4 to 9.

The Thymes, 11 Main St., Kingston.

Not long after opening, chef Daniel Smith and his year-old restaurant walked off with seven awards, including the Grand Award, in the Taste of the Hudson Valley culinary competitions. It came as no surprise to those who knew him, for he also had swept the competition two years earlier when he was chef at the Beekman Arms across the river in Rhinebeck. Earlier, this graduate of La Varenne Cooking School in Paris had won a medal in the 1980 Culinary Olympics in Frankfurt.

Awards alone weren't responsible for making this uptown Kingston establishment one of the better restaurants in the Hudson Valley (and the launching pad for a newer endeavor, the more casual **Jake Moon Restaurant and Cafe** in nearby Big Indian). A comfortable, convivial atmosphere pervades the front bar and dining room beyond. Sixty patrons can be seated in both rooms at tables covered with white linens at night. The turn-of-the-century decor includes a beautiful mahogany bar, dark wood wainscoting, mauve mini-print wallpaper, a brick wall, brass sconces, high ceilings and other vestiges of the building's heritage as the City Hotel, circa 1905.

All that rich wood gives off a rosy glow after dark, as we found during a leisurely November dinner. The menu is reasonably priced for the area: soups, appetizers, salads and sandwiches for $2.75 to $7.95 and entrées from $10.95 for fettuccine with mushrooms and toasted almonds to $17.50 for rack of New Zealand lamb slivered with garlic and roasted with pinot noir demi-glace. Our meal began with good, crusty rolls and scoops of three different butters – basil, tomato-garlic and lightly salted – inspiring spirited debate over which was best. Next came a huge "cup" of seafood minestrone that was unfortunately light on seafood and four skewers of spicy chicken satay, spiked like stalks into a lemon resting in a pool of peanut sauce crossed with a ribbon of onions. Main courses were pan-seared arctic char bearing a superior mushroom sauce and robust pork medallions with cara-melized apples and roquefort cream. The plates were artfully presented with slivered beets, beans and carrots plus a timbale of rice. An $18 bottle of Markham sauvignon blanc accompanied from a short, expensive wine list priced up to $200. Desserts were pumpkin bread pudding and a plate of intense homemade sorbets – pineapple-orange, green tea and mixed fruit.

A Pacific Rim wine dinner was on tap at our latest visit. "I also can make French, German, Chinese, Italian or Mexican food and I'm free to call it modern American," says Dan. His legion of fans calls it wonderful.

(914) 338-0434. Lunch, Tuesday-Friday 11:30 to 3; dinner, Tuesday-Saturday 5 to 10.

Cafe Tamayo, 89 Partition St., Saugerties.

The dining scene on the west bank of the Hudson has been enhanced by this large, sprightly restaurant in a restored 1864 downtown tavern in the rustic riverfront village of Saugerties. James Tamayo, a CIA graduate who worked in New York at the Russian Tea Room, the Plaza and Green Street Cafe, sought a smaller venue of his own. He and his wife Rickie, who ran a theater in Woodstock, had summered in the area and "wanted a hometown." Their double storefront is a surprisingly large, somewhat theatrical space with bare floors, pine wainscoting, high molded ceilings, green trim and stenciling here and there. More than 100 patrons can spread out at well-spaced, white-linened tables facing the original massive walnut bar, a couple of rear dining sections, a more formal side dining room and an outdoor patio alongside.

Support from the local community was a long time coming, Rickie said. The couple survived with a contingent of regulars from Manhattan, who liked to feast on such delicacies as pompano (obtained from New York's Fulton Fish Market and served with an herb vinaigrette and saffron rice), braised rabbit, confit of duck and pan-roasted venison. The menu changes nightly, but the price of the main courses ($14 to $19) always includes a salad (red-leaf with balsamic vinaigrette) to appease the locals.

Of Mexican descent, James adds the spicy bite of chile peppers to such favorite dishes as capellini tossed with tomato, garlic, gaeta olives and pecorino cheese or mussels in an olive-oil, garlic and tomato broth. Other starters ($5 to $6.50) could be grilled shrimp and cannellini bean salad, rabbit bolognese, and an acclaimed grated potato pancake encasing slivers of house-smoked salmon.

Among desserts are crème brûlée, chocolate-truffle cake with raspberry sauce, biscotti and homemade sorbets – blackberry, pineapple and melon, when we were there. An expanding wine list is priced mainly in the teens and twenties.

Many of the appetizers turn up on the lunch menu ($5.50 to $8.50), which ranges widely from a gruyère and mushroom omelet to a hot roast pork sandwich.

Upstairs, the couple offer two simple B&B rooms with brass beds and private baths for $75 a night.

(914) 246-9371. Lunch, Thursday-Sunday 11 to 2; dinner, Wednesday-Sunday 5 to 9:30 or 10; Sunday brunch, 11:30 to 3.

The Would Bar & Grill, 120 North Road, Highland.

A former gin mill – her words – with a curious name winning the grand prize among restaurants in the Northeast in a national ranking by Restaurants & Institutions magazine? "I was just overwhelmed," said Claire Winslow, the chef who turned her parents' neighborhood bar around and firmly implanted it on the local culinary map.

Claire, a 1985 Culinary Institute grad, had planned to return to California to work for noted chef Brad Ogden, with whom she had done her externship. She decided instead to stay in her home area and apply her cooking talents to changing the image of the Applewood Bar, located in a complex of two old and undistinguished apartment buildings seemingly at the edge of nowhere. "We started small and now it's grown around us," Claire said of her restaurant's locally high profile and its inordinate number of Taste of the Hudson Valley culinary awards.

The derivation of the restaurant's shortened name from Applewood is obscure, but there's no mistaking the quality and creativity of the food served in the main barroom, from which Claire and her partner removed the TV set and pool table, and the adjoining dining room, nicely upgraded with white tablecloths, modern oil lamps and fresh flowers.

The fairly ambitious dinner menu is the kind that makes choosing difficult. For starters ($7.25 to $8.25), how about fried escargot and forest mushroom wontons with a tarragon-roasted garlic sauce, oysters poached in Guinness and served on napa cabbage slaw or grilled smoked quail with arugula pesto and pomegranate molasses? Or a salad ($3.75 to $5.95) of oriental field greens with Chinese noodles in a safflower dressing, or another with mesclun greens tossed with Peekskill Pyramid cheese, pinenuts and fig vinaigrette?

Entrées range widely from $14.95 for penne with locally smoked chicken in saffron-fennel sauce to $23.95 for grilled noisettes of lamb. Manila clams might be teamed with mussels and andouille sausage over linguini, and curried grilled shrimp with pineapple-citrus salsa and mango puree. Expect innovations like medallions of venison wrapped with spinach, roasted red pepper and rice paper and served with Asian wild mushroom salad.

The pastry chef knows what she's doing. Terrific breads (perhaps pesto, raisin and nut, focaccia and cinnamon swirl) start the meal. White chocolate heath bar cheesecake, carrot cake with apple/sweet-potato puree and chocolate/peanut-butter pound cake with caramelized bananas and banana crème anglaise are worthy endings.

New dimensions are given to the bar and grill's lunch menu ($5.50 to $12.95) with such offerings as oriental chicken salad with roasted almonds and Chinese noodles, a salmon gravlax BLT on toasted oat bread, and grilled salmon with roasted shallots and black currant sauce..

Honored by Wine Spectator, the wine list features boutique offerings from Rhode Island to Oregon as well as imports. Most are in the $16 to $30 range. A reserve list is priced up to $150.

(914) 691-9883. Lunch, Monday-Friday 11:30 to 2; dinner nightly, 5 to 9 or 10.

The Inn at Osborne Hill, 150 Osborne Hill Road, Fishkill.

Geese seem to be the theme at this country restaurant, from the sign outside to the simple but pretty decor inside. The food is far from simple, and since Michele and Frank Nola set up business in 1988, their reputation has spread far and wide. Thomas Hoving, no less, wrote in Connoisseur magazine that they had created one of America's top restaurants. Both CIA grads, they'd had experience in Fairfield County restaurants in Connecticut. Along with devising a sophisticated menu, Frank, a native Californian, has built a 6,000-bottle wine cellar that earned the restaurant a three-page spread in Wine Spectator.

Except for stale rolls, we were quite impressed with a weekday lunch. The blackboard menu ($6.50 to $9.95) yielded a superb linguini with rock shrimp, scallions, mushrooms and tomatoes in a lobster-cream sauce and a potent sweet-and-sour oriental pheasant soup, which we teamed with an appetizer of shrimp and crab cakes, small and precious with squiggles of sauce and flecks of herbs. The small appetizer left one of us hungry, so we shared the dessert sampler plate. It turned out on the bill to have been a $7.95 indulgence of white-chocolate mousse on a designed bed of raspberry coulis, chocolate-pecan mousse cake, the specialty profiteroles and a couple of scoops of cassis and lemon-mint sorbet.

At night, the understated menu might list such appetizers ($4.95 to $7.95) as duck confit quesadilla with cranberry-cumberland sauce, chilled seafood sausage with cucumber relish, and sea scallops and dried tomatoes in phyllo bowls. Entrées ($14.95 to $22.95) could include brook trout with crisp pancetta and provençal sauce, grilled salmon with Tex-Mex salsa and corn cakes, calves liver with prosciutto and red onions, strip steak with oriental butter and wonton crisps, and loin of veal with artichokes and shiitake mushrooms. Accompanying starches might be nut pilaf, minted barley or red bliss potatoes. The salad is a mix of exotic greens. Dessert could be apple dumpling with warm caramel sauce or a frozen mango soufflé.

All this good eating takes place in two small beamed and wainscoted rooms with sleek black lacquered chairs, cream-colored linens, tiny oil lamps and bare floors. A small outdoor deck beckons in good weather.

As for his award-winning wine list, Frank says it features "my favorites, hard-to-find varieties or both." The father of two young sons, he refers to his wine cellar as "my third child."

(914) 897-3055. Lunch, Monday-Friday 11:30 to 2:30; dinner, Monday-Saturday 5 to 9 or 10.

Le Pavillon, 230 Salt Point Tpke. (Route 115), Poughkeepsie.

A brick Victorian house on the outskirts of town is home to an intimate, country-French restaurant run by chef-owner Claude Guermont, who was born in Normandy and apprenticed himself to a French chef at age 14. After a stint as an instructor at the CIA's Escoffier Restaurant, he opened Le Pavillon in 1980 against the prevailing

Frank and Michele Nola have won acclaim for their Inn at Osborne Hill.

wisdom that a fine restaurant could not survive in the area. In 1985, he wrote *The Norman Table*, an acclaimed cookbook of 200 regional recipes from his native land.

You enter through a vestibule lined with clippings ("Chef has never really left Normandy," headlines one) into a brick and beamed bar. Dining is by candlelight in two intimate front dining rooms, each accommodating thirty. French posters and art, white service plates bearing a discreet Le Pavillon logo, black candles in small hurricane lamps and white linens contribute to a charming setting.

The French menu is pleasantly priced, $17.50 to $21.50 for entrées or $30 prix-fixe for three courses. "I try to stay with local products, make everything here and try to be a little contemporary – but not entirely classic or nouvelle," Claude says.

Among appetizers ($6.50 to $7.50), his crisp frog's legs with burgundy garlic sauce and escargots baked in brandy-garlic sauce are highly rated. So are his Normandy-style onion soup and the shrimp bisque with sherry.

The dozen or so entrées could include salmon fillet niçoise, dover sole meunière, sautéed sweetbreads with capers, veal kidneys in spicy mustard sauce and roast duck with honey-bigarade sauce. New Zealand venison, quail au poivre, rabbit with mustard sauce and other game dishes are offered when available.

Desserts ($5 to $6) are hot soufflés and crêpes suzette, as well as French pastries, profiteroles, homemade sorbets and the like. Le Pavillon's wine list ranges widely from Hudson Valley vintages to French châteaux.

A blackboard menu offers cassoulet, grilled swordfish with pesto, pheasant sauté and other items in the $8.95 to $14.95 range for lunch.

(914) 473-2525. Lunch, Tuesday-Friday noon to 2, September-June; dinner, Monday-Saturday 5:30 to 10.

California Spirit

Cascade Mountain Winery & Restaurant, Flint Hill Road, Amenia.

Why is a winery listed under dining choices? Because this out-of-the-way place is a gem, known as much for its creative food prepared from local ingredients as for its award-winning wines and a funky, California kind of spirit. In fact, we almost felt we were on a Napa Valley hillside the first sunny autumn day we lingered on one of several decks overlooking the apple orchards, enjoying a bottle of seyval blanc and some appealing luncheon fare.

The food is the work of chef David Viertel, who returned in 1996 from, of all places, the Napa Valley. Both he and his wife Donna, the hostess and bread baker, are CIA grads who had been at the famed Sonoma Mission Inn and Spa. David prepares candlelit wine-tasting dinners on Saturday nights in the winery's homey dining room to "show off our local wines and food products." Dinner is à la carte, with entrées from $15.50 for grilled pork tenderloin with cherry vignoles sauce to $19.50 for grilled veal chop with sage brown butter.

We got a tantalizing taste of the fare at a recent lunch. Our party of four enjoyed a thick butternut-squash soup, a gingered carrot soup, a clear leek soup with roasted garlic and a foie gras pâté with cranberry chutney. Then we dug into an excellent smoked-trout plate, a pâté and goat-cheese plate, a mustardy maple chicken salad with green and red grapes, and grilled chicken breast – grilled right on the deck – stuffed with Coach Farm goat cheese (all in the $8.50 to $9.50 range, although prices go up to $13 for grilled ahi tuna with herb pesto). An apple-pear crisp, a plum tart with lavender crème anglaise, spiced maple cheesecake with gingersnap crust and a chocolate-raspberry marjolaine ended a leisurely, memorable meal. The bill was written on the back of a wine label.

After lunch, we stepped gingerly around workmen to enter the main winery downstairs, an unexpectedly small and primitive affair, considering the merit of its output (it made the strongest showing of any winery east of the Rockies at a couple of wine competitions). The chief workman at our first visit turned out to be William Wetmore, owner-winemaker and author of four novels, a jack-of-all-trades who produces almost as many red wines as whites because of his grape-planting decisions more than two decades ago.

A couple of typewritten sheets inside cellophane wrappers point out salient facets of winemaking for self-guided tours. Visitors taste wines in the crowded and convivial downstairs setting, where no one takes things too seriously. How could they, at a place where a couple of favorite bottlings were called "Le Hamburger" and "Pardonnez-Moi," the latter billed as a dry red wine "for social emergencies" but also a play on the word chardonnay.

Such is the homespun fun of Cascade Mountain Vineyards, a place full of integrity. *(914) 373-9021. Lunch daily except Wednesday, 11:30 to 3; light menu, 3 to 5 (also Wednesday 11:30 to 3); dinner Saturday by reservation, 6 to 9. Closed in March.*

More Dining Choices

Le Canard Enchaîne, 278 Fair St., Kingston.

Chamonix in the French Alps was home for chef Jean Carquillat, who trained in Paris and New York before marrying the daughter of Catskills restaurateurs and launching his own ever-so-French bistro in 1996 in uptown Kingston. "Welcome to the South of France," proclaimed their opening menu. "Delicious," advised one local connoisseur when asked what she thought of the low-key newcomer.

Jean and his wife, Jennifer Madden, have created a bistro that looks as if it belongs on the main street of Avignon. Two side-by-side storefront rooms have high ceilings and lace curtains in the windows. A small bar anchors the end of one room. Center stage in the other, larger dining area is taken by a display case, revealing everything from assorted pâtés to salads to dessert pastries for a make-your-own gourmet picnic.

Local folks come in for a continental breakfast of homemade croissants and cafe au lait, served as it is in France in "a big bowl," Jean notes. Lunch could be a sampling from more than a dozen salads or a sandwich, perhaps grilled cajun chicken with watercress on a baguette.

The namesake duck is the specialty at dinner, offered in three presentations varying from grilled with orange-fennel sauce on braised endives to roasted with grilled sweet potatoes. Other entrées are priced from $15 for grilled free-range chicken with basil and garlic mashed potatoes to $18.50 for sautéed rack of lamb on a pyramid of spiced broccoli puree. Start with mussels meunière or fricassee of escargots with asparagus and shiitake mushrooms flamed in cognac. Finish with crème brûlée, tarte tatin or another of the specialty fruit tarts.

(914) 339-2003. Open daily, 10 to 10, weekends to 11.

Le Petit Bistro, 8 East Market St., Rhinebeck.

Yvonne and Jean-Paul Croizer were at Auberge 32 in Kingston before they moved to Rhinebeck in 1986 to open an establishment held in high esteem by locals. The space used to be occupied by a Greek restaurant, and the Croizers didn't have to do much to the pine walls and floors to give it a country-French theme. Except for globe lamps inside wooden frames, the decor is simple and the atmosphere convivial and intimate. There are 40 seats in the dining room and a half-circle bar at the side.

From Jean-Paul's classic French menu, start with onion soup, pâté maison, smoked trout or escargots ($4.75 to $7.25). Entrées go from $14.75 for the chicken special that changes weekly to $19.95 for dover sole meunière. Sea scallops with crushed black peppercorns and cream sauce, duck with orange sauce, veal piccata, frog's legs, rack of lamb provençal and steak au poivre are other choices.

Desserts include crème caramel, mocha mousse, raspberry frappe and peach melba. "People tell me the lemon pie is the best around," says the chef. The fairly extensive wine list mixes French and domestic at prices from $12 to $85.

(914) 876-7400. Dinner, Thursday-Monday 5 to 10, Sunday 4 to 9.

Bois d'Arc, 29 West Market St., Red Hook.

A small and snazzy cafe, the former Green & Bresler was taken over in 1994 by James Jennings, a CIA grad from eastern Texas, who oversees the kitchen with a couple of CIA-trained assistants. They added a side patio for seasonal use, but most of the dining takes place in a subdued storefront space with gray walls, white-clothed tables and black chairs. About the only visual color comes from the flowers painted on a mural above the bar at the far end.

Plenty of color emanates from the dinner menu, which changes weekly. It's short but sweet and carries a southern accent. Expect main courses ($16.95 to

$20.95) like seared sesame-crusted salmon with ginger-garlic sauce and scallion potato pancakes, house-smoked pork chop with cheddar gratin potatoes and collard greens, and pan-seared black angus filet mignon wrapped in bacon with fried zucchini. Appetizers range widely from chilled corn soup with oregano and chives ($5.50) to poached lobster and mussels on pea spaetzle with baby carrots ($11.95). Venison carpaccio and crispy smoked sweetbreads with a potato web are among the choices. An appropriate wine is suggested for each. Desserts ($5) include a shortcake with fresh fruit, a changing cheesecake, homemade ice cream served in a tuile and fallen chocolate soufflé cake.

Many of the appetizers turn up on the lunch menu. The with-it compendium ($8.95 to $12.95) ranges from Jim's favorite East Texas pulled pork barbecue sandwich to pan-fried salmon cakes and sautéed crawfish with andouille sausage over homemade pasta. Accompaniments include cheddar gratin potatoes, collard greens, corn-crusted okra and others of the "sides" from the evening menu. The herbs come from the young chef's garden in back.

(914) 758-5992. Lunch, Friday-Sunday 11:30 to 2:30, spring through fall; dinner nightly, 5:30 to 9:30.

Santa Fe, 52 Broadway, Tivoli.

Margaritas are a claim to fame of this restaurant in a colorful burnished plum building at the only intersection in the one-horse riverside hamlet of Tivoli. It's long been held in high regard by aficionados of serious Mexican fare. So much so that owner David Weiss, who has traveled extensively in Mexico and knows well its cuisine, has expanded from 25 seats to 150 in three dining areas on the main floor and another upstairs. The decor is colorful: woven rugs adorn the salmon-colored walls and the ceiling has been painted blue. Votive candles flicker in brandy snifters.

Margaritas come by the glass or pitcher and in flavors from peach to raspberry to cuervo to blue curaçao, served up with gusto from the ornate bar. Although Santa Fe started with strictly authentic Mexican food made from scratch, as its reputation grew, David added "eclectic Southwestern fare" and an emphasis on grilling.

Now you'll find the tried-and-true Mexican standbys supplemented by an appetizer of sundried-tomato and goat-cheese quesadilla or a shrimp chimichanga, rolled up like a spring roll and served with a homemade ginger broth. Among entrées ($7.95 to $15.95), the Oaxacan taco is a corn tortilla with grilled chicken, cheddar, cilantro and homemade molé made with thirteen kinds of dried chiles. The spicy Baja shrimp satay comes with a peanut sauce, sweet plantains and curry. The grilled pork tenderloin is marinated in Dos Equis dark beer and served with mango salsa. The grilled strip steak might come with a chipotle pepper and goat cheese sauce. The vegetarian stew pairs Santa Fe black beans with melted Wisconsin cheddar. Save room for dessert, perhaps homemade flan, ginger crème brûlée or key lime pie.

(914) 757-4100. Dinner, Tuesday-Sunday 5 to 10. Closed in January.

The Church Street Cafe, East Church Street, Pine Plains.

Richard Reeve left as chef at Cascade Mountain Winery to open his own cafe in a former deli in his hometown. He and partner Maya Karrol outfitted the place in country-rustic white and blue, with ten tables in front and a large open kitchen in back. They initially served lunch, "but that didn't work out," according to Richard. So now they concentrate on dinner.

The contemporary menu features such appetizers ($5 to $6.50) as crostini with caramelized onions and Coach Farm goat cheese, a stacked warm roasted eggplant and red pepper salad, smoked duck with cranberry chutney and frisée and smoked trout mousse with pickled onions and gaufrettes, a delicacy that we had enjoyed earlier at Cascade. One of those and a pasta dish ($9.50 to $12.95) makes a fine meal.

But most diners choose a main course ($12.50 to $15.50), particularly a seafood choice from the blackboard: salmon en brodo, pan-seared and served with wilted greens over mashed potatoes with aioli the night we were there. Other possibilities could be a signature roasted local chicken with cider-shallot-bacon sauce, beef bourguignonne, and grilled rib-eye steak with madeira and wild mushrooms.

Typical desserts are caramelized apple tart with whipped vanilla fromage blanc, chocolate bouchée with chocolate brandy glaze, and old-fashioned gingerbread with pumpkin crème brûlée ice cream from Ronnybrook Farm Dairy. Local wines are featured, nicely priced in the teens and twenties.

(518) 398-6755. Dinner, Thursday-Monday 5:30 to 9 or 10; Sunday brunch, 11:30 to 2.

Calico Restaurant & Patisserie, 9 Mill St. (Route 9), Rhinebeck.

A perfect five-star rating from the Poughkeepsie restaurant reviewer followed the opening of this intimate little charmer in a twenty-seat storefront across from the famous Beekman Arms. The stars were for the food offered by CIA grad Tony Balassone, an alumnus of Le Pavillon in Poughkeepsie, and the baked goods of his wife Leslie.

The patisserie in front opens at 7 a.m. for croissants and brioche. Come lunch time, the kitchen offers a handful of interesting choices ($6.95 to $8.95), perhaps seafood chili with cornbread, house-smoked salmon fillet served on a mixture of greens and roasted porcini mushrooms, pizza of the day and sliced flank steak on a toasted baguette. The gratinéed vidalia onion soup laced with Anchor Steam ale makes a good starter. So does the roasted garlic soup with crème fraîche and herbed brioche croutons.

At night, Tony prepares such entrées ($14.95 to $17.95) as bouillabaisse, seafood risotto, seared Asian-marinated salmon fillet over warm rice salad, breast of duck with cranberry-champagne cream sauce and wild rice pancakes, and breast of chicken stuffed with spinach and goat cheese.

Artifacts and calico items adorn a shelf above the pale blue wainscoting of this pure and simple place beloved by the locals. It has a full liquor license.

(914) 876-2749. Lunch, Wednesday-Sunday 11 to 3:30; dinner, Wednesday-Sunday 5:30 to 9:30 or 10:30.

Budget Gourmet

Cafe Pongo, 69 Broadway, Tivoli.

This began as the Tivoli Bread Co., an offshoot of the well-known Santa Fe restaurant up the street. When the bakery expanded into an all-day cafe, co-owner Valerie Nehez sold her share of Santa Fe to David Weiss and concentrated her efforts here.

Bakers start at 3 a.m., making up to ten kinds of organic breads from scratch as well as interesting pastries, everything from chocolate-espresso torte to cranberry-walnut tea bread to focaccia incorporating goat's-milk ricotta. The cafe serves breakfast fare both ordinary (granola and scones) and exotic (salmon benedict, huevos rancheros) for weekend brunch. Robust lunches, mainly sandwiches and a few salads and plates (salmon, hummus or fruit and cheese), are offered at midday.

The kitchen comes into its own at night, when the fare ranges from healthful to indulgent, with plenty of it. Upon being seated, you're served a basket of homemade breads and three accompaniments: infused olive oil, a vegan chipotle sauce and shaved cheese.

There arc a few appetizers and salads, but perhaps you had better go easy on them. For ahead are entrées ($8 to $13) like half a roasted chicken, marinated flank steak and broiled shrimp with rice and shaved romano. Or Pongo pastas: perhaps stewed chicken with penne and sundried tomatoes over sautéed garlic kale, or pan-seared penne with spinach, toasted pinenuts, braised savoy cabbage and shrimp. Or "steam pots" served in pewter pots: the house-smoked fillet of salmon, served Thai style with coconut milk, crispy leeks, steamed greens and angel-hair pasta, or Moroccan-style lamb with couscous and more in a wine-cinnamon-cumin broth. Incredibly, even most of the meat items on this earthy, vegetarian-friendly menu are $10 or under.

Desserts from the bakery follow suit, but only the seriously hungry have room. One of us sat at the bar/counter and lunched on a tarragon chicken sandwich served on a hefty baguette with roasted rosemary potatoes ($5.95) that proved to be a meal and a half. The coffee comes in bottomless white mugs, there's a full license and you may sit, as we did, next to Valerie's dog Pongo leashed at the bar. The casual, convivial place has a decidedly hip (or hippie) air. The day's baguettes are available for $2 to go.

(914) 757-4403. Lunch, Tuesday-Friday 11 to 3; brunch, Saturday-Sunday 8 to 4; dinner, Tuesday-Sunday from 5:30.

Gourmet Plus

Harris & Monogue, Front Street, Millbrook.

Two Canadian sisters, Deborah and Chippie Kennedy from Ottawa, took over this eclectic coffee and tea shop in 1996. Chippie, who'd been a customer, knew it was for sale and, fearing no one would buy it, prevailed upon Deborah to move to Millbrook and acquire it.

Retaining the original name "because we couldn't think of anything better," they offer a variety of fresh-roasted coffees and full-leaf teas, but are perhaps best known for their lunches. The sisters offer a variety of specials ($5 to $7.95), from cream of asparagus soup and Greek chicken salad to beef bourguignonne, four-cheese macaroni and cheese, pork and stilton pie, and scotch eggs. On weekends, you might order french toast with sausages and fried tomatoes. The sisters do all the cooking, which explains why we found only soup and sandwiches on the Wednesday we visited, their day off. There are fine pastries like chocolate croissants and raspberry linzertortes for dessert or to accompany tea or coffee.

And there's an eclectic mix of gifts in the retail shop, from dishware and amusing dog dishes to books, puzzles, juggling balls and pieces of art, plus teas and coffees. We liked a gourmet chess board with assorted salt and pepper shakers as players.

(914) 677-0067. Open Monday-Friday 8:15 to 4; Saturday, 9:30 to 5.

Offbeat Gourmet

The Texas Taco, Route 22, Patterson.

Rosemary Jamison, who hails from Texas, began selling tacos in front of the Plaza Hotel in Manhattan in 1968 "before anyone even knew what they were," she says with a laugh. Within a week she had lines down the block. Moving to Patterson

in 1971, she proceeded to fill her small house with flea-market objects and now not an inch is left uncovered and barely a blade of grass outside, either. Even the curbs, paving stones and driveways are painted in wild colors to match the exterior of the house.

Cooking from her old New York cart that's ensconced in what must have been a dining room off the kitchen, she serves tacos, burritos, tostadas, chili, guacamole and fiesta pups ($1.15 to $2.50) and that's it. "Very simple, and I don't have to do a lot of ordering," she explains. With a rhinestone on her front tooth and long green hair ("I change it to fit my mood"), Rosemary is someone you can't miss.

Tiny dining rooms are filled with small tables, with hundreds of business cards displayed under their glass tops. Old toys, Marilyn Monroe collectibles, posters, jewelry – there's so much to look at you

Rosemary Jamison at The Texas Taco.

can't begin to take it all in. The bathroom is unique – Rosemary thinks it gives one a feeling of being in an aquarium, with a huge shark on the ceiling. On the front lawn are a bunch of pink flamingo statuettes and the most motley collection of lawn chairs we ever saw. Even Rosemary's pickup truck is decorated to the max with stickers and jewelry. The Patterson flea-market people understand her tastes and bring to her door things they know she'll buy. Now an icon in the area, she lives in the cellar and rarely goes out except to cater parties. "I have no family," she volunteers, "so this is my life."

Her place sure has character. We think her tacos are pretty darned good, too. *(914) 878-9665. Open daily, 11:30 to 9.*

Dining and Lodging

Le Chambord, 2075 Route 52, Hopewell Junction 12533.

Here, thanks to the eighteen-hour days of versatile innkeeper Roy Benich, is a distinguished restaurant, a shop and an expanding inn and conference center focused on a pillared, glistening white Georgian Colonial mansion with dark green shutters and an ornate statue on the front patio. The dining rooms are posh, the guest rooms quite European, and romance permeates every nook and cranny. "New Yorkers love this," says Roy, who was previously at the city's Tavern on the Green. "They're only an hour from downtown but way out in the country."

First things first. The contemporary French food overseen by executive chef Leonard Mott is superb, from the duck pâté and green salad with all kinds of julienned vegetables that began our dinners to the almond pastry shell filled with whipped cream and luscious fresh raspberries that was the crowning touch.

A complimentary plate of small canapés (two like an egg salad and four of salmon mousse with golden caviar) and a small loaf of sourdough bread came with drinks. For appetizers ($7.95 to $16.95), expect such exotica as carpaccio of venison with a black bean and mango chutney, timbale of lobster and sole with morels, and braised artichokes stuffed with shrimp and crabmeat.

Among entrées priced from $19.95 for sautéed sweetbreads and pasta or roast cornish game hen to $28.95 for tournedos rossini, the veal chop sautéed with diced onions and a touch of paprika proved a standout. One of us tried the tasting menu, which changes weekly. It brought mesquite-smoked flank steak carpaccio with corn relish, sea scallops in puff pastry with ginger and oregano, medallions of pork in calvados sauce, steamed salmon with carrots, and breast of chicken with broccoli and fennel, plus a trio of chocolate desserts and excellent decaf coffee.

All this was served with polish in one of the two intimate dining rooms, where the tables for two were so large that we had to slide our chairs and place settings closer together to avoid shouting. Lighting is fairly bright from a crystal chandelier as well as candles, plus the lights illuminating each work in a collection of art worth quite a bundle, we were told. The bound wine list, complete with table of contents, starts in the high teens and rises rapidly to $2,200. Roy had recently sold for $4,100 an 1891 port from Portugal, one of the oldest available in the world and one of more than 30 vintage ports he had obtained on trips to Portugal and Madeira and displays proudly on a hallway credenza. Our more modest Parducci chardonnay was poured into champagne flute glasses.

Upstairs on the second and third floors are eight spacious guest rooms, each with private bath, television and telephone. They're furnished in different periods with European and American antiques.

Out back in a pillared Georgian Colonial structure that Roy had built and named Tara Hall are sixteen large guest rooms with sitting areas and what he calls a "Gone with the Wind" theme. Imported tapestries adorn the sofas and chairs, the queensize beds include canopies and four-posters, and toiletries await on faux-marble vanities in the large bathrooms. The mahogany furniture includes a European-style desk and a full-length, free-standing mirror in each room. An outdoor terrace with a sitting area goes off the fireplaced lobby.

Ensconced in front of Le Chambord is **Rajko's,** the innkeeper's suave gourmet and gift shop (see Gourmet Treats).

Guests are served a complimentary continental breakfast (fruit, juices, and croissants and scones baked by the inn's two pastry chefs) in the main restaurant. Downstairs in the cozy Marine Bar at night, exotic coffees and cordials are offered in front of the fireplace.

(914) 221-1941. Lunch, Monday-Friday 11:30 to 2:30; dinner, Monday-Saturday 6 to 10, Sunday 3 to 9. Doubles, $105.

Old Drovers Inn, Old Route 22, Dover Plains 12522.

The sense of history is palpable in this out-of-the-way, white wood inn, built in 1750 to serve the cattle drovers traveling to New York City on the post roads. It's been in continuous operation ever since, but never so grandly as since it was acquired

Innkeeper Roy Benich in front of patio at Le Chambord.

in 1989 by New York film producer Kemper Peacock and Nantucket restaurateur Alice Pitcher. Kemper had been coming here for 25 years and leapt at the chance to buy "my favorite place." Theirs was only the third deed transfer since 1750 – the Preston family had it until 1937, when they sold to hotelier James Potter's family, from whom the new innkeepers bought. "We're the four P's – Preston, Potter, Pitcher and Peacock," quips Kemper.

He and Alice have breathed new life into the old inn, refurbishing and lightening up the colors and making it more comfortable – to the point where they became the world's smallest Relais & Châteaux property in 1993. "They call us their littlest angel," declares Alice.

Upstairs they offer four guest rooms with private baths (with two more in the planning stage on the third floor). Three have fireplaces and guests in each are provided with fluffy terrycloth robes. Largest is the Meeting Room, so-called because it served that function for the Town of Dover in the 19th century. Long and fairly wide, it boasts the only known barrel-shaped (rounded) ceiling in New York State. Two upholstered chairs face the fireplace and double beds flank the side walls. Nightly turndown service brings a plate with an apple, chocolate mints and truffles.

Under construction in 1997 for a summer opening were six luxurious cabins hidden in the woods to the south of the inn's main entrance. These were planned as the premium accommodations, each with kingsize bed, fireplace, TV/VCR, double jacuzzi and outdoor deck.

The inn's museum-quality main floor houses a fireplaced parlor/TV room, a long reception hall and the grand Federal Room with five remarkable Edward Paine murals of local and valley scenes. This was the original dining room (the drovers imbibed in the Tap Room downstairs). Now it's the romantic setting in which to enjoy a continental breakfast on weekdays and a leisurely, substantial breakfast ordered from a blackboard menu on weekends.

Few rooms anywhere feel more historic and romantic than the Tap Room, site of the inn's acclaimed restaurant. Forty-two diners can be seated in a stone and beamed room lit almost entirely by candles that fairly sparkle inside hurricane chimneys day and night. (An outdoor courtyard also is popular in summer.) Tables, dressed in gray and burgundy linens, are set with red and white service plates bearing pictures of the inn. More hurricane chimneys etched with eagles top the bar and brass utensils adorn the fireplace.

Chef Christopher Brooks from England took over in late 1996 the kitchen headed for six years by Jeff Marquise, who left for Australia. He retained such traditional favorites as cheddar-cheese soup and the signature browned turkey hash with mustard sauce, and added new twists. His first winter menu offered starters ($6.50 to $9.50) like roasted carrot and parsnip soup with crème fraîche, coriander-crusted rare tuna with shaved fennel and tangerine soy dressing, and carpaccio of local venison with huckleberry chutney. These may be superfluous given the small squares of toasted black bread, the dishes of crudités and deviled eggs, and the hot popovers that arrive at every table.

Among main courses ($16.75 to $33) are pan-seared halibut with lemon-thyme beurre blanc, breast of free-range chicken with light ginger nage and beef tenderloin with port sauce and stilton polenta. Desserts ($6) are unusual, perhaps walnut crostini with chèvre and pear salad, sticky toffee pudding, and warm caramelized apple soup finished with calvados, vanilla ice cream and oatmeal cookies.

(914) 832-9311. Fax (914) 832-6356. Lunch, Friday-Sunday, noon to 3; dinner nightly except Wednesday, 5:30 to 9, Saturday 3 to 10, Sunday noon to 8:30. Doubles in inn, $150 to $230 B&B weekdays, $320 to $395 MAP weekends; cabins, $400 B&B.

Beekman Arms, 4 Mill St. (Route 9), Rhinebeck 12572.
Dating from 1766, America's oldest continuously operating inn now is decidedly up to date, from the new American cuisine emanating from its restaurant leased to celebrity New York chef Larry Forgione to its Delamater Courtyard rooms with color TV, air-conditioning and working fireplaces. In fact, from the outside, as you gaze upon the striking, contemporary greenhouse restaurant at the side of the main entrance, you might think history is deceiving.

But you can have your history and eat it, too, in the dark and beamed, low-ceilinged Tap Room, the Pewter Room and the Wine Cellar Room, with wooden tables and many private booths, all lit by candles, even at midday. Or you can feel more contemporary in the greenhouse room facing the center of town, which can be opened to the outside on nice days.

The restaurant, now named **The Beekman 1776 Tavern,** reopened to unprecedented fanfare after it was leased in 1991 to Forgione, owner of An American Place in Manhattan, who was familiar with the area as an early CIA graduate. The inn's owner of 35 years "wanted to pull back and this was the perfect match," said the manager – "America's oldest inn and An American Place's country restaurant." Forgione, who since has opened a third restaurant in Miami Beach and seldom is in the kitchen here, regularly updates a menu that incorporates American classics and regional ingredients. A chef from Argentina, Tony Nogales, executes his commands.

A recent autumn menu listed such appetizers ($6.95 to $9.95) as a local Brittany Hollow potato and Coach Farms goat cheese terrine wrapped in applewood-smoked bacon, crispy fried calamari with spicy rémoulade sauce and a deviled Maine Jonah crab cake spring roll with ginger-soy dipping sauce .

The trendy, American-to-the-max roster continues with such main courses ($14.95 to $22.95) as cedar-planked Atlantic salmon atop a soft corn pudding and chanterelles with a white wine sauce, Eastern yellowfin tuna garnished with bok

Tap Room has been in continuous use since 1750 at Old Drovers Inn.

choy and steamed sticky rice, lacquered confit of Adirondack free-range duck on a stone-ground corn cake, and Colorado leg of lamb with mint pesto. Those with lower aspirations can try glazed country-style meatloaf, Pennsylvania Dutch free-range turkey pot pie or a Traphagen burger on a fresh sesame bun ($9.95).

Desserts ($4.50 to $5.50) include old-fashioned double-chocolate pudding, individual farmstand fruit crisp, homemade ice cream and sorbet of the day, and something endearingly called a campfire s'mores ice-cream sandwich, a throwback to one's youth but with *homemade* marshmallows and graham crackers.

Obviously, the menu implies excitement, many of the accompaniments are interesting and unusual, and the prices are far lower than they would be in Manhattan. But the food critics' raves seem to exceed ordinary customers' reality. The local food community has mixed reactions and some find the welcome less than warm.

Elsewhere in the main inn, history is palpable. We marveled over the glass-enclosed replica of an old tavern in the far main-floor parlor, an incredible table-top display complete with miniature glasses and liquor bottles behind the bar and the most intricate little chairs and bar stools we ever saw. The specialty foods of Larry Forgione's American Spoon Foods line are featured in a small store off the lobby.

The thirteen guest rooms upstairs were remodeled and redecorated with folk art accents in 1995, but remain modest and historic. More luxurious are those in the Delamater complex a long block up the street from the main inn. The gingerbread-trimmed 1844 Delamater House, a rare early example of an American Gothic residence, offers a B&B experience. Television sets are hidden in the armoires of its eight rooms, sherry awaits in decanters, and front and rear porches are great for relaxing. Behind it are top-of-the-line rooms in the cathedral-ceilinged Carriage House and the Delamater Courtyard area. Altogether the inn's ten buildings offer 57 rooms and two suites, all with private baths and 23 with working fireplaces.

(914) 876-7077. Lunch daily, 11:30 to 3; dinner, 5:30 to 9 or 9:30; Sunday, brunch 10 to 2, dinner 3:30 to 9. Doubles, $90 to $110 in inn; $85 to $140 in Delamater complex.

Belvedere Mansion, Route 9, Box 785, Rhinebeck 12572.

Erected in 1900 on a hilltop overlooking the Hudson, this Greek Revival mansion is named for its beautiful view. Most recently it had been the Pawling Health Center, a fasting spa, but in 1995 it took on quite a different life as an elegant restaurant and an inn in progress.

The restaurant on the main floor quickly earned good reviews under auspices of owners Nikola and Patricia Rebraca, who have run Panarella's restaurant on Manhattan's West Side since 1979. Here they imported as chef Lawrence Chu, a CIA grad and veteran of some of New York's best restaurants, to provide contemporary regional cuisine. They seat 60 diners in three high Victorian dining rooms of the chandelier, fireplace and gilt-framed painting variety. Forty-five more can be accommodated at tables beneath green umbrellas on a spacious side deck in season. There's also an odd but romantic table for two or four in a little tea room at the head of the stairway landing.

It's an elegant, formal, almost pretentious setting for food that is not at all intimidating. The short dinner menu is straightforward and quite affordable. Appetizers ($5.95 to $7.95) vary from citrus-cured gravlax with capers and red onion to a complex napoleon of scallops, swiss chard and mushrooms, served in a soup bowl atop a coating of porcini consommé. Entrées ($16.95 to $18.95) could be grilled Atlantic salmon with roasted red pepper vinaigrette, grilled yellowfin tuna with mango and nectarine salsa, pan-seared muscovy duck with red onion marmalade and – when did you last see these items for $18.95 in a dining room of this caliber? – rack of lamb and tournedos of black angus beef. Interesting vegetables and starches accompany. Homemade desserts include a great rhubarb and strawberry tart with chantilly cream, crème caramel with almond lace and a trio of sorbets.

Upstairs are five guest rooms of mansion proportions, appointed with the Gilded Age in mind. The rear Roosevelt Room with an English Tudor canopy bed is masculine and mysterious in chocolate brown with gold trim. "There are a lot of pictures to get crooked around here," Patricia noted as she straightened a couple while showing us around. All rooms have private baths with abundant marble, ceiling fans and matching French Empire queen beds and mirrored armoires. The Astor and Lafayette in front offer fireplaces and river views.

Behind and to the side of the mansion is a motel-like lineup of accommodations with separate entrances. Euphemistically called cottages, they're decorated differently with as much pizzazz as their simplicity and space would allow (a handpainted bureau here, a wicker chair there). Six have king beds and four "cozies" each have a double bed tucked away in an alcove, a bathroom and not much more. They're perfectly serviceable, but not exactly the kind of place where you'd want to hang out and, at any rate, most have no places to sit.

Breakfast in the dining room generally includes a choice of omelets with Coach Farm goat cheese and oven-dried tomatoes, walnut-crusted french toast or Hudson Valley pear pancakes.

The ten-acre property includes a rear pool with new cabanas, a tennis court and a pond. "We have a long way to go," Patricia acknowledged after three years of restoration. But they're off to a promising start.

(914) 889-8000. Dinner, Wednesday-Sunday 5:30 to 9:30; lunch service planned for 1997. Doubles, $175 to $195 in mansion; cottages, $85 and $125 to $145.

Hilltop Belvedere Mansion is named for its beautiful view of mountains and river.

Lodging

Inn at the Falls, 50 Red Oaks Mill Road, Poughkeepsie 12603.

Hard to find but worth the effort is this elegant bed-and-breakfast hotel beside a picturesque stream in suburban Poughkeepsie.

Owners Arnold and Barbara Sheer, who previously ran a nearby motor inn, liked to visit New England inns and B&Bs, "but we didn't like bathrooms down the hall or sharing the house with its owners," Arnold explained. So they decided to create in their hometown a combination of what they felt were the best features of a hotel and a B&B.

An unusual architectural scheme, a Boston decorator and $3 million produced a curving, two-story, residential-style building following the path of the stream. Opened in 1985, it has 22 rooms and suites, beautifully decorated in seven themes from English country to oriental to contemporary. A California artist did the striking paintings that enhance the rooms. Our suite had a comfy sitting room with extra-high ceilings, good reading lights, a dining table and kitchen sink with wet bar, plus two TV sets, three telephones and a canopied kingsize bed. It also had one of the biggest bathrooms we've seen, with an oversize tub and a huge walk-in shower. Floor-to-ceiling mirrors, bottles of toiletries and a marble-topped sink added to the imposing effect.

The marble floors of the lobby lead to a large living room with a soaring ceiling, a gigantic chandelier, luxurious seating areas and a wall of windows onto the stream. Here, cocktails are available at night and a complimentary continental breakfast is waiting in the morning (you also can have it sent to your room). French doors open to a terrace, where chairs and tables are put out in summer.

The Sheers pamper guests with nightly turndown service, chocolate mints on the pillow and a mini-safe in every closet. They even provide cards with explicit written directions to each of their favorite restaurants.

(914) 462-5770 or (800) 344-1466. Fax (914) 462-5943. Doubles, $110; suites, $127 to $150.

Bykenhulle House, 21 Bykenhulle Road, Hopewell Junction 12533.

A fifteen-room Georgian manor house built in 1841 for a Dutch silversmith was opened as a B&B in 1990 by Florence Beausoleil. Listed on the National Register and located on six acres off an exurban residential street not far from Le Chambord, the house has seven fireplaces and double living rooms that are decorated with imported crystal chandeliers. A new chandeliered ballroom in the Greek Revival style with parquet floors and fourteen doors is used for weddings, and a few B&B guests have been known to have danced there at night.

We were particularly impressed with the plant-filled side sun room with a marble floor, outfitted in chintz and wicker and yielding a view of the patio and vast lawn. Beyond the 20-by-40-foot swimming pool, a stone path edged with thyme leads through Florence's perennial gardens to a fountain and gazebo. Guests enjoy viewing a rare buffalo farm nearby.

On the second floor are three large bedrooms, two with fireplaces and all with private baths. Four-poster beds and antique furniture are the rule. The third floor has two large bedrooms with sitting areas and jacuzzi baths.

A full country breakfast is served on fine china in the formal dining room, the table set with crystal candelabra. The innkeeper prepares things like cheese frittata, french toast, eggs benedict, apple pancakes and other recipes from her studies at the Culinary Institute. On busy weekends, husband Bill, an IBM engineer, helps serve.
(914) 221-4182 or 227-6805. Doubles, $125 to $145.

Captain Schoonmaker's B&B, Route 213, High Falls 12440.

Seven-course breakfasts and early evening wine parties are executed with flair and personality here by Sam and Julia Krieg, retired educators-turned-antiques dealers. The festivities, the antiques, interesting common spaces and an eclectic clutter more than compensate for a shortfall of private baths in this fourteen-bedroom operation scattered across four buildings.

Most activity evolves around the Kriegs' good-looking 1760 stone house, nestled along a hillside between the road and a creek. The couple's antique furnishings add to the early American ambiance throughout. A porcelain chandelier graces the entry hall. The guest living room displays quilts, old crocks, a wagon full of stuffed animals and a bunch of stuffed mice atop a cabinet. Baskets hang from the ceiling of the fireplaced sun room, furnished with wicker and warmed in season by a potbelly stove. The Kriegs offer local wines, cider, popcorn and cheeses from 6 to 8 in the evening here or, in summer, on the terraces outside.

The heart of the house – literally – is the fireplaced dining room, through which guests generally pass to reach other areas. It holds a long antique table for twelve, where the Kriegs serve legendary breakfasts at 9 (a couple of tables in the living room are pressed into service when the house is full). One day's repast began with orange juice, poached pears with raspberry sauce and whipped cream, and home-made breads. The main event was spinach-cheese-dill soufflé, with sausage on the side. Blueberry-banana-walnut strudel and apricot-honey danish concluded ("we always have two desserts," explains Julia). Sam is known for his broccoli quiche that's like a frittata; another favorite is silver-dollar pancakes flavored with crème de cacao or amaretto. Julia, a former grade-school teacher, may lead guests in serenading birthday or anniversary celebrants.

The guest rooms seem almost secondary in the Kriegs' house-party atmosphere. First to be rented are four rooms sharing two baths in a cottage in the woods

Breakfast room at Inn at the Falls looks out onto passing stream.

behind the main house. One with floor-to-ceiling windows opens onto a deck built around a tree beside the creek. Those upstairs have timbered walls and vaulted ceilings. They're outfitted with feather beds and hooked rugs. Six more rooms are rented in two guest houses in the nearby village. An 1870 Victorian house contains two large bedrooms with the only private baths. The 1840 Towpath House adds four large rooms with double and twin beds; they share two baths and one has a fireplace. Four small bedrooms upstairs in the main house share one bath and are rented last.

(914) 687-7946. Doubles, $80 to $90.

Veranda House, 82 Montgomery St., Rhinebeck 12572.

An attractive 1845 Federal house that started as a farmhouse and once was an Episcopal church parsonage took on a new life in 1993. Ward and Linda Stanley of Philadelphia, who bought the place to run as a B&B, offer four air-conditioned guest rooms with private baths. Three have a variety of queensize beds, from four-poster Shaker with lacy canopy to antique brass, and one has old-fashioned wood twin beds convertible to king. Two bedrooms, one downstairs in what had been a dining room and the other above, are architecturally notable for their bay windows attached to a five-sided bay.

The Stanleys have outfitted the common areas with rather modern furniture from their Philadelphia home. The living room opens onto a breakfast room as well as a TV room/library. The original parquet floors and nice glassware are on display throughout. Ward, who recently retired from a university job teaching the history of architecture and design, hosts lively wine and cheese hours for guests on the wicker-filled front veranda or on a new terrace off the dining room.

Linda serves a full breakfast, starting with a fruit plate and a homemade pastry, perhaps sour-cream coffee cake. Orange-yogurt pancakes, sweet and savory crêpes – ham and mushroom paired with ones filled with jam – or eggs Veranda (her own elaborate version of eggs benedict with portobello mushrooms) could be the main course. Apple or pecan strudel might follow. Linda says she gave out the recipe

several times in the first month for her sausage and tomato tart, made with tomatoes from their garden.
(914) 876-4133. Doubles, $95 to $120.

Wine Tastings

Millbrook Vineyards & Winery, Wing Road off Route 57, Millbrook.

The Hudson Valley's first winery dedicated exclusively to the production of vinifera, Millbrook occupies 130 remote, hilly acres, somewhere in the back of beyond. It's blessed with dramatic views of vine-covered hillsides, three ponds, a picnic area and an unparalleled vista toward the Catskill Mountains. Owner John Dyson, former New York agriculture and commerce commissioner, converted a former dairy barn into the winery.

He and winemaker John Graziano produce 16,000 cases of fine wine a year, including award-winning chardonnays, pinot noirs, cabernet sauvignons and merlots (most in the $10.99 to $16.99 range) that some find as spectacular as the setting. Everything is state of the art, from the manmade ponds that help moderate temperatures to a patented "goblet" trellis system that lets his pinot noir grapes get more sun and air for better ripening. Dyson, who also has purchased two California vineyards, grows and experiments with about 25 European grape varieties, more than anyone in the East. By example he has proved two claims: that the Hudson Valley can produce world-class viniferas, and that grapes provide a better return for farmers than cows, hay or corn.

You can follow his interesting story during a twenty-minute winery tour. Sample the results in a small sales room holding literature and a tasting counter barely big enough for two. A fine olive oil from Dyson's Italian estate also is on sale here.
(914) 677-8383. Open daily, noon to 5.

Benmarl Vineyards, 156 Highland Ave., Marlborough-on-Hudson.

One of the first of the Hudson Valley's farm wineries, this is particularly interesting for its seasonal **Benmarl Bistro,** a rakish cafe that has served some extraordinary lunches over the years, depending on circumstances and chefs, most from the Culinary Institute. At a recent visit we found a less exciting menu: french bean soup, a pesto burger and four entrées ($8.95), including barbecued ribs and grilled chicken. Sit inside or out at a table with a grand view of the Hudson as you sip a $7.50 bottle of seyval blanc.

Another distinction for the winery, founded in 1957 by artist Mark Miller, is that it also represents (and sells) wines from other farm wineries, two from Long Island and five from the Finger Lakes. On hand are nearly 35 varieties, from blush to cabernet. The winery operation seems to have been upstaged lately by its Gallery in a Vineyard, which displays Miller's collection of art.
(914) 236-4265. Open daily, noon to 5. Bistro open Friday-Sunday, 11:30 to 3:30.

Gourmet Treats

The Corner Bakery, 10 Charles Colman Blvd., Pawling, (914) 855-3707. This is one of the new breed of bakeries, featured in a New York Times magazine article and described by Redbook magazine in 1993 as one of the five finest bakeries in America. Shannon McKinney and Brian Doyle, who studied with Swiss dean of pastry Albert Kumin, opened in smaller quarters in 1986 (they expanded in 1992 with the Fine Foods Cafe and a large takeout-food operation.) Using all natural ingredients, they bake exquisite cakes, pastries and pies (how about eggnog chiffon?), Irish soda bread that was written up in Food & Wine magazine, gingerbread houses and stollen. We can vouch for their blueberry muffins and a scone, which we enjoyed with a latte from the espresso bar. They also bottle their own dijon herb dressing, English mint sauce and preserves made on site by Shannon's mother, and offer a large selection of soups, salads, appetizers and entrées to go. Open daily from 6:30 or 7 a.m.

Slammin' Salmon Fish & Charcuterie, Franklin Avenue, Millbrook, (914) 677-5400. Run by CIA grad Thomas Rose, this is a fish store of the old school, a funky but neat place where specialty foods are crammed on the shelves amid fishing gear. The sausages are made right here, and the fish is first-rate. From the counter you can order lunch: the day's soups might be sour cherry and jambalaya, the salad smoked salmon on greens. Sandwiches are a steal: $3 for a half-pound burger, $5.95 for a smoked salmon BLT or prosciutto with goat cheese. The day's entrées could be seared tuna with rice pilaf and steamed clams with pasta (both $6.95). Shop open Tuesday-Sunday 10 to 5:30 or 6; lunch, 11:30 to 3.

Rajko's at Le Chambord, 2075 Route 52, Hopewell Junction, (914) 221-1941. Billed as the Hudson Valley's "most unique gift shop," this gem is a must stop in the area. It features a variety of Le Chambord's gourmet food products, from balsamic vinegar with capers ($10.50) to chocolate-covered raisins, plus a line of handmade gourmet pastas (lobster fettuccine, $8 a package). Also part of the repertoire are exquisite porcelain and ceramics, handmade jewelry from Greece, stunning Italian silk neckties designed by innkeeper Roy Benich, handpainted fused glass, island imports and more.

Joyous Kitchen, 307 Wall St., Kingston, (914) 339-2111. Here is the ultimate kitchen shop and a well-stocked gourmet store, where we admired fantastic teapots and a Ghirardelli concoction billed as the world's largest chocolate bar (five pounds, $40.95). We sat at the counter in the cafe along one side and breakfasted on latte, a glass of carrot-beet-ginger juice, a toasted bagel with scallion-cream cheese and an order of eggs with oven-roasted potatoes and toast, for a combined bill of $8.50. The gourmet-to-go deli case is full of salads, entrées and baked goods. Interesting classes are offered in the evenings in the cooking studio.

Also worth a stop in uptown Kingston is **Schneller's Fine Foods,** 63 John St., (914) 338-2337. Next to the old-world German restaurant of the same name, this European-style food market is billed as the only full-service butcher in the valley. More than 100 homemade food items, from salads to sauerbraten, are featured. Cheeses, caviars, sauces and seasonings are among the choices.

Adams Fairacre Farms, 195 Dutchess Tpke. (Route 44), Poughkeepsie, (914) 454-4330. Founded in 1919, this is a farm market like few others – really a one-stop supermarket sprawl of produce, gourmet foods and garden items. The produce section is bigger than many a grocery store, dwarfing even the Adams grocery section. Besides a gift shop and The Chocolate Goose for chocolates and ice creams, there is a Pastry Garden bake shop, where the aromas fairly overwhelm. Fresh rabbit was $2.99 a pound at the Country Butcher shop when we were there. The country deli and cheese shop offers all kinds of interesting goodies. Ralph Adams and company have opened a somewhat smaller branch along Route 9W just north of the Kingston-Rhinecliff bridge.

In Hyde Park, **The Uncommon Caffé,** Route 9, is the place to stop for espresso and cappuccino, specialty drinks and light fare, served inside or on an outdoor patio. The retail shop sells specialty coffees and teas, gourmet accessories and country gifts. Nearby is the **Eveready Diner,** Route 9, a gleaming 10,000-square-foot tribute to yesteryear, serving everything from breakfast to diner classics. The **Hyde Park Brewing Co.,** 514 Albany Post Road, offers four brews plus an interesting menu that includes Asian vegetable salad with grilled chicken and wok-seared salmon fillet ($6.50 to $14.50) to go with.

Gourmet Producers

McEnroe Organic, Route 22/44, between Millerton and Amenia. (518) 789-4191. The area's only certified organic produce market, this is also the biggest, with an almost overwhelming selection. The farm plants 6,000 heads of exotic lettuces a week from March through October, selling them off at $1 a head. Here is a paradise of produce: mesclun, coriander, garlic, walla walla onions, leeks, fingerling potatoes. A garlic festival was on when we were there, and pies, breads, jellies and vinegars are among the sidelines. Open daily, 8 to 5, May-December.

Coach Farm, Mill Hill Road off Route 82, Pine Plains. (518) 398-5325. America's premier producer of goat cheese, this is the brainchild of Miles and Lillian Cahn, who gave America the classic Coach leather handbags from their New York City factory. In 1984, the Cahns imported a French cheesemaker and a Californian who owned the nation's largest goat herd to their 700-acre farm in the remote town of Gallatin. Within a few years, they had 1,000 goats, 40 employees and a goat cheese "that is the equal of any French chèvre sold in this country," according to the New York Times. Already they are the largest American producer, "though that doesn't mean much," Miles quips. The music of Bach plays during milking, from 3 to 7 daily, and the milk from each goat yields about one pound of cheese a day. Coach goat cheese comes plain or with herbs or pepper, and the farm also produces yogurt and Yo-Goat, a natural yogurt drink with no preservatives or sugar added. The farm shop is open occasionally in summer, and tours of the milking parlor during the milking may be arranged. Since he wasn't selling cheese on the premises at the time, Miles directed us to the nearby General Store in Ancramdale, where we bought Coach Farm yogurt and peppered chèvre.

Ronnybrook Farm Dairy, Ancramdale, (518) 398-6455. A family farm that has overcome the ups and downs of the dairy business, this produces dairy products in demand at the area's finest restaurants, and you can't spend any time in the valley without coming across the name Ronnybrook. The Osofsky family has revived the old-fashioned glass bottle to showcase its now-famous milk, which it delivers to grocery stores across the region. There's little to see at the 1,000-acre farm, other than more than 100 award-winning Holsteins, but seek out one of its exotic ice creams produced in the old gelato factory behind the Xe Sogni restaurant in Amenia, where chef-owner Jason Thomas develops their flavors. A Ronnybrook retail store was scheduled to open in 1997 in a side section of the Xe Sogni restaurant complex, and another was planned for New York's Chelsea Market.

Keuka Lake provides backdrop for wines on Bluff Point.

Finger Lakes
The Pleasures of the Grape

Anyone who has indulged in the pleasures of the grape in the California wine country yearns to return, especially when the harvest is at its height. But Easterners no longer have to go out West. Closer to home, the Finger Lakes region of upstate New York embraces a cluster of vineyards and wineries that are producing wines of international distinction.

The New York Times headlined an article posted later at many a local winery: "Sorry, France. Too Bad, California. Some New York Wines Outshine Even Yours." At last count, 47 wineries were located in an area about the size of Connecticut. It is a landscape of rolling hills, lakes and vineyard vistas that are not only the match in terms of scenery of any in California but often exceed them because of their proximity to water.

The Finger Lakes wineries range from venerable Widmer's, which attracts hundreds of tourists on busy days, to tiny Standing Stone Vineyards, a precocious new winery with a tasting room fashioned from an old chicken coop behind a farmhouse. Most are clustered along the hillsides rising sharply from the southern ends of Cayuga, Seneca and Keuka lakes.

The wine boom has spawned related ventures, far beyond the winery visits that beckon more than 300,000 tourists annually to the Finger Lakes, most in the late summer and fall.

Foremost, of course, is the sale of grapes – pick-your-own, or available by the basket or in juice for wine. Grape pie is a staple on traditional dessert menus. Fire hydrants are painted purple in Naples for the annual Grape Festival in September.

Good restaurants, most featuring Finger Lakes wines, have emerged, particularly in the Ithaca area. So have a handful of new or refurbished inns and a multitude of B&Bs.

Also emerging lately is a cottage food industry. "We're at the same point with foods today that we were twenty years ago with wine," said Michael Turback, whose Ithaca restaurant celebrates upstate New York food ingredients. "It took time for people to understand the renaissance in winemaking, and it's going to take some time with the food, too." Particularly noteworthy is the local cheese industry. Ithaca was the site for the first annual meeting of the American Cheese Society, and the Ithaca Journal reported the Finger Lakes were "becoming known as the wine and cheese region of the country." Ithaca's Farmers' Market, marking its 25th anniversary in 1998, is known across the country as a model of the genre.

These days, a tour of the Finger Lakes wine country is much more than a one-day affair, and involves far more than simply touring a winery or two. On a leisurely trip, all the senses are at once heightened and lulled as you sample wines and indigenous foods on a sun-bathed deck overlooking one of the Finger Lakes, particularly in autumn when the hillsides are ablaze in color.

Tippling Through the Wineries

Canandaigua Wine Co. is the biggest, Widmer's the most picturesque and Bully Hill Vineyards the most controversial of the larger Finger Lakes wineries.

But others are more interesting for visitors with an interest in winemaking and an appreciation for finer wines, especially those who seek personalized, informal tours that follow the dictates not of the leader but of the led.

For orientation purposes, start at one of the larger wineries, whose guided tours offer a comprehensive if perfunctory overview of the winemaking process followed by a quick short course on the proper way to taste wines and a commercialized pitch to purchase your favorites on the way out. Then head for the smaller wineries, where the tours, if any, are intimate, the conversations spirited, the tastings more varied and the guide may be the winemaker or the owner. The tastings are usually free, although some wineries charge $1 or more. Since they tend to be clustered at the southern ends of three lakes, you can visit the wineries along one lake each day. Locally available brochures group them under the Cayuga and Seneca Lake wine trails and the Keuka Lake Winery Route.

Because the wineries are so central to the Finger Lakes and their appeal is so special, we begin this chapter with a guide to some of the best and most interesting.

Dr. Konstantin Frank/Vinifera Wine Cellars, 9749 Middle Road, Hammondsport.

This is where the "new" Finger Lakes wine tradition was launched in 1962. Dr. Frank was the first to plant European vinifera grapes successfully in the Finger Lakes. His son Willy and grandson Fred continue his tradition. The Frank wines have been served at the White House and have consistently outscored French wines in blind tastings.

The low-key tasting room along an unpaved side road is the place to go for world-class pinot noir ($17.95) and cabernet sauvignon ($22). "We could spend a quarter of a million dollars and make this a very attractive tourist destination," says Willy. "We prefer instead to make the best wines that can be made from our grapes." They produce 10,000 to 14,000 cases a year, exporting internationally to countries as far away as Japan.

Willy also has opened **Chateau Frank** in the cellar of the Frank home for the

Wine Garden Cafe deck at Glenora Wine Cellars overlooks Seneca Lake.

making of methode-champenoise sparkling wines, including a flagship brut in the French style that sells for $17.95.

(607) 868-4884. Daily, 9 to 5, Sunday noon to 5.

Hermann J. Wiemer Vineyard, Route 14, Dundee.

Hermann Wiemer, whose family has grown grapes and made wine for more than three centuries along the Mosel River in Germany, ranks as today's icon of Finger Lakes vintners.

Wiemer, then the winemaker for Walter Taylor, acquired an abandoned soybean farm on a slope on the west side of Seneca Lake in 1973 and began planting viniferas as well as the traditional hybrid grapes. Fired by Taylor six years later as disloyal to the hybrid cause, Wiemer set up his own winery and never looked back. His soaring barn winery, renovated to state-of-the-art condition, is low-key and very serious, as befits a producer of award-winning chardonnays and rieslings that command top prices. Wiemer established a nursery that has become one of the country's most important sources for top-quality grape vines, a business that in its way dwarfs his vineyard and winery. He produces about 12,000 cases of wine annually, samples of which can be tasted in a rather forbidding tasting room where the solo visitor senses that the staff has other priorities. Prices range from $6.75 for a dry rosé or bin chardonnay to $16 for the reserve chardonnay or late-harvest riesling. In its annual pick of the world's finest wines, Wine Spectator gave Wiemer's semi-dry riesling ($10) the top rating.

(607) 243-7971. Monday-Friday 10 to 5; also Saturday 10 to 5 and Sunday 11 to 5, April-November.

Glenora Wine Cellars, 5435 Route 14, Glenora-on-Seneca.

Among medium-size Finger Lakes wineries, this is a pace-setter with a commanding view from the west side of Seneca Lake. Glenora has been winning awards since it opened in 1977. Its Johannesburg riesling was rated the best in America two years in a row, and its reserve chardonnay was served at President Bush's inauguration. Glenora long ago abandoned variety in order to concentrate on premium white viniferas and French-American varietals, plus premium sparkling wines. Wine Spectator ranks it among the world's 70 top producers of fine wines.

Glenora's merger with the smaller Finger Lakes Wine Cellars of Branchport doubled output to 60,000 cases a year. A large, two-story addition has expanded the production facility as well as the upstairs tasting area and added an impressive new showroom with an outdoor dining deck (see below).

After viewing a video presentation, visitors sample up to five wines. Questioners who linger may get to try a few others, as is the case at most smaller wineries. Glenora has launched the Trestle Creek label for table wines ($4.99 to $5.99), but we always pick up a few of the dry rieslings ($7.99), which we think are about the best anywhere. Also great are the brut and blanc de blanc ($12.99) and the merlot ($14). Glenora sponsors occasional Sunday jazz concerts on its lawn. The Wine Garden Cafe (see below) offers lunches and snacks with a stupendous view.

(607) 243-5511. Daily, 10 to 8 in July and August, 10 to 6 in June, September and October; 10 to 5 (Sunday noon to 5), rest of year.

Wagner Vineyards, 9322 Route 414, Lodi.

This is another favorite among the larger estate wineries, thanks both to its for-tuitous location on the eastern slope overlooking Seneca Lake and to the myriad endeavors of owner Bill Wagner, a dairy farmer-turned grape grower-turned winemaker. One of his most appealing endeavors is the Ginny Lee Cafe (see below), but he's no doubt proudest that the winery has been ranked among the world's top 70 by Wine Spectator.

Wagner differs from some in that he grows all his grapes ("my philosophy is that good wine is made out in the vineyards, which makes winemakers shudder, but I like that full-time control over the grapes," says its owner), the amount of research ("more than the rest of the wineries put together"), and the proportion of red wines (at one point nearly 50-50, but scaled back lately). Wagner produces about 35,000 cases a year.

He and his staff host hundreds of visitors on busy weekends in the octagonal building he designed himself. After guided tours, visitors are offered a tasting of wines and then browse through a large and busy shop. The limited-release chardonnays and pinot noirs have been much honored; ditto for a couple of dessert ice wines. We came home with a good gewürztraminer for $7.99.

(607) 582-6450. Daily 10 to 4:30, weekends to 5.

Lamoreaux Landing Wine Cellars, 9224 Route 414, Lodi.

In its construction stage, passersby thought this striking structure atop a hill commanding a panoramic view of Seneca Lake was going to be a cathedral. It turned out to be a temple – a temple glorifying some of the best wines in the Finger Lakes region. Owner Mark Wagner's "neo-Greek Revival barn" houses the region's most exciting new winery. California architect Bruce Corson, a friend whose father was president of Cornell University, designed a four-level masterpiece of open spaces, oak floors, floor-to-ceiling windows and cream-colored walls hung with changing artworks.

 The elegant showroom provides a perfect backdrop for the tasting of premium viniferas, including a 1995 semi-dry riesling that won best of class at the 1996 San Diego National Wine Competition. Mark, a distant cousin of Bill Wagner of the adjacent Wagner Vineyards, had been growing classic vinifera grapes on his 130 lakeside acres for other wineries before opening his own winery in 1992. His early rieslings won a total of 30 medals in the first four years. The 1990 blanc de noir

Lamoreaux Landing Wine Cellars occupies neo-Greek Revival barn above Seneca Lake.

was Wine Spectator's highest rated sparkling wine in New York. We savored the barrel-fermented chardonnay ($12) and cabernet franc ($14). At our latest visit, Lamoreaux was looking forward to outstanding red wines – merlot, pinot noir, cabernet sauvignon and cabernet franc – aging in oak barrels from the exceptional 1995 harvest.

Mark explains that some of his wines may not be at their best as stand-alone tasting wines, "but I drink wines with food so those are the kind I'm producing here." He plans to remain small and aim for the ultra-premium market. The first of two wings on either side of the slender building was added in 1996 for increased production space. A concert pavilion with a hillside view of the lake is planned.

(607) 582-6011. Monday-Saturday 10 to 5, Sunday noon to 5.

Standing Stone Vineyards, 9934 Route 14, Valois.

Who'd expect a year-old winery open only on weekends to win the Governor's Cup (best of show) at the 1995 New York State Wine and Food Classic? With a red wine, no less? The best-in-state award for its ruby red cabernet franc put Standing Stone quickly on the connoisseur's map.

Owners Tom Macinski, a chemical engineer with IBM, and his wife Marti, a litigation lawyer, commute on weekends from Binghamton to their vineyard along the eastern shore of Seneca Lake. Even before their winery opened in 1994, their first gewürztraminer had won a gold medal at the New York State Fair and their riesling and dry vidal also had won awards. The part-time winemakers won awards for every wine they produced in their first two harvests. Each year, they had to close before Christmas because their wines were sold out.

The winery is in a restored barn and the tasting room is in an old chicken coop enhanced by a covered outdoor deck. The Macinskis have increased their output from 800 cases in 1993 to 7,000 in 1996, still operating weekends only but hiring a winemaker. Their stylish chardonnay, riesling, merlot and cabernet franc offerings are priced from $8.99 to $14.50 a bottle.

They also offer catered monthly winemaker dinners ($42 per person) in season at tables for eight on the lake-view deck or inside the tasting room.

(607) 582-6051. Open Saturday 10 to 6, Sunday noon to 5.

Knapp Vineyards, 2770 County Road 128, Romulus.

A vaguely California air pervades this winery, a growing family operation on 100 acres of a former chicken farm above Cayuga Lake. There's a large, airy

Vines grow over trellised terrace at Three Seasons Restaurant at Knapp Vineyards.

tasting room with a California-like veranda, but the prize addition is the Three Seasons Restaurant at Knapp Vineyards at the rear of the winery (see below). Winery owners Doug and Suzie Knapp have been joined in the venture by his daughter, Lori, a winemaker, and Suzie's son Jeff Adema, the chef.

The Knapps say theirs is one of the few wineries producing "methode-champenoise" champagne. It also is one of the growing handful doing red viniferas, including pinot noir and cabernet sauvignon. Total production is 10,000 cases a year, and its late-harvest riesling is a gold-medal winner. Newly released at our latest visit was a velvety ruby port, fortified with brandy from the Knapp still. The new grappa had won a gold medal and, aging slowly in oak, a cognac-style brandy was due in 1997. Wines are priced from $5.95 to $17.99 (for the brut champagne).

(607) 869-9271. Monday-Saturday 10 to 5, Sunday noon to 5.

Swedish Hill Vineyard, 4565 Route 414, Romulus.

Straddling farmlands almost midway between upper Seneca and Cayuga lakes, this vineyard dates to 1969 but has vaulted into the forefront lately with quite a variety of award-winning wines totaling about 30,000 cases a year. Champagnes produced by Richard and Cynthia Peterson garnered gold medals in three national and international competitions in 1995. Their 1994 dry riesling, 1994 late-harvest vignoles and Svenska red each won gold medals at the San Francisco Fair International Wine Competition. Among the 25 varieties "there's something for everyone," according to Cynthia, from a semi-dry riesling for $8 to a prize-winning blanc de blanc for $11. Non-vintage blends are Svenska whites and reds for $5.50 each. Horse-drawn wagon tours of the vineyard are offered on nice afternoons.

(315) 549-8326. Daily, 9 to 6, Sunday 10 to 5. Guided tours, weekdays at 1 and 3, weekends at noon, 2 and 4, May-October.

King Ferry Winery, 658 Lake Road, King Ferry.

Peter and Tacie Saltonstall (he's a grandson of the Boston Saltonstalls) release 5,000 cases a year of their award-winning Treleaven wines at their small winery on the former Treleaven farm along the east shore of Cayuga Lake. Aged in oak casks in the French tradition, the chardonnays are highly rated, selling for $11.99 a bottle (the reserve is $15.99). The rieslings and merlots are other good offerings, and the winery's new "melange" blends merlot and pinot noir. An innkeeper-friend tried to buy a case of the first release of merlot, but it already had sold out. *(315) 364-5100. Monday-Saturday 10 to 5, Sunday noon to 5, May-December. Also weekends, February-April.*

Special Winery Treats

Three Seasons Restaurant at Knapp Vineyards, 2770 County Road 128, Romulus.

Pair a chef trained at the Culinary Institute of America with a scenic winery setting for a gastronomic success in the Finger Lakes area. Jeffrey Adema and his wife Louise joined his family's business in 1992, launching a full-service restaurant at the rear of the winery. It opens onto a trellised outdoor terrace where vines grow above, herb and flower gardens bloom beyond, vineyards spread out on three sides, you can see or hear wild turkeys and pheasants, and bluebirds fly all around. It's a delightful setting for some inspired meals. Jeff changes the menus with the seasons to take advantage of local ingredients.

The dinner menu produces a choice of eight entrées ($15.95 to $19.95), including perhaps poached salmon with a sundried tomato and artichoke compote, wood-roasted duckling with a mango tea sauce and peppercorn-grilled ribeye steak with a shiitake mushroom sauce. Jeff gets creative with appetizers of smoked salmon, offering smoked salmon cheesecake with whole wheat chips and crème fraîche on the spring menu and changing to smoked salmon tamales with a roasted tomatillo salsa in summer. Other starters could be thick garbanzo bean soup with three compotes of roasted peppers, avocado and onion, and caesar salad with sliced smoked duck breast. Desserts include Jeff's ultimate flourless chocolate cake made with belgian chocolate and topped with whipped cream and raspberry sauce, fruit cobblers, peach ice cream and passionfruit sorbet.

Lunchtime brings similar innovation at lower prices ($6.95 to $9.25). You might try a pesto-crust pizza with smoked turkey and Vermont cheddar, a pork and black bean quesadilla, curried tuna salad on a toasted baguette or Thai red curry chicken and pineapple on basmati rice.

Pastel watercolors lend a bit of color to the interior dining room, fairly stylish in black and white. But we'd opt for the outdoor terrace, a seasonal retreat that draws folks from Syracuse and Rochester for a leisurely meal amid the peace and quiet. *(607) 869-9481. Lunch, Monday-Saturday 11 to 3, Sunday noon to 4; dinner, Thursday-Saturday 5:30 to 8; no lunch Monday-Wednesday and no dinner Thursday in April and November. Closed December-March.*

Ginny Lee Cafe, Wagner Vineyards, 9322 Route 414, Lodi.

With its reasonably priced wines and charming setting (a panoramic view of its vineyards and Seneca Lake), the Ginny Lee has long been a treat. The expansive deck has been enclosed to better weather the elements and to extend the season. Now there's a vast interior space with cathedral ceiling, white walls and white garden-type furniture. A section of the outdoor deck remains. Although dinner no longer is served and the cuisine is scaled down from its original heights, lunch here is a must at each of our visits.

Wagner wines and Aurora grape juice by the bottle, half carafe and glass are available at winery prices at the cafe, which was the first at a Finger Lakes winery and was named for the owner's then-infant granddaughter.

Chef Laurie Marsh has added vegetarian fare and expanded the menu. You can order anything from a turkey club, Philly steak or Danish smørrebrød sandwich to a cobb or shrimp caesar salad to a Mediterranean or Southwestern pizza ($4.50 to $6.95). Or you can make lunch an event with appetizers like spinach polenta and oriental turkey dumplings and entrées ($5.25 to $9.95) like vegetable and cheese strudel, grilled salmon and sautéed twin tenderloins with grilled vegetables. At various visits we've enjoyed a Greek salad, shrimp salad on a croissant, chicken salad on a kaiser roll and a fruit and cheese platter with French bread. We won't soon forget the fuzzy navel peach pie and the strong cinnamon-flavored coffee, which after lunch with a bottle of wine was the only way we managed to make it through the afternoon.

(607) 582-6574. Lunch, Monday-Saturday 10 to 4:30; Sunday, brunch 10 to 2, lunch 2 to 4. Open May-October; also weekends off-season.

Wine Garden Cafe, Glenora Wine Cellars, 5435 Route 14, Glenora-on-Seneca.

Starting small by serving sandwiches on a side deck in 1993, this quickly evolved into a classy, full-service restaurant. The operation has been leased to restaurateur Doug Thayer, owner of the Wildflower Cafe in Watkins Glen. He experimented with dinners for a receptive but too-small market in 1995 and, sadly, dinner was discontinued in 1996. The lunch menu ($4.95 to $8.95) remained as enticing as ever.

The view of the lake and vine-covered hillsides here is arguably the most spectacular of any in the Finger Lakes. Green and white molded chairs are at tables beneath a canopy on the 50-by-50-foot deck, whose side curtains can be raised or lowered according to the weather.

This is the place to relax and savor the wines and the view over a cheese and sausage board, a platter of baked brie with fresh fruits or a bowl of peel-and-eat shrimp with fresh-baked bread. Sandwiches tempt: smoked salmon, crab cake, broiled portobello mushroom or California BLT. Entrées might be shrimp and mussels scampi over angel-hair pasta, torta rustica or seafood of the day. Chicken with wild mushrooms, served over red pepper angel-hair pasta, accompanied by the winery's stellar dry riesling for $7.95, made a zesty meal. Finish with a dessert pastry and cappuccino or espresso.

(607) 243-5511. Lunch daily, 11:30 to 4:30, May-October.

Castel Grisch, 3380 County Route 28, Watkins Glen.

An enormous wine cask at the entry – with the Louis Pasteur quote, "Wine rejuvenates," emblazoned on the far end – welcomes visitors to this winery-cum-restaurant and a B&B in the manor house. Tom and Barbara Malina carry on the traditions of the original Swiss owners, who sought to provide a touch of Europe in the Finger Lakes. The setting is special: two large dining rooms dressed in burgundy and pink with full-length windows onto a partly canopied, partly open deck strung with tiny white lights. Down steep hillsides is a view of Seneca Lake.

The cooking bears a European accent. The lunch menu ($5.95 to $11.95) offers unusual stews (Hungarian goulash) and salads (duck) along with burgers and traditional sandwiches ($5.95 to $8.95). Swiss fondue ($13.95) is a specialty, and there also are open-face New York strip, wiener schnitzel and chicken sandwiches.

The dinner menu adds shrimp scampi, grilled swordfish, duck à l'orange, Swiss veal dishes and filet mignon, priced from $12.95 to $21.95. Roesti potatoes and spaetzle may accompany. Desserts include fruit strudels. The Malinas keep things hopping with Friday-night German-Swiss buffets and Sunday buffet brunches.

Inside the nearby timbered and vine-covered Manor House, the Malinas offer three upstairs bedrooms with private baths for overnight guests ($89 to $109). The master room in shades of rose has a kingsize bed and its own little balcony overlooking the vineyards and the lake, A queen-bedded room also has a private balcony; the other room has twin beds. The sitting room in the turret has rattan furniture. Guests are welcomed with wine and fruit in their rooms, and are served fresh fruit, muffins and a main course like quiche or waffles in the morning.

(607) 535-9614. Lunch daily, 11 to 4; dinner nightly, 4 to 9 or 10; Sunday, brunch 11 to 2, dinner 3 to 9, May-October. Also weekends in April and November.

Dining

The Best of the Best

Rosalie's Cucina, 841 West Genesee St., Skaneateles.

A plaque on the wall in the rear foyer says this was "built with great love for my sister" and, after listing the architectural credits, adds "with way too much money." Both the love and the money are manifest in the chic new Tuscan-style restaurant, wine cellar and bakery – a testament to Rosalie Romano from Phil Romano, the restaurant impresario who started the Fuddrucker's chain.

It seems that Phil, who grew up in nearby Auburn and lives in Texas, still summers on Skaneateles Lake and "wanted a nice place to eat," in the words of general manager Gary Robinson, a part-owner. "He'd been all over Italy, so he built this the way he wanted it for himself."

His reported investment of more than $1.5 million includes a stylish 120-seat restaurant backing up to a designer's dream of an open kitchen, a downstairs wine cellar and the upstairs Romano Room for family reunions and private parties, a bakery, an outdoor bocce court, a small vineyard for show, and an elaborate herb layout and vegetable garden for real.

The result: The hottest culinary establishment in the Finger Lakes at our 1996 visit. Without advertising, no press kit and not even a listing in Skaneateles or Finger Lakes promotional materials, the place was mobbed nightly, and up to two-hour waits were the norm on weekends. The bocce court, the wine cellar and a delightful Mediterranean-style courtyard – all holding areas for the waiting crowds, who are given breads, olives and cheese – were getting quite a workout.

Inside the salmon-colored building identified by a sign so small we missed it on the first pass is a dark and spacious dining area understated in white and black. Black chairs flank well-spaced tables covered with white butcher paper over white cloths. A few columns break up the expanse. The white walls are enlivened with hundreds of splashy autographs of customers, who pay $25 each to charity to enshrine their name and the date for posterity. Most of the color comes from the open kitchen at the end of the room, where cooks work amid hanging ropes of garlic, arrangements of bounty and chickens roasting on the rotisserie.

Executive chef Robert Fasce, a Culinary Institute of America grad with experience in five-star restaurants, changes the menu daily. The specialty is prime meats, as in aged New York strip steak, prime rib (roasted and then grilled) and grilled veal loin chop. The roasted pork with oregano and garlic and the lamb loin with white wine and garlic are done according to family recipes. So is the scampi alla Rosalie (with garlic and lemon butter). Prices range from $13.50 for linguini with mussels to $27 for the strip steak, with pastas and chicken dishes in the $14 range and most of the meats and fish around $17.

Antipasti include steamed mussels, pizza margherita, cannelloni with ground meat and ricotta, carpaccio and grilled portobello mushrooms. Of the insalata, the one with arugula, prosciutto, reggiano and lemon is special.

Homemade desserts vary daily. The pastries and breads come from **Crustellini's,** the bakery at the rear of the establishment, where a dozen varieties of "hand-made breads" are for sale daily from 9 a.m. to 10 p.m. for $2.40 to $4.95 a loaf.

Oh, yes. You may well get to meet Rosalie. She comes in most nights to be hostess in her cucina that love built.

(315) 685-2200. Dinner, Monday-Saturday 5 to 10, Sunday to 9.

Daño's on Cayuga, 113 South Cayuga St., Ithaca.

Daño Hutnik had quite a background before opening in 1990 a small downtown Ithaca restaurant that quickly became one of the area's best. Born in the Ukraine, he grew up in Czechoslovakia and was a ballet dancer for fifteen years in Vienna before embarking on a restaurant career in New York and San Francisco. A classified ad in the New York Times led him to Ithaca and this old space that he and his wife, artist Karen Gilman, transformed into a chic French-style bistro in peach and blue-gray. There's seating for 44 at white-linened tables topped with white paper against a backdrop of her artworks on the walls and a spotlit alcove showcasing the fabulous desserts.

Chef Daño (pronounced Dan-yo) changes his menu of contemporary central European, French and northern Italian fare seasonally. Those in the know go for such specialties as oxtail stew with black and green olives or veal sausage with braised red cabbage and spaetzle. One autumn night we sampled an appetizer of melted raclette cheese with boiled potatoes, cornichons and pearl onions, the classic version and enough for two, and the house terrine of chicken, pork, duck, veal "and everything – a little cut here, a little there," according to the chef.

Among main courses ($14.95 to $19.95), we were delighted by the sautéed chicken breast with artichoke hearts and smoked mozzarella, served with incredibly good polenta sticks, and the linguini with shrimp, peas and scallions. Other tempters included seared sea scallops served in a warm vegetable gazpacho with saffron potatoes, haddock basquaise on a bed of garlic-mashed potatoes and grilled veal flank steak with a wild mushroom risotto. We liked the Hermann J. Wiemer dry riesling ($16), the only Finger Lakes choice on an excellent little wine list specializing in imported wines and rarely seen Californias. Crème brûlée and a bittersweet-chocolate gâteau with raspberry sauce were worthy endings to one of our better meals in a long time. The occasion was made more enjoyable as congenial chef Daño, table-hopping at night's end, proved to be quite the talker and philosopher.

(607) 277-8942. Dinner, Monday-Saturday 5:30 to 9:30 or 10.

Renée's Bistro, 202 East Falls St., Ithaca.

This appealing American bistro was opened by Renée Senne, who had been sous chef at L'Auberge du Cochon Rouge and chef at the Greystone Inn here,

Flowers and pastries are displayed in niche at Daño's on Cayuga.

upon her return to Ithaca from studying at La Varenne in France and teaching in New York City.

Ficus trees and hanging plants thrive in the airy dining room and a small bar, both with a wall of windows across the front. It was in the former that we enjoyed a fine spring lunch: an excellent cream of onion soup, a slice of French bread topped with fresh mozzarella, sundried tomatoes and basil, and a special of fettuccine with grilled shrimp and garlic-cream sauce.

Alas, lunch has fallen victim to the restaurant's success, as Renée decided to concentrate on dinner. Dining is at tables dressed in white linens topped with butcher paper. Innovative seafood preparations are highlighted on a short menu supplemented by myriad specials, priced from $16.25 for chicken with shallots and garlic, served with egg noodles, to $21.50 for beef tenderloin. You might find broiled salmon served with yellow pepper coulis, smoked potatoes and scallion mashed potatoes; swordfish seared with garlic and olive oil resting on spinach linguini or grilled and served with shrimp-filled ravioli; or grilled halibut on steamed spinach with beurre blanc, garnished with roasted red peppers, pink peppercorns and basil.

Renée's repertoire includes such starters as escargots in a grilled portobello mushroom, smoked salmon quesadilla, polenta with artichoke hearts and chèvre, and shrimp cakes served with roasted-pepper sauce. How we'd like to graze through a couple of those, a salad of new potatoes served warm with chèvre on baby greens, and one of the pasta dishes, perhaps squid ink linguini with sautéed calamari. The owner's background as a pastry chef shows in the desserts, which run from mille-feuille to peach shortcake, and include lots of ices and granités.

(607) 272-0656. Dinner, Monday-Saturday 5:30 to 10.

John Thomas Steakhouse, 1152 Danby Road (Route 96B), Ithaca.

For some years, a restaurant has been ensconced in this farmhouse on a hillside overlooking the Cayuga Lake valley about a mile south of the Ithaca College campus. Alas, a kitchen fire closed the long-popular L'Auberge du Cochon Rouge, a French restaurant of renown, in 1994. When owner Walter Wiggins rebuilt, he surprised almost everyone by turning the country-French landmark into a New York-style steakhouse. He also surprised local skeptics, some of whom were persuaded that this was even better than its predecessor. The beef is prime and the prices lofty, since everything is à la carte.

The restaurant's original French theme had run its course and its traditionally masculine decor lent itself to the steakhouse concept, explained manager Mike Kelly, who had overseen a similar venture in Roslyn, Long Island. The interior of the farmhouse remains basically the same, although the inner Red Room was enlarged following the fire. The upstairs L'Auberge Lounge retains links with the past.

Former L'Auberge sous chef William Peterson stayed on as chef, presenting a predictable menu priced from $12.95 for roasted half chicken to $24.95 for T-bone steak. The specialty is porterhouse steak, $39.90 for two. There are grilled or blackened tuna, broiled swordfish, broiled salmon, shrimp scampi, a vegetarian platter and a couple of chicken dishes for non-beef eaters. Salads, vegetables and the usual side orders cost extra, from $2.50 for vegetable of the day to $8.50 for sautéed wild mushrooms. Appetizers include smoked trout, baked deviled crab, shrimp cocktail and clams casino. Desserts range from crème brûlée and puff pastry with Italian cream and blueberries to assorted ice creams and triple berry strudel.

The fire destroyed L'Auberge's acclaimed wine cellar, but management planned to rebuild it slowly.

(607) 273-3464. Dinner nightly, 5:30 to 10 or 11.

More Dining Choices

The Heights Cafe & Grill, 903 Hanshaw Road, Ithaca.

Ensconced next to Talbots in the Community Corners shopping plaza in tony Cayuga Heights, this new storefront operation is plainer than plain. Black upholstered chairs are at mottled gray tables, each topped with a votive candle in a little flower pot. A few paintings on the white walls above gray wainscoting, dim lighting from wall sconces and a couple of ceiling fans, and that's it for decor.

Chef-owners James and Heidi Larounis are known for good American-Mediterranean fare at reasonable prices. Dinner entrées run from $10.95 for grilled pork chops with a dijon-wine sauce to $14.95 for veal roulade. In between are grilled salmon with a feta, black olive and sundried tomato compote, baked Boston bluefish Greek style, grilled leg of lamb and strip steak seasoned with herbed peppercorns. Downright bargains are the pasta dishes, from $9.95 for pesto grilled chicken to $12.95 for cioppino. Three brick-oven pizzas are offered for $8.25. Everything comes with choice of Greek or caesar salad.

Starters could be tomato-basil bruschetta, taramosalata (a carp roe spread) with baked pita chips or grilled octopus. Desserts range from baklava to crème brûlée.

The short wine list, mainly from the Finger Lakes and California, is pleasantly priced from the low teens to the mid-twenties.

(607) 257-4144. Lunch, Monday-Saturday 11 to 3; dinner, Monday-Saturday 5 to 9 or 10.

Trattoria Tre Stelle, 120 Third St., Ithaca.

This striking Italian trattoria is the home of wood-fired pizzas and a winning Mediterranean decor. The owners are designer-architects who did the sculptures in the corners of the dining room, rag-rolled the walls, designed the metal chairs,

Plants thrive in dining room at Renée's Bistro.

orchestrated the marble look on the bar and fashioned a charming outdoor courtyard, which is the dining venue of choice in summer. One also is a mushroom expert who picks the chanterelles that turn up in various dishes.

The changing printed menu is short but sweet: a couple of antipasti, six pizzas ($7.50 each), a couple of side dishes, two specials and four desserts. Chalkboard entrées ($8.50 to $11.50) might include herb and cheese lasagna, braciola (flank steak rolled around sausage and egg) and an acclaimed rabbit dish simmered in white wine and bearing a smoky taste from the wood oven. Many folks start with the Tuscan platter of sweet sopressata salami and air-cured coppa ham or the salad of chanterelles on a bed of bibb lettuce, both served with focaccia. The favorite of the pizzas is the della casa (wild mushrooms with sundried tomatoes, caramelized onions and parmesan). Desserts include almond biscotti, neopolitan chocolate-walnut cake with whipped cream and ricotta cheesecake with blueberries.

Although prices are modest, some Ithacans complain that so are the portions. The kitchen, for better or worse, has a heavy hand with the garlic. There's an excellent all-Italian wine list, priced mostly in the teens.

(607) 273-8515. Dinner, Thursday-Monday 5 to 9:30 or 10:30.

Thai Cuisine, 501 South Meadow St., Ithaca.
The best Thai food in New York State, including New York City – that's the opinion of many knowledgeable Thai-food lovers. It's served up in a serene, white and pink linened, L-shaped dining room and a new front solarium in a commercial plaza by a Thai family in the kitchen and a mainly American staff out front. All is overseen by gregarious manager Sunit ("call me Lex") Chutintaranond.

A large choice of starters at dinner ($2.95 to $11.95) includes a couple of exotic soups for the former price and for the latter, yum talay, a salad of shrimp, clams, scallops, mussels, Bermuda onions, mint leaves and ground chile peppers on mixed greens. There are six rice and noodle dishes; pad Thai is $8.95.

You'll have a hard time choosing among such entrées (all served with jasmine rice) as panang-neur, sliced tender beef simmered in panang sauce with sweet basil and pineapple, served with a side of pickled cauliflower, and gaeng goong, shrimp simmered in Thai green curry with coconut milk, sliced eggplant, bamboo shoots, baby corn, fresh chile peppers and kaffir lime. The selection is enormous, with ten shrimp dishes, for example. Nothing is over $13.95, except for a few specials.

Sunday brunch is the Thai equivalent of a dim sum meal, offering more than 30 exotic little plates for $1.95 each. Thai Cuisine has a fairly good wine list and, of course, Thai beer.

(607) 273-2031. Dinner nightly, 5 to 9:30 or 10; Saturday lunch, 11:30 to 2:30; Sunday brunch, 11:30 to 2.

Just a Taste, 116 North Aurora St., Ithaca.

Opened by the owners of Thai Cuisine, this is billed as Central New York's largest wine and tapas bar. They since have sold it to one of their former cooks, Jennifer Irwin, and Stan Walton, who have made it better than ever with a carousel of treats that change daily, sometimes twice a day.

Sleek in gray, black and white with black lacquered chairs, the small downtown establishment also has a tiny outdoor courtyard to the rear.

More than 30 wines are offered by the glass – in 2½-ounce or 5-ounce sizes or by the "flight," which means a sampling of 1½ ounces in a particular category, say five chardonnays for $7.50 or six local wines for $7.75. There are also Spanish, Italian and sherry flights, as well as a "big red" flight of heavy reds, three for $4.75. Assorted beers are available from a beer bar.

We know folks who like to order a couple of flights and a selection of international tapas ($3.50 to $6.50) and while the night away here. We had to settle for a quick lunch, sharing a breaded oyster served on a bed of spinach, a chicken teriyaki kabob with an array of vegetables, and a pizza of smoked salmon and brie (the most expensive item at $5.95). The last was great; the other two were marred by the missing house sauce (so spicy when we finally got it that one of us wished we'd done without) and no semblance of an "array" of vegetables. Cappuccino and a terrific pineapple cheesecake made up for the lapses.

The dinner hour brings tapas in appetizer and larger sizes, as well as pastas and entrées ($9.50 to $13.75). Expect tapas like flatbread with roasted squash and goat cheese, and salmon gravlax tostada with cannellini hummus, cucumber-citrus relish and tobiko caviar. You can order treats like crispy fried quail legs with Chinese sausage in oyster sauce and grilled tuna with starfruit-melon salsa in both tapas and larger sizes. Or try the penne with wild mushrooms, onions and romano or the grilled filet of beef with fried masa cake, grilled scallions and pasilla salsa.

(607) 277-9463. Lunch/brunch daily, 11:30 to 3:30; dinner, 5:30 to 10 or 11.

Turback's, 919 Elmira Road (Route 13 South), Ithaca.

Entrepreneur Michael Turback makes a name promoting New York State foods and wines. That is what sets apart his confection of a Victorian restaurant with its soaring eleven-gable roof and vivid cinnamon-colored facade with green trim, rebuilt following a fire. He has closed his downtown Made in New York Store, but was launching a Made in New York mail-order catalog for those interested in regional products.

The food always has been novel, often at the expense of consistency and taste. Lately, the food is said to have been much improved under new chef Jekabs (Yeppi) Pulsts, a Latvian native who returned in 1996 to the Ithaca area where he grew up after 30 years on the East Coast cooking circuit. He continued the unique dedication to "New York First," but backed it up with consistency and successful execution.

His new wood smoker produces a highly rated "yeppatizer" called "my brother Andy's field and stream" – a beautifully presented platter of smoked salmon, smoked turkey and tiny quail eggs, served with red pepper curls, mesclun, cranberry-orange relish and garlic toasts. Other starters include grilled sliced portobello mushrooms with bordelaise sauce and ethereal onion straws and a roulade of New York mozzarella with toasted pinenuts and walnut oil. Main courses range widely from $10.95 for turkey pot pie with baked cornbread crust to $21.95 for angus sirloin steak. Among the possibilities: grilled tuna with tomato and cucumber salsa, chicken yepina with artichoke hearts and brie, smoked and grilled breast of Long Island duck with honey-champagne sauce and roasted rack of local lamb. On the dessert menu are dense and creamy brownies topped with raspberry sauce. Other possibilities vary from white chocolate mousse cake and strawberry cream cake to rice pudding and eight kinds of ice cream sundae.

The all-New York wine list is modestly priced, and the house wine bears the label "The Painted Lady of Ithaca." Tables are decked out in green and white checked cloths beneath Tiffany-style lamps and a jungle of hanging plants in a ramble of rooms, upstairs and down.

The annual August garlic festival features a gartini (one of Turback's fourteen kinds of martini), garlic soup bubbling with provolone, garlic-marinated local rabbit, garlic shrimp scampi, even garlic ice cream.

(607) 272-6484. Dinner nightly, 4:30 to 10, Sunday from noon.

Wildflower Cafe, 301 North Franklin St., Watkins Glen.

Light, innovative food and a menu spanning a spectrum from vegetarian to game dishes are hallmarks of this storefront cafe. The effort proved successful, owner Doug Thayer having branched out with Lily's Emporium and Doug's Homemade Ice Cream next door and operating the Wine Garden Cafe at Glenora Wine Cellars.

The cafe's gourmet pizzas are the rage. We can vouch for the California pizza special ($6.50), big enough that three shared it as an appetizer and still took part home in a doggy bag.

Among entrées ($13.95 to $24.95), we liked the salmon alfredo and a special of fettuccine with anchovies and mushrooms, and wished the flame-roasted vegetables served with the charbroiled chicken hadn't been the same kinds as those that had graced both the pizza and an appetizer of fresh vegetables with dip – a bit of veggie overkill. The Glenora Glen seyval blanc was a bargain and the apple crisp with whipped cream, the pear-almond tart and the chocolate-hazelnut ice cream were fine. The price was right, the atmosphere spirited and casual, and the menu more interesting than others in the Watkins Glen area. Folks like the sautés of veal, pork and chicken, and the grills, among them halibut steak, pork anjou, New York strip steak and mesquite buffalo strip steak. Venison with wild mushrooms over lemon pepper linguini was on the docket at our latest visit.

A Swiss pastry chef has added dessert delicacies like amaretto cheesecake, chocolate fudge espresso torte, kirsch torte and St. Honoré, a cream puff filled with vanilla rum custard.

(607) 535-9797. Lunch daily, 11:30 to 4; dinner, 4 to 10 or 11.

Pasta Only, 258 Hamilton St., Geneva.

How can a little restaurant and wine bar in a shingled house make a go of it, open only a few hours for dinner five days a week? "That's the reason we're successful," answers owner Sue Cohen. "We're consistent because we've got the same two guys in the kitchen and the same wait staff all the time we're open. And besides, I need a couple of nights off!" Taking over a small pasta restaurant with an antiques shop in 1992, Sue turned the shop into a wine and espresso bar, expanded dinner service from three to five nights, and now seats 40 people in two small dining rooms dressed with floral tablecloths on the main floor and 40 more in three rooms for overflow upstairs. A small brick patio in front beckons in summer.

Sue tablehops to chat with patrons when she's not in the kitchen, but leaves the cooking chores to chef Rob Teed and crew, who produce the most interesting Italian fare in the area. All the pastas and classic sauces are homemade, as are many desserts. The extensive menu details basic pastas ($7.95 to $10.95) and adds chicken, seafood, veal and beef categories ($10.95 to $16.95), all teamed with pastas and including salad and homemade breads. Possibilities range from cioppino with linguini and salmon pomodoro to chicken pesto, hickory-smoked filet mignon and veal sorrentino. Crab cakes and stuffed portobello mushrooms are among the appetizers. The primarily local wine list is remarkably priced in the single digits and teens, and a dozen wines are available by the glass.

(315) 789-8498. Dinner, Thursday-Monday 5:30 to 9:30.

Old World Choices

Giovanni's, 124 North Aurora St., Ithaca.

"Original Italian specialties," says the sign at the entry to this new downtown storefront called an "osteria paesana." Giovanni Freesia from Italy runs a tiny but ambitious place that's true to his homeland.

Prices are from yesteryear. Fresh breads and salad come with dinner dishes, which start at $10 for sautéed rainbow trout apulia or chicken breast sautéed with garlic, honey and vinegar and top off at $13 for New Zealand mussels over linguini. In between are swordfish siciliana, sliced tuna steak sautéed with fennel and white beans, and three leg of lamb dishes, the apparent specialty. There are a dozen or so pasta dishes ($10 to $13), including ravioli stuffed with lobster, shrimp and crab for a mere $11.

Start with the antipasti for two ($6.50), pheasant, rabbit and venison pâté with marinated artichoke hearts and giardiniera. End with the dolci, perhaps tirami su or tart cherries soaked in barolo wine with custard. Accompany with a choice from the all-Italian wine list, priced in the teens. You'll be hard pressed to spend more than $50 for two.

The setting is bare wood tables set with paper napkins and dollar-store chairs in a narrow room with a few plants on pedestals, a glass divider separating the server preparation area and a mirror at the end of the room to make it look bigger.

(607) 273-2818. Dinner nightly, 5 to 10, Sunday to 9.

Handl's European Cuisine, 105 West 8th St., Watkins Glen.

A former automobile dealer's showroom is an unlikely place for a restaurant, as is Watkins Glen for some authentic Eastern European home-style cooking. Marta Handl, a few years out of Slovakia, has endeared herself to those into ethnic foods with this venture that opened in 1992 and was back on track here after a brief, ill-fated move to Ithaca.

A onetime broadcast journalist in Brataslava, she and her family left

Czechoslovakia in 1986 and eventually settled in the countryside near Dundee. Her children wait on tables while their mother prepares her creations, "old-fashioned and pure European, everything done like in my grandmother's kitchen." Expect such dinner dishes ($7.95 to $16.95) as baked trout stuffed with salmon mousse, pierogi dumplings, chicken paprikash, beef stroganoff and wiener schnitzel. They come with cabbage or beet salad. Start with garlic soup, potato pancakes or grilled chicken salad with roasted red pepper relish. Finish with one of the dessert crêpes, a raspberry éclair or walnut coffee cake.

(607) 535-4676. Open Wednesday-Saturday 11:30 to 8:30 or 9:30, Sunday noon to 8:30. No credit cards. BYOB.

A Landmark for Vegetarians

Moosewood Restaurant, 215 North Cayuga St., Ithaca.

Small and plain, this establishment on the lower level of the quirky Dewitt shopping mall is known to vegetarians around the country because of the *Moosewood Cookbook,* written by a former owner of the co-op operation, which had twenty owners last we knew. Now there are six cookbooks associated with the operation, all for sale along with other Moosewood memorabilia at the entry. Alas, the legend surpasses the reality, according to some who have trekked to Ithaca from afar to eat at Moosewood and been disappointed.

Recent remodeling has produced a lighter look in blond pine, with yellow-sponged walls and wooden banquettes all around. The covered sidewalk cafe out front is pleasant and obviously popular in season.

Original and natural-food cuisine is featured, although purists are skeptical. ("Beware," warns a printed vegan and vegetarian guide to the area. "This well-known vegetarian restaurant is no longer vegetarian and has virtually no vegan courses" – a charge disputed by the restaurant, which says it always has at least one soup and one entrée that are dairyless.)

"We're lazy about changing prices," one owner told us, and indeed they are quite modest, with lunch entrées at $5.50 and dinner $9.50 to $11.50. Tofu burgers, pasta primavera and Hungarian vegetable soup are frequent choices – the menu changes with each meal to take advantage of what's fresh. A mushroom-cheese strudel, a plate of Middle Eastern salads, cauliflower-pea curry and flounder rollatini are regulars. The blackboard menu lists an imaginative selection of casseroles, curries, ragoûts, salads and luscious homemade desserts like lemon-glazed gingerbread, peach trifle and a pear poached in wine with whipped cream. We liked the tagine, a Moroccan vegetable stew simmered with lemon and saffron on couscous, at one visit, when folks were lined up in a row of chairs in a corridor, waiting for tables at 1 o'clock. Also tempting was a Chesapeake platter – baked catfish with old Bay seasoning, salt potatoes and stewed corn and tomatoes. The pasta al calvofiore with cauliflower and Italian cheeses and the Japanese braised eggplant appealed to others. The food is said to vary, depending on which of the rotating chefs is in the kitchen.

Fresh pasta is featured Wednesday or Thursday nights, fish is served Thursday through Sunday, and Sunday nights are devoted to varying ethnic or regional cuisines. Yuengling Brewery beer and Finger Lakes and organic wines are available.

(607) 273-9610. Lunch, Monday-Saturday 11:30 to 2; light cafe menu, 2 to 4; dinner nightly, 5:30 to 8:30 or 9, summer 6 to 9 or 9:30. No smoking.

Dining and Lodging

The Rose Inn, 813 Auburn Road (Route 34), Box 6576, Ithaca 14851.

Charles Rosemann, who had moved to Ithaca to manage the Cornell University hotel school's Statler Inn, gave it up to join his wife Sherry full-time in running their own inn. The large and classic Italianate mansion they bought in 1983, known locally as "The House with the Circular Staircase," was built around 1850 on twenty acres in the hilly countryside ten miles north of Ithaca.

Working constantly to improve and expand the guest quarters, they now have twelve rooms with private baths, plus five glamorous suites with fireplaces and jacuzzis for two. A parlor with a game table, a Victorian living room with TV, outdoor terraces and a rose garden also are available for guests.

In a short time, the Rosemanns built the Rose Inn into New York State's only four-diamond, four-star country inn, as rated by AAA and Mobil, and one of the nation's ten best inns, according to Uncle Ben's. Those accolades tell only part of the story, for this is one great, friendly place that's haute without being haughty. From the minute you enter (through the kitchen, where dinner likely is being prepared) to your departure following an exceptional breakfast, you are in for a treat.

Rooms are individually decorated by Sherry, and those in a recent two-story addition capture the classic flavor of the rest of the house. They are luxurious, with everything from lace curtains, ceiling fans and fresh flowers to luggage racks, terry robes, Vitabath and other amenities. In two, the bathroom fixtures (including a stretch-out tub) are from the Eastman House in Rochester. Folk art and antiques abound. Our rear suite came with a sunken jacuzzi in a garden-like space filled with plants off the bedroom, a majestic kingsize bed and antique furnishings in the bedroom, a large closet and a modern bath. Even the smallest room is no slouch, with beautiful wall coverings and borders coordinated with the bedspread and the bathroom, an Empire desk and a plaster bust of King Tut on the wall. At nightly turndown, a candle is apt to be lit beside the bed, the towels replenished, your toiletries neatly lined up on the bath vanity and your clothing hung in the closet. A thank-you note bids "Sweet Dreams."

The Rosemanns' latest addition is a casual restaurant and jazz club in their conference center, located out of the way on the main floor of a restored carriage house at the side of the property. The carriage house is like no other, its original walls and hand-hewn oak beams enhanced by handsome furnishings and oriental rugs on the floors. Even the rest rooms here are ultra-elegant.

Breakfast, served in the parlor, dining room, carriage house or foyer with its beautiful parquet floors, is an event worthy of the rest of the inn experience. Rose mats are on the polished wood tables, as are white baskets filled with seasonal flowers. The juice glasses sport the Rosemann crest. Because fifteen varieties of apples are picked from their apple orchard, homemade cider is often poured. Also on the table are Sherry's homemade jams and preserves – maybe black currant/red raspberry, mirabelle plum or gooseberry/red currant. Local fruit is served from early June to mid-September (we loved the raspberries), often with the Rosemanns' own crème fraîche. There's always a choice of two main dishes. One day it might be a custard french toast with bananas foster and a smoked salmon and dill quiche; the next, eggs sardou and Charles's extra-special puffy Black Forest apple pancake, which we can attest is absolutely yummy. The coffee is his own blend of beans, including Kona from Hawaii.

Sherry and Charles Rosemann in front of The Rose Inn.

The Rosemanns set an elegant dinner table as well, with candles, flowers, sterling silver and sparkling wine glasses. A many-course feast fit for a king costs $55. The dinner is optional and must be ordered in advance, but it could turn out to be your most memorable meal in the Finger Lakes area.

You might start as we did with smoked oysters in a puff pastry and hot artichoke strudel accompanied by smoked artichokes and mango-artichoke salsa. The colorful salad was a work of art: boston lettuce with snow peas, radicchio, watercress and sprouts, dotted with red and yellow peppers and red and yellow tomatoes, and enhanced with a raspberry-dijon vinaigrette. The rack of lamb (cooked on an outdoor grill, even in winter) or grilled loin of venison might be garnished with baby ears of corn. Scampi Mediterranean style is served on a bed of acini, the sauce including a touch of curry and pinenuts on top. And the béarnaise sauce on the châteaubriand is first rate. Our favorite vegetable was the potato basket, which the Rosemanns do with every dinner. Individual grand-marnier soufflés with either chocolate or a foamy brandy sauce are a perfect end to the meal, but perhaps you'd prefer fresh raspberries with cointreau? The mostly French wine list is selective as well, with several dozen carefully-put-together choices priced from the teens to $150.

On Friday and Saturday nights, the hunt-themed Carriage House restaurant is open to the public. The à la carte menu offers eight entrées ($13.95 to $18.95), perhaps grilled tuna in a pink peppercorn cream sauce, osso buco milanese and pecan-crusted filet mignon with a pinot noir sauce. The roasted garlic, goat cheese and mushroom strudel is a favorite appetizer. Live music is offered from 7:30 to 11:30.

With the expansion, the Rose Inn has added a full-time manager, a chef and two cooks. The owners' goal was to offer first-class lodging and a fine dining experience. They have succeeded in spades.

(607) 533-7905. Fax (607) 533-7908. Dinner by reservation, Tuesday-Saturday at 7; also Carriage House, Friday and Saturday 6 to 10. Doubles, $125 to $175; suites, $200 to $275. Two-night minimum on weekends.

Morgan-Samuels Inn, 2920 Smith Road, Canandaigua 14424.

Actor Judson Morgan, not J.P. Morgan as was first thought, built this rambling stone mansion in 1810, and eventually it became the home of industrialist Howard Samuels, who ran unsuccessfully for governor of New York a couple of decades ago. The house was acquired in 1989 by Julie and John Sullivan, who left jobs in Geneseo to convert it into a very special inn. They named it the J.P. Morgan House, but later learned they were in error and, honest and perfectionist types that they are, they renamed it the Morgan-Samuels in 1993. Remotely situated on 46 rural acres and run ever so personally by the Sullivans, it offers one of the more peaceful, utterly relaxing situations we know of.

One fastidious innkeeper of our acquaintance said she had the best breakfast ever here. Ours certainly was a triumph, and so pretty we wished we'd brought along a camera for a color photograph, although this was an instance where a photo could not do it justice.

The meal – for some the highlight of a stay at this sophisticated and enchanting B&B – is taken in the beamed dining room, in a glass-enclosed breakfast-tea room with potbelly stove or outside on the rear patio. John is in charge of cooking – he and eight-year-old son Jonathan make an early-morning run to the supermarket to pick out the perfect fruit for the first course. We counted 26 varieties on the exquisitely put-together silver platter, including local Irondequoit melon, mango, two kinds of grapes, papaya, persimmon, figs, kiwis and prunes sautéed in lemon sauce. Preceding the platter was fresh orange juice served in delicate etched glasses. Following were huge and delicious carrot muffins and a choice of buckwheat pancakes with blackberries, blueberries or pecans (or all three), scrambled eggs with herbs, french toast or a double-cheese omelet. The last was one of the best breakfast treats we've had. It looked like a pizza with slices of tomato, scallions, red peppers, jalapeño peppers, mushrooms, herbs and parsley. Monterey jack, mozzarella, parmesan and blue cheeses were on top. Spicy sausage patties and sunflower-seed toast accompanied this breakfast worthy of a Morgan, as did hazelnut coffee.

The Sullivans join their guests for hors d'oeuvres and beverages in the late afternoon, which helps break the ice so "everybody is friends when they get together for breakfast the next morning," says Julie. The treats range from John's homemade sauces on chicken wings to cheese and crackers. They accompany hot or iced tea, cider or sparkling grape juice from local vineyards.

John will prepare dinners by advance reservation for six or more guests ($30 to $50 each, depending on number and selection of courses). Guests bring their own wine and enjoy togetherness in the dining room or the enclosed garden porch, or privacy in five separate dining areas. The birds were chirping, the fountains trickling and classical music playing as we dined by candlelight with fine silver and china on the garden porch. Our meal, which John said was typical, produced a procession of whitefish with horseradish sauce, pasta shells in a hot Bahamian sauce, garlic bread, a fabulous chilled peach soup and a mixed salad bearing everything from strawberries and apples to beets, snow peas and artichoke hearts, dressed with raspberry vinaigrette studded with bacon and capers. The main course was filet mignon with a sherry-herb sauce, accompanied by green beans, mushrooms, cauliflower, potatoes, and broccoli and cheese. Dutch apple pie with ice cream ended a spectacular meal. "I cook the way I like to cook," says John, who has no formal training. He certainly cooks the way we like to eat, although we would have had to be super-human to finish it all.

John and Julie Sullivan serve sumptuous breakfasts on terrace at Morgan-Samuels Inn.

Although food is obviously a passion here, the five guest rooms and a suite and the common areas are hardly afterthoughts. The Morgan Suite is lavish with early 18th-century French furniture, a kingsize bed, an over-length loveseat in front of the TV and a double jacuzzi in a corner of the bathroom. A fountain sounds like a babbling brook beneath Evy's Chamber, a Victorian fantasy with a rosewood queensize bed. The Antique Rose Room has a fireplace, a floral carpet and one of the first kingsize beds ever made. Our room on the third floor, small but exquisitely done, featured an interesting Gothic window beneath a cathedral ceiling and a kingsize bed awash with fourteen pillows. All rooms are air-conditioned, have private baths and are equipped with reproduction radios and tape cassettes.

Soft music is piped throughout the house and across the grounds, and candles glow in the common rooms. Besides the aforementioned garden porch where we like to relax, there are a well-furnished living room, an intimate Victorian library with a TV and one of the mansion's eight fireplaces, and fine oil paintings all around. Outside are no fewer than four landscaped patios (one with a trickling fountain and another with a lily pond and waterfall), a tennis court and gardens. Ducks and chickens and a heifer or two roam around in the distance. You could easily imagine you were at a house party in the country with *the* J.P. Morgan et al.

(716) 394-9232. Fax (716) 394-8044. Doubles, $119 to $179; suite, $220. Dinner for house guests by reservation, Thursday-Sunday at 7 or 7:30.

Geneva on the Lake, 1001 Lochland Road (Route 14), Geneva 14456.

If you want to pretend you are in a villa on an Italian lake, stay a night or two at this onetime monastery, now a European-style resort hotel beside Seneca Lake.

Built in 1910 as a replica of the Lancellotti Villa in Frascati outside Rome, with marble fireplaces and symmetrical gardens, the original Byron M. Nester estate was the home from 1949 to 1974 of Capuchin monks, who added a chapel, dormitory and dining room. Influenced by the Algonquin Hotel in New York, designer William J. Schickel of Ithaca turned it first into apartments and then into a deluxe resort with 30 rooms and suites in 1981.

The Schickel family sold in 1995 to Alfred and Aminy Audi of Syracuse, who had saved the ailing Stickley furniture company and put it in an expansion mode. The Audis kept a low profile, telling the staff they would build on the Schickel legacy and "share in the vision that will make Geneva on the Lake the crown jewel of all resorts."

Gradual refurbishing was under way for all accommodations. They range from studio bedrooms to suites with fireplaced living rooms and two-story townhouses. The bigger ones like the Landmark one-bedroom suite with kitchen and elegant living room in which we last stayed were already were quite luxurious in an understated way. The Landmark made the small studio in which we first stayed (a combination living-bedroom with a queensize murphy bed and a small kitchenette) seem cramped and a bit dated. Some of the dormitory vestiges inevitably remained, although under the new ownership, one suspected, not for long.

The setting is spectacular. Manicured grounds dotted with marble statues stretch to the swimming pool on a bluff at lake's edge. A trail leads down to the lake, where guests may swim, fish or use a paddle boat, or charter a private sailboat skippered by a semi-retired orthopedic surgeon. A colonnade provides a lovely shaded area for breakfast, lunch or cocktails on the rear terrace, which converts to a skating rink in winter.

Guests are treated to a complimentary bottle of wine in their room and, on Friday nights, a tasting of New York State wines and cheeses.

A light continental breakfast of fresh juice and croissants is included in the rates. A full breakfast is available. The scrambled eggs with cream cheese and the shirred eggs with Canadian bacon are excellent.

Candlelight dinners with live music are offered to guests and the public Friday through Sunday in the romantic Lancellotti Dining Room that could well be in Rome; it's the former chapel with carved wood ceilings, marble fireplaces and tapestries. A 17th-century Mexican tin-crafted mirror and Italian chandeliered sconces are among its treasures.

A singer and a pianist or a cellist entertain as guests partake of appetizers like dilled jumbo shrimp cocktail (featured in Bon Appétit magazine), and such entrées ($21.95 to $39.80) as veal scampi diane, mesquite-grilled tournedos béarnaise and Australian lobster tail. We enjoyed a dinner of chicken Jacqueline in port wine and heavy cream with sliced apples and toasted almonds and the night's special sherried shrimp dejonghe, both with crisp beans and mixed rice, followed by pumpkin cheesecake and a grand-marnier mousse. A $21.50 Hermann J. Wiemer riesling was one of the more affordable accompaniments from a pricey wine list.

New in 1996 were midweek dinners on Wednesday and Thursday nights. The prix-fixe menu ($34.50) offers four courses with a choice of six entrées and three desserts.

Locals who object to the dinner prices are quite smitten with summer lunches on the shaded Colonnade Pavilion terrace. Prices range from $6.60 for a vegetarian delight to $12.95 for chicken provençal. We liked the garlicky and chunky vegetable gazpacho with a curried chicken and avocado plate, the carrot-ginger soup with a curried chicken in pita sandwich, followed by a cheesecake with blueberries and a delectable frozen grand marnier coupe.

Geneva on the Lake resort accommodates guests in Italian-style villa.

The resort is expensive, but worth it for special occasions. Spring for a Landmark suite ($332) with a four-poster bed and a lovely view or a deluxe suite with fireplace and balcony ($289).

(315) 789-7190 or (800) 343-6382. Fax (315) 789-0322. Lunch in summer, Monday-Saturday noon to 2; dinner seatings, Wednesday and Thursday at 6:30 and 7, Friday and Saturday at 7 or 7:30, Sunday at 6:30 or 7. Sunday brunch, 9 to 11:30. Doubles, $225; suites, $261 to $481.

Benn Conger Inn, 206 West Cortland St., Groton.

A restaurant of distinction and fastidious attention to detail in accommodations draw people to this 1921 classic Revival mansion in out-of-the-way Groton. Chef-owner Peter van der Meulen mans the kitchen, while his wife Alison does the baking and oversees the front of the house.

The main floor of the Colonial Revival mansion holds a cozy library/lounge and three elegant dining rooms enhanced by fine artworks done by a family friend. Along the side is a smashing porch/conservatory in white and green, where tables are set with white linens and fresh flowers. The colorful candlesticks and flower pots that grace each table, handpainted by a local artisan, are for sale.

Peter's Mediterranean-inspired cuisine includes appetizers like gravlax, coquilles St. Jacques and marinated artichoke hearts served hot with gruyère and chèvre. Pastas, available as appetizers or main courses, include fish-shaped ravioli filled with smoked salmon and served in a light tomato cream sauce, and spicy crayfish ravioli with sausage, tomato and garlic salsa.

Main dishes ($17 to $24) are as varied as shrimp, scallops and mussels in cognac cream, served over black lobster-filled ravioli; roasted cornish game hen stuffed with grapes and wild mushrooms, grilled flank steak provençal, and grilled veal chop with blackberry demi-glace and wild mushroom ragoût.

Peter's desserts include an acclaimed crème brûlée with blackberries, a classic French cheesecake with mascarpone and cream cheese, and marjolaines. The wine list holds the Wine Spectator award of excellence.

The treats for overnight guests continue in the morning with a five-course breakfast in the pretty conservatory dining room. Expect a choice of juices, fruit (crenshaw melon with mixed berries at our visit) and a pastry course, perhaps Danish aebleskiver, crêpes or blueberry-buttermilk pancakes. Then – can you stand it? – comes the main course. It could be eggs benedict or a frittata with three kinds of wild mushrooms, cheddar and chèvre. The last course is breakfast meats (surely you weren't expecting dessert).

Guests stay upstairs in three suites and one bedroom, all with private baths and television. The largest is the Dutch Schultz suite, named for the infamous bootlegger and racketeer who found this a safe haven following the departure of original owner Benn Conger, a state senator, banker and founder of the Corona Corporation (later Smith-Corona). The kingsize brass bed is outfitted with 310-count percale sheets and down or feather pillows, and the TV is hidden in an armoire. You may get lost in the bathroom, surely one of the world's biggest – it seemingly goes on forever in assorted rooms and alcoves. Though very different in feeling, each accommodation contains period furnishings appropriate to the 1920s. Guests gather in a small, wicker-furnished common area in the hallway at the head of the stairs, or join outside diners in the cozy library/bar with fireplace and piano.

(607) 898-5817. Dinner, Wednesday-Sunday 5:30 to 9. Double, $120; suites, $145 to $220.

Sherwood Inn, 26 West Genesee St., Skaneateles 13152.

This landmark inn of the old school, dating to 1807, commands a prime site at the head of the clearest and what some consider the loveliest of the Finger Lakes. It's as famous in its own right as the Krebs restaurant just up the street, but the Sherwood has better adapted with the times.

William B. Eberhardt, who bought the inn in 1974, has undertaken extensive refurbishing lately. Several of the thirteen guest rooms and six suites on the second and third floors are quite distinctive. Many offer lake views and all come with private baths, telephones and antique furnishings. Some have queensize beds, fireplaces and TVs, and several have whirlpool baths or, in one case, a hot tub. Rates include a continental breakfast.

The main floor has turned into a community focal point, and its fireplace lobby with a gift shop, recently expanded corner tavern, formal dining room and a long, summery dining porch are favorite gathering spots. We enjoyed the view of Skaneateles Lake across the street as we lunched on the enclosed porch, newly renovated with a radiant-heated flagstone floor and dressed in pristine white with vases of freesia on the tables and Jeffersonian windows that open to let in the breeze. The extensive tavern menu is used at lunch, with salads and sandwiches in the $4.95 to $10.95 range.

For dinner ($14.50 to $24.95), traditional favorites like fillet of scrod baked in a cracker-crumb crust, chicken piccata and prime rib with pan gravy vie for attention with more updated items like grilled swordfish with a preserved ginger and onion jam and grilled pork medallions with onion and apple jam. Starters include a pâté of duck liver mousse with port and truffles, wild mushroom feuillette and baked brie wrapped in phyllo. Radicchio and grilled portobello mushrooms jazz up the spinach salad. Dessert could be country inn cobbler, crème caramel or fresh berries and cream.

(315) 685-3405 or (800) 374-3796. Fax (315) 685-8983. Lunch, 11:30 to 3:30; dinner, 5 to 9 or 10; tavern, 11:30 to 9 or 10. Doubles, $75 to $145; suites, $95 to $225.

Lodging

Hanshaw House B&B, 15 Sapsucker Woods Road, Ithaca 14850.

She loves country inns, decorating and entertaining, so the wife of an Ithaca College dean put it all together in a sumptuous country B&B. Helen Scoones, who used to work for a decorator, did the decorating herself in this restored 1830 farmhouse with a second-story addition and a new rear wing for the couple's living quarters.

Furnished with flair and an eye to the comforts of home, Hanshaw House offers four air-conditioned guest rooms, all with private baths and two with sitting areas. We lucked into the second-floor suite, with a queensize feather bed, down comforter and pillows, English country antique furnishings, a modern bath and plenty of space to spread out. We didn't need all that space, however, for we had the run of the house – a classy living room outfitted in chintz and wicker with dhurries all over, a side room with TV, and a lovely yard backing up to a small pond and woods full of deer, woodchucks and other wildlife.

Always upgrading her rooms, Helen showed the newly tiled bathroom, the floral sheets and the new curtains in a main-floor bedroom that she decorated in "MacKenzie-esque style," a reference to the colorful pottery from the nearby MacKenzie-Childs studio.

Gardens are now on view on both sides from the refurbished television room. Beyond it in the new wing is "my pièce de résistance," a formal dining room with a crystal chandelier, oriental rugs on pegged floors and french doors opening onto the rear patio and gardens

Helen greets guests with iced lemon tea or mulled cider and cookies in the afternoon. Early-risers are pampered with a choice of exotic coffees, perhaps taken at a table in the country kitchen as Helen and a Culinary Institute-trained assistant prepare a gourmet breakfast. Ours included fresh orange juice, an orange-banana yogurt frappe and Swedish pancakes puffed in the oven with peaches and crème fraîche. Other main courses could be quiche, frittata with homemade popovers, baked french toast with caramel sauce, baked eggs and heart-shaped waffles.

Breakfast is served in the new dining room on blue and white china. The table is set with crocheted lace mats and field flowers in colorful MacKenzie-Childs pottery. The candles are dressed with MacKenzie-Childs lamp shades and the glasses are handpainted with rosebuds. They epitomize the interesting touches that abound at Hanshaw House.

(607) 257-1437 or (800) 257-1437. Fax (607) 266-8866. Doubles, $77 to $120.

Buttermilk Falls B&B, 110 East Buttermilk Falls Road, Ithaca 14850.

A huge painting of the Buttermilk Falls gorge graces the stairway landing at this attractive, white brick 1825 house, which is the closest private building to Buttermilk Falls. Margie Rumsey came to the home of her late husband's grandfather as a bride in 1948. The couple ran it as a tourist home until they had children. When their youngest son graduated from Cornell in 1983, she reopened it as a B&B and has been improving it ever since.

Now all five guest rooms have private baths, though some are down the hall, and some retain a homey look (built-in cupboards like those one of us grew up with). But good art of Finger Lakes scenes, oriental rugs and early American antiques enhance each room. The luxurious downstairs bedroom in which we stayed has a wood-burning fireplace and a double jacuzzi surrounded by plants in the corner, from which we could glimpse Buttermilk Falls through the hedge.

Classical music plays throughout the public rooms. These include a parlor with games like chess and checkers and collections from Margie's world travels, a plant-filled dining room notable for a long cherry table flanked by twelve different styles of windsor chairs made by her son Ed, a large kitchen and a comfortable screened porch with a garden in one corner.

Breakfast is an event, starting perhaps with a frozen orange concoction that includes a whole banana and is spiced with fresh ginger. Margie invites guests to build "a cereal sundae" with a variety of fruit and nut toppings on her hot whole-grain cereal. Next might come a cheese soufflé with a hot local salsa, served with yogurt to cool it down. "I never serve muffins; everyone else has them," says she. Instead she features toasted sourdough-rye bread or popovers, with intense peach-ginger, raspberry and rhubarb-raspberry jams that we found sensational. Guests in the dining room barter with those on the porch – and vice-versa – for exchanges on jams, seconds and what not, with loquacious Margie encouraging it all as she cooks up a storm on her AGA stove in the kitchen in the midst of all the fun.

A rear carriage house includes a simple two-room cottage good for families. It's not far from the large maple tree up which the hostess sometimes climbs in good weather to sleep out in an open-air tree house.

(607) 272-6767. Doubles, $85 to $145; jacuzzi room, $150 to $250.

The Federal House, 175 Ludlowville Road, Lansing 14882.

Antiques collector Diane Carroll closed her former Decker Pond Inn south of Ithaca and reopened north of town in the rural mill hamlet of Ludlowville. Here, instead of a pond, she has Salmon Creek Falls within earshot, plus a park-like setting. Diane has fashioned a great side yard, complete with prolific flower gardens, a gazebo and a white garden swing beneath a trellis canopy. There's an expansive wicker-filled side porch from which to take it all in.

The interior of the gracious 1815 house was stripped to its original woodwork and floors before Diane decorated it elegantly in the Federal style. Candles flicker by day in the handsome living room and at breakfast in the formal dining room.

Any cook would covet Diane's enormous country kitchen that stretches across the back of the house and includes a center island and a dining area. Here she prepares lavish breakfasts for guests. One day it might be fresh orange juice, an apple-banana crisp with sour cream sauce, banana bran muffins and stuffed french toast with cream cheese and peach marmalade with sautéed peaches on top. The next day could bring cantaloupe with lime-yogurt sauce and fresh mint, blueberry muffins and oven-baked eggs with vegetables. Individual vegetable soufflés are served with steamed asparagus and broiled tomatoes on the side.

Upstairs in the rear of the house is the new Seward Suite, named for William Seward of nearby Auburn, secretary of state under Abraham Lincoln. He courted his future wife in this, her uncle's summer house. The accommodation of choice comes with a sitting room with gas fireplace, TV and a day bed, and a large and airy high-ceilinged bedroom decked out in wicker with a queen bed, plush carpeting and spiffy white and green decor. Also with air-conditioning and private baths are two more bedrooms reached by a steep rear staircase. Each is decorated with flair and appointed with antiques. The front Lincoln Suite has a queensize canopied four-poster bed, fireplace and TV.

Diane sells antiques and gifts in her little Blueberry Muffin Gift Corner. Every guest leaves with a tiny loaf of banana bread, wrapped with a blue ribbon.
(607) 533-7362 or (800) 533-7362. Doubles, $120 to $125; suites, $135 and $175.

The Red House Country Inn, 4586 Picnic Area Road, Burdett 14818.

Innkeepers Joan Martin and Sandy Schmanke and their guests are the only humans in this preserve in the Finger Lakes National Forest, full of birds and wildlife. Leaving careers in Rochester, they opened their charming B&B inn in an 1844 farmhouse. Three dogs and four goats are part of the entourage.

Five upstairs bedrooms, all lovingly furnished with antiques in a quaint country style, share four baths, two up and two down, nicely outfitted with perfumes, powders and soaps. Guests sip sherry by the fireplace in the old-fashioned parlor and sometimes play board games. A stunning scene of the area, hand-stitched with 60 kinds of material by a guest from Canada, graces the wall of the main dining room. Country items are offered in the good little gift shop. There are a kitchen for making drinks or snacks and a wicker-filled front veranda to relax on, as well as berries to be picked and miles of trails awaiting in the forest.

And not long ago, for her 50th birthday, Sandy treated herself and guests to a great new swimming pool, flanked by a patio and cabana where guests can lounge and barbecue. The last is a good thing, as it's a bit of a trek into Watkins Glen or Ithaca for dinner.

In the off-season from November through April, for an astonishingly low $18 a head, the owners sometimes prepare country dinners for house guests with advance notice. Ours started with a great composed spinach salad and homemade rolls. The main course was a whole roasted chicken with a rice and pecan stuffing, green beans with mushrooms and delightful pattypan squash. Banana-cream pie capped a meal that was nicely paced and graciously served. Other entrée possibilities might be duck garnished with fresh raspberries in vodka and accompanied by wild rice, or poached salmon steaks with dill sauce on the side. A frequent guest brings saffron to put in the rice pilafs and paellas. Meals often begin with Red House chowder, which has a potato and leek base and adds cream and fresh vegetables. Warden tarts made with local warden grapes, butter-pecan-rum cake, chocolate-chestnut cake with kahlua-butter cream, and fruit pies and tarts are among desserts.

Breakfast, served in the main dining room with its pressed-oak chairs and lace cloths or in a smaller adjunct to the side, always includes juice and a fruit course, which in our case was a dish of peaches, blueberries and raspberries, garnished with mint from the owners' garden. Butter scones with black currants, pecan popovers, banana pancakes and cottage french toast are some of the goodies. We were quite happy with scrambled eggs, ham and toast.

"Our raspberries are as big as most strawberries," says Sandy. We know. She led us up the road to her favorite haunts to pick blueberries and black raspberries, and then directed us to a pick-your-own raspberry patch. We enjoyed assorted berries from the Finger Lakes for days afterward.
(607) 546-8566. Doubles, $60 to $85.

Gourmet Treats

There's a growing regional awareness of what one booster calls the "foods of the Finger Lakes," a reference to the diversity of locally produced foods, from goat cheese to exotic produce. Having returned from California, where he had spent ten years in the food business, a restaurant manager in Ithaca contended that "some of the foods being produced here are as good if not better than their more publicized California counterparts."

A national model, the **Ithaca Farmers' Market** is a joy for fresh produce, local crafts and odds and ends (free kittens, bluegrass music, hand-stenciled shirts and such). Fresh egg rolls or falafel sandwiches washed down with homemade raspberry juice are one local innkeeper's Saturday lunch of choice. The market operates at Steamboat Landing off Route 13 north of downtown on Saturdays from 9 to 2 and Sundays from 10 to 2. A smaller version operates Tuesdays from 9 to 2 in Dewitt Park downtown at Buffalo and Cayuga streets.

Another market is **The Windmill,** the first rural farm and craft market in New York State and now with more than 225 vendors. Likened to the Pennsylvania farm markets (Mennonite foods are available), it's off Route 14 between Penn Yan and Dundee. Wineries are among the booths that operate Saturdays from 8 to 4:30 from late April through mid-December.

Ludgate Produce Farms, 1552 Hanshaw Road, Ithaca, is where you can get an idea of the variety and magnitude of the local food phenomenon. It is a produce stand without peer, as well as a purveyor of fresh herbs (eight kinds of mint; seven kinds of thyme), edible flowers for garnishes, wild game and a potpourri of specialty items. Linda Ludgate and her brother Michael started two decades ago with a card table along the road, selling produce from their father's fields. Today, the stand is an enclosed store open 365 days a year. Local restaurateurs shop here for hard-to-find foods, exotic lettuces and rare vegetables.

The Brous and Mehaffey families have cornered a good share of the specialty-foods market in Ithaca since they bought **Collegetown Bagels** at 413 College Ave. in 1981. Now with a branch downtown at 203 North Aurora St., this is where local folks go for twelve varieties of bagels, baked fresh daily. Bagel sandwiches and a fourteen-foot-long salad, soup and baked-potato bar are attractions. (The downtown outlet has a new adjunct called **Basics – Soup, Salad & Bread** at 201 North Aurora.) A few years later they opened **CTB Appetizers**, which calls itself "Ithaca's ultimate gourmet takeout," in Triphammer Mall. There are tables in back for enjoying the fare, from exotic salads to "outrageous sandwiches" to bagels to desserts like almond tarts. In 1989 they purchased the **Ithaca Bakery** at 400 North Meadow St. to create a flagship store with the best of all their operations in a single location. Here is a gourmet paradise, where we've often found the makings for a fabulous picnic or a dinner at home. We have a tough time deciding between salads and roasted chicken items, but that's nothing compared to our dilemma in front of the pastry counter. The scope of the possibilities is unbelievable.

Now You're Cooking at 124 Cayuga St. carries unusual aprons, many regional and other cookbooks, dishes painted with colorful fruits and vegetables, fine flatware and napkins. Along with classic cookware are hard-to-find gadgets and an enormous collection of cookie cutters.

North Side Wine & Spirits boasts the largest selection of Finger Lakes wines in the world. It may be an idle boast, although the owner says he checked around. The selection is mind-boggling and nicely priced. The toughest part is finding the place, which actually is on the south side of town in the Ithaca Shopping Plaza off Elmira Road, where the sign calls it Discount Beverage Center.

A supermarket for gourmets? You bet, in Ithaca. In fact, there are two almost side by side on Route 13 south. Some folks like **Tops,** but we prefer **Wegmans,** an outgrowth of the Wegmans markets we frequented many years ago when we lived in Rochester, its headquarters. The updated Wegmans in Ithaca, and to a lesser extent the one in Canandaigua, are heaven on earth for food lovers. The Ultimate Coffee Adventure, a coffee bar and shop at the entry, sets the stage for the wonders to come. We enjoyed a medium latte for $1.69 as we ogled pastry delectables and pondered the choices at the bakery and the gourmet salad bar (from broccoli slaw to caesar with shrimp or chicken), the deli quiche, chicken fajita and muffuletta pizzas, shrimp egg rolls and an array of chicken dishes (from herbed to fried to ribs to sweet and sour wings). With choices like these to eat here or to go, who'd ever cook at home? But if you want to, Wegmans will oblige. The 26 checkout counters at the front await.

In Watkins Glen, **Sullivan's** at 309 North Franklin St. is the place for home-made fudge, hand-dipped chocolates and butter crunch. Head for the **Glen Mountain Market** at 200 North Franklin for fine sandwiches ($3.75 to $5.95). The Blues Brother is turkey breast with sliced apples and blue cheese on homemade bread. Vegetarians will find a good selection of salads and sandwiches as well as a tofu burger. You can eat at one of the market's picnic tables.

Glen Mountain Market owners Shari and Brud Holland branched out in 1996, opening **Seneca Valley Kitchens** up the west side of Seneca Lake at 5438 Route 14 in Glenora. Here they started selling specialty foods and dispensing salads, deli sandwiches, cheese and "vegetarian salami" platters at rustic tables inside and out. Over the winter, they used the expansive kitchen to produce their new vegan food line called Salami della Terra, incorporating seitan with sundried tomatoes, Southwest hickory and the like for distribution nationally. Look for it to show up in sandwiches, salads and pizzas. Also look for their new full-service lunch and dinner restaurant, planned to operate here May-October daily from 10 to 8 starting in 1997.

In its first year, a new house on a hilltop just north of Penn Yan became something of a destination. **Miller's Essenhaus Restaurant & Bakery** at 1300 Route 14A offers wholesome foods and breads, prepared by local Mennonites. Sandwiches, Amish stew and country platters are featured at lunch in the $2.50 to $5.95 range. The dinner menu is priced from $6.95 for church supper ham loaf to $10.95 for grilled New York strip steak. The bakery alone is worth a stop. Open Monday-Saturday 7 a.m. to 9 p.m.

Canandaigua has two special shops of interest to gourmets. **Renaissance – the Goodie II Shoppe at 56 South Main St.** stocks all the socially correct gifts, from jewelry to porcelain dolls, Port Merion china and lovely Christmas ornaments. Cookbooks (we picked up Linda McCarthy's for a vegetarian son) and nifty paper plates and napkins abound. At **Cat's in the Kitchen,** 367 West Ave., Laurel Wemett has collected, from tag sales and auctions, all the things our mothers and grandmothers used in the kitchen. She specializes in the Depression era to the 1960s, and it's fun to check the old canisters, cookie jars, china, pots and pans and more. New items are mixed in.

Skaneateles has become a mecca for shoppers lately, and the feeling in shops backing up to Skaneateles Lake is palpably upscale. **Pomodoro,** our favorite gift shop here for many years, now has two locations – one in a landmark bank with a vault museum and a branch of Syracuse's Everson Museum Shop at 2 East Genesee St., and the other an older ramble of rooms in a house at 61 East Genesee. Cookbooks, a few specialty foods, dishes and placemats are among the wares. **Rhubarb** at 59 East Genesee is a small but select kitchen and garden shop, where everything from gadgets and gourmet foods to espresso makers is chosen with great taste and nicely displayed. Friendship pays, says owner Kay DiNardo, for **Vermont Green Mountain Specialty Co.** at 50 East Genesee is the only retailer to whom Albert Kumin sells his famed Green Mountain Chocolate Co. candies. His luscious chocolates vie for attention with Green Mountain coffees and Vermont specialty foods at this most unlikely place for a Vermont shop.

Gourmet China

MacKenzie-Childs Ltd., Route 90, Aurora.
You may have seen the fanciful handpainted china of the MacKenzie-Childs studio in fine gift shops and department stores across the country. Their design and production studio is in the area – a wonderful estate called Highbanks on 55 acres above Cayuga Lake, a couple of miles north of Aurora. Until lately, two rooms of great fantasy in the Victorian home of Victoria and Richard MacKenzie-Childs showed their furniture, china, painted floor rugs and trimmings, all noted for their intricate stripes, dots, checkerboards, fish and pastoral landscapes. In 1996, the shops were merged into an old barn relocated to the grounds. Ninety-minute tours of the studios are given weekdays at 10, and there are a couple of shops where seconds are sold. The couple invite visitors to picnic on their beautiful grounds; and provide a pushcart where you can buy a hot dog, ice cream or lemonade.
(315) 364-7123. Showroom and shop, Monday-Saturday 10 to 5; studio tours, Monday-Friday at 10.

Gourmet Gardens

Sonnenberg Gardens, 151 Charlotte St., Canandaigua.
Restored in 1973 after 40 years of neglect, the Victorian gardens here are recognized by the Smithsonian as some of the most magnificent ever created in America. The 50-acre estate around their 40-room summer home was planned at the turn of the century by Mary Clark Thompson, who traveled the world to create nine formal gardens, an arboretum, a greenhouse complex and more as a memorial to her husband. We were quite taken by the Japanese hill garden and tea house, the Pansy Garden in which even the bird bath is shaped like a pansy, and a rock garden with streams, waterfalls and pools fed by geysers and springs. Marvelous, too, are all the accompanying statues, gazebos, belvederes, arbors, a temple of Diana, a sitting Buddha and even a Roman bath. The mansion, a testament to the extravagances of the Gilded Age, has its own delights, among them the Lavender & Old Lace gift shop. The greenhouse in which Mrs. Thompson raised peaches and nectarines is now the Peach House, a jaunty little luncheon spot (open daily in season, 11:30 to 2). There's also a Widmer's Wine Tasting Room.
(716) 394-4922. Gardens and mansion daily, 9:30 to 5:30, mid-May to mid-October. Adults, $6.50.

Roadside stands testify to nature's bounty all around Niagara fruit belt.

Niagara-on-the-Lake
Wine, Orchards and Shaw

We first met Niagara-on-the-Lake in the late 1960s when it was Sleepy Hollow, as Canadians sometimes called it.

With a set of parents in tow, we had driven to Ontario from our home in Rochester, N.Y., so a visiting father could see "The Devil's Disciple" by one of his favorite playwrights, George Bernard Shaw. After a matinee performance at the Court House Theatre, we browsed through the few shops worth browsing, ate dinner at the quaint Oban Inn and headed home under a full moon. It was the historic night when man first landed on the moon, and that extra-terrestrial feat remained etched in our consciousness long after the Niagara outing had been forgotten.

Now, many moons later, we regard Niagara-on-the-Lake much more fondly. This Sleepy Hollow has awakened, spread its wings and come of age. The opening in 1973 of the Shaw Festival Theater sparked a renaissance in culture and tourism on a scale perhaps unmatched in eastern North America.

It was quite a change for this charming, tree-lined town located where the Niagara River meets Lake Ontario. The first capital of what was called Upper Canada, it played a pivotal role in the War of 1812 – still called "the war" in local circles today. But the capital was moved to safer ground in Toronto and business languished as the Welland Canal bypassed Niagara to the west.

Spared the onslaught that an economic boom can wreak, Niagara's Old Town was an architectural treasury of early buildings awaiting revival. The home-grown Shaw Festival provided that impetus, attracting a clientele that demanded good lodging and good eating. Niagara-on-the-Lake now offers both with charm and style.

Geography has afforded the area natural advantages. Old military reserves and farmlands provide a greenbelt around the town. The Niagara River Parkway cuts through 35 miles of the prettiest park lands and scenery you'll ever see. The Niagara fruit belt yields an abundance of fresh fruits and vegetables. And wineries have flourished in what Canadians call "the Napa of the North."

We're always struck by the British ties of so many innkeepers and restaurateurs in this most English of Canadian towns, which traces its roots to the Empire Loyalists who fled to Canada during the American Revolution. Many an inn and restaurant goes all-out for afternoon tea, a daily ritual here.

There are no chain stores or hotels, beyond a large Crabtree & Evelyn branch that seems very much at home and a newer Dansk outlet that doesn't. There is only one traffic light (at the edge of town). A clock tower in the middle of Queen Street is the dominant landmark of the flower-bedecked downtown.

Come along and see why Niagara-on-the-Lake is such a choice getaway for the gourmet.

Dining

The Best of the Best

On the Twenty Restaurant & Wine Bar, 3638 Main St., Jordan.

Ontario's first full-service winery restaurant draws food lovers from miles around. Housed in the old Jordan Winery dating to 1870, the restaurant has an elegant country air and food to match.

"You can't imagine what it's like for a cook to come into an area like this," said young executive chef Michael Olson, who trained in Toronto and Ottawa restaurants. Upon arrival at the ambitious food and catering venture launched in 1993 by the owners of the adjacent Cave Spring Cellars, Michael took off on his mountain bike to scout out local purveyors. His forays turned up growers who provide him with everything from mesclun to mushrooms. With Angelo Pavan, Cave Spring's winemaker, he set about matching wines and foods for adventuresome palates. He bottles his own vinegars and preserves, and bakes the incredible breads that accompany every meal.

His lunch and dinner menus are among the area's most innovative. The winemaker's prix-fixe lunch ($20) might start with chilled potato and leek soup, offer a choice of local trout with honey mustard or quail in a maple-raspberry vinaigrette, and include a dessert of fruit cobbler, beverage and a glass of chardonnay or riesling. À la carte possibilities range from a goat cheese and potato terrine ($7) to the daily sandwich with soup or salad ($10) to grilled Atlantic salmon on red and yellow pepper sauces or beef strip loin with yukon gold potato fries and mushroom ragoût (both $17).

At dinner, our party of four was impressed with both the tastes and presentations. A bruschetta of toasted sourdough bread with herbed tomatoes barely made it around the table, so good was each morsel. Among other starters ($5 to $10), the Hamilton Mountain mushroom bisque with chardonnay cream and sourdough croutons was a work of art and the salad of roasted sweet bell peppers on greens with baked olives and feta cheese was sensational. The pan-fried chicken livers with sour cherries atop greens and toasted pumpkin seeds was an interesting if not wholly successful combination, and the chilled cucumber soup with smoked trout

Dining room at On the Twenty Restaurant & Wine Bar looks onto wooded ravine.

and chives turned out a bit bland. For main courses ($17 to $24), we were delighted with the Pacific halibut with sweet-corn salsa, grilled trout with golden plum and mint salsa, roast lamb with red and black currants, and fresh spaghettini with roast chicken, leeks and apricots in a riesling-olive oil sauce. Each plate came with chef Michael's trademark decoration, squiggles of pureed beets blended with yogurt, as well as simple steamed vegetables.

The night's desserts included blueberry/sour-cream cake with maple hard sauce, chocolate-espresso torte with caramelized orange glaze and cardamom cream, and a selection of standard ice-cream flavors. All of us passed in favor of a sample of Cave Spring's riesling icewine, which winemaker Angelo correctly described as "dessert in a glass" – a heavenly ending to a most pleasing meal.

Dining is at white-linened tables in a couple of airy rooms with sponged pale gold walls, floors and columns of travertine marble, striking art works and floor-to-ceiling windows onto a garden terrace along the ravine shielding Twenty Mile Creek from view below. Cave Spring wines are featured at little markup. The restaurant has a full liquor license and carries the best of other local winery offerings.

(905) 562-7313. Lunch daily, 11:30 to 3; dinner, 5 to 10. Closed Mondays, January-April.

Hillebrand's Vineyard Cafe, Highway 55, Niagara-on-the-Lake.

Big money went into the new restaurant at Hillebrand Estates Winery, and it shows. Interesting architectural lines delineate the handsome, high-ceilinged establishment on two levels. A wall of windows opens onto the barrel aging cellar along one side, while taller windows in back yield views of the vineyard. Cushioned wood chairs are at well spaced, white-linened tables, each topped with a different potted herb; a few dramatic artworks and the odd ficus tree add color. Canvas umbrellas top the tables on the sunny outside patio.

Prominent chef Antonio de Luca was lured from Toronto to oversee the kitchen. Menus neatly bound with grapevines detail some fairly exotic fare. To start the meal, a changing array of breads arrives in a grapevine basket with a daily spread – at our lunch, an unusual black bean spread to soothe an assertive olive focaccia, corn bread with peppers and fennel-seed bread. One of us sampled the day's cold cucumber soup "garnished" with an awkward-to-handle hunk of smoked salmon ($4.50) and the salad of arugula and radicchio with a confit of tomatoes, smoked scallops and dill ($7.50). The other was impressed with the penne pasta tossed with caramelized vidalia onions, smoked chicken and roast garlic with a spicy tomato sauce. At $9.50, it was the least expensive among main courses priced up to $15.95 for ancho chile-glazed breast of free-range chicken stir-fry with snow peas and sweet and sour sauce. The highly touted mango and cardamom crème brûlée with fresh berries ($5.50) lacked any hint of mango or cardamom.

Dinner may be a better bet, both for value and for sampling the kitchen's prowess. We hear great things about the Tour of Niagara tasting platter as an appetizer ($12.50), which combines a confit of tomatoes with roast garlic, fresh asparagus fritters and savory sugar snap pea pastries with three varieties of wine. Main courses run from $16.95 for papardelle noodles with black tiger shrimp and scallops with double smoked salmon cream to $23.95 for roast Ontario lamb on eggplant, portobello mushrooms and roasted shallots with rosemary new potatoes and a fava-cabernet reduction.

Besides turning up in some of the sauces, Hillebrand wines make up the entire wine list, nicely varied (particularly the whites) and priced from $13.95 to $79.95. *(905) 468-3201 or (800) 852-8412. Lunch daily, 11:30 to 5; dinner, 5 to 11.*

Lola, 17 Lock St., St. Catherines.
Opened in 1995, this little spot near the water in resorty Port Dalhousie made a mark among trend-setters for international/fusion cuisine and funky surroundings.

The place is named for a vintage World War I aircraft and each of the dining room walls is painted a different color. The ceiling lights are wrapped in bags and paper stamped with the name Lola covers the tables. A few tables are set outside on a front porch, which every car in town seemed to pass with radios blaring on the summer evening we were there.

It's a laid-back setting for the hearty contemporary fare of head chef Selena Bennett who, in her mid-twenties, is considered something of a prodigy. Hers is the vertical style, in which foods stand tall rather than rest horizontally on the plates.

The ice water bore a lemon slice and the basket of breads came with olive oil flavored with thyme and garlic. The lofty spinach salad ($6) appeared with grilled onions, gorgonzola and pancetta on a large white plate sprinkled with herbs. Among entrées ($15.95 to $18.95), we tried the osso buco with garlic mashed potatoes and the lamb chops with sweet pepper risotto, both accompanied by grilled vegetables rising like teepees. We have to say that dinner gets very messed up when one must dig down through several layers to get to the mashed potatoes, for example. Other choices included curried halibut in a tandoori-coconut lime sauce, pork tenderloin with maple-smoked beans and matsu applesauce, and willy choi steak with a peppercorn and black rice vinegar glaze.

Desserts were of the tarte tatin, chocolate-orange bread pudding and double-chocolate cheesecake variety. For a refreshing sorbet or frozen yogurt, the waiter suggested the ice-cream stand across the street.

The lunch menu yields interesting salads, sandwiches and pastas. How about a club sandwich with snow crab, grilled chicken, pancetta and greens, dressed with honey-dijon? *(905) 646-8917. Lunch, Thursday-Sunday 11:30 to 3; dinner nightly, from 5.*

Dining room at Hillebrand's Vineyard Cafe looks onto patio and vineyard.

The Wine Deck and Boardwalk Room, Vineland Estates Winery, 3620 Moyer Road, Vineland.

Ontario liquor authorities have finally allowed wineries to open on Sundays, accept credit cards and serve food on the premises. Vineland Estates, which with its hilly country setting is probably the area's most picturesque winery, was the first to oblige. It enclosed the front porch of its original 1845 estate house and opened a bistro-style restaurant named for the wooden beams in the floor. The side deck was later expanded to seat 100 under cover and outside, where on a clear day you can discern the Toronto skyline through the grapevines. In 1995 a major kitchen expansion allowed the winery to offer lunch and dinner year-round.

The menus are short but select, perfect for sampling the winery's offerings. At one lunch, we lingered on the deck over a bottle of premium dry riesling ($13.50) as three of us shared platters of assorted cheeses and fruits ($8.95) and assorted pâtés ($9.95). The first yielded brie, cream cheese, cheddar and havarti with fruit, tomato and vegetable garnishes. The second contained garlic and red-wine pâté, shrimp and lobster mousse, and black-peppercorn and country pâtés, garnished with pickled mushrooms, vegetables and eggs. Both came in vine-basket trays decorated with asters and containing assorted breads and big soft pretzels. A fresh peach tart and steaming coffee were worthy endings.

The setting turns fancy at night, when classical music plays, cloths cover the tables and splashy floral arrangements add color. There's even a private table set for four at the side of the tasting room. You can dine well on entrées like poached salmon, pork calvados or châteaubriand ($15.95 to $18.95). Or you can be more casual, sampling bruschetta, an excellent caesar salad with Canadian bacon and crunchy croutons, and a platter of smoked salmon garnished with celery, carrot sticks, sprigs of mint and a clover blossom. We sat on the covered deck at a sturdy picnic table dressed in mauve and watched the sunset paint a changing palette across the western sky.

The setting could not be more bucolic and, if you linger, you may want to stay the night. The little stucco cottage across the way is a B&B called **Wine 'n Recline.** It harbors a fully equipped kitchen, living room, bathroom and sleeping accommodations for four. There's a TV set for contact with the outside world, you can barbecue on the deck, and the refrigerator is stocked with a bottle of wine as well as the fixings for the next day's breakfast.

(905) 562-7088. Lunch daily, 11 to 5; dinner, 5 to 9. B&B, $135 for two.

Breakers Waterfront Restaurant, 2793 Beacon Blvd., Jordan.

The best wide-angle, up-close view of Lake Ontario from any area restaurant is the claim of Alan Manjos, owner-operator of the newly renovated restaurant in the Beacon Harbourside inn/motel at Jordan Harbor. Beyond the family-style Beacon Diner lies a 180-seat expanse of white-linened tables with banquettes above and behind, all facing windows onto the water.

Mark Walpole, longtime chef at the Prince of Wales Hotel in Niagara-on-the-Lake, moved here in 1996 for a piece of the action and brought with him some of his customers. His menu, billed as "wine country cuisine," is one of the area's more interesting and reasonably priced.

Consider dinner dishes ($15.50 to $19.50) like pan-fried trout on acini pasta with sweet corn relish, seared quail with red wine risotto and portobello mushrooms, and roasted whole rack of lamb with minted couscous and vegetable noodles. Start with chipotle grilled shrimp on a spicy slaw or sesame chicken satay with balsamic plum sauce and a vegetable spring roll. Or try a thin-crust pizza topped with grilled vegetables and goat cheese. Finish with a chocolate and pistachio pavé or walnut- rhubarb strudel with dried cherry ice cream.

Early reviews were mixed, but the chef was considered to be up to the challenge.

(905) 562-3133. Lunch daily, 11 to 3; dinner, 5 to 9 or 10.

Other Dining Choices

Fans Court, 135 Queen St., Niagara-on-the-Lake.

"We serve gourmet Chinese food only – no chow mein," proclaims the sign at the door. In the opinion of local gourmands, this unpretentious Chinese restaurant is one of the town's better places to eat.

There's a pleasant outdoor patio for dining in front. Inside are a couple of nondescript rooms, where tables are set simply with silverware and chopsticks atop peach cloths. Oriental art and music provided a soothing backdrop as we nursed an Inniskillin brae blanc ($13.50) from a short list featuring Canadian wines and Chinese beers.

The menu advised that "sharing is one of the biggest enjoyments of a Chinese meal." Yet orders were not served in typical, help-yourself Chinese fashion, but rather on small dinner plates that made sharing difficult.

For starters, we chose deep-fried wontons ($2.80) and an intriguing-sounding radish and pork soup ($2.80) that arrived without much evidence of radish. For main courses ($9 to $16.80), the shrimp and scallops in a phoenix (crisp noodle) nest and double-cooked pork tenderloin were fine. But we were astounded that steamed rice (rice!) cost extra, as did tea – the first time we have encountered this

Niagara River lies far below dining terrace at Queenston Heights Restaurant.

in a Chinese restaurant. For that matter, there were no Chinese noodles and plum sauce to nibble on, as in most Chinese restaurants, and the service, while correct, was icy. *(905) 468-4511. Daily, noon to 10. Entire menu available for takeout.*

The Queenston Heights Restaurant, Queenston Heights Park, Queenston.
Operated by the Niagara Parks Commission, this restaurant is a cut above – if no longer in culinary aspirations, still at least in location, commanding a panoramic view down the Niagara River toward Lake Ontario.

The menu mixes traditional and contemporary cuisine, though not at the heights we enjoyed at our first visit. Then, one of us made a wonderful lunch of two appetizers: a tomato and eggplant salad, served on a black octagonal plate brightened by corn kernels and colorful bits of peppers, and smoked-salmon carpaccio, garnished with shavings of romano cheese, herbs and tiny purple edible flowers. The other enjoyed smoked turkey with cranberry mayonnaise on a whole-wheat croissant. From the dessert cart we picked a super chocolate-strawberry charlotte with curls of chocolate and savored both it and the afternoon sunshine on the capacious outdoor terrace.

The menu has since been toned down, although caesar salad with grilled chicken and a lamb burger enticed for a recent lunch. At night, entrées run from $15.95 for roast Ontario pork loin to $18.95 for Atlantic salmon with strawberry-champagne hollandaise and prime rib with Yorkshire pudding. One of the more interesting starters is a camembert spring roll with spicy fruit chutney. Desserts run to strawberry mousse, chocolate cheesecake and local peaches. The extensive wine list contains a page of Niagara whites and another of reds.

The formal main dining room is Tudor in feeling with a high timbered ceiling, armchairs at well-spaced tables and a painting of Niagara Falls above a huge stone fireplace. The view down the length of the river, while sitting at a table by the expansive windows, gives one the sense of being on an airplane.

(905) 262-4274. Monday-Saturday 11:30 to 9; tea, 3 to 5; Sunday brunch, 11 to 3. Closed November to mid-March.

The Buttery Theatre Restaurant, 19 Queen St., Niagara-on-the-Lake.
After the obligatory dinner at the Oban Inn, our second meal in town years ago was lunch at The Buttery. We were attracted by the casual menu and a conspicuous outdoor terrace fronting on the main street, perfect for watching the world go by.

Said menu includes a trio of Colonial soups served with homemade bread, salads, sandwiches and such diverse fare as welsh rarebit, cornish pasties, salmagundi and croques monsieur. The tavern menu, served daily from 11, also includes crêpes, curries, steak and kidney pie, and spareribs, priced from $7 to $15.50 (for filet mignon).

Inside are several dimly lit dining rooms notable for pierced-copper tables. One is a banquet hall that hosts weekend medieval banquets, four-course theatrical events called Henry VIII feasts ($45 per person). The regular dinner menu ($14.95 to $19.50) is a mix of Canadian and continental entrées ranging from crêpes à la reine and shrimp curry to grilled red snapper and prime rib with yorkshire pudding. Desserts "of a Colonial nature" include blackberry and apple crumble and key lime pie.

(905) 468-2564. Tavern menu, daily from 11; afternoon tea, 2 to 5; dinner, 5:30 to 10; after-theater menu, Thursday-Sunday 10 to midnight.

The Epicurean, 84 Queen St., Niagara-on-the-Lake.
Pick up your own food here to take out back to the shaded patio or eat inside a colorful blue and buttercup yellow dining room. Soups like Mexican chicken or gazpacho are $2.95, or you might get chicken and feta pie or seafood quiche ($7.95). Good-looking gourmet salads, served with homemade bread, are $2.95 for one, $6.95 for your choice of three. Sandwiches range from tuna to seafood and avocado or eggplant with roasted peppers and chèvre.

The Epicurean also prepares "pampered picnics" ($11.95 to $12.95), packed in a hamper with utensils and wine glasses. Salads and desserts accompany a choice of poached salmon, sliced filet mignon or grilled chicken with lime and ginger.

You'll also find a selection of specialty foods and culinary books in a section called **Kitchen Accents.**

(905) 468-3408. Daily, 9 a.m. to 11:30 p.m.

Dining and Lodging

Gate House Hotel, 142 Queen St., Niagara-on-the-Lake L0S 1J0.
This sleek, mirrored hotel in black and white emerged from the simple, old Gate House Inn – tastefully on the outside, contemporary Italian and showy on the inside.

A marble entry leads to the reception desk, where guests are directed to the two-tiered dining room (considered the fanciest in town) or upstairs to nine guest rooms on the second floor. We were shown a very modern room done in teal and black with two double beds, German and Italian furnishings, and a bathroom with double sinks, a bidet and Auberge toiletries. Rooms have TVs and all the usual amenities in contemporary European style. A continental breakfast is included.

The hotel's **Ristorante Giardino** is the gem of the operation. Chef Remo Penasa presents a trendy menu in a dining room that's ultra-chic. Huge windows look onto the gardens and lawns (and passersby look in as well). Generally well-spaced tables are set with black-edged service plates, white napkins rolled up in black paper rings, pink carnations in heavy crystal vases, votive candles and two long-stemmed

Expansive windows bring outside in at Ristorante Giardino in Gate House Hotel.

wine glasses at each place. All the plates and water glasses are octagonal. Masses of flowers brighten the room's dividers and good art hangs on the walls.

The modern Italian fare is on the expensive side (dinner entrées, $20 to $29.50; antipasti, $7 to $12, and desserts, $8). The possibilities range from consommé of capon with homemade tagliolini and celery mirepoix to strozzapreti sautéed with a julienne of roast duck, sage and aged parmigiano leaves to Canadian black angus tenderloin with foie gras and port wine sauce.

Not wishing to break the bank, we settled for lunch, which at the time was a relative bargain at $13 for salad, main course and dessert. A plate of crusty Italian bread arrived along with two glasses of the house Inniskillin wine (brae blanc and brae rouge). One of us started with an intensely flavored and silken shrimp bisque, followed by a rolled pasta with spinach and ricotta cheese. The other sampled a trio of pastas: spaghetti with pancetta and parmesan-cream sauce, tagliatelle sautéed with salmon and chives and a house specialty, eggplant Giardino, baked with mozzarella, basil and tomato sauce. Dessert was a thin slice of carrot cake with vanilla ice cream and fresh strawberries – imported from California, which seemed strange, given all the fresh peaches, pears and plums in season at the time around Niagara. Good cappuccino and coffee finished a memorable repast. The prix-fixe menu lately has been dropped in favor of à la carte selections: antipasti and pastas $5.50 to $8, main courses $11 to $13.50. The extensive wine list is especially strong on Niagara and Italian vintages.

(905) 468-3263. Doubles, $150 to $170. Lunch daily, noon to 2:30; dinner nightly, 5 to 9. No lunch in off-season. Closed January and February.

Prince of Wales Hotel, 6 Picton St., Niagara-on-the-Lake L0S 1J0.
When Henry Wiens took over a 127-year-old hostelry in the center of town in 1974, "it was a dive," recalled daughter Angelika Whitham, a partner in this family-run

enterprise with her parents, brother and sister. Through property acquisitions and thoughtful restorations, they have expanded from the original sixteen rooms to 100 on three floors behind a meandering brick facade that looks more residential than commercial.

Period furnishings, brass beds and floral chintzes enhance all the guest rooms, which vary in size from standard double through deluxe and superior to the Windsor, an enormous suite with two television sets. High ceilings, mini-refrigerators and gleaming bathrooms with bidets and hair dryers are the norm.

The layout is enough of a maze that guests are given a floor plan to help find their rooms, the indoor pool, the basement health club and the rooftop sun deck.

Light fare is available in the **Three Feathers Cafe** and the **Queen's Royal Lounge**. The former opens onto a new side veranda that's sought after for its view of the passing scene. The latter is a sumptuous space with a fireplace on one side and a solarium in which to enjoy the $8.75 luncheon buffet or a new cafe menu.

Royals, the main dining room favored by locals for special-occasion meals, is known for consistently good food – a commodity in somewhat short supply in a town in which restaurants turn tables according to curtain times. The room is a study in restrained elegance, the walls covered in rusty-pumpkin suede-like fabric, the tables set with silver octagonal service plates, and full-length windows facing the hotel's lush flower beds and Simcoe Park.

During a pre-theater dinner, countless well-heeled pedestrians passed outside our window table amid zillions of plants in the solarium, providing diversion and a reminder that this is a strolling town for pleasure-seekers.

A small salmon and spinach terrine, "compliments of the chef," preceded our appetizers, a good spinach and endive salad with goat cheese and pancetta and an oversize portion of sliced smoked venison with English cucumbers, tomatoes and a roasted-garlic vinaigrette. Among entrées ($19.50 to $25) were a superior roasted rabbit with prosciutto, spinach, garlic and tomatoes and a more ordinary dish of medallions of beef tenderloin bathed in a cognac and peppercorn cream sauce. Cauliflower, crisp green beans and potatoes au gratin accompanied.

The dessert list covered everything from macaroon-lemon cheesecake and a duet of frangelico and chocolate mousses to Bailey's ice-cream fudge cake and frozen neapolitan mille-feuille. A "regal sampler" of several costs $8. A plate of raspberry sorbet with three ice creams (vanilla, pistachio and caramel), garnished with fresh blueberries and raspberries, was plenty for two.

In March 1997, the hotel was purchased by Si Wai Lai, owner of the Pillar and Post. A spokeswoman said some renovations and changes were planned after the 1997 season.

(905) 468-3246 or (800) 263-2452. Fax (905)468-5521. Doubles, $129 to $235; suites, $275. Lunch daily, 11 to 2:30; dinner nightly, 5 to 9; Sunday brunch, 11 to 2:30.

The Kiely House Inn & Restaurant, 209 Queen St., Box 1642, Niagara-on-the-Lake L0S 1J0.

Large verandas on two stories, front and back, dominate this imposing, pillared Georgian house built in 1832, set on an acre of lawns backing up to a golf course overlooking Lake Ontario. The rear veranda is so big it contains both a screened porch and an open porch facing spectacular gardens, where roses bloom into November and English ivy and other exotica grow as they do nowhere else in eastern Canada.

Meandering brick structure houses Prince of Wales Hotel.

One large guest room with a canopy bed is in the original kitchen. Note its kitchen-size fireplace, rich wood paneling and deep-toned wallpaper, and a loveseat looking out at the gardens. Room 8 upstairs is lighter with a 1930s art-deco look, a fireplace and a private veranda. The upstairs rear balcony slopes a bit – the better to catch the breezes off Lake Ontario, says innkeeper Heather Pettit, with a trace of an English accent.

Of the eleven guest rooms, six have fireplaces and all have private baths. The five smallest are in a wing at the side.

Heather and husband Ray have converted the handsome double parlor with its crystal chandeliers and a cheery Victorian breakfast room into a fine-dining restaurant, offering lunch and dinner daily. Chef Rob Egan prepares contemporary French cuisine with an accent on local produce and wines. Look for a short selection of dinner entrées ranging from $14.95 for half a roasted grain-fed chicken with yukon gold potatoes to $24.95 for seared medallions of venison with spiced quince and pear coulis.

Some of the dinner appetizers turn up on the lunch menu ($7.95 to $12.95), best taken on the front veranda or in a cozy side room done up in mauve and hunter green. We hear good things about the smoked salmon with a tangy cracked wheat salad, the house-made chicken and duck liver terrine with mesclun and vegetable crisps, and the terrace sampler of smoked meats, cheese and other charcuterie items.

In the afternoon, Heather serves a proper English tea ($6.95) in two versions: Victorian with finger sandwiches and pastries, or cream tea with scones, preserves and "genuine double Devon cream." She even teaches novices the proper way to eat scones.

Overnight guests enjoy a continental-plus breakfast of juice, seasonal fruits, cereal, scones and muffins.

(905) 468-4588. Doubles, $75 to $175. Lunch daily, 11:30 to 2:30; dinner, 5:30 to 9.

The Oban Inn, 160 Front St., Box 94, Niagara-on-the-Lake L0S 1J0.

This landmark facing Lake Ontario across a strip of golf course has been around since 1824 and looks it. Which is quite remarkable, given that it was destroyed by fire on Christmas Day 1992 and was rebuilt to its original specifications for re-opening the following November.

Guests now have an elevator to reach the second and third floors, where nineteen rooms go off narrow corridors adorned with a multitude of ornate paintings. The best are those in front facing the lake; they are larger and have queen or twin beds, antique furnishings, gas fireplaces and plush armchairs or a loveseat facing a TV set. A second-story balcony, outfitted with tables, chairs and many plants, goes off the rooms at the back of the inn and is available to all house guests. Vivid wallpapers, terrycloth robes, a clock-radio and a phone in each room are the rule. Guests enjoy a new library/sitting room upstairs with TV, gas fireplace and lots of books and games.

Besides rooms in the main house, the inn offers three that are highly prized in the adjacent Oban House.

The waiters and bartenders are in tartan plaids in the formal dining rooms and the ever-so-British **Shaw's Corner** piano bar full of festival memorabilia. The place is abuzz day and night, for the bar is a popular gathering place and the inn is considered the quintessential Niagara experience.

The same no longer could be said at our latest visit for the dining situation, the service in particular having slipped over the years, according to local consensus. The dinner fare includes such English specialties as dover sole with tartar sauce and prime rib with Yorkshire pudding and horseradish among entrées ($18.50 to $27.50). Starters include potted shrimp (blended with spices and butter and served with toast points), and deep-fried camembert with English crackers and homemade red-pepper jelly. Desserts run from meringue chantilly and hot fudge sundae to English trifle and frozen grand-marnier soufflé.

Steak and kidney pie, fried salmon fish cakes, and cold pork pie with piccalilli relish and potato salad are included on the lunch menu. These and other English specialties are featured on the lounge menu in winter.

(905) 468-2165. Doubles, $136 to $185; suite, $200. Lunch daily, 11:30 to 2; tea, Sunday-Friday 3 to 5; dinner nightly, 5 to 9.

New Life for an Old Standby

The Pillar and Post, 48 John St., Box 1011, Niagara-on-the-Lake L0S 1J0.

This campus-like hostelry with 123 guest rooms, a variety of dining rooms, a glamorous spa and health center and a gift shop dates to the 1890s when it began life as a canning factory. The building was converted in 1970 into a restaurant, inn and crafts center to launch Niagara's inn boom. Vastly expanded to ramble across a square block, it now reflects the taste, energy and money of new owner Si Wai Lai, who fled China 30 years ago by swimming to Hong Kong and now is equally fearless as she buys up much of Niagara-on-the-Lake.

Si Wai moved to Canada in 1980 and started as a desk clerk at the Niagara Falls Sheraton. She slowly acquired small properties, using her own resources and, it's reported, those of her twin brother, a Hong Kong clothing magnate and publisher. Niagara-on-the-Lake first took notice when she brought the quirky and quaint

Kitchen staff at work in Cannery dining area at The Pillar and Post.

Pillar and Post out of bankruptcy in 1994, pouring $12 million into renovations and a new wing for additional rooms and a European health spa. She soon acquired The Buttery restaurant, purchased the larger and more conference-oriented Queen's Landing Inn here for the highest price per room ever paid for a Canadian hotel, and planned to exercise her option to buy the Oban Inn in 1998. At our visit, she was about to open the casual Shaw Corner restaurant in a Queen Street retail complex she was building. In 1997 she contracted to purchase the Prince of Wales Hotel for an even higher room price than the Queen's Landing..

Her mark is everywhere evident at the Pillar and Post, to which she initially devoted most of her resources. She enlarged and opened up the formerly cramped lobby, reconfigured the gift shop area into a fancy dining room, and glamorized the **Vintages Wine Bar and Lounge** with a wine mural (said to be the largest hand-painted mural in Canada) and a huge, gently curving oak bar. The lower level of the new wing holds an indoor pool flanked by stuffed Florida palm trees, a Hundred Fountain spa with lion's heads spewing water, an outdoor hot spring pool and waterfall surrounded by tiers of lush begonias, and eight salons, each individually themed to represent an exotic country. You might think you were in the Roman baths, not Niagara.

The 32 new rooms and suites follow suit. Si Wai picked all the furnishings and fabrics, from the pink and raspberry colors of Suite 251 to the handpainted wash basin from Spain in 247. Kingsize four-poster and crown canopy beds, sumptuous sitting areas, antiques, rich woods and dark colors prevail. Twenty-seven have whirlpool tubs, and many have fireplaces. Most are turned into themselves in a cozy and dark way that may appeal more in winter than in summer.

Guests partake of complimentary hors d'oeuvres in the evening. An extensive breakfast buffet is available for $10.95 in the morning. The plates and the wildflower placemats used for breakfast are for sale in the **Country Treasures** gift shop.

The renovated Carriages restaurant is elegant and formal in one section, less so in the beamed and pillared Cannery areas and in the lounge. Si Wai is proud to have hosted for dinner 26 members of the prestigious Club des Chef des Chef, the international association of chefs to reigning royalty and heads of state during its annual meeting in Toronto in 1995. Under less regal circumstances, the dinner menu ($17.95 to $23.95) is contemporary and regional, from an appetizer of seared rare yellowfin tuna with wasabi cream on sesame snaps to a main course of grilled angus filet on a vegetable tortilla with yukon mashed potatoes and double smoked bacon. Cappuccino-cinnamon mousse and chocolate-cherry kirsch pâté are typical desserts. The extensive wine list is strong on Niagara vintages and rather pricey, except for the sampler flight of five local chardonnays for $12.95. An interesting, less expensive all-day menu is offered in the Vintages wine bar and lounge.

(905) 468-2123 or (800) 361-6788. Fax (905) 468-3551. Doubles, $170 to $220; suites, $195 to $250. Lunch daily, noon to 2:30; tea, 3 to 5:30; dinner, 5 to 9, winter 6 to 8, lounge to midnight.

Lodging

Besides the larger inns and hotels, Niagara-on-the-Lake had 149 B&Bs at last count – more than double the number only three years earlier and increasing every year. By zoning ordinance, most offer three or fewer guest rooms. The most choice:

Lakewinds, 328 Queen St., Box 1483, Niagara-on-the-Lake L0S 1J0.

Pristine white with dark green trim, this substantial Victorian manor sits amidst an acre of trees and gardens facing Lake Ontario across the golf-course fairways. Besides a scenic residential location, it offers Niagara-on-the-Lake's most elegant B&B accommodations and culinary treats, and was the setting in 1996 for a country-inn scene in the Bette Midler movie, "That Old Feeling."

You'd never suspect that "the house was falling down," as owner Jane Locke put it, when she and her husband Stephen from nearby Hamilton bought it in 1994 with the idea of turning the front section into a B&B . "We're trying to make a silk purse out of a sow's ear."

The main floor is devoted to a formal living/dining room in which the Lockes serve breakfasts to remember, an ample games room for billiards or cards, and an airy solarium that becomes a working greenhouse in the winter to produce the seedlings for the lavish flower, vegetable and herb gardens that grace the grounds. The solarium opens onto a back-yard swimming pool much enjoyed by guests.

Upstairs are four guest rooms, three with queensize beds and one with a king. All have private baths. The Venetian suite with jacuzzi and separate shower is so named for all the silver and glass and the handpainted mirrored furniture. Others bear furnishings appropriate to their names: Florentine, Singapore and the Algonquin, in which we found the most comfortable of beds and a guest diary whose entries embellished on three themes: sumptuous surroundings, delicious breakfasts and personable hosts.

Guests are greeted with tea and sherry, and help themselves to mixers in a bar area off the solarium. The Lockes, whose family quarters are in the rear of the house, often mingle with guests and provide turndown service at night.

The highlight is the morning repast, a communal sit-down affair at 9 o'clock. Ours began with apple-cassis juice, cantaloupe harboring port and berries, and five varieties of breads, from orange-date muffins to muesli baguettes to croissants. The main event was a melt-in-your-mouth leek and sage quiche with roasted red pepper coulis, teamed with a crostini bearing sautéed mushrooms, pesto, tomato

Horse and carriage arrives for Christmas festivities at Lakewinds.

and goat cheese. On tap the next morning was honeydew melon marinated in lime and gin, followed by orange-cointreau french toast. Crêpes, often incorporating asparagus or smoked salmon, are a specialty. Five of Jane's recipes are included in the new Canadian edition of the *Rise and Dine* inn cookbook.

Jane, who was preparing a batch of rhubarb-ginger jam at our arrival, runs culinary workshops with visiting chefs at Lakewinds on ten off-season weekends ($495 per couple, including two dinners, breakfast and brunch; BYO wines to share). She attributes her cooking talents to training in a private yacht club and corporate travels around the world with her husband. Both love to entertain, and treat their guests royally.

(905) 468-1060. Fax (905) 468-1061. Doubles, $135; suite, $155.

The Vintner's Inn, 3845 Main St., Jordan L0R 1L0.

Plush accommodations join the expanding Cave Spring Cellars winery, restaurant and shopping equation with this new B&B fashioned from an old sugar warehouse. Helen Young, wife of winery owner Leonard Pennachetti, offers ten suites with sitting areas, gas fireplaces, whirlpool tubs and kingsize or two double beds. Eight are double-deckers with powder rooms and sitting areas downstairs and loft bedrooms and baths up. The other two are bigger with two double beds and television sets; the Garden Suite overlooks a demonstration garden, while the skylit Deluxe Loft adds a wet bar, refrigerator and a sofa so deep you can barely get up.

Handsomely decorated in restful Mediterranean tones, each suite contains a colorful painting (for sale) by local artist Jane Kewin, whose works adorn the restaurant. You'd never guess that some of the furnishings took on new life after resting in Buffalo junk shops. Helen mixed refurbished castoffs with antiques, chintz fabrics and old marble vanities to create "an eclectic country look," simple but stylish.

Although the kind of place that you might not want to venture forth from your room, you can gather by the fireplace in the soaring, fashionably furnished lobby.

Complimentary breakfast is available at the inn's companion On the Twenty restaurant across the street.

Six more suites were in the planning stages for the inn's main floor.
(905) 562-5336 or (800) 701-8074. Fax (905) 562-3232. Doubles, $195; deluxe loft, $225.

The Varey House, 105 Johnson St., Box 1675, Niagara-on-the-Lake L0S 1J0.
Canadian history and fine art emerge behind the roughcast stucco exterior of this Regency residence built in 1837. Now an Ontario heritage house, it's a stylish B&B with a distinctive welcome given by Lorraine Delisle, a Quebec City native, and her husband, Toronto art dealer Geoffrey Joyner, president of Sotheby's Canada.

Lorraine, who maintains the home front, offers four comfortable upstairs bedrooms with private baths and king or twin beds. Good reading lamps, designer sheets, duvet comforters, hair dryers and bathrobes in each closet are the rule. Local chocolates on the pillows at nightly turndown and a hand-woven stairway runner from Quebec testify to Lorraine's attention to detail. The patterns of the window treatments and wallpaper borders are repeated on the lamp shades.

Canadian art graces the walls of two small guest parlors on either side of the front entry. Four round tables in the dining room are set for breakfast. In summer it tends to be an elaborate cold buffet of fresh fruits, ham, turkey, smoked salmon, tomatoes, deviled eggs and assorted breads and cheeses. The Niagara fruit belt provides the ingredients for Lorraine's specialty crêpes. Strawberries, raspberries, cherries, apples – "this is the best place in the world to make fruit crêpes," she says.
(905) 468-3252. Fax (413) 323-9249. Doubles, $115. Closed January-March.

The Stable, 243 Mississauga St., Niagara-on-the-Lake L0S 1J0.
"Proprietor and bon vivant" is how the brochure for this neat, three-room B&B describes its owner and inspiration, Roy W. Clark. Business teacher and management consultant are other titles for the personable and energetic Roy, whose favorite sideline is his B&B. "I opened on a whim," says he. "Everyone else in town – the lord mayor, the Chamber of Commerce president – has one, so why not me?"

His is a private residence converted from an 1887 carriage house and stable. The large, open living room, library and dining area reflects Roy's tastes: contemporary yet historic, "eclectic, you might say." Three sofas are grouped as sectionals near the wood-burning stove and upright Mason & Risch piano. The rear windows look onto a shady, secluded back lawn harboring a swimming pool.

The antique dining room set was a wedding gift from his grandparents to his parents in 1936. "I remember playing under the table as a child," he says. Now it's the setting for a breakfast to remember, the fare posted daily on a printed menu. Cheese soufflé was the main dish the day we were there. Fresh fruit cocktail, homemade muffins and breads, Florida red grapefruit, assorted cereals, preserves and "homemade sweet salsa" – otherwise known as chili sauce – accompanied.

The laundry room doubles as a hospitality center, with a refrigerator, microwave and such available for guests. The former stable was being restored and converted into a games room and cozy lounge.

Upstairs are three guest rooms with private baths and television sets. Shaw's Corner holds some of the playwright's memorabilia and a kingsize bed. The queen-bedded China Room revives memories of Roy's travels in Asia.
(905) 468-4140 or (800) 335-6877. Fax (905) 468-3113. Doubles, $88 to $99.

Bottle of wine is available for guests in suite at The Vintner's Inn.

Rogers-Harrison House, 157 Queen St., Niagara-on-the-Lake L0S 1J0.
Significant dates in its history are posted in a display case beside this restored 1817 Georgian beauty at the edge of the business district. Peter and Marilyn Marchesseau took over "a tired old place" in 1995. He and two young assistants spent nearly a year renovating and upgrading before opening a three-room B&B with private baths and queensize beds. They converted a rear sun porch into a living room to create the Harrison Suite with gas stove and clawfoot tub. The front Blake Room has a lacy canopy four-poster bed, six-foot-long jacuzzi tub and fireplace, while the original master bedroom called the Rogers Room holds a sleigh bed and a jacuzzi.

Antique and period furnishings abound upstairs and in the formal parlor, notable for both an upright piano and an 18th-century double harpsichord. A brass chandelier is a focal point of the elegant dining room, where breakfast is served at 9. The fare could be eggs benedict, stuffed crêpes, french toast raphael or scrambled eggs with smoked salmon.

(905) 468-1615. Doubles, $95; suite, $100.

Cranberry House, 169 Gate St., Niagara-on-the-Lake, L0S 1J0.
Building from the ground up allows would-be innkeepers the opportunity to create the kind of B&B in which they like to stay. That's what Justin Venhuizen, an IBM early-retiree, and wife Fran did in 1995. Buying a small vacant lot from the owner of an adjacent residence, they built a cheery Queen Anne-style home that feels new but looks as if it's been there forever.

The requisite wraparound porch, the front of the house and the upstairs are the domain of overnight guests. Three bedrooms, each with private bath, are named after the couple's mothers and their daughter. Nicole's has a whirlpool and separate shower. Carnelia's reflects Justin's mother's Dutch background with Delft blue tones and kingsize bed.

Breakfast is served in a garden dining room with a notable hand-stenciled ceiling or on the porch. Fran employs 30 recipes, including strata, asparagus quiche, strawberry-stuffed french toast and cottage cakes (small pancakes made with cottage cheese). Sherry and port are offered later in the day.

Guests also enjoy a parlor and a basement entertainment room with TV, fireplace, dart board and pool table.

(905) 468-4966. Doubles, $115.

Grand Victorian, 15618 Niagara Pkwy., Niagara-on-the-Lake L0S 1J0.

Very grand and very Victorian is this new B&B, occupying an imposing mansion that's a landmark for all to notice next to the Reif Estate winery vineyards. The inside is in transition, as ex-Torontonian Eva Kassel seeks to furnish the place. Meanwhile, guests rattle around in huge, high-ceilinged rooms reminiscent of a century ago.

Rich wood, stained-glass windows, heavy antiques and wide-open spaces characterize the interior. Upstairs are five guest rooms and a suite, all bearing fireplaces and fancy and ornate queensize beds. The beds and much of the furniture, loaned by a Queenston antiques dealer, are for sale. Romantics might enjoy the ornately carved but cramped-looking Chinese wedding bed in the front room, or the honeymoon suite in back with the original sleeping porch along the side offering a view of the Niagara River. These and another room come with private baths; the other three share two.

There's plenty of space for guests to spread out in the main-floor common rooms, the flower-bedecked front veranda or around the much-used swimming pool and tennis court, which is flooded in winter for ice-skating. The facility lends itself to the weddings and corporate seminars that Eva seeks to attract to build her business.

Eva, assisted by her nine-year-old daughter "who sets a mean table," offers a "European brunchy breakfast" in the dining room and conservatory. Cold cuts, cheeses, salads, fruits, deviled eggs and muffins are the fare. In winter, Eva might add crêpes or soufflés. Wine from the Reif Estate is offered in the afternoon.

(905) 468-0997. Doubles, $100 to $125; suite, $140.

The Old Bank House, 10 Front St., Box 1708, Niagara-on-the-Lake L0S 1J0.

The first Bank of Upper Canada branch was converted into the town's largest B&B, facing a lakefront park with a glimpse of Lake Ontario through the trees from the shady front veranda. Inside is a formal living room so spacious that tables can be set up to seat sixteen for breakfast with room to spare.

Rooms vary widely. Four upstairs with wash basins in the room share one bathroom with a separate w.c. We were ensconced in the Gallery Suite with its own entrance off the veranda, a double-bedded room containing the only private bathroom with combination shower-tub, a small sitting area and a dressing room that doubled as a kitchenette with a mini-fridge, an electric kettle, supplies of coffee and tea, and even a teapot with a tea cozy. Two other rooms also have private baths with showers and private entrances, and the Rose Suite has two bedrooms, a sitting room and "four-piece bathroom ensuite," as full private baths connected to the rooms are called in Ontario.

Breakfast here is hearty. It might start with fruit crisp or mixed fresh fruit in crème fraîche, plus a choice of juices and a basket of muffins and toast. One morning we had scrambled eggs, bacon, fried tomatoes and potatoes, and the next, crêpes filled with corned beef topped with cream sauce, accompanied by sautéed yellow and red peppers and sausage.

(905) 468-7136. Doubles, $90 to $135; suite, $225.

Moffatt Inn, 60 Picton St., Box 578, Niagara-on-the-Lake L0S 1J0.

The 22 rooms here are individually decorated, up-to-date and arranged for privacy. Considering the in-town location and the amenities, they're a good value, too. Dating to 1834 and successively a private residence, house, offices and apartments, the structure was renovated in 1983 by Jim and Vena Johnstone, who have run it as an inn ever since. The two buildings flank a garden solarium that doubles as a guest lounge with a fireplace in the winter. At other seasons it is part of the **Moffatt Restaurant & Pub,** a separate operation where breakfast and other meals are available.

Our room on the second floor front had a queen bed, a pleasant sitting area with TV and telephone, and a modern bath with Finesse toiletries and hair dryer. It was very quiet until our next-door neighbors showered in the morning, when it sounded as if they were in our room. We also liked the four rooms on the main floor sharing a side patio and garden. All rooms have private baths, queensize or two double beds, brass headboards and unusual carved wood doors.

What one of us felt was the most appealing room (the other disagreed) is kept for walk-ins. It's a basement conference room, which is convertible to an extra-spacious guest room with high windows and a murphy bed for $80. One couple so liked it that they stayed a week.

(905) 468-4116. Doubles, $95 to $110.

Touring the Wineries

Geographically, one would not think of Canada as a wine-producing country. The Niagara Peninsula has changed that perception in a big way.

Shortly after New York's Finger Lakes region started proving that European viniferas could be grown in the Eastern climate, Niagara followed suit, scrapping acres of concord and niagara grapes in favor of chardonnays, rieslings and pinot noirs. Today, vineyards are everywhere around Niagara-on-the-Lake, interspersed among more orchards of diverse fruit trees than we've ever seen in close proximity. Both are the area's distinguishing features, yielding mile after mile of beauty and bounty.

Vineyards proliferated in recent years to the point where Niagara-on-the-Lake boasted a Group of Seven, borrowing a well-known name from the Canadian art world. That became the Group of Seven Plus One with the opening of another winery in 1993, and still another was in the works for 1997.

The grape-growing region is wedged between Lake Ontario to the north, the Niagara River to the east and the picturesque Niagara Escarpment to the south. The escarpment – a long, tiered ridge shaped something like a bench – separates the flatlands along Lakes Erie and Ontario. (The land along the seat of the bench is considered the most fertile, giving rise to the local phenomenon of "the Bench," whose growers put down the flatlands below as "the Swamp.") The escarpment is responsible for making this so prolific a fruit belt, both in terms of the rich minerals eroded into its soil and the micro-climate created by its sheltering effect and the moderating influence of Lake Ontario.

Its location near the 43rd-degree latitude places Niagara in the same position as such wine-growing regions as northern California, southern France and northern Italy. Some increasingly acclaimed wines, particularly rieslings, are the result. "For an area our size," says Cave Spring Cellars winemaker Angelo Pavan, "we probably win more awards in international competitions than any other region in the world."

The Niagara region also has become the world's leading maker of icewine (eiswein), a rare, sweet, almost chewy dessert wine whose miniscule production formerly was centered in Germany and Austria. Riesling and vidal grapes for icewine are left to freeze on the vine and are pressed frozen in winter to yield a wine that will age for ten or fifteen years. The limited supply fetches $30 to $50 or more a half bottle, and one wine writer predicted icewine could become "as Canadian as ice hockey."

Connoisseurs enjoy following the scenic, marked Wine Route, spending a day touring the wineries in the flatlands around Niagara-on-the-Lake and another day touring those along the Bench.

Inniskillin Wines Inc., Line 3 Road off Niagara Parkway, Niagara-on-the-Lake.

In 1975, Inniskillin was granted the first Ontario wine license since 1929 and became Ontario's first cottage winery, specializing in viniferas. Karl Kaiser, winemaker who learned the art in Austria as a monk, and Donald Ziraldo, promoter, are co-owners of what some consider to be Canada's finest winery, seller of 120,000 cases annually, nearly half from its own 60 acres of vineyards.

Visitors may take a twenty-station self-guided tour or a 45-minute guided tour and taste wines in a 1930s barn, the ground floor of which has been transformed into a sparkling showroom. The large second floor remains more rustic, the better for changing art exhibits, sit-down "festival tastings," and four theme dinners a year at $75 per, including wine (the one at our visit featured Thai cuisine). A menu at the door shows that Inniskillin's cabernet sauvignon reserve was served at former Prime Minister Mulroney's 1993 dinner for Mikhail Gorbachev. Successive vintages of icewine made from vidal grapes won a record three gold medals in a row, culminating in the Grand Prix d'Honneur at Vinexpo in France. Tastings of three wines are free; others cost 50 cents an ounce.

(905) 468-3554. Tours, daily at 2:30, also weekends at 10:30, June-October; weekends at 2:30 only rest of year. Showroom, daily 10 to 6, to 5 in winter.

Hillebrand Estates Winery, Highway 55, Niagara-on-the-Lake.

Billed as Canada's most award-winning winery and top producer of premium Vintners Quality Alliance (VQA) wines, this is the nation's largest estate winery, producing more than 300,000 cases a year and running more than 150 retail stores across Ontario.

The frequent tours here are said to be the most lively and informative of any Niagara winery. Indeed, it's the only winery to give regular tours year-round and they last an hour or longer.

A new welcome center and gallery provides directions to the expanding complex, which includes a new 110-seat restaurant. Complimentary tastings are offered in the large retail boutique, which looks like a wine store and purveys a selection of regional gourmet foods, Hillebrand's Vineyard Cafe specialties and wine-related items. Local watercolorist Angie Strauss designed labels for some of the blush

Inniskillin has grown far beyond its beginning as Ontario's first cottage winery.

wines. The superb Collector's Choice chardonnay and cabernet-merlot (both $13.95) bear the labels of some of Canada's famed Group of Seven artists. We coveted the poster of their labels, but left empty-handed because they sell faster than they can be produced.

(905) 468-7123. Tours daily on the hour, 10 to 6; showroom daily, 10 to 6.

Château des Charmes, 1025 York Road, Niagara-on-the-Lake.

This was touted by a Finger Lakes winemaker as Niagara's "best of the bunch" and owner Paul Bosc is considered Ontario's foremost winemaker. The winery is known for estate chardonnays, aged in oak barrels imported from France for $550 each. Its brut sparkling wine is widely considered to be Canada's best, and its recent cabernet and merlot releases are quite good. The winery was Canada's first to experiment with the French barrels, and its 60-acre vineyard was the first in Canada planted entirely with European vinifera vines.

Another 85 acres have been planted lately around the pretentious, $6 million French château built in 1994 seemingly in the middle of nowhere beneath the St. Davids Bench to house the winery, a champagne cellar, a banquet facility and a showroom and reception area. A $2 ticket gets you a video presentation, a tour, a visit to the underground cellars and a wine tasting. The place does catering and special events, including a luncheon prepared by seven top Canadian chefs for the 1995 meeting of the international Club des Chef des Chef. You might stumble onto one of the periodic Taste of Niagara lunches, featuring visiting chefs each week, under the tent. With a facility like this and the Bosc family's avowed desire to "marry food and wine," one would not be surprised to find a full-fledged vineyard restaurant here soon.

(905) 262-4219. Tours daily on the hour, 11 to 4; showroom daily, 10 to 5.

Konzelmann Estate Winery, 1096 Lakeshore Road, Niagara-on-the-Lake.

Wines in the German style are made here by Herman Konzelmann, his wife and son Mattthias, who returned from studying in Germany to join his parents as winemaker – the fifth generation involved in a family winery founded in Germany in 1893. Rows and rows of grapes, all labeled, grow primly on 40 acres along the shores of Lake Ontario, which has particularly beneficial effects for the vineyard.

The winery bottled its first harvest in 1986, has won 33 gold medals in national and international competitions since, and now produces 275,000 bottles a year of 29 different wines. The dry riesling is especially good, as is the gewürztraminer. Konzelmann's vidal icewine won the grand gold award at the VinItaly competition in 1993. A couple of pinot noirs and a gamay noir show Niagara's potential in red wines.

(905) 935-2866. Tours, Wednesday-Saturday at 2. Boutique, Monday-Saturday 10 to 6, Sunday 12:30 to 5:30, May-December; Tuesday-Saturday 10 to 6, rest of year.

Marynissen Estates, Concession 1 off Line 3, Niagara-on-the-Lake.

Red wines are the forte of winemaker John Marynissen, who started planting vinifera grapes in 1974 and won amateur winemaking competitions for years before opening an estate winery in 1991. The exceptional 1995 growing year allowed the production of 9,000 cases of wine, double that of a year earlier. The winery's 1994 cabernet franc won an award as the best red wine at Cuvée 96, and the 1994 cabernet sauvignon won fifth place. Other leading Marynissen red wines are pinot noir. gamay and petit syrah. At our visit, everyone was awaiting release of the outstanding 1995 vintage reds.

(905) 468-7270. Daily, 10 to 6, May-October; 10 to 4 or 5 rest of year.

Vineland Estates, 3620 Moyer Road, Vineland.

This small, personal winery is Niagara's most picturesque – situated in the rolling countryside along the Bench, with a view of Lake Ontario to the northwest. Lots of trees and hills make for a pleasant break from the sameness of the flatlands scenery below (follow Route 81 and the Niagara Winery Route along the Bench and you may think you're in the upper vales of California's Napa Valley).

German wine grower Hermann Weis had to prove to skeptical Canadian growers that his riesling grapes could be cultivated so far north, so he established a vine-yard of his own here. Today, his original 45 acres produce 12,000 cases annually of mostly riesling and some chardonnay. They have put the expanding operation, now owned by Hamilton wine connoisseur John Howard, in the forefront of Bench wineries. The new owner acquired 50 more acres, planting cabernet, merlot and pinot noir vines and planning to double production to 25,000 cases. He vastly expanded the wine deck and patio off the original 1845 estate house, creating a full-service restaurant, and opened a rear carriage house for craft shows, art auctions and a series of monthly theme dinners pairing the food of area chefs and Vineland Estates wines. Vineland's premium dry rieslings are decisive proof that Niagara rieslings are "better than anything outside the Rhine-Mosel axis itself," one writer proclaimed. Brothers Allan and Brian Schmid, the winemakers, are also known for gewürztraminers, pinot noirs and icewines.

(905) 562-7088. Tours daily in summer at 11, 1 and 3; showroom daily, 10 to 5:30.

Cave Spring Cellars, 3836 Main St., Jordan.

Serious, prize-winning wines from vinifera grapes are the specialty of this bou-tique winery on the Bench, housed in a lineup of buildings that comprised the defunct Jordan Winery, Ontario's oldest winemaking facility. The small, elegant wine-tasting and sales room is as stylish as the owner's On the Twenty restaurant at the other end of the complex.

Chardonnays and rieslings are featured here, the elegant and oaky chardonnay reserve selling for a cool $21.95 and the smooth, award-winning riesling icewine commanding $49.95 a half bottle. The venture headed by Leonard Pennachetti also produces rosé, cabernet-merlot and gamay noir varietals among its 15,000 cases annually in an effort to put Cave Spring in the vanguard of small North American wineries. Winemaker Angelo Pavan says the bone-dry riesling reserve is his personal favorite.

The Cave Spring enterprise has inspired nearly a dozen one-of-a-kind shops (from clothing to Inuit and Canadian native art to New Mexican furnishings to antiques) leased to the owners in its buildings along both sides of Jordan's Main Street. They help make Jordan a special destination.

(905) 562-3581. Open Monday-Saturday 10 to 5, Sunday 11 to 5. Tours, Saturday and Sunday at 1, May-October.

Other wineries worth a visit:

Reif Winery, Niagara Parkway, Niagara-on-the-Lake, the closest to town and river, opened in 1983 and is known for wines in the German style. All North American grapes were uprooted in favor of European vinifera and premium French hybrids on the 135-acre estate behind the winery. Klaus W. Reif, 13th generation of a winemaking family in Germany, still selects only the best 40 percent of the harvest for his own wines, selling the rest to other wineries. The dry riesling and gewürztraminer are standouts here. The winery stages functions in conjunction with the adjacent Grand Victorian B&B. Tours daily at 1:30, May-September; showroom, daily 10 to 6, to 5 in winter.

Henry of Pelham, 1469 Pelham Road, St. Catherines, has a small winery with quite a history. Located in the heart of the Bench, the hilly vineyard has been owned by a single family since Henry Smith planted the first grapes in 1794. We sampled a variety from the Loyalist house red to an elegant reserve chardonnay in the stone basement of an inn dating from 1842. Its chardonnays, rieslings, sauvignon blancs and icewines are considered some of the best in Ontario, but president Paul Speck held out promise for red wines following the great 1995 vintage. The baco noir already had won awards. Tours daily in summer, 11:30, 1:30 and 3:30; showroom daily, 10 to 6, to 5 in winter.

Pillitteri Estates Winery, 1696 Highway 55, Niagara-on-the-Lake, opened in 1993, adding wines to owner Gary Pillitteri's traditional farm and fruit offerings. The 14,000-square-foot winery houses a farm market known for good values and a bakery where we were pleased to find real butter tarts for 45 cents – half the cost of ersatz butter tarts we'd bought earlier at another market. A trellised **Wine Garden** overlooking a cherry orchard offers a daily special, perhaps tuna salad on a fresh croissant with cheese, olives and a glass of wine for $5.95. The wine labels picture a stylized Sicilian donkey cart, the original of which stands amid a gallery of art works in the winery's reception area and has been in the family for generations. The winery's early production included a couple of rieslings and chardonnays, plus rosé and cabernet sauvignon. A tractor-drawn caravan of covered carriages takes visitors on tours of the vineyards and orchards. Open daily, 10 to 8.

Fruit Stands

In harvest season, the fruit fairly drops off the trees, evidence of how prolific the Niagara Peninsula orchards are. They represent 90 percent of the fruit raised in Ontario, and Niagara is a major fruit bowl for much of Canada. Country markets, some of them run by local Mennonites, stand chock-a-block between orchards along every road. Prices naturally are lower the farther you get from the Queen Elizabeth Way and population centers. Some of the best are around Niagara-on-the-Lake.

Rempel's Farm and Flower Market, 1651 Lakeshore Road, is a favorite with locals and markets its own fruits and vegetables grown on a 50-acre farm. The selection is limited and choice. A sign said the peaches were "washed and defuzzed, so you can eat them right away," and the radishes were the biggest we ever saw. Debbie Rempel's bakery produces great strudels, cappuccino nanaimo bars and raspberry squares; we took home a rempelberry pie ($6.99) baked with raspberries, blackberries, rhubarb and apples, and a sample of Mennonite platz. Frozen yogurts (even a rempelberry), made with their own fruits, are especially popular at Rempel's downtown bakery and frozen-yogurt outlet on Queen Street. Out back is a huge greenhouse where roses are grown for cutting year-round.

Harvest Barn Country Market, Highway 55 at East-West Line, is a large country market selling everything from fresh produce to home-baked breads, pies, cornish pasties, and steak and kidney pies; two of the last made a good dinner back home. We also made a picnic lunch out of the fantastic salad bar ($3.19 a pound, supermarket style), with ever-so-fresh ingredients set out on ice in about 50 separate dishes.

Kurtz Orchards Country Market, Niagara Parkway at East-West Line, is the biggest and most commercial market, but don't be fazed by the tour buses out front. Jean and Ed Kurtz started more than 25 years ago with one table under an umbrella and still maintain the family touch. There are varieties of jams, maple syrups, honeys and plum butter with crackers for sampling, many specialty foods, baked goods like almond-raisin bread (a local specialty with marzipan in the middle) and huge cookies, drinks like cherry cider and peach nectar, and a sundae bar.

Gourmet Treats

Angie Strauss, 125 Queen St., has become the town's best-known shopping destination for with-it visitors, thanks to the artist's watercolors and her vibrant floral designs. They're on everything from high-fashion sweatshirts in the $50 range to gifts, cards, wine labels and kitchen accessories, among them placemats, coasters, bibs and oven mitts. We acquired a couple of refrigerator magnets and a large print at a fraction of the cost of one of her lovely originals ($2,000), and thus qualified for a pair of free sweat pants at the **Angie Strauss Fashion Outlet** store at 183 Victoria St., where discontinued patterns are sold. Angie's is quite a story – previously a potter, she injured her left elbow in a roller-skating accident and started dabbling in watercolors with her good right arm, painting the flowers that husband Hartley brought her each week. People admired her paintings, asked to buy them and the rest, since the early 1980s, is history. All the designs are Angie's, created in the back-yard studio and stunning gardens behind her house at 178 Victoria St. But the copies and products are the work of 25 Mennonite women whom Angie employs around town. Ever the entrepreneur, she rents a one-of-a-kind studio apartment known as **Victoria Cottage** for $120 a night in the coach house built by her husband next to their home.

Imagine an entire downtown store in a prime corner location devoted to jams. **Greaves Jams & Marmalades,** 55 Queen St., looks just as it must have more than 50 years ago. This is where the Greaves family retails its jams, marmalades and preserves. Bins of jams, shelves of jams, boysenberry, peach, raspberry, red and black currant – you name it, they have it, and they use no pectin, preservatives or coloring. We picked up six mini-jars for $6.30, as well as some special mustards (these they don't make).

Niagara is known for its fudge, and **Niagara Fudge** at 92 Picton St. is where you can choose from 35 kinds, including chocolate-ginger studded with chunks of fresh ginger. It's $7.98 a pound, and produced right there on the marble table. Irish cream is the most popular flavor.

The **Niagara Home Bakery** at 66 Queen St., the oldest business is town, operates as it did half a century ago. The bread is still baked in an old stone oven and the Easter chocolate is made by hand. Scones, tea biscuits, almond tarts, sausage rolls, quiches and more are for sale.

Taylors at 69 Queen is the place to stock up for an old-fashioned picnic. You could get a submarine for $3.95, but why not try a schnitzel on a bun or a cornish pastie? Sandwiches come on a choice of breads or "balm" cakes, which are large rolls. Have a date square or an Empire biscuit for dessert, or one of the 30 flavors of ice cream, including Laurentian vanilla.

For more up-to-date fare, head for **Niagara À La Carte,** 38 Market St., a new gourmet takeout food shop. Besides the usual, owner Christa Hale offers gourmet pizzas and sushi. You might try the chilled watercress soup and a sandwich of goat cheese, roasted peppers, black olives and pesto.

Yes, Niagara keeps up with the times. **Monika's Coffees,** a coffee and pastry shop at 126 Queen St., sells espresso, cappuccino, caffe mocha and caffe latte, along with strudels, muffins, broccoli-cheese puffs, spinach pies and, a new one for us, smoked-salmon cheesecake.

The facade of **The Shaw Shop** "doesn't exactly shout shop," conceded the manager, which may be why we missed it the first time around. With a location at 79 Queen St. next to the Royal George Theatre, the Shaw Festival's memorabilia shop features books, festival posters, music, gifts and ShawWear.

Gourmet Theater

Shaw Festival, Box 774, Niagara-on-the-Lake L0S 1J0.
No report on Niagara-on-the-Lake would be complete without mention of the Shaw Festival. Eleven productions of George Bernard Shaw and his contemporaries are staged in three theaters from April through October. Artistic director Christopher Newton and one of the world's largest permanent ensembles of actors explores classic plays in a modern way for contemporary audiences. The 861-seat Festival Theater, built in 1973, contains the larger epic works. The 345-seat Court House Theater presents smaller Shaw works and the more intimate American and European dramas of the period. The 353-seat Royal George Theater houses musicals and perhaps an Agatha Christie mystery.
(800) 511-7429. Regular ticket prices range from $21 to $60.

In midst of Saratoga Spa State Park, stately Gideon Putnam Hotel is a Saratoga icon.

Saratoga Springs
The Summer Place to Be

The party's really hopping these days in that grand dowager of American resorts, Saratoga Springs. The small town that mineral springs, horse racing and society summers made famous had nearly died in the 1950s and 1960s. It re-emerged slowly in the 1970s and now is back on track, as it were, with a five-and-a-half-week racing season that extends through Labor Day, live performances almost nightly in July and August at the Saratoga Performing Arts Center, and a summer social scene that brings back the good old days. Little wonder that Saratoga proclaims itself "the summer place to be."

Something of a gourmet renaissance has added dimension to what U.S. News and World Report termed "the August delirium of Saratoga, for generations America's symbol of high living." In a single square block below Broadway around Phila Street are the new Palmetto's and Putnam Street markets, the restaurant lineup of Four Seasons Cafe, 43 Phila Street, Hattie's and Beverly's Specialty Foods, the Chocolate Moose and Ben & Jerry's, not to mention a tavern and a sports bar.

The result is a uniquely Saratoga spirit and panache, one that gives it an odd parochialism as if encased in its own cocoon with a north-south focus on Albany and New York, oblivious to points east and west.

The romance of the old Saratoga was evident in its grand, long-gone hotels with their sprawling porches along Broadway, the wide main street. Herbert A. Chesbrough, longtime executive director of the SPAC, which was instrumental in the city's rejuvenation, says "the romance of the new Saratoga is in the small cafes, unusual restaurants and the boutiques that have opened in some of the community's oldest buildings."

Food has become a big – and expensive – business in Saratoga, and some restaurants stay open in August until 3 a.m. to accommodate the after-the-concert or after-the-race crowds. In fact, scoffs one former restaurateur, "even the clothing stores sell food. Everything and anything becomes a restaurant for two months." In a bit of local hyperbole, she claims the town has more restaurants and bars per capita than any other in the United States.

Most of the year, Saratoga is "very low key," says Linda G. Toohey, former Daily Saratogian publisher who became executive vice president of the local Chamber of Commerce. "We think we're the best-kept secret in the world."

The pace picks up in late June with racing at the Saratoga Raceway harness track, the Newport Jazz Festival-Saratoga and performances of the New York City Ballet and New York City Opera at SPAC, and the opening of the party season that culminates in socialite Marylou Whitney's grand entrance in a horse-drawn carriage at her annual ball.

Come August, the crowds converge for the height of Saratoga's storied racing season and the Philadelphia Orchestra series at the Saratoga Performing Arts Center. Prices double and even triple, but many are the people who are willing to pay them.

Where else would a Holiday Inn change from a range of $74 to $99 for eleven months to a base of $195 in August?

That's Saratoga for you, a curious anomaly of a world-class resort with a shiny gold sheen and a hand out for the big bucks. Especially in season.

Dining

Serving days and meal hours vary widely in Saratoga, especially off season. To avoid disappointment, check ahead.

The Best of the Best

43 Phila Bistro, 43 Phila St., Saratoga Springs.

Winner of top culinary honors in Saratoga is this suave American cafe-bistro run by Michael Lenza, an ex-South Jersey chef who cooked locally at Sperry's before launching his own venture in 1993. "I might as well own a place if I'm working so hard," he figured.

Sixteen-hour days have paid off for Michael, who spent eight months gutting and remodeling the former Mother Goldsmith's cafe. He and his staff earn rave reviews for their contemporary fare served with finesse. His wife Patricia oversees the 50-seat dining room, lovely in peach and terra cotta. The bar and banquettes are custom-made of bird's-eye and tiger's-eye maple. Caricatures of local businessmen brighten one wall. Tables, most of the deuces rather close together, are covered with white linens topped with paper mats bearing the 43 Phila logo (a curious but attractive touch that we far prefer to glass). Atop each are fresh flowers, a lucite pepper grinder and a bottle of red wine – a different label at each table.

Arriving almost as we were seated for dinner was a dish of assorted spicy olives marinated in olive oil – the oil useful for soaking the accompanying bread from Michael London's Rock Hill Bakery, an area institution. Featured among starters ($6.50 to $12.50) is an Absolut Maryland crab martini, jumbo lump crabmeat served with citron vodka, lettuce and an olive in a chilled martini glass. Others are a smooth chicken liver pâté served with crostini and cornichons, a terrific trio of smoked seafood (with capers in a little carrot flowerette and roasted red-pepper crème fraîche) and an enormous pizzetta on Italian bruschetta, a meal in itself.

Had we eaten more than a sliver of the pizzetta we never would have made it through the main courses, a choice of a dozen ($18 to $26) ranging from sesame-crusted sea bass marinated in tequila and served with a papaya-melon salsa and a ginger-scallion noodle cake to skillet-fried filets of beef with a smoked jack cheese polenta and a yucatan-poblano coffee sauce. The Tuscan chicken pasta with roasted peppers, olives and white beans was a lusty autumn dish; the fillet of sole in parchment on a bed of julienned vegetables and rice, a signature item, turned out a bit bland. A $16 bottle of our favorite Hogue Cellars fumé blanc accompanied from a varied, well-chosen wine list.

The pastry chef is known for her distinctive desserts, including an acclaimed 43 Phila chocolate cake soaked in kahlua and covered with a brandied chocolate ganache, deep-dish peach crumble pie, and white chocolate raspberry tart. We settled for a dish of plum-port sorbet, a refreshing ending to an uncommonly good meal.

(518) 584-2720. Dinner nightly, 5 to 10 or 11. Sunday brunch in off-season.

Chez Sophie Bistro, 2853 Route 9, Malta Ridge.

Long considered the Saratoga area's finest restaurant, Chez Sophie reopened in 1995 after a decade's absence. Sophie and Joseph Parker turned up south of town in a sleek silver diner that once housed Sam's Place, and her coterie of fans could not have been happier.

Inspired French fare and a seasonal schedule had been Sophie's trademarks over the years, first in the rural restaurant that was an addition to their home north of town in Hadley, then in an elegant Saratoga townhouse and finally back at the Hadley retreat. That ultimately closed, and Sophie took a break for a few years as she sought a more urban, year-round venue.

The diner was offered in a tax-foreclosure sale. The Parkers bought it and their son Paul moved from Long Island to help manage. They did some renovation and rechristened it a bistro. Some bistro. This has black booths and banquettes, white tablecloths and lacy cafe curtains on the windows, through which the setting sun casts colorful streaks of light. The bar holds some of Joseph's fantastic wire sculptures, produced in his Hadley gallery, and his sketches serve as menu covers.

Sophie has discarded her traditional prix-fixe format in favor of à la carte. "The menu is basic, but we always have specialties such as salmon, lamb, duckling, and different appetizers and desserts," depending on availability, she says. Born of Polish parents in northern France, she cooks in the classic French style.

Look for appetizers ($7 to $8) like escargots en cassoulet, house-cured smoked salmon, roasted sweet peppers marinated in extra-virgin olive oil and, if she has it, a dynamite rabbit pâté with prunes and armagnac and a coulis of blueberries, an odd combination that tastes simply wonderful. Main courses ($21 to $27) vary from fillet of sole in lobster sauce to roast duckling madagascar to steak au poivre. Dessert could be a light crème caramel, rich chocolate mousse, fresh lemon cheese pie or our old favorite, vacherin, a meringue filled with vanilla ice cream and served with raspberry puree and chocolate sauce.

(518) 583-3538. Dinner, Tuesday-Sunday from 5:30; nightly in August. Closed January to mid-February.

Artworks are backdrop for diners at 43 Phila Bistro.

Eartha's, 60 Court St., Saratoga Springs.

This small grill and wine bar has been on everyone's list of best restaurants since it was opened in 1985 as Eartha's Kitchen, serving assertive fare in congenial surroundings. Carolyn Male, a chef who prefers to be in the front of the house, took over the restaurant in 1996. The dining experience slipped, according to the local consensus, although only those who had been there before recognized the difference.

The name, incidentally, derives not from the chef but from the half-ton, cast-iron wood stove and grill the founder called Eartha. From it come eight or nine entrées, mostly grilled but with an occasional sauté or pasta dish combining grilled vegetables and chicken or shrimp. Seafood is stressed, and the menu changes often.

When we were there, the huge wood stove was ready for mesquite, charcoal and applewood. It produced a super grilled mahi-mahi with avocado mousseline and a remarkable grilled catfish with pickled ginger and a mango glaze, among entrées from $18 to $23. They were accompanied by good rice and the best zucchini we've tasted in a long time. Preceding these were appetizers of salmon roulade with horseradish cream sauce and grilled belgian endive with basil aioli, served on nasturtium leaves.

The new owner has added such starters ($6 to $12.50) as smoked salmon fallen soufflé and grilled portobello mushroom with vegetable salsa and goat cheese. Recent main dishes included grilled jerk pork medallions with a lime-roasted red pepper and scallion sour cream and grilled black angus strip steak with a red onion jam and mushroom ragoût.

Desserts include chocolate timbale with a hint of Bailey's on a hazelnut tuile, blueberry-oatmeal crumb pie, fresh fruit terrines and a homemade ice-cream sandwich. We enjoyed a creamy cheesecake with strawberry puree on top.

A choice, expensive wine list harbored a fine Hidden Cellars sauvignon blanc ($18), served in delicate pink-stemmed glasses and stored in a lucite bucket.

Carolyn has brightened up the decor a bit, painting the walls, adding salmon-colored tablecloths and comfortable chairs with cushioned seats.

(518) 583-0602. Dinner nightly in season, 5:30 to 10. Closed Monday and Tuesday rest of year.

Sperry's, 30 Caroline St., Saratoga Springs.

Only in Saratoga could what "looks like a gin mill" (a local booster's words) pass itself off as a good restaurant. Everyone we talk with, from top chefs to hotel desk clerks, mentions Sperry's among their favorites.

It's certainly not for the decor – peek through the window and you might not venture inside. A long bar with a black and white linoleum floor takes up about half the space. At either end of the room are dark old booths and tables covered with blue and white checked cloths. On one side is a small new dining addition, similarly outfitted and used for overflow. Beyond is a covered patio for outdoor seating in season.

Chef-owner Ridge Qua is known for consistently good food at reasonable prices. The menu rarely changes, but the preparations and specials do.

For lunch, one of us enjoyed a great grilled duck-breast salad with citrus vinaigrette ($7) and the other a cup of potato-leek soup with an enormous open-face dill-havarti-tomato sandwich ($6.25), served with a side salad. Service on a slow day, unfortunately, was so slow as to be interminable. We had to go to the bar to request – and later to pay – the bill.

At night, when we assume service is better, the menu runs from $13.95 for jambalaya to $18.95 for steak au poivre. Fillet of sole sautéed with malt vinegar, an extra-garlicky shrimp scampi, grilled salmon fillet over warm sesame noodles with Thai sauce and wasabi, and veal chop with mushroom and port demi-glace were among choices at our latest visit. The day's pasta was sautéed rock shrimp, escarole, snow peas and roasted red peppers over angel hair.

Appetizers ($6.25 to $7.95) like escargots, chicken liver pâté, wasabi shrimp and grilled portobello mushrooms with chèvre and garlic toast are better than run-of-the-gin-mill offerings. Desserts include tortes, cheesecakes, seasonal fruit tarts, crème caramel, and lemon and chocolate mousses.

The wine list is reasonably priced, a further attraction for locals who gravitate here when outsiders take over their other favorites.

(518) 584-9618. Lunch daily except Sunday in season, 11:30 to 3; dinner nightly, 5:30 to 10 or 11.

Gourmet for the Soul

Hattie's, 45 Phila St., Saratoga Springs.

After 55 years as Hattie's Chicken Shack, this well-known institution changed hands, shortened its name and raised its culinary aspirations. Hattie Austin, still doing the baking here at age 93, sold in 1993 to Christel Baker, then a 33-year-old Wall Street investment banker. "We're old friends," she explained. "Our families go way back."

Personable Christel, who was making apple butter in the kitchen at our first visit, has gradually broadened the emphasis from soul food to southern home cooking to "bayou" cuisine with a distinct New Orleans bite. She kept the homey,

Food entrepreneur Christel Baker takes break in dining room at Hattie's.

cozy, checkered-tablecloth decor, but added a brick patio surrounded by a southern-style garden "just like one I saw in New Orleans" out back. She expanded the hours, added po'boys for lunch and live blues in season, offered the traditional side dishes à la carte and won a liquor license, featuring southern drinks like mint juleps (with mint picked from her garden). She also offers specialties through her new **Hattie's General Store,** based on the premises and featuring mail-order chutneys, pies and free-range pork and pasture-raised aged beef from her 110-acre farm near the Vermont border.

The whole enterprise is decidedly with-it and upbeat, the ambiance appealing and the food sensational. And what value! At night, you can order Hattie's famous southern fried chicken with two sides (perhaps collard greens and candied yams), a green salad and homemade biscuits for $11.25. The new bayou specialties – creole jambalaya, low-country crab cakes, bourbon shrimp mandeville, shrimp étouffée and blackened farm-raised strip steak – go for $11.95 to $14.95. Four of the southern side dishes with a salad and biscuits make a vegetarian sampler ($9.50). Christel urges patrons to mix and match appetizers, soups and salads for a light meal.

Try an oyster po'boy ($6.25) for lunch, or the fried chicken or barbecued spare ribs if you will. Finish with the peach cobbler or sweet-potato pie.

(518) 584-4790. Open Wednesday-Sunday, 11 to 10:30 or 11; daily in summer and breakfast, 8 to 11:30 in race season.

Two for the Season

The Lodge, 1 Nelson Ave., Saratoga Springs.

A striking green summer mansion beside the harness track at the Saratoga Equine Sports Center, built by the founders of the harness track and once known as Cedar Lodge, is now open to the public as a restaurant in season. Mike and Esther Viggiani and Tony Testo, restaurateurs from the Albany area who made The Elms a local culinary landmark for nearly a decade, returned from Florida in 1995 to operate this summery restaurant owned by the track. It's a perfect addition to the Saratoga scene.

The interior is a stunner. Built around a great hall full of rich cedar soaring two stories high, it spreads out in a variety of smaller dining rooms and an enclosed porch overlooking the verdant grounds. Each area, dressed in white linens, has a subtle horse-related theme. The great hall, now home to a bar, a grand piano and a couple of dining tables, is the majestic focal point.

Known for their complex Italian cuisine and homemade pastas, the Viggianis have broadened the Lodge's offerings to appeal to diverse tastes. Mike is executive chef, but he brought with him the head chef and other staff from the Asti restaurant the trio run the rest of the year in Naples, Fla.

Though the continental menu is understated, the fare isn't. Consider such main courses ($24 to $39) as grilled shrimp spiced with Caribbean jerk seasonings, served atop julienned tropical vegetables and lobster potstickers, and roasted sesame-seed-crusted salmon fillet served on a bed of napa cabbage with wasabi cream, soy sauce and California rolls. The grilled venison chops, with a juniper berry and wild black currant glaze, are served with dauphine potatoes and julienned vegetables; the filet mignon béarnaise, with baby vegetables and sweet potato pancakes. Osso buco, the house specialty, comes with Italian parsley and risotto milanese.

You could start with rigatoni alla vodka, sautéed gulf shrimp around goat cheese polenta or sautéed foie gras on a bed of baby field greens tossed with raspberry vinaigrette, sundried cranberries and roasted pumpkin seeds ($8 to $18). Or settle for one of the exotic salads, perhaps orange and fennel with pistachios or endive and celeriac with toasted walnuts. Desserts ($7 to $10) are no letdown: chocolate soufflé served with grand marnier anglaise, orange coconut semifreddo, tarte tatin or warm berries with homemade cinnamon ice cream.

The select wine list starts at $20 and goes way up. Single-malt scotches and premium dessert wines and cognacs also are offered.

(518) 584-7988. Dinner from 5, Wednesday-Sunday, late June to late July; nightly, late July to Labor Day. Jackets recommended.

Siro's, 168 Lincoln Ave., Saratoga Springs.

Imagine a fancy restaurant next to the race track, open a mere five weeks a year (for the racing season) and considered an institution. Only in Saratoga could such a place survive. Siro's has not only survived but thrived since the 1930s.

Siro's occupies a little white house that sports blue awnings and canopies. There's a tent at the side for jazz, a prominent bar inside the front entry and a couple of medium-size dining rooms dressed in white linens with white candles standing tall.

Expect to spend upwards of $200 (or more) for dinner for two. The menu changes

Horse-drawn procession arrives for dinner at The Lodge.

nightly, but the contents are always inventive, the product acclaimed and the delivery polished.

High-rollers like to start with exotic hors d'oeuvres ($8.50 to $14.50), perhaps piña colada tiger shrimp with grilled pineapple, local chanterelles with shaved reggiano and pancetta, or lobster tortilla with corn relish and spiced avocado. Then it's on to a second course ($5 to $14), say black pepper linguini alfredo with oysters and tasso, local beefsteak tomato salad with fresh mozzarella or Siro's romaine salad with anchovy, reggiano shards and caesar dressing. Typically, the half dozen main courses run from $33 for roast free-range chicken with spinach-tomato napoleon and grilled corn or crusty baked flounder with caramelized banana and tropical fruit salsa to $34 for rack of lamb with roasted garlic, root puree and oyster mushrooms. Executive chef Ken MacEachron's cooking background in Hawaii is often evident.

(518) 584-4030. Dinner nightly, 6 to 11, late July to Labor Day.

More Dining Choices

The Wheat Fields, 440 Broadway, Saratoga Springs.

A pasta machine in the front window attracts passersby to this restaurant, which features "unique pasta dining." The original owners from New York decorated the two long, narrow storefront rooms with taste and pretty wallpaper accented with baskets of wheat. Glass-topped tables in one room and white linens over pale mauve in the other, modern blond tweedy chairs and Saratoga mineral water bottles filled with dried pasta topped with dried flowers complete the decor. A new raised platform adds outdoor dining on the sidewalk out front.

Every main dish contains pasta and all the pastas and breads are made in the "viewing room."

The 30 pasta entrées are priced at night from $7.95 for spaghetti and meatballs to $16.95 for sliced Tuscan flank steak on a bed of spinach and egg fettuccine with a tomato-mushroom sauce. The chicken breast stuffed with asparagus mousse is served over tomato fettuccine, while the shrimp and mushrooms with fresh snow peas comes on a bed of linguini. Starters include a hearty soup of pasta and beans, stuffed pasta sticks with dipping sauce and a sampler of three special pastas and sauces of the day. Even the quiche of the day has a unique angel-hair pasta crust, topped with imported cheeses.

At lunch, one of us tried the cream of artichoke soup (delicious) and the fiesta Italiano – chilled pasta salad, garnished with edible nasturtiums. The other chose the pasta sampler ($7.95), an uninteresting cavetelli with house sauce, a better spinach fettuccine with herb butter and a tasty tomato-basil rotelle with sweet basil cream. Good, chewy bread with a sesame-seed crust and a generous glass of the house chardonnay accompanied. The sugar that came with coffee was flavored with anise.

Pumpkin-pecan cheesecake, a killer chocolate cake described as like fudge, and cappuccino pie are favored desserts.

(518) 587-0534. Open daily for lunch and dinner, 11:30 to 10 or 10:30.

The Olde Bryan Inn, 123 Maple Ave., Saratoga Springs.

All gray stone and flanked by tubs full of geraniums and white petunias, this is the oldest building in Saratoga (1773). It's jammed day and night, no doubt because of its moderate prices (the same menu is served all day) and fare that is considered better than average. Inside is a pleasant atmosphere of brick, brass and booths. There's also a covered outdoor terrace that we found torridly uncomfortable on a sunny day.

For lunch, try a grilled-chicken BLT or a roasted garlic philly cheese steak sandwich (both $6.95), or one of the five salads ($5.95 to $7.95) served with a homemade nut muffin or garlic bread.

Dinner could be a burger or a light entrée, perhaps scallops florentine, stir-fried chicken maui or petite sirloin. Heartier dishes range from an old-fashioned turkey dinner for $10.95 to blackened steak or New York sirloin for $16.95, with plenty of options in between. Chocolate oblivion, a fudge-like creation topped with whipped cream and resting on a pool of raspberry sauce, is the signature dessert.

Success spawns success. Owner Steve Sullivan first opened **The Old Homestead** (same format, same menu) on Route 50 in nearby Burnt Hills. In 1996, he went more upscale when he took over the old Caunterbury Restaurant way out Union Avenue, enhanced the Federal decor in the ramble of former theme rooms, and created an appealing steak and seafood grill called **Longfellows at Saratoga Farms.** Some said it was upstaging Eartha's in terms of hickory grill cuisine.

(518) 587-9741. Open daily, 11 a.m. to 11 or midnight.

The Original Saratoga Springs Brew Pub, 14 Phila St., Saratoga Springs.

The warehouse for an old tin manufacturer became the home in 1995 of a brew pub serving highly regarded food in interesting surroundings. All brick and dark wood, the space soars more than two stories high with tables perched on catwalks along a mezzanine around a bar and open kitchen. The upper tables provide a good vantage point for watching the cooking action and the brewing of four stouts and ales for on-premises consumption.

The all-day pub menu has the predictable contents. The dinner fare is quite a cut above. Look for appetizers ($6 to $7.50) like baked escargots en croûte, grilled portobello mushrooms, pan-seared oysters over crostini and baked buffalo mozzarella in phyllo with a chunky tomato ragoût. Typical entrées ($11.50 to $19.50) are scallops gratin, Mediterranean chicken stuffed with sundried tomatoes and feta cheese, grilled pork tenderloin and steak au poivre. The night's specials might be maple-glazed salmon with lemon crème fraîche and farm-raised rainbow trout stuffed with shrimp and scallops served on top of a sweet potato-apple-onion hash with seasoned orzo and heishu vegetables. Even the salads are unusual. The grundy comes with hearts of palm, artichoke hearts, marinated mushrooms, kalamata olives and chèvre croûtes. The spinach, endive and radicchio salad with grilled apples is dressed with toasted walnut vinaigrette.

(518) 583-3209. Open daily, from 11:30.

Scallions, 404 Broadway, Saratoga Springs.
What started as a gourmet takeout with a few tables has grown like topsy. Now it has doubled in size, with a multitude of jaunty, peach-over-white-under-glass-covered tables for dining. Dinner hours have been extended. Breakfast and the thriving Scallions take-out operation have been removed to the former Saratoga Sweets space at 480 Broadway, now christened **Hungry Spot Cafe.**

"We pack a lot of picnics on a busy day," says owner James Morris, who oversees both operations with his wife Kerry. Gourmet picnic selections include vegetarian pitas and hearty sandwiches ($10.95 and $11.95) and the Parisian, an indulgence of pâtés, all-butter croissants and shrimp salad ($16.95).

Chilled peach soup – a secret recipe with a hint of sherry – is a refreshing starter, as are gazpacho and one of the hot soups of the day. Besides sandwiches, exotic salads and light meals such as curried chicken and rice casserole, beggar's banquet and quiche with soup or salad are on the docket ($7.75 to $10.95) for lunch. Dinner ($13.95 to $16.96) brings more of the same plus additions like wild mushroom chicken, grilled Maryland crab cakes and grilled shrimp with linguini. The combination salad plate along with a sampling of pâtés turned our late supper at home into a special occasion.

Wine, beer, cappuccino and espresso are available.

(518) 584-0192. Open daily in summer, 11 to 10; rest of year, Monday-Saturday 11 to 9, Sunday noon to 5.

Beverly's Specialty Foods, 47 Phila St., Saratoga Springs.
Baskets on the ceilings, shelves full of gourmet foods, a deli case and a handful of tables typify this cafe and catering service that serves up some of the more assertive food in town. Beverly Cone took over the small space vacated when Eartha's Kitchen moved to Court Street. Catering, baked goods and specialty foods comprise the bulk of her business, but there's space for half a dozen tables that are filled day and night plus, of course, the ubiquitous Saratoga restaurant patio for outdoor dining.

Stop in for breakfast – anything from cinnamon buns and croissants to omelets, Irish oatmeal, french toast, belgian waffles and Beverly's own pancakes with a touch of wheat germ.

Sandwiches, salads, platters and specials like New Mexican chili (with green peppers), chicken stuffed with prosciutto and ricotta, and pork medallions with rosemary, sherry and onions are featured at lunch. We enjoyed a fall vegetable soup with a Greek salad ($6.25) and a salad platter bringing a choice of three (pasta with tuna and pesto, curried chicken, and sesame snow peas, very good but very niggardly for $6.95). The sandwiches, served on the Rock Hill breads made by Michael London, looked to be much more filling.

Bailey's Irish Cream cheesecake, chocolate-chambord torte, carrot cake with cream-cheese frosting and apple-bourbon cake with bourbon sauce are among the desserts, which Beverly prepares for customers here and at other restaurants.

(518) 583-2755. Breakfast and lunch daily, 7 to 4, Sunday to 3.

Cafe Panini, 371 Broadway, Saratoga Springs.

The soups and the panini sandwiches are terrific at this new cafe with a handful of tables spilling onto the sidewalk in front of the Adelphi Hotel. With little background but great desire, Beverly and Peter Williams opened the kind of place they like to find when they go out: good food, nicely priced, in a casual setting.

The sweet pea is the favorite among soups, selling out every day. The carrot-dill and sherried brie and mushroom alo are popular. The panini on focaccia (from $4.50 for swiss chard, ricotta, plum tomato and sundried tomato to $6.50 for the classico with prosciutto, artichoke hearts, sundried tomatoes and provolone) are to die for. We took one look at the hefty slice of vegetable frittata that crossed our path and knew it was a winner. The server took our minds off it with a whiff of the cookies. There are other delectable pastries and desserts, Italian sodas, teas and espressos.

(518) 583-7134. Breakfast, lunch and light dinner daily, 9 to 8.

A Sweet Homecoming

Mrs. London's, 464 Broadway, Saratoga Springs.

The pastries made famous by Michael and Wendy London came back in style in 1997 to the town in which they got their start two decades earlier on Phila Street.

The Londons acquired a more prominent storefront location along Broadway to purvey their Rock Hill Bakehouse breads and pastries in what Michael likened to a French patisserie and espresso bar. A larger retail area than before, a stylish cafe done in the Neo-Classical style of New York of the 1820s, and an open pastry and demonstration kitchen occupy the main floor. A bakery is planned eventually in the basement. The unusual cafe decor showcases Federal period pieces and the Londons' collection of early American silk embroideries. The kitchen is a showcase for Michael and Wendy, who were happy to get back to baking, and is a teaching facility for their licensees. The onetime Skidmore College professor-turned-world-class-baker expected to revive memories of such Mrs. London's favorites as lemon tarts and chocolate whiskey cake as rich as fudge, with bitter chocolate curls on top.

In the decade since their Phila Street bake shop closed, the Londons had concentrated on baking fabulous sourdough and natural grain breads at their Federal farmhouse outside Greenwich, producing a ton of bread a day for delivery to fine stores and restaurants around the East. They also had licensed fourteen bakers to produce Rock Hill breads across the country, and now produce Rock Hill reserve breads from a unique, enormous wood-fired oven made of volcanic rock in a new bakehouse addition in Greenwich.

Wendy and Michael London prepare Rock Hill Bakehouse breads at home in Greenwich.

Scheduled to open in phases starting in April 1997, the new Saratoga operation offers espresso, teas and light sandwiches as well as their trademark pastries. *(518) 692-2943. Open Tuesday-Sunday, 7 to 6.*

Lodging

The Mansion, 801 Route 29, Box 77, Rock City Falls 12863.

About seven miles west of Saratoga in an old mill town is a 23-room Venetian, villa-style mansion that has been carefully turned into a fine Victorian B&B. Built as a summer home in 1866 by self-made industrialist George West, known as the Paper Bag King for his invention of the folded paper bag, the imposing white Victorian house with cupola on top was acquired in 1986 by Tom Clark, a former college president who had restored four other houses in Saratoga.

He and partner Alan Churchill opened the house for guests, who luxuriate in grand parlors, four bedrooms and a suite amid priceless Victoriana, and enjoy four acres of landscaped grounds across from the mills. Off the central hall with its deep green rug and an unsigned Tiffany chandelier is a double parlor with recessed pocket doors and an old hand pump organ. One parlor is furnished in Empire furniture and the other in Eastlake.

Upstairs is a small, plant-filled area, where you can sit on bentwood rockers and admire the river and falls across the road, plus four spacious guest rooms, all with private baths and the original inside shutters. Armoires, wing chairs and puffy comforters are among the furnishings. A selection of hard candies is in each room, as are fresh flowers and plants that attest to Alan's green thumb as well as his talent for arranging the results in his collection of 200 vases.

A suite on the main floor has a sitting room with a Victorian couch from

Saratoga's old Grand Union Hotel, parquet floors, marble fireplaces and a pink marble sink.

Classical music from Alan's extensive collection of tapes plays in the front library, a fascinating room with a life-size carved wood statue of St. Francis in a window area and so full of coffee-table books and magazines that one of us could hardly be pried away for breakfast.

The gourmet feast quickly tempered any reluctance. A bowl of exotic fruits centered by an alstroemeria blossom was followed by fresh orange or grapefruit juice. Next came a platter with half a dozen breads: lemon, zucchini, banana-bran, pumpkin, applesauce and six-grain toast. Cooked to order was a hot dish of one's choice. We relished a masterful eggs benedict and a vegetable omelet with a slice of ham. Chocolate-almond coffee was poured throughout at individual linen-covered tables topped with fresh roses and tulips (this in January). A flame flickered from an Aladdin's lamp in front of the mirror on the fireplace mantel.

Always pampering their guests, the innkeepers are known to serve picnic brunches (cold soups and seafood salads) on the side porch, and a glass of wine or milk with cookies in the afternoon. The cupola is open for a rooftop drink, if you'd like.

The house is full of striking details, among them the six fireplaces with massive mantelpieces, brass and copper chandeliers with Waterford glass shades, etched-glass doors, parquet floors of three woods, and Currier and Ives prints. Brass doorknobs detailed with classical heads – including a dog with one paw outstretched – greet you at the front door.

(518) 885-1607. Doubles, $95, $185 in racing season; suite, $120, $210 in racing.

The Batcheller Mansion Inn, 20 Circular St., Saratoga Springs 12866.
Saratoga's most spectacular, conspicuous and architecturally fanciful landmark is now an urbane city inn. Built in 1873 and patterned after a Bavarian castle, the 28-room edifice sports Moorish minarets and turrets and reflects what has been variously called flamboyant French Renaissance and High Victorian Gothic styles. It had been condemned and abandoned as a rooming house when a bachelor attorney bought it for $25,000 in 1972 and started a restoration that culminated in 1994 in its conversion into one of the grandest B&Bs of all.

Guests enter through arched mahogany front doors. Off one side of the hall is a living room with gilt-edged mirrors and an enormous crystal chandelier. Off the other side is a mahogany-paneled library with plump red velvet sofas beside the fireplace and towering ficus trees by the tall windows in the bay. The dining room is large enough to hold a long table for twelve and four side tables for two. The dream of a kitchen is a breathtaking space, long and narrow and 26 feet high – contemporary and stark white except for an extravagant display of colorful culinary artworks and three soaring, twenty-foot-high arched windows that bring the out-doors in.

All nine guest rooms on the second and third floors come with private baths, queen or kingsize beds, fancy wallpapers and coordinated fabrics, oriental rugs atop thick carpeting, writing desks, television sets, telephones, mini-refrigerators, monogrammed bathrobes, thick towels and Haversham & Holt toiletries. Some have gas fireplaces. They vary widely in size from two small front rooms with hall baths to the enormous third-floor Diamond Jim Brady Room, outfitted with a billiards table in the middle, a kingsize iron canopy bed, a sitting area and a huge bathroom with an oversize jacuzzi, large stall shower and mirrored wall.

Double parlor is a feature of The Mansion, once an industrialist's summer home.

An elaborate continental breakfast is prepared by the staff. Set out buffet style on the kitchen counters, it includes fresh fruit (perhaps melon wrapped in prosciutto), cheeses, cereals and homemade granola as well as homemade muffins, scones and croissants.

(518) 584-7012 or (800) 616-7012. Fax (518) 581-7746. Doubles, $115 to $230; racing, $230 to $360. Two-night minimum most weekends, four nights racing weekends.

The Westchester House, 102 Lincoln Ave., Box 944, Saratoga Springs 12866.

One of Saratoga's oldest guest houses, this Queen Anne Victorian structure has been taking in guests for more than 100 years. But never so lovingly as since Bob and Stephanie Melvin of Washington, D.C., realized a dream by restoring the abandoned house into an elegant yet welcoming B&B in which guests' comfort is paramount.

All seven guest rooms have handsomely tiled private baths and king or queensize beds except for one with two three-quarter beds. Each is attractively furnished to the period. On the chest of drawers you'll find fresh flowers and chocolates embossed with the raised Westchester House logo. Handsome woodwork, blue tiles, two elaborate fireplaces and distinctive wainscoting are all original. The couple collect antiques, which are scattered throughout the house, along with "old" and modern art.

Guests gather on a wraparound porch overlooking old-fashioned gardens for tea and cookies or wine and cheese. The side and rear gardens contain six distinct sitting areas, where guests also can relax. Or they can enjoy two main-floor parlors, one with a great suede sofa and a grand piano (upon which Stephanie practices, when no guests are around, for her performances as an opera singer).

The Melvins serve a continental breakfast stylishly amid fine linens, china, crystal mugs and stemmed glasses in the dining room or on the porch. Juice, fresh fruit salad, baked goods from the nearby Bread Basket and sometimes cheese are the fare, enhanced by Stephanie's homemade peach butter and apple preserves. After breakfast, Bob snaps photos of guests, which are forwarded to their homes with a thank-you note to remind them of their stay.

(518) 587-7613 or (800) 581-7613. Doubles, $95 to $150; racing, $195 to $250.

Saratoga Bed & Breakfast, 434 Church St., Saratoga Springs 12866.

Some of Saratoga's most luxurious B&B accommodations are offered by Noel and Kathleen Smith in their recently opened 1850 House. The four sumptuous suites there are a far cry from the simpler 1860 farmhouse in which they got their start as Saratoga's first B&B, or their basic motel that gives them an unusually broad range of accommodations and prices.

Let Kathy lead a tour of her pride and joy, the brick Federal structure whose modest facade belies its plush interior. First comes the President Grant Suite, named for her husband's distant cousin (who died not far from here), which harbors a partial-canopy kingsize bed and beautiful oriental rugs. Next is the Roberts Room, done up in 1920s masculine style. Beyond is the McKinley Room, where one of the accessories is an Irish cradle from which Kathy first saw the world, her mother having brought it from Ireland. To the rear and upstairs is the Irish Cottage Suite, very quiet and private with two queensize beds and two curved loveseats facing the TV and fireplace. The Waverly Sweet Violets fabrics match the curtains and wallpaper; even the clawfoot tub is painted violet. All the suites have gas fireplaces, splashy coordinated fabrics, walnut and mahogany antique furniture, glistening hardwood floors, TVs and bottles of Saratoga water. There are a main-floor sitting room and an enclosed side porch, where breakfast is served at tables for four and eight in the summer.

The four lodgings in the farmhouse vary from a couple of small rooms with double beds and maple and oak furniture to two larger rooms with fireplaces, wicker furniture and queensize beds topped by colorful quilts made by local church women. All have private baths.

Breakfast is an event, staged on the porch in season and in the farmhouse in winter. Noel handles the cooking while Kathy converses with guests. The fare might be blueberry-walnut pancakes one day and cream-cheese omelets with bacon the next. Juice, fresh fruit and corn muffins or toast accompany.

(518) 584-0920 or (800) 584-0920. Doubles, $65 to $95, racing $85 to $145; suites, $110 to $145, racing $160 to $225.

The Adelphi Hotel, 365 Broadway, Saratoga Springs 12855.

Built in 1877, the Adelphi had been closed for four years when Gregg Siefker and Sheila Parkert started its ongoing restoration into a fantasy of Victoriana. "It was a complete wreck, but we were lucky because it was never modernized," said Sheila, who made the curtains, sought out the antiques and now arranges the spectacular flowers that grace the lobby.

Thirty-four air-conditioned rooms and suites come with private baths, telephones and televisions. All are spacious and feature lofty ceilings, ornate woodwork, antiques, rich wallpapers and lavish doses of Victoriana. We've never seen quite so much lace or so many crazy quilts all around. Check out the Adirondack Mission Room with its twig furniture, a sitting room in Stickley arts and crafts style, and a bathroom paneled in dark wood slats. Across the hall is a suite furnished in French country style.

Dining room is stylish setting for breakfast at The Westchester House.

Lately, the owners completed a total overhaul of the elaborate Victorian lobby, bar and upstairs parlor. The lobby is an extravaganza of palms, crystal chandeliers, and plush sofas and chairs. The walls and ceiling have been hand-stenciled in an exotic Neoclassic style. Cocktails, tea, supper, dessert and coffee are offered seasonally in the Cafe Adelphi, a Victorian bar incorporated into the back of the lobby and extending onto a rear porch and a lush courtyard garden. The latest addition here is a small swimming pool surrounded by an elaborate pergola and flagstone terrace.

Complimentary continental breakfast is served in bed, on the second floor in the High Victorian Parlor or outside on the Grand Piazza, the geranium-bedecked porch overlooking Broadway.

(518) 587-4688. Fax (518) 587-0851. Doubles, $90 to $145, racing $145 to $225; suites, $115 to $190, racing $225 to $310. Three-night minimum on race weekends.

A Hotel in the Park

Gideon Putnam Hotel and Conference Center, Saratoga Springs 12866.
Deep in the heart of the Saratoga Spa State Park, the huge, red-brick and white-columned Gideon Putnam Hotel – its front outdoor cafe almost walled in by colorful hanging plants and window boxes – looks as if it's been there forever. It's owned by the state, operated by a new concessionaire and on its way up. About $5 million invested in the hotel in recent years has produced new and renovated bathrooms, better air-conditioning and heating, and new carpeting and lighting.

Each of the 132 guest rooms has at least a glimpse of part of the 1,500-acre park. Rooms are furnished in Colonial reproductions and wicker in rose or blue color schemes. Because two double beds didn't fit well, most rooms have one queensize and an extra-long twin bed. All have enormous closets, televisions and telephones. Guests who spend the season usually snap up the eighteen parlor and porch suites.

The latter come with large screened porches furnished in bamboo overlooking a forest.

The Sunday buffet brunch ($14.95 each, $17.95 with unlimited bloody marys) draws mobs of people. We know traditionalists who come here regularly for lunch, savoring the quiet and majestic setting, the sensitive refurbishing and the restored murals in the main dining room, the modestly updated menu and service by "real" waitresses. Nachos supreme, taco and chicken caesar salads, vegetarian melts and grilled reubens go for $5.50 to $8.95, and oldtimers lament the passing of such standbys as welsh rarebit and chicken pot pie.

At night, the menu ($17.50 to $24.95) takes on international overtones. Expect the (for the Gideon) unexpected: shrimp and scallop jambalaya, grilled pork tenderloin with minted couscous and hummus, roast duck Chinatown style with shiitake fried rice, and grilled sirloin with brandy-peppercorn sauce and sweet-potato fries.

The outdoor Cafe in the Park is particularly popular before and after events at the nearby Saratoga Performing Arts Center.

(518) 584-3000 or (800) 732-1560. Fax (518) 584-1354. Doubles, $140 EP, racing $270; suites, $160 to $180, racing $440 to $455.

A Gourmet Excursion

New Skete Farms, Cambridge 12816. (518) 677-3928.

The smoked chicken we noticed years ago on many area menus prompted us to ask where it came from. "The monks at New Skete," we were told.

We learned that the monastery east of Cambridge near the Vermont border had a gift shop, and on our next trip – with cooler and ice in the trunk – we set out to find it. You take East Main Street (Route 67) out of Cambridge and drive about five miles to a dirt road, where you turn right after you see the monks' distinctive sign of white with a red cross. Up and up a road you go until 1,500 feet up, you finally arrive at the Russian Orthodox Monastery.

We were there on a Sunday morning when services, open to the public, were just ending. The only sounds we could hear were the birds and the mixed choir of monks and nuns singing.

Besides smoking bacon, sausage and hams and making many flavors of cheddar-cheese spread, the monks paint icons and the traditional Easter eggs, which they also sell. Their main source of income, however, is the breeding of German shepherds – a story told in their well-known book called *How to Be Your Dog's Best Friend* – and the training and boarding of all dogs.

They also sell maple syrup and acclaimed cheesecakes made by the nuns who live five miles away. The cheesecakes appear on the tables of some first-rate restaurants, in flavors of amaretto and cream, chocolate and kahlua.

We departed with a few pounds of chicken, smoked over apple and hickory wood, and some delicious horseradish-cheese spread that we served at a gathering soon after. The memories of an utterly peaceful place linger still.

The Breakfast Tradition

Breakfast is a Saratoga tradition, from the buffet at the Saratoga Race Course thoroughbred track to Sunday brunch at the Gideon Putnam Hotel. On the porch

Russian Orthodox monastery at New Skete.

outside the historic clubhouse at the track, watch the horses take their morning exercise as you sip the Saratoga Sunrise – a concoction of vodka, orange and cranberry juices, and a slice of melon – and pick your way through a selection of à la carte breakfast items. Breakfast is served from 7 to 9:30 every racing day.

The Bread Basket at 65 Spring St. is where many innkeepers in town obtain their breakfast breads. Proprietor Joan Tallman bakes daily "from scratch – no mixes used" in a basement bakery beneath her retail showroom. There's also a front room with help-yourself coffee, tables and chairs, and at our latest visit her husband was building an addition for more retail and eating space. Besides at least 30 varieties of breads, Joan offers muffins, walnut sticky buns, coffee cakes, apple-raspberry and peach pies, coconut-apricot dessert bars, raspberry mousse brownies, cookies and a triple-layer chocolate cheesecake that's to die for. There's an off-price bin for "yesterday's temptations." Plus – would you believe? – dog biscuits.

Wonderful coffees and pastries are featured at **Uncommon Grounds,** 402 Broadway, a long cavern of a room with bags of coffee beans inside the entrance and more than 40 bulk coffees and teas. Pick out a cranberry-orange muffin or a slice of English toffee cheesecake to go with a café au lait or iced latte.

Another refuge for coffee lovers is **Madeline's Espresso Bar,** 350 Broadway, a European-style coffee house with antique parlor, book exchange, board games and live entertainment. Sink into one of the stuffed chairs or sofas in back and you may never want to get up.

Coffee and Cabaret

Caffé Lena, 47 Phila St., (518) 538-0022, is a coffeehouse par excellence. The first of its type in the country, it was run from 1960 until her death in 1989 by Lena Spencer, and friends have continued the tradition since. Her legacy remains in the small upstairs room full of atmosphere as patrons enjoy the music along with good coffees, teas and homemade pastries (no alcohol served). Many are the name folk and cabaret singers who have entertained here. Open Thursday-Sunday evenings.

Gourmet Treats

Two exceptional new specialty-food markets have opened within a block of each other near Phila Street's Restaurant Row. The **Putnam Street Market Place,** 63 Putnam St., is upscale in the fashion of Dean & DeLuca. Sisters Cathy Hamilton and Gloria Griskowitz converted an old beer warehouse (note the old Ballantine Ale sign still on the wall) into a wondrous emporium centered by a fabulous deli. You'll find delectable sandwiches (regular or big) employing Rock Hill breads, a butcher featuring beef from Christel Baker's Hill Rock Farm and grill-ready kabobs to go, organic produce, focaccia from Bruno's and even an "olive station."

As purposely old-fashioned as Putnam Street is au courant, **Palmetto's Market** at 42 Phila St. occupies another old warehouse that dispenses good vibes along with meats, seafood, baked goods, deli items, coffee, Wheat Fields pastas, antiques and more. A bookstore-boutique and a sewing store are adjacent. Owner Peter Marquis even carries groceries to your car.

Across the way at 33 Phila is **Four Seasons Natural Foods Store & Cafe,** providing health foods and vegetarian fare inside and out in the space once occupied by Mrs. London's Bake Shop.

For a break, indulge in homemade ice cream, sorbets or frozen yogurt from **Chocolate Moose,** 63 Putnam St. Owner Sue Parry's favorite flavors include cappuccino chip, french silk, peaches and cream, raspberry treasure (with chocolate chunks) and moose tracks (vanilla with caramel fudge and chocolate chunks). Cones come in four sizes.

If you're into gourmet pizzas, check out **Bruno's,** a transformed 1950s roadhouse full of character and good aromas – not to mention pastas, burgers and salads – at 237 Union Ave. Closer to downtown, the new generation of owners at **D'Andrea's** offers deep-dish pizzas, stuffed breads (one is chicken cacciatore, $4 a loaf), and focaccia sandwiches in a colorful old paint store at 33 Caroline St.

Worth a side trip is **Sutton's Country Store and Cafe,** Lake George Road (Route 9), Glens Falls, a favorite gourmet shop hereabouts. It has an abundant selection of Crabtree & Evelyn gourmet foods and bath items, handmade chocolates (even a chocolate sheep with a white-chocolate bow), delectable baked goods, produce, zillions of cookbooks, a line of Adirondack coffee cups that look as though they're made of birch bark, and all kinds of gifts and accessories. Hearty, homemade food is served in the large, contemporary cafe at down-to-earth prices. We sometimes take out a couple of Sutton's hefty sandwiches ($4.25 to $5.50) for a picnic. Breakfast, 7 to 11:30 (noon on Sunday); lunch, 11:30 to 3; Friday dinner, 5 to 8.

The Roosevelt Mineral Baths, Saratoga Spa State Park, (518) 584-2011. The Roosevelt 1 Bathhouse is a good place in which to relax after over-indulging in Saratoga's good life. Stress and pain float away as you sink into a deep tub of hot, bubbly, brown mineral water in a private room, $14 for twenty minutes; for $26 more, a masseur will massage you from head to toe and then wrap you in hot sheets before you nap for a half hour. This and the other two architecturally grand mineral baths that drew thousands to Saratoga in years past for the cure are being upgraded by the concessionaire that runs the Gideon Putnam Hotel. Roosevelt 1 Bathhouse is open from 8:30 to 5 Wednesday-Sunday year-round, also Tuesday in summer; make reservations several weeks in advance in summer.

Downtown and Mount Royal are on view from Altitude 737 restaurant atop Place Ville Marie.

Montreal
A Tale of Two Cities

What can one say that hasn't already been said about Montreal, that changing, cosmopolitan slice of the continent just north of the Canadian border?

It's the city and the heritage in which one of us was raised, and it's been a home away from home ever since. But it's very different from the Montreal we once knew, the French-Canadian majority having asserted itself to give the city and the province in which it is located a singular, strong sense of place.

More than any other, Montreal is a city of duality. Which side one sees depends on the eye of the beholder.

The reigning duality is, of course, the "French fact." After Paris, Montreal is the world's second largest French-speaking city, and Canadian bilingualism translates in Quebec into French, down to the street names, store signs and restaurant menus.

Its English heritage has given parts of Montreal a British character. The mix of British and French in North America makes Montreal unique – solid, sedate and sophisticated but also surging, swinging and sensual.

We do not aspire here to give a definitive guide to Montreal, which has been well defined since it hosted two international extravaganzas, the Expo 67 World's Fair and the 1976 Summer Olympics. Instead, we share our personal observations of a city that always surprises our friends as being so near, yet so far – never more than a six-hour drive or an hour's flight from where we've lived but a world apart from the one most Americans know.

As a destination for fine dining for every taste and pocketbook, Montreal takes a back seat to no city in North America. Haute cuisine competes side by side with more casual fare in thousands of cafes and bistros. The ethnic enclaves span the spectrum of the world's cuisines. There's also a sampling of the hearty regional Quebeçois fare.

To the casual visitor along the main streets, all Montreal appears to be one vast emporium of food and drink, from boucherie to bistro. There are four principal concentrations of restaurants: for urban sophisticates, the downtown hotels and the Crescent-Mountain street area off Sherbrooke Street West; for tourists, the mixed bag of haute and honky-tonk that is Old Montreal; for the young and young at heart, the swinging Left Bank bistro row along Rue St.-Denis and St. Laurent Boulevard, and for the real thing, the enclave of chic spots in Outremont, where many of the more affluent French-Montrealers go.

Be advised: you don't need to know French (almost everyone can speak some English). But it certainly helps – if only to read visitor brochures, signs and menus. In the mysteries of translation, "essence de col-vert en surprise" in the Sheraton Centre Hotel dining room becomes "duckling consommé."

Be advised also that prices in Montreal, as elsewhere, run the gamut from bargain to rip-off (liquor and wine prices are unduly high). When the currency exchange rate is in Americans' favor, as it has been recently, food items can be cheap – American money stretches about 25 percent farther than the Canadian prices quoted here. Much of that difference may be negated by Canada's wide-ranging Goods and Services Tax, however.

Finally, be advised to look beyond the Basilica-Wax Museum-calèche on Mount Royal tourist circuit of the Montreal of yore. Look beyond the glittering skyscrapers, shiny shopping concourses, the underground city and subways that are the monuments of new Montreal.

Savor the spirit and style of the real Montreal, the joie de vivre that makes it so special. Especially when it comes to culinary pleasures.

Dining

Most restaurants offer several-course, table-d'hôte meals that are good values compared with the à-la-carte prices if ordered separately. On Montreal menus, "entrées" are appetizers, "pâtes" are pastas and "plats" are main courses. The barbecued chicken you'll find at a host of places is some of the best in the world, and the brochetteries offer marvelous meals on a skewer.

The Best of the Best

Toqué! 3842 St. Denis St.

Young chef Normand Laprise from eastern Quebec gained quite a following at the former Citrus restaurant on St. Lawrence Boulevard. He created a further stir when he and his former sous-chef, Christine Lamarche, opened their own place in the heart of the St. Denis restaurant row in 1993. In 1996, he was the first Montrealer invited to cook at the James Beard Foundation in New York, and now is widely considered the hottest young chef in town.

The quality and presentation of food are foremost to Normand – not a restaurant's decor or its reputation for preparing classic dishes. Indeed, at our recent late-afternoon visit, he was shopping at the fish market, and would send that night's dinner menu to the computer at 5:55, which was given as the reason it comes out in French only with inexplicable complexities and verbiage that requires lengthy translation. Imagine a Wolfgang Puck or Lydia Shire menu written in French, and you get the idea.

Chef Normand Laprise and partner Christine Lamarche at Toqué!

The place is suave and stylish, all the more so since it closed for a month in 1996 for a total renovation that replaced the open kitchen beside the front entry with a bigger one in the basement (the floor had to be lowered two feet). The freed-up space on the main floor added ten more seats but, more importantly, a more spacious feeling in two rear dining areas separated by a wall upholstered in red velvet. The banquette serving close-together tables has been relegated to the bistro section up front.

The name, a play on the name for a chef's hat, means crazy or nuts when it takes on the accent, advised Christine, the engaging and omniscient hostess. We didn't know whether it referred to the spirit or the food, but our initial lunch (since discontinued) was one of the nuttier we've had – pricey, oddball and not at all what we had expected having perused the dinner menu a few weeks earlier. We could not believe we'd eaten in the same restaurant when we read the restaurant's rave review in the next day's Montreal Gazette.

Discontinuing lunch service to concentrate on dinner in a more spacious and refined setting has helped establish Toqué! as the city's best restaurant. Even the AAA dining evaluators, seldom in the vanguard of things culinary, rank it up there with the four-diamond standbys that some consider has-beens.

The short menu changes nightly. It offers original main courses ($19 to $26) like grilled salmon with a ragoût of red beans and peppers; braised Charlevoix veal with thumbelina carrots, haricots and potatoes; grilled halibut served with mushroom risotto and a confit of cabbage, peas and tomatoes, and chilled foie gras of Quebec duck, topped with slices of duck breast, resting on caramelized eggplant caviar and topped by fried rice noodles. Appetizers are priced from $6 for a salad of garden lettuces and herbs to $12 for sashimi of peppered char with pickled daikon, pineapple ketchup and soy-balsamic reduction. Desserts ($6 to $9) range widely from a caramelized peach tart with strawberry sorbet to chocolate mille-feuille with pineapple sorbet. The presentations are as dazzling as the ingredients.

Those really out for a meal to remember can select a five-course dégustation menu ($58), with two starters, a choice of main courses (at our visit, grilled swordfish or roasted venison with too many obscure accompaniments to translate here),

a cheese platter and selection of desserts. For $68, Normand also will prepare a dégustation menu of five courses with foie gras "pour les aventuriers."
(514) 499-2084. Dinner, Monday-Saturday 6 to 11.

Les Caprices de Nicolas, 2072 Drummond St.

The chef is in his late 20s, and les caprices reflect the whims of his ingredients and cooking style. Nicolas Jongleux, who trained in France with renowned chefs George Blanc and Alain Chapel, settled into his own place here in 1996 with partner Daniel Medalsy, a genial host and the business half of the team. They offer exciting French haute cuisine in a stunning yet refined setting.

Located on the ground level of a downtown rowhouse, the welcoming restaurant seats 50 at large tables spaced well apart – a rare attribute in Montreal – in a garden atrium, an intimate library/salon and a serene dining lounge with an antique marble

and oak bar. In fact, the ambiance was so appealing and the menu so enticing that when we dropped by to check it out, we decided on the spot to stay for lunch.

It proved a good decision. We were seated beside a trickling fountain in the garden courtyard, an idyllic space soaring three stories to a skylight, with vines hanging down the sides. Tables were dressed with pale yellow linens and antique china from Nicolas's family business in France.

Lunch was table d'hôte, two courses varying from $17.75 to $27 with a choice of four main dishes. Ours began with a "teaser" from the chef, a complimentary treat that changes with the meal. This day it was an exquisite poached quail egg on a baby potato with tomato confit and balsamic dressing. Excellent French bread preceded the appetizers. One was a fabulous white bean cappuccino soup with

Garden atrium at Les Caprices de Nicolas.

enoki mushrooms and gnocchi made of guinea hen (the cappuccino label turned out to be self-explanatory upon its frothy arrival). The other was a classic salad of lettuces and herbs "from Monsieur Homer's garden." Main courses were veal kidneys with salsify and tiny potatoes in a rich sauce, covered with a huge, sliver-thin piece of parmesan cheese that had been melted and hardened, and arctic char topped with a teepee of chives and teamed with yellow tomatoes, asparagus and snow peas. Desserts were a crispy meringue with fresh figs and homemade vanilla ice cream, and chocolate cake with warm honeyed bananas and a sherbet of pure cocoa. Perfect cafe filtre followed. Service was correct and detailed and we had the place almost to ourselves, few business people being able to linger over a two-hour-plus lunch, no matter how memorable.

This is really a refuge for a serious dinner, co-owner Daniel advised. Nicolas, whose sensitivity to product reflects his upbringing in a small town in Burgundy, "spends almost more time at the market than here." A typical night might offer the

Artworks and flowers enhance dining experience at Le Passe-Partout.

starters that we experienced at lunch, plus liver mousse surrounded by snails and soya emulsion and topped with angel-hair katafi, celery root and goat cheese profiteroles, and a salmon and caviar potato crêpe inspired by Georges Blanc. Main courses ($19 to $34) could be roasted guinea fowl in liqueur wine with a puree of sweet potatoes and pearl onions in a truffle broth, roasted buck with a risotto of barley, watercress and confit shallots, and filet of Alberta beef with ravioli of wild mushrooms and smoked bone marrow.

Few can resist the magnificent cheese board, considered the city's best and offered at $17 per. But save room for the sweets ($7.50) – Nicolas credits his dessert touch to his training with Alain Chapel. They include a hot soufflé-like chocolate torte with homemade vanilla ice cream, warm cabernet cake with roasted black figs and basil ice cream topped with chopped nougat, and a classic Lyon gaufrette (a waffle-like cookie) with a puree of chestnuts and an ice milk preserve.

Upon departure, check out the shelves in the front window displaying flavored oils, herbs, dried morels, antique teacups and such. They're caprices reflecting attention to detail in a place that cares.

(514) 282-9790. Lunch, Monday-Friday noon to 2; dinner Monday-Saturday 6:30 to 10:30.

Le Passe-Partout, 3857 Decarie Blvd.

Call this a bakery, a restaurant, an art gallery. It's a classic Parisian-style neighborhood establishment of the old school, lovingly tended by ex-New Yorker James MacGuire, the chef and baker par excellence, and his French-Canadian wife, Suzanne Baron-Lafrenière, the art enthusiast and printmaker.

After closing for a couple of years when the rent tripled on their simple, unsigned Monkland Avenue quarters that had packed in serious gourmands, the couple resurfaced in larger, signed quarters with a bakery of note, a small and serene dining room, and a new gallery downstairs. The name reflects the link, Suzanne explains. Passe-partout means both the soft brush with which bakers remove excess flour from dough and the cardboard matte used to frame artworks on paper.

The bakery tends to upstage the restaurant in its new incarnation (a loyal patron and newspaper columnist called its bread the best in America, noting travelers from all over make it their last stop on their way home). Although famous for his breads, his compatriots consider James one of the top French chefs in the city. "I'm here at the bakery anyway," he says, "so I might as well be cooking in the kitchen."

And cook he does, as attested by a sensational lunch at our latest visit. The meal is basically table d'hôte, $18.50 for three courses with two or three choices changing daily, although there are a few à-la-carte options. A suave carrot soup and an ethereal mussel soup were auspicious starters. Three kinds of perfect breads from the adjacent bakery accompanied, inspiring us to return the next day to buy a loaf to take home. One of us concluded with smoked salmon (a generous portion) accompanied by a savory cucumber salad ($8.75), while the other continued on the table d'hôte journey with poulet basquaise, a boneless chicken with tomatoes, peppers and delicate white rice. That route led to the dessert du jour, a fabulous dense almond cake with homemade vanilla ice cream incorporating vanilla from Madagascar. We passed on the proffered cheese tray, including "two imported specially for us," but munched on a sampling of sugar-coated almonds, bite-sized maple sugar candies and chocolate orange rinds that came with the coffee. With a glass each of the house white wine (Suzanne opens a fresh bottle and pours "whatever we think goes well with the food"), the luncheon tab came to a rather memorable $60, including tax and tip.

Parisian prices and style extend to the bakery counter and deli, which you pass both on entering and leaving the dining room. Suzanne notes it specializes in the two items that go well with bread – cheeses and pâtés, both of which they have in abundance. A couple of each and a loaf of bread to go and, voilà, another $30 charge to the good life.

White damask linens and vases of alstroemeria dignify the eleven tables in the romantic peach-colored, high-ceilinged dining room. There are artworks on the walls and a showy spray of gladioli at the entry. The fare changes daily and provides what James says is a choice between simple and complex. While regional food (cooked meals from the baker's oven) is featured at lunch, dinner gets more sophisticated with individual preparations. Start, perhaps, with cream of celery soup, a terrine of duck or a special of raviolis of sweetbreads with asparagus and mushrooms. Main courses ($24.50) could be supreme de vivanneau with eggplant caviar, tomato concasse and fresh basil, and saddle of lamb with moutarde de meaux and haricots verts. Refresh with a perfect little salad or a plate of unpasteurized French cheeses. Finish with chocolate mousse, floating island, puff pastry with Italian plums or homemade orange-banana sorbet or grand marnier ice cream.

"We're not à la mode to appeal to the magazine critics and the twenty-somethings in their BMWs," says Suzanne of their restaurant's low profile. The seasoned food cognoscenti know better.

(514) 487-7750. Lunch, Tuesday-Friday 11:30 to 2;30; dinner, Thursday-Saturday 6:30 to 9:30.

Claude Postel, 443 St. Vincent St.
This elegant restaurant in Old Montreal is not widely known, but three of the

Patrons enjoy dinner on front porch at Claude Postel.

city's leading restaurateurs tipped us off to its existence. It's owned by Claude Postel, a chef from Chartres, who had made Bonaparte one of the best restaurants in the old city.

Here he makes the rounds to describe for early patrons the day's selections before he gets too busy in the kitchen. He'll likely recommend the salmon and scallops from his own smokehouse, the salad of mesclun and smoked duck, the lamb's lettuce and goat cheese seasoned with truffle-flavored oil, and the terrine of venison and foie gras for starters ($8.50 to $17). Main courses on the all-day menu are priced from $22.50 for grilled scallops with fennel on a bed of vegetables to $29 for dover sole meunière or lobster grilled with chives. The emphasis is on seafood (rack of monkfish from the Grenadine Islands, porgy fillet with tapenade, oriental sea-perch fillet, Atlantic salmon with citrus fruits), although you'll also find seasonal treats like (in the fall) magret of barbary duck with pears and cinnamon, bison tournedos with wild berries, and caribou garnished with marrow. A short, three-course table-d'hôte menu is priced from $23.95 to $25.95. Three découverte menus incorporating favorite dishes in five courses are available for two at $48 each. The pastry cart is known for its lemon-meringue tart and chocolate-hazelnut cream cake, but traditionalists opt for the showy crêpes suzette or liqueured soufflés.

Full of history, the structure was built in 1861 as the Hotel Richelieu, in which actress Sarah Bernhardt once stayed. It served as a morgue before it was transformed by Claude Postel.

Dining is in two masculine-looking rooms with dark wainscoting, high beamed ceilings, wrought-iron light fixtures, deep-set windows with fresh flowers on each sill, and flowers in gleaming copper planters. A canopied porch adds dressy tables above the sidewalk in summer.

(514) 875-5067. Lunch, Monday-Friday 11:30 to 3; dinner nightly, 5:30 to 11.

Quelli della Notte, 6834 St. Lawrence Blvd.

This is a showplace of a restaurant, worthy of the revolving searchlights that pointed the way for the 2,500 invitees who turned out for its October premiere in 1996. Thanks to a tip from one who was there, we visited two weeks later without benefit of a precise address and before it even had a sign out front. There was no mistaking the building, its facade trimmed in bronze, in the heart of Little Italy. But it did take three tries before we got the right entrance – a circular aluminum affair that opens like a revolving door into a tube-like red velvet vestibule with a velvet door that revolves into a two-story space bespeaking its multi-million-dollar renovation price tag.

The establishment seems larger than its 120 seats, partly because dining takes place on the main level in two distinct areas separated by a two-story space open to a sunken lounge. All is plush as can be in pale yellows and reds accented with aluminum railings and sculptures. Large circular glass lights on the walls with mirrors in the middle serve as art, as do stylish grappa bottles in a couple of mounted displays. The well-spaced tables are topped with white linens, heavy cutlery and feather topiaries and flanked by suave brown Bertoni leather chairs from Italy. Mod lights hang from the ceiling over the lounge, where heart-shaped blue velvet stools face a curving redwood bar.

The food and beverages are affordable and first-rate. A sushi bar at the rear serves up some fabulous looking treats. The glamorous downstairs bar offers Montreal's first cigar lounge, complete with Cuban cigars, and rest rooms more mod than any we've seen. The kitchen is a beauty, too. One section has bouquets of impeccably fresh herbs, each in its little pot of water.

Salvatore Donato, the host and manager, heads a team of five owners who came from local Italian hot spots, Le Latini, La Sila and Primadonna. Against the trends toward California and fusion fare, Salvatore said, "we're going back to our roots." That means regional Italian fare, featuring a guest chef from each of Italy's twenty regions every two months, and a menu del mercato of seasonal specialties obtained from the famed Jean Talon Market nearby. These and the sushi offerings are in addition to the regular menu, a not overwhelming compilation of contemporary Italian treats at refreshing prices.

Primi plates yield sophisticated pastas and risottos in the $12.75 to $18.25 range. Secondi are priced from $15.50 for grilled veal livers marinated in sage and lemon to $25.75 for roasted veal chop or a crown of grilled shrimps around a fried saffron rice cake. Antipasti ($8.75 to $12) include carpaccio of sea bass, shredded crabmeat in its shell, marinated salmon with mint and red pepper coulis, and grilled pork slices on a bed of pumpernickel croutons spread with mascarpone and goat cheese and topped with blueberries. Desserts ($4.50 to $6.50) range from feuilleté de chocolat to assorted glacés and sorbets. The bill comes with dessert biscotti, imported Italian candies and a complimentary liqueur.

The breads and pastas are housemade, the olive oils are imported from Umbria and the cappuccino is some of the best we've tasted. Two sommeliers help Salvatore with the wine list, which is heavily oriented to the regions of Italy with a nod to California, Oregon, Spain, Chile and South Africa. The prices are fair, and France is almost ignored.

At lunchtime, when the scene is quieter, the menu is table d'hôte. A three-course meal with coffee goes for $9.50 to $15, depending on choice of main course.

(514) 271-3929. Lunch, Monday-Friday noon to 3; dinner nightly, 5:30 to midnight or 1.

Feather topiaries and circular wall lights are part of dining scene at Quelli della Notte.

Mediterraneo, 3500 St. Lawrence Blvd.

Commanding a rare corner space along the Main (as Montrealers call St. Lawrence Boulevard) near Sherbrooke Street, this hot newcomer differentiated itself as a California-style grill and wine bar with a plush, urbane look. Floor-to-ceiling windows look out onto the streets, and the interior is a sea of well-spaced tables in blue and white.

A serpentine bar running the length of one side echoes the curves in the ceiling, a huge white disc designed to resemble a space ship.

Chef Claude Pelletier, acknowledged as one of Montreal's best, presents imaginative fare at affordable prices. The logo and menu covers convey a beachy theme, and seafood takes top billing ($16.75 to $18.75).

Expect striped bass steamed in an oriental broth, seared scallops with grilled bok choy, blackened swordfish with taro chips and rare grilled tuna with a tomato and caper tombée. Grilled meats go up to $20.75 for chanterelle-crusted veal chop and pecan-crusted rack of lamb. Saddle of rabbit, mignonette of venison and guinea fowl stuffed with foie gras are among the choices, each with different accompaniments, from a barbecued root vegetable quartet to wild mushroom-mashed potatoes to spaghetti squash timbale.

Start with sashimi tuna, grilled octopus in a chive and yogurt sauce, escargot spring rolls or breast of duck prosciutto. Finish with crème brûlée, assorted sorbets or a caramelized banana split consisting of vanilla and chocolate ice creams, diced fruits, peanut brittle and two sauces. The food is considered as fabulous as the presentation.

The extensive California-Italian wine list starts at $29, and includes a number of grappas.

(514) 844-0027. Dinner nightly, 6 to midnight or 1 a.m.

Globe, 3455 St. Lawrence Blvd.

"Cuisine du monde" is featured at this beauty of a place in the midst of the hottest restaurant block along The Main. Originally housed in the second-floor loft of a warehouse, it moved downstairs for better visibility and a more urbane setting of white-clothed tables spaced nicely apart, stunning red brocade fabric chairs and walls in varying shades of gray. Accents include a twelve-foot-high banana tree in the rear and brightly striped red and green banquettes along a wall of the side lounge.

Co-owner Matteo Yacoub, who opened this as an adjunct to his first love, Buona Notte, up the street, leaves the cooking here to chef Robert Haumont "et sa brigade." Maki and sushi take starring roles on the culinary stage, along with such starters ($6 to $9.50) as Vietnamese spring rolls, vegetable and Alaska crab terrine, salmon and smoked scallops tartare with roasted sesame seeds, fried calamari and Montreal's seemingly ubiquitous summer tomato and bocconcini salad with balsamic dressing.

More substantial dishes include homemade pastas and risottos ($12.50 to $16), perhaps fusilli with salmon and grilled onions or seafood risotto with Alaskan crab. Among meat and fish dishes ($16.25 to $23.50), look for Thai salmon with sesame spinach, grilled tuna with a pyramid of shrimp tabbouleh, braised pork loin in a cashew and raisin sauce, roasted veal chop with prosciutto and mushrooms, and grilled cognac pepper steak.

Desserts might be crème brûlée, fruit tarts and bananas flambéed with tequila and coconut.

(514) 284-3823. Lunch, Monday-Friday 11:30 to 3; dinner nightly, 5 to 11 or midnight.

Le Latini, 1130 Jeanne Mance St.

From a modest beginning in 1979, Moreno de Marchi and two partners have built quite a culinary establishment. They rebuilt this original with a spectacular, two-story glass addition and an incredible wine cellar below. Around the corner at 205 Viger St. they added a complex of Italian eateries with a wine bistro and a moderately priced restaurant called **L'Altro.**

Ebullient Moreno gave us a tour of Le Latini, which is indescribably handsome with pillars, arches, untold kinds of custom-made chairs (he changes them every year) and damask-covered tables, each with a bottle of Manciuti extra-virgin olive oil as a centerpiece. We were mighty impressed by the dining rooms up and down with views from soaring windows, the canopied dining patio, the three fireplaces, the entry facing extensive antipasto counters and display shelves for fruits, cheeses and more. To say nothing of the 85,000-bottle wine cellar, with a table for sixteen set with seven glasses at each place for a wine-tasting dinner (the all-Italian cellar is one of the biggest of its kind in North America, with prices starting in the thirties). Not to mention the gleaming kitchen, where seven chefs man the stations at every meal "and they all can do everything." A stickler for detail, Moreno imports bread from his hometown in Italy – "I'm crazy, they say."

As for the food, he showed his computer, which itemized 154 hors d'oeuvres, 231 pasta dishes, 121 beef and veal dishes and 99 fish entrées at the time ("more now," he said at our latest visit). He changes 75 items on the menu twice daily. Appetizers were priced from $6.25 for brodino with tortellini or capelli d'angelo

Interior dining room at Le Latini.   **Outside porch dining at Le Latini.**

to $14 for grilled shrimp with citron linguini; pastas from $13.50 for penne all'arrabiata to $22.75 for tagliolini with mushrooms and truffles, and "plats résistances" from $19.75 for veal piccata to $37 for filet mignon with morels (not counting a filet of bison in salsa saporita for $58.50). The table-d'hôte dinner has six choices, from grilled salmon ($24.75) to entrecôte ($33.25); appetizer and dessert come with. A menu gastronomique offers five predetermined courses for $42.

Unlike most Montreal restaurants, Le Latini posts no reviews at the entry – except for one in French, which is accompanied by Moreno's typewritten reply in French. It seems he disagreed with what was said. But the Montreal Gazette reviewer hailed its "spectacular makeover and superb food," and an Outremont restaurateur praised this as a knockout place, which it certainly is.

(514) 861-3166. Lunch, Monday-Friday 11:30 to 3; dinner, Monday-Saturday 5:30 to 11:45.

The Best Bistros

Laloux, 250 Pine St. East.
A high-ceilinged storefront formally done up in striking black and pale yellow and an inspired, reasonably priced menu recommend this classic bistro, considered tops in the city. It's run by chef André Besson, who trained with Paul Bocuse and proclaims his membership in the Academie Culinaire de France.

The decor is modern Parisian bistro, simple and stark: bare floors, white linens, black banquettes, hanging globe lamps and a wall of mirrors – not even flowers to intrude on the prevailing black and white theme.

The cuisine is nouvelle and the chef's reach far-ranging. With the menu comes a little bowl of assertive chicken-liver mousse to spread on homemade bread crisps. Changing three-course, table-d'hôte dinners are priced from $16.95 for pan-fried skate with capers and lemon to $25 for sweetbreads with chanterelles and port wine. Ordered à la carte, the dozen main courses at our latest visit ranged from $9.95 for orecchiette with mushrooms, tomatoes and oregano to $19.50 for filet mignon au poivre. Other choices were scallops of salmon with essence of carrot, chervil and ginger; doré in pastry with vermouth and lobster cream sauce, and lamb filet with eggplant marmalade and sweet peppers.

Appetizers run from $3.75 for soup du jour (seafood, at our visit) to $11.75 for charlotte of lamb with fresh mint and tomato coulis. The crab ravioli with orange sauce, the sweet and sour dim sum with ginger and the duck neck stuffed with foie gras intrigued. Salads might be papaya and watercress, mesclun and grapefruit, or "toute verte" (all green).

Desserts are delectable: genoise with pralines, chocolate and crème anglaise; an acclaimed chocolate mousse topped with coconut, ginger and chocolate shavings; candied pear on grand-marnier ice cream, and crêpes with pralines. André suggests the grand dessert ($8.50), a selection of three and "better to share." He's also proud of his platter of assorted French cheeses.

Many wines are available by the glass. The wine list is comprehensive and rather pricey.

(514) 287-9127. Lunch, Monday-Friday noon to 2:30; dinner nightly, 6 to 10:30.

L'Express, 3927 St. Denis St.

No sign identifies this chic bistro, only the name discreetly inscribed in white tiles on the front sidewalk. But L'Express, as authentic a French bistro as it gets, is generally packed day and night with Montreal's trend-setters, media types and restaurateurs. Everybody who's anybody seems to turn up to see and be seen – a phenomenon enhanced by the squeezed-together tables and the mirrors on the walls.

So we were rather surprised to have the place completely to ourselves for a weekday continental breakfast of cafe au lait, flaky croissants (purchased from a bakery) and a couple of slices of grilled brioche. With jam and cheese on the side, the bill came to a rather continental $10-plus, but, hey, isn't this the good life in Montreal?

The waitress was chatty, the white paper tablecloths rolled out like gift wrap and printed with Perrier bottles, and the no-smoking signs appreciated in a city that has few non-smoking dining rooms. The fare is simple and ever-so-French.

Bistro interior glitters at L'Express.

The only egg dish at breakfast was basic egg with sausage or ham. No one comes to be dazzled by the food, although it is reputed to be quite good.

They come for the ambiance, the conviviality and a short menu of typical bistro fare, all available à la carte. The menu strikes the adventurous as somewhat old-hat, as in appetizers of soupe paysanne, jellied egg, celeriac rémoulade and quiche du jour. But reviewers consider the chicken-liver mousse with pistachios the city's best; ditto for the terrine of duck foie gras (at $19.75 the most expensive item on the menu, except for the three caviars).

More substantial dishes start with cold roast beef sandwich with legendary fries ($9.95) and top off at $16.95 for roast lamb with rosemary. Pickled duck salad, fillet of doré amandine, grilled salmon on a bed of spinach, pan-fried veal livers with tarragon and grain-fed chicken in mustard sauce are among the standbys. Specials are simply inserted in the plastic-covered menus diner style, as in "six oysters."

Desserts include a floating island that our waitress called "the bomb," chocolate mousse cake, raspberry charlotte and a couple of "frozen logs" made of pear and raspberry sorbets or black cherry and chocolate ice creams with crème anglaise.

(514) 845-5333. Open daily, 8 a.m. to 1 or 2 a.m.

Le Persil Fou, 4669 St. Denis St.

This "adorable" little prize, as headlined over a French newspaper review, is typical of many a neighborhood bistro in Montreal, but enough of a cut above in food, style and price to make it a destination. We have fond memories of the place when it was Citron-Lime, with a bit of California flair. Now it's even better and truly French with a chef from Alsace and two caring young owners, Pierre Gauthier and France Grenier, he mostly in the back of the house and his wife up front.

The shoestring decor reflects her artistic touch. Fabric swagged along a rod dresses the top of a fieldstone wall; vines twist around the bar, and masses of artificial flowers turn up in unexpected places. Why not, with a name that means "crazy parsley." Pierre says it stands for freshness, and for affordable cuisine de marché.

Affordable it certainly is, with the printed menu listing five pastas for $7.50 to $13.50 (for smoked salmon) and four main dishes from $9.95 (for supreme of chicken with "sauce confuse") to $15.50 for loin of lamb with goat cheese. The choices are few but the variations multiple, in that you can order à la carte and add side dishes (the menu suggests artichokes with the goat-cheese pasta and hearts of palm with the vegetarian pasta). Six more choices are available nightly à la carte or table d'hôte, the latter going from $13.95 for fillet of salt cod to $19.70 for veal scaloppine with avocado and chèvre, and including soup or salad and beverage. Fancier appetizers cost extra, as do desserts like chocolate praline and tirami su.

The best deal is a three-course dinner including dessert for $12.95, offered before 7 o'clock and geared to patrons headed for the Le Théâtre du Rideau Vert across the street.

(514) 284-3130. Lunch, Tuesday-Friday 11:30 to 2; dinner, Tuesday-Sunday 5:30 to 10; Sunday brunch, 11:30 to 2.

Gastronomic Landmarks

Chez la Mère Michel, 1209 Guy St.

For thirty years we've been directing friends heading for Montreal to this intimate downtown restaurant we first visited during the summer of Expo 67, shortly after it opened. None has been disappointed, nor have we on subsequent trips.

Inside a typical Montreal graystone townhouse are three small dining rooms, plus a massive downstairs wine cellar and a skylit courtyard that's exceptionally pleasant for dining year-round.

Decor is elegantly rustic: high ceilings with dark beams and stuccoed arches, shiny hardwood floors, stained-glass windows, walls of showy fabric above mottled gray and copper pots here, there and everywhere. White lace over bright red linens and lovely arrangements of roses and lilies grace the tables, and candles inside graters cast fascinating shadows. Brilliant enamel paintings add to an already colorful scene.

The crowning glory is the atrium courtyard, lovely with banquettes and high-back chairs, antique tables, a Delft-tiled fireplace and a sixteen-foot enamel mural.

Seasonal and contemporary specialties enhance the traditional fare from the kitchen of Micheline Delbuquet. She bestowed her childhood nickname Michel on her "little house" in the city and her French Riviera restaurant background on her cuisine, which has become increasingly lighter and more refined over the years.

Micheline Delbuquet at Chez la Mère Michele.

Over the years, we've enjoyed, among other appetizers ($6.50 to $12.50), a light and fluffy sweet onion pie, a pâté en croûte with pistachios, baked pheasant and mushrooms au gratin, and asparagus and sweetbreads in puff pastry. Each of the dozen or so entrées ($22 to $27.50, except $34.50 for grilled scampi) comes with garnishes and vegetables – purees of celery root and carrot on one visit, brussels sprouts and carrots with rosettes of potatoes, whipped and then sautéed on another. At dinner, many dishes are finished tableside and served on piping-hot plates.

The veal kidneys flamed in armagnac, which we've always recommended, are as good as when we first had them in the 1960s. We've also liked sweetbreads with wild mushrooms en croûte, noisettes of lamb with tarragon sauce, the specialty lobster soufflé nantua and, at our latest fall visit, a tender caribou steak with sauce poivrade.

At lunch, when a three-course meal runs from $13.50 to $16, we've enjoyed a wonderful vegetable terrine that was a mosaic of colors, a tender noisette of beef with bordelaise sauce, chicken with coconut sauce and an interesting special of skate fish.

Such desserts as a smashing strawberry napoleon, grand-marnier soufflé, fresh fruits with kirsch and black-currant sorbet are refreshing endings. The chocolate delice with grand marnier, kiwi and raspberry sauce is a work of art. So is a whole poached pear, its cavity filled with black-currant sorbet and served atop an almond tuile.

A special five-course dégustation menu is offered nightly for $38.

The wine list is handsome and extensive, as you'd guess when you look at Micheline's husband René's wine cellar, which he ranks among the four or five best in the city. His was the city's first restaurant to add a trio of wines from three new Quebec vineyards to its offerings. We sampled a couple and found them surprisingly good.

Micheline and René, a widely traveled photographer, are caring hosts. They've had only two chefs over the years, and the staff welcomes returning customers by name. The cozy French provincial ambiance, consistently fine food and value combine to make La Mère Michel a good bet for visitors in this city where more trendy establishments can be pricey, pretentious and perhaps short-lived.

(514) 934-0473. Lunch, Tuesday-Friday 11:30 to 2:30; dinner, Monday-Saturday 5:30 to 10:30.

Les Halles, 1450 Crescent St.

Following the departure of its longtime chef and one of the original partners, Les Halles has slipped a trifle since the lofty years when it was considered the best restaurant in Montreal. In the mid-1990s it remodeled and repositioned itself and, for traditionalists and big spenders, still ranks right up there.

The two-story lineup of rooms is patterned after the old market in Paris. We were shown to a table in one of two main-floor dining rooms, not far from the working boucherie/charcuterie/pâtisserie that is a focal point of the room with its colorful awnings. The rooms are small and bright, and the tables so close together that a friend says you can eavesdrop and hear everything going on in Montreal, if you understand French.

The menu is extensive, expensive (even the three-course table-d'hôte is $29.75 to $43) and somewhat intimidating. So was our waiter, who rattled off the daily specials at some length from memory until the female half of our party interrupted to ask the price of the duck. "Twenty-five dollars," he could barely let out through his clenched lips, affronted by both the question and its source. He condensed the rest of his recital and departed. We were left wanting to know more about the specials, which are reputed to be the high points of the kitchen, and their prices, which are usually quite a bit more than dishes on the regular menu.

For appetizers ($12.95 to $16.95), one of us settled for the cold assortment of cochonouilles and terrines from the menu, a lunch-size plate of salamis and three pâtés from the boucherie. The other tried a special appetizer, St. Peter's fish – an entrée-size portion of rather boring European white fish in a superior sorrel sauce and garnished with green beans (later priced on our bill at $14).

For main courses ($22.25 to $31.50), we had sliced guinea hen with red cabbage, artfully arranged in a swirl with carrots, beans and turnips, and sweetbreads in a raspberry-vinegar sauce with the same vegetables plus cauliflower. Both were sensational.

With our meal we had the least expensive bottle we could find on the lengthy wine list, $29 for a smooth Château Mondetour bordeaux. Prices are mainly in the three figures and we noticed that the wines of those more selective than we were poured in extra-large balloon glasses. (We all got the same white Les Halles bags on departure. We had thought they were doggie bags, but they contained an apple and an orange to go.)

Desserts are fairly classic French. We shared a plate of homemade sorbets – orange, raspberry and pear, served with kiwi, tangerine, fresh mint and a red sauce notable for its herbs, including rosemary.

After dinner, we looked upstairs at three other dining rooms, which were more formal and quiet, lacking the market flavor. There we happened to bump into owner Jacques Landurier, who was making the rounds to talk with regulars. He recommended that next time we try the $60 menu gastronomique, which includes two substantial appetizers, a sorbet, a small main course, dessert, coffee and sweets. Unlike many such feasts, chef Dominique Crévoisier ensures that each person at the table has a different dish for each course and that most of his specialties are presented. And we wouldn't have to ask the price.

(514) 844-2328. Lunch, Tuesday-Friday 11:45 to 2:30; dinner, Monday-Saturday 6 to 11.

Les Chenets, 2075 Bishop St.
This relative old-timer, with an awesome wine cellar and a collection of copper that's out of this world, also is one of the coziest, warmest restaurants we've seen. It's doubly so on a wintry Yuletide afternoon, when the copper pots and pans that cover every available bit of wall space reflect the glow of candles and even the Christmas tree behind the reception table is trimmed mostly in copper.

Chef-owner Michel Gillet, a Frenchman who opened the restaurant in 1973 after a stint at Le Chambord in Westport, Conn., employs one person full-time just to keep all that copper gleaming. Copper service plates top the white-linened tables in two dining rooms, and there's a mix of semi-circular banquettes and chairs upholstered in velvet.

Wine connoisseurs marvel at two weighty tomes of wine selections mounted on a bookstand behind the reception table. They list 1,200 choices representing 30,000 bottles at prices up to $15,000 for an 1890 Château Lafite-Rothschild. The pricier bottles are too old to drink, our waiter advised; instead, they are sold as collector's items. He led us upstairs (yes, up) to the wine cellar on the second floor, where he hoisted himself to the top shelf to retrieve the 1890 Lafite, which, we must say, looked much like any other. Michel, who's partial to white wines himself, also has an outstanding collection of cognacs – more than a hundred kinds, we're told.

His menu is quite traditional, but the preparation is innovative. The soup du jour might be a delicate cream of watercress swirled with crème fraîche and centered with croutons. The seafood feuilleté comes in puff pastry shaped like a little fish; the terrine of rabbit is enhanced by anisette. House specialties are fish with two sauces (salmon with beurre blanc and halibut with hollandaise and a dollop of caviar, the two separated by a puree of broccoli over slivered carrots), pheasant with morels (accompanied by a pastry barque filled with beans, carrots and potato sticks), and filet mignon with goose liver.

Dinner appetizers are priced from $6.25 to $12.50 (for smoked salmon) and main courses from $19.50 (chicken in wine sauce) to $26.50 (filet mignon in green peppercorn sauce). The best bet may be the menu gastronomique, five courses with choice of beef filet or saddle of rabbit for $35. That includes such desserts as grand-marnier parfait, pears hélène and raspberry-mousse cake.

Although this is considered a place for a splurge, you also can find good value. The $14.50 lunch special is said to be one of the best bargains in the city.

(514) 844-1842. Lunch, Monday-Friday noon to 3; dinner nightly, 5 to 11.

Altitude 737, 1 Place Ville Marie.
One of our early memories of a gala night out in Montreal involves the rooftop restaurant on the 44th floor of the city's first major skyscraper, circa 1960. After being closed for a dozen years, it reopened under new owners in 1995 and looks

much as we remembered it – a stylish refuge with white-clothed tables, black chairs and little to detract from the drop-dead views of Mount Royal and the city's skyline spread out beyond the floor-to-ceiling windows. Not to mention the considerable privacy afforded by tables wrapping single file around the perimeter. Most of the kitchens, including an open grill and a sushi bar, are on view on the outside of the service core in the center.

Three distinct venues – the sophisticated restaurant on the highest level, a disco club one floor below and a lounge and terrace a floor below that – offer something for everyone who wants to be on top of the city, especially at night.

The oversize menu is contemporary French with California and Italian accents and an unexpectedly extensive selection of sushi, sashimi, maki, spicy rolls and teppanyaki. Newspaper critics swoon over the Japanese offerings, from the assorted sushi and sashimi plate offered for an $8.50 surcharge on the table-d'hôte menu to those who go oriental all the way with maki rolls and Japanese grills (up to $35 for lobster tail). The rest of the menu includes the usual suspects, plus such Pacific Rim touches as miso soup, California salad (with avocado, orange chicken and exotic fruits), shrimp ravioli with peanut sauce, salmon tartare and, among main dishes ($16 to $27), capellini with assorted seafood, lobster ravioli, veal ribs with fruit chutney, duck breast with three sauces and rack of lamb gremolata or szechuan.

The best bet may be to stick with the quite large table-d'hôte menu, which yields soup or salad and beverage along with main course, $17 to $35 for lunch, in the $35 range for three courses at dinner. Desserts are extra and change daily.

(514) 397-0737. Lunch, Monday-Friday 11:30 to 3; dinner nightly, 5 to 10 or 11.

The Best of Outremont

When in Montreal, do as the knowing Montrealers do – which is to say, the with-it French-Canadian gourmands emulating Parisian style in their own neighborhood. Head around Mount Royal for Outremont, the residential bastion of French chic, with its changing array of bistros, outdoor cafes and serious small restaurants. Be forewarned: you may be the only English-speaker in the crowd.

La Chronique, 99 Laurier Ave. West.

A small pumpkin or gourd on each table typified the season at this inspired bistro that's considered one of Montreal's best. Belgian-born chef-owner Marc de Canck, who trained at Michelin restaurants in his native land, moved to Quebec and worked at our old favorite Hovey Manor in North Hatley before opening his own place in 1994.

The storefront setting is suave in pale yellow and black, with white butcher paper over white cloths on the tables, black patterned banquettes, and black and white art photos on the walls. Marc calls his "fine fusion cuisine," a blend of French, Asiatic and Southwest in particular, and presents it in the trendy architectural style.

Dinner is table-d'hôte, $22.50 to $29.50 for three courses (not including dessert). You might start with a traditional South of France fish soup garnished with croutons, rouille and saffron or a more exotic yam soup with bocconcini cheese and coriander. Other starters vary from confit of duck with herbs and greens to shrimp in tempura with a julienne of yams and wasabi sauce.

A salad or petite "soupière du moment" precedes the main course. Typical choices are grilled swordfish with shiitake sauce, pan-fried shrimp coated in cajun spices and served with a salsa of avocado and jalapeño peppers, a "conjugaison" of sweetbreads and marinated salmon with miso sauce and tempura of yams, and tender lamb chops grilled in spicy honey, flambéed in Jack Daniels bourbon and served with caramelized vegetables on a small bed of couscous. The chef also employs Jack Daniels in his rich pecan tart, the signature dessert.

The best value may be the nightly prix-fixe menu for $26.95. The fare at our visit included an antipasto of Italian sausage, haricots and goat cheese, the yam soup, southwest salmon with cajun spices and the pecan tart. Table d'hôte lunches are available from $8.50 to $16.50.

(514) 271-3095. Lunch, Monday-Friday 11:30 to 2:30; dinner, Monday-Saturday 6 to 10.

Le Club des Pins, 156 Laurier Ave. West.

The South of France is the theme at this cheery little bistro with a stunning hand-stenciled design of fish and vegetables accenting one of the walls. It's colorful in yellow and red-orange. Owner Danielle Matte acquired the unusual yellow and green waxed fabric tablecloths in France, and chef Natalie Major hews to the theme with a short menu of specialties from Provence.

The dinner menu is basically à la carte, with four main courses priced from $17 for fillet of salmon with olives to $19.50 for saddle of hare. Confit of duck and scallops of sweetbreads perfumed with vanilla are the others. You might start with a classic Marseillaise fish soup or three versions of duck, from foie gras to aiguillettes. Desserts ($6) vary from chocolate fondant with crème anglaise to tarte tatin and fruit gratin.

Consider also the nightly table d'hôte, three choices for $22 to $24. Veal kidneys with tarragon, leg of lamb and a mille-feuille of swordfish layered with eggplant were offered at our visit. Starters

Arty accents at Le Club des Pins.

were cream of spinach soup, grilled oysters with rouille and quail provençal.

The wine list, nicely priced in the twenties and thirties, is oriented to the South of France as well, with an emphasis on young vintages ready to drink without aging.

A short table d'hôte menu offers a three-course lunch with four choices of main course, $12 to $15. Tables are nicely spaced and the ambiance inviting.

(514) 272-9484. Lunch, 11:30 to 4; dinner, 5:30 to 10. Closed Sunday.

Exotica, 400 Laurier Ave. West.

Here's a new cafe/lounge/restaurant that must be seen to be believed. You can tell from the entry. Just past the palm trees, a small produce and specialty-foods market opens into a coffee bar with individual CD players at each seat for those who wish to imbibe with their choice of music.

La Chronique dining room is suave in pale yellow and black.

Head up the stairs to the second-floor lounge, a dark and jungly space with custom-made chairs incorporating zebra skins, reptiles coiled around the columns and individual TVs housed in oval affairs that we thought looked like explorers' helmets and our informant likened to eggs. This is the place for light meals, coffee and dessert, afternoon tea and drinks, with live jazz on weekends.

Continue on to the third-floor dining room, a drop-dead scene resembling an African village. There are a three-dimensional mural of tribesmen along one wall, a desert-colored floor, napkins bearing jungle animals folded wildly on the tables with miniature palm trees beside, a fountain in the center, and a pair of large stained-glass eyes peering out from either side of the wine bar.

The food is upstaged by the show, we understand, but that may be simply because of the novelty and the resulting crowds. When Exotica launched Sunday brunch a few months after opening in 1996, the sixteen-member kitchen staff expected a few dozen takers and were overwhelmed with 500.

The menu is quite extensive and exotic. The usual French suspects are trendied up with all the latest ingredients. How about carpaccio of ostrich with orange and wasabi, or medallions of alligator sauced with peanuts and braised pineapples? Guinea fowl is grilled with apricots and papaya, and the veal stuffed with lichees and onions. Appetizers are priced from $6 to $14, and main courses from $11 to $23. Six prix-fixe dinner options with a travel theme range from $26 to $109.

Success spawns expansion, and the team of six local owners was planning to open a smaller Exotica (without the restaurant) on Decarie Boulevard and looking for two sites downtown.

(514) 273-5015. Open daily, from 9 a.m.; Sunday brunch, 9 to 3.

Le Bernardin, 387 Bernard Ave.

Sheaves of wheat provide accents and dividers in this light and airy bistro with brass rails, brass chair backs and mirrored walls. There's a bar on one side, and dining is on two levels in the main room, attractive in yellow and burnt red. White butcher paper tops the white linened tables, spaced generally well apart.

The menu choices here are more varied than others in Outremont, perhaps because

Le Bernardin is larger and caters to a neighborhood and family trade. Seven salads, twelve pasta dishes ($7.75 to $9.75) and four sandwiches are available à la carte. The luncheon special offers soup or salad, main course and coffee or tea for $7.95.

Duck is featured on the dinner menu, which reflects the South of France. It comes in stew, cassoulet, confit or magret. Other choices on the evening table d'hôte ($12.95 to $22.95) include whitefish, grilled chicken, mixed grill, entrecôte and rack of lamb. Start with the fish soup with rouille, feuilleté of escargots, terrine du chef or pan-fried eggplant with balsamic vinegar and bocconcini cheese.

Save room for the specialty tarte tatin, or the panache of sorbets, chocolate gateau or profiteroles.

(514) 948-1981. Lunch, Monday-Friday 22:30 to 3; dinner, Monday-Saturday 5:30 to 10 or 11.

Da Marcello, 825 Laurier Ave. East.

This hideaway in a nondescript yellow building is considered by many to be the premier Tuscan restaurant in Montreal. Opened by Marcello Banini, a chef devoted to the food of his native Siena, the place changed hands following his death but the tradition continues.

Tiny and true, the L-shaped room sports Italian posters on the walls, maroon and white cloths on the tables and little fluted lights overhead. The menus vary, but expect first-rate specialties from Tuscany along with dishes from the rest of northern Italy.

Menus are presented à la carte ($11.95 to $30.95), although a table-d'hôte option is offered evenings for $22.95 to $23.95. Highly rated are the rolled rabbit stuffed with veal and fried eggplant, the scallops of veal with porcini mushrooms, sautéed sweetbreads with porcini and hazelnuts, and breast of chicken with chanterelles.

Starters could be liver pâté with chestnuts, ragoût of wild boar on polenta and bocconcini agrumi, the fresh white cheese alternated here with slices of tomatoes and blood oranges. Among desserts are zuccotto, cassata and frangelico almond cake. The wine list features choice Italian vintages. Almond-studded biscotti come with the bill.

(514) 276-1580. Lunch, Monday-Friday 11:30 to 2:30; dinner, Monday-Saturday 5:30 to 10:30.

La Moulerie, 1249 Bernard Ave. West.

Mussel dishes done every way imaginable, served with french fries and mustardy mayonnaise, are the theme of this high-tech bistro with an all-glass front and a color scheme of black, grays and moss green. Water trickles down a corner marble wall. Starting small, La Moulerie quickly doubled its size and, in summer, there are 150 more seats outside on what the manager proclaimed "the nicest and busiest terrace in town."

Mussel out on mussel soup with saffron ($5.25), hot mussels with garlic cream ($5.75), and any of twelve varieties of main courses ($13.95 to $15.95), from mussels Madagascar, Italian or Indian style (with ginger and coriander) to mussels roquefort and jardinière. No, there are no mussel desserts, but there are plenty of pies, cakes, profiteroles, sorbets and fancy coffees. Six shrimp dishes, steak tartare, pastas and a handful of other items are offered in a section of the menu with a drawing of a glowering character exclaiming "I hate mussels!"

(514) 273-8132. Open daily, 11:30 a.m. to midnight.

Ritz Garden is a traditional favorite for outdoor dining at the Ritz-Carlton.

Hotel Dining

In the European tradition, Montreal is a city in which the hotel dining rooms are among the foremost. The best:

Société Café, Loews Hotel Vogue, 1415 Mountain St.

Executive chef Eric Foaudau from Acapulco moved over from the Ritz-Carlton to continue the theme of Eurasian cuisine that earned this a reputation as the city's top hotel dining room. He calls it "cuisine actuelle, a step up from nouvelle."

At dinner, you might start with a tuna carpaccio with tomato chutney and provolone, a crab and avocado terrine with corn chutney or sautéed sea scallops with duck foie gras, artichokes and truffle oil. The seven main courses ($17 to $28) include grilled red snapper fillet with polenta, baked veal chop with wild mushrooms and rack of lamb provencal. Among desserts are a refreshing lemon and raspberry pie, the signature dessert, as well as an unusual apple and rosemary pie.

A limited table-d'hôte menu is available for $18 to $24.

The stunning, split-level room includes lots of stainless steel and gray with accents of reds and yellows, white tablecloths and napkins, and a rich carpet in apricot and terra-cotta hues.

(514) 987-8168. Open daily, 7 a.m. to 11 p.m.

Ritz-Carlton Kempinski, 1228 Sherbrooke St. West.

In a city that becomes more French every year, the Ritz is a tradition to be treasured. It is a nostalgic reminder of the days when Sherbrooke Street West was a bastion of English institutions and tastes, although we must say we were a bit taken aback to find the Ritz to have been taken over by a European hotel chain.

Its restaurants have been favorites of anglo-Montrealers for years. One of us remembers having the businessman's lunch in the Ritz Café for about $3.95 for three courses back in the late 1950s; it was there she was introduced to such unfamiliar dishes (because her mother certainly never cooked them) as calves brains in black butter.

The charming **Ritz Garden** has been the scene of family celebrations. Tables on a covered terrace on two sides of a courtyard look out over an oasis of lawns, flowers and a duck pond. Here, Sunday brunch is an event, as it should be for $39.95.

At night, the extensive menu for the **Café de Paris** offers an entire page of caviars, including two dégustation options of beluga, ossetra and sevruga, $250 for 30 grams each and $405 for 50 grams. For appetizers ($8.25 to $16.50), chef Michel Lanot mixes the classic and the trendy: consommé or fresh duck foie gras with a fig chutney; shrimp cocktail or deer raviolis with poivrarde sauce and blueberries. Silver cloches are raised in unison to reveal the main courses, priced from $25 for sautéed frog's legs to $48 for lemon dover sole. Sample some Canadian Oka cheese for dessert with a glass of vintage port, or try some of the marvelous French pastries.

New at our latest visit was a martini hour in the Grand Prix piano bar, offering a selection of seventeen kinds of martinis with complimentary snacks, more substantial hors d'oeuvres and piano music. Each $7.50 and served in an oversize martini glass, they vary from Russian with vodka, cointreau and lemon to Greek with ouzo and a black olive.

(514) 842-4212. Lunch daily, noon to 2:30; dinner, 6 to 10; Sunday brunch, 11:30 to 2. Jackets required.

Restaurant Zen, 1050 Sherbrooke St. West.

The first North American venture for the Zen restaurant chain, originating in Hong Kong and London, operates in the depths of Le Westin Mont-Royal Hotel. The two-tier, circular space is dramatic in white and black. It has a curved bar, an elliptical pit in the center and raised tables bearing stunning oriental floral service plates all around. Chopsticks and soup spoons are ready for exotic fare.

The lengthy menu makes for fascinating reading. You'll want to peruse the entire epistle, unless you opt for "the Zen experience" – three special pages detailing 44 signature dishes from all the Zen restaurants. It's an incredible bargain for $25, and you can choose as many items as you like. The menu reflects chefs from China, Thailand, Malaya and Indonesia as well as Montreal.

The regular à-la-carte offerings ($10.50 to $20) run from sweet-and-sour pork filet to sautéed shrimp with chili sauce and glazed walnuts to roasted szechuan duck.

(514) 499-0801. Lunch daily, 11 to 3; dinner, 5:30 to 11.

Champs Elysées, 1800 Sherbrooke St. West.

A chef from southwest France teams with Germain Villeneuve, a Cornell University Hotel School graduate, to run this highly regarded restaurant in the Versailles Tower, the hotel opened by Germain's parents. The gray and peach room seats 120 in Louis XV chairs so comfortable that you might never want to get up.

The straightforward menu is priced from $14.50 for chicken breast sauced with apple cider to $27.50 for breast of duck with honey and lime. In between are a trio of fish with fresh basil, fillet of sole in mustard sauce, a casserole of curried mussels and scallops, and filet mignon madeira. Start with the house-smoked salmon or the sautéed shrimp provençal. Finish with the tulipe of sorbets, the chocolate profiteroles or the bananas flambéed for two.

Good values are a couple of table-d'hôte menus, three courses with three choices

each for $23.50 and $29.50. Germain is proud of the wine list, mostly French but with a nod to California.
(514) 939-1212. Lunch, Monday-Friday noon to 3; dinner nightly, 6 to 10 or 11.

Lodging

Of the multitude of choices, we suggest a few with special appeal:

Ritz-Carlton Kempinski, 1228 Sherbrooke St. West, Montreal H3G 1H6.
Splendidly posh and comfortable in the Old World sense, Montreal's oldest hotel is still favored by many knowledgeable travelers over the more glitzy newcomers. "The grand dame of Sherbrooke Street" is the city's symbol of elegance and service, with 230 high-ceilinged guest rooms and suites, a lobby that is refreshingly clubby and old-line Montreal, and noted restaurants.

Renovated and grandly updated over the years, the hotel has preserved much of its cherished interior. Lately it has added an exercise room to keep up with the times and each guest room comes with three telephones. Twenty rooms contain fireplaces and many have original moldings, embossed ceilings and chandeliers.

Afternoon tea from 3:30 to 5 is an event at the Ritz, offered seasonally in the Ritz Garden or beside the fireplace in the gold-trimmed Palm Court amid crystal chandeliers, marble floors and palm trees. A dozen loose-leaf teas are offered (Russian Caravan, Prince of Wales and Green Gunpowder are some). "English style" finds your tea presented with tea sandwiches, scones with devonshire cream, petits fours and sweets ($13.75); or you can order individually from the sweets table.
(514) 842-4212 or (800) 426-3135. Fax (514) 842-3383. Doubles, $220 to $250.

Le Westin Mont-Royal, 1040 Sherbrooke St. West, Montreal H3A 2R6.
If the Ritz is Montreal's grand, understated hotel, the Westin is arguably its most sumptuous high-rise.

Built by the Four Seasons chain for the Summer Olympics in 1976, it has 300 large, tastefully appointed rooms and suites, an indoor-outdoor pool, saunas and an exercise room full of Universal equipment. Each guest room has a stocked minibar, most have sitting areas with sofas, and the bathrooms offer bidets, hair dryers and terrycloth robes.

The main dining room was in transition in 1997, the new Westin ownership having closed its predecessor's mod Le Cercle to transform it into an upscale Parisian bistro with a sidewalk cafe at the corner of Peel and Sherbrooke streets. Across the way, Restaurant Zen continued as ever.
(514) 284-1110. Fax (514) 845-3025. Doubles, $225 to $240.

Hotel Inter-Continental Montreal, 360 St. Antoine St. West, Montreal H2Y 3X4.
In the heart of the Financial District and close to Old Montreal is this 26-story hotel, which opened in 1991. A towering atrium connects the hotel with the World Trade Center and hotel function rooms, as well as shops and restaurants in an underground complex.

The lobby is full of rich wood paneling and potted palms. The 357 rooms are as up-to-date as can be, with in-room coffee machines and hair dryers. Guests take advantage of a fitness center with sauna, exercise room and indoor pool.

The plush main dining room, **Restaurant Les Continents,** with big windows looking onto St. Antoine Street, was the setting for a month-long oyster festival when we were there.

(514) 987-9900 or (800) 361-3600. Fax (514) 847-8550. Doubles, $139 to $255.

Loews Hotel Vogue, 1425 Mountain St., Montreal H3G 1Z3.

This boutique-style downtown hotel, opened in 1991 as an independent but lately acquired by Loews, is the ultimate in luxury. It's geared toward the business traveler (with a fax machine in every room), but tourists will find it an exceptional place to stay, too.

Each of the 126 rooms, done in soft greens, creams and pinks, and sixteen suites has a king or queen bed, dressed in duvet comforters and pillows and some with canopies, and in each marble bathroom there are a telephone, a remote-controlled TV facing the whirlpool bath and a separate shower. The suites, in deep jewel tones, are decorated in late Empire style by internationally renowned Stanley J. Friedman.

Of course, there are a 24-hour concierge, room service and turndown service, and a workout room with exercise equipment is on the ninth floor. The **Opera Bar** in the intimate and stylish lobby atrium is the place for afternoon tea and desserts for post-theater snacking. Hotel Vogue's location is terrific, just off St. Catherine Street and across from Ogilvy's, our favorite department store.

(514) 285-5555 or (800) 465-6654. Fax (514) 849-8903. Doubles, $255 to $305.

Hotel Château Versailles & Tower, 1659 Sherbrooke St. West, Montreal H3H 1E3.

Starting as newlyweds with one house and 23 rooms in 1957, André Villeneuve and his late wife Mary-Louise developed a choice for those who value small, European-style inns and hotels. The château has 70 comfortable rooms fashioned from four old four-story graystone townhouses on the western edge of downtown. Exteriors have been restored, the only change being an illuminated yellow sign bearing the hotel's name. The once-humble pension now has antique furnishings, walls that look like those in an art gallery, bedrooms with floral draperies and matching spreads, halls dotted with sofas and a small, manicured yard. All rooms come with private baths and cable TV; one deluxe room with windows onto Sherbrooke Street has a large velvet sofa, two armchairs, a non-working fireplace and an armoire.

A few years ago, the Villeneuve family invested $5 million in a fourteen-story apartment building across the street, turning it into a 107-room hotel called the Tower. Twenty-two corner rooms have jacuzzis, microwaves and wet bars; all have mini-refrigerators, full-size work tables and computerized safes. Rooms are light and airy, with big windows screened by roman blinds; "when the blinds come down at night," said André, whose wife did the decorating, "they become the art." Italian marble is plentiful in the bathrooms. All the toiletries are custom-made; the Villeneuves found the soap at a health-food store, had it reproduced for their hotel and put it out in soap dishes crafted by a Laurentian potter. Even the luggage racks here match the furniture.

The difference between the château and the tower is the difference between old-world charm and state-of-the-art sophistication.

(514) 933-3611 or (800) 361-3664 in U.S., 361-7199 in Canada. Fax (514) 933-6867. Doubles, $119 to $169.

Rooftop cafe at L'Hôtel de la Montagne.

Food hall at Le Faubourg Ste.-Catherine.

L'Hôtel de la Montagne, 1430 Mountain St., Montreal H3G 1Z5.

Backing up to Ogilvy's, an historic enclave of anglo merchandising, this apartment building-turned-hotel represents another part of the diverse spectrum that is Montreal. It caters to business people, couples and singles, many of them French. Welcoming guests in the lobby is a prominent nude sculpture with stained-glass butterfly wings, perched atop a gurgling fountain. The 138 rooms and suites on nineteen floors are decorated in five styles. They contain original art, plush seating, bathrobes and fruit baskets, and beds are turned down nightly at sundown.

That's when the action really picks up in **Le Lutecia,** the hotel's Greco-Roman-Victorian dining room bedecked in palms, sofas and table lamps. We know English Montrealers who take their maiden aunts here for lunch, despite (or because of?) hotelier Bernard Ragueneau's claim that his restaurant is "a place for intrigue." So is the rooftop cafe and outdoor swimming pool, where some of the lithesome sun-bathers go topless. A tunnel from the hotel leads to a multi-level ramble of disco and drink, plants and people called **Thursday's,** part of an evolving enterprise that includes a club called **Crocodile.**

(514) 288-5656 or (800) 361-6262. Fax (514) 288-9658. Doubles, $129 to $139; suites, $195 to 225.

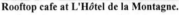

Bed and Breakfasts

Les Passants du Sans Soucy, 171 St. Paul St. West, Old Montreal, H2Y 1Z5.

The first real B&B in Montreal, located at the edge of Old Montreal, is as authentic as all get-out. Daniel Soucy, a French-speaking Quebecker, and partner Michael Banks from Ontario offer seven bedrooms and a suite on three floors of an old fur trading warehouse dating to 1773.

Each has the requisite beamed ceilings, brick and stucco walls and European ambiance you'd expect, as well as all the comforts of home and then some. All rooms have private baths (four with jacuzzis), bedside telephones and TVs ensconced in armoires made by a Quebec craftsman and painted a distressed green. Beds (most of them queensize) are made up in the European fashion, with pillows showing. The wood floors are left bare, but colorful bed covers, draperies and, in some rooms, paisley sofas add warmth. Petunias brighten the window boxes facing the street, and we loved the colorful Parisian glass sconces in varied colors in the halls and bedrooms. They're a pricey $500 a pair, and Michael says he has sold quite a few. A ground-floor suite contains a living room with sofabed, a queen bed in the rear bedroom and a marble bath with jacuzzi.

You enter through a lobby also serving as a gallery showcasing Quebec art and crafts. To the rear is an open, skylit living room with a fireplace and a dining area, where Michael serves a breakfast cooked to order by Dan. A choice of seven kinds of juices, flaky croissants (some with chocolate filling), feta-spinach and ham and cheese omelets, bottled mineral water and cafe au lait served in big bowls made ours a breakfast to remember.

(514) 842-2634. Fax (514) 842-2912. Doubles, $95 to $115; suite, $160.

La Maison Pierre du Calvet, 405 Bonsecours St., Old Montreal H2Y 3C3.

Montreal's oldest private house (1725) open to the public is this charmer, which had four years as a restaurant under its belt before adding a B&B in 1995. The sense of history is palpable in the residence of Calvet, a wealthy merchant and patriot, located in the heart of Old Montreal across the street from the historic Notre-Dame-de-Bonsecours Chapel. Behind the Breton-style facade of thick stone walls, French windows and heavy chimneys lies a complex of five baronial suites and a bedroom, with four more under construction in 1997.

The accommodations are large, luxurious and decidedly masculine except for the 18th-century costumes on a hook here and an old pram in a corner there. Otherwise they're all fieldstone walls, rich walnut paneling, dark wood floors and high, step-up queensize canopy beds with oversize bedding made up in the European style. Expect gas fireplaces, Canadian art and tapestries on the walls, a mix of sturdy Quebec antiques and apparent hand-me-downs, and, in at least two cases, carved bed headboards fashioned from church pews. Lord & Mayfair toiletries enhance the marble bathrooms.

Resident innkeeper Martin Ortiz from New Mexico prepares a hearty breakfast of fruit, croissants, and bacon and eggs for guests to take in a plant-filled greenhouse with three parrots or outside in a tiny garden courtyard.

Guests also may join the public for dinner by candlelight in the plush main-floor restaurant of the same name, an elegant, living-room-like affair with leather sofas grouped around a fireplace in the center and tables around the perimeter. Classic French cuisine is offered à la carte (five choices from $23.50 to $28.50) or table d'hôte (three courses from $31.95 to $33.95), Tuesday-Saturday 6 to 10.

(514) 282-1725. Fax (514) 282-0456. Doubles, $150 to $195.

Auberge du Vieux Port, 97 De la Commune East, Old Montreal H2Y 1J1.

Dan Soucy and Michael Banks always wanted to have an inn on the waterfront in Old Montreal, but satisfied themselves with Les Passant du Sans Soucy (see above) in the interim. Their chance came in 1996, when they and some partners gutted a five-story leather factory and created a deluxe 27-room auberge facing the St. Lawrence River.

They opened to four straight weeks of 100 percent occupancy, thanks to overflow from Sans Soucy. Nearly half the rooms in this urbane small European-style hotel have kingsize brass beds; the rest are queens or two doubles. All but four come with single or double jacuzzis in the bathrooms. Each has a TV and a minibar in the armoire, Canadian pine doors and handsome maple floors "with as many knots as we could find," in the words of resident manager Douglas Thompson.

Guests have a choice of bagels with cream cheese, omelets or waffles with all the trimmings for breakfast in **Cafe Parigi,** a full-service restaurant on the main floor of the building.

(514) 876-0081. Fax (514) 876-8923. Doubles, $95 to $140.

A Country Retreat

Hostellerie Les Trois Tilleuls, 290 Rue Richelieu, St. Marc sur Richelieu, J0L 2E0.

About a twenty-minute drive southeast of Montreal is this Relais & Châteaux property, a delightful refuge beside the quiet Richelieu River, situated at a particularly scenic spot where the river seems to go in three directions. "It's a calm retreat for Relais & Châteaux types" who want to be close to Montreal, but not there all the time, advised a manager.

It takes its name from the three gnarled linden trees at the entrance. Although the front is smack up against the road, the hotel is oriented to the rear to take advantage of the riverside setting.

We first came here for a luncheon outing. The hotel's lovely restaurant spills across several different areas with large picture windows looking onto an outdoor patio, a gazebo and the tree-lined river. The rooms are notable for Canadian art on the barnwood walls, comfy chairs that looked hand-crafted, pink linens and handsome pottery plates.

The table-d'hôte lunch cost $17.75 each ($22.75 on Saturday), but with three glasses of wine, coffee, taxes and tip, the tab came to about $70 for two. The springtime splurge started with a delightful cream of celery soup, a large salad of boston lettuce with roquefort cheese, and great melba toasts and French breads. One of us had poached halibut with wine-sabayon sauce; the other enjoyed calves liver with a brown sauce and chanterelles. Both came with roast potatoes, cauliflower, carrots and snow peas. A divine chocolate-mousse cake was a worthy ending. Service verging on the supercilious and some tarnished silverware were the only negatives.

Dinner for the public is à la carte. Guests normally dine table d'hôte. A typical dinner involves a choice among four soups (perhaps venison consommé with wild mushrooms or armagnac lobster bisque) and eight appetizers (among them foie gras and sweetbread terrine, duck tartare and a rosette of escargots with apples and calvados). The main course ($28.50 to $34.50) could be halibut and shrimp with tarragon cream, skewered sesame and aniseed scampis with vanilla butter, veal medallions with chanterelle cream sauce or flambéed sirloin steak with peppercorn sauce. Desserts ($7.50) include chocolate marquise, crêpes suzette and frozen grand marnier soufflé.

Three prix-fixe dinner menus – traditional, gourmand and discover – offer six or more courses for $62 to $76.

Window table at Hostellerie Les Trois Tilleuls looks onto gazebo and Richelieu River.

Between meals, overnight guests swim in the pool, play tennis or simply relax in Adirondack chairs beside the gardens.

The 24 guest rooms are spread out on three floors, and each has a patio or balcony looking onto the river. Decorated in what could be described as Quebec rustic style, they are outfitted with hand-crafted, custom-made furniture, queen or kingsize beds, two swivel chairs, thick carpeting, TV and telephone. Bathrooms come with hair dryers, terrycloth robes and lots of amenities and two have whirlpool tubs. The enormous Royal Suite is breathtaking, what with loveseats on all sides of a central fireplace, a sofabed beside a TV, a kingsize canopied bed and a dining area in the solarium. Its bath contains a sauna and a whirlpool for four, which is almost big enough for swimming.

(514) 856-7787 or (800) 263-2230. Fax (514) 584-3146. Restaurant open daily, 7:30 to 10 a.m. and 11 a.m. to 10 p.m. Doubles, $115 to $150 EP, $245 to $280 MAP; suite, $390 EP and $520 MAP.

Gourmet Treats

More than any place we know, all Montreal seems passionate about food. In a city where there is a bakery or charcuterie or cafe issuing forth delectable aromas at almost every corner, we can do no more than cite a few favorites.

Le Faubourg Ste.-Catherine, 1600 St. Catherine St. West. This is the ultimate food hall, a block-long stretch of stalls, markets and eateries on two floors, with some of the eating areas on floors suspended between. The $40 million renovation of a downtown block is a frenchified version of Boston's Faneuil Hall Marketplace. You can find places like Le Hamburger, Crêpes Maison, Le Wok, La Creole, Pasta Villa, Istanbul Express and Sushi Plus. After scouting the choices, one of us settled on a filling (but mediocre) lunch of steak teriyaki with salad and rice for $3.99.

If you find Le Faubourg rather dizzying, cross Guy Street to our favorite Montreal store, **Ogilvy's,** the born-again department store, spiffed up with boutiques and specialty shops (including Crabtree & Evelyn and Godiva). In the basement are a small kitchen shop offering jams and relishes, a pâtisserie and the sprightly Café Romy, which dispenses quiche, sandwiches, salads and such.

Another good food court is on the lower level of **Les Cours Mont-Royal,** 1455 Peel St., near St. Catherine. At our visit, it looked like most of working Montreal was here for lunch, but we wandered around and found **Cafémania,** a little out of the main stream, where we had delicious panani, Italian grilled sandwiches. Great cookies, soups and all kinds of fancy coffees are offered here. **La Boutique du Terroir** is a shop full of Quebec products like fiddlehead ketchup and silkweed vinaigrette, and, of course, the ubiquitous maple sugar candies. There are interesting crafts as well. **Guy et Dodo** is a full-service popular restaurant in this complex; you could make a good lunch of lobster bisque and salade niçoise.

There is probably not a Montrealer who hasn't at some time in his or her life had a smoked meat sandwich at **Bens Delicatessen,** 990 Maisonneuve Blvd. West. Although it has expanded and now has a liquor license, it hasn't changed much since one of us, who attended nearby McGill University in the 1950s, would stop in late at night after parties to sit with other students under dreadful fluorescent lights that made faces green and nosh on the inch-high smoked-meat creation (now $3.95). The Kravitz family have operated this institution since 1908, and one of them is always around to keep an eye on things. Also on the menu are potato latkes, blintzes, corned beef and cabbage, borscht, Bens famous strawberry cheesecake and – would you believe? – smoked-meat egg rolls with plum sauce. Bens opens at 7 a.m. for breakfast and stays open until 4 or 5 a.m.

Just to make your smoked-meat choice more difficult, our Canadian nieces say Bens is passé, left behind by **Schwartz's Hebrew Delicatessen** at 3895 St. Lawrence Blvd., a favorite of the younger generation.

Les Paradis du Gourmet

The really suave food emporium du moment is **Le Marché Westmount Square** at St. Catherine Street West and Greene Avenue in uppercrust Westmount. Starting as an underground retail complex in the 1960s, it has evolved into a first-rate market and food court. The freshest produce, baked goods, seafood (including sushi) and ready-to-heat take-out items, from delectable looking pizzas to vegetarian tortes, are close at hand from several vendors. Pick out your treats and find a table in one of the little alcoves, or take something out for a picnic or dinner. Many of Westmount Square's stores seem to have vanished, but **Ma Maison** is a good kitchen and pottery shop next to the market.

Across the street at 1250 Greene Ave. is **Les 5 Saisons,** an anglicized version of the original at 1180 Bernard Ave. West in Outremont. We've shopped both, but are partial to the Outremont store for exotic vegetables, fresh salmon pies, pastas, beautiful steaks and seafood, a salad bar with hot soups and café filtre, a charcuterie with fantastic pâtés, and a pastry shop with adorable animals made out of marzipan. Here is the ultimate gourmet paradise.

Or so it seems until you find **Patisserie de Gascogne.** There are three, but the most handy is at 4825 Sherbrooke St. West. From platters loaded with delectable little tea sandwiches, to the fanciest ice-cream desserts we have seen, this is a treasure. Brioche, croissants, an incredible selection of cheeses (some made with raw milk), quiches with all kinds of fillings, pâtés, mini-pizzas, pastries – no wonder Westmount's elite love this place. There are a coffee bar and a few little tables where you could have one of the made-up sandwiches or a fancy dessert and a cafe au lait. We took home one of the vacuum-packed dinners for two – poached salmon in a citrus sauce with rice – and it was about the best salmon dish we have ever had. And all we had to do was stick it in the microwave.

Two huge indoor/outdoor markets in Montreal, **Jean Talon Market** in the East End and **Atwater Market** on the edge of downtown, are well worth a visit. Jean Talon is bigger and has more produce stands and Italian items; Atwater more indoor shops and butchers. We are more familiar with the Atwater Market, and frequently fill our cooler with things like stuffed quail or boned rabbit, and exotic cheeses and olives, as well as the most impeccable of vegetables, to take home to Connecticut for a dinner to remind us of "La Belle Province."

Healthful Gourmet

Optimum, 630 Sherbrooke St. East at Union, is billed as Montreal's largest all-natural supermarket and department store. It's full of a wondrous variety of natural foods, a takeout counter, vitamins, minerals, healthware appliances, juicers and such – the biggest selection we've seen in Canada.

Also of interest to those into healthful eating is the local chain called **Le Commensal,** specializing in "gastronomie végétarienne." We were surprised by the number of lunchers lined up at the cafeteria-style buffet on the second floor of the sleek downtown outlet, a glass-enclosed solarium running for nearly a block at 1204 McGill College St. From couscous to vegetable pizzas to ginger tofu, the midday spread had something for everyone. It's open daily from 11 to 10.

Gourmet Chic

For the authentic French experience, tour the shops along Laurier Street in Outremont. Before you get there, you can smell the coffees at **Cafe GVH (Gerard Van Houtte)** at 1042 Laurier, a large grocery store specializing in coffees, health foods, gourmet items and cookware; it also has a bakery and a cafe. The tiny smoked-salmon rolls and kiwi cakes are delicious. There are GVH cafes all over Montreal.

Anjou Quebec at 1025 is about the most authentic charcuterie/boucherie we've seen, a paradise of terrines, wild mushrooms, exotic fruits and more. The tiny haricots verts are flown in from France.

La Maison d'Emile at 1073 is an excellent kitchen and bath shop. **La Pâtisserie Belge** at 1075 has display cases full of pastries, and the windows are full of exotic breads at **Au Pain Dore** at 1145, one of a local chain.

Across Park Avenue on Laurier is **La Petite Ardoise,** a contemporary boutique gourmande with fabulous-looking desserts, salads and sandwiches.

Burlington's Church Street Marketplace is a smorgasbord of carts and cafes.

Burlington
A Culinary Sense of Place

Few areas exude such strong feelings of pride and place as Vermont, and nowhere are these more pronounced than in Burlington, the state's Queen City, poised along a slope above Lake Champlain. From a university town that once had little more than college hangouts and greasy spoons, Burlington has blossomed into the culinary mecca of northern New England.

A dozen restaurants of distinction have opened in the last decade in the city, as well as south along the lake toward Shelburne. "They seem to spring up every other day here," reports the manager of one of the better ones, the Daily Planet. "This town is ripe."

At the edge of downtown Burlington, one short block of Church Street has a lineup of side-by-side eateries that run the gamut from Tex-Mex to Pacific Rim, including vegetarian, multi-Asian and roasted chicken. Countless more are within a block or two of this culinary centerpiece.

The main shopping area, the Church Street Marketplace pedestrian mall, is a smorgasbord of carts and cafes dispensing everything from chicken wings to chimichangas. Coffee à la Carte pours espressos and lattes as long as the temperature is above 20 degrees.

Ben & Jerry, the gurus of fancy ice cream, got their start in Burlington in 1978. Since 1979, the New England Culinary Institute in nearby Montpelier has focused attention on regional cuisine, and moved closer to the action when it opened restaurants in the new Inn at Essex outside Burlington.

In Shelburne, the Webb family's Shelburne Museum is renowned as a remarkable "collection of collections" of Americana. Another part of the Webb family operates Shelburne Farms, which is known for its farm programs and cheddar cheeses, and lately has received national recognition for its majestic Inn at Shelburne Farms. The area claims the Lake Champlain Chocolates factory, New England's largest cheese and wine outlet, the Harrington ham company headquarters and a showplace bakery, plus countless gourmet food shops and growers or producers of Vermont-made products.

Almost every restaurant in the Burlington area offers al fresco dining in season, and tables spill onto sidewalks and decks at every turn. This is a casual, outdoors city, where people go for interesting food with a Vermont-made theme.

Dining

The Best of the Best

Cafe Shelburne, Route 7, Shelburne.

This prize among small provincial French restaurants has been going strong since 1969, but never better than under chef-owner Patrick Grangien, who trained with Paul Bocuse and came to Vermont as part of the short-lived Gerard's Haute Cuisine enterprise in Fairfax.

Talk about happy circumstance: after twenty years, owners André and Daniele Ducrot offered the cafe for sale in 1988, Patrick was available, and he and his wife Christine bought it and moved in upstairs. Knowing diners seeking inspired food and good value have been flocking to the place ever since.

The copper bar and the dining areas with their black bentwood chairs and white-linened tables topped with tiny lamps retain much of the Ducrot ambiance. Patrick covered and screened the rear patio, a beauty with lattice ceiling and grapevines all around. It's a good choice for dinner on a pleasant evening.

Patrick calls his cuisine "more bistro style than nouvelle." Seafood is his forte (he won the National Seafood Challenge in 1988 and was elected best seafood chef of the year). His prize-winning fillet of lotte on a bed of spinach and mushrooms in a shrimp coulis is a fixture on the menu. Try his steamed fillet of Atlantic salmon with a zucchini and basil flan, lasagna St. Jacques layered with sea scallops, spinach and cheddar cheese, or the panache of assorted steamed seafood with champagne-chervil sauce. Other entrées ($17 to $19.50) include sautéed rabbit with wine-sage sauce and homemade fettuccine, duck breast with garlic flan, roasted veal tenderloin and, a staple on the menu here, steak tartare, seasoned at tableside.

Soups are a specialty, and all of the night's four offerings are usually triumphs. Among them are chilled cucumber-dill garnished with curried shrimp and water chestnuts, creamy mussel with saffron, and the two vichyssoises – creamy leek and potato and cold asparagus soups served in the same bowl. Tempting appetizers ($5.50 to $7) include house-smoked salmon sliced over grilled polenta, carpaccio of tuna, sliced lamb salad with a mushroom and walnut oil puree, and warm oysters and baby vegetables in a champagne sauce.

Crème brûlée is the favorite dessert. Others from the changing but always delectable repertoire in the $5 range include warm chocolate cake soufflé, raspberry mousse, profiteroles, assorted fruit sorbets and a trio of chocolate ice creams – semi-sweet, white and cacao.

Chef-owner Patrick Grangien at entrance to Cafe Shelburne.

The heavily French wine list, priced from the low twenties to the triple digits, harbors considerable variety. Quite a few are wines available by the half bottle.
(802) 985-3939. Dinner, Tuesday-Saturday 6 to 9:30, also Sunday from Labor Day to mid-October.

Pauline's Cafe & Restaurant, 1834 Shelburne Road, South Burlington.

One of the earliest of the Burlington area's fine restaurants, this unlikely-looking roadside place has been expanded under the ownership of Robert Fuller.

The original downstairs dining room is now an attractive, clubby cafe paneled in cherry and oak. A new side addition adds bigger windows for those who like things light and airy. The original upstairs lounge is now a ramble of small, elegant dining rooms. All is serene in sponged yellow and green beneath a striking green ceiling. The walls are hung with handsome artworks, heavy draperies obscure the view from the windows of busy Route 7, and the nicely spaced tables are topped with small oil lamps and, at our spring visit, vases of tulips. Outside is a hidden brick patio enveloped in evergreens and a latticed pergola decked out with small international flags and tiny white lights.

These are versatile settings for some of the area's best food. There are set cafe and changing dinner menus. Both are offered in the cafe and on the patio, which makes for unusual range and variety.

With the cafe menu you can make a mighty good meal of appetizers and light entrées ($7.50 to $11.95) for the likes of salads, pastas, crab cakes, grilled pork tenderloin, chicken with Shelburne Farms cheddar-cream sauce and seafood mixed grill.

The changing dinner menu is the kind upon which everything appeals. Entrée prices typically run from $14.95 to $22.95. You might start with roasted garlic soup or a sauté of wild mushrooms and move on to baked bluefish provençal, salmon Siciliana or Mediterranean veal.

Our spring dinner began with remarkably good appetizers of morels and local fiddleheads in a rich madeira sauce and a sprightly dish of shrimp and scallops in ginger, garnished with snow peas and cherry tomatoes. A basket of oh-so-good steaming popovers and so-so bread accompanied, as did salads with zippy cream dressings and homemade croutons that redeemed the tough curly endive lettuce.

The entrées were superior: three strips of lamb wrapped around goat cheese, and a thick filet mignon, served with spring vegetables and boiled new potatoes. The glasses bearing the house Père Patriarche white wine, generous and good, were whisked away for the proper globes when it came time for a Rutherford Hill merlot. A honey-chocolate mousse from Pauline's acclaimed assortment of desserts (Bon Appétit magazine requested the recipe for the bananas foster) and a special coffee with cointreau and apricot brandy ended a fine meal.

(802) 862-1081. Lunch daily, 11:30 to 2:30; cafe menu, 2:30 to closing; dinner, 5 to 10; Sunday brunch, 10:30 to 2.

The Iron Wolf, One Lawson Lane, Burlington.

If you're one of the few who know about this tasty little secret, you're apt to spend two or three hours for dinner – "or longer if you choose," says Lithuanian hostess Danny Bockwoldt. She and her German husband Claus, the chef, moved here from San Francisco for a quieter life. They started serving appetizers at what basically had been an elegant Victorian bar hidden away at the rear of an office building and "got forced into dinner and a restaurant" by a receptive clientele.

The place takes its name from the symbol for the capital of Lithuania. The nine tables plus seats at the bar are filled by word of mouth, and Claus, who cooked all across Europe, prepares every dish from scratch, one by one. That makes for a leisurely dining experience, as does the couple's insistence upon showering attention on every customer.

"We want this to be like going to a friend's house for dinner," says Danny, who seems to have developed many friends and enjoys catering to them. Lest the house analogy mislead: this is more like an intimate private club, in feeling as well as in decor. The handsome bar facing the kitchen is flanked by tables on three sides amid much dark wood paneling and etched-glass windows.

Claus calls his fare "basically classic French, with a select wine list to go with. I buy daily, and the sauces are very important." His wife writes the brief menu by hand on little white cards.

A typical evening might produce appetizers ($5 to $6.50) of country pâté, carpaccio, roasted red peppers and goat cheese, and smoked salmon. Only the watercress and endive salad with roquefort and caramelized walnuts gets a description. Entrées ($14 to $16) are listed with their accompaniments: salmon with watercress sauce and corn pancakes, filet of pork with wild mushrooms and madeira sauce, leg of duck braised in red wine with mushrooms and spaetzle, and filet of beef marchand de vin. Dessert could be sorbet, crème caramel, chocolate mousse or soufflé glacé.

Linger over an after-dinner drink, and you'll know why The Iron Wolf has such a loyal and protective following. They want to keep it for themselves.

(802) 865-4462. Dinner by reservation, Tuesday-Saturday 6 to 9 or 10.

Canopied terrace offers outdoor dining at Isabel's on the Waterfront.

Isabel's on the Waterfront, 112 Lake St., Burlington.

This cafe with a canopied terrace, not far from Lake Champlain, is one of a kind. Started as a catering business and cooking school, it began serving lunch and brunch, and now also offers dinners with great panache. About 50 diners can be seated in the high-ceilinged room, and perhaps 50 more on the outdoor terrace with a view of the lake. (Those who really want to get close to the lake can do so at **Whitecaps,** Isabel's ultra-casual new bar and grill at the Community Boathouse.)

Isabel's is the happy brainchild of Beverly Watson, who ran a catering service out of her home for nine years before moving in 1987 to the Waterfront Place complex of offices fashioned from an old lumber yard. Isabel is her middle name, and good food her raison d'être.

The spaciousness of the main room surprises the first-time visitor, as do the well-spaced, cloth-covered tables and the bouquets of field flowers. In the rear is a short blackboard menu, a self-service counter upon which samples of the lunch-time offerings are displayed on show plates (which makes the choice really rending), and a small, open kitchen.

The blackboard menu changes daily, but you can be assured that everything is good. We enjoyed a piquant platter of shrimp and snow peas oriental with egg fettuccine, plus a build-your-own salad with the biggest fresh croutons ever and a choice of four dressings. We also were enticed by the Mexican pizza, a luscious-looking pan-fried pork with maple-mustard sauce, a wild mushroom and lobster alfredo, an omelet with olives, onions and artichokes, and a grilled turkey sand-wich with cheddar and apples. Prices are not inexpensive ($5.95 to $8.50, with salad), but the value is received.

On another occasion we were too late for the lunch spread but were served from a light grill menu, outside on the terrace. The grilled chicken sandwich with mango chutney and the chilled blueberry soup and sausage quiche (both $5.95) were quite satisfactory.

At night, the menu changes often and the price of main courses ($10.95 to $19.95) includes soup or salad. Among the possibilities might be orange-sesame glazed salmon with a creamy ginger sauce, smoked cheddar baked scallops, Caribbean chicken with mango chutney, sautéed lamb with basil-walnut pesto and chive polenta, and filet of beef with a mustard-thyme sauce. Starters could be Maine crab cakes with sweet tomato salsa, chèvre-stuffed polenta, sweet and sour shrimp with Vietnamese vegetable wonton cups, and baked brie topped with almonds and homemade cranberry-apple chutney, served with seasonal fruit.

For weekend brunch, try the banana and walnut pancakes, the broccoli benedict or "Old MacDonald Goes to France," a croissant topped with two poached eggs, sausage patties, mushrooms, brie and hollandaise ($7.95).

(802) 865-2522. Lunch, Monday-Friday 11 to 2; light grill menu, 2 to 5:30; dinner, Tuesday-Sunday 5:30 to 9; Saturday and Sunday brunch, 10:30 to 2.

The Yellow Dog Restaurant & Cafe, 10 West Canal St., Winooski.

"I have a yellow Lab," says Rick Damalouji in explaining the name for his trendy new bistro beside the Champlain Mill in blue-collar Winooski. And the moose head, the stuffed pheasant, the antlers and such scattered here and there along the walls reflect "everything my dog barks at." Black cushioned chairs are at pine tables spaced around the long storefront dining room and the rear bar. Local artworks add color to the pale yellow walls beneath a black ceiling.

The restaurant we first knew as Forest Hills had lapsed into a succession of bars until Rick and two chefs from NECI arrived on the scene in 1996. They offer a contemporary menu with prices honed to the nickel to reflect appropriate value.

For dinner, you might order "cafe items" like grilled salmon with mozzarella, cherry tomatoes and greens ($8.65) or grilled chicken breast with roasted corn and black bean salsa ($10.85). Appetizers ($3.95 to $6.15) include gravlax with garlic toast and crème fraîche, Asian shrimp kabob with tamari dipping sauce and grilled portobello mushroom with fresh mozzarella and baby tomatoes. Main courses range from $11.15 for asparagus and risotto cakes with garden vegetables to $18.35 for grilled beef tenderloin with sherried mushrooms. Pan-seared salmon with lemon-caper salsa and grilled pork loin chop with apple-calvados chutney are favorites.

Lunch items are priced from $5.45 for grilled cheese and tomato on crispy Italian bread to $7.35 for angel-hair pasta with sautéed shrimp and basil pesto.

(802) 655-1703. Lunch, Tuesday-Friday 11 to 2; dinner, Monday-Saturday from 5:30.

Five Spice Cafe, 175 Church St., Burlington.

This spicy little prize occupies two floors of a former counter-culture restaurant at the edge of downtown. Since 1985, chef-owner Jerry Weinberg has won a host of followers for his multi-Asian menu of unusual, tantalizing dishes from Thailand, Vietnam, Indonesia, China and Burma.

We had the upstairs dining room almost to ourselves for a Wednesday lunch, but our waitress said it would be packed that night.

Our meal began with a bowl of hot and sour soup that was extra hot and a house sampler ($9.45) of appetizers, among them smoked shrimp, Siu Mai dumplings, Hunan noodles, Szechuan escargots and spicy cucumbers. The less adventurous among us passed up the Thai red snapper in black-bean sauce for a blackboard special of mock duck stir-fry in peanut sauce (the vegetarian dish really does taste like duck, just as, we were assured, the mock abalone really tastes like abalone). Sated though we were, we simply had to share the ginger-tangerine cheesecake, which proved denser and more subtly flavored than we had expected.

Chef Weinberg's wizardry in the downstairs kitchen is apparent on a chatty, wide-ranging dinner menu that boasts that some of the items and spices have been imitated locally but never matched. Prices of the main courses run from $7.95 for spicy Hunan noodles to $14.95 for Thai red snapper and a trio of shrimp dishes, one an eye-opener called Thai fire shrimp ("until this dish, we had a three-star heat rating. Now we have four").

A drunken chocolate mousse laced with liqueurs and a blackout cake drenched with triple sec are among favored desserts. The aforementioned ginger-tangerine cheesecake won Jerry a first prize somewhere, and the ginger-honeydew sorbet is extra-appealing. A dessert sampler teams the chocolate mousse with three other sweets for $13.25.

Oil lamps flicker on each table even at noon. Beige cloths and flowers in green vases comprise the decor. Above the serving sideboard is a collection of Five Spice T-shirts emblazoned with fire-breathing dragons and the saying, "Some Like It Hot." Yes, indeed.

(802) 864-4505. Lunch daily, 11:30 to 2:30; dinner nightly, 5 to 9, 10 or 11; Dim Sum brunch, Sunday 11 to 3.

Leunig's Bistro, 115 Church St., Burlington.

The garage doors go up in the summer to open this European-style bistro and grill to the sidewalk. The high-ceilinged interior is pretty in peach with black trim. In season, much of the action spills onto the sidewalks along the front and side. People pack the tables day and night, sipping drinks and espresso and savoring the appetizers and desserts, but they also come for full meals.

New owners Kathryn and Attila Keller, he a Hungarian chef and former manager of the Four Seasons restaurant in New York, have expanded the menu and elevated the fare into the forefront of contemporary cuisine locally. The day's soup could be gazpacho with cilantro crème fraîche or roasted eggplant, tomato and garlic soup with feta cheese. Grilled pizzas and pastas are featured at lunch ($4.95 to $7.95). So are sandwiches like grilled yellowfin tuna with red onions and wasabi mayonnaise, prime rib lavasch with horseradish mayo, and applewood-smoked turkey with provolone cheese and cranberry chutney. Entrée choices could be Mediterranean chicken salad, calamari stew or pan-roasted salmon with caramelized red onions and greens.

The Mediterranean-inspired dinner menu adds more pastas and entrées priced from $10.75 for poached chicken with rosemary goat cheese, sundried tomato pesto and mesclun salad to $19.95 for herb-crusted rack of lamb with garlic mashed potatoes. Among the possibilities are soft-shell crabs with lemongrass coconut broth and ginger steamed rice, seared sea scallops with caramelized fennel, and roasted duck with pears, honey-ginger sauce and couscous salad.

Among homemade desserts are espresso chocolate nougat, fresh fruit crisps and pumpkin crème brûlée.

(802) 863-3759. Breakfast daily, 7:30 to 11; lunch, 11:30 to 4; dinner, 5 to 10.

The Daily Planet, 15 Center St., Burlington.

Creative food at down-to-earth prices is the forte of this quirky place, advertised in the alternative press as an "inner city playground."

The name reflects its "global fare – ethnic and eclectic," in the words of the staff. Casual, innovative and a favorite local watering hole among knowledgeable noshers, it has a large bar with a pressed-tin ceiling, a solarium filled with cactus and jade plants plus a jukebox, and a lofty, sun-splashed dining room where the pipes are exposed, the walls are covered with works of local artists, and the oil-cloth table coverings at noon are changed to white linens at night.

The chefs, most trained at the Culinary Institute of America or the California Culinary Academy, are known for turning out some of the most imaginative fare in town. For lunch, how about spicy orange and beef salad, a grilled mushroom sandwich, a Korean vegetable pancake, cold and spicy Chinese noodles or a sundried tomato tapenade with flatbread (all under $6.50)? The stellar salad encircles a slab of goat cheese with small mounds of spaghetti squash, spinach, roasted red peppers and toasted walnuts.

At night, the Daily Planet sparkles with appetizers and light entrées like smoked-salmon flatbread pizza, spicy Moroccan mussels, and corn cakes with black bean and chipotle salsa and cilantro crème fraîche. Entrées ($9.95 to $18.50) might include Greek seafood pasta, pink sea bass with spicy crust and pineapple salsa, grilled Yucatan-style pork and roasted chicken stuffed with goat cheese. When was the last time you saw rack of lamb for $18, rubbed with North African spices and served with crisp couscous cakes, no less? Have you even heard of pork vindaloo, an Indian hot and sour pork loin sautéed with tomatoes and chick peas and served with a scallion flatbread?

Desserts that change daily intrigue as well. Some are pear-blueberry pie, white chocolate-apricot cheesecake, southern nut cake with bourbon crème anglaise, fresh plum ice cream, and baked apples with figs and cranberries.

As you might expect, the wine list, though small, is well-chosen and offers some incredible steals.

(802) 862-9647. Lunch, Monday-Friday 11:30 to 3; dinner nightly, 5 to 10 or 11; Saturday and Sunday brunch, 11 to 3, September-May.

Sài-Gòn Cafe, 133 Bank St., Burlington.

This authentic, highly rated establishment was opened in 1994 by Phi Doane, who had married an American soldier in Vietnam. Here she connected two houses by enclosing the driveway between them and offers several dining areas with the look of a Victorian residence, a Vietnamese market and a lounge.

A little pricier than most Vietnamese restaurants of our acquaintance, the menu is extensive and lists appetizers in the $3 to $5.95 range and salads from $4.95 to $6.50. Start, perhaps, with the steamed imperial rolls, which another restaurateur touts as the freshest ever. Your salad might be layers of shrimp, cucumber, carrots, onion and mint leaves, topped with peanuts and shrimp chips. Pho Ha Noi, a traditional soup, is served in three sizes; the extra large ($7.50) is a meal in itself. There are several other regional soups; one is asparagus and crabmeat topped with cilantro and scallions.

Beef, pork, chicken and seafood entrées are in the $8.50 to $11.95 range, with vegetarian options somewhat less. We like the sound of the grilled chicken with lemongrass, served with lettuce, cucumber, cilantro, mint and rice noodles. Rice paper, to make little packets of the dish, is served upon request. Under special entrées is hu tieu xao, rice noodles stir-fried with vegetables in an oyster sauce, with choice of pork, shrimp or chicken.

(802) 863-5637. Lunch, Monday-Saturday 11 to 3; dinner, 5:30 to 9:30 or 10.

Budget Gourmet

The Blue Seal Restaurant, Bridge Street, Richmond.
The old Blue Seal feed granary beside the railroad track in rural Richmond had a checkered past – from dance hall to pharmacy – before Debra Weinstein converted it in 1995 into a modest cafe for the budget-conscious gourmet. The University of Vermont grad returned to the area she loved after a stint as chef in the cafe at famed Arizona 206 in New York City. She dressed the pale yellow interior with collections of birdhouses, pitchers and such from her travels. "My home is empty because everything is here," she says. Yet the ambiance remains plain, with windsor chairs at bare tables set with paper napkins and votive candles. The "banquette" along a side wall is actually a bench with no back other than the wall.
Trains may rumble by as patrons dine on interesting contemporary and vegetarian fare, remarkable for its low prices. Main courses start at $8 and top off at $14 for pan-roasted salmon with garlic mashed potatoes and corn mushroom salsa, or mixed grill of spicy shrimp, pork loin and garlic sausage with basmati rice and roasted tomatillo salsa. The chile-rubbed chicken comes with potato fritters, peas and carrots; the marinated portobello mushroom with grilled new potatoes, sautéed spinach and goat cheese, and the charred steak salad with romaine lettuce, cheese and toasted New Mexican chiles.
A local farmer grows her vegetables and produce, which turn up in innovative ways: a snap pea salad with cucumbers, green beans, pickled onions and feta cheese; spring rolls of julienned vegetables, and roasted stuffed tomato with grilled vegetables and sautéed field greens. Other starters include grilled salmon rolls with cucumbers, chile peppers and a wasabi dipping sauce, and warm artichoke salad with grilled zucchini, chick peas and garlic-ginger vinaigrette.
Expect desserts like a classic lemon meringue tart, blueberry-rhubarb cobbler with cinnamon biscuit crust and vanilla ice cream, and chocolate pound cake with chocolate-praline mousse and coffee crème anglaise. The choice little wine list is remarkably priced, starting at $10 and most bottles in the low teens.
(802) 434-5949. Dinner, Tuesday-Saturday 5:30 to 9:30.

More Dining Choices

Sweet Tomatoes Trattoria, 83 Church St., Burlington.
Borrowing a page from their smash-success restaurant of the same name in Lebanon, N.H., Robert Meyers and James Reiman opened a carbon copy here and, at our latest visit, were about to launch another in downtown Rutland.
From Burlington's first wood-fired brick oven come zesty pizzas like the namesake sweet tomato pie, a combination of tomato, basil, mozzarella and olive oil ($8.75). From the rest of the open kitchen that runs along the side of the surprisingly large downstairs space emerge earthy pastas, grills and entrées at wallet-pleasing prices – $10.95 is the highest for a mixed grill or skewers of lamb. For a quick dinner, we were quite impressed with the cavateppi with spit-roasted chicken ($8.95). Less impressive was a special of linguini infused with olive oil and mushrooms ($7.75), rather bland and desperately in need of more pecorino romano cheese, the container of which the waitress sprinkled less than liberally and guarded as if with her life until we finally asked for (and received) our own container full to

rescue the dish. A huge salad topped with romano, a basket of bread for dipping in the house olive oil and a $14 bottle of Orvieto accompanied.

The stark decor in white and black is offset by brick arches and stone walls with a neon strip over the kitchen. It's a convivial and noisy setting for what Robert calls "strictly ethnic Italian cooking, as prepared in a home kitchen."

The sidewalk cafe on the Church Street Marketplace out front is an even busier setting in summer. We were floored to see all the people waiting for tables for a late lunch here on an August weekday.

(802) 660-9533. Lunch, Monday-Saturday 11:30 to 2; late lunch, 2 to 4; dinner, 5 to 9:30 or 10, Sunday to 9.

The Village Pumphouse Restaurant, On the Green, Shelburne.

The hand-written menu changes frequently at this much-loved but not widely known restaurant, with 35 seats in two intimate dining rooms and an enclosed porch.

Assisted by his sister in the prep department, chef David Webster prepares some exciting fare. Dinner entrées, served with soup and a green salad, run from $18.95 to $22. One night's offerings were Thai shrimp sautéed with scallions and ginger, baked striped bass with a roasted tomato puree, veal madeira with shiitake mushrooms and dried cherries, and sautéed loin of lamb finished with port and shallots. Four "suppers," with salad but no soup, produced crab cakes, poached fillet of sole, pork tenderloin with dried cherry chutney and broiled New York sirloin for $15.25 to $17.95.

Start with smoked trout cheesecake, black bean cakes with salsa and sour cream, or mushrooms stuffed with sausage and parmesan. Finish with a raspberry-peach crisp, chocolate-hazelnut meringue tart, maple crème caramel or cream-cheese crêpes with apricot sauce.

Decor is country simple, with a stress on the simple, according to David. Most of the assorted oak and maple chairs came from his parents' barn.

David's partner, host-bartender David Miner, is responsible for the large beer list. It's as lengthy as the wine list, and includes seven on draft.

(802) 985-3728. Dinner, Tuesday-Saturday 5:30 to 9:30 or 10.

Trattoria Delia, 152 St. Paul St., Burlington.

Relatively new and well-received is this authentic Italian establishment with something of an old-world ambiance and an updated menu. Tom Daley, who used to cook at Mr. Up's in Middlebury, and his wife Lori took over the old What's Your Beef steakhouse and transformed it into a trattoria. The beamed and timbered room is comfortable and good-looking in deep red and green, with a long bar along one side.

Homemade pastas are featured as primi dishes ($7.95 to $12.95). Tagliatelle with porcini mushrooms and pappardelle with braised wild boar and wild mushrooms are favorites. Among secondi ($9.95 to $14.50) are wood-grilled fish of the day with a garlic-pepper sauce, salt cod simmered with raisins in a sweet tomato sauce, rabbit cacciatore, wild boar braised in barolo wine and served on a bed of saffron risotto, veal saltimbocca, osso buco and wood-grilled angus sirloin finished with sage and olive oil.

Antipasti ($3.50 to $6.50) include bruschetta, deep-fried calamari, carpaccio and the traditional sampling of imported Italian meats, cheeses and roasted vegetables. Among desserts are profiteroles filled with gelati and homemade crème caramel with golden raisins and vin santo.

The Wine Spectator award-winning wine list is extensive and fairly priced. Digestives at the end of the dinner menu include sweet Italian dessert wines. Also offered are cappuccino and caffe latte.

(802) 864-5253. Dinner nightly, 5 to 10.

Bourbon Street Grill, 213 College St., Burlington.

Art and Manon O'Connor had never been to New Orleans when they opened this small and intimate cafe. You wouldn't know it from the decor: a comfortable and warm rendition of a Bourbon Street prototype, nicely outfitted in pink and yellow with a tile floor, artworks, plants and a parasol hanging from the ceiling. Nor would you know it from the menu, which is patterned after those of restaurants there.

Chef Art had been dabbling in cajun food as executive chef for the Mount Mansfield Corporation after restaurant stints in Connecticut. Here he went all out with specialties like gumbo, jambalaya, red beans and rice, and barbecued shrimp. He drew on other cuisines for the Southwest raviolis filled with jack cheese and jalapeños, the Jamaican jerk chicken and shrimp, and the grilled pork tenderloin with Asian barbecue sauce. Favorites entrées ($12.95 to $15.95) include grilled catfish, cajun sauté, seafood mixed grill and cajun grilled flank steak, a house specialty that's also available as an appetizer. The dessert tray yields bourbon-pecan torte, chocolate cheesecake and chocolate-praline crêpes.

A shelf above the bar holds some of the restaurant's specialty foods for sale, among them Big Art's Jazz Sauce for chicken wings, caesar salad dressing and a fire sauce for those who like things extra-hot.

In 1996, the O'Connors opened **Mona's** beside the lakefront at 3 Main St. A large, two-story establishment with an elegant Mediterranean look and water-view decks, it offered an extensive, contemporary menu for lunch and dinner to decidedly mixed early reviews. The local consensus indicated that our mediocre lunch was not an exception, but everyone hoped Mona's would eventually get its act together.

(802) 865-2800. Lunch, Monday-Saturday 11:30 to 4; dinner nightly, 5:30 to 10; Sunday brunch, 10:30 to 3.

Offbeat Gourmet

Pepper's Memphis Barbecue, 1110 Shelburne Road, South Burlington.

Here is a must-stop for those into Memphis music and barbecue.

There's a lot to look at and listen to in the old diner section, where huge glasses of iced tea are the drink of choice at lunch time, and in a small, memorabilia-filled dining room, where musical instruments and photos of jazz musicians line the walls.

Legendary BBQ chef Robert Moye came from Memphis to prepare the real thing: hickory-smoked ribs, chicken, beef and turkey, all served in the authentic Southern barbecue tradition. We liked his signature pulled pork sandwich ($4.95) topped with zippy coleslaw and the corned-beef brisket. The pork shoulder is smoked for fourteen hours in a closet-size rotisserie, yielding such treats as dry ribs ($8.95) and a sampler platter ($11.50). There are munchies, soups and salads to go with.

(802) 864-7427. Open daily from 11

Dining and Lodging

The Inn at Shelburne Farms, Shelburne 05482.

It's hard to imagine a more luxurious inn, albeit in an old-school way, or a more spectacular setting than the summer mansion built by Dr. William Seward Webb and his wife, Lila Vanderbilt Webb, high on a promontory surrounded on three sides by Lake Champlain.

Their 1,400-acre Shelburne Farms agricultural estate was planned by Frederick Law Olmsted, the landscape architect who designed New York's Central Park. The focal point is their incomparable summer home, a lakeside landmark completed in 1899 for $10 million and converted in 1987 into an inn and restaurant of distinction.

The rambling, towered and turreted, Queen Anne-style mansion has 24 bedrooms and suites, seventeen with private baths. It retains the original furnishings, although Old Deerfield Fabrics created for the inn a Shelburne House line of fabrics and wall coverings reproduced from original designs dating to the turn of the century.

Most guest rooms on the second and third floors are awesome in size, some with three windows onto the water and non-working fireplaces. Each is done in its own style, but four-poster beds, armoires, settees, lavishly carved chairs, writing tables and such barely begin to fill the space. Fresh flowers adorn the bathrooms, mostly original and some with skylights. Guests' names are on the doors and bowls of fruit in the rooms upon arrival.

For their spaciousness and aura of royalty, we would choose to stay in Lila Webb's south corner sitting room with its twin pencil-post beds and a fine view of forests and lake from mullioned windows, or Dr. Webb's room with William Morris wallpaper setting off a massive double bed, a two-story bathroom and spiral stairs up to his valet's quarters (now the White Room full of wicker and containing one of the inn's few queensize beds). Other choices would be the Overlook bedroom in between, or the Rose Room with a canopy bed, silk moiré wallpaper and a view of sunsets over mountains and lake that defies description. Although they represent good value, we would not care to stay in some of the smaller rooms with shared baths and hard-to-climb-in double beds up against the wall.

The main floor is a living museum reflecting the graciousness of another era. There are porches full of wicker, a library with 6,000 volumes, several sitting rooms (one for afternoon tea and pastries), a dark and masculine game room harboring an 1886 billiards table, and a formal dining room in which breakfast and dinner are served. Telephones in the guest rooms, TV sets on request and a tennis court are among the few concessions to modernity.

Meals are quiet and formal at twelve tables dressed with white linens and Villeroy & Boch china in the spacious Marble Room, quite stunning with black and white tiled floors and walls covered in red silk damask fabric. Favored in summer are outdoor tables on the adjacent veranda with views of Lake Champlain.

The public may join house guests by reservation, paying $6.75 to $9 for appetizers, $22 to $28 for entrées, and $4.75 to $5.50 for desserts.

Chef Tom Bivins, a New England Culinary Institute graduate, started as pastry and sous chef with the inn in its early days. He incorporates produce from the farm's gardens and uses local purveyors in keeping with the Shelburne Farms mission of sustaining local agriculture. Complimentary canapés, perhaps truffle

Dinner is served with a view of Lake Champlain on veranda at Inn at Shelburne Farms.

mousse or salami with Shelburne Farms cheddar, begin the meal. Then there could be a choice of vichyssoise with chives and cheddar croutons, salmon tartare with caperberries or grilled garlic-rubbed bruschetta with garlic marmalade, tomato and sheep's milk cheese. Salads could be miskell tomato with shaved romano, fresh arugula and strawberries, or spicy Louisiana caesar with tasso-wrapped shrimp and cornbread croutons.

For main courses, how about pan-roasted sea bass with grilled mushrooms, roasted breast of duck with blueberry-vodka-lime sauce, or roasted rack of lamb with a sundried tomato crust and caramelized garlic demi-glace?

Desserts vary from assorted fruit sorbets and seasonal fruit cobblers to a compote of summer berries with champagne sabayon and a chocolate mousse torte with hazelnut ganache, cherry amaretto, white peach brandy and raspberry sauces.

Breakfast for overnight guests is à la carte. Main courses are priced from $7.25 for homemade granola with low-fat yogurt to $9.50 for zucchini fritters with poached eggs and a tomato-tarragon hollandaise sauce. Unusual items include orange-yogurt pancakes with maple-ginger syrup and crème fraîche, and grilled sweet flatbread with raspberry sauce, sweet Vermont chèvre and roasted mango.

Guests can walk the grounds, enjoy the superb gardens, swim at a small beach, play croquet on a manicured lawn and hike up Lone Tree Hill for a 360-degree view of the lake and mountains, says Alec Webb, president of Shelburne Farms and great-grandson of the original owners. The quiet and sense of privacy are overwhelming.

The house was opened as an inn "to preserve the structure and generate revenues," adds Alec, who spent summers in the house as a teenager before his father bequeathed it to a non-profit foundation. "It's an appropriate use since it was basically a guest house originally."

(802) 985-8498 (late May to mid-October); 985-8686 (mid-October to May). Dinner nightly by reservation, 6 to 9. Doubles, $90 to $250, EP. Open mid-May to mid-October.

The Inn at Essex, 70 Essex Way, Essex Junction 05452.

"We have a chef for every room," says innkeeper Jim Lamberti of this elegant small country hotel that emerged in the midst of a large field on the commercial outskirts of Essex Junction. That's because Jim and his wife Judy, who built the inn with the help of Hawk Mountain Corp., approached the New England Culinary Institute for advice on a leasee for their planned food and beverage operation at the very time NECI was seeking a teaching kitchen in the Burlington area. NECI decided to run the inn's two restaurants with faculty and students. The Lambertis devoted their personal touch to the inn, from inspiration to decor to training of the exceptionally welcoming staff.

Now owned by the Lambertis in partnership with Eurowest Inns of California and other investors, the inn has overcome early challenges. It opened as the recession hit, its original developer went bankrupt and the out-of-the-way location made the task of filling its 97 rooms daunting, to say the least. The economy bounced back, funding was restructured and the first part of the planned Route 289 circumferential highway opened with an exit near the inn. A designer outlet center opened in 1996 across the highway interchange, and the Lambertis began to talk of expansion.

The white, three-story main structure is one of several built around what Jim likens to a New England village green. Furnishings and wallpapers in each room are different, and decor varies from Shaker to Queen Anne, from canopy to pencil-post to brass beds. Each room has a sitting area with comfortable upholstered chairs, a TV hidden in the armoire and a modern bath. Thirty have working fireplaces. An attractive new outdoor swimming pool beckons beneath a large fountain/rock sculpture chiseled on the property by a Vermont artist.

At one end of the main inn are two restaurants: the formal, 50-seat **Butler's** with a Georgian look in pale green and lavender, upholstered Queen Anne chairs, heavy white china and windows swagged in chintz, and the more casual **Birch Tree Cafe,** where woven mats on bare tables, dark green wainscoting and small lamps with gilt shades create a Vermont country setting. There's considerable creativity in the huge kitchen, thanks to fifteen teaching chefs and a hundred student assistants.

The cafe was where we had a fine Christmastime lunch: sundried-tomato fettuccine with scallops and a wedge of pheasant pie with a salad of mixed greens, among entrées from $5.75 to $7.25. Although the portions were small and the service slow, we saw signs of inspiration, on the menu as well as in a dessert of chocolate medallions with mousseline and blueberries in a pool of raspberry-swirled crème fraîche, presented like a work of art. Two pieces of biscotti came with the bill, a very reasonable tab. Interesting meals and theme dinners at bargain prices are served in the cafe at night. The all-you-can-eat dessert buffet here is $3.75.

Dinner in Butler's, NECI's temple to haute cuisine, is a study in trendy food prepared and served by second-year students. A specified four-course prix-fixe dinner is available for $27. The rest of the menu is à la carte, $4.50 to $7.75 for starters and $16 to $21 for entrées. A pre-wedding party added festivity the summer night we dined. Piano music emanated from the lounge as one of us made a meal of three starters: a subtle duck and chicken liver pâté garnished with shredded beets and wild mushrooms, pan-seared scallops with potato-garlic coulis and a salad of organic greens with a cilantro-lime dressing. The other enjoyed an entrée of crispy-skin salmon with wilted greens, tomatoes and risotto. A complimentary canape of mushroom duxelles in pastry preceded, and a scoop of honeydew melon sorbet appeared between courses. From the delectable looking desserts on display

Inn at Essex is home of two New England Culinary Institute restaurants.

at the entry we shared the trio of sorbets – mango-passionfruit, strawberry daiquiri and peach champagne – spilling from a cookie cone, and splurged for an eau de vie for a bargain $5. Four little pastries and candies accompanied the bill, $77 for a highly satisfactory experience.

(802) 878-1100 or (800) 727-4295. Fax (802) 878-0063. Butler's, dinner, Monday-Saturday 6 to 10. Birch Tree Cafe, lunch, Monday-Saturday 11:30 to 1:30; dinner nightly, 5:30 to 9:30; Sunday brunch, 11 to 2. Doubles, $109 to $190.

Lodging

The Willard Street Inn, 349 South Willard St., Burlington 05401.

Enter the cherry-paneled foyer of this 1881 brick mansion in the city's Hill Section to reach Burlington's first historic B&B-style inn. Beverly Watson, the restaurateur who runs Isabel's on the Waterfront, and husband Gordon bought the property that had been a retirement home in 1996 and became resident innkeepers. The house was in beautiful shape, Beverly said, needing only some fresh paint and wallpaper. A mere three weeks transpired between closing the purchase and opening in time for fall foliage and the first guests.

The fifteen guest rooms on the second and third floors are furnished in traditional style with period antiques and reproductions, plus TVs and phones. Seven have private baths, two share an adjoining bath and the rest share one on each floor. Rooms vary widely, from large master bedrooms with handsome ornamental fireplaces to a few small ones with in-room sinks. Those on the west side yield views of Lake Champlain in the distance.

Guests share the high-ceilinged living room, dining room and a plant-filled solarium looking onto beautiful gardens in back, reached by a marble staircase. Afternoon tea and breakfast are offered in the solarium. The latter is continental on weekdays, more substantial on weekends, when french toast casserole or vegetable frittata might be the fare.

(802) 651-8710 or (800) 577-8712. Fax (802) 651-8714. Doubles, $75 to $150.

Radisson Hotel Burlington, 60 Battery St., Burlington 05401.

When it opened in the late 1970s as part of the Burlington Square office/commercial complex, it was billed as northern New England's most urbane hotel (it's still urbane, but the competition is increasing). The seven-story, 255-room hotel occupies a choice piece of real estate between downtown and the lakefront, and the most desirable rooms, of course, are those that face a broad vista of Lake Champlain, with the Adirondacks rising in the distance.

The lobby is a bit austere by Burlington standards, but our room was spacious and subtly decorated in golds and browns. The seventh-floor Plaza Club has concierge service, a complimentary continental breakfast, afternoon wine and other amenities. There's a great jacuzzi on one side of the indoor swimming pool, which is surrounded by poolside cabanas.

The **Oak Street Cafe** and lobby/bar offers three meals a day at moderate prices. The former Gerard's gourmet restaurant has given way to **Seasons on the Lake**, an elegant dining room advertising creative international cuisine for dinner, open Friday and Saturday only from 5 to 10.

(802) 658-6500. Fax (802) 658-4659. Doubles, $143 to $164..

Two Outlying B&Bs

The Inn at Charlotte, 1188 State Park Road, Charlotte 05445.

The immediate Burlington area is lacking in good B&Bs, but this newcomer to the south of town is a good bet. Located just off Route 7 near the foot of Mount Philo, it started as a boutique in an old schoolhouse with the owner's living quarters behind. You'd never know it today, such is the transformation into a rambling, contemporary, chalet-style house with six guest rooms, all with private baths. Most also have private entrances via sliding doors onto a tiered rear garden around a swimming pool and tennis court. We're partial to the two rooms at the far end, one with a kingsize bed and full bath and the other with twin four-posters and a closet-size shower. Another favorite is a detached cottage with twin beds. A thermos of Vermont spring water is in every bedroom.

Besides the pool, tennis court and garden area, guests enjoy a large and comfortable living room and a dining room in which owner Letty Ellinger, a caterer, serves dinner to guests by reservation (she was making delectable-smelling Chinese egg rolls at our visit). A typical $25 prix-fixe meal might involve oriental soup or green salad, chicken teriyaki or New York strip sirloin (grilled outside on the barbecue), a homemade pie, a glass of wine and gourmet coffee. A $30 tab gets you a full Asian dinner with several appetizers, three main dishes with rice, and choice of dessert.

Letty serves a full breakfast in the morning, perhaps ham and eggs, quiche, french toast or blueberry pancakes.

(802) 425-2934 or (800) 425-2934. Doubles, $75 to $95.

Thomas Mott Homestead, with raspberry bushes in foreground and lake in background.

Thomas Mott Homestead, Blue Rock Road, Alburg 05440.

This lakeside prize at the top of the Champlain Islands north of Burlington is one of our favorite B&Bs anywhere. Ex-California wine distributor Pat Schallert transformed an 1838 farmhouse into a homey B&B with five spacious guest rooms and a secluded lakeside location with panoramic water and mountain views that won't quit. Three porches invite lounging, the fireplaced living room is stocked with books and magazines, and a massive collection of cookbooks and wine books flanks the stairway. Each of the five guest rooms with private baths is furnished with antiques and quilts from different states. The ultimate is Ransom's Rest, nestled beneath a cathedral ceiling with a queen bed, two chairs in front of a fireplace and a balcony looking across Ransom's Bay to Mount Mansfield.

Pat cooks up a hearty breakfast amid much camaraderie in the kitchen open to the dining room. The french toast stuffed with cream cheese and five kinds of nuts, served with warm maple syrup, and the crab omelet proved stellar during our visit. Other special touches that make this place a winner: chocolates from the local Shoreline Chocolates put out at turndown, a help-yourself stash of at least ten varieties of Ben & Jerry's ice cream in the refrigerator, a lakeside gazebo and boating dock, a barnyard pen where Pat raises quail and a patch of what he calls "stealing" raspberries. We were surprised they were still producing in late September and gladly would have picked a few quarts to take home – but that would have been stealing!

(802) 796-3736 or (800) 348-0843. Doubles, $69 to $89.

Gourmet Destinations

Shelburne Museum, Route 7, Shelburne.

The incredible collections of Electra Havemeyer Webb, wife of a Vanderbilt heir, became the Shelburne Museum in 1947, and the resulting 37 exhibit buildings spread across a 45-acre heritage park fascinate young and old. The almost overwhelming display of Americana, unrivaled in New England, spans three centuries and a multitude of interests. People into things culinary will enjoy the kitchens in four restored homes, each with large open hearths full of gadgets that our ancestors used. The Weed House has a remarkable collection of pewter and glass, and the dining-room tables in the side-wheeler Ticonderoga are set with Syracuse china. A free shuttle tram transports visitors from the new visitor center to the far ends of the grounds every fifteen minutes.

(802) 985-3346. Daily 9 to 5, mid-May to mid-October; rest of year, guided tours, daily at 1. Adults, $17.50; second consecutive day free.

Shelburne Farms, 102 Harbor Road, Shelburne.

The 1,400-acre agricultural estate of Dr. William Seward Webb and Lila Vanderbilt Webb has been opened to the public lately as a working farm. Blessed with one of the more spectacular lakeside-mountain settings in the Northeast, Shelburne Farms combines an active dairy and cheesemaking operation, a bakery, a market garden, furniture-making and other leased enterprises in a working-farm setting that has a Camelot-like quality. Guided tours leave every 90 minutes from the Visitor Center after a free multi-media slide introduction. You board an open-air wagon to view the enormous Farm Barn, the Dairy Barn, the formal gardens and the exterior of the Shelburne House. You may see grazing along the way the fine herd of Brown Swiss cows, descended from stock raised for cheesemaking in Switzerland. Their Shelburne Farms farmhouse cheddar (some of the best cheddar we have ever tasted) is sold in the Visitor Center, where a fine shop also stocks other Vermont farm products and crafts and is open daily year-round.

(802) 985-8686. Tours daily at 9:30, 11, 12:30, 2 and 3:30, late May to mid-October. Adults, $6.50.

Gourmet Treats

In Burlington, **Lake Champlain Chocolates** at 431 Pine St. produces some of the best chocolates in the Northeast. It's an outgrowth of Jim Lampman's original Ice House restaurant, where partner Richard Spurgeon was the baker and produced truffles that generated such demand that they branched into the chocolate enterprise in 1983. You can view the production area from the windows of a small showroom that smells like chocolate heaven. Richard starts with Belgian chocolate but the addition of Vermont heavy cream and sweet butter and intense natural flavoring puts their creations "on a par with the best in the world," according to Cuisine magazine. Among the latest treats are Vermints, and factory seconds are offered at 40 percent off. A sampling is available downtown at the **Copper Kettle Fudge** on the Church Street Marketplace.

"Custom-built coffees" are the trademark of **Speeder & Earl's,** a high-tech, high-ceilinged space in black and white at 412 Pine St. Its boutique roastery and coffee bar are located here, while a small Speeder's coffee bar is situated downtown on the Church Street Marketplace. You'll find rare coffee roasts that are served plain, with foam and/or with flavored syrups. What are custom-built coffees? The menu answers: "Simply put, if you want hazelnut Italian syrup in a nonfat latte, with nonfat whipped cream topping, sprinkled with mint-flavored sugar, don't be shy. Just ask." Ask also for teas, Italian sodas, biscotti and pastries. It seems enough people have asked that owners Gordon and Jeannie Blankenburg have opened a 50-seat restaurant and espressso bar purveying their Speeder's premium blend in the Copley Square Hotel in Boston.

Bennington Potters North, a multi-level emporium at 127 College St. in downtown Burlington, carries everything from the popular pottery to aprons to egg cups. Housed in a restored warehouse, it's enormous, and so is the selection.

Two enterprises are of particular interest along the Church Street Marketplace: a **Lindt of Switzerland** chocolate factory store and **Kiss the Cook,** a good kitchen store.

The **Cheese Outlet/Fresh Market** at 400 Pine St. has evolved into a gourmet emporium with the Twirlybird Cafe, a bakery, a section of local produce, a specialty deli featuring good-looking salads, and a case of all kinds of pasta, some with interesting fillings, where you can take as much or as little as you want. It remains northern New England's largest cheese and wine warehouse, with an excellent selection of pâtés and cheeses, quiches and cheesecakes at bargain prices.

Shelburne is home to the **Shelburne Country Store,** opposite the village green. It still sells penny candy but also offers an upscale assortment of country things, accessories, kitchenware, fudge and specialty foods, including its own line of chowders and finnan haddie. All kinds of mustards and sauces are opened for tasting.

"The world's best ham sandwich" ($4.75) is advertised at **Harrington's of Vermont,** Route 7, next to Cafe Shelburne. Headquartered in nearby Richmond, this has a cafe as well as everything for the kitchen from cookbooks to Cuisinarts. It sells a panoply of gourmet foods, including every kind of cracker imaginable. The cob-smoked ham, turkey and pheasant are famous, and you also can find delicious country sausage, Canadian bacon, air-dried beef and smoked salmon.

Gourmet Bakers

The best breads in town come from **Klinger's Bread Company**, headquartered at 10 Farrell St. in South Burlington and with a small downtown outlet at Church and College streets. Designed to resemble a European village courtyard, complete with murals and a tiled roof, the bakery's Disneyesque display area dispenses countless varieties of breads, sandwiches and salads. There's even a retail wine cellar. Big windows open onto the bakery area launched in 1993 by Judy Klingebiel, who learned the trade as accountant to master baker Michael London of Rock Hill Bakehouse near Saratoga Springs, N.Y. At last count, Klinger's 21 varieties ranged from jalapeño-cheddar to chocolate-cherry to Jewish rye, some made only on certain days and best reserved in advance.

Desserts and pastries that turn up at the swishest parties in town come from **Mirabelles,** 198 Main St., a terrific bakery and deli created by Alison Fox and Andrew Silva and named for the golden plums grown on the Continent, where both had worked. Sandwiches are inspired, perhaps black forest ham and brie, artichoke pesto with vegetables or goat cheese with Mediterranean tapenade and vegetables, served on homemade wheat, sourdough, honey oat breads or a baguette for $3.95 to $4.95. The ploughman's lunch ($5.95) is a sampling of cheeses, breads, fruits and a sweet. Finish with a raspberry butter tart, chocolate-raspberry mousse cake or a slice of cappuccino-truffle cake. More of the same, plus afternoon tea, is offered at **Mirabelles Cafe** in the new Wing Building on Burlington's waterfront.

MIDDLE BRIDGE · WOODSTOCK VERMONT

Woodstock and Hanover
Quintessential New England

Woodstock, which has been called one of America's prettiest towns by National Geographic, is the quintessential New England village. Across the New Hampshire state line is Hanover, the quintessential New England college town.

Put them together and you have an extraordinary destination area for those who seek the real New England, relatively unspoiled, even if highly sophisticated. Happily, both towns have escaped the commercial trappings that so often accompany tourism. The Rockefeller interests have enhanced much of Woodstock, even burying the utility wires in the center underground for a picture-perfect Currier and Ives look. Dartmouth College sets the character of Hanover. Both towns exude an aura of culture and class.

The attraction of the area is epitomized by historic Woodstock, where America's first ski tow was installed in 1934, propelling it into a winter sports mecca called "the St. Moritz of the East – without the Ritz." There's still no Ritz, although the Woodstock Inn and Resort built in 1969 by Rockefeller interests and the Twin Farms luxury hideaway that emerged in 1993 could qualify.

The Rockefeller connection with Woodstock began in 1934 when Laurance Rockefeller married Mary Billings French, the granddaughter of railroad magnate Frederick Billings. Now the town's largest landowner and employer, he lives about two months of the year in the mansion north of town that was once the home of George Perkins Marsh, the 19th-century ambassador and a founder of the Smithsonian. The Rockefellers are preserving the family heritage – and that of Vermont – in their Billings Farm Museum with its thousands of 19th-century farm implements. Their home and 550 acres of surrounding gardens and woodlands have been given to the National Park Service for preservation as the new Marsh-Billings National Historical Park.

A generation ago, chowders, boiled dinners and pumpkin pies were the fare served at the White Cupboard Inn – which closed in 1967 – and at the old Woodstock Inn, which was razed to make way for the new showplace. "Had a patron requested chocolate mousse he probably would have been told that the pharmacy didn't carry those but they did have maple sugar candies shaped like Indians," a local magazine once wrote.

Today, the Woodstock and Hanover region abounds with fine restaurants and inns appealing to diverse tastes. The area also has more than its share of casual restaurants serving creative fare at down-to-earth prices.

Dining

The Best of the Best

Barnard Inn, Route 12, Barnard, Vt.

Its red-brick facade accented by four white pillars and surrounded by mighty trees, the Barnard Inn is a handsome, two-story structure dating to 1796. It really is out in the country, ten miles north of Woodstock almost at the "back of beyond." But its fans consider the distance a trifle to be put up with for a meal at a restaurant they tout as one of the best in Vermont.

The Barnard has held that lofty status since 1975, so Marie-France and Philip Filipovic from Quebec knew they had a lot to live up to when they purchased it in 1994. They came with impeccable credentials. Self-taught Yugoslav chef Philip, who started as a waiter in Montreal's Ritz-Carlton Hotel, and his wife owned a four-star restaurant called simply Marie Philip in the Laurentian resort town of St. Sauveur. It had been rated the best in the province by the Quebec government in one of its annual awards competitions.

Moving to Vermont for "quality of life," Marie said, they took over a going concern and began adding their imprimatur. They hung their favorite paintings, put down oriental rugs, added more French wines to an already choice cellar and started smoking their own salmon. We, who enjoyed several great meals here previously, were pleased to find that the new Barnard Inn was equal to, if not better than, the old.

A fire blazes in the hearth in the biggest of four small dining rooms in the elegant, late-Colonial inn. Dusky rose cloths, gold-rimmed china, candles in hurricane chimneys and sparkling wine globes dress the well-spaced tables. The only lighting is from the candles and the wall sconces. It's an altogether charming backdrop for leisurely dining.

The menu is à la carte (appetizers, $6 to $7, and entrées, $19 to $25). A five-course tasting menu ($33) represents good value.

Choosing the latter, we began with a couple of complimentary hors d'oeuvres: tastes of prosciutto and melon and a cherry tomato stuffed with French boncoccini cheese. Next came the house-smoked salmon, a signature presentation shaped like a rose and served with endives, and a zucchini blossom bearing lobster and shrimp mousse over lemongrass beurre blanc. Crusty sourdough bread and perfect green salads preceded the main courses, noisettes of Green Mountain lamb wrapped in spinach mousse and tenderloin of rabbit with wild mushrooms. Everything was beautifully presented on dramatic square plates and garnished with flowers. Snap peas, baby squash, beets and potato gaufrette accompanied.

A plate of four cheeses arrived bearing one of the Barnard's decorative trademarks, in this case a swan carved from an apple, with a clove for its eye. (The house potatoes are shaped and coated to look like a pear, with a clove at the bottom and a pear stem on top.) Dessert was a crème brûlée laced with orange and ginger, and an assortment of remarkable sorbets (chocolate, papaya, peach and raspberry) looking like an artist's palette. The bill came in a lacquered box with two truffles on a doily.

Lingering over coffee and eau de vie in the cozy bar, we felt mesmerized by the setting as well as by the exceptional meal. We can't wait for a return engagement.

(802) 234-9961. Dinner, Tuesday-Sunday from 6. Also closed Sunday in winter.

Hemingway's, Route 4, Killington, Vt.

The restored, 19th-century Asa Briggs farmhouse has been earning culinary accolades since Linda and Ted Fondulas moved over from Annabelle's in Stockbridge in the early 80s.

Antiques, locally crafted furniture, fresh flowers from Linda's gardens and original oil paintings, watercolors and sculpture enhance the decor in each of three dining rooms. A European feeling is effected in the formal dining room with velvet chairs and chandeliers, a garden room done up in white and pink with brick floors and pierced lamps on the walls, and a charming wine cellar with stone walls, lace tablecloths and elaborate candlesticks.

These are diverse settings for ever-changing food that made Hemingway's the first four-star, four-diamond restaurant.in northern New England. An added accolade came a few years later when Food & Wine magazine ranked it among the top 25 restaurants in America. Hemingway's also is known for its monthly food and wine tastings featuring wine experts as guest speakers. The Fondulases stock more than 175 wine selections, at prices from the high teens to $200.

Dinner is prix-fixe, available in three formats: $42 for four courses, plus hors d'oeuvre, coffee and confection; $65 for five tasting portions, each served with a glass of selected wine, champagne or port, and $40 for a four-course vegetarian menu.

About six choices are available in each category for the first option. For starters you might find bundles of applewood-smoked salmon with lemon and seaweed, lobster soup with fennel and garlic toast, roasted duck liver with grilled mango and brioche, and napoleon of wild mushrooms with tarragon phyllo pastry. The fish course could be fillet of halibut with vanilla, sweet corn and chives or seared diver scallops with truffled potatoes and caramelized onions. Main courses include pepper-crusted yellowfin tuna with mesclun greens in a crispy potato basket, panroasted poussin with basmati rice, oven-roasted lamb chops with spinach-stuffed eggplant, and grilled tenderloin of beef with potato galette and shallots.

Desserts could be caramelized napoleon of pear with star anise, black and white chocolate sandwich with pistachio sauce, fresh fruit charlotte with a vanilla and raspberry web, coconut ice cream under a caramel cage with mango and banana, or "local anything," says Linda, whose husband oversees the kitchen. The chef gets his herbs from a garden out back, and scented geraniums might turn up as a garnish.

(802) 422-3886. Dinner, Wednesday-Sunday 6 to 10. Closed mid-April to mid-May and early November.

All is elegant and historic in Barnard Inn's main dining room.

La Poule à Dents, Main Street, Norwich, Vt.

Texas chef Barry Snyder and his wife Claire gave up an innkeeping stint at the Parker House in nearby Quechee to open their own restaurant. When the former Carpenter Street Restaurant became available in 1990, they jumped at the chance to take over. Knowing diners have been applauding their fare and sense of culinary adventure ever since.

Both Culinary Institute of America graduates, the Snyders cook in the classic French style and change their short, contemporary menu every few weeks. They're known for their monthly wine theme dinners and, at our latest visit, had just completed a series of Taste of the City dinners, based on Barry's adaptations of his solitary dining forays at some of New York's finest restaurants. After which he concluded, "The quality of food we present here is equal to that of New York City. It's just that our presentations are not as complicated, with only two of us in the kitchen."

Dinner is prix-fixe, $39 for three courses plus a substantial complimentary hors d'oeuvre, a half-portion of, say, smoked salmon with caramelized onion salad. Appetizer choices range from cream of chestnut soup with chive blossoms to Chilean sea bass with saffron risotto and lemon-thyme sauce. Typical main courses are grilled Norwegian salmon on angel-hair pasta with three sauces, loin steak of pork "African" with curried couscous and apple chutney, breast of guinea hen with pinot noir sauce, and lamb chops with cabernet sauce.

With Texas bravado, Barry calls his wife's dessert tarts the best around. Other possibilities could be coconut-chocolate torte with mango puree, apple tarte tatin with crème anglaise, and griotte sorbet in an almond tuile with a kiwi-lime coulis. A little tray of hand-dipped or molded chocolates arrives with coffee.

All this is served in three dining rooms. A beautiful oak bar flanks a more casual, post and beam, cafe-style dining area with high-back, windsor-style chairs. Two smaller dining rooms are more formal, the Burgundy Room outfitted in floral wallpaper and the Bordeaux hung with royal purple swags and jabots. The latter harbors a couple of romantic recessed alcoves, barely big enough for two. The tables are set with crystal from Judot, Villeroy & Boch china and three forks at each place, face down.

We got a taste of this talented pair's work a few years ago at lunch, which since has been discontinued. Three of us enjoyed various soups – a velvety puree of butternut squash with dill chantilly, an intense wild-mushroom broth with porcini and shiitakes, and the winner, a hearty zuppa di pasta e fagioli. Then we tackled a charcuterie plate with pâté and goat cheese, breaded salmon anglaise with herb vinaigrette, and estockificada, a bouillabaisse of shrimp, scallops and mahi-mahi on a plate with saffron sauce and a bowl of broth topped by garlic toast on the side. Salads of exotic greens followed, a bit spare but painstakingly prepared. The meal whetted our appetites to return for dinner.

Oh yes, the French name? Loosely translated, Barry says, it means "as scarce as hen's teeth." It's their way of noting that the best things in life, at least in terms of food and wine, are rare indeed.

(802) 649-2922. Dinner, nightly, from 6.

The Prince and the Pauper, 24 Elm St., Woodstock, Vt.

Walk up the brick walkway alongside one of the area's oldest buildings, open the green door, pass the pubby bar and enter the L-shaped dining room. You're in what is considered to be the best restaurant in Woodstock proper.

Oil lanterns cast shadows on beamed ceilings and white-clothed tables are surrounded by Hitchcock chairs or tucked away in high, dark wood booths, the ultimate in privacy. Antique prints decorate the white walls, one of which has a shelf of old books.

Chef-owner Chris Balcer calls his cuisine "creative contemporary" with French, continental and international accents. The prix-fixe menu ($34, for appetizer, salad and main course) changes nightly. The pasta of the day could be with scallops, shrimp and sundried tomatoes; the soup, charred carrot garnished with crème fraîche, and the pâté, Vermont pheasant teamed with orange chutney. Conch fritters, Vietnamese spring rolls and homemade lamb sausage in puff pastry might be other appetizers.

Entrées at our last visit included grilled swordfish with mango-horseradish sauce, roast duckling with a sauce of kiwi and Meyers's rum, filet mignon au poivre and the house specialty, boneless rack of lamb baked in puff pastry with spinach and duxelles.

Spend some time reviewing the interesting wine list (strong on California chardonnays and cabernets), priced from the high teens to more than $100 for Château Lafite. But save room for dessert – maybe a fabulous raspberry tart with white chocolate mousse served with raspberry-cabernet wine sauce, pumpkin cheesecake with pecan topping, walnut-apricot linzertorte or a homemade sorbet like Jack Daniels-chocolate chip. Finish with espresso, cappuccino or an international coffee.

A bistro menu is available in the elegant bar. It offers half a dozen entrées (including perhaps grilled salmon with Thai ginger sauce, sirloin strip steak or Maine crab cakes) for $11.95 to $15.95. Also served here are five kinds of hearth-baked pizzas for $9.95.

(802) 457-1818. Dinner nightly, 6 to 9 or 9:30; bistro menu, 5 to 10 or 11.

Arched windows give diners view of waterfall outside Simon Pearce Restaurant.

Simon Pearce Restaurant, The Mill, Quechee, Vt.

Irish glass-blower Simon Pearce's intriguing mill complex includes an exceptional restaurant serving Irish and regional Vermont specialties in a smashing setting beside the Ottauquechee River. We think the enclosed terrace with retractable windows almost over the waterfall is great for lunch, and the Pennsylvania friends to whom we recommended the restaurant liked it so much they took relatives back the next day. Countless others have been directed here and, captivated by the magic of a special place, now make it a point to stop for a meal whenever they're in the vicinity.

The interior dining areas, vastly expanded since its opening, reflect the exquisite taste of the entire complex. Sturdy ash chairs are at well-spaced wood tables outfitted with small woven mats by day and dressed with white linens at night. The heavy glassware and the deep brown and white china are made by Simon Pearce and his family at the mill. Plants, dried flowers in baskets and antique quilts lend a soft counterpoint to the brick walls, bare floors and expansive windows.

The chefs train at Ballymaloe in Ireland, and they import flour from Ireland to make their great Irish soda bread and Ballymaloe brown bread. They change the menu periodically, but there are always specialties like beef and Guinness stew (which we tried at lunch – for $9.25, a generous serving of fork-tender beef and vegetables, plus a small side salad of julienned vegetables). We also liked a pasta salad ($7.75) heaped with vegetables and a superior basil-parmesan dressing. One of us nearly always orders the mouth-watering house-smoked coho salmon. For dessert, the famed walnut meringue with strawberry sauce and a mountain of whipped cream is the crowning glory. A menu fixture, it's crisp and crunchy, and melts in the mouth. Irish apple cake and cappuccino cheesecake are other possibilities.

Candlelight dinners might start with Maine crab cakes with rouille, marinated grilled chicken with a spicy peanut sauce or grilled portobello mushrooms with shaved parmigiana, fennel and watercress. Entrées run from $15.50 for grilled breast of free-range chicken on field greens to $21 for sesame-seared tuna with noodle cakes, wasabi and pickled ginger. Other choices might be chile-cured pork tenderloin with corn and black bean salsa, roasted duck with mango chutney, Tuscan grilled sirloin steak with rosemary and arugula, and grilled leg of lamb with garlic, rosemary and balsamic vinaigrette

The wine list printed on the menus, short but choice, is supplemented by a longer list priced from $16 to $48. Naturally, you can get beers and ales from the British Isles.

In 1997, Simon Pearce was expanding its nearby Windsor manufacturing facility to include a restaurant in a renovated dairy barn.

(802) 295-1470. Lunch daily, 11:30 to 2:45; dinner nightly, 6 to 9.

More Dining Choices

Sweet Tomatoes Trattoria, 1 Court St., Lebanon, N.H.

Pizzas from a wood-burning oven, pastas, and entrées from a wood and char-coal grill at wallet-pleasing prices. These are the hallmarks of a sleek but casual, New Yorkish place that quickly became the dining sensation of the Upper Valley, despite an unlikely location fronting the green in oft-overlooked Lebanon.

Occupying the key front-corner space of a new downtown commercial complex, this is the brainchild of James Reiman, who was formerly at the Prince and the Pauper and opened Spooner's in Woodstock, and Robert Meyers, a builder whose experience was pivotal in putting the space together. And it's quite a space. Seats for 100 are at tables placed well apart under mod California spotlights, their neon-like rims echoing the neon encircling the exposed metal grid beneath a high black ceiling. A black and white tiled floor, a few indoor trees, a mural along one wall, a tin mobile and plants hanging on pillars complete the minimalist decor.

Excitement is provided by the totally open kitchen, where the owners sometimes join the cooks at the grills, wood-burning oven and work counters amidst garlic ropes hanging from on high. Theirs is what Robert calls "strictly ethnic Italian cooking, priced for the 1990s." You'll find pastas ($6.95 to $10.95) like linguini with shrimp and sweet peas or fusilli with chicken and artichoke hearts and pizzas ($7.95 to $8.95) from the namesake sweet tomato pie to one with fresh clams, all accessorized with mozzarella, olive oil and garlic.

Entrées ($8.75 to $10.95) include grilled chicken with herbs, skewers of marinated lamb, mixed grill, rainbow trout stuffed with bay shrimp and crabmeat, and, our choice, grilled swordfish with basil pesto, served with a side salad of red potatoes, sweet peas, leeks, garlic and extra-virgin olive oil.

You can sample most of the menu at lunchtime, when prices are in the rock-bottom $4 to $6 range. We thoroughly enjoyed the cavatappi with roasted chicken, plum tomatoes and arugula, a memorable concoction served with two slices of herbed sourdough bread and cheese sprinkled liberally from a hand grater. The enormous clam pizza, its thin crackly crust weighted down with clams and mozzarella, proved too much to eat. We had to forego the delectable desserts, which included chocolate-espresso cake, cannolis and dacquoise.

Success here led the partners to open carbon copies in downtown Burlington and Rutland, Vt.

(603) 448-1711. Lunch, Monday-Friday 11:30 to 2; dinner, Tuesday-Sunday 5 to 9 or 9:30.

Cafe Buon Gustaio, 72 South Main St., Hanover, N.H.

The owners of Peter Christian's restaurants (Hanover and New London) teamed up with a chef from Harvest in Cambridge to open this engaging Italian bistro. Murray and Karen Washburn transformed a decrepit eatery into a picture-pretty room of intimate tables outfitted with white linens, carafes of alstroemeria and votive candles. A bottle of extra-virgin olive oil is on every table, ready to pour into a saucer for dipping the crusty Tuscan bread. Candles flicker in the wall sconces, and tiny white lights twinkle on the beams in the adjacent bar.

The restaurant lives up to its name, which means "good eats." The menu changes nightly and is categorized by appetizers, salads, pastas, pizzettas and entrées.

You might start with pan-fried polenta with grilled wild boar sausage, rabbit stew or sautéed eggplant with tomatoes, pancetta and chèvre. Pizzettas ($8 to $10) could include sundried tomatoes with roasted peppers and brie or grilled chicken with cilantro pesto and button mushrooms. How about a calzone of pepperoni, salami, tomatoes, onions and mozzarella?

Expect pasta dishes ($12 to $14) like farfalle with chicken and spinach in fontina cream sauce, linguini with shrimp and leeks, and cannelloni of crabmeat, red and green peppers, mushrooms and ricotta. Typical entrées ($18 to $19) are grilled red snapper with lemon-garlic vinaigrette and baby greens, sautéed veal medallions with porcini-marsala cream sauce and asparagus, and grilled beef tenderloin with a fennel mushroom sauce and roasted garlic. Desserts include toffee-lime tart, napoleons and chocolate lover's cake topped with chocolate-dipped strawberries.

(603) 643-5711. Dinner, Tuesday-Saturday 5:30 to 9 or 9:30.

Wild Grass, Gallery Place, Route 4, Woodstock, Vt.

Multi-regional cuisine – from Pacific Rim to island jerk – is offered by Steve and Gail Buckley at this new place fashioned from the former Rachel's Deli on the lower level of a gallery/office complex. The chef is Paul "Shultz" Langhans, who attracted a wide local following at Simon Pearce and The Prince and the Pauper before leaving for the Pacific Northwest, only to be enticed back in 1996 for this venture.

The cream-colored decor with hunter green and mauve accents is sleek yet simple. Bare pine tables seat 85 people inside an open dining room and bar, with more seating outside on a seasonal terrace beside Route 4.

The short dinner menu ranges widely from $10.75 for jerk chicken with sweet potato puree and wilted greens to $14.25 for cioppino served over linguini with garlic-rubbed crostini. Among the choices: peppered grilled ahi tuna on spicy buckwheat soba noodles, roasted pork loin marinated in juniper berries and cumin, and grilled adobo-rubbed lamb with black bean cakes and plantain fritters. Starters might be crispy sage leaves with assorted dipping sauces, carpaccio with arugula, parmesan and roasted shallot vinaigrette, and scallops wrapped in smoked salmon with wasabi cream sauce.

Desserts include pear galette with crème anglaise, chocolate ganache with espresso sauce and locally produced Blue Moon sorbets.

(802) 457-1917. Dinner nightly, 5:30 to 9:30.

Bentleys, 3 Elm St., Woodstock, Vt.

A rather funky and casual spot at the prime corner in Woodstock, Bentley's caters to every taste at every hour. It serves lunch, dinner and Sunday brunch, has dancing on weekends, and there's a great bar to visit in cold weather for a hot buttered rum or a Bentley burner (hot apple cider, ginger, cinnamon and brandy).

On two levels with bentwood chairs, jungles of plants and cozy alcoves with Victorian sofas, it offers at lunch all kinds of burgers, sandwiches (some in croissants), chili, Mexican dishes and salads in the $4.95 to $8.95 range. We enjoyed torta rustica, a hot Italian puff pastry filled with prosciutto, mozzarella and marinated vegetables, and a fluffy quiche with turkey, mushrooms and snow peas, both accompanied by side salads. For dessert, a delicate chocolate mousse cake with layers of meringue was served with good Green Mountain coffee in clear glass cups.

At brunch, try a bellini (champagne with the essence of peaches) before eggs benedict, a woodlands frittata of wild mushrooms and shallots, or salade niçoise.

Dinners are priced from $12.95 for pasta athena to $19.50 for Jack Daniels strip steak, flamed tableside, with hand-cut french fries. Choices include chicken and scampi pescatore, sautéed trout with toasted almonds and champagne sauce, maple-mustard chicken and roasted duckling with chambord-black raspberry glaze.

Partners Bill Decklebaum and David Creech also run **FireStones,** featuring a wood-fired oven, in Waterman Place at Quechee. Recently transformed from their former Rosalita's, a Southwestern bar and grill, this offers flatbreads, pastas and grills ($13.95 to $17.95) in an Adirondack lodge atmosphere.

(802) 457-3232. Lunch, daily 11:30 to 3 (late lunch menu, 3 to 5); dinner, 5 to 9:30 or 10; Sunday brunch, 11 to 3.

Dining and Lodging

Twin Farms, Barnard, Vt. 05031.

The secluded farm once owned by writers Sinclair Lewis and Dorothy Thompson is now the crème de la crème of small, luxury country hotels, ranked among the finest in the world. One of a kind, it offers six suites and eight cottages, superb dining and a full-time staff of 30 to pamper 28 guests.

The tab? A cool $700 to $1,500 a night for two, including meals, drinks and recreational activities, but not tax or service charge. The clientele? A moneyed international crowd that likes to travel. Twin Farms is deluxe, of course, but understated and not at all ostentatious – not nearly as drop-dead showy as one might expect. "The idea is you're a guest at somebody's country estate for the weekend," says Beverley Matthews, innkeeper with her husband Shaun, both of whom are British and who come with impeccable resort-management credentials.

The idea evolved after the Twigg-Smith family of Honolulu acquired the estate's main Sonnenberg Haus and ski area as a vacation home in 1974. In 1989, Laila and Thurston Twigg-Smith acquired the other half of Twin Farms, returning the estate to its original 235 acres. Son Thurston (Koke) Twigg-Smith Jr. and his wife Andrea, twenty-year residents of Barnard, managed the development phase of Twin Farms. Andrea and Ibby Jenkins of Woodstock, Koke's sister, assisted with the interior design and product selection.

Their resources and taste show throughout the property, from the electronically operated gates at the entrance to the fully equipped fitness center and separate Japanese furo soaking tub beneath a pond-side pub reached by a covered bridge. In the main house, three living rooms, each bigger than the last, unfold as the innkeepers welcome their guests. One with a vaulted ceiling opens onto a neat

Vaulted ceiling, chandeliers and fireplaces enhance dining room at Twin Farms.

little library loft and soaring windows gazing onto a 30-mile view toward Mount Ascutney. Decor is elegantly rustic and utterly comfortable.

Upstairs are four bedrooms bearing some of the Twin Farms trademarks: plump kingsize feather beds, tiled fireplaces, comfortable sitting areas, fabulous folk art and contemporary paintings, TV/VCR/stereos, tea trays with a coffee press and Kona coffees from the family-owned corporation, twin sinks in the bathrooms, baskets of all-natural toiletries, and unbleached and undyed cotton towels. They impart a feeling of elegant antiquity, but come with every convenience of the perfect home away from home.

Less antiquity and even more convenience are found in the newly built stone and wood guest cottages, each with at least one fireplace, a screened porch or terrace, a twig-sided carport and its own private place in the landscape. The Perch, for instance, is situated above a small stream and beaver pond. It harbors luxuriant seating around the fireplace, a desk, a dining area, a refrigerator with ice-maker, a bed recessed in an alcove and shielded by a hand-carved arch of wooden roping, a wicker-filled porch where a wood sculpture of a shark hangs overhead, and a bathroom with a copper tub the size of a small pool and a separate shower stall, both with windows to the outdoors.

Good food and drink (from well-stocked, help-yourself bars) are among Twin Farms strong points. Guests meet at 7 o'clock for cocktails with one or the other of the Matthewses in a changing venue – perhaps the wine cellar, one of the living rooms or, the night before our first visit, in the Studio, the largest cottage. A set, four-course dinner is served at 8 in a baronial dining hall with vaulted ceiling and fieldstone fireplaces at either end. Tables for two are flanked by luxurious bent hickory and Guatemalan leather chairs. Although the hefty 32-page, four-color book that serves as the inn's brochure initially noted that guests "are often inspired to dress for dinner," the reality is that more casual attire is encouraged.

The talented chef is Neil Wigglesworth, who came from The Point on Saranac Lake in the Adirondacks, a smaller but similarly grand inn that some think has been upstaged by Twin Farms. A typical dinner might start with medallions of lobster with avocado relish and angel-hair pasta, followed by warm red cabbage salad with slices of smoked chicken. The main course could be veal mignon with timbales of wild rice and xeres sauce, and dessert, fresh figs with beummes de venese ice cream and peach-caramel sauce. Coffee, cheeses and a glass of aged port might round out the evening.

A visit to the glittering new professional kitchen is instructive – and Neil says he likes to have guests in to "talk and dabble." We enjoyed seeing the three patterns of Wedgwood china (one each for breakfast, lunch and dinner), the pantry wall of table linens in every color and material (there were about 25 sets of placemats and it was like being inside a well-stocked linen shop), the fiestaware used exclusively for picnics, the fine sterling-silver pieces, the pottery from Miranda Thomas and the glassware from Simon Pearce.

Breakfast is continental if taken in the guest rooms and cooked to order in the dining room from a small menu – raspberry pancakes or eggs benedict with lobster the day we visited. The property is a registered American natural organic farm, and Neil and his kitchen staff of five make their own oils, vinegars, breads and preserves, some from raspberry bushes planted by Dorothy Thompson 60 years earlier.

Lunch is a movable feast, depending on the day and guests' inclinations. It could be a sit-down meal in the dining room, a picnic anywhere, or a barbecue beside the inn's seven-acre trout pond or at its own ski area, where there's never a lineup for the pomalift. Afternoon tea is a presentation worthy of the Ritz, complete, perhaps, with little gold leaves on one of the five kinds of tea pastries.

The pub, incidentally, is nearly a museum piece with its collection of beer bottles from around the world. Beer-bottle caps cover the light shades over the billiards table, outline the mirror and sconces above the fireplace, and cover the candlesticks on the mantel. Even a pub chair is dressed in beer caps – a dramatic piece of pop art from the Twigg-Smiths' renowned art collection. Such are some of the delights and surprises encountered by guests at Twin Farms.

(802) 234-9999 or (800) 894-6327. Fax (802) 234-9990. Doubles, $700 and $850; cottages, $1,050 and $1,500. All-inclusive, except for 15 percent service charge and 8 percent state tax. Two-night minimum on weekends, three nights on holidays.

Woodstock Inn and Resort, 14 The Green, Woodstock, Vt. 05091.

Sitting majestically back from the village green, the three-story, Vermont-white Woodstock Inn built by Rockresorts in 1969 replaces an older inn that was torn down. The lobby is warmed by a ten-foot-high stone fireplace, where in chilly weather guests congregate on sofas in front of the always-burning fire. Later renovations and additions created a number of other cozy sitting areas, including an inviting library for card-playing and a rear wicker room where afternoon tea and cookies are served.

The 144 luxurious guest rooms are among the most comfortable in which we have stayed, with peppy color schemes, handmade quilts on the beds, upholstered chairs, TV sets, three-way reading lights, and large bathrooms and closets. Nightly

Spring flowers brighten entrance to Woodstock Inn and Resort.

turndown service brings chocolates and fresh, fluffy towels. Paintings and photographs of local scenes decorate the walls. The latest addition is the Tavern Wing, designed as three attached townhouses. It features 34 deluxe rooms with built-in bookcases and desks, fine cabinet work, mini-refrigerators, safes and double marble vanities in the bathrooms. Many come with fireplaces, and three have sitting-room porches overlooking the putting green.

Besides an eighteen-hole golf course, ten tennis courts, an outdoor pool and an indoor sports center, hundreds of acres of forests managed by the inn are available to guests for hiking, horseback riding and cross-country skiing. The woods also contain troves of fiddlehead ferns, morels and wild leeks, which the chef incorporates into his menus in season.

The glamorous main dining room is characterized by pillars, graceful curves and large windows onto a spacious outdoor terrace overlooking the putting green and gardens. Vases of lavish flower arrangements, wine glasses and the inn's own monogrammed, green-rimmed china sparkle on crisp white linens. Off each side of the main room are smaller, more intimate dining areas.

Dinner entrées are priced from $19.95 for Atlantic salmon or roasted chicken to $26.95 for Vermont rack of lamb. Choices range from pan-seared sea scallops with madras curry, wilted spinach, pappadums and grilled bananas to provimi veal tenderloin with Maine crabmeat, asparagus and black peppercorn hollandaise. Seasonal specialties include an appetizer of Green Mountain fiddlehead terrine, entrées of sautéed veal with Vermont cheddar cheese and fresh morels and roast loin of pork glazed in maple syrup with apple-prune stuffing, as well as a dessert of flambéed pineapple with maple syrup.

The elaborate Sunday buffet brunch, a good value at $22.95, is enormously popular.

You can dine well and quite reasonably in the **Eagle Cafe,** transformed from the old coffee shop and more attractive than most in both decor and fare. At lunch

($6.95 to $9.25), we've enjoyed interesting salads – chef's, grilled steak, chilled bouillabaisse and seared tuna with wild rice – and, most recently, the smoked chicken and green onion quesadillas and a grilled chicken sandwich with melted jack, roasted peppers and herbed mayonnaise on toasted focaccia, a knife-and-fork affair accompanied by assertively seasoned fries. The varied dinner menu repeats some of the lunch offerings and adds entrées from $11.95 for beef or chicken satay to $19.95 for black angus strip steak.

Linger with an after-dinner drink in the sophisticated **Richardson's Tavern,** as urbane a night spot as you'll find in Vermont.

(802) 457-1100 or (800) 448-7900. Fax (802) 457-6699. Doubles, $149 to $285, EP. Lunch, 11:30 to 2; dinner, 6 to 9, jackets requested; Sunday brunch, 11 to 1:30.

The Hanover Inn, Main Street, Box 151, Hanover, N.H. 03755.

As its advertising claims, this venerable inn is really a "small, fine hotel." Facing the Dartmouth College green, the five-story, 19th-century brick structure contains

92 Colonial-style rooms decorated with period furniture, handmade lampshades and eiderdown comforters.

The older East Wing has been remodeled to make the rooms larger and more comfortable, like those of the West Wing. An expanded lobby and a new front entrance are the latest in a continuing series of renovations that have helped make the inn the area's only four-diamond hotel and restaurant.

Dining is in the elegant Daniel Webster Room or the more intimate **Ivy Grill,** a most New Yorkish-looking spot. The two-level grill has a sleek contemporary style with lacquered chairs, murals of seasonal Dartmouth scenes, huge clay pots spilling over with ivy and Vermont-made hanging lamps.

Daniel Webster Room at Hanover Inn.

Executive chef Michael Gray, whose credentials include the old Rarities in Cambridge and Seasons in Boston, oversees a menu of contemporary American cuisine, described as "simply prepared but with adventurous twists."

For dinner in the Ivy Grill, start with Tuscan antipasto, steamed dim sum with Thai peanut sauce or Thai-spiced duck satay on grilled vegetable salad. Entrées ($12.50 to $17.50) include lobster and crab ravioli with sweet garlic butter, five-spice Chinese pork with hoisin sauce and fried rice, and grilled venison paillards with hunter's sauce. Desserts could be white chocolate-cashew cheesecake and apple crisp with whipped cream..

More formal meals are served in the gracious, gray and white **Daniel Webster Room,** a vast space in the Georgian style with potted palms, brass chandeliers and changing food and wine displays at the entry. Typical among dinner entrées ($19 to $26) are yellowfin tuna with caramelized onions and toasted pinenuts, crispy five-spice sweetbreads with an oriental vegetable slaw, olive-crusted rack of lamb with roma tomatoes and garlic-whipped potatoes, and grilled medallions of venison

Sideboard is laden with goodies at Jackson House Inn at Woodstock.

with a wild rice cake. Honored by Wine Spectator, the wine list is among New Hampshire's more extensive. The room also hosts a series of wine dinners featuring visiting chefs every other month.

In summer, meals from both restaurants are available on a shady outdoor terrace overlooking the Dartmouth green. Canvas umbrellas, planters and tiny white lights in the trees make it a most engaging spot.

(603) 643-4300 or (800) 443-7024. Fax (603) 646-3744. Daniel Webster Room, lunch, Monday-Friday 11:30 to 1:30; dinner, Tuesday-Saturday 6 to 9; Sunday, brunch 11 to 1:30. Ivy Grill, open Monday-Saturday 11:30 to 10, Sunday 1:30 to 10. Doubles, $207; suites, $277.

The Jackson House Inn at Woodstock, 37 Route 4 West, Woodstock 05091.

It's hard to tell what we like best about the Jackson House: the marvelous guest rooms worthy of coverage in an antiques magazine, the sumptuous breakfasts, or the wine and champagne with fancy hors d'oeuvres in the early evenings.

We didn't think a B&B could get much better than this three-story Victorian house on three acres of beautiful grounds west of the village. But new owners Juan and Gloria Florin, former Argentineans by way of Connecticut, had other plans. Taking over in 1997, they were adding four luxury suites, a 45-seat dining room open to the public, and a level of service for potential affiliation with Relais & Chateaux. "We're not going to change the inn," Juan emphasized. "We're just going to add to it."

The Florins acquired a going concern with nine guest rooms and two suites, a distinctive gourmet emphasis, a basement exercise facility, and lavish lawns and gardens, complete with a stream and pond with a little beach of crushed white marble. Each guest room is eclectically furnished with such delights as an 1860 cannonball post bed, a Casablanca ceiling fan, antique brass lamps on either side of the bathroom mirror, a marble-topped bedside table, a night table fashioned from an old sewing stand of tiger maple, steam radiators painted gold and handmade afghans coordinated to each room's colors. Decor varies from French Empire to British Oriental to old New England.

Most prized are two third-floor suites, about twice the size of the other rooms. Both contain queensize cherry sleigh beds, Italian marble baths and french doors onto a rear deck overlooking the gardens in back. We found plenty of room here to spread out, what with a leather sofa and an upholstered wing chair, plus two lounge chairs on the deck beyond. The mirrored, marble bathroom sparkled as if it had never before been used – an attribute that fellow guests agreed was characteristic of this special place.

The Florins were building a side carriage house to add four larger suites with whirlpool tubs and wood stoves. Another addition was under construction in the rear for a dining room to offer dinner to inn guests and the public. Juan was looking to hire a top chef to provide classic French cuisine, with complete dinners in the $50 range. Meanwhile, he was continuing the Jackson House tradition of serving champagne or wine and a buffet of hors d'oeuvres in the elegant front parlor. He also was hiring a pastry chef to add to the extravagant breakfast repertoire. The first course might be baked apple with mincemeat in rum and wine. Croissants and muffins come next. Poached eggs on dill biscuits with smoked salmon and hollandaise sauce highlighted one of our best breakfasts ever.

(802) 457-2065 or (800) 448-1890. Fax (802) 457-9290. Dinner by reservation, nightly 6 to 9. Doubles, $150 to $165; suites, $195 and $250.

Lodging

The Maple Leaf Inn, Route 12, Box 273, Barnard, Vt. 05031.

Guests are showered with hospitality at this inn built from scratch by Texans Gary and Janet Robison. They couldn't find the perfect old New England inn in their search among existing buildings. So they built it – a brand new, meant-to-look-old Victorian structure with the requisite gingerbread and gazebo – in a clearing amid sixteen acres of maples and birches in tiny Barnard.

Crackers and a homemade Texas chili cheese log – incorporating pecans grown in her yard by Gary's aunt and sent as "a CARE package from home" – are served arriving guests on the wraparound front porch with its corner gazebo and Tennessee oak rockers, or inside in the library or fireplaced parlor. Light suppers of soup, bread, salad and dessert are served by request in winter. Two chocolates are placed at bedside at nightly turndown, and a personalized maple leaf wood Christmas ornament is hung on the door knob. And effervescent Janet is apt to send you on your way with a farewell package of pumpkin bread or muffins for midday sustenance. Between arrival and departure, guests are cosseted with unusual warmth and creature comforts, the latter the result of "being able to build what we wanted from the ground up," in Gary's words.

Most of the five luxurious bedrooms are positioned to have windows on three sides. All have modern baths (four with whirlpool tubs), kingsize beds, wood-burning fireplaces with antique mantels, sitting areas with swivel club chairs, TV/VCRs secreted in the armoires, ceiling fans and closets. Janet spent a week in each room doing the remarkable hand stenciling. She stenciled an elaborate winter village over the fireplace and around the doors and windows in the Winter Haven room in which we stayed. Birds are the stenciling theme in the Spring Hollow Room; foliage the theme in Autumn Woods.

The Robisons' attention to detail continues throughout, from the maple leaf engraved in the window of the front door to the "pasta-hair angels" that Janet

Maple Leaf Inn was built from scratch to resemble an old New England Victorian inn.

fashioned from angel-hair pasta and placed atop bud vases as centerpieces in the dining room. The love stamps that she needlepointed and framed on the dining-room walls were anniversary gifts to Gary and, by extension, to their guests, who take breakfast by candlelight at individual tables near the fireplace.

And what a breakfast! Ours began with buttermilk scones garnished with flowers. The accompanying orange and cranberry-apple butters were shaped like maple leaves, and the preserves were presented in leaf dishes. The fruit course was sautéed bananas with Ben & Jerry's ice cream, an adaptation of bananas foster at Brennan's in New Orleans. The main event was stuffed french toast with peach preserves and cream cheese, garnished with nasturtiums.

For 1997, the Robisons added two more rooms on their third floor, each with king bed, sitting area and two-person soaking tubs. They carry lower price tags, so getaway couples on tighter budgets may also enjoy the hosts' abundant hospitality. *(802) 234-5342 or (800) 516-2753. Doubles, $100 to $160.*

The Charleston House, 21 Pleasant St., Woodstock, Vt. 05091.

Barbara and Bill Hough from Maryland run this handsome, 1835 Greek Revival townhouse, named for the hometown of its former owner. Although it's listed in the National Register of Historic Places and is elegantly furnished with period antiques and an extensive selection of art and oriental rugs, the Houghs don't consider their B&B a museum piece. Barbara, a former flight attendant, and Bill, a sales and marketing executive, are quite outgoing, and are now back on the scene after a period of semi-retirement when others ran the B&B for them.

Back with upgrades, we hasten to add. At our latest visit, the Houghs were building a substantial addition in back to produce two deluxe guest rooms with jacuzzi tubs, fireplaces and TVs. One has a queen bed; the other has a kingsize four-poster bed and its own patio – a gazebo in summer, convertible to a carport in winter. The Houghs also renovated the third floor to produce a suite with double shower, king bed and futon. Four other rooms on the second floor have queen beds and private baths.

Stunning floral arrangements and lovely needlepoint pillows adorn the dining room and the comfortable living room.

Breakfasts here are such an attraction that Barbara put together a cookbook of her recipes, called *Breakfast at Charleston House*. Among her specialties are puffed pancakes, "sort of like a popover and filled with fruit;" a cheese and grits soufflé, and Charleston strata, an egg dish with sausage and apples. Other favorites are chipped-beef eggs, California omelet, and macadamia-nut waffles with papaya and strawberries.

Bill laughs when he tells the story of a new B&B owner on Cape Cod. She was worried about what to serve for breakfast until a guest gave her Barbara's cookbook. Now, he says, her breakfasts are the talk of the Cape.

(802) 457-3843. Doubles, $110 to $175.

Ardmore Inn, 23 Pleasant St., Woodstock, Vt. 05091.

The guest book at this new B&B is full of raves about the breakfasts prepared by innkeeper/chef Giorgio Ortiz. Served at an English mahogany banquet table inlaid with rosewood and seating ten, the main dish might be pumpkin pancakes, stuffed french toast or vegetable frittata. His masterpiece is the "Woodstock Sunrise," flatbread bearing baked spiced eggs, Vermont cheddar, smoked apple sausage and asparagus with béarnaise sauce. It's designed to look like a sunrise.

In the afternoon, tea biscuits and cheesecake are offered with tea and cider on the rear screened veranda, richly furnished in wicker and oriental rugs.

The guests' raves also cite the hospitality dispensed by Giorgio and Bill Gallagher, owner of the impressive white Georgian Greek Revival house that for years was the home of the well-known F.H. Gillingham family. Father Bill, as he's known to Woodstockers, bought the house with its distinguished palladian windows as "a nice place for my aunts and me" when he retires from Our Lady of Snows church across the street. He called it Ardmore, which means "Great House" in the Irish tradition.

In his booming baritone voice, the ebullient priest likes to point out prized features of the house, including the etched glass in the solid mahogany front door, the circular moldings around the original light fixtures on the ceilings and the recessed pocket windows screened with Irish lace curtains in the living room. The five bedrooms, all with small private baths, are painted in light pastel colors. "That's my grandmother's bed," says Bill of the carved black walnut headboard in the mint-green front bedroom, which is accented with Waverly fabrics and hand-hooked area rugs. "My father was in the marble business," so the bathroom floors are enhanced with marble. The biggest bedroom is in the rear. Called Tarma, Irish for sanctuary, it lives up to its name with a kingsize bed, a loveseat facing a marble coffee table and guardian angels as night lights. The inn's own toiletries are placed in little white baskets.

In 1996, Bill added a couple of fireplaces and a jacuzzi to his guest-room repertoire.

(802) 457-3887 or (800) 497-9652. Fax (802) 457-9006. Doubles, $110 to $150.

Quechee Bed & Breakfast, Route 4, Quechee, Vt. 05059.

From the front of this rambling 1795 Colonial, you'd never guess that the back is atop a cliff looking down onto the Ottauquechee River, with a wide sloping side lawn and a wraparound veranda taking full advantage. Susan and Ken Kaduboski, transplanted Boston accountants, converted it into a luxurious B&B, offering eight spacious, air-conditioned bedrooms with private baths.

Guests congregate in a large living/dining area with sofas gathered around a huge brick and granite fireplace, a television set and individual breakfast tables topped with dusky rose clothes and potted flowers. An interesting art collection is on display, and a large cactus stands in one corner.

A smaller parlor leads through heavy doors into the original house, where the guest quarters are nicely secluded and private. Three rooms are on the first floor and five on the second, including two with beamed, vaulted ceilings. Each is furnished with king or queensize beds (one has twin mahogany sleigh beds), antique dressers, two wing chairs, large baths with colorful towels, and decorative touches like swags and stenciled lamp shades.

Susan serves a full breakfast starting with juices, baked apple or broiled grapefruit, and homemade Swedish breads with different jams. The main dish at our latest visit was scrambled eggs with Vermont cheddar and chives from the garden. Other favorites are apple pancakes and french toast stuffed with cream cheese and walnuts. *(802) 295-1776. Doubles, $109 to $139.*

Gourmet Treats

The Woodstock area has a couple of good bakeries as well as two excellent farm markets. **Dunham Hill Bakery,** 61 Central St., is where local folks go for sensational baked goods – anything from mocha torte to ganache cake to apple turnovers. You also can get a few breakfast and lunch items, the latter priced from $3.75 to $5.75. The sandwiches are fine, but the bowl of cream of potato and leek soup was so lukewarm we had to ask that it be reheated. **Chumley's Bakery** at 9 Main St., Quechee, right across the street from Simon Pierce, is a good place to pick up a sandwich. We liked one of lemon-pepper chicken and hickory ham with melted provolone and tomato, served on a basil roll with tomato and pepper-parmesan dressing. Or you could get an apple-walnut roll, a raspberry bear claw, or some of the colorful icebox cookies. There are a few tables where you can eat, or take out to have by the Quechee River.

Bet you've never heard the strains of Vivaldi's "Four Seasons" emanating from a farm stand. We did at **The Green Market,** Route 4, Quechee, a farm stand extraordinaire. Here is a trove of produce, coffee beans, specialty foods, breads, cheeses, clay pots and bird houses, to name a few. At our latest visit, it had a traffic-stopping lineup of wooden cows grazing along the crest of the hillside. Not the usual transient farmers' market, the **Woodstock Farmers Market,** west of the village, is a permanent fixture where you can find not only fruits and vegetables but Vermont food products, baked goods, seafood, deli sandwiches and more.

For your morning coffee fix, head for **The Caffé Mill,** 47 Central, a laid-back place beside Kedron Brook, which serves some of the best coffees and teas in town. Try the Vermont latte, flavored with maple syrup and topped with whipped cream and crystallized maple sugar. The place also dispenses baked goods (delicious scones, popovers and cookies) and light fare, including carrot soup with ginger and orange and Italian panini sandwiches.

Woodstock is chock full of elegant stores – just stroll along Central or Elm streets. The most fun shop of all is **F.H. Gillingham & Co.** at 16 Elm, a general store owned by the same family for more than a century and reputed to have been a favorite of Robert Frost's. It's now run by Jireh Swift Billings, great-grandson of the founder. His is an incredibly sophisticated and varied emporium, with everything from spa dessert sauces produced in nearby Norwich to trapunto aprons (embroidered with blue jays, rabbits or squirrels). Fresh fruits (even baskets of lichee nuts) and vegetables, wines, cooking equipment, Vermont cheeses, Bennington pottery, dozens of mustards, cloudberry preserves from Scandinavia, Black Jewel American sturgeon caviar – you want to cook with it? They probably have it.

Next door is **The Village Butcher** with wines, a deli and gourmet items. Across the street is **Bentleys Coffee Bar and Florist Shop,** which has lovely flowers and twelve flavors of cappuccino, which you can drink at little marble tables amid the plants. **Aubergine,** a good kitchenware shop, is a few doors away. You'll probably find a thermos of the day's coffee flavor to sample, as well as a whole lineup of jams, relishes and salsas to try on various crackers. We particularly like the majolica pottery here. If you're looking for natural foods, head for **18 Carrots,** a market with deli at 47 Pleasant St.

The historic **Taftsville Country Store,** an 1840 landmark in tiny Taftsville, has the requisite general store and post office in back. Up front are all kinds of upscale Vermont foodstuffs, including jams, chutneys, mustards, wines and maple syrups from South Woodstock. The selection of cheeses is exceptional, and the cheddars are cut to order off 38-pound wheels.

The old mill built in Quechee has been turned into a nationally known glassblowing center and shop known as **Simon Pearce.** Simon Pearce, the Irish glass maker, moved here in 1981. It's worth a visit just to see how space is used in his tremendous mill, but it's also fascinating to watch the glass blowers by the fiery furnaces on the ground floor. You can see the water roar over the dam outside from a floor-to-ceiling window on the second floor, and you can buy seconds of the handsome glass pieces, pottery and woolens from Ireland. The table settings are to be admired. Shop is open daily, 9 to 9.

In Hanover, hidden behind the Rosey Jekes clothing shop at 15 Lebanon St., is **Rosey's Cafe,** a European-style coffee emporium where eleven versions of grilled Italian panini (all $4.95) are dispensed at the counter. We liked the sound of the Provence (pepper brie and watercress on a baguette) and sampled some of the ginger cookies and cranberry-pistachio biscotti. Enjoy at one of the marble-top tables, the stuffed armchairs in the corner, or outside on a sunny patio.

Chez Françoise at 44-48 South Main St., Hanover, is a nifty patisserie named for the former owner, a Paris native, who sold to young Paris-trained baker Stephane Crocher and his American wife, Christine. Stephane's family had numerous bakeries in France, which explains his expertise in producing the two dozen individual-size pastries showcased in the front display case. The Crochers added a boulangerie and doubled the seating area, so now offer a variety of pâtés, cheeses, sandwiches and a small salad bar, to eat here or to go.

To our minds, the area's ultimate grocery store is the off-the-beaten-path **Hanover Consumer Co-op,** a consumer-owned supermarket at 45 South Park St. The selection of prepared foods is enormous, and we picked up the makings for an elaborate dinner to cook for our weekend hosts at a nearby lake.

Pristine white facade of The Equinox is symbolic of Southern Vermont.

Southern Vermont
Old Inns, New Style

As verdant as the Green Mountains and as New England as they come. That's the area from Dover to Dorset, names that have an English ring to them, but that are the heart of old New England – or is it old New England, new style?

The fairly broad area embraces such storybook Vermont towns as Wilmington, Newfane, Weston and Manchester. It ranges from unspoiled Dorset, a hamlet almost too quaint for words, to changing West Dover, where condominiums and resorts thrive in the shadow of Mount Snow ski area.

This is a land of mountains and lakes, ski and summer resorts and, because of its fortuitous location for four-season enjoyment within weekend commuting distance of major metropolitan areas, a center for fine inns and restaurants.

Some of the East's leading inns were established here before people elsewhere even thought of the idea. In an era in which new inns and B&Bs seem to be popping up everywhere, most of those featured here have been around a while, the better to have established themselves in the vanguard of lodging and culinary success.

The food here is far more than Vermont cheddar cheese and maple syrup, as adventuresome diners have known for the last twenty years or so. Many of the area's better dining rooms are found in its inns. Several country restaurants are dining destinations as well.

Dining and Lodging

The Inn at Sawmill Farm, Route 100, Box 367, West Dover 05356.

For a country inn, the Inn at Sawmill Farm is one of the more sophisticated and luxurious that we have seen. Owned by architect Rodney Williams, his interior-decorator wife Ione, daughter Bobbie Molitor and son Brill, who is the talented chef, it is the epitome of country elegance and a worthy member of Relais & Châteaux.

Admiring the old barn and farmhouse during ski expeditions to Mount Snow, the Williamses bought the property in 1967 and spent the next few years turning it into a decorator's dream.

The rates here are MAP and such that, for many, this is a special-occasion destination: up to $400 for suites with fireplaces in four buildings called cottages. However, the indulgences lavished in any of the twenty accommodations are considerable – queen and kingsize beds, comfortable upholstered chairs with good reading lights, little gold boxes of Lake Champlain Chocolates, good dinners, incredible breakfasts, even afternoon tea with nut bread and ginger cookies by the fire in the living room. Not to mention a splashy decor of color-coordinated fabric and chintz that nearly overwhelms in one inn room with busy pictures on the walls, but proves more restful in the outlying Spring House and Cider House. The ten outlying rooms come with fireplaces and three with jacuzzis.

The large brick fireplace in the cathedral-ceilinged living room, festooned with copper pots and utensils, is the focal point for guests who gather on chintz-covered sofas and wing chairs and read magazines that are spread out on a gigantic copper table. Other groupings are near the huge windows, through which you get a view of Mount Snow. Upstairs in a loft room are more sofas, an entire wall of books and the lone television set in the inn, which does not seem often to be in use.

The three attractive dining rooms display the owners' collection of folk art. One, off the living room, also has a cathedral ceiling, with large wrought-iron chandeliers and Queen Anne-style chairs contrasting delightfully with barnwood and fabric walls. We like best the Greenhouse Room in back, with its indoor garden and rose-papered and beamed ceiling. In winter, you almost think you're outside; in summer, it opens onto the pool area.

You can pop into the cozy bar between the dining rooms for a drink before dinner; crackers and cheese are set out then. The dining rooms at night are dim and romantic: tables are set with heavy silver, candles in pierced-silver lamp shades, napkins in silver napkin rings, fresh flowers and delicate, pink-edged floral china.

A large selection of appetizers and entrées awaits. For non-house guests, the former are priced from $9 to $13 for delicacies like a terrine of smoked salmon and spinach with anchovy butter, or a sauté of chicken livers with an onion brioche and a quail egg. The dozen entrées are priced from $27 for pan-seared salmon with saffron sauce or breast of chicken with Indonesian curry sauce to $32 for lobster savannah, grilled veal chop with rosemary sauce or steak au poivre.

Guests are served canapés and a basket of good hot rolls and crisp homemade melba toast. That will hold you while you pick a wine from Brill Williams's re-markable and quite costly wine compendium (selected annually by Wine Spectator as one of the 100 best in the country and ranked in the top five as winner of its Grand Award). The house wine is French, bottled specially for the inn, and the côtes du rhône rouge we tried has been acclaimed better than many a châteauneuf du pape. Prices rise steeply, with only a few in the high teens and twenties. Those with a special interest can descend to the wine cellars, where more than 900 selections and 36,000 bottles reside. Brill says he does this "more as a hobby than a business," but manages to sell $4,000 to $6,000 worth of wine a week.

We liked an appetizer of thinly sliced raw sirloin with a shallot and mustard sauce and the salads of crisp lettuce topped with blue cheese. Fresh rabbit chasseur and sautéed sweetbreads were hearty autumn dishes, and the garnish of french-fried parsley on the sweetbreads was both unusual and delicious. Creamed salsify and onion with sautéed cucumber, squash stuffed with pinenuts and maple syrup, and wild mushroom or spinach and tomato timbales might accompany the entrées, every presentation being different.

Main dining room at The Inn at Sawmill Farm is country elegant.

Game specialties – of which Brill says he is doing more than in the past – include pheasant, partridge and venison with a foie-gras sauce. A game consommé with diced smoked goose and marrow is sometimes on the fall soup list.

Dessert lovers will appreciate whiskey cake with grand marnier sauce, fresh strawberry tart or bananas romanoff. Coffee lovers will like the strong espresso or better-than-usual decaffeinated coffee served in a silver pot.

Breakfast lovers will be in their glory in the sun-drenched greenhouse, watching chickadees at the bird feeders and choosing from all kinds of fruits, oatmeal and fancy egg dishes (eggs buckingham is a wonderful mix of eggs, sautéed red and green peppers, onions and bacon seasoned with dijon mustard and worcestershire sauce, placed on an English muffin and topped with Vermont cheddar cheese and baked). Scrambled eggs might come with golden caviar, and poached eggs with grilled trout. Don't pass up the homemade tomato juice; thick and spicy, it serves as a base for the inn's peppy bloody marys.

(802) 464-8131. Fax (802) 464-1130. Dinner nightly by reservation, 6 to 9. Doubles, $340 to $400, MAP. Closed Easter to mid-May.

The Equinox, Route 7A, Manchester Village 05254.

In a class by itself is the grand old Equinox, a resort hotel dating to 1769 and renovated to the tune of $20 million in 1985 and another $12 million in 1992. The finishing touches were applied by a partnership whose majority owner is Guinness, the beer company that owns the noted Gleneagles Hotel in Scotland. The Equinox was closed for three months in 1992 to correct shortcomings in the previous renovation. This one, which really made a difference, involved all 141 guest rooms and eleven suites, a new lobby, a vastly expanded Marsh Tavern and the formal Colonnade dining room.

The classic, columned white hotel now opens into a world of lush comfort, starting with a dramatic, two-story lobby with a view of Mount Equinox, converted from what had been nine guest rooms. All bedrooms have been winterized, equipped with modern baths, TVs and telephones, and dressed in light pine furniture, new carpeting, and coordinated bedspreads and draperies. Rooms come in five sizes (standard, superior, deluxe, premium and suite), and anything smaller than deluxe could be a letdown.

The former lobby gave way to the **Marsh Tavern,** now attractive in deep tones of dark green, red and black. The tavern is four times as big as before with a handsome bar and well-spaced tables flanked by windsor and wing chairs and loveseats. We found it too bright one winter's night with lights right over our heads, although the hostess said that was a new one on her – most folks thought the place too dark. We also found the dinner menu rather pricey and lacking in depth, given that it was the only restaurant open in the hotel that evening. Witness a caesar salad with a few baby shrimp for $8, a simple mesclun salad for $5, a good lamb stew with potato gratin for $14 (it was called shepherd's pie but wasn't) and a small roasted cornish game hen for $16. With a shared cranberry-walnut torte and a bottle of Hawk's Crest cabernet for $21, a simple supper for two turned into something of an extravagance for $80. Our reaction, we should point out, does not seem to be shared by the loyal clientele, who sing the plaudits of the tavern and its food priced from $8.75 for a burger to $19.50 for charbroiled sirloin with grilled shrimp.

The barrel-vaulted ceiling in the enormous **Colonnade** dining room was stenciled by hand by a latter-day Michelangelo who lay on his back on scaffolding for days on end. It's suitably formal for those who like to dress for dinner and pay $21 to $25 for the likes of salmon wellington with lobster caviar or napoleon of beef with plum tomato and garlic roësti potato. The short menu details such appetizers as lobster and roasted red pepper bisque, trio of chilled salmon, and glazed duck breast and charred sweetbreads with blackberry vinaigrette. Desserts might be chocolate-grand marnier cake, a trio of cheesecakes with berries, and raspberry-lemon pavé with coconut anglaise.

Work off the calories at the Equinox Spa in an adjacent building, which contains a pool, steam rooms, an exercise room with Nautilus equipment, massage therapy, aerobics programs, the works. The challenging Gleneagles Golf Course has been improved as well, and there's no better setting for a summer's lunch than the seasonal **Dormy Grill** on the veranda at the clubhouse, where the evening lobster fest and cookout also is a draw Friday-Sunday from 5:30 to 8:30 in summer.

If you really want to splurge, settle into one of the suites in the Equinox's new **Charles Orvis Inn,** the famed fisherman-innkeeper's former home and inn renovated in 1995 for $2.8 million. From the fly-fishing gear framed in the "lift" to the game room with not one but two billiards tables next to the cozy Tying Room Bar, it takes club-like luxury to new heights. The three sumptuous one-bedroom and six two-bedroom suites come with king or queen beds, stereos and TVs in armoires in both bedroom and living room, gas fireplaces, marble bathrooms, full cherry-paneled kitchens, and rich colors and furnishings in the English style. Charles Orvis "would have approved," according to its elaborate brochure.

(802) 362-4700 or (800) 362-4747. Fax (802) 362-4861. Marsh Tavern: Lunch, Monday-Saturday noon to 4; dinner nightly, 6 to 9:30. Colonnade: Dinner nightly at peak periods, 7 to 9:30; weekends only, rest of year; Sunday brunch, 11:30 to 2:30. Doubles, $169 to $299, EP; suites, $379 to $559. Inn suites, $569 to $899. Add $60 per person for MAP, $80 per person for full AP.

Handsome new dining room at Windham Hill Inn looks onto lawns and pond.

Windham Hill Inn, West Townshend 05359.

Gourmet dining is a major part of the appeal of this elegant but remote inn on a hill overlooking the West River Valley. Once here, you tend to stay here, which is why innkeepers Grigs and Pat Markham go out of their way to make their guests' stays so comfortable and satisfying.

Five-course dinners of great distinction are served nightly to guests and, increasingly, the public, as the innkeepers capitalize on their newly expanded dining room and on the talents of chef Cameron Howard, who studied at the French Culinary Institute in New York and trained with celebrity chef Daniel Boulud. Guests gather for drinks and hors d'oeuvres in a new bar off the parlor. Then they adjourn to a dining room dressed in pale pink, with oriental scatter rugs, upholstered chairs at well-spaced tables, and views onto lawns and Frog Pond.

Dinner is prix-fixe ($35), with up to four choices for each course. Typical starters are smoked salmon en croûte, ravioli with goat cheese and sundried tomatoes, and grilled wild mushrooms in herbed phyllo. Saffron mussel bisque, a salad of mesclun greens and French nut bread come next. Main courses might be grilled tuna with a soy-ginger vinaigrette, grilled medallions of veal with apricot-sage sauce and black angus beef tenderloin with a rosemary-merlot sauce. Refreshing desserts include lemon charlotte, blackberry clafoutis and various sorbets.

Grigs is as proud of his wine selection as Pat is about the accommodations, which have been expanded and upgraded since we stayed here a few years back.

All eighteen air-conditioned rooms have private baths, telephones and a stuffed animal from the local Mary Meyer factory store on the bed, and nine have fireplaces. They're furnished with a panache that merited a six-page photo spread in Country Decorating magazine. We've always been partial to the five rooms fashioned from nooks and alcoves in the White Barn annex, particularly the two sharing a large deck overlooking the mountains and the renovated Taft Room with fireplace, bay window and floor-to-ceiling bookshelves. Even these have been upstaged by three deluxe rooms carved out of the former owners' quarters in the south wing. These come with kingsize beds, two armchairs in front of the fireplace, and jacuzzis or free-standing soaking tubs. Since our stay in the Tree House (so named because it gives the feeling of being up in the trees), it has gained a Vermont Castings stove and an idyllic deck from which to enjoy the view.

The Markhams pamper guests with gourmet touches, from complimentary juices and Perrier in baskets in each room to candy dishes at bedside and Mother Myrick's chocolates on the pillows at nightly turndown, when small votive candles are lit.

Besides the new bar room off the living room, common areas include another sitting room and a rear game room. Outside are a new heated gunite swimming pool and clay tennis court, as well as 160 acres of woods and trails.

Full breakfasts are served amid a background of taped chamber music, antique silver and crystal: fresh orange juice in champagne flutes, a buffet spread of granola, breakfast pastries and fresh fruits, and a main dish like lemon pancakes with blueberry syrup or scrambled eggs with chives and sausages.

(802) 874-4080 or (800) 944-4080. Fax (802) 874-4702. Dinner nightly, 6 to 8:30. Doubles, $195 to $230, MAP. Closed Christmas week and month of April.

The Reluctant Panther, West Road, Box 678, Manchester Village 05254.
Creature comforts. Fine food. Urbane atmosphere. Intimate setting.
Innkeepers Robert and Maye Bachofen have made the most of these attributes,

Dining area at Reluctant Panther.

parlaying the venerable Reluctant Panther into one of the fine small inns of the Northeast since they took over in 1988.

Creature comforts they provide aplenty in twelve rooms in the main inn, striking for its lavender facade with yellow trim, and in four suites in the stark-white Mary Porter House next door. All rooms have air conditioning, private baths, TVs and telephones. Twelve come with fireplaces and all but one with king or queensize beds. During our tenure in the Seminary Suite we were enveloped in comfort, although we wished we could open some of the windows on all sides to let in that fresh Vermont air and we rued the lack of good reading lights in the places we wanted to read, namely the sofa and the armchair. The bathroom was deluxe, if not quite as showy as the one we'd observed earlier in a suite downstairs. That has a double jacuzzi in the center of one of the largest bathrooms we've seen, with a fireplace opposite, two pedestal sinks and a separate shower. Sparkly Maye, who hails from Peru, has redecorated most of the rooms in a mix of styles, each with splashy wallpapers, fabrics and window treatments, and down comforters on the beds.

Guests find a half-bottle of wine in their room upon arrival. That's a mere preliminary to what's to come in the attractive dining room, crisply dressed in white linens and fine china, and harboring a plant-filled solarium at one end. Robert, who is Swiss and has an extensive background in the food and beverage business, changes the ambitious menu daily. The contemporary fare is so highly regarded that fully two-thirds of the diners, on average, are not house guests.

Award-winning Waverly Room looks onto deck and pool at Deerhill Inn & Restaurant.

The room was full and pleasantly vibrant the Monday night we were there. An amuse-gueule – lobster salad in a hollowed-out cucumber slice – preceded our appetizers, an excellent terrine of pheasant with sundried-cherry chutney and an assertive caesar salad topped with three spicy grilled shrimp. Main courses were priced from $18.95 for broiled haddock with dill cream to $25.95 for peppered New York strip steak with truffled port wine reduction. We enjoyed the medallions of New Zealand venison finished with green peppercorns and Beefeater gin and, one of the chef's favorites, the fricassee of Vermont rabbit with local chanterelles and pearl onions – good but rather rich and more than we could eat. An array of new potatoes, sautéed baby carrots, broccoli and zucchini accompanied. Among the delectable desserts ($4.95) were a fan of berries in sparkling wine around homemade apricot sherbet and plums baked in a light cointreau custard. Maye oversees a dining room in which the ambiance is sophisticated and the service friendly but flawless. She and Robert have put together an exceptional, and quite reasonable, wine list.

The couple serve breakfast at round marble tables topped with floral mats in a fireplaced breakfast room. Fresh orange juice, a baked apple stuffed with nuts and raisins, and corn muffins preceded a plate of blueberry pancakes topped with powdered sugar and garnished with blueberries, blackberries and raspberries.

We left feeling well fed and well taken care of. The New Yorkers who make up much of the inn's clientele consider the experience quite a bargain.

(802) 362-2568 or (800) 822-2331. Fax (802) 362-2586. Dinner, Thursday-Monday from 6; weekends only in winter. Doubles, $178 to $258, MAP; suites, $278 and $288, MAP.

Deerhill Inn & Restaurant, Valley View Road, Box 136, West Dover 05356.

The former owners of Two Tannery Road Restaurant spent seven years traveling and catching their breath before deciding "it was time to be grown up and responsible again." Michael and Linda Anelli purchased this inn on a hillside overlooking the Mount Snow valley and injected it with the warmth and style that made Two Tannery such a hit.

The restaurant is the star here, thanks to Michael's cooking talents and Linda's passion for art and flowers. Both turn up in abundance in two dining rooms in the country garden style. There's a lot to look at, from a garden mural and floral paintings to ivy and tiny white lights twined all around.

The fare is contemporary continental-American. Our leisurely dinner began with potato and leek soup and a portobello mushroom stuffed with lobster and crab, a couple of tasty treats at either end of the appetizer price range ($3.50 to $9.50). A good mixed salad followed.

The dozen entrée choices were priced from $17 for sliced grilled chicken breast with apple and sweet onion relish to $23 for black peppered sirloin steak. The sliced grilled leg of lamb with a wedge of saga bleu cheese and the five-layer veal with roasted red pepper sauce were exceptional. A $25 Forest Glen merlot accompanied from what Linda called "our NAFTA wine list," all North and South American from Chile to Virginia to Oregon, pleasantly priced in the teens and twenties. Desserts were a refreshing lemon mousse parfait and peanut-butter/banana ice cream in a decorated pastry shell.

The culinary treats continued at breakfast, available from a full menu. Juice and strawberries with cantaloupe, garnished with a pansy, preceded a poached egg in one case, a mushroom and cheese omelet with homefries in the other.

Overnight, we stayed in one of the front rooms with a long, full-length balcony built by Michael and equipped with wicker rockers to take in the view. The queen canopy bed was outfitted with fancy sheets and pillows – "one of my things," explained Linda, who switches to flannel sheets in winter. Two armchairs flanked the fireplace, a pastoral mural graced one wall, and bowls of fruit and candy were at hand. Behind was a swimming pool, surrounded by cutting gardens that furnished the bouquets for guest rooms and restaurant tables.

Others of the inn's fifteen guest rooms and suites, all with private baths and bright and cheery decor, can best be described as eclectic. The Waverly room, named for its decor and winner of Country Inns magazine's annual Room of the Year award in 1996, has a king bed with a picket-fence headboard and a deck facing the pool. Two rear rooms with vaulted ceilings and kingsize beds open onto private decks. A fan is displayed on the wall and the queen bed has a canopy of mosquito netting in a room with an oriental theme. Common areas include a couple of fireplaced living rooms, their walls hung with a veritable gallery of local art for sale, a comfy library with TV, and a small bar called The Snug.

(802) 464-3100 or (800) 993-3379. Fax (802) 464-5474. Dinner nightly except Tuesday, 6 to 9:30. Doubles, $110 to $175 B&B, $180 to $245 MAP; suites, $220 B&B, $290 MAP.

The Four Columns Inn, 230 West St. on the Common, Box 278, Newfane 05345.

Chef Gregory Parks, a fixture at this venerable inn for twenty years since he started as sous chef under famed owner Rene Chardain, has free rein in the kitchen and a reputation for inventive regional cuisine.

The dining room is in a white building behind the white clapboard 1832 structure containing guest rooms and the four Greek Revival columns that give the inn its name. With beamed ceilings and a huge fireplace, the dining room is country charming and full of antiques and folk art. Fresh white organdy curtains and pink tablecloths topped with white overcloths contribute to a country look.

French country look prevails in dining room at Four Columns Inn.

Behind the dining room is a charming lounge, with an old French pewter bar, decorated with things like calico hens. Cider was simmering in a crock pot here at one autumn visit. An armoire displays wines.

The dinner menu is supplemented by blackboard specials. "Greg's an artist," says his mentor, "so the menu is constantly changing."

Starters ($6 to $9.50) are exotic: perhaps tuna tartare with American sturgeon caviar and wasabi cream served in a crisp taro nest with a leek vinaigrette, warm sea scallops crowning a salad of baby greens with white truffle oil and saffron, and grilled sweetbreads and artichoke bottoms with fried polenta and chipotle mayonnaise. The night's "soup whim" could be leek and onion with herbed biscuits or potato and spinach with shrimp and green-chile salsa.

Entrées run from $19 for grilled pork chop with an apple-scotch bonnet sauce to $24 for grilled sirloin with tomato-horseradish demi-glace. Others could be sauté of scallops and shrimp with a Thai lemongrass and coconut broth, pistachio-crusted swordfish fillet with a saffron-citrus sauce, and roasted young chicken stuffed with foie gras.

The dessert repertoire here has long been famous. It might include pumpkin cheesecake, chocolate pâté, raspberry torte, hazelnut layer cake with mocha cream, and homemade sorbets and ice creams. You can stop in the lounge to enjoy one from the cart, even if you haven't dined at the inn.

New innkeepers Gorty and Pam Baldwin from Manhattan, who took over in 1996 for a life-style change, have upgraded some of the fifteen guest rooms, all with private baths. Most have king or queensize beds, and all are decorated colorfully with hooked rugs, handmade afghans and quilts. Room 3, with a four-poster bed, comes with a jacuzzi for two in a marble bathroom that's larger than the bedroom. Room 18 is newly equipped with a gas fireplace, kingsize sleigh bed and a free-standing soaking tub in a corner near the bathroom. Another favorite is the third-floor hideaway, with trim of old wood and Laura Ashley fabrics in shades of deep rusts. It has a canopied bed set into an alcove, plush beige carpeting and a sitting room with a private porch overlooking the Newfane green. A center chimney that divides the room gives it unusual spaces.

The Baldwins continue to serve what their predecessor called "a healthy, new age, country breakfast" for overnight guests. The buffet table contains fresh orange juice, lots of fruit, yogurt, homemade granola, hot oatmeal in winter and an assortment of homemade muffins and croissants. The inn also has a swimming pool, trout pond, lovely gardens and spacious lawns on which to relax in country-auberge style.

(802) 365-7713 or (800) 787-6633. Fax (802) 365-0022. Dinner nightly except Tuesday, 6 to 9. Doubles, $110 to $130; suites, $140 to $195.

The Dorset Inn, Church and Main Streets, Dorset 05251.

Built in 1796 and the oldest continually operating inn in Vermont, the Dorset has been upgraded in both lodging and meals by innkeepers Sissy Hicks and Gretchen Schmidt.

All 29 rooms on the two upper floors have been redone over the years with wall-to-wall carpeting, modern baths with wood washstands, print wallpapers and antique furnishings, although they retain a distinctly historic feel. Two newer suites, one with a double bed and one with twins, each have a sitting room with a pullout bed. In 1997, renovations were planned to create some larger, deluxe rooms with sitting areas, TVs and telephones.

Dressed-up bears in the lobby greet guests, who have use of a sitting room with comfortable furniture around a fireplace. Vermont-woven mats top wood tables in a cheery breakfast room, its green floral curtains framing small-paned windows that extend to the floor. Out back is a pleasant tavern with a large oak bar that is favored by locals.

The main dining room has been redecorated in hunter green with white trim and wainscoting. A focal point is a spotlit glass cabinet displaying cups and horse figurines along one wall. Chef Sissy, an early practitioner of the new American cuisine, has joined the previously separate tavern and dining-room menus into one that serves both areas. Now you'll find a classic burger ($8) on the same menu as grilled loin lamb chops with roasted shallots and garlic confit ($20), to say nothing of spicy chicken wings, crisp potato skins and the "original warm chicken tenderloin salad." The emphasis lately seems to be on more downscaled, tavern fare. Seven vegetarian items, including garbanzo croquettes and baked eggplant crêpes, also are available.

We found the smoked-trout mousse with avocado sauce and a few slices of melba toast a fine appetizer, big enough for two to share. How could we pass up the calves liver ($15), which we'd heard was the best anywhere? Served rare with crisp bacon and slightly underdone slices of onion, it was superb. The trout ($16.50), deboned but served with its skin still on, was laden with braised leeks and mushrooms. These came with a medley of vegetables, including red skin potatoes with a dollop of sour cream and crisp cauliflower, broccoli and yellow squash.

Among delectable desserts are fruit pies, bread pudding with whiskey sauce, white-chocolate cheesecake with raspberry sauce and – when did you last see this on a menu? – tapioca with whipped cream. We chose a kiwi sorbet, wonderfully deep flavored and with the consistency of ice cream, accompanied by a big sugar cookie.

The inn serves a hearty, prix-fixe breakfast and interesting lunches tuna and herb bruschetta, welsh rarebit, baked eggplant crêpes and apple-smoked chicken ($6 to $10.50), with enough selection to appeal one fall day a few years ago to all in our party of seven youngsters and adults.

(802) 867-5500. Fax (802) 867-5542. Lunch daily in summer and fall, 11:30 to 2; dinner nightly, 5:30 to 9. Doubles, $200, MAP; suites, $300.

The Four Chimneys Inn and Restaurant, 21 West Road (Route 9), Old Bennington 05201.

New owners are enhancing this 1910 landmark mansion, which had been restored by recent chef-owner Alex Koks to its heyday of the 1950s and 1960s. Ron Schefkind, who was an executive in the corporate food business in Connecticut, and wife Judy took over in late 1996. "We're making cosmetic changes in terms of

freshening up the paint and wallpaper," said Ron. "But the restaurant had a tremendous reputation and we wouldn't change a thing."

Scott Hunt, who had been Alex's chef, maintains the culinary tradition. The seating recently was reduced from 160 to 96. Dining is concentrated in the old lounge that was expanded, and the bar relocated to a former dining room. The west porch opens onto restored gardens. Both rooms are handsomely appointed in shades of pale mauve, pink and rose, from the velvet seats of the chairs to the brocade draperies and matching panels on the walls, the heavy linens and the carnations on the mantel above the fireplace. Flickering oil lamps in hurricane globes and classical background music complete the romantic, formal atmosphere for what is billed as "estate dining in a park-like setting."

We've enjoyed many a meal here and at Alex's former establishment, the old

Dining area at Four Chimneys.

Village Auberge in Dorset. At a recent lunch, the creamed spinach soup and an order of home-cured gravlax were simple and superb, while the roasted quail came with a complex brown game sauce, wild rice and a side dish of asparagus scented with nutmeg. Hazelnut-praline mousse in a chocolate shell and a trio of refreshing sorbets (raspberry, blueberry and strawberry) ended a memorable meal for two for under $30.

The French fare with a touch of nouvelle continues at dinner, which is prix-fixe ($32.50 for three courses). The meal is preceded by complimentary cheese fritters, a house trademark. To begin, go for the cream of mustard soup that Alex was famous for, a galantine of poultry or escargots in puff pastry. A new section of the menu labeled "lighter fare" offers shrimp and fettuccine, chicken julienne, salmon quenelles with scallops and a terrific duck salad. Among main courses are poached salmon with an herb sauce, roast duckling with amarena cherries, beef wellington for two and, the house specialty, rack of lamb with honey and thyme sauce. Good sourdough bread and salad with a champagne vinaigrette come with. Creamed fennel and celery root with rice or a creamy swirl of pureed and rebaked potato might accompany.

A chocolate marquise with raspberry sauce, peach cheesecake, frozen chocolate-mocha parfait torte, Bailey's Irish Cream cake and those sparkling homemade sorbets are among desserts.

The inn's accommodations have been expanded as well. A former dining room was converted into two handicapped-accessible guest rooms with queen beds, fireplaces and TVs. Two more deluxe rooms with sitting areas and whirlpool tubs are found in out-buildings in back. The original brick ice house with vaulted ceiling has a queen bed, fireplace and a spiral staircase to a skylit loft with a sofabed and TV. The restored carriage house with a front veranda holds a cozy room with kingsize bed, a TV in a niche over the fireplace and a nifty English garden bench upholstered in bunny needlepoint. The seven commodious guest rooms upstairs in the main house are bright and airy in off-white and rose, four with fireplaces and porches and two with jacuzzis. Continental breakfast is delivered on a tray to one's room or served in the restaurant.

(802) 447-3500 or (800) 649-3503. Fax (802) 447-3692. Lunch, Tuesday-Saturday 11:30 to 2, July-October; dinner, Tuesday-Sunday 5:30 to 9; Sunday brunch, 10:30 to 3. Doubles, $100 to $175.

The Arlington Inn, Route 7A, Box 369, Arlington 05250.

A pillared, cream-colored Greek Revival mansion with dark red shutters houses the reborn Arlington Inn, which has been expanded by new owners and with a dining situation on the way back toward its glory days under former acclaimed chef-owner Paul Kruzel.

After a few faltering years with interim owners, the Arlington has been revived by new owners Mark and Deborah Gagnon, he a former financial analyst with Fidelity Investments and she an accountant for Omni Hotels. "So we knew what we were getting in to," Mark said.

One of their priorities was to re-establish the inn's dining reputation. The kitchen was put under the direction of Tom Dolivo, former chef at the Birkenhaus at Stratton.

Off a grand entry hall is a pretty fireplaced dining room with windsor chairs at white-clothed tables bearing glass oil lamps. It leads into an appealing wraparound solarium, all burgundy and green against a marble floor.

The setting is elegant for contemporary continental fare with Asian accents. Typical among the half-dozen starters ($7.50 to $8) are smoked trout, escargots with pernod butter, pork and ginger dumplings with mango and sesame sauce, and pan-seared Maine crab cakes with creole rémoulade sauce. Main courses ($16.50 to $20) could be lemongrass and lime chicken, filet of pork normande, roasted duck with a game sauce of port and currants, veal osso buco and a signature rack of lamb with changing sauces. Dessert could be key lime pie or fresh berries with cream, the berries picked from the extensive blackberry and raspberry bushes behind the inn. The outstanding wine list is quite expensive.

In addition to dining, the Arlington offers nineteen air-conditioned guest rooms in a wide variety of sizes, all with private baths and outfitted with the heavy furniture typical of the 1848 era in which it was built.

Upstairs in the main inn are six guest rooms ranging from cozy with double beds to a suite with queen bed, fireplace and jacuzzi. Another fireplaced suite with

Pillared, Greek Revival mansion is site of Arlington Inn.

king bed had been the prime accommodation of the four in the rear carriage house. These have been equaled by some of the six new rooms that the Gagnons added in the Old Parsonage next door. They have TVs hidden in armoires, telephones and four have fireplaces. Among them is the Justin James Room with kingsize poster bed (plus a daybed in an anteroom), complete with a library of books and National Geographics dating to 1925. The decor in the Zadok Hard Room with queensize bed is coordinated from comforter to wallpaper border to swag draperies. The sitting room in the rear Old Squire's Gable suite still bears the shelves attesting to its former status as a kitchen; it also comes with a queen sleigh bed and a clawfoot tub, plus a platform bed in an alcove.

Included in the rates is a full breakfast – perhaps omelet of the day, pancakes or french toast – served in the bright and airy conservatory.

(802) 375-6532 or (800) 443-9442. Fax (802) 375-6534. Dinner, Tuesday-Sunday from 6. Doubles, $80 to $150; suites, $150 to $160.

The Inn at Long Last, Main Street, Box 589, Chester 05143.

The route to Jack Coleman's "inn at long last" was circuitous. The former president of Haverford College and of a New York charitable foundation, he caused a stir when his book, *Blue Collar Journal,* traced his experiences as a garbage man, short-order cook and ditch digger. He later worked on a Southern chain gang, served as a voluntary inmate in five prisons and as a guard in two others, and lived with the homeless in Manhattan during a record cold spell. He finds that running an inn is the most difficult challenge he has encountered so far.

Patrons at the 30-room hostelry he opened in 1986 in the abandoned Chester Inn facing the village green would never guess. "The inn displays the story of my life," remarked the man who always wanted an inn and tirelessly transformed a rundown building into a showcase for his personality and memorabilia. "My son told me, 'Dad, this is just your apartment made larger.'"

Indeed, the furnishings from his New York apartment have plenty of room to spread out in the three-story inn. The rooms are named for either an aspect of Jack

Coleman's life, authors he admires or famous Vermont personages. They are decorated accordingly, from the Fair Winds Farm Room reflecting his best friends in his native Ontario to the Grand Opera Room in which framed opera programs adorn the walls. They vary considerably, but all have private baths and are endearingly kooky, if not charming.

Cocktails are served in a fireplaced parlor that holds Jack's personal library, including a collection of travel magazines shelved as in a periodical room and "the largest collection of books on prisons of any inn in Vermont," he quips. The main living room houses illuminated shelves of miniature soldiers, mostly marching bands, arranged in a dozen European scenes.

The mirrored back of a twelve-foot-long bar obtained from a razed Maine hotel is the focal point of the dining room, in which a changing menu of regional American cuisine is offered by chef Ross Jones.

The dinner menu changes seasonally. It began at our summer visit with beef bouillon with fresh peas and aioli crouton and chilled gazpacho with cilantro cream and tortilla sticks. Other starters ($4.25 to $7) were smoked salmon mousse wrapped in a dill crêpe with chive beurre blanc, spicy lamb and goat cheese baked in phyllo with minted yogurt, and gulf shrimp and pancetta with grilled pineapple relish and black mignonette.

The seven entrées are $13.50 to $22.50 for the likes of catfish with black bean sauce and corn-okra relish, hazelnut-crusted pork loin chop with papaya and tangerine, veal roulades with sundried tomatoes and enoki mushrooms, and grilled ribeye steak with roasted shallot-garlic ragout. The Vermont lamb might be roasted with fresh thyme and Vermont goat cheese or grilled with caramelized pistachios. A green salad with a secret dressing, sourdough rolls and vegetables accompany.

Banana or pumpkin-ginger cheesecake, Williamsburg orange cake, blueberry pie and almond-pecan tarts are among the luscious desserts. The innkeeper's favorite, although he cannot always prevail upon the chef, remains a Shaker lemon pie made with whole lemons. The short wine list is affordably priced.

Jack prepares the breakfasts, taken in a sunny room overlooking the tranquil rear lawn and garden. The fare when we visited included his own six-grain hot cereal following juice and cantaloupe, apple and anise muffins, oatmeal scones with apricots, and a choice of scrambled eggs with corn cob-smoked ham and sharp cheddar cheese, strawberry pancakes and shirred eggs ("like Portuguese, but without the anchovies," says Jack). He compiled favorite recipes, each accompanied by a morning reflection, in a good little cookbook called *Breakfast...At Long Last.*

To go with these gourmet feasts, the inn decorates for the season: a Christmas tree decked out with guests' personal greetings and a collection of 96 Santas helped the inn win the town's annual Yuletide decoration contest – a fitting reward for a special place.

(802) 875-2444. Dinner, Tuesday-Sunday 6 to 8 or 9. Doubles, $160, MAP. Closed in late November and month of April.

The Red Shutter Inn, Route 9, Box 636, Wilmington.

This hostelry nicely blends the old and new: a main Colonial house and adjacent carriage house dating to 1894, a homey restaurant, and contemporary guest rooms and amenities.

The blend was achieved by new owners Renée and Tad Lyon, who were in the restaurant business in Baltimore. They offer five rooms in the main house with queen or kingsize beds and private baths. The burgundy showing through a crocheted white bedspread is repeated in the wallpaper in one of the handsomely decorated rooms. We like best the rear two-room suite with fireplaced sitting room with TV, vaulted ceiling and bay window, its bedroom with queensize brass bed and full-length windows opening onto a private deck.

Also impressive are the four rooms in the reborn carriage house, especially the fireplaced suite with queensize bed, sitting room with loveseat and armchair, and a bathroom with two-person jacuzzi beneath a skylight. A vintage radio here is juxtaposed beside a new color TV.

Comfortable as the accommodations are, it is dining for which the Red Shutter is best known, thanks to chef Graham Gill from London, who trained in Europe in the French style and whose good food we sampled earlier when he was at the Doveberry Inn. Working alone in the inn's small, homey kitchen, he has so enhanced the restaurant's reputation that, despite Renée's background as a commercial chef, the Lyons were not about to change. The pine-paneled main dining room is appropriately Vermonty with shelves of books, caneback chairs, cloth mats and candlelight. Tables in the narrow back room sport floral cloths, and there's a canopied outdoor dining deck in front.

The blackboard menu lists entrées from $15 for baked scrod to $21.50 for lamb noisette with port wine glaze. Among the dozen possibilities might be horseradish-crusted salmon with lemon butter, native trout topped with dill pesto, pork tenderloin with garden peppers, Long Island duck with raspberry sauce, veal orloff and prime rib with lemon-pepper crust. Accompaniments one night we were there were broccoli with cheese sauce, oven-roasted potatoes and butternut squash (so good that a guest from Texas phoned afterward for the recipe).

Appetizers might be cream of celery soup, three-fish pâté with lemon-dill sauce, crabmeat-stuffed mushrooms and lobster ravioli with pesto and sundried-tomato sauce. Homey desserts include apple crisp and maple-pecan pie, both with ice cream, and berry cobblers. Tad has expanded the wine list, most in the $18 to $28 price range. There's a small honor bar off the cozy living room.

Inn guests partake of a hearty breakfast cooked by Renée, perhaps western omelet with bacon or blueberry pancakes with sausage.

(802) 464-3768 or (800) 845-7548. Dinner, Tuesday-Sunday 6 to 9, July-September; Wednesday-Saturday in winter. Doubles, $105 to $145; suites, $165 and $170. Closed April and early May.

Three Clock Inn, Middletown Road, South Londonderry 05155.

French chef Serge Roche from Marseilles took over this classic continental restaurant in a homey Colonial inn that had garnered quite a following under long-time owner Heinrich Tschernitz, who retired in 1992. After a few shaky years under an interim owner, things were on the way up with the arrival in 1996 of Serge, who had been supervising executive chef for the famed enterprises run by Restaurant Associates of New York. Here, with his American wife Marcie, he was back in the kitchen and on his own for the first time.

Two centuries old, the little white house with black shutters harbors a cozy parlor where guests can relax near the hearth with a drink before dinner, three small dining rooms seating 56 people (plus three tables on a porch in summer) and three B&B guest rooms and a suite, two with private baths.

Their principal interest – and claim to fame – being food, the Roches were slowly upgrading the decor and the menu. They stripped the floors, painted the walls in vanilla colors and added antiques to the country-pretty dining rooms. Tables are set with white cloths, brass service plates and hand-blown glassware.

The formerly solid continental fare was updated as well, blending classics with seasonal and local ingredients for more of a brasserie theme. The menu is à la carte and, while not quite the steal of the prix-fixe, four-course meals of the past, still a relative bargain.

Main courses start at $10 for chicken fricassee provençal, a signature dish along with the braised lamb shank for $12. Prices top off at $21 for black angus sirloin steak with peppercorn sauce and $22 for roast rack of lamb. In between are things like soft-shell crabs with lemon-caper butter, grilled Atlantic salmon with horse-radish potatoes, orrechiette with manila clams and chorizo, and roast duckling with Vermont berries. Extra vegetables are now $4 as side dishes.

Starters range widely from $4 for chilled roasted pepper soup or mushroom and wild-rice bisque to $9 for shrimp cocktail, crab cake with mustard sauce and feuilleté of frog's legs. Desserts include profiteroles, wild berry charlotte and lemon sorbet, and a crêpe soufflé with mango and passion-fruit sauce. The Roches were expanding the wine list, small but serviceable with California and French vintages starting in the high teens.

The upstairs accommodations vary. Homey and simply furnished, one room with private bath offers a queensize bed and a fireplace, and a suite has two bedrooms and a sitting room. The other two rooms, one queensize and one with twins, share a bath.

(802) 824-6327. Dinner, Tuesday-Saturday 5:30 to 8:30, Sunday 5 to 7. Doubles, $70 to $95; suite, $85 ($140 for four).

Doveberry Inn, Route 100, West Dover 05356.

Glowingly described by a fellow innkeeper as "a diamond in the rough, like us," this small inn under new ownership offers a pleasant restaurant and eight comfortable guest rooms. Michael Fayette, the young chef-owner who trained at Paul Smith's College in New York and 21 Federal in Nantucket, and wife Christine, the baker, offer acclaimed northern Italian fare. They also have added a wine bar in the common room, and attract the public for dessert and cappuccino as well as dinner in the evening.

They seat 30 guests at tables covered with her mother's handmade quilt overcloths that change with the seasons in a two-part, beamed dining room with mint green walls and swag curtains. The menu changes weekly. Typical starters ($4.95 to $9.50) might be garlic and corn soup, grilled shrimp with tomato-chive risotto and the evening's bruschetta. Main courses range from $17.95 for sautéed chicken served over a hash cake with orange-tapenade sauce to $27.95 for wood-grilled veal chop with wild mushrooms. Pan-seared salmon on a bed of risotto, a sauté of lobster and mixed peppers with polenta, and grilled maple-glazed pork chop are among the possibilities.

Christine might prepare mascarpone cheesecake, a plum napoleon or frozen tirami su with bittersweet chocolate for dessert.

Overnight guests order a complimentary breakfast from a full menu. Choices range from belgian waffles to eggs benedict with a crab cake.

Some of the renovated inn's guest rooms, all with private baths and TV/VCRs,

Window tables overlook Bromley Brook outside Mistral's at Toll Gate.

convey a contemporary air. A few rooms have skylights and one luxury suite adds a kingsize bed, a private deck and a sitting area with TV. The spacious East Room had a queensize and a double bed, and a basket of apples at our fall visit. A typical smaller double has two cat pillows on the chairs, floral curtains matching the wallpaper (which also covers the ceiling) and a bathroom with copper in the sink and shower.

Overstuffed sofas and armchairs are grouped around the open brick hearth that warms the large common room. Tea and cookies are served here in the afternoon.

(802) 464-5652 or (800) 722-3204. Fax (802) 464-6229. Dinner nightly except Tuesday, 6 to 9. Doubles, $75 to $130.

Dining

The Best of the Best

Mistral's at Toll Gate, Tollgate Road, Manchester Center.

The old Toll Gate Lodge was a classic French restaurant of the old school, one of Vermont's original Travel-Holiday award winners with a tuxedoed staff and lofty prices. Brown with bright blue trim and looking a bit like grandmother's cottage out in the woods, it was reborn in 1988 by young chef-owners Dana and Cheryl Markey, who live upstairs and have given it a personal, less formal touch. Both local, they met as teenagers at the Sirloin Saloon and worked their way through area restaurants before buying the Toll Gate.

Although the two dining rooms seating 80 are country pretty with dark woods, lace curtains, blue and white linens, and gold-edged white china, it is the views through picture windows looking onto the trickling flume of Bromley Brook that are compelling. At night, when the brook and woods, accented in summer by purple petunias and brilliant impatiens, are illuminated, the setting is magical.

The menu offers a choice of about a dozen starters and ten entrées, most classic French with some nouvelle and northern Italian touches. Tempting starters ($6.25 to $8.25) include crab cakes grenobloise, smoked salmon crêpes with golden caviar, escargots persillade and French onion soup gratinée.

Main courses run from $17.75 for stuffed breast of chicken marsala to $24 for grilled filet mignon roquefort, except the specialty châteaubriand béarnaise and rack of lamb rosemary for two, $52 and $54 respectively. They could be crispy sweetbreads dijonnaise, sautéed Newfane trout stuffed with scallop mousse, grilled pork tenderloin moutarde, and medallions of veal zingara with prosciutto, mushrooms, artichoke hearts and a lemon-wine sauce. Homemade bread and house salad with a choice of dressings accompany.

The signature dessert ($6.50) is coupe mistral (coffee ice cream rolled in hazelnuts with hot fudge sauce and frangelico). Others choices include a complex chocolate godiva cake, praline cheesecake, linzertorte and assorted fruit sorbets.

While Dana is in the kitchen, Cheryl oversees the front of the house and a growing wine list, honored recently by Wine Spectator.

(802) 362-1779 or (800) 279-1779. Dinner nightly except Wednesday, from 6.

Chantecleer, Route 7, Manchester Center.

Ask anyone to name the best restaurants in the Manchester area and the Chantecleer usually heads the list – absolutely tops, says an innkeeper whose taste

Country decor at Chantecleer.

we respect. One of Swiss chef Michel Baumann's strengths is consistency, ever since he opened his contemporary-style restaurant in an old dairy barn north of town in 1981. The rough wood beams and barn siding remain, but fresh flowers, oil lamps, good art, hanging quilts, shelves of bric-a-brac, and navy and white china atop white-over-blue calico tablecloths lend elegance to the rusticity. A pig tureen decorates the massive fireplace.

The contemporary continental menu has Swiss and American touches and changes bi-weekly except for staples like rack of lamb.

Our party of four sampled a number of offerings, starting with a classic baked onion soup, penne with smoked salmon, potato pancakes with sautéed crabmeat and a heavenly lime-butter sauce, and bundnerfleisch, the Swiss air-dried beef, fanned out in little coronets with pearl onions, cornichons and melba rounds. Escargots, peppered Scottish salmon roulade and a terrine of eggplant and roasted peppers with goat-cheese mousse are other favorites among appetizers (most $7.95 to $9.25).

Entrées are priced from $19.50 for wiener schnitzel to $28 for grilled prime veal chop citronate. We savored the specialty rack of lamb roasted with fine herbs, veal sweetbreads morel, sautéed quail stuffed with duxelles and the night's special of boneless local pheasant, served with smoked bacon and grapes. Fabulous roësti

House once owned by Pearl Buck now offers stylish dining as Danby Village Restaurant.

potatoes upstaged the other accompaniments, puree of winter squash, snow peas and strands of celery.

Grand marnier layer cake, bananas foster, Swiss tobler chocolate mousse and trifle were memorable endings to a rich, expensive meal. A number of Swiss wines are included on the reasonably priced wine list, and yodeling may be heard on tape.

In late 1996, Michel added another restaurant to his entourage that already included **The Little Rooster Cafe** in Manchester Center (see Gourmet Treats). Taking over the old Park Bench Cafe just down Route 7A from the Rooster, he and partners opened **Jasper's,** a casual establishment offering a mix of Southwest and eclectic American fare for lunch and dinner. Thin-crust pizzas, paella, cowboy steak and roast rack of pork Meditteeranean were on the initial dinner menu, with most entrées in the $14.25 to $17 range.

(802) 362-1616. Dinner by reservation, nightly except Tuesday from 6.

Danby Village Restaurant, Main Street, Danby.

The previous entry in the guest book at the door raved: "Fabulous food. What a find!" That and a tip from a Dorset innkeeper prompted us to proceed inside for lunch a month after the Danby Village opened in 1996, and our experience matched the consensus.

Caterer Debbie Andrew, she part Greek and Irish, and partner Dana Cole, he a native Vermonter, teamed up to offer a short menu of assertive international fare in a little white house once owned by Pearl Buck. Debbie visits her sister near Athens a couple of times a year, which prompts such Greek specialties as shrimp with artichoke hearts, sundried tomatoes and feta cheese; seafood stew, pork shish kabob and lamb shanks braised in red wine, garlic and tomatoes on a dinner menu priced from $13.95 to $19.95. A Mediterranean platter, pita pizza and spanakopita pies are among the appetizers ($3.95 to $5.95).

We were introduced to the partners' cuisine on the trellised rear patio shaded by a towering maple tree. Dana was in the kitchen as we lunched on a fabulous, garlicky chilled cucumber-dill soup and the Mediterranean platter of hummus and pita triangles, stuffed grape leaves, marinated artichoke hearts, feta cheese, tazatziki and Greek olives ($5.95), a worthy midday spread. Debbie, who works the front of the house by day and trades places with her partner at night, recommended the grilled smoked chicken and apple sausage ($4.95), a meal in itself with sautéed onions and mushrooms and a zesty honey-horseradish mustard. The signature chocolate pâté with golden raisins made a worthy ending.

On a pleasant day, the patio is the place to be, and there's a small lounge with a couple of tables. The 24-seat dining room is stylish in light olive green with dark trim, white-linened tables, good art on the walls and a white pressed-tin ceiling. The striking cushioned chairs with cross-hatched backs were declared surplus by the Colonnade Room at the Equinox and were acquired for $20 each, about fifteen times less than their original price five years earlier.

(802) 293-6003. Lunch in season, 11:30 to 2; dinner, 6 to 9; Sunday brunch, 11:30 to 2:30. Closed Wednesday and Christmas to Memorial Day.

Two Tannery Road, 2 Tannery Road, West Dover.

The first frame house in the town of Dover has quite a history. Built in the late 1700s and moved "stick by stick" from Marlborough, Mass., it was the summer home in the early 1900s of President Theodore Roosevelt's son and daughter-in-law, and the president is said to have visited. In the early 1940s it was moved again to its present location, the site of a former sawmill and tannery. It became the first lodge for nearby Mount Snow and finally a restaurant in 1982.

Along the way it also has been transformed into a place of great attractiveness, especially the main Garden Room with its vaulted ceiling, a many-windowed space so filled with plants and so open that you almost don't know where the inside ends and the outside begins. A wall of windows looks onto the Garden Room from the Fireplace Room, which along with two smaller interior dining rooms has beamed ceilings, barnwood walls and wide-plank floors dotted with oriental-patterned rugs. Charming stenciling and folk art are everywhere. A pleasant lounge contains part of the original bar from the Waldorf-Astoria.

Longtime chef Brian Reynolds stayed on when Karen and Steve Steinfeldt took ownership. Dinners start with a hot or cold soup du jour (hot cauliflower and cold cucumber with dill the night we were there) and more than a dozen appetizers in the $8 range. The house antipasti, grilled cajun steak tips, and Acadian pepper shrimp are popular, and we enjoyed duck livers with onions in a terrific sauce.

Seventeen entrées plus nightly specials range from $17.50 for four chicken dishes to $24 for filet mignon. Veal is a specialty, so we tried veal granonico in a basil sauce as well as grilled New Mexican chicken with chiles, herbs and special salsa, accompanied by a goodly array of vegetables – broccoli, carrots, parsley and boiled new potatoes in one case, rice pilaf in the other. Shrimp lyonnaise or bangkok style, roast duckling and grilled lamb chops with a pear-mint compote are frequent choices on the changing menu.

A four-layer grand marnier cake with strawberries was enough for two to share and testified to the kitchen's prowess with desserts. They include a renowned mud pie, frozen black and white mousse with raspberry sauce, and apple crêpes.

Colombian-blend coffee and espresso end a pleasant, reasonably priced meal. And if the dining room is a wondrous garden retreat with rabbits running around the lawn in summer, think how lovely it must be when the lawn is covered with snow in winter.

(802) 464-2707. Dinner nightly except Monday, 6 to 10.

Bistro decor at Main Street Cafe.

Table for two at Le Petit Chef.

More Dining Choices

Le Petit Chef, Route 100, Wilmington.

Although the renovated 1850 Cutler Homestead looks tiny from the outside, it is surprisingly roomy inside, with three dining rooms and an inviting lounge. The chef is Betty Hillman, whose mother Libby is the noted cookbook author and food writer. Betty studied in France for a year and her menu is rather classic with contemporary accents.

Appetizers ($6.50 to $10.50) include a tomato and goat cheese tart, roulade of smoked salmon with salmon caviar, and ragoût of escargots and shiitake mushrooms. Among entrées ($19.50 to $25), you might find fillet of salmon baked in a horseradish crust on a bed of mashed potatoes, a crab cake with confetti shrimp on a julienne of vegetables bordered by a Mexican corn sauce, shrimp à la grecque, free-range chicken roasted with garlic and lemongrass, filet mignon with green peppercorn sauce, rack of lamb and noisettes of venison with sundried cherry sauce.

Homemade lemon sorbet and ice creams, fresh fruit tarts, apple cake, crunchy meringue and chocolate torte are among desserts.

Tables are covered with white linens, blue napkins, handsome and heavy white china and cutlery, and oil lamps. Oriental rugs, grapevine wreaths and cabinets filled with antique china and glass are accents.

(802) 464-8437. Dinner nightly except Tuesday, 6 to 9 or 10.

Main Street Cafe, 1 Prospect St., North Bennington.

This storefront cafe has attracted such a coterie of devotees that it expanded into a small room in the rear, adding fourteen seats in 1996. The main room is stylish with sponged peach walls under a deep burgundy pressed-tin ceiling. Cafe lights, one hanging over each table, cast a flattering glow.

Owner Jeff Bendavid, who used to be at the late great Sam's Place in Saratoga Springs, handles the cooking chores. His wife Peggy takes care of the perfect dried-flower arrangements. Each table sports bottles of red and white house wine that you may open and pour as much or as little as you like into delicate, pink-stemmed glasses (and be charged only for what you drink). It's all quite jolly and "like coming to our home," says Jeff.

Tuxedo-clad waiters serve the northern Italian fare. The short menu might begin with mozzarella in carozza, mussels arrabiata, grilled sea scallops over smoked salmon with a tarragon-dill-lemon sauce, and vegetable cannelloni, among appetizers from $5.95 to $6.95. Entrées ($15.95 to $17.95) might be rock shrimp sautéed with sweet onions and sundried tomatoes in garlic-basil cream sauce on linguini, chargrilled sea scallops with artichoke hearts and plum tomatoes on spinach linguini, chicken and spicy Italian sausage sautéed with braised onions and mushrooms over rigatoni, and chicken with green peppercorns and portobello mushrooms over angel-hair pasta and steamed spinach.

Among desserts are Italian lemon sponge cake, chocolate-kahlua cheesecake and tirami su with tia maria and dark rum. The wine list is nicely priced from $12 to $40, with many in the teens. Some of the more choice come from Jeff's private cellar.

(802) 442-3210. Dinner nightly except Monday, 6 to 8:30 or 9. Closed some Sundays in winter.

T.J. Buckley's, 132 Elliot St., Brattleboro.

"Uptown dining" along a side street in Brattleboro is how chef-owner Michael Fuller bills this choice little black, red and silver diner with tables for up to twenty lucky patrons. The setting is charming; the food, creative and highly regarded. The city slicker from Cleveland, who came to Vermont eighteen years ago to ski and to apprentice with Rene Chardain at the Four Columns in Newfane, does everything here himself, except for some of the prep work, the desserts and serving.

He usually offers four entrées a night at a fixed price of $23, which he's quick to point out includes rolls, vegetables and a zippy salad of four lettuces, endive, radicchio and marinated peppers dressed with the house vinaigrette. At a recent visit, Michael was preparing a neat-sounding shrimp and clam dish with a puree of roasted plum tomatoes and dill oil with shaved fennel and slices of reggiano, to be served with polenta. Other choices were poached Norwegian salmon topped with a puree of Maine rock shrimp and coriander, roasted duck with foie gras sausage, and grilled beef tenderloin with portobello mushrooms and red wine sauce.

Typical appetizers include a country pâté of veal and pork, a colorful vegetable terrine and a four-cheese tart that resembles a pizza. For dessert, look for a lime-macadamia tart that's very tart, white peach croustade and a trio of sorbets: kiwi, blood orange and pineapple. Only beers and wines are served, the latter priced from $20 to $58.

Red roses grace the linen-covered tables in wintertime, and other flowers the rest of the year. They add a touch of elegance to this tiny charmer.

(802) 257-4922. Dinner, Tuesday-Sunday 6 to 10. No credit cards.

Brasserie, 324 County St., Bennington.

A cafe with quite a European flair and an expansive, shaded outdoor terrace paved in marble, Brasserie was opened in the 1960s by the late great chef, Dionne Lucas, and still bears her mark under Sheela Harden, who took over in the 1970s.

Funky and bright, the restaurant has quarry tiles on the floors and plain white walls and ceilings (even the old rough beams have been painted white). Tables are set with Bennington pottery from the Potter's Yard next door.

The all-day menu was innovative ahead of its time. Our favorite item – something we seldom see in New England – is pissaladière ($6.25), a Provence snack of sweet onions cooked until they are almost jam, topping thick French bread, with anchovies and oil-cured olives forming a pattern on top.

Another fine lunch is the Yard special ($6.75), a crock of Danish pâté sealed with clarified butter, with French bread and a salad of delicate boston lettuce with a fabulous dressing of olive oil, tarragon vinegar, garlic, lemon juice, dijon mustard and a pinch of salt, bound with eggs.

A friend says she never orders anything here but the baked onion soup, considering it the best anywhere. We liked the soup of the day, cream of watercress and potato, as well as the house quiches, lorraine and spinach, both of the melt-in-the-mouth variety. The chef's salad was a masterpiece of smoked ham and turkey, gruyère cheese, dilled cucumbers, tomatoes and lettuces, so good it almost didn't need the house dressing. A relatively new item is called "the best and simplest," a slab of goat cheese, a small loaf of whole-wheat/sunflower-seed bread, and the house tomato salad with kalamata olives ($6.95).

Nine omelets, salads, pâtés and antipasto plates are offered daily, as are changing specials for heartier appetites, among them grilled duck salad, sautéed chicken breast with a sauce of exotic mushrooms and grilled mako shark served with corn, organic baby potatoes, beans and cherry tomatoes ($7.95 to $11.95).

Favored desserts ($3.25) are roulade leontine, a sponge roll filled with chocolate soufflé and topped with ice cream, and an Austrian nut roll – except for the chunks of nuts, this could have floated away, it was so light and good. The "virtuous chocolate and apricot torte" is said to have less than two milligrams of cholesterol. Brasserie has a full license but a disappointing wine selection. The beers and ales are more interesting.

(802) 447-7922. Open daily, 11:30 to 8, May-October; rest of year, Sunday-Thursday to 3:30, Friday and Saturday to 8.

Alldays & Onions, 519 Main St., Bennington.

This casual cafe with a prominent deli counter was named for an obscure manufacturer of early British cars, and it sums up the free-wheeling spirit of young owners Matthew and Maureen Forlenza. The aspirations have been scaled down since the early days when this was more of a gourmet store offering specialty foods and fine wines, and weekend dinners featured innovative cuisine amid stylish trappings.

The early spirit shone in a weekday lunch that included a delicate cream of golden squash soup and a delightful dish of nachos made with organic blue corn chips, all kinds of chopped vegetables (happily, no refried beans), spicy salsa and melted jack cheese. Another winner was a trio of salads: fettuccine with smoked chicken, tortellini with basil and red potato. The emphasis these days seems to be on create-your-own sandwiches in the $3.95 range.

The menu expands at night, when chef Matthew, who trained in Holland and cooked at the old Village Auberge and the Barrows House in Dorset, prepares dishes like striped bass with garden pepper sauce, scallops with spinach and mushrooms in asiago sauce over pasta, veal sweetbreads with wild mushrooms, roasted chicken with lingonberries, and southwest cowboy steak with skillet corn sauce. Entrée prices are modest, mostly $10.95 to $14.95.

For starters ($3.95 to $6.95), consider bruschetta, the house caesar salad with smoked trout or smoked salmon cakes. Desserts could be dark chocolate cheesecake with raspberry ganache, nectarine-plum crisp, coffee ice cream and oatmeal-fudge bars (for which Gourmet magazine requested the recipe, but the Forlenzas wouldn't give it out). The interesting wine list harbors good values.

(802) 447-0043. Open Monday-Saturday 8 to 5; dinner, Wednesday-Saturday 6 to 9.

Artistic Gourmet

The Artist's Palate Cafe, West Road, Manchester.

Halfway up a mountain, this seasonal cafe at the Southern Vermont Art Center is a great place for lunch with a view of the sculpture garden as well as birch trees, valleys and hills.

Dine inside or on the outdoor terrace on ice-cream parlor chairs. The cafe, newly run by The Equinox, offers a changing menu. At our visit, the menu, attached to an artist's palette, offered choices ($7 to $9.50) like crab and asparagus melt over a toasted English muffin, warm ham and cheese croissant, seafood caesar salad (with smoked shrimp and scallops), poached salmon and vermicelli, and a burger topped with Vermont cheddar. We remember a fantastic tomato-orange soup and a good chicken salad with snow peas. Dessert could be crispy apple tart or melon with berries.

(802) 362-5223. Lunch, Tuesday-Saturday 11:30 to 3, Sunday noon to 3, June to early October.

Mexican Flair/Budget Price

Casa del Sol, Main Street, Putney.

Here is a place purer than Ivory Snow, with prices from never-never land, which never advertises and which fills up through word of mouth. We only found out about it when we read a small article in a local weekly. It's owned by Susana and Richard Ramsay – she, the cook, from Mexico City and he, an anthropologist, who grew up in Georgia and who met her in Peru.

From her small kitchen, Susana turns out some of the best Mexican food we have ever tasted, from her tortilla soup to her flan de leche. The tostada sampler, five small tostadas with toppings of tinga, mole, picadillo, cochinita pibil and refried beans, makes a superb lunch for $5.25. A taco with a choice of toppings (maybe steamed green beans and guacamole or sautéed green peppers with corn and sour cream) is only $2.50. And the suizas, a chicken casserole with green tomatillo sauce, sour cream and cheese, served with refried beans, would satisfy the heartiest of eaters for $7.65.

Complete dinners, including soup or salad, two tostadas of refried beans, Mexican rice, vegetable and tortillas will set you back only $9.75 to $11.50. We took home pork tenderloin in salsa verde and pollo en mole rojo and savored every bite.

The small dining room with its cathedral ceiling is decorated with fine Mexican crafts (some are for sale in a little gift shop). It contains only a dozen or so tables but there are quite a few picnic tables in a garden outside. Bring your own beer or have a bottle of Penafiel, the Mexican mineral water, and end with one of Richard's plates of pecan balls, chocolate-walnut squares and lemon curd ($2.25). If you've indulged in the mixiotes (barbecued lamb in a very hot chile guajillo), you might like some non-fat frozen yogurt with fresh berries.

A lazy susan on the table holds five of Susana's homemade salsas, pickled jalapeños, serrano chiles and marinated onions. This food is dynamite!

(802) 387-5318. Lunch, Tuesday-Sunday 11:30 to 2; dinner, Tuesday-Sunday 5 to 8, Friday to 9. BYOB.

Lodging

Cornucopia of Dorset, Route 30, Dorset 05251.

The personality and hospitality of effervescent innkeepers Bill and Linda Ley shine at this, one of the more deluxe and comfortable B&Bs we've encountered.

The four guest rooms in the main house, each with private bath, are handsomely outfitted with poster or canopy beds, ranging in size from queen to king. We found the Mother Myrick Room particularly comfortable with a kingsize bed against a wall of shelves containing books and family photos. All rooms are lusciously decorated with down comforters and pillows and merino wool mattress pads, chairs with good reading lights, artworks and pieces from the Leys' assorted collections (check the lovers' bench that really isn't). Bowls of fresh fruit, terrycloth robes, telephones and Crabtree & Evelyn toiletries are standard equipment. A rear cottage suite with cathedral-ceilinged living room, fireplace, kitchenette and a loft bedroom is a private retreat. Champagne is served at check-in and a decanter of brandy is ready to be poured in the upstairs hall. Upon your return from dinner, you'll find your bed turned down, the lights off and an oil lamp flickering, and perhaps that yummy buttercrunch from Mother Myrick's Confectionery on the pillow.

Delightful as the bedrooms are, they are nearly overshadowed by the common rooms. The Leys turn over the entire first floor of the house to guests. The small front parlor has bare wide-plank floors, a leather chair with hassock and a built-in backgammon board. The fireplaced living room holds overstuffed sofas and a Tracker organ. The large dining room has a family-style table on a huge oriental rug and opens onto a contemporary sun room with bird feeders attached to the windows and comfy seating where we'd gladly while away the hours. More than 100 movies are available for the VCR here. Outside are lounge chairs on Dorset's obligatory marble patio, set near the colorful gardens.

The Leys pamper their guests with everything from scrapbooks displaying mounted restaurant menus to lavish breakfasts, the menu for which is detailed on a personalized card left in your room the night before. The meal starts with a fruit course, perhaps warm spiced applesauce topped with granola, toasted almonds and crème fraîche; a melon boat filled with berries, blackberry-raspberry cobbler, or kiwi, sliced bananas and blueberries arranged on a strawberry-raspberry sauce. Berry and pecan muffins follow. For main courses, how about apple-cinnamon pancakes with sausage, baked french toast with ham, cream cheese blintzes with warm fruit topping and sour cream, quiche lorraine with tomato and dill, or baked ham and egg cup with Vermont cheddar served with a petite croissant? The baked raspberry pancakes were so good that we asked Linda for the recipe.

You won't leave the table hungry or the Cornucopia unimpressed.

(802) 867-5751 or (800) 566-5751. Fax (802) 867-5753. Doubles, $115 to $155; cottage suite, $225.

The Inn at Ormsby Hill, Route 7A, Manchester Village 05254.

Chris and Ted Sprague, who turned the dining room at the Newcastle Inn in Maine into a destination for gourmands, now lend their considerable innkeeping talents to this expanded B&B backing up to Robert Todd Lincoln's Hildene estate.

Chris, who cooked six nights a week at their Maine inn, found she could not keep up the pace. "The change has rejuvenated me," she advised after they acquired the Ormsby Hill in her native Vermont in late 1995. "I'm able to do more creative breakfasts here, and we've reached a level of elegance that would have been impossible at Newcastle."

The elegance comes in five new luxury rooms they added in an unfinished wing of this sprawling manor house long owned by Edward Isham, an Illinois state legislator and senior partner in a Chicago law firm with Abraham Lincoln's son, whom he entertained here. Each has a gas fireplace, whirlpool tub and handsome decor. Rooms come with interesting angles – "we don't like squares," says Chris – and novel touches, a see-through fireplace between the bedroom and corner jacuzzi in one, a jacuzzi accessed through cupboard doors in another.

The main house already offered five comfortable guest rooms, four with two-person whirlpool baths and separate showers. All contain king or queen canopy or four-poster beds, plush armchairs, antique chests, artworks and oriental rugs. Some prefer the main-floor library room, beamed and dark with well-stocked bookshelves and a woodburning fireplace. We're partial to the rear Hildene Room, light and airy in yellow and white, where ivy is twined around the bed canopy.

The best part may be the common rooms and the culinary treats. The foyer leads to a front parlor furnished with antiques. From here one looks to the rear through a spacious fireplaced library into a conservatory dining room extending 40 feet back. At first glance, the total depth, in what is a strikingly wide house, takes the breath away. So does the view across the terrace, back yard, gardens and Hildene to mountains through the many-paned windows.

Breakfast is usually a lavish buffet, taken in the conservatory or on the outdoor terrace. The sideboard holds three kinds of cereal including homemade granola, a bowl of assorted fruit, a basket of English muffins and two kinds of pastries (perhaps espresso-white chocolate coffee cake and blueberry-lemon pound cake). The main dish could be cheese strata, blueberry bread pudding, leek-bacon-gorgonzola polenta or wild mushroom risotto. Dessert is the icing on the cake, so to speak: perhaps peach or apple-cranberry crisp with vanilla ice cream.

The treats continue on weekend evenings. The Spragues offer a light supper on Friday night for arriving weekenders ($20 a couple). "It's like coming home to Mom's," Chris says. Guests go into the kitchen and are served something like a stew and salad and then clear their own plates for dessert. Saturday night revives memories of four-course Newcastle dinners ($60 a couple, BYOB), the menu hand-written on a card. Our meal started with skewers of five large shrimp laced with dill and garlic. Cream biscuits accompanied an exotic salad of many lettuces and a creamy dressing. The main course was juicy rack of lamb with an elegant sauce incorporating shiitake mushrooms, tender as could be and teamed with barely cooked snow peas and pattypan squash. A very large slice of satiny chocolate-hazelnut terrine was a super ending.

From welcoming macaroons upon arrival to a doggy bag of white-chocolate pound cake to take on your way, food is the star at this charming B&B.

(802) 362-1163 or (800) 670-2841. Fax (802) 362-5176. Doubles, $115 to $205.

Conservatory dining room at The Inn at Ormsby Hill is site for creative meals.

1811 House, Route 7A, Manchester Village 05254.

Bowls of popcorn and no fewer than 49 single-malt scotches – the biggest selection in Vermont, they say – are available in the intimate pub of this elegant B&B full of antiques, oriental rugs and charm.

The pub (open nightly from 5:30 to 8) is where owners Marnie and Bruce Duff offer McEwan's ale on draught or one of their rare scotches, $4 to $7 a shot or three for $10 for a wee dram of each, if you're into testing. Although it's supposed to be a reproduction of an early American tavern, it looks just like a Scottish pub with its McDuff tartan seats and horse brasses. Nearby are the elegant yet comfortable parlor and library with stenciled flowers of the British Isles (the thistle, shamrock, rose and daffodil), dark wood paneling, fine paintings and porcelains.

All eleven guest rooms in the main house are spacious, air-conditioned and come with private baths. Five have fireplaces, and a corner suite has a kingsize canopy four-poster bed and a fireplace. The fabrics in the draperies and bedspreads are exceptionally tasteful. The bedroom of Mary Lincoln Isham (Abraham Lincoln's granddaughter, who lived here for a short time) contains a marble enclosure for the bathtub that she had put in.

An addition in a rear cottage has produced three deluxe rooms with kingsize beds, fireplaces and private baths.

In the big kitchen with a commercial stove, Marnie Duff whips up hearty English breakfasts, perhaps including fresh scones, fried tomatoes, eggs any style or special french toast soaked overnight with pecans. Guests partake in the dining room or pub amid Villeroy & Boch china and the family sterling.

(802) 362-1811 or (800) 432-1811. Doubles, $110 to $180.

Gourmet Treats

The Little Rooster Cafe, Route 7A south of Manchester Center, is an offshoot of the Chantecleer restaurant. It offers interesting breakfast and lunch fare. For breakfast, the Rooster tops an English muffin with poached egg, creamed spinach and smoked salmon in a light mustard sauce. For lunch ($6.95 to $8.95), we've enjoyed the crab cake baguette, the leg of lamb sandwich and the grilled tuna niçoise salad.

Across the street is the **Buttery at the Jelly Mill,** upstairs in a fun collection of shops selling gourmet foods and kitchenware, among other things. It offers many sandwiches, including smoked salmon on a toasted croissant with capers. The Buttery special is ham, cheese, artichoke hearts and hollandaise on toasted rye. Snacks like nachos, soups, salads and specials such as a tomato, bacon and cheddar quiche are listed, and you can end with neapolitan mousse torte or amaretto bread pudding. Weekend brunches are served from 10 to 1.

More exotic sandwiches and salads are available at **The Village Fare Cafe & Bakery,** Union Street, Manchester Village. Guests at the nearby Equinox resort take a break from high living to lunch on a tuna rollup, a roast beef and boursin sandwich, or quiche of the day in the $4.50 to $6.25 range. A choice of four deli salads with a side of bread goes for $5.50. The pastries change daily, but they always include the biggest muffins you ever saw. Stop here in the morning for espresso and the pita eggwich (scrambled eggs, peppers, onions and diced tomatoes with provolone, $4.25). Or come on weekend nights for a fancy dessert, wine or beer, and live entertainment.

Up for Breakfast, Main Street, Manchester Center, is just what its name says: upstairs above a storefront, and open for breakfast only (weekdays except Tuesday 6 to noon, weekends 7 to 1). You'll find sourdough pancakes, cajun frittata, huevos rancheros and belgian waffles in the $5 to $7.25 range. We chose "one of each" – one eggs benedict and one eggs argyle (with smoked salmon). These proved hearty, as did the heavy Irish scone, both dishes garnished with chunks of pineapple and watermelon. Only after we'd eaten did we see the blackboard menu around the side, listing some rather exotic specials like rainbow trout with eggs and mango-cranberry-nutmeg pancakes.

Mozzarella and More

Al Ducci's Italian Pantry, Elm Street, Manchester Center. For superior fresh mozzarella, drop into this little Italian grocery and meet Al Scheps, who has been making his own since he was eight years old. The name is a takeoff on Balducci's in Manhattan. "We have a lot of fun here," says Al, who jokes back and forth with his customers. A one-pound ball of mozzarella is $4.49 and, as Al suggests, it is delicious cut into cubes and mixed with ripe tomatoes, red onions, fruity olive oil, balsamic vinegar and cubes of homemade Italian bread, all of which he sells. Good sandwiches ($4.50 to $5.50) are also made with the bread; you can have additions like grated carrots, sundried tomatoes. roasted peppers and fresh basil. Homemade sausage, cannoli and sfogliatelle (a flaky pastry with ricotta cheese) are other goodies. At our latest visit, chef Victor Gentile was planning to open **Vittorio's Trattoria** next door, offering a four-course dinner of "whatever I make that day" for $24.99.

Peltier's Market on the Green in Dorset has been the center of Dorset life since the early 1800s. A true country store with all the staples, it also caters to the upscale. You might pick up a sandwich from the refrigerator – perhaps smoked salmon or avocado, cheese and tomato. Caviar, good wines, Vermont products like cheese from Shelburne Farms, exotic vegetables and prime meats can be found here. So can worms and night crawlers, close by the pesto and sundried tomatoes in the chilled produce case.

Billed as "a true factory store," **Adams Gourmet Woodware** on Route 30 just south of Dorset has a fine selection of cheeseboards, spice racks, butcher blocks, and the like made of native hardwoods. On the second floor, seconds are sold at substantial savings. There's a smell and sound of woodworking in the air, and you can see some of the action through a factory-viewing window.

Two large stores in tiny Weston are worth a visit. Almost across the street from each other, the **Vermont Country Store** and the **Weston Village Store** are chock full of those wonderful Vermont items we all love to shop for. The Country Store is more upscale in three buildings, including the West River Jewelry Company and Bandstand Books & Art. Check the candy counter at the Country Store for a fantastic selection of old-fashioned candy. How about a log cabin made of maple sugar? The Village Store is an old-fashioned, jumbled-up emporium from yesteryear. It has a good selection of Vermont cheeses.

The essence of Vermont, in food as well as decor, is served up at **The Bryant House Restaurant,** part of the Vermont Country Store complex. Here you can get a grilled Vermont cheddar sandwich plate with shoestring french fries or, a Vermont standby from days gone by, Vermont Common crackers and milk with a hunk of cheddar cheese, eaten with a spoon from a bowl. Most lunch items are in the $6 to $7 range. Or stop in the **Ice Cream Parlor** for Indian pudding, a root-beer float, ice-cream sodas or an Ovaltine milk frappe.

As if Weston visitors needed more food, the **Grafton Village Apple Co.** moved from Grafton into the thick of the Weston action. "Come taste Vermont," it beckons. Indeed you can. All kinds of Vermont foods are for sale and you get to sample some, including salsas, horseradish-pepper jelly, vinegars, apple butter, mustards, cheeses and biscuits. There were oodles of kitchen gadgets, but no apples – we were there before apple season.

Along Route 100 to the south, **Partridge Feathers** at Tollgate Village, West Dover, is where well-known chef Brill Williams of The Inn at Saw Mill Farm hangs his hat by day. It's an interesting pottery, glassware and woodenware shop where he stocks a few choice and expensive lines by Vermont artisans, among them Simon Pearce glass, Monroe Salt Works stoneware and wood-turned bowls by Luke Mann.

Taddingers, Route 100 at the Haystack Access Road, is an expansive new country store with seven unusual shops under one roof. We especially liked the Vermont specialty foods section, with quite an array from horseradish jam to hot sauces and bread mixes, the Wilcox Ice Cream parlor and the Nature Room full of more kinds of birdhouses than we thought existed.

Wilmington is home to **Bean Head's,** an espresso bar and bagelry that serves soups and sandwiches as well as gourmet coffees. Two good gift shops here are **For All Occasions** and **The Incurable Romantic.**

A gaggle of wooden Canada geese on the roof identifies the woodworking showroom of **John McLeod Ltd.** along Route 9 west of Wilmington. The Scotsman produces fabulous bowls, spoons, chopping boards and such. Adjacent is **The Eclectic Eye,** with specialty foods and gourmet jewelry (spatula and teapot pins) among its gift items.

Bennington Potters at 324 County St., Bennington, is the place to head for a great selection of the familiar pottery at discount prices. Also part of the Bennington Potters Yard complex is **Cinnamons,** specializing in kitchen ware.

Fine produce, fruit, plants, fresh pies and more are featured at **Dutton Farm Stands,** a fixture along Route 30 in Newfane and with an expanded second ocation along Routes 11-30 in Manchester Center. Wendy and Paul Dutton grow the produce on their 105-acre Newfane farm and apples on a 30-acre orchard in Brattleboro. In melon season, they offer slices of many kinds to sample – an instructive touch, and refreshing, too.

Gourmet Sweets

Mother Myrick's Confectionery and Ice Cream Parlor, Route 7A, Manchester Center.

Here is paradise for anyone with a sweet tooth. Jacki Baker and Ron Mancini have operated Mother Myrick's (named for a famous midwife) since 1977 and their chocolates and candy are known across the East.

It's fun to watch the confections being made. Using old-fashioned equipment wherever possible (like a two-foot cream beater from the 1940s for fondant), they make a myriad of chocolates, truffles, fudge, apricots hand-dipped in dark chocolate, fancy molds and their most popular candy, buttercrunch, rolled in roasted almonds and cashews, $17.95 a pound and worth every penny.

The best fudge sauce we have tasted (even better than mom's) comes out of the kitchen here. Several flavors of ice cream changing by the season (Irish coffee and bittersweet-pumpkin at a recent fall visit), pies and much more are for sale. The couple's scones are a hot item; the coffee-hazelnut-chocolate chip is delicious. Stop by for sour cream-chocolate chunk coffee cake and superior cappuccino in the morning or anytime for a myrtle (their kind of turtle) or a piece of blueberry-raspberry pie or Vermont maple cheesecake with fresh berries.

These are served to go or to have in the charmingly art-deco cafe or outside on the front deck. You can send for Mother Myrick's little newsletter and catalog, The Scoop (Box 1142, Manchester Center 05255) and order some of these things by mail.

(802) 362-1560. Open daily 10 to 6, weekends to 9.

Champagne awaits special-occasion celebrants in guest room at Wheatleigh.

The Tri-State Berkshires

A Tradition of High Tastes

Country inns may seem more historic in Vermont, but they have reached their pinnacle in the Berkshires, an area whose name is inseparably linked with country inns and summer tradition in the national perception.

That may be a result of Norman Rockwell's depiction of the Red Lion Inn and Main Street in Stockbridge, a scene that has come to epitomize the essence of New England for anyone west of the Hudson River.

Indeed, when friends from Switzerland visited us one foliage season and asked to "see" New England in a day, we headed off to the Berkshires and Stockbridge so they could sense what New England is all about. They shot two rolls of color film before departing for Texas.

Had their visit been in the summer, we would have taken them to Tanglewood in Lenox, where the elaborate picnics complete with tablecloths and candelabra on the lawns beside the Music Shed are as delightful a tradition in which to partake (and observe) as the Boston Symphony Orchestra is to hear.

The inns in the Berkshires are keeping up with the times, both in quality and in numbers. And although the area has had good restaurants longer than most resort regions, thanks to its early and traditional status as a destination for summer visitors, new restaurants pop up every year.

As with the inns, the dining situation reflects the sophisticated tastes and often the prices of a noted resort and cultural area close to metropolitan centers.

But there also are rural, rustic charms to be discovered amid the luxury of Lenox or Lakeville and the sophistication of Stockbridge or Salisbury. Seek them out as well, to savor the total Berkshire experience.

Dining and Lodging

The Berkshires are such a popular destination that three-night (and even four-night) stays are the minimum for weekends in summer and foliage season at many inns. Prices quoted here are for peak weekends; midweek and off-season often are considerably lower. Restaurant hours generally vary from daily in summer and fall to part-time the rest of the year.

Old Chatham Sheepherding Company Inn, 99 Shaker Museum Road, Old Chatham, N.Y. 12136.

Consider the contrast: The 1790 Georgian Colonial manor house was formerly occupied by the man whose renowned Shaker collections are housed in the Shaker Museum across the street. Today it's the home of an exceptional restaurant and country inn, the focal point of an expanding dairy and food operation, and a delightful destination for gourmets.

The inn has embellished the Shakers' stress on "simple pleasures," conveying the ultimate in the good life in an utterly bucolic setting: 500 acres of forested hillsides, rolling pasturelands, grazing sheep and hardly a sign of civilization in sight.

The inn with the unusual name fulfills a dream of Tom Clark, head of an investment firm in Greenwich, Conn., and his wife Nancy, an interior designer. They bought the property in 1993 for a sheep dairy farm, which quickly became the nation's largest with more than 2,000 head, and thought the manor house might become a modest B&B. But graduate students from the School of Hotel Administration at Cornell University, to whom they turned, recommended otherwise. More than $1 million later, the inn opened in 1995 with six comfortable guest rooms, two cottage suites and a 48-seat restaurant of great charm. At our stay coinciding with its first anniversary, two more suites were about to open in a carriage house, as was a bakery and a retail shop dispensing the farm's breads, cheeses and meats. Plans included three more bedrooms and a meeting site in a barn.

The stylish restaurant is a showcase for the sheepherding farm's products. A mural of the house, grounds and a foxhunt wrapped around the room in which we dined. Chippendale chairs flanked well-spaced tables set with white linens and cobalt blue water glasses. Beyond was a smaller room done in Colonial colors and beyond that a handsome tavern dining area

A team of young, apron-clad waitresses in khaki pants, striped shirts and ties provided friendly and flawless service. One presented a crock of butter and poured olive oil and pepper into a dish to accompany crusty wheat and rye bread and melt-in-the-mouth cheddar-scallion biscuits. Another arrived with a complimentary amusé, a spicy little lamb sausage with couscous. The farm's output also turned up in two appetizers. One was the signature camembert crisp ($8.50) in flaky phyllo

Chef Melissa Kelly holds baby lamb raised at Old Chatham Sheepherding Company farm.

with venison prosciutto, cherry-gooseberry chutney, mesclun and crisp walnut levain croutons. The other was grilled fresh sheep's cheese wrapped in grape leaves, again with mesclun, olives and homemade toast points.

The best was yet to come. Among the six changing entrées ($17 to $24), the grilled leg of lamb with white bean salad, tapenade, grilled fennel and roasted peppers was as close to lamb lovers' heaven as we may ever get. Two delicate quail stuffed with Szechuan sausage carried a distinct bite, leavened a bit by wilted oriental greens and a puree of mashed potatoes. For dessert ($5 to $6.50), the perfect crème brûlée with black raspberries was nearly upstaged by the plate of three sheep's milk ice creams and sorbets (chocolate-vanilla, strawberry verbena and toasted almond) and a sampling of four different cookies. A glass of the house Millbrook chardonnay and a bottle of Beaulieu Vineyard Rutherford cabernet ($26) accompanied from a select wine list on the pricey side.

Executive chef Melissa Kelly, who's known for flavorful contemporary dishes with Mediterranean and Asian accents, made the rounds after dinner. After graduating first in her class at the Culinary Institute of America, she became enamored with the area's agricultural bounty during her two years as executive chef for Larry Forgione's Beekman 1766 Tavern in Rhinebeck. After a year with the legendary Alice Waters at Chez Panisse in California, she came home at age 30 to make her mark at a restaurant on a working farm.

When we returned to our overnight quarters in the Cotswold suite, sheep-shaped cookies had been placed beside the next day's weather forecast on a tray at turn-down, and two small sheepskin rugs (for toasty tootsies) appeared on either side of the queensize bed. The vaulted, two-story accommodation in a side cottage was country-chic with an Adirondack look. Beneath the frame of a kayak resting on the rafters, a toffee-colored leather sofa and two matching chairs, faced a large fireplace in the spacious sitting area. Half an old rowboat placed upright made a neat corner case for books and creels. Ingenious tiny track lights on wires illuminated the space. The big sunken bathroom contained a racy red clawfoot soaking tub with sleek chrome legs, a bidet, an oversize corner shower with heavy glass door, Neutrogena toiletries, thick white towels, and washcloths rolled up in a Shaker basket. As we relaxed on comfortable wicker chairs on the expansive rear deck that overlooks the hillsides, enjoying the sounds of the sheep and birds, we wished we never had to leave.

The Cotswold and the adjacent, smaller Hampshire Suite are the most choice accommodations, although two new fireplaced rooms in the bakery building rank right up there. Like the others, the six smaller rooms in the main house are handsomely appointed with queen beds, Brunschwig & Fils draperies and fabrics, oriental rugs and a mix of traditional country pieces and antiques. Two rear inn rooms open onto individual porches, and the nicest of these also comes with a loveseat and a fireplace. A couple of front rooms and one downstairs opposite the entry are on the small side and lack places to sit. Guests share with dinner guests a handsome living room in which the ubiquitous (but understated) sheep motif is slyly interrupted by red fox heads at the ends of the curtain rods. A large screened porch is outfitted in dark green wicker with overstuffed pillows and a two-person swing.

The New York Times was at our door before breakfast, when the inn's culinary treats continued in the tavern room. Fresh orange juice was poured and a sideboard held breakfast pastries and a large bowl of tiny berries (golden raspberries, black-berries and blueberries) to mix with sheep's milk yogurt. The main courses were blueberry corn cakes and a grilled vegetable omelet with sheep's milk ricotta, toast made from the previous evening's wheat and rye bread, and lamb sausage with a curiously sweet taste. The heaping plate was garnished with edible sun-flower sprouts and slices of kiwi, pineapple, orange and cantaloupe. Our only quibble, after two memorable meals, was that the morning coffee was lukewarm.

That was a surprise, as was the appearance of Melissa back in the kitchen cooking breakfast after so late a dinner the night before. Surprises abound at this eden of an inn, however. Innkeeper George Shattuck III, a Cornell hotel school grad with credentials beyond his years, answers the telephone, shows guests to their rooms, prints the night's computer-generated menus and seats dinner patrons. Nancy and Tom Clark mingle with diners on weekends as if they were hosting a country house party. The entire staff is service-oriented and inordinately friendly, and there's not a whit of pretension or intimidation. "We want to be a luxury inn but not take ourselves too seriously," explains George. The Shakers' "simple pleasures," he means, delivered quite grandly.

(518) 794-9774. Fax (518) 794-9779. Doubles, $150 to $225; suites, $250 and $350. Dinner nightly except Tuesday, from 5:30; Sunday brunch, 10 to 1:30.

New Gallery Cafe at Gedney Farm.

Table for two at Old Inn on the Green.

The Old Inn on the Green and Gedney Farm, Route 57, New Marlborough, Mass. 01230.

Bradford Wagstaff bought this abandoned 1760 inn on the old Hartford-Albany stage route in 1973 and it took ten years to get it back into shape. The result was initially a six-room B&B and a dining room of distinction. He's since opened eleven luxurious rooms and suites in a great Normandy-style barn called Gedney Farm down the road, and lately added a sculpture park and farm gallery, with a cafe for lunch that's positively idyllic.

Brad's wife, Leslie Miller, a baker who used to supply area restaurants, and chef Christopher Capstick oversee gourmet dinners served totally by candlelight in as historic a setting as can be conceived. About 50 people are seated in the tavern room, a formal parlor or at the harvest table in the dining room. In each, the original wainscoting, stenciling, antiques and windows draped in velvet are shown to advantage. Pamela Hardcastle's unique handmade wreaths using branches and bark are fascinating, the large mural of cows grazing on the New Marlborough green is wonderful to see, and it's easy to imagine yourself transported back a couple of centuries for the evening.

While the inn once served only prix-fixe dinners on weekends, it now offers à-la-carte menus the rest of the week in the tavern or on the canopied outdoor terrace in summer, as well as weekend lunches in that great new Gallery Cafe or outside overlooking the sculpture park. Even with its bold new contemporary dimensions, its culinary claim to fame continues to be the Saturday prix-fixe dinners ($48) with a set menu except for a choice from two entrées and two desserts. Arranged three months in advance for mailing to 2,000 regulars, the quarterly menu makes for delicious reading and is guaranteed to make you think about getting yourself to New Marlborough pronto.

Chèvre and almond puff-pastry sticks accompany drinks, served in delicate stemmed glasses. From a mushroom and herb soup that is the essence of mushroom to the final cappuccino with shredded chocolate on top, things go from great to greater. We can't say enough for either the food or the experience. A summer meal might start with a caviar terrine with a trio of black caviars, lemon crème fraîche and frozen vodka soufflé. The main dish could be grilled arctic char with smoked tomato sauce, pesto fritters and chèvre malfatis or herb-crusted rack of wild boar with tomatoes à la marseillaise, spaghetti squash gratin and rosemary gremolata. For dessert you might find riesling wine sorbet or white chocolate-pistachio mousse.

Besides Leslie's breads and desserts, the couple's specialties are lamb and veal raised on their Willow Creek Farm. Brad's wine list is extensive and expensive, with most bottles $30 and up.

The candlelit bar area and rear terrace are popular for casual dining. The terrace/fireside à-la-carte menu is short but appealing, from rock shrimp and potato brandade, alsacian tarte and marinated octopus and pomodoro charlotte to lobster timbale, wine-poached skate, and veal breast and loin roulade. Appetizers are in the $6 to $8 range and entrées, $17.50 to $22.50.

Upstairs are six rather spare guest rooms, two with private baths, authentically furnished with old armoires, hooked rugs and crewel bedspreads. The second-floor veranda across the front of the inn is a serene spot from which to view the passing scene. A generous continental breakfast – including fresh fruits, cereals, pastries, coffee cake, croissants and homemade preserves – is served on the terrace or in the tavern.

The Gedney Farm restoration is a sight to behold. Beneath the barn's soaring, 30-foot ceiling is a lineup of six guest rooms and six two-level suites, their second floors fashioned from the old hayloft and reached by private staircases. Most have fireplaced sitting rooms. The modern baths are outfitted with Neutrogena amenities; some have deep, two-person whirlpool tubs under glass ceilings open to the roof structure. Leslie has decorated each room with panache in styles from French provincial to Moroccan. Oriental and kilim rugs are on the floors, woven or fabric coverlets are on the beds, and Pamela Hardcastle's exotic wreaths adorn the walls.

And now, crowning glory, comes the Gedney Farm Gallery in a restored Normandy horse barn. Fantastic paintings, sculptures, furniture and other artworks are displayed against the white painted interior walls. The barn door is open onto a trellised stone terrace and the green fields, where the outdoor sculptures are strategically placed for viewing. White-clothed tables are set here and there for lunch in the **Gallery Cafe.** From the abbreviated menu we liked the sound of the Gedney Farm salad with mesclun, roasted peppers and house-made ricotta. Start perhaps with toasted corn and shellfish soup. Continue with grilled sirloin steak au poivre with sautéed mushrooms on a crispy sourdough baguette, torta rustica or a vegetable brioche ($8 to $12). After a piece of fruit pie or a refreshing sorbet in that pastoral setting, you may be lulled into buying some art to remember the place by.

(413) 229-3131 or (800) 286-3139. Fax (413) 229-2053. Lunch, Saturday and Sunday 11 to 3, summer-foliage. Dinner by reservation, prix-fixe, Saturday 6 to 9; à la carte, nightly except Saturday 5:30 to 9. Closed Tuesday and Monday-Wednesday in winter. Doubles, $120 to $160 in inn; $175 to $285 at Gedney Farm.

Aubergine, Intersection of Routes 22 and 23, Hillsdale, N.Y. 12529.
Classic French chef Jean Morel and his L'Hostellerie Bressane, a culinary landmark since 1971, had a tradition to uphold. So when he and his wife Madeleine

Chef-owner David Lawson checks out stock in wine cellar at Aubergine.

decided in 1995 to retire, they approached David and Stacie Lawson. David, a native Minnesotan who had trained in London in the French tradition with Albert Roux, had earned his spurs in the Berkshires as executive chef at the Old Inn on the Green and at Blantyre. There was only one remaining step – a restaurant he could call his own. He found it in this rosy brick inn, built in 1783 by a Revolutionary War soldier in the Dutch Colonial style, across the Massachusetts/New York state line at the crossroads of Hillsdale. "I learned this was a thriving corner at the gateway to the Berkshires," says David. "And it certainly was a going concern."

With a change in name to the easier-to-pronounce Aubergine (French for eggplant) and some dramatic changes in the entry, the establishment barely skipped a beat. The lightened-up foyer now focuses on a stunning display (at our late summer visit) of huge sunflowers in a vase, and eggplants, runner beans and squashes on a table. The walls of the men's room are still papered with wine labels and the four smallish, fireplaced dining rooms retain a quaint, somewhat dated look. The fare continues to reflect the French tradition, but the menu is in English and blends contemporary nuances and techniques that quickly earned it a four-diamond AAA rating as a destination restaurant. In the planning stages were smoker dinners for cigar buffs, wine tastings and a "Berkshire chef's roundtable" featuring guest chefs.

Three accomplished cooks assist David in the kitchen, while wife Stacie and three of L'Hostellerie's senior wait captains oversee the dining rooms. The silver forks and spoons are set upside down in the European style beside Villeroy & Boch service plates on tables spaced decently apart. Fresh flowers, pretty wallpapers and curtains, and ladderback or round-backed velvet chairs in a plum color convey French country charm. A few tables are set up for overflow in the lounge with its copper bar, where we were seated.

Dinner begins with a complimentary amusé, perhaps a slice of rich country pâté, served on a crouton with cornichons, or triangles of duck confit and scallions wrapped in an Algerian feuille-de-bric. Among starters ($5.75 to $10) are a classic caesar salad garnished with crispy fried onions and what has become a signature dish: three Maine scallop cakes with shiitake mushrooms, scallions and bean sprouts, dressed with a warm ponzu vinaigrette. Soups (perhaps creamy mushroom bisque with croutons or onion with madeira and cognac) are served from a silver tureen at tableside.

Typical main courses run from $18 for pan-seared salmon with wilted organic greens, white bean puree and saffron sauce to $24 for filet mignon with stilton and herb crust, baked grits, pinenuts and port-plumped raisins. Two specialties are roasted loin and confit leg of local rabbit with potato flan, French green lentils, mushrooms and bacon lardons, and roasted breast of squab with honey-vinegar jus, creamy Minnesota wild rice and mirepoix.

The most special desserts here have always been the soufflés, hot or cold, and we'll never forget the frozen coffee soufflé with kirsch, ringed by figs and candied chestnuts. David continues to offer grand marnier and hazelnut soufflés ($7), "as much for theater as anything else." He prefers a classic tarte tatin with calvados-caramel sauce, orange crème brûlée or what he calls a Roux Brothers' lemon tart "in the style of my mentors."

To the distinguished, mostly French wine cellar he inherited, David has added a number of American offerings at fair prices. Rare wines command up to $400 and fine ports up to $200, but a decent muscadet and beaujolais can be had for $20, and our favorite Millbrook chardonnay from the Hudson Valley goes for about $15.

Aubergine offers two plain but comfortable guest rooms, each with queen bed and private hall bath, on the second floor. On the third are two more luxurious bedrooms with private baths. One is done in soft lavenders with a queensize bed and one is in coral shades with twins. Continental breakfast (an artfully arranged fruit plate, muffins and scones, and strong French coffee) is available for $10 each. The price is a bit of a deterrent. But, David explains, this is not an inn: "we're adamantly a restaurant with rooms."

(518) 325-3412. Dinner, Wednesday-Sunday 5:30 to 10. Doubles, $85 and $110.

Blantyre, Route 20 and East Street, Lenox, Mass. 01240.
Past a gatekeeper and up a long, curving driveway in the midst of 85 country acres appears the castle of your dreams. In fact, the 1902 Tudor-style brick manor built as a summer cottage for a millionaire in the turpentine business as an authentic replica of the Hall of Blantyre in Scotland used to be called a castle. It's full of hand-carved wood ornamentation, high-beamed ceilings, crystal chandeliers and spacious public rooms, plus turrets, gargoyles and carved friezes – just as in the English country-house hotels that innkeeper Roderick Anderson, speaking with a trace of a Scottish accent, seeks to emulate. And emulate it does rather success-fully, as attested by membership in the prestigious Relais & Châteaux group.

Faithfully restored by owner Jane Fitzpatrick of the Red Lion Inn in nearby Stockbridge, Blantyre houses guests in eight elegant rooms and suites in the mansion, twelve more contemporary quarters in a distant carriage house and three scattered about the property in small cottages (one a relative bargain at $175 a night).

The public rooms and guest rooms are so luxurious in a castle kind of way as to defy description – take our word or that of those who pay up to $650 a night for the

Blantyre is a Tudor-style replica of a castle in Scotland.

Paterson Suite with a fireplaced living room (complete with a crystal chandelier over a lace-covered table in the middle of the room), two bathrooms and a large bedroom with a kingsize four-poster bed. A typical bathroom has a scale, a wooden valet, heated towel racks, embroidered curtains and more toiletries than one ever hoped to see. With handpainted tiles and marble floors in the bathrooms, newly renovated rooms in the carriage house have balconies or decks and wet bars. Some have lofts or sitting rooms, and all are near the pool.

A continental breakfast of croissants and muffins is served in Blantyre's sunny conservatory. Tables topped with mustard jars full of flowers are set beside windows overlooking gnarled trees and golf-course-like lawns. Additional breakfast items can be ordered for a charge.

Country-house cuisine, lately lightened up in style and made more contemporary by chef Michael Roller, is available to house guests and the public in the formal dining room or two smaller rooms. The tables are set with different themes, the china and crystal changing frequently as Jane Fitzpatrick adds to the collection. Investing in its kitchen, Blantyre added a barbecue for grilling purposes and new and adventurous dishes for what chef Michael, who returned to Blantyre after a stint at Restaurant Million in Charleston, S.C., considers a savvy clientele with high expectations. Dinner is prix-fixe, $68 for three courses with many choices.

A typical dinner starts with a "surprise," perhaps foie gras or veal sweetbreads with sauternes and carrot sauce. Just a couple of bites to whet the appetite for what's to come – perhaps oyster and spring onion broth with a chive potato cake, Maine lobster and somen noodle salad with spicy ginger sauce, lightly cured salmon with cucumber and seaweed salad, or sautéed foie gras and green lentils with shiitake mushrooms and leeks. Main courses could include herb-layered sea scallops with grilled asparagus and chive sauce, seared pepper-crusted tuna with leeks and chanterelles, roast saddle of rabbit and foie gras with a basil and bell pepper confit, and pan-roasted breast and ravioli of wild mallard duckling with zucchini.

For dessert, how about bitter Swiss chocolate cake with sour orange compote and blackberry sorbet, white chocolate mousse and plum roulade with ginger-lime sauce, or lemon meringue tart with blueberry compote and passionfruit coulis? The wine list is strong on California chardonnays and cabernets and French regionals, priced up to $220. After dinner, guests like to adjourn to the Music Room for coffee and cordials, Blantyre having the atmosphere of a convivial country house.

Lunch on the terrace ($13 to $25) is a sybaritic indulgence. Walk it off around the gorgeous property. Play tennis on one of four Har-Tru courts or croquet on the only bent-grass tournament lawn in Massachusetts. The oversize guest book in the entry hall is full of superlatives written by happy patrons. The consensus: "Perfect. We'll be back."

(413) 637-3556 (November-April, 298-3806). Fax (413) 637-4282. Lunch in July and August, Tuesday-Sunday 12:30 to 1:45; dinner by reservation, nightly in summer and foliage season, 6 to 9; otherwise, Tuesday-Sunday. Jackets and ties required. Doubles, $250 to $435; suites, $300 to $650. Closed November-April.

Wheatleigh, Hawthorne Road, Lenox, Mass. 01240.

People who expect the height of luxury seek it in this Italian palazzo built in 1893 as a wedding gift for the Countess de Heredia. It's romantic, extravagant, dramatic and ornate. Wheatleigh's food ranks with the best in the Berkshires, and the area food cognoscenti covet the experience, if not the expense.

The imposing entrance of the honey-colored brick building framed in wrought iron leads into a pillared great hall with parquet floors, fireplace, a grand piano, a majestic staircase and formal sitting areas. For its centennial year in 1993, owners Susan and Linwood Simon redecorated the entire place, "bringing in antiques we've been collecting for years," in Susan's words. Window treatments now match the bed canopies, and bathrooms sport new tiles and fixtures. All seventeen air-conditioned guest rooms are different. Seven are huge, two merely large, two medium and the rest, frankly, small. Nine have fireplaces and some have terraces or balconies. Susan's aim was to be "true to the period of the house and its architectural style" (it took her five years to find the right pattern of English axminster for the carpeting in the halls). The period can be austere; some guests think the larger rooms could use more furniture and more of a cozy feeling. Having seen all the rooms, we would go for the best; the small rooms seem claustrophobic in comparison.

Finishing touches have been added under general manager François Thomas, a suave young Parisian who had managed a four-star hotel in Bordeaux. Each room now has a TV/VCR and – a first in our experience – a portable telephone for those who want to be in touch wherever they are. He redid seven rooms, added $50,000 worth of artworks and, crowning glory, turned a portion of the basement into a state-of-the-art fitness room with computerized equipment that tallies how you're doing as you watch the overhead TV. Adjacent is a massage room with a masseur on call, and next on the agenda was to be a wine cellar for tastings or casual dinners.

Outside are the joys of a 22-acre property within walking distance of Tanglewood, a tennis court and a heated swimming pool hidden away in a glade.

Like the French châteaux, says François, the pride of Wheatleigh is its restaurant. It includes a handsome chandeliered dining room and a large enclosed portico, their round tables set with white linens, service plates in three patterns, delicate wine glasses and vases of fresh flowers. Three tile murals from England, each weighing 500 pounds, dress the walls and acquire a luminescent quality in the candlelight.

Executive chef Peter Platt, a 1980 Williams College history graduate, trained at the Cordon Bleu in London and worked under Jasper White and Lydia Shire at the Parker House in Boston before moving to Wheatleigh in 1986. Lean and lanky, he's articulate and as down-to-earth as his food prices and aspirations are lofty. He oversees a cooking staff of fourteen, some of whose foreign backgrounds give an international flavor to what he calls "new French classic cuisine."

Three four-course tasting menus ($68 each) are offered each evening – regular, low-fat and vegetarian – and substitution between tasting menus is encouraged. The entire table may sample treats from a special dégustation menu of the chef's choice for $90 per. A less exotic but highly regarded à la carte menu ($16.50 to $24.50) is available in summer in the Grill Room.

One recent night's offering opened with seared Hudson Valley foie gras with squab breast, chanterelles, French green lentils and black truffle sauce. The fish course teamed "line-caught Maine halibut" with lobster, shaved fennel, sweet corn and ossetra caviar sauce. The main dish was roast loin of veal with tiny vegetables, celery root and lemon-thyme sauce, but you could have substituted roast rack of South Texas antelope with a trio of vegetable purees, tiny vegetables and black huckleberry sauce from the low-fat menu. Dessert was warm Valhrona chocolate soufflé with maple ice cream, or poached bosc pear with coconut sorbet from the low-fat menu, or lemon gratin with peppered blackberry coulis from the vegetarian menu.

A wine list complete with table of contents presents selections worthy of the feast. It used to start in the thirties – "that's the level that begins to fit in with our food," the mâître-d informed – and rises to more than $1,000. François has added choices in the mid to high twenties in an effort to make the Wheatleigh experience more affordable.

He also has added Evian water and bowls of fruit in guest rooms upon arrival, and chocolates at nightly turndown. Also new was a series of food theme weekends. One of the first featured truffles – for a cool $1,450 a couple.

(413) 637-0610. Fax (413) 637-4507. Lunch in summer, Tuesday-Saturday noon to 1:30; dinner nightly by reservation, 6 to 9; Grill Room, 5 to 9, July and August only; Sunday brunch in summer, 10:30 to 1:30. Doubles, $195 to $535, EP.

Mayflower Inn, Route 47, Washington, Conn. 06793.

"Stately" is the word to describe this renovated and expanded inn, as styled by owners Robert and Adriana Mnuchin of New York and general manager John Trevenen. They took a venerable inn, once owned by The Gunnery school and hidden away on 28 wooded acres, and – with a Midas touch – renovated it in 1992 into one of the premier English-style country hotels in America.

No expense was spared in producing seventeen guest rooms and eight suites that are the ultimate in comfort and good taste. Fifteen rooms are upstairs on the second and third floors of the main inn. Ten more are in two guest houses astride a hill.

Fine British, French and American antiques and accessories, prized artworks and elegant touches of whimsy – like the four ancient trunks stashed in a corner of the second-floor hallway – dignify public and private rooms alike. Opening off the lobby, an intimate parlor with plush leather sofas leads into the ever-so-British gentleman's library. Across the back of the inn are three handsome dining rooms and along one side is an English-style piano bar.

Chef Christopher Freeman is known for high-caliber regional country cuisine.

Mayflower Inn dining room is appointed in English country-house style.

He changes the menus daily. For dinner, expect starters ($6.75 to $13.25) like smoked salmon with potato-chive cake and crème fraîche, seared diver sea scallops on a parsnip puree with steamed spinach and truffle oil, and grilled shrimp on a soba noodle salad with ginger shoyu vinaigrette. Main courses ($16.50 to $28) might be grilled salmon on french green lentils with lobster mushrooms and savoy cabbage, sautéed black sea bass on a fingerling potato, leek and littleneck clam stew, and grilled pheasant breast and braised thigh on sage polenta with roasted artichokes, cipollinis and carrots. The extensive list of desserts (most $7.25) varies from the simple (tapioca pudding with fresh berries or warm apple pie with vanilla ice cream) to the complex (blueberry and raspberry crème brûlée or milk and dark chocolate mousse cake with coffee ice cream). The house favorite is the plate of Mayflower cookies, a tasty assortment including perhaps macaroons, thick butter shortbreads and chocolate chip with cocoa. The expensive wine list has been honored by Wine Spectator.

The setting for meals is exceptional, especially the outdoor terrace with its view of manicured lawns and imported specimen trees.

Each guest room is a sight to behold and some are the ultimate in glamour. We like Room 24 with a kingsize canopied four-poster featherbed awash in pillows, embroidered Frette linens and a chenille throw. An angled loveseat faces the fireplace and oversize wicker rockers await on the balcony. Books and magazines are spread out on the coffee table, the armoire contains a TV and there's a walk-in closet. The paneled bathroom, larger than most bedrooms, has marble floors, a double vanity opposite a glistening tub, a separate toilet area and a walk-in shower big enough for an army. Even all that didn't prepare us for a second-floor corner suite with a spacious living room straight out of Country Life magazine, a dining-conference room, two bathrooms, a bedroom with a kingsize canopied four-poster, and a porch overlooking the sylvan scene. The rear balconies and decks off the rooms in the two guest houses face the woods and are particularly private.

Across from the entrance to the main inn, a magnificent tiered rose garden tiptoes up a hill to a heated swimming pool and a tennis court. On the inn's lower level is a state-of-the-art fitness center. Such amenities, along with a pampering staff, contributed to the inn's speedy elevation to the ranks of Relais & Châteaux, the prestigious international hotel group whose clientele appreciates the finest.

(860) 868-9466. Fax (860) 868-1497. Lunch daily, noon to 2:30; dinner nightly, 6 to 9. Doubles, $240 to $395, EP; suites, $420 to $580.

Williamsville Inn, Route 41, West Stockbridge, Mass. 01266.

Gail Ryan, a chef from New York, and her mother Kathleen took over this quiet and remote country inn, built in 1797 but feeling considerably newer. "We ate here and it was exactly the inn we wanted to buy," said energetic Gail. "It was 18th century, a farmhouse, out in the country but still close to Lenox and Stockbridge."

Ten acres of nicely landscaped grounds stretching toward Tom Ball Mountain include a sculpture garden with some stunning pieces, a swimming pool and a clay tennis court. Sixteen rooms with private baths are in the main inn, a remodeled barn and two cottages. The spacious rooms are air-conditioned and furnished in period decor. Two armchairs are in front of the fireplace in one we saw with a queen canopy bed; newer rooms on the third floor have skylights.

A tavern off the front entry is most inviting, with a copper hood over the fireplace, stenciled walls and colorful fabrics on the chairs.

With her cooking background, Gail takes special interest in the inn's four pretty, candlelit dining rooms. Her mother's dining-room table graces the fireplaced party room for twelve in the rear, where, Gail says, "you feel like you're dining in a home, not a restaurant." The fireplaced library, where we once ate, has tables on old sewing-machine bases and walls of books. We're also partial to the garden room, with windows on three sides. It's perfect for breakfast, and thus the site for a buffet of homemade muffins, pastries, fresh fruit, cheeses, and quiche or a casserole for house guests.

Although Gail handles breakfast and might cook up a holiday dessert treat, she leaves the dinner chores to chef Susan Donaghey, formerly of the Boiler Room Cafe in Great Barrington. Her crispy red snapper with salsa verde and couscous, balsamic-roasted veal chop, and grilled black angus steak with potato fries and homemade ketchup starred on her early menus. Other possibilities among entrées ($16.95 to $23.95) ranged from seared halibut on a bed of zucchini noodles with tomato coulis and corn pudding to barbecued pork ribs with mashed potatoes.

An antipasto plate and crab cakes with tomato-corn salsa make good starters. Dessert could be grand marnier crème brûlée, oatmeal tart with lemon curd and berries or fruit pies topped with the great Berkshire Ice Creams produced in West Stockbridge.

(413) 274-6118. Dinner nightly in summer, 6 to 9, Thursday-Sunday rest of year; Sunday brunch. 11:30 to 2. Doubles, $120 to $150; suite, $185.

White Hart Inn, Route 44 & Route 41, Salisbury, Conn. 06039.

A wide white porch full of wicker and chintz provides the entry to the venerable White Hart Inn, now nicely restored by Terry and Juliet Moore, owners of one of our favorite restaurants, the Old Mill in South Egremont, Mass. The Moores, who said they couldn't bear to see the century-old Salisbury landmark vanish from the scene, acquired the property at a foreclosure auction and poured big bucks into its renovation.

Given their track record, we knew the food would be first-rate. The overnight accommodations turned out first-rate as well. The Moores reduced the original 33 rooms on the second and third floors to 26, all with private baths, pedestal sinks and new plumbing. Vivid floral wallpapers with matching comforters are their trademark. Mahogany reproduction furniture, TV sets in armoires and canopy four-poster beds are the rule.

The porch and main-floor public rooms are showplaces. On the porch, flowers are handpainted on the pillars; the floor is stenciled and the curtains – yes, curtains – are swagged. Off the lobby on one side is the clubby Hunt Room for functions. On the other side is the historic **Tap Room,** full of dark wood with green curtains and print wallpaper. Breakfast is offered in the airy **Garden Room,** where upholstered rattan chairs flank white faux-marble tables.

The Moores commissioned a South Egremont friend to do the paintings of fruits and vegetables that grace the tangerine and green walls of **The American Grill,** the pristine main dining room; they tie in with the tapestry fabric from Italy. Splendid floral arrangements provide colorful accents to an L-shaped room serene with white over mint linens, floral upholstered chairs and banquettes, and widely spaced tables seating a total of 80.

Chef Robert Corliss, who had been sous chef at the five-star Williamsburg Inn in Virginia, presents a contemporary American menu at affordable prices. Typical dinner dishes ($16 to $19) are miso-rubbed salmon with fennel-leek compote, grilled duck breast with gingered peaches and braised lamb shank with mushroom-barley risotto. Look for such starters ($4 to $7.50) as grilled seafood chowder with crab cake, vegetable spring rolls with mustard plum sauce and grilled squab with mache and black currant vinaigrette. Desserts are unusual: perhaps clichy cake (chocolate genoise and ganache with coffee buttercream, crème anglaise and raspberry coulis), ladyfinger and mascarpone terrine with espresso sauce, buttermilk and vanilla-bean brûlée, and ricotta-lemon tart with honey-fig-caramel sauce. The primarily American wine list starts in the mid-teens.

Interesting salads, sandwiches and pizzas are offered for lunch and light dinner (up to $15) in the casual Tap Room.

(860) 435-0030. Fax (860) 435-0040. Lunch daily, 11:30 to 2:30, to 5 on weekends; dinner in Grill, Wednesday-Sunday from 5:30; Tap Room, nightly 5 to 9:30 or 10:30. Doubles, $90 to $190, EP.

The Red Lion Inn, Main Street, Stockbridge, Mass. 01262.

As far as one of our relatives from Montreal is concerned, there is only one place to stay and eat when he's on business or pleasure in the Berkshires. It's the Red Lion, the quintessential New England inn that is a mecca for visitors from near and far.

For more than two centuries, it has dominated Stockbridge's Main Street, its guests rocking on the wide front porch or sipping cocktails in the parlor. Antique furniture and china fill the public rooms, and the Pink Kitty gift shop is just the ticket for selective browsers. The 91 rooms and twenty suites in the rambling inn, four outbuildings and the Stevens House (formerly the Berkshire Thistle Inn) are furnished in period decor. All have telephones and air-conditioning, 80 have private baths and most have color TV. The Red Lion also rents a two-bedroom apartment called **Meadowlark,** part of sculptor Daniel Chester French's summer studio at Chesterwood, for $350 a night, May-October.

Handpainted flowers, curtains and wicker grace porch at White Hart Inn.

Dining is formal in the Red Lion's bright and spacious main dining room, where New England favorites are featured on a continental-American menu. Entrées range from $17.50 for chicken breast stuffed with Monterey chèvre to $26 for filet mignon with a peppered madeira sauce. They run the gamut from broiled scrod and roast turkey with the trimmings to pan-seared pork loin with bing cherries. The menu has been updated, but you can still start with shrimp cocktail and finish with Indian pudding for a meal out of yesteryear.

More intimate dining takes place in the dark-paneled Widow Bingham Tavern, everyone's idea of what a Colonial pub should look like. In season, the shady outdoor courtyard lined with spectacular impatiens is a colorful and cool retreat for a drink, lunch or dinner. The same menu is served inside and out. A smaller menu is available downstairs in the Lion's Den, which offers entertainment at night.

For lunch ($9.75 to $15), you can order almost anything from burgers to baked meatloaf or creamed chicken and biscuits. The aforementioned relative always gets the caesar salad, which he says is terrific.

(413) 298-5545. Fax (413) 298-5130. Lunch daily, noon to 2:30; dinner, 6 to 9 (summer, 5:30 to 9:30), Sunday, noon to 9. Doubles, $94 to $159, EP; suites, $350.

Dining

The Best of the Best

West Street Grill, 43 West St., Litchfield, Conn.

Two of the best meals we've ever had were served at this jaunty establishment, which, we think, offers the most exciting food in Connecticut. It's the subject of universal adulation from food reviewers and the perfect foil for the Litchfield Hills trendoids who make this their own at lunch and dinner seven days a week.

The two dining rooms were full the winter Saturday we lunched here, and the manager rattled off the names of half a dozen celebrities who had reserved for that evening.

Lunch began with a rich butternut-squash and pumpkin bisque and the signature grilled peasant bread with parmesan aioli that was absolutely divine ($4.95). Main dishes were salmon cakes with curried French lentils ($10.95) and a special of

grilled smoked-pork tenderloin with spicy Christmas limas ($9.95). Among the highly touted desserts, we succumbed to an ethereal crème brûlée and a key lime tart that was really tart. With two generous glasses of wine, the bill for lunch for two came to a rather New Yorkish $50.

That was nothing, however, compared to the special tasting dinner that Irish owner James O'Shea presented to showcase his summer menu. The meal began with beet-green soup, grilled peasant bread with parmesan aioli and roasted tomato and goat cheese, corn cakes with crème fraîche and chives, roasted beet and goat cheese napoleons with a composed salad, and nori-wrapped salmon with marinated daikon, cucumbers and seaweed. A passionfruit sorbet followed.

Dining room at West Street Grill.

By then we felt that we had already dined well, but no, on came the entrées: tasting portions of pan-seared halibut with a beet pappardelle, spicy shrimp cake with ragoût of black beans and corn, grilled ginger chicken with polenta and ginger chips, and grilled leg of lamb with a ragoût of lentils, spicy curried vegetables and fried greens, including flat-leaf spinach. A little bit here, a little there, and next we knew came a parade of desserts: a plum tart in a pastry so tender as not to be believed, a frozen passionfruit soufflé, a hazelnut torte with caramel ice cream and a sampling of sorbets (raspberry, white peach and blackberry). How could we be anything but convinced, if ever there were a question, of West Street's incredible culinary prowess?

Talented French chef Frederic Faveau from Burgundy continues the tradition. Recent dinner entrées ($17.95 to $22.95) included roasted codfish with a balsamic-shallot reduction, pan-seared chicken with a tomato-ginger coulis, and grilled leg of lamb with a lightly roasted garlic cream sauce.

The long, narrow dining room is sleek in black and white, with a row of low booths up the middle, tables and mirrors on either side, and a back room with trompe-l'oeil curtains on the walls. Lavish floral arrangements add splashes of color.

(860) 567-3885. Lunch daily, 11:30 to 3, weekends to 4; dinner nightly, 5:30 to 9 or 10.

John Andrew's, Route 23, South Egremont, Mass.

"Innovative and spectacular" are words that area chefs and innkeepers employ when describing this culinary star fashioned by Dan and Susan Smith. The Smiths

Sponged walls and tiled fireplace add warmth to John Andrew's.

met in Florida while he was cooking at the Ritz-Carlton in Naples. She wanted to return to her native Berkshires and named their restaurant after her grandfather, John Andrew Bianchi.

The sponged walls are a romantic burnt red, the ceiling green and the striking chairs that came from the Copacabana in New York have been reupholstered and repainted green. Metal wall sconces and a tiled fireplace add warmth. At night, the walls "positively glow – like copper," says Susan. The enclosed rear porch is mod in cane and chrome and overlooks an outdoor dining deck.

Chef Dan favors Northern Italian and Mediterranean cuisine on his straightforward menu, which changes seasonally and represents good value. Favorite starters ($6.50 to $9.50) include peasant bread with roasted garlic, goat cheese, sundried tomatoes and black olives; pan-fried oysters with mesclun greens and anchovy-mustard vinaigrette, and napoleon of grilled shrimp with spicy semolina crisps and oven roast tomatoes. The homemade pastas ($13) might pair black pepper fettuccine with shiitake and porcini mushrooms, pinenuts and parsley cream, while grilled white cornmeal pizzas ($9) are topped with smoked salmon and mascarpone or prosciutto and fontina.

Entrées start at $16 for charred spiced leg of lamb with a pilaf of dried cherries and sweet corn or skewered chicken with lime, cilantro, avocado and a black bean sauce. Top price is $19.50 for grilled ribeye steak with shredded corn crêpes and grilled corn relish. In between are five-spice seared tuna with scallion dumplings, crisp duck confit and sautéed breast with garlic mashed potatoes, and garlicky roast pork with a fondue of onions and a straw potato pancake.

Desserts include plum crisp with vanilla ice cream, fresh berry lemon tart, chocolate torte with white chocolate chip ice cream and caramelized apple tart with cider crème anglaise. The lengthy boutique wine list, heavily American, is priced from $18 to $90.

In 1996, the Smiths and several partners opened the casual **Union Bar & Grill** (see below) at 293 Main St. in Great Barrington.

(413) 528-3469. Dinner nightly, 5 to 10; Sunday brunch, 11:30 to 3.

Church Street Cafe, 69 Church St., Lenox, Mass.

This is the casual, creative kind of American bistro to which we return time and again for an interesting lunch whenever we're in Lenox. Owners Linda Forman and Clayton Hambrick, once Ethel Kennedy's chef, specialize in light, fresh cafe food, served inside by ficus trees and eclectic paintings and outside in season on a canopied deck.

Blackboard specials supplement the seasonal menus. Clayton once worked at a creole restaurant in Washington, a background that shows in his Louisiana gumbo and a special of blackened redfish. But expect innovative international twists. Dinners might start with fiery Asian grilled beef and vegetable salad with lemongrass vinaigrette or a corn, zucchini and grilled red onion quesadilla with spicy tomato salsa. Summer entrées ($16.50 to $21.95) include sautéed Maine crab cakes with dilled rémoulade sauce, cold poached salmon with gazpacho salsa, grilled Jamaican jerk chicken with black beans and tropical fruit salsa, and crispy roast duckling with an orange-honey-ginger sauce. One of the pasta dishes ($15.95 to $17.50) incorporates garlic roasted shrimp and vegetables with cold Thai noodles and a peanut-curry dressing.

A recent lunch included a super black bean tostada and the Church Street salad, a colorful array of mixed greens, goat cheese, chick peas, eggs and red pepper, with a zippy balsamic vinaigrette dressing on the side. The whole wheat-sunflower seed rolls were so good that we accepted seconds.

For dessert, try the chilled cranberry soufflé topped with whipped cream, if it's available. Frozen rum-raisin mousse, white-chocolate crème brûlée and bittersweet chocolate-espresso torte with vanilla crème anglaise are other possibilities. The house Georges Duboeuf wine is $11.50 a bottle. Two dozen other wines are priced in the teens and twenties.

There are fresh flowers on the white-linened tables and white pottery with colorful pink and blue flowers in three dining areas. Track lights illuminate artworks on the walls at night.

(413) 637-2745. Lunch, Monday-Saturday 11 to 2; dinner nightly, 5:30 to 9; Sunday brunch in summer. Closed Monday and Tuesday in winter.

La Bruschetta, 1 Harris St., West Stockbridge, Mass.

Steven and Catherine Taub – both young alumni of Wheatleigh and Blantyre, where he last was executive chef and she pastry chef – opened their own winner of a place in 1992. Sticklers for making almost everything from scratch, they offer contemporary and traditional Italian cuisine at down-to-earth prices to an appreciative clientele.

The short but complex menu is strong on pastas ($14.50 to $17.50), perhaps straw and hay with a sauté of rock shrimp and asparagus, rigatoni with roasted chicken and braised escarole, and trenne with a ragu featuring domestic spring lamb. Main courses ($16 to $17.50) could be grilled organic trout with salsa verde,

Artifacts decorate walls of beamed dining room at The Old Mill.

pan-roasted pork tenderloin encrusted in toasted fennel, and grilled New York strip steak with garlicky escarole, gorgonzola polenta, vidalia onions and spicy house ketchup. The grilled sausage sampler yields a spicy house garlic sausage, Gunter's veal brat and a house mushroom sausage, served with garlic whipped potatoes, rappini and mustard.

The namesake bruschetta might come with chèvre, grilled radicchio and basil-olive oil. Other starters include a salad of Merrimac smoked sturgeon and baby organic arugula, gravlax with potato crostini, and Venetian ravioli filled with Maine crab, spinach and herbs with a coulis of plum tomatoes and roasted peppers.

By all means save room for one of Catherine's incredible desserts, perhaps chocolate-hazelnut cake, a rich chocolate-orange crème with caramel-liqueur sauce, or assorted gelati. The Taubs have fun with their wine list, which is layered in sheets with "our latest finds" on top.

The decor in two small rooms consists of white linens, upholstered rattan chairs, glass vases full of fresh flowers and sheer French curtains draped over the windows. Two big wine globes are part of every setting.

(413) 232-7141. Dinner nightly except Wednesday, 6 to 8:30 or 9, Sunday 5:30 to 8:30.

The Old Mill, Route 23, South Egremont, Mass.

In the charming and oft-overlooked hamlet of South Egremont, the Old Mill (which really is an old gristmill and blacksmith shop) has been impressing diners since 1978. The atmosphere is a cross between a simple Colonial tavern and a European wayside inn, warm and friendly, yet sophisticated.

The large, L-shaped main dining room has wide-planked and stenciled floors, beamed ceilings, pewter cutlery and bottles of olive oil as centerpieces on the nicely spaced tables, and a collection of old mincing tools on the cream-colored walls. Reflections of candles sparkle in the small-paned windows. An addition to a sunken rear dining room provides large windows onto Hubbard Brook.

A few nightly specials supplement the dozen entrées on the seasonal menu. The bulk are in the $17 to $19 range, and the most expensive at $24 is roast rack of lamb in pecan crust with rosemary-mascarpone pilaf. All come with vegetables and house salad.

The black-bean soup is a treat – hot, thick with pieces of spicy sausage and garnished with scallions. Other starters might be country-style pâté with peppered apple and fennel salad, crêpes filled with Maryland crabmeat, and grilled polenta with portobello mushrooms. Three kinds of rolls are served in a handsome basket. The salad is a mixture of greens, tomatoes and sliced mushrooms with a creamy, tangy oil and vinegar dressing.

Of the entrées, which always include the freshest of fish, we have enjoyed broiled red snapper, sesame-crusted mahi-mahi and baked bluefish with ginger and scallions. Veal piccata with a lemony sauce was sensational, and calves liver with apple-smoked bacon superior. Other possibilities include black soy-seared loin of tuna with green curry sauce and roasted moulard duck with cranberry-cabernet sauce.

Appetizers and smaller portions of some of the entrées turn up on the bar menu ($8 to $13).

The interesting wine list, reasonably priced, is split in origin between California and France, with nods to Italy and Australia. There's a cozy parlor bar for drinks while you wait for a table, a not unlikely occurrence since reservations are not taken for less than five.

Of the desserts, we think the mocha torte and the meringue glacé with cointreau and strawberries are most heavenly. Others include profiteroles au chocolat, crème brûlée, apricot charlotte and flourless chocolate cake.

Owners Terry and Juliet Moore – he is British and trained as a chef on the Cunard Line ships –reopened the White Hart Inn in Salisbury, Conn., where they now make their home and spend a good bit of their time. But the Old Mill carries on, and its 65 seats may turn over four times on busy nights.

(413) 528-1421. Dinner nightly, 5 to 9:30 or 10:30. Closed Monday or Tuesday in off-season.

Castle Street Cafe, 10 Castle St., Great Barrington, Mass.

The locals cheered when Michael Ballon, who used to cook at the Williamsville Inn in West Stockbridge, returned to the Berkshires to open his own cafe after several years at upscale restaurants in New York City.

Other restaurants had not had much luck in this space beside the Mahaiwe Theatre, but Michael succeeds with his bistro, especially on nights the theater is busy. Artworks are hung on the brick walls of the long narrow room with white-linened tables and windsor chairs. Michael puts out goodies like pâté and cheese at the bar at the rear. The wine bar dispenses a number of select choices by the glass.

With appetizers ($5) like grilled shiitake mushrooms with garlic and herbs, fried shrimp dumplings, and mesclun and goat-cheese salad and entrées like a Castle burger with straw potatoes ($9) or eggplant roulade stuffed with three cheeses ($12), there is something for every vegetarian and carnivore. Other main courses ($16 to $22) include grilled salmon with coriander salsa, sautéed sea scallops with sundried tomatoes and garlic on fettuccine, grilled cornish game hen, grilled filet of lamb with cannellini bean salad and steak au poivre with straw potatoes.

The dessert list is headed by the world's best chocolate-mousse cake, as

Chef-owner Michael Ballon at Castle Street Cafe.

determined by the late New York Newsday. Others include crème brûlée, warm apple crisp with vanilla ice cream and frozen lemon soufflé.

Michael makes a point of buying from Berkshire farmers and purveyors, whom he nicely acknowledges on the back of his menu.

(413) 528-5244. Dinner, Wednesday-Monday 5 to 9:30 or 10:30.

Boiler Room Cafe, 405 Stockbridge Road (Route 7), Great Barrington, Mass.

Michelle Miller, once a chef at Alice's Restaurant of Arlo Guthrie fame and founder of Suchèle Bakers, moved her restaurant and catering service from an old boiler room at the out-of-the-way Southfield Outlet and Craft Center into the thick of things along Route 7 in Great Barrington. She transformed an old farmhouse into three colorful rooms – one red, one gold and one olive green – joined by arched doorways, and recently opened an airier and lighter upstairs room for overflow. Mismatched chairs are at tables covered with white cloths. Twiggy branches are arranged artfully here and there, as are wood sculptures by Michele's husband, Peter Murkett. Although she has turned over some cooking chores to assistants, Michele still does most of the baking, which is fortunate, for her dacquoise is about the best we've tasted.

Michelle calls her food "cuisine locale" and, instead of being categorized, everything on the changing menu is lumped together roughly in the sequence you would expect to order. The menu might start, for instance, with shrimp and lobster chowder, spicy pumpkin soup with black pepper crouton and salad of curly endive with toasted walnuts and duck liver crouton, in the $4 to $8 range. The list continues with things like corn pizza with yukon gold potatoes and grilled portobello mushrooms, clam and corn fritters with roasted pepper sauce, chèvre-stuffed grape leaves with roasted grapes and walnut sauce, and linguini with chard, olives and pinenuts (these in the $6.50 to $13 range). Next in order are what other menus would consider main courses ($16 to $22) perhaps cedar-smoked salmon with corn pudding, grilled moulard duck breast with red wine risotto and roast rack of lamb with zucchini and roast tomato.

Desserts are on a separate list, as they should be, given the repertoire of their creator. You might find apple-blackberry crumb pie, apple calvados crêpes, toasted-pecan cheesecake and "drowned" vanilla ice cream with scotch and espresso. Interesting wines and beers are offered.

(413) 528-4280. Dinner, Tuesday-Saturday from 5:30.

The Cannery, 85 Main St., Canaan, Conn.

This little American bistro retains the name of its predecessor in which canning jars were the theme. New chef-owner William O'Meara lightened up the formerly homey decor with pale yellow walls bearing gold stars. A paneled divider with a windowed arch separates the small front dining room and the rear bar. White cloths, votive candles and fresh flowers in tall, thin glass vases dress the tables and a handful of booths.

Bill's imaginative contemporary American fare is highly regarded across the tri-state Berkshires. A basket of Italian and sourdough breads with a tasty spread of eggplant caponata arrives with the menu. At our fall visit, we were tempted by starters ($6.50 to $9) like figs stuffed with mascarpone cheese and toasted walnuts, a grilled portobello mushroom with endive salad and stilton cheese, and arugula salad with pinenuts, pancetta and shaved parmigiano-reggiano.

Main courses ranged from $16 for curried free-range chicken with sautéed pears and couscous to $20 for grilled sirloin with garlic chive mashed potatoes and red pepper coulis. Especially appealing were the salmon crusted with black pepper and pistachio and served with watercress salad and crystallized ginger, and the sautéed lamb with straw potato cake and wild mushrooms over salad greens.

Desserts included apple brown betty with calvados crème anglaise, chocolate mousse terrine with raspberry sauce and pear-almond tart with caramel sauce. Except for a few tokens for connoisseurs, the choice wine list is priced in the teens.

In late 1996, the owner purchased the century-old Village Restaurant on the green in Litchfield. He retained its traditional menu and planned to go back and forth between the two establishments, with a chef at each site.

(860) 824-7333. Dinner nightly except Tuesday, 5 to 9 or 10; Sunday brunch, 11 to 2.

The West Main Cafe, 13 West Main St., Sharon, Conn.

Hotshot young area chef Matthew Fahrner, who earned his spurs at Litchfield's West Street Grill, makes the kitchen sing at this snug little cafe in small house near the Sharon green. He and co-owner Susan Miller left the great but short-lived Bee Brook restaurant in Washington Depot, Conn., to open their own place.

Their quarters could not be more simple and intimate, a small room with about 40 seats at tables covered with white butcher paper over white cloths, white walls brightened by a few watercolors and glass plates of assorted pastel colors.

The zip comes from the kitchen, where Matt proved – as he had in earlier venues – to be a master of innovation and assertive flavors. Our latest lunch began with an appetizer of crisp vegetable rolls served with sweet pea shoots and pickled cucumber salad, all bursting with intense tastes. One of us went on to an appetizer of lightly fried oysters served with garlic, mustard and anchovy mayonnaise. The other had an entrée of Asian chicken salad, piled high in the architectural style on a Japanese tray with spicy peanuts and crisp wontons. We dipped the rosemary and black olive breads in olive oil, and finished with a fabulous banana napoleon that literally melted in the mouth.

Many of the lunchtime treats turn up at dinner. Expect appetizers ($6 to $8) like hoisin duck and vegetables with scallion pancakes, cornmeal-crusted calamari with lemon-caper aioli, and seared tuna with sweet pea shoots and warm sesame drizzle. For main courses ($15.95 to $17.95), how about pan-roasted Moroccan spiced salmon with curry, ginger and fall vegetable stew; garlic and lemon chicken with sweet walla walla onion puree and crisp hominy polenta, and grilled herb-encrusted pork loin with roasted garlic? Codfish is jazzed up with wasabi and orange-ginger sauce, and strip steak with cracked pepper, scallion and gorgonzola sauce. Cool off with one of Susan's refreshing desserts, perhaps hot and cold chocolate torte with berry coulis, ginger crème brûlée or sorbet with pomegranates. The tastes will linger in your memory.

(860) 364-9888. Lunch, Wednesday-Monday 11:30 to 2:30; dinner, Wednesday-Monday 5:30 to 9 or 10. Also closed Wednesday in off-season.

Doc's, Flirtation Avenue at Route 45, New Preston, Conn.

Celebrity weekenders love to lose themselves in the convivial crowd that packs into this roadside stand gone upscale across the street from Lake Waramaug. Adam Riess, a Californian fresh out of the University of Pennsylvania, named the Italian cafe, pizzeria and bakery his grandfather, a physician who summered on the lake for 40 years.

Although on the scene only periodically while pursuing cooking and graduate studies in New York, he has a team of chefs who continue his tradition: dynamite pizzas in the $7.50 to $8.75 range, super salads from $4.75 to $7.25 and a smattering of robust pastas and entrées ($13.75 to $17.75), among them penne with shrimp and tomatoes, seared salmon with rosemary, chicken roasted with rapini and garlic, and New York strip steak with wild mushroom sauté.

You might start with the house antipasto, grilled portobello mushrooms or smoked mozzarella with roasted tomatoes and basil. But most opt for one of the new-wave pizzas, perhaps the funghi with crimini, portobello and shiitake mushrooms or the scampolini with shrimp, tomatoes, garlic and rosemary. Desserts could be apple crisp, pumpkin creme caramel, peach sorbet or hazelnut biscotti.

The ever-so-rustic dining room contains chairs painted pea green, spartan tables bearing butcher paper, votive candles and big bottles of extra-virgin olive oil (plus metal containers that the menu notes contain salt, not cheese), and a handful of posters and plants for accents.

(860) 868-9415. Lunch in summer, Friday-Sunday noon to 2; dinner, Wednesday-Sunday 5 to 10. BYOB. No credit cards.

More Dining Choices

Cafe Lucia, 90 Church St., Lenox, Mass.

Authentic northern Italian cuisine is served up by Jim Lucie at this serious little cafe, which has evolved from its days as an art gallery with a cafe. Jim opened up the kitchen so patrons could glimpse the culinary proceedings and lately replaced the artworks with family photos on the exposed brick walls. A spiral staircase remains the focal point of the main dining room. Especially popular in season are the outdoor cafe and garden bar, their tables topped with umbrellas.

An antipasto table with the day's offerings is showcased at the entry. Fans praise the carpaccio with arugula and shaved reggiano, pastas ($12.95 to $18.95) like imported linguini with shrimp in a seafood veloute, and such entrées ($13.95 to $25.95) as herb-roasted free-range hen, paillard of chicken with Italian salsa, baked calamari Genoa style, veal milanese and a signature osso buco with risotto, so good that it draws New Yorkers back annually.

Desserts include fresh fruit tarts, flourless chocolate torte and gelatos. Those desserts, a fine port or brandy, and cappuccino can be taken on warm evenings on the flower-bedecked patio. A few Californias augment the basically Italian wine list.

(413) 637-2640. Dinner nightly from 5; closed Sunday and Monday in winter.

Helsinki Tea Company Cafe and Bistro, 284 Main St., Great Barrington, Mass.

Owner Deborah McDowell's mother was from Helsinki, which accounts for the name and some of the theme at this colorful new establishment hidden behind a shopping arcade, beside a parking lot and across from a movie theater. But the exotic treats that emanate from a pint-size kitchen are more international, and all kinds of local foodies seem to have found it.

Live jazz on Thursday evenings and the fact that tea cups and pots are for sale indicate that this is not your ordinary cafe. The interesting food, the combination of teas and wines, and the laid-back service prove it.

Seated for lunch in the back dining room at one of the burgundy velvet booths (more comfortable than the usual), the table topped with a cloth like our grand-mothers had, we enjoyed listening to music from the '40s on tape, with teapots on ledges all around us. One of us liked Emma's Hymyilla, a chef's salad of sorts – greens topped with ham, chicken, swiss and havarti cheeses, broccoli, a boiled egg and olives, and tamari-basil dressing. The other lucked out with Anni's Plate, "little bits from the land of the midnight sun." Marinated herring, a generous serving of gravlax, cucumber-dill salad, havarti, smoked gouda and finlandia swiss cheeses, cucumber-dill salad, shredded beets and cherry tomatoes were some of the bites, and we also loved our side order of mango-chipotle coleslaw. Soups of the day included Tuscan vegetable and chilled fruit, and every table was served a high metal contraption containing ryevita and French bread. We split an ethereal lemon tart with berry compote and whipped cream. Service was lethargic and, while we had heard that Helsinki was quite reasonable, our lunch tab totaled more than $30.

At dinner time, appetizers like three-onion tart and a roasted portobello mushroom topped with goat cheese, roasted garlic and sundried tomatoes are in the $4 to $7.95 range. There are blinis with changing toppings, gravlax and salads. Entrees run from $9.95 for vegetarian chili to $17.95 for chicken tournedos (wrapped in turkey bacon with apricot-walnut stuffing). Also available are a meatloaf made with tofu (a tad pricey at $14.95, we thought), seafood frittata and the "Mad Russian," potato latkes with gravlax, caviar and sour cream.

Changing desserts ($4.95) might be a strawberry-lemon-hazelnut torte, coffee meringue with chocolate mousse, or a vanilla and chocolate checkerboard cake.

(413) 528-3394. Open daily, 11 to 10.

Union Bar & Grill, 293 Main St., Great Barrington, Mass.

The latest Berkshires hot spot was this casual dining place opened in 1996 by Dan and Susan Smith of John Andrew's restaurant in South Egremont and three partners. Taking over the storefront space vacated by the late La Tomate, they fashioned what Susan called a light industrial look in purple, silver and black, with a bar along one side and dining areas along the other. The name reflects a union of partners as well as the fusion cuisine bearing the unmistakable influence of Dan Smith.

An opening specialty of his chef here was an appetizer of barbecued duck, roasted and shredded like South Carolina pulled pork, served with chiles, cumin and peppercorns in a blue corn tortilla. The all-day menu is perfect for those who like to mix and match. For starters ($3 to $7), how about a basket of house baked and grilled breads with extra-virgin olive oil, clam and corn fritters with Chinese dipping sauce or a caramelized onion and goat cheese tart with peppery arugula salad?

Under "next" come salads and sandwiches ($4 to $6), among them caesar with garlic croutons, spicy grilled chicken with tomato jam on flatbread and grilled shiitake mushrooms, charred onions and arugula on toasted sourdough.

Six with-it versions of pizza and pasta are offered for $9 to $11. "After 5" choices for dinner dishes ($11 to $13) range from lacquered salmon with vegetable spring rolls and wasabi shrimp with peanuts, bean sprouts and portobello mushrooms to charred lamb on garlic naan and grilled garlic flank steak with tomatillo salsa.

(413) 528-8226. Open daily except Wednesday, 11:30 to 11.

The Hamilton Inn, Route 44, Millerton, N.Y.

The French aspect of the old New Yorker restaurant gave way in late 1996 to this reincarnation fashioned by the former owner, Sharon cattleman James Metz, who is widely known for his black angus beef. Borrowing the name of his Hamilton Inn in central New York, he did an extensive renovation, producing several chic dining rooms and a bar/lounge with pale yellow walls and cream-linened tables flanked by upholstered armchairs. Worldly chef Flavio Manzoni, originally from the Lake Como section of Italy, joined the venture from Hawaii.

The fare is contemporary American with Italian, Asian and South African overtones, reflecting the chef's travels. The initial dinner menu offered a dozen entrées from $14.95 for free-range chicken with parma ham and asiago cheese to $21.95 for veal chop with yogurt-cilantro sauce. Choices included saffron risotto with shrimp and scallops, blackened yellowfin tuna with tamarind honey sauce, and medallions of tenderloin in balsamic syrup with pearl onions. Appetizers ranged from $3.95 for the chef's special bruschetta to $10.95 for porcini mushrooms sautéed with white truffle oil and aged balsamic vinegar. The soup could be cream of golden lentil and barley with garlic croutons; the salad, poached baby calamari with julienned vegetables. Four pastas were available as appetizers or main courses.

Desserts included a chocolate walnut soufflé in a brandy mascarpone sauce and a golden apple terrine in a tangerine custard sauce.

(518) 789-9399. Dinner nightly, 5:30 to 9:30.

Offbeat Gourmet

Thelma's Roadside, 107 Stockbridge Road (Route 7), Great Barrington, Mass.

This wouldn't normally warrant mention, but the new 1950s-look diner is, as its card says, "not your ordinary diner." A large space outfitted in gaudy green and red booths and tables, it holds an old-fashioned soda fountain featuring Berkshire Ice Cream. The kitchen dispenses predictable diner fare, blue-plate specials ($7.86) and unexpected specials like escargots bourguignonne, onion tarts, steamed mussels in wine, seafood risotto and grilled salmon raifort. Apple and blueberry crêpes and croissant eggs benedict are typical brunch fare. The French touch comes from the chef, Jean Claude Vierne, veteran of New York landmarks, who transferred some specialties from his late La Tomate in downtown Great Barrington

(413) 528-0880. Open weekdays, noon to 9 or 10, weekends from 8.

Hickory Bill's Bar-B-Que, 405 Stockbridge Road, Great Barrington, Mass.
For an authentic taste of Texas, head to this fun place behind the Boiler House Cafe. "The best barbecue north of the Mason-Dixon" is typical of comments in the guest book. Genial proprietor William C. Ross Jr., a former social worker, and staff sport red shirts as they turn out pork, chicken, brisket and ribs from the special indoor Oyler hickory-wood barbecue pit in the kitchen. Barbecue platters ($8.50 to $10) like spareribs or fancy brisket are served with a choice of two side dishes, perhaps collard greens and baked beans, along with the delicious Mexican cornbread, dotted with jalapeños. Mrs. Evelyn's sweet potato pie is a fitting dessert. Partake in the no-frills, luncheonette-style dining room or at picnic tables out back.

(413) 528-1444. Open Tuesday-Saturday 11:30 to 9, Sunday noon to 7.

Blue Heaven Rotisserie, 30 Church St., Lenox, Mass.
The old Blue Heaven Turkey Farm took on a new incarnation in 1996 as "home of the best turkey sandwich." Make that seven kinds of turkey sandwich ($3.75 to $4.25), cooked on the rotisserie and paired with pesto or roasted red peppers or hummus or what-have-you. Bill Harrington, grandson of the farm's founder, prepares picnics for two ($22.50) as well as cooked turkeys, chickens and stuffed ducks to go. In the cooler months he offers sandwiches and a variety of side dishes associated with the traditional Thanksgiving meal.

(413) 637-3204. Open daily, 11 to 7 or 8.

The Pub & Restaurant, Route 44, Norfolk, Conn.
International cuisine and beers are offered here by a former owner of the famed Stonehenge restaurant in Ridgefield, Conn. David Davis created what he called "an English-style pub with good food in a relaxed setting." The menu varies from seven kinds of burgers in the $7 range to grilled chicken, flank steak and dinner specials ($12.50 to $15.95) like poached salmon with watercress salad and couscous, Greek lamb moussaka, poached chicken Chinese style, New Age salad with gravlax, and fettuccine with roasted garlic, red peppers, radicchio and snow peas. Of special interest is the list of 160 beers from across the world. David says it's the most extensive selection in Connecticut and, he reports, he's tried them all.

(860) 542-5716. Lunch, 11:30 to 5; dinner, 5 to 9 or 10. Closed Monday.

Lodging

Cliffwood Inn, 25 Cliffwood St., Lenox, Mass. 01240.
Joy and Scottie Farrelly walked in the door of this gorgeous Belle Epoque mansion built in 1904 in the Stanford White style for a former ambassador to France and said, "this is it." The Ralston Purina Co. executive and his wife had been looking

Former ambasssador's Belle Epoch mansion accommodates guests as Cliffwood Inn.

for a retirement activity and a place to house the furnishings they had collected
while living in Montreal, Brussels, Paris and Italy. Cliffwood was the perfect find.

Seven luxurious guest rooms (all with private baths and six with fireplaces, one
of them in the bathroom) are beautifully furnished with the fruits of the Farrellys'
travels. Each is named for one of their ancestors, and a scrapbook describing the
particular ancestor is on the bed – an illustrious lot they were. Joy had a bookcase
and hutch designed and built in Vermont to fill a space in the second-floor hall and
to pick up the pattern of the rounded windows nearby. It holds books from sixteen
different countries. A gaily painted lunch pail is a decorative accent in one room;
Joy has done folk-art boxes for Kleenex in the others. The Farrellys also are dealers
in Eldred Wheeler 18th-Century American furniture and 24 of the prized pieces
are in the rooms (and for sale). Notable at a recent visit were the queensize canopy
Sheraton field bed and side tables in the Nathanial Foote room, enlarged by re-
moving a wall between two rooms and sporting two wing chairs in front of the
fireplace.

Guests gather in the magnificent living room, foyer and dining room, much as
they would as house guests in a mansion. A full-length back porch overlooks a lap
swimming pool with hammocks nearby. And, for those who want their swimming
exercise year-round, the Farrellys have installed a counter-current pool and spa in
a new cedar-walled enclosure underneath the porch. Wine and hors d'oeuvres –
things like marinated olives, cheeses and a hot artichoke dip – are served in the
late afternoon. "Dinners in a party atmosphere" are offered occasionally in the
spring. "Sharing our house is a great way to keep busy and have fun," Joy explains.

A buffet-style continental breakfast in the elegant dining room brings homemade breads and muffins, Joy's homemade granola for which she shares the recipe,
and a special hot fruit compote with nuts and crème fraîche. Wonderful popovers
emanate from her prized new AGA cooker.

(413) 637-3330. Doubles, $119 to $210.

Applegate Bed & Breakfast, 279 West Park St., RR 1, Box 576, Lee, Mass.
01238.

A pillared porte cochere hints of Tara at this majestic, sparkling white Georgian
Colonial, built by a New York surgeon in the 1920s as a weekend retreat. Surrounding it are six tranquil acres bearing venerable apple trees, towering pines,

flower gardens and a beckoning swimming pool. Inside are elegant common rooms, six guest rooms with private baths and an effervescent welcome by Nancy and Rick Cannata, she an airline flight attendant and he a pilot, who decided to alight here in 1990 and convert their large home into a B&B. They planned their flight schedules so at least one of them was always on hand before she "retired" in 1996.

Off a grand entry foyer are a fireplaced dining room, its three tables each set for breakfast for four, and a large living room equipped with a grand piano. To its side is a sun porch, newly enclosed for use as a reading and TV room. Off the dining room is a screened back porch facing the pool and rose gardens.

A carved staircase leads to the four main guest rooms, one the master suite with a kingsize poster bed, old family wedding photos on the mantel above the working fireplace, a sitting area with a sofabed and two chairs, and a great steam shower. "What a treat to sit in there and steam away," advises Nancy. The other rooms are slightly less grand in scale, holding queensize beds. One has Shaker-style pine furniture, another a walnut sleigh bed and a third an antique white iron bed and white and blue wicker furnishings. Recently, talented Rick has redone two rooms in a far wing of the house. One is a corner space swathed in pale lavenders and greens with a tiger-maple four-poster, a sitting area and the best view of the grounds. The other is a smaller room done up in Victorian style with an antique bed and matching marble-topped dresser and a hat rack holding an opera cape and granny hats. A rear carriage house has been renovated into a two-bedroom, condo-style apartment, available for $330 a night, three-night minimum.

Godiva chocolates and decanters of brandy are in each room. The Cannatas offer wine and cheese around 5 p.m. The continental-plus breakfast, including cereal and yogurt, is served amid stemware and antique cups and saucers.

Having run out of ways to improve Applegate, the Cannatas have taken to wall-papering the closets. And he tends to the rose gardens.

(413) 243-4451 or (800) 691-9012. Doubles, $110 to $195.

Devonfield, 85 Stockbridge Road, Lee, Mass. 01238.

The former summer home of George Westinghouse Jr. is now a comfortable, traditional New England-style B&B run with fun and flair by Ben and Sally Schenck, old friends who surprised us when they turned up as innkeepers. They purchased it in 1994 from Gerhard Schmid, former chef-owner of the Gateways Inn in Lenox, who had shared his family's home with overnight guests in a low-key B&B known as Haus Andreas.

Theirs is a handsome Federal mansion dating to the late 1700s, looking across 40 pastoral acres toward Beartown State Forest. Manicured lawns surround a tennis court and a swimming pool flanked by a showy new flower garden designed by a house guest.

The Schencks are slowly upgrading the accommodations, which had been outfitted in European florals and traditional furnishings. Do not expect yet a "deco-rated" inn with canopy beds and fancy window treatments. The emphasis here is on relaxed comfort, spacious bedrooms and common rooms, and warm hospitality.

The ten guest lodgings, all with private baths, include six rooms with queen or king beds, one with a canopy and two with fireplaces. Two more are suites with sitting areas and TVs, one with a fireplace. Top of the line are a couple of apartment-size areas that were the personal quarters of the former innkeepers and a set of parents. The third-floor "penthouse" holds a modern living room, a king bed facing

Circular Colonial bar (left) is in corner of breakfast room at Merrell Tavern Inn.

a skylight under the eaves, and a skylit jacuzzi with a shower. A pool-side guest house comes with a kingsize bedroom, an open living room with a pullout sofa facing a corner fireplace, a kitchenette and dining area, a jacuzzi tub in the bathroom and pleasant patios beckoning on two sides.

The main house includes a large living room and library, a cozy television room, a guest pantry off an enormous dining room and a great side porch, with enough wicker furniture to seat everyone in the house and then some. This is the setting for festive weekend breakfasts in summer, starring cooked-to-order omelets featuring such add-ins as goat cheese and grilled vegetables. Otherwise, breakfast is taken at individual tables in the dining room. Guests help themselves to a buffet of fruit, granola, yogurt, muffins and such before a hot dish of scrambled eggs or blueberry pancakes is served.

(413) 243-3298 or (800) 664-0880. Fax (413) 243-1360. Doubles, $155 to $195; suites and cottage, $205 to $260.

The Inn at Richmond, 802 State Road (Route 41), Richmond, Mass. 01254.

Sumptuous breakfasts, elegant accommodations with modern amenities and a secluded country setting are hallmarks of this stylish new B&B. In their restored 18th-century farmhouse, Jerri and Dan Buehler offer three guest rooms and three suites, each with king or queen bed, modern bath, thick carpeting, cable TV and telephones. The largest is the front Federal Suite with king poster bed, a sitting room, and a clawfoot tub and shower. An ornate iron queen bed dignifies the Victorian Suite. An unusual louvered headboard graces the queen bed in the Nantucket Retreat. Accommodations in a rear carriage house and a cottage are more like mini-apartments and are rented by the week.

What seems to be every Copenhagen plate ever issued joins books and games on the shelves of the comfy library. Other common rooms are a small parlor, a garden room looking onto a reflecting pool and a greenhouse.

The breakfast menu, posted on the sideboard in the six-table dining room, conveys the day's treats. At our visit, the meal began with choice of three juices, granola and yogurt, cranberry-lemon and banana-yogurt breads, old-fashioned rice pudding and a compote of nectarines, pineapple and plums. The main course was sesame-cornmeal pancakes with wild blueberry-lemon sauce. Other main dishes could be frittatas, stratas and maple-walnut french toast with Canadian maple syrup. Port and sherry are complimentary in the evenings.

The rear of the 27-acre property is a breeding and training farm for Morgan horses. The location is utterly rural and requires a bit of a trek for dinner, although Lenox is just over the mountain and West Stockbridge not far down the road.

(413) 698-2566. Fax (413) 698-2100. Doubles, $135 to $165; suites, $195 to $225.

Historic Merrell Inn, 1565 Pleasant St. (Route 102), South Lee, Mass. 01260.

History buffs particularly like this elegantly restored inn, one of the first properties in the Berkshires to be listed in the National Register of Historic Places. Saved early in the century by Mabel Choate of Naumkeag in Stockbridge, the 1800 building a mile east of Stockbridge was acquired by Faith and Charles Reynolds of Rochester, N.Y., who carefully created nine guest rooms on three floors in 1981 and undertook a complete redecoration a dozen years later.

All with private baths and some with fireplaces, the bedrooms are furnished with canopy or four-poster beds and antiques the couple have collected over the years. They have been upscaled lately with telephones, Gilbert & Soames toiletries, tiled floors in the bathrooms, comfy sitting areas, fancy window treatments, and color-coordinated linens and towels. The owners even ignored the period to furnish a couple of bedrooms in fancy Victorian style, based upon customer requests. An air of luxury is created by decorator fabrics and oriental rugs throughout as well as by prized possessions like an 1800 grandfather's clock. Guests register in the old tavern room at the birdcage bar, the only surviving circular Colonial bar still intact. They relax over lemonade or hot cider in a guest parlor with a beehive oven, fashioned from the old keeping room. A small room adjacent, formerly a guest bedroom, has been converted into a TV room.

The tavern is where Faith serves breakfast of the guest's choice, remarkably cooked to order by Chuck in what he calls the world's smallest kitchen. The room is a beauty, with pale yellow tablecloths, handmade Bennington pottery, well-aged woodwork and a fireplace of Count Rumford design. Chuck decorates each breakfast plate – perhaps a mushroom and cheese omelet, blueberry-walnut pancakes or french toast with raspberry syrup – with parsley and johnny jump-ups from his garden. He also painted the incredible murals in the front hall, and built the screened gazebo down by the Housatonic River in the deep back yard.

(413) 243-1794 or (800) 243-1794. Fax (413) 243-2669. Doubles, $115 to $135.

Manor House, Maple Avenue, Box 447, Norfolk, Conn. 06058.

One of the grander estates in a town of many is an elegant Victorian B&B run by Diane and Henry Tremblay, self-styled "corporate graduates" from the Hartford insurance world. Theirs is an eighteen-room, Tudor-style manor home built on five acres in 1898 by Charles Spofford, architect of London's subway system and the son of Abraham Lincoln's Librarian of Congress.

Huge stone fireplace is feature of living room at Manor House.

The eight guest rooms on the second and third floors come with private baths, one with a double jacuzzi and another with a double soaking tub. All are furnished to the period with fine antiques, French armoires and antique sleigh, spindle, canopy or four-poster beds covered with duvet comforters. The Lincoln Room contains a reclining couch and a carved walnut sleigh bed that belonged to Diane's great-grandmother. The Spofford Room boasts a kingsize bed and a fireplaced sitting area. Always upgrading, the Tremblays were planning at our latest visit to add a fireplace and a private deck to the jacuzzi room.

The original Tiffany and leaded-glass windows, cherry paneling and stone fireplaces enhance the main floor, where guests can spread out in a small library, a baronial living room with a gigantic stone fireplace and a view onto the back gardens, a sun porch with a wood stove, a little barroom with stereo and TV, and two dining rooms, where the Tiffany windows represent fish on one side and fowl on the other.

In the afternoons, Diane puts out popcorn, cheese and crackers, and serves tea from her collection of teapots. In the morning, the good coffee is laced with cinnamon. The Tremblays cook a couple of breakfast entrées each day, among them scrambled eggs, blueberry pancakes, french toast stuffed with raspberries, orange waffles with honey and maple syrup, and poached eggs with a sauce of lemon, butter and chives on muffins. The honey comes from their beehives and the herbs from their garden.

(860) 542-5690. Doubles, $95 to $190.

Greenwoods Gate, 105 Greenwoods Road East (Route 44), Norfolk, Conn. 06058.

A welcome card greets you and a bag of potpourri with a farewell sends you on your way. In between are all kinds of pampering touches of the kind that appeal particularly to romantics and gourmands at this unusual B&B offering a luxury country experience.

Much of the furnishing of the handsome white Federal-era home with black shutters was done by the former owner, but the T.L.C. is lavished by George Schumaker, who retired as executive vice president of the Hilton hotel chain.

The experienced hotelier, whose wife is a nurse and is not involved in the B&B operation, offers tea in the afternoon, wine and cheese or snacks ("whatever inspires me") before the dinner hour and after-dinner liqueurs, not to mention cookies and candies. In the morning, what he calls "a long and leisurely breakfast" begins with coffee, followed by a buffet of fruit compote, pastries, blended granola, cereal and juice. Next comes "a plated breakfast:" perhaps featherbed eggs, cranberry-raspberry baked puffed pancakes or grand marnier-stuffed croissants with orange marmalade and whipped cream cheese. Little wonder that some guests spend the rest of the morning lounging around this very comfortable house.

Guests find aloe vera shampoo, conditioner and perfumes among the amenities in the bathrooms. A furnished dollhouse is in a corner of the Trescott Suite, gorgeously decorated in china blue and white. The dramatic, three-level Levi Thompson suite in the rear has a lovely sitting area, a stained-glass window above the queensize cherry bed fashioned by a local craftsman, and a double whirlpool and steam bath. A single room for "the very special third person in your party" adjoins the Captain Phelps Suite with its two double beds. George's pride and joy is the new Lillian Rose Suite, which he created as "the ultimate in country living" from quarters of the former innkeeper. It has two bedrooms (one with wall-canopy twin beds and the other with a queen brass bed and white fabric wall canopy), connecting to a den/library and a large bath.

The formal living room in pale yellow is furnished in antiques and oriental rugs and retains its original fireplace. So does the intimate breakfast room, where the host's breakfasts are served in all their glory.

(860) 542-5439. Doubles, $175 to $235; two-bedroom suites, $280 and $330.

Gourmet Treats

This entire area is a hotbed of food activity, with Great Barrington increasingly the focal point. Its railroad station is the site of a farmers' market Saturday mornings in season.

Focus on Great Barrington

Guido's Fresh Marketplace, established in 1979 along Route 7 at the Pittsfield-Lenox line, is a fascinating complex of small food markets. It now has a branch at 760 South Main St. (Route 7) in Great Barrington, to which we'd gladly repair to turn marketing chores into fun. There were samples of crenshaw melons at the entry at our recent visit, and a wondrous assortment of exotic produce. Pasta Prime dispenses eight varieties of homemade pasta and many zippy sauces. A seafood wholesaler and Mazzeo's Meat Center showcase their wares. But we always head to our favorite gourmet takeout emporium, **The Market Place Kitchen**, which moved its retail store here. It's fun to browse, but you'll likely be tempted to take home some of their terrific breads (the olive bread is sensational), salads (perhaps lo mein with shiitake mushrooms), quiches, dinner entrées and desserts. We couldn't resist picking up a special of lamb rolled with pinenuts and spinach, new potatoes with dill and grilled vegetables for a fancy dinner at home.

Owner John Campanale didn't realize it at the time, but he came to "smoked fish heaven" when he moved his **Merrimac Smoked Fish** wholesale and retail operation from eastern Massachusetts to 955 South Main St., Great Barrington. Seafood is smoked on the premises, resulting in superior Scotch-style Atlantic salmon, Idaho rainbow trout, mussels, bluefish, catfish and sea scallops, among others. Smoked fish is popular for takeout (we enjoyed the salmon at a Tanglewood picnic) and turns up on many a local restaurant menu. It also complements the H&H Bagels, imported from New York City (with cream cheese and smoked salmon, $5.95). Olives, Greek olive oil, smoked sturgeon from California and some interesting sauces made by a local caterer are other offerings.

Main and Railroad streets in Great Barrington have been the happening retail sites lately in the Berkshires. Billing itself as "Provence in the Berkshires," **Mistral's** offers a fine selection of kitchenware along with perfumes and bed and bath accessories. **T.P. Saddle Blanket,** the most colorful store we've been in recently, stocks hot sauces along with rugged mountain and western apparel and furnishings. **Berkshire Cottage Kitchen** is a good kitchen shop.

The Berkshire Coffee Roasting Co. at 286 Main St. (with an offshoot in Lenox) offers all the right coffees, teas, fresh juice, muffins and croissants at a handful of tables or to go. Adjacent is **Baba Louie's Sourdough Pizza Co.,** where the wood-fired oven produces organic and San Francisco sourdough pizzas. Breakfast is served all day at **Martin's Restaurant,** an L-shaped storefront at 49 Railroad St., where former Waldorf-Astoria chef Martin Lewis whips up incredible omelets along with luncheon salads and sandwiches.

Locke, Stock and Barrel, just north of Great Barrington at 265 Stockbridge Road (Route 7), is more than a large gourmet store with a nifty name. Sophisticated as all get-out, it supplies a great selection of English cheeses, salsas and a remarkably extensive supply of preserves, conserves and jellies from all over the world (as in apricot jam from Lebanon). Owners Pat and Locke Larkin must have a lot of fun finding the dozens of hot sauces (oink ointment is a barbecue sauce), the hundreds of olive oils, the exotic cheeses and hams, rice from Thailand, the glazed violets, the chutneys, the nutmeg syrup – you get the picture. Locke sells granola made from his own recipes, too.

Life's Little Luxuries – in Lenox and Beyond

In Lenox, **Mary Stuart Collections,** 81 Church St., carries fine china and glass, exquisite accessories for bed. and bath, hand-woven rugs, imported needlepoint designs, potpourris and fragrances, adorable things for babies, beautifully smocked dresses for little girls and hand-painted stools. The owners know their food and steered us to **Moore Fine Foods,** 62 Church St., caterer for some of the best parties in town. From Megan Moore's brim-full display cases you can share in the good life and assemble a fancy picnic to go.

Bev's Homemade Ice Cream, 38 Housatonic St., is the place to head for an ice-cream fix. Ex-Californian Beverly Mazursky opened this establishment after graduating from the Culinary Institute of America in 1989. She and sons Dan and Jeff make all the wonderful flavors in two machines behind the counter. They're known for their raspberry-chocolate chip and their margarita sorbet, served in sugar cones ($1.90 and $2.70). You can order gelatos, frappes, smoothies, sherbet coolers and even a banana split ($5.50), as well as espresso, cappuccino and cafe latte. Soups and sandwiches are available except in summer, when their popular Jamaican patties (different kinds of Caribbean breads with such fillings as beef, mixed veggies and broccoli-cheese) are about the only things that get in the way of the ice cream.

At **Suchèle Bakers,** 31 Housatonic St., the breads of the day might be sourdough, anadama, beer rye, toasted sunflower or white potato. We picked out some oatmeal-raisin lace cookies from the pastry case, full of sticky buns and gorgeous tarts, cakes and fruit pies, including peach and plum.

Seldom have we seen so many kitchen resources, so enticingly displayed, as at **Different Drummer's Kitchen,** on the north side of Lenox at 374 Pittsfield Road (Route 7). Everything you could ever want for kitchen or dining room is here, from the best cookware to gadgets galore. If we were getting married today, this is where we would register. Since we've been married 36 years, there isn't much we need (but how we'd love a new set of pots). We did come away with a little gizmo for making gyozas (Joyce Chen, and it really works) and a practical thing for peeling garlic cloves, a tube that you put the garlic into, roll it and the skin comes right off.

The Store at Five Corners, an 18th-century general store gone upscale, is worth the jaunt to the junction of Routes 7 and 43 south of Williamstown. Ex-New Yorkers Stuart Shatken and his wife Andy offer select lines of specialty foods. Rather than carry 30 lines of jam, for instance, they stock a couple of their favorites. "We sell as many French St. Dalfour as we do jams from the lady down the street," says Stuart. You'll find Mendocino pastas, Epicurean spices, interesting wines, homemade fudge and Italian biscotti along with an espresso bar, baked goods from the store's bakery, "real NYC bagels," and an assortment of breakfast and lunch items from the deli.

Connecticut's Cornucopia

In Connecticut, Lakeville is the home of **April 56 Extreme Cookery,** which carries gourmet foods, Junior League cookbooks and original gifts; we liked the ceramic pie plates with lids topped with berries and apples. At **Riga Mt. Coffee Roasters,** you can sample the internet on computers as well as many kinds of coffee, pastries and panini sandwiches.

Head to Salisbury for **Habitant,** a good kitchen store ensconced in a house at 10 Library St. Everything from crab cakes to baba ghanoush to four-cheese lasagna and wonderful salads is available in another little house called **Harvest Bakery & Prepared Foods,** a fabulous bakery and deli at 10 Academy St. Two alumni of the White Hart Inn, Leslie and Tom Eckstein, offer San Francisco sourdough, baguettes, peasant bread and other baked goods that are much in demand in the area. There are a handful of tables upon which to partake.

More good foods are available in Norfolk at **Greenwoods Market & Cafe,** 32 Greenwoods Road West. Good values are the sandwiches ($3.75) and the deli salad plate ($5.25, for a sampler of three plus a roll). The breakfast sandwich of egg, bacon and Swiss cheese with a dab of mayo on a Portuguese roll gets the day

Michael, John and Paul Harney in new tasting room at Harney & Sons.

off to a good start for $2.50. Enjoy all at umbrella-covered tables on a rear deck overlooking the town meadow.

Two Northwest Connecticut wineries are of interest to visitors. At **Hopkins Vineyard** in New Preston, Bill and Judy Hopkins produce a superior seyval blanc ($8.99), which has won many awards, among nine varieties from their twenty acres of French-American hybrid grapes. Recently they expected their new cabernet franc plantings to develop into one of their signature wines. An excellent and much-expanded gift shop sells wine-related items like stemware and grapevine wreaths. You can picnic with a bottle of chardonnay or Vineyard reserve white and bask in the view of Lake Waramaug below. The winery is open daily from 10 to 5 May-December, Friday-Sunday rest of year. **Haight Vineyards and Winery** near Litchfield, the first farm winery in New England's biggest wine-producing state, is Connecticut's largest. The Haight family take pride in their covertside white and red award-winners as well as their chardonnay and riesling labels. There's an informative vineyard walk and guided tours are available in the Tudor-style winery, which is open daily 10:30 to 5.

Two for Tea

Harney & Sons, 23 Brook St., Salisbury.

Master blender John Harney, former innkeeper at the White Barn Inn here, sells exotic teas by the bag or tin at his packing factory with a new tasting room. All the teas – ordered through a catalog by discriminating customers and purveyed by Williams-Sonoma and Ritz-Carlton hotels across the country – can be sampled here. Loose teas, flavored iced teas and tea bags, as well as accessories like mesh tea balls and silver infuser spoons, even a "tea-shirt" are on display. So are preserves, mixes for scones and lots of information about tea, including the Harneys' book on tea leaf reading. John is a genial host as he shows novices the proper way to taste tea. At his small counter, he makes it more fun to sample teas than we could have imagined. And the teas come in an amazing variety of flavors and hues. After sampling three or four, meticulously timed by little timers to just the right flavor and served in small handle-less white cups, we left with some Indian spice tea and some wonderful (and expensive) Japanese green tea. At our close-to-Christmas visit, local folks kept coming in for a stash of holiday tea, spiced with citrus, almond, clove and cinnamon. All the teas in the catalog are rated for smokiness, added flavors, body, aroma and astringency.

(860) 435-5044 or (800) 832-8463. Open daily 10 to 5, Sunday noon to 5.

Chaiwalla, 1 Main St., Salisbury.

Tea lovers have discovered Chaiwalla (which means teamaker in Sanskrit) and flock in for owner Mary O'Brien's pots of rare tea. They sit at gate-leg tables with mismatched chairs in her dining room and a three-seat counter facing the open kitchen. Mary serves morning fare ("offered whenever it is 'morning' for you"), tiffin (midday fare) and tea. A stunning selection of perfectly brewed teas, using local spring water, is served in clear glass pots on warmers and poured into clear glass mugs. You also may try Chaiwalla's own granola, eggs en cocotte, fruit-filled french toast, perhaps a soup like corn chowder or tomato-kale, pot stickers or a sandwich like "scholar's delight," roast beef with watercress and homemade herb mayonnaise, all in the $3.50 to $6 range. At tea time, Scottish shortbread, crumpets and scones with lemon curd are among the goodies. When we stopped in, plum kuchen and three-berry cobbler were a couple of the desserts.

(860) 435-9758. Open daily, 10 to 6.

New York Treats

The Millerton area of New York is becoming a mecca for culinary-related activity. The venerable McArthur's Smoke House at Railroad Plaza has given way to a lineup of food places, including **The Health Food Store,** which opens into an espresso bar, bakery and deli that operate as a retail adjunct to the stark white **Farm Country Cafe,** specializing in "simple, rustic" contemporary American fare. Across the street is **Gilmor Glassworks,** the sparkling new showroom for the colorful handblown glassware created by John and Jan Gilmor at their studio in nearby Pine Plains. The train depot is the seasonal home of **Steed's Ice Cream Parlour,** a confection in pink and green, where you can order anything from a frappe or soda to a cappuccino freeze and a banana split. Just up Main Street is **Pasta at Large,** a retail shop where founder Sofia Okolowicz prepares her wonderful pastas, sauces and breads to go.

Well worth a side trip is the **Hammertown Barn,** an antiques store plus much more at 4027 Route 199 in Pine Plains, N.Y. Owner Joan Osofsky's expanding sideline is gourmet foods and dishware. We reveled in all the preserves and salsas, the handpainted pottery, suave placemats and latest cookbooks. The old Gatehouse in front is furnished like a house and everything is for sale. On weekends, its working kitchen is opened for tastings of soups (perhaps mixed bean or potato-leek), salad dressings and mulling juices. Joan's husband Sid, a principal in the nearby **Ronnybrook Farm Dairy** that the New York Times called "the Dom Perignon of Dairy," may offer samples of some of his ice creams. We tasted his green apple and pumpkin ice creams and headed off to buy some at the new Ronnybrook store in Amenia.

Rural pond with swan and geese is an attraction at Stonehenge inn and restaurant.

Ridgefield
An Enclave of Elegant Eateries

For its size, no town in Connecticut – perhaps even in all New England – enjoys the reputation that Ridgefield has for fine dining. "Some people think that Ridgefield was put on the map by our restaurant," claims the brochure for Stonehenge. The same could be said by a couple of other restaurants after the rural charm of Ridgefield was discovered by New Yorkers in the post-war era.

For three decades or so, Stonehenge, the Inn at Ridgefield and The Elms had things pretty much to themselves. In recent few years, more first-rate restaurants have sprouted in Ridgefield and just to the west across the New York State line.

That there is such a concentration of great establishments in one small area does not surprise the restaurateurs. "It's like opening a fine shoe store," said one. "You don't want to be the only good store around."

Lately, the early emphasis on haute has been superseded by a proliferation of bistros and cafes that specialize in everything from Southwest fare to bagels. "This town has really taken to gourmet takeout," says Lynelle Faircloth of the Ridgefield General Store, whose cafe caters to the luncheon crowd as well as the takeout trend.

That trend was noted by the folks from Hay Day, the Westport-based, country-chic farm market, as they opened a new market with an extensive takeout section, a coffee bar and a cafe in Ridgefield in 1991. Successful beyond expectations, it served as a prototype two years later for the expanded Westport operation.

The Hay Day concept was tailor-made for Ridgefield. This is, after all, a town where a sidewalk vendor dispenses gourmet hot dogs and a store called Bone Jour advertises gourmet treats for pets.

The burgeoning of the restaurant business extends to lodging, with a fine B&B next to the Inn at Ridgefield, upgraded and expanded accommodations at Stonehenge and The Elms, and a private B&B suite with a 30-mile view.

But food remains foremost in Ridgefield, an enclave of creative cuisine.

Dining

The Best of the Best

Elms Restaurant & Tavern, 500 Main St., Ridgefield.

They were high-school sweethearts at Ridgefield High, Class of 1976. Twenty years later, they returned to take over the restaurant in Ridgefield's oldest (1799) operating inn.

It was a happy homecoming for Brendan and Cris Walsh. The pioneer in new American cuisine had got his start "flipping crêpes" at Stonehenge and was a waiter at The Elms and the nearby Le Chateau while attending the Culinary Institute of America. At age 26 after working in the California kitchen of Jeremiah Tower, he made a national name as opening chef at Arizona 206 in New York City. Three Long Island restaurants of his own and three children later, he got a phone call from his old boss, Robert Scala, of The Elms: "I'm retiring. Do you want the restaurant?" It was a godsend, recalls Cris. "All our family was still here." They negotiated to take over the restaurant operation, added a more casual tavern concept and launched a new cooking style.

Brendan, the master of innovative Southwestern cooking who helped create the trend of small plates called "grazing," took inspiration from 18th-century food associated with New England. He elevated stews, roasts, spoonbreads and puddings to new culinary heights and quick acclaim in the national media (Esquire magazine named The Elms one of the ten best restaurants of 1996). His renowned "food of the moment" now is refreshingly familiar, its presentation new and exciting.

For starters ($6 to $12), consider shepherd's pie, masterfully done here with lobster, peas and chive mashed potatoes. Braised lamb, celery root and goat cheese embellish the corn cake, and the potted duck salad comes with caramelized pear, frisée and toasted barley.

Among main courses ($18 to $27) are a tasty skillet-roasted organic chicken, accented with a sausage made of its leg and paired with sweet-potato spoonbread, creamed collards and truffle whipped potatoes. The grilled Montauk swordfish with mango relish is as good as swordfish gets. Other early favorites were Connecticut seafood stew, rib loin of veal and maple-thyme grilled loin of venison with buttered brandy glaze.

Desserts in the $5 range are new twists on traditional themes. The apple pandowdy with granny smith apples is teamed with Tahitian vanilla yogurt. The pumpkin

Chef-owner Brendan Walsh with wife Cris in dining room at the Elms.

mousse comes with cranberry granité and cinnamon cookies, and the pear-ginger charlotte with a spiced wine glaze.

A more casual tavern menu ($7.95 to $13.95) is offered for lunch and dinner in the handsomely refurbished, Tudor-look tavern. Atmospheric as all get-out, it has a beamed ceiling, sturdy dark wood tables seating 30, a neat birdcage bar with four seats, a big fireplace with a roaring fire in season and windows onto a covered, stone-floored deck with a cottage garden in one direction and a park in the other. Here you can order pasta with organic chicken, chard and goat cheese; citrus-spiced hangar steak with potato cake and wilted spinach or an alderwood smoked-salmon club sandwich that an admiring local chef says is to die for.

Cris Walsh, an interior decorator and graphic artist, stenciled the four small dining rooms in 18th-century patterns, painted the walls white with "lantern-glow yellow" trim, cloaked the well-spaced tables in white over 18th-century fabric, and added simple Colonial plaid curtains for the windows. It's a stylish, updated setting for food that's the last word in New England dining.

(203) 438-9206. Dinner by reservation, Wednesday-Sunday 5 to 9 or 10; tavern, Wednesday-Sunday 11:30 to 9 or 10.

Stonehenge, Route 7, Ridgefield.

The famed Swiss chef Albert Stockli of Restaurant Associates in New York put Stonehenge on the culinary map back in the 1960s. Since his death, owner Douglas Seville has survived changing dining habits and a disastrous fire, adding a variety of settings for dining as well as upgrading and expanding the overnight accommodations. And, in something of a coup, famed chef Christian Bertrand – former executive chef at Lutece in New York – took over the kitchen in 1996 following the closing of the restaurant bearing his name in Greenwich.

Rebuilt following a 1988 fire, the restaurant could not be more sophisticated in a country way. Slightly smaller than the original early 19th-century, Colonial white edifice upon which it is modeled, it has a new side entrance and a layout that gives almost every table a view of the property's tranquil pond. The main dining room is light and airy in a peachy coral, green and white color scheme. Fresh flowers and small lamps are on the widely spaced tables flanked by upholstered Chippendale-style chairs. Handsome swagged draperies frame the large end window onto the pond, and french doors open into a recently enclosed Terrace Room adding 60 seats for overflow on the former flagstone cocktail terrace. More masculine is the cozy tavern in hunter green, where English sporting prints cover the walls and the sconces are made from hunting horns.

The ambiance is sheer luxury, but not pretentious. "Stonehenge has left no stone unturned," a fellow restaurateur pointed out, no pun intended. "Everything is perfection."

Chef Bertrand cooks in the classic continental style with nouvelle accents and is known for subtle sauces. Stonehenge's famed beer-batter shrimp, a mainstay for 30 years, has been retired from service. So have the complimentary canapés that traditionally helped justify the expense of an extravagant meal.

Generous drinks are served in pretty, long-stemmed goblets. The half American, half French wine list is short and somewhat pricey, mostly in the $30 to $60 range. A page of rare vintages is priced from $150 to $1,200, for a magnum of 1970 Château Latour.

Among dinner appetizers ($9 to $16), we found the snails with hazelnut and garlic butter and the mushroom crêpes with a mornay sauce and gruyère cheese out of this world. Although the menu changes, keep an eye out for the house-smoked fish, perhaps smoked and marinated salmon with ginger over cucumber and vegetable angel-hair pasta. The terrines are terrific, and a recent offering was a lobster medallion with warm artichoke heart, poached egg and coral vinaigrette.

The short list of entrées is priced from $18 for sautéed chicken breast with tarragon vinegar to $30 for roast or poached Maine lobster. Specialties include dover sole in two services (sautéed meunière and poached in bouillon), crisp duck confit in "a surprise bed" of ground pork-filled cabbage, and roast rack of lamb with tarte niçoise, an artfully created pastry basket, complete with handle and holding diced tomatoes, zucchini and other vegetables. We can vouch for the veal scallops savoyarde with wild mushrooms and the tournedo of grilled salmon with ginger-chive beurre blanc.

The selection of desserts ($7.50) is luscious-looking. House favorites are the three versions of soufflés (pistachio, hazelnut and grand marnier), tarte tatin, and chocolate marquise with lady fingers. Ours was a strawberry tart with an abundance of fresh berries on a shortcake crust and topped with a shiny glaze. We're also partial to the ginger crème brûlée. Requests for Stonehenge's chocolate recipes arrive almost weekly from across the country. Such is the stature of the restaurant.

(203) 438-6511. Dinner nightly except Monday, 6 to 9; Sunday, brunch 11:30 to 2:30, dinner 4 to 8.

Chez Noüe, 3 Big Shop Lane, Ridgefield.

The decor is whimsical. The service without pretension. And the food is somewhat offbeat and represents good value.

Such is this worthy successor to Le Coq Hardi and later Sam's Grill, unfortunate victims of changing culinary times. After the demise of Sam's, a shrine to modern international and Pacific Rim fare tested by the wife of a onetime co-owner of Stonehenge, the former cave-like space returned to its French roots under brothers

Christian deNoüe uses sword to open champagne bottle in Napoleonic tradition at Chez Noüe.

Christian and Jehan deNoüe, early emigrés from France where their father's roots trace back to 900 A.D. and their mother was a Cabot (their uncle was Henry Cabot Lodge, ambassador to France). Christian, a cook who oversees the front of the house, leaves the business side to Jehan.

Pale yellow walls alternate with whitewashed fieldstone beneath a beamed ceiling, creating a country French setting. Brocade floral banquettes and bleached cane-seat chairs flank close-together tables dressed in white over blue linens. Shelves display copper pans and bottles of vinegar. High stools are at faux marble tables in the airy bar in front.

You won't find swordfish or tuna on the menu here "because everybody else has them," Christian says. Instead their country French menu (printed in English on one side, French on the reverse) goes for the unusual: a stew of the day (perhaps rabbit, cassoulet, vol-au-vent), choucroute or beef bourguignonne. With the exception of a few sandwiches at lunch and more substantial entrées at dinner, the menus for both meals are similar. Main courses are $8.95 to $10.95 at lunch, $16.95 to $21.95 at dinner.

Start with (or make a meal of) warm garlic sausage in puff pastry, mussels marinière, ratatouille baked with grated cheese or salade niçoise. The main course could be sole grenobloise, poached salmon with confit of leeks, sautéed calves liver with apples and onions, pork loin with apple compote, and escalope of veal with mushrooms in a cognac and cream sauce.

Desserts vary from chocolate mousse, fruit crêpes and crème caramel to pear-walnut tart and apple-cinnamon bread pudding with hard rum sauce.

Christian also chooses French and California wines that are "off the beaten path" with an eye to value. Most are priced in the teens and twenties. "I'd rather sell them than have them collect dust," he says. But the effort is serious. He sponsors periodic wine dinners: Joseph Phelps and Veuve Cliquot were on tap at a recent visit.

He also likes to have fun. He opens champagne bottles in the Napoleonic tradition with a saber, pulling out a hefty sword and popping a cork fifteen feet.

(203) 438-1946. Lunch, Monday-Saturday 11:30 to 2:30; dinner nightly, 6 to 10 or 11; Sunday, brunch 11:30 to 2:30, dinner 5 to 9.

Auberge Maxime, Ridgefield Road, North Salem, N.Y.

The charming white Normandy-style house at the intersection of Routes 116 and 121 is named for Westchester chef Maxime Ribera, who opened it in 1977 and sold a couple of years later to Bernard Le Bris, who arrived in this country from France in 1976. Bernard, a practitioner of contemporary French cuisine, is thoroughly at home in this picture-perfect French provincial restaurant, which now has a new herb and vegetable garden that strolling diners like to inspect. "We have the ambiance of a real French auberge," says Bernard, who was negotiating with the town in hopes of offering four or five bedrooms for overnight guests.

Dinners are $49 prix-fixe, but also can be ordered à la carte (entrées, $19 to $25). Tables in the 45-seat main-floor dining room are booked far in advance on weekends. A pleasant new room in the walk-out lower level takes care of overflow. It looks out onto a patio where lunch and cocktails are served beside tranquil gardens, fields and hillsides.

You enter through a small lounge graced with a mass of fresh and silk flowers, and panels of etched glass depicting a bevy of ducks over the bar. The rectangular dining room has a mirrored rear wall that makes it seem larger. Chairs upholstered in a striped fabric, chintz draperies, dark paneling, candles in tall silver candlesticks, custom-designed white china from France bearing the restaurant's logo, and gleaming table settings present an elegant country flair. Carved ducks handpainted by a woman from Sherman, Conn., grace each table and are available for purchase ($110 each).

Duck is the specialty of the house, served in five versions from traditional l'orange to roasted with ginger or green peppercorns or wild blueberries. Pressed duck à la Tour d'Argent is available with 48 hours' notice.

The six other entrées might include grilled salmon with mustard vinaigrette, grilled chicken with morels, veal chop marsala and rack of lamb provençal.

Meals begin with appetizers like snails in a curry oil with apples and raisins, smoked salmon with blinis and cucumber-lime salad, grilled lamb sausage on a bed of pasta, and a timbale of vegetables with smoked mozzarella. Salads of mesclun or endive are served with a cheese of the day.

Chef Bernard offers nightly specials – soft-shell crabs with saffron, baby pheasant with wild mushrooms and a heavenly sounding blueberry soufflé one spring evening we visited. Although soufflés are the specialty, other worthy desserts include banana mousse crêpe with walnut and rum ice cream, cappuccino-apple bread pudding with Belgian chocolate sauce, and orange-flavored crème brûlée.

The wine list, strong on champagnes, runs from $20 to $840 and is notable for its grid chart signifying the year. The chef makes his own vinegars and cherries in vodka and gives small bottles to regular customers at Christmas. He also will prepare a dégustation menu for two or more with advance notice. It's priced at $70 for eight small courses and includes "foie gras, lobster and all that fancy stuff," says Bernard.

Some lunch patrons like to start with the special house cocktail, a glass of champagne with passion-fruit liqueur, a dash of campari and a scoop of sorbet. Then they might try soup or one of the evening's appetizers, an omelet ($10.50) or entrée ($14.50 to $16.50) like confit of duck or entrecôte au poivre, and finish with one of those marvelous soufflés.

(914) 669-5450. Lunch, weekdays noon to 3; dinner, 6 to 9; Sunday, noon to 3 and 3 to 9. Closed Wednesday.

Heidi and Bernard Le Bris in dining room at Auberge Maxime.

The Inn at Ridgefield, 20 West Lane (Route 35), Ridgefield.

Masses of azaleas and rhododendron in spring brighten the canopied entrance to this elegant restaurant founded in 1947, the same year as Stonehenge. The entrance is lined with the sides of wine crates from across the world. Inside are a small cocktail lounge, three fireplaced dining rooms and a piano bar where a pianist entertains. There's a lovely summer garden cafe, where lunch and dinner are served on the side lawn.

The main dining room, with the grand piano at the entrance, is our favorite. Some tables have window views of surrounding lawns and all focus on a huge spotlit painting of Monte Carlo. The upholstered chairs are comfortable, tables are well spaced, and the eye-catching pewter service plates are emblazoned with a picture of the inn.

Partners Ray Kuhnt and Johannes Brugger cater to the wants of a regular clientele. The ambitious, oversize dinner menu is prix-fixe at $38 for one side that mixes old classics with representatives of the new French cuisine and à la carte for the traditional continental side, now also with contemporary touches.

Chef Brugger peppers the inn's traditional dishes like escargots bourguignonne and filet of beef wellington with such surprises as gulf shrimp on spiced mango puree with ginger and black angus steak from a granite stone grill, prepared tableside and served with two dipping sauces. Main courses run from $18 for grilled and steamed vegetables to $29 for dover sole meunière. New on the 50th anniversary menu were zarzuela, a fishmonger's kettle from Spain, and grilled free-range chicken basted with tarragon. Maryland crabmeat with a chile and pepper coulis and a medley of scallops and shrimp with mushrooms au gratin are among appetizers ($8 to $16).

Dessert could be raspberry mousse cake, chocolate or grand marnier soufflé, crêpes suzette or a trio of cranberry, quince and melon sorbets.

The lunch menu has a smattering of the dinner items, priced from $10 to $21. Recent offerings included steak tartare, shrimp in beer batter, a vegetarian plate with a poached egg, and (doesn't *this* sound archaic?) "for my lady – blinis à la Reine," petite crêpes with mixed green salad. The tuxedoed staff outnumbered the customers at our latest midday visit.

(203) 438-8282. Lunch, Monday-Saturday noon to 2; dinner nightly, 6 to 9:30 or 10:30, jackets required; Sunday, brunch noon to 3, dinner 3 to 8.

Le Château, Route 35 at Route 123, South Salem, N.Y.

Drive through the gate and up the winding, dogwood-lined road to the baronial stone mansion built by J. Pierpont Morgan on a hilltop in 1907 for his former minister and you'll get one of the most majestic views of any restaurant – a sylvan

panorama across the northern Westchester valley. The entry hall is paneled in rare chestnut, hand-hewn and held together by butterfly pieces. Dining is in high-ceilinged rooms, a couple facing onto the garden patio and all with expansive views. No wonder Le Château does such a lively wedding and function business.

Despite the numbers, dining is correct and quiet. It's well regarded locally, a credit to Joseph Jaffré, son-in-law of the original owners who came here from Le Coq au Vin in New York in 1974, and his longtime staff. The fabulous array of appetizers and desserts, on display buffet-style on either side of the entry foyer, are enough to make the most diet-conscious succumb.

New chef Claude Moreau has imparted more colorful and dramatic presentations

Window table at Le Chateau.

to the continental fare, which received a rare excellent rating recently from the New York Times. Entrées go from $23 for fillet of sole stuffed with lobster and truffles to $30 for lobster fricassee with porcini mushrooms and truffle sauce. Fillet of Pacific turbot with lime sauce, sautéed shrimp with curry and mango over basil linguini, roasted muscovy duck with cherry sauce, sweetbreads with capers, veal medallions with walnuts and roquefort, and rack of lamb with rosemary sauce are among the choices. Appetizers range from $8.50 for an eggplant and salmon charlotte with tomato-butter sauce to $19 for fresh foie gras. Desserts include grand marnier soufflé, crème brûlée and a creamy chocolate-kahlua terrine. The wine list is well-chosen and rather expensive, although the price-conscious can find a few in the $20s.

It's idyllic in summer to have cocktails on the lawn, enclosed by gray stone walls as in a castle. And it's great any time to tarry at the bar, its windows offering the best view around.

(914) 533-6631. Dinner, Tuesday-Saturday 6 to 9:30; Sunday, 2 to 9; jackets required.

L'Europe, 407 Smith Ridge Road (Route 123), South Salem, N.Y.

With the demise of a couple of French restaurants and the slippage of others, this sprightly establishment has found a niche. Beautiful gardens flank the front entrance of a small gray house converted in 1988 by Rui Toska of Danbury. Lovely moss-green rugs, nicely spaced tables set with white damask and pots of flowers beautify the interior as well. A New York Times reviewer said a meal here is like dining in a private club.

Chef Jeff Toska, the owner's nephew, offers a traditional French menu upon which only the penciled prices seem to change from year to year. Dinner entrées ($21.50 to $29.50) include fillet of Norwegian salmon with champagne caviar, ragoût of lobster and scallops, braised sweetbreads madeira with wild mushrooms, roasted baby chicken with morel sauce, escalope of veal with shiitake mushroom sauce, and filet mignon with mushrooms and port wine sauce.

Among appetizers ($7.50 to $13) are escargots in puff pastry, duck salad with raspberry vinaigrette and smoked salmon, trout and bluefish with Scandinavian garnishes. Beluga caviar with imported vodka is $45.

Soufflés ($8) are the dessert forte, always grand marnier and chocolate and often a seasonal special like raspberry. Lemon cheesecake, zabaglione with fresh strawberries or raspberries,, crème brûlée and walnut parfait are other favorites. The wine list is primarily French, starting at $19.50 for a beaujolais and rising rapidly into the hundreds.

Lunch is an abbreviated version of the dinner menu (entrées from $13 for pasta of the day to $22 for filet mignon with green peppercorn sauce).

(914) 533-2570. Lunch, Tuesday-Saturday noon to 2:30; dinner, 6 to 9:30, weekends to midnight; Sunday brunch, noon to 3. Closed Monday.

More Dining Choices

Thirty Three & 1/3, 125 Danbury Road, Ridgefield.

Everything comes up threes in this jaunty newcomer known for innovative American cuisine. Culinary Institute-trained chef Arthur Michaelsen, his sister Nancy Burke, the hostess, and their mother (Josephine Connelly, who we're told arranges the flowers) took this approach because each has a one-third interest.

Fashioned from a storefront pizzeria in a shopping plaza, the place is fresh and fun, from decor to food. The family gutted the kitchen and produced a long and narrow dining room behind the front bar. A few paintings and murals brighten white walls above mottled gray vinyl wainscoting, and much of the scene is reflected in big mirrors. A mural of Art, Nancy and one of their chefs running across the countryside, food in hand, starts at the kitchen door and sets the theme.

From the kitchen comes a variety of treats, all with prices ending in 33. The dinner menu offers more than a dozen entrées from $15.33 for a sauté of sweet and hot sausage over penne pasta to $19.33 for grilled black angus steak with a southwest pepper jelly and cornmeal-fried vidalia onion rings. The pecan-crusted Idaho brook trout might come with a mango puree, the grilled yellowfin tuna on a bed of a garlicky spinach, the pan-seared sea scallops with a candied ginger risotto cake, and the grilled free-range chicken on a sundried tomato pesto with five-onion ragoût.

Expect starters ($5.33 to $7.33) like grilled beef and scallion rolls with sesame-ginger sauce, a sauté of wild mushrooms, a smoked chicken and arugula pizza, and a grilled vegetable antipasto.

Desserts are predictable, from chocolate-chip cheesecake to crème brûlée.

Despite the stylish digs, this is a community hangout kind of a place, where you can order a hamburger for dinner and a cobb salad for lunch. There's a lively happy hour in the open bar up front, and a late-night happy hour with a bar menu on weekends.

(203) 438-3904. Lunch and weekend brunch, 11:30 to 3; dinner nightly from 5.

Biscotti Food Company, 3 Big Shop Lane, Ridgefield.

The simple, casual Cafe Naturel gave way to this more ambitious and expanded Italian eatery where chef Silvia Bianco-Anthony lends authenticity to the operation run by her husband, Corwyn, and Stephen Herman.

Glass cases and counters display some of the day's offerings, including wonderful panini, salads and luscious desserts. We picked up an oversize chunky chicken salad platter ($8.95), tasty and filling, for a quick lunch on the run, after considering the fajita omelet and ogling the array of three-berry and pear-cranberry tarts that beckoned near the entry.

The restaurant has expanded into an adjacent space, doubling the size of its dining room. A country bistro look in pink and white was produced, with stucco walls and netting swagged around the ceiling, trailing vines to the windows. The netting holds colored leaves in fall, balloons in winter, and flowers in spring for a whimsical effect overhead.

The extensive dinner menu ($9.95 to $16.95) harbors all kinds of pasta treats as well as such entrées as broiled fillet of salmon on a sauce of roasted red peppers and tomatoes with arborio rice and steamed vegetables, chicken marsala and caponata, and medallions of pork with mozzarella in a tomato-wine sauce. There's no beef, but the "roasted eggplant meatloaf" incorporating ground turkey and pork may suffice.

Sautéed smoked mozzarella, several versions of wild mushrooms, grilled vegetables and bruschetta are featured among antipasti ($4.95 to $11.95, according to size). Most opt for a sampling platter, $9.95 for two.

(203) 431-3637. Lunch, Tuesday-Saturday 11:30- to 3; dinner, Tuesday-Saturday 5:30 to 9:30 or 10; Sunday, brunch 9 to 3, dinner 5 to 9.

Ridgefield General Store Cafe, Copps Hill Common, 103 Danbury Road, Ridgefield.

In the basement of a marvelous country store is this cafe, redecorated in English tearoom style by store owner Lynelle Faircloth, an interior designer. Although the whole store is her bailiwick, the cafe with its demonstration kitchen is her pride and joy. In it her staff serves everything from Sunday brunch through creative lunches to formal English tea.

The blackboard lists soups, salads, sandwiches and quiches (most $6.95 to $8), to eat at one of the 36 seats or to take out. Everything's made fresh on the premises and is oh-so-good, from deep-dish chicken pie and Texas cornbread casserole to desserts like double chocolate fudge cake, pumpkin-spice cheesecake, raspberry pie and fresh fruit tarts, $2.50 to $4.50. The smoked turkey, apple and melted brie on oat bread is her most popular sandwich, Lynelle says, although she seems to devise a new twist for the menu every day and lately has added a number of vegetarian items.

The British tea involves three courses – scones and sandwiches, crumpets and

Cheery dining room at Thirty Three & 1/3 is reflected in mirrors.

sweets. It comes on doilies atop Portuguese floral pottery, the presentation being done with as much flair here as the food.

(203) 438-1740. Lunch, Monday-Saturday 11:30 to 3; British tea, Wednesday-Saturday 3 to 5; Sunday brunch, 10 to 3.

Gail's Station House, 378 Main St., Ridgefield.

One of the endearing and enduring places in Ridgefield is this offshoot of Gail's Station House in nearby West Redding. Original partners Gail Dudek and Nancy Broughton converted the old Brunetti's Market into a lively, casual arena for good, basic food at affordable prices. They sold recently to John Finnegan, their original chef, and his wife Patty, who expanded the dinner hours and offerings.

Gail's is known for its baked goods, and all the baking is done downstairs at the Ridgefield location. It's also known for its breakfasts, featuring a variety of pancakes and omelets in the $3.95 to $5.50 range (for corn and cheddar or banana-pecan pancakes). The skillet specials are something else: Texas Pink combines red-skinned hash browns, jalapeño peppers, scrambled eggs topped with salsa and sour cream with a wedge of pink grapefruit for $5.75; Leo's brings scrambled eggs, Nova Scotia lox, green onions, hash browns and a bagel with cream cheese for $7.75.

At lunch time, burgers range from $3.75 to $7.25, depending on size and accessories. Standard sandwiches, salads, veggie casseroles and blackboard specials go for a range of $3.95 to $7.25.

The changing dinner menu lists appetizers and light fare ($3.75 to $6.95) like jalapeño-cheddar crab cakes, goat cheese and green chile chimichanga, and oriental chicken salad. Main courses ($9.95 to $17.95), served with bread and salad, could be vegetable lasagna, rainforest stir-fry (vegetables and tropical nuts over brown rice), lemon sole, chicken enchiladas, veal ragoût and New Zealand lamb. New York-style cheese cake, fruit pies, fruit squares and freshly baked cookies are some of the good desserts.

The ambiance is a mix of baked-goods displays, a counter with stools, and mismatched chairs at tables dressed up at night with floral cloths under glass. Assorted hats decorate one wall. A small rear dining room (once the market's store room) is perked up with a huge window and floral wallpaper above the wainscoting. Three layers of linoleum were removed to expose the original wood floors.

The establishment conveys a 1960s feel as "a home away from home," a frequent customer volunteered. "It's a Cheers kind of place." It also keeps up with the times. Gail's was about to host a wine and cigar dinner at our latest visit.

(203) 438-9775. Breakfast daily, 8 to 3; lunch, 11:30 to 3; dinner, 5:30 to 9:30, Sunday to 8.

Southwest Cafe, 109 Danbury Road at Copps Hill Common, Ridgefield.

A simple cafe with black and white tile floors and nine tables is where Barbara Nevins dishes up lunch and dinner and lots of takeout orders. Barbara, who used to live in Taos, N.M., is known for her green chile sauce. It's the base for a hearty green chile stew of carrots, celery and new potatoes, topped with melted cheese and served with a warm flour tortilla. Barbara also employs the sauce in many of the dinner dishes, such as cheese, chicken, seafood or beef enchiladas (the last layered New Mexican style and topped with a fried egg), chicken or beef chimichangas, chalupas, shrimp tostadas, quesadillas and huevos rancheros, all $13.95 or under. It's not often you find huevos on both lunch and dinner menus, or Colorado tostadas with chicken or shredded beef and New Mexican red-chile sauce, for that matter.

Much the same menu is available at lunch, as are sandwiches ($4.95) and salads ($6.95), varying from chicken and artichoke to shrimp and vegetables. Southwest dishes include a bowl of green chili ($2.95) and green chile chicken, vegetable or beef stew, $6.95. Start with tortilla soup and end with Mexican flan or kahlua-pecan pie. Mexican beers and Spanish wines are featured.

(203) 431-3398. Lunch daily, 11 to 4; dinner nightly, 4 to 9:30 or 10.

Offbeat Gourmet

Steve's Bagels, 483 Main St., Ridgefield.

Ex-Vermont restaurateur Steven Grover saw a need for a good bagel shop in his new hometown. He went to New York and "tasted all the bagels in Manhattan. When I found the ones I liked, they said to cut the sugar and increase the malt. So I did." The rest is history. Steve's bagels took the town by storm, and he quickly had to expand, both in space and offerings.

The bagels (55 cents) are the foundation, upon which his friendly crew builds sandwiches. They range from $4.25 to $6.50 (for smoked salmon, cream cheese and onions) and include tuna, hummus, turkey, chicken salad and roast beef with watercress and horseradish. Or you can have said sandwiches on Steve's caraway rye or whole wheat breads. There are vegetarian sandwiches (sundried tomatoes with brie; hummus with cucumbers and sprouts) as well. Accompany with one of the soups, the daily vegetarian, chicken and beef or sweet potato and kielbasa.

Steve's CIA-trained baker is also the chef, overseeing production of wonderful pastries, oversize cookies, pecan squares and the like. The deli case displays salads to go. There are tables at which to eat in this spare but spiffy place, or you may take out.

Is there life after bagels? " We toyed with the idea of gourmet pizzas in the evenings," said Steve, "to fill out the other side of the day." They eventually decided to stress espresso and cappuccino instead.

(203) 438-6506. Open daily, 5:30 a.m. to 7 p.m.

Chez Le Hot Dog

Chez Lenard, Main Street, Ridgefield.

We can't give you a proper address for this operation, which he officially calls "Les Delices Culinaires de la Voiture," but it's usually near the corner of Prospect Street. Anywhere else but in Ridgefield it would be merely a hot dog cart, but this one has chutzpah, or we should say its pusher, Michael Soetbeer, who changes his hats with the seasons, has. Year-round on even the chilliest days, the "voiture" dispenses le hot dog, le hot dog supreme, le hot dog choucroute alsacienne, le hot dog garniture Suisse (topped with cheese fondue), and le hot dog façon Mexicain, $1.50 to $3.50.

Michael says he has "the first gourmet hot dog rolls in the world," made for him at Martin's Bakery with semolina flour and potato water. We thought le hot dog supreme with the works ($2) was the best we'd ever had. Beverages to go with these elegant hot dogs are cold sodas Americaines ($1) and Perrier with lime (de rigeur in the area), $1.25. For dessert, chocolate-chip cookies from

Michael Soetbeer at Chez Lenard.

O'Carmody's ("out of this world – they would put Famous Amos out of business," says the proprietor) are 75 cents.

Open year-round, Monday-Saturday 11 to 4, sometimes later and sometimes on Sunday.

Lodging

Stonehenge, Route 7, Box 667, Ridgefield 06877.

Instead of a country inn, this is now a fine inn in the country, stresses owner Douglas Seville of the "new" Stonehenge, southwestern Connecticut's grand old inn. He was showing some of the sixteen redecorated guest rooms – six in the inn, six in the Guest Cottage and the rest in a large new outbuilding called the Guest House – and a grand job has been done indeed.

Fashioned in 1947 from a country farmhouse into an English inn by a World War II veteran who had been stationed on the Salisbury Plain near the ancient monument of the same name, Stonehenge has been synonymous with fine food for many years. Since the guest rooms were refurnished and more were added in 1984, it has been a place for country getaways as well.

Each room has its own style, from the corner Windsor Room in the inn with a bookcase, antique dresser, wing chairs and ornamental fireplace to the spacious bridal suite with large living room and kitchenette in the Guest House. The two master bedrooms and two suites can sleep four, and are particularly sumptuous and comfortable. All rooms have private baths, air-conditioning, telephones and TV.

Picnic hampers containing continental breakfast and the New York Times are delivered to the rooms each morning. In season, guests like to take them to the pond to watch the antics of the geese, ducks and swans. Guests also enjoy a cozy, fireplaced parlor in the main inn, full of the latest magazines and books.

(203) 438-6511. Fax (203) 438-2478. Doubles, $120 to $160; suites, $200.

West Lane Inn, 22 West Lane, Ridgefield 06877.

Beside the Inn at Ridgefield restaurant, this quiet inn is much favored by corporate types moving into the area or visiting on business. The comfortable rooms in the early 1800s home are decorated in soft colors, two with working fireplaces. All have two queensize or a kingsize bed, upholstered wing chairs and/or sofas, private baths, telephones and remote-control TVs. The sheets are 100 percent cotton and there are scales in the bathrooms.

Fourteen rooms are in the main inn; six more are out back in a converted garage named "The Cottage on the Hill." Each of the latter has a kitchenette and a private rear balcony looking onto emerald-green lawns. Three suites have been fashioned from the former home of innkeeper Maureen Mayer, hidden behind green plantings and a redwood fence between the inn and the restaurant.

Off the inn's rich, oak-paneled lobby is a cheery breakfast room for continental breakfast (fresh juice and danish). You can choose to have it in summer on the wide front porch with its inviting wicker furniture.

(203) 438-7323. Fax (203) 438-7325. Doubles, $115 to $165.

The Elms, 500 Main St., Ridgefield 06877.

At Ridgefield's oldest operating inn, parts of the original 1760 structure look appropriately ancient, although the restaurant has been dramatically updated by new owners Brendan and Cris Walsh. But the adjacent inn, totally refurbished in 1983, is up to date and continues under the thumb of the Scala family

Thirteen rooms and three suites are located on three floors of the inn. They are spacious, carpeted and outfitted with television and telephones; many of the bathrooms have dressing areas. Antique furnishings, a few four-poster beds and striking wallpapers add a feeling of tradition and luxury. Two rooms and two suites above the restaurant in the original inn are redecorated but retain their historic look, even to sloping floors. Two have stenciled bluebirds on the walls.

"The annex had reached the point where we either had to knock it down or build it up," said innkeeper Violet Scala, who decided on the latter and is justifiably proud of the results.

A continental breakfast with croissants is served in guests' rooms.

(203) 438-2541. Doubles, $105 and $115; suites, $140.

Far View Manor, 803 North Salem Road, Ridgefield 06877.

Bed and breakfasts come and go in Ridgefield, but remain few and far between. This was the only one operating at our latest visit.

Jack and Ann Gilchrist offer by reservation a B&B suite with a private entrance on a former working farm. The 1,200-square-foot space includes a high-ceilinged great room with fireplace, a bedroom with kingsize bed and a full bath. Barns,

Early 1800s residence now houses West Lane Inn in Ridgefield.

horses and wildlife remain on five pastoral acres with a 30-mile view. Built in 1911, the manor was once the Ridgefield Boys School and was considered as a site for the United Nations. Continental breakfast is included.

(203) 438-4753. Double, $100 to $125. No credit cards.

Gourmet Treats

Hay Day, The Country Farm Market, 21 Governor St., Ridgefield. (203) 431-4400. Hidden behind Main Street in the old Grand Central supermarket is this branch of the Westport-based market par excellence. When it opened in 1991, it was the biggest and most diverse of the Hay Days with a "real marketplace atmosphere," in the words of a principal. The 10,000-square-foot facility – which became the model for a 1993 relocation and expansion of the original Westport store – is a food lover's paradise of produce, bakery, fish store, butcher shop, gourmet shelf items and a deli to end all delis, plus a wine shop, a coffee-espresso bar and a small pastry cafe. Best of all for noshers: you can sample your way through the store, tasting perhaps a spicy corn chowder and an addictive chunky clam and bacon dip at the deli, exotic cheeses at the cheese shop, hot mulled cider and Connecticut macoun apples, and French vanilla coffee at the door. Hay Day conducts cooking classes, publishes a monthly newspaper chock full of recipes and food tips that formed the nucleus of the wonderful *Hay Day Cookbook,* and does an extensive mail-order business. Open daily, 8 to 8, Sunday to 7.

The Ridgefield General Store in Copps Hill Common, 103 Danbury Road, is a nifty contemporary place full of all kinds of gourmet goodies, from exotic vinegars and its own line of jellies to good-looking china and cooking paraphernalia. Owner Lynelle Faircloth calls hers "a mini-department store" with fifteen departments stocking antiques and "gifts for all reasons." A large area of children's toys and a great selection of paper items from cards and wrapping to invitations are attractions.

Catering to the coffee craze is the **Ridgefield Coffee Co.,** a new espresso cafe and gourmet shop at 419 Main St. The European-style cafe has a tile floor, marble-top tables and a few tables on the sidewalk. The pastry cases display black and white espresso cakes, ebony and ivory tarts, and more to accompany omelets, salads and fancy sandwiches in the $8.95 to $10.95 range. The treats, including gelati and sorbets, upstage the coffees.

Some think the best ice cream around is served at **Mr. Shane's Homemade Parlour Ice Cream,** 409 Main St. Energetic John Ghitman bought the former branch of Dr. Mike's, a well-known Bethel operation, where he learned how to make ice cream. Now he serves up dozens of flavors, from a rich chocolate ("very powerful," says John) to spiced apple, pumpkin and eggnog. We can vouch for his pralines 'n cream (cones, $1.50, 2.25 and $3), as well as his new twix caramel swirl ice cream "that's been flying out the door." John also offers frappes (milkshakes, to those not familiar with the Massachusetts variety), brown cows (root beer with two scoops of ice cream) and frozen yogurt he doctors up from Columbo.

Consider the Cook, Route 35, Cross River, N.Y., is an excellent kitchen shop in the interesting Yellow Monkey village shopping complex west of Ridgefield. Quimper plates, fabulous table settings and all the latest gourmet foodstuffs are among the offerings. The shop opens into **Sweet Expectations,** a small candy and chocolate shop.

The village also contains a branch of **Wm. Nicholas & Co.** of nearby Katonah, caterer and purveyor of fine foods. We've seldom seen so sophisticated an array of salads, sandwiches and baked goods in so rustic a country setting. You could order half a ham and swiss pita sandwich for $2, a curried chicken rollup for $5.95 or a sampler plate of three salads (pesto shrimp, penne with roasted eggplant and zucchini, and dijon rice with sweet peas) for $6.95. There are wonderful muffins and triple berry tarts for the sweet tooth. You can eat at tables here or take out.

A Destination for Cooks

The Silo, 44 Upland Road (off Route 202), New Milford.

No report on culinary affairs in this section of Connecticut would be complete without mention of the fabulous cookery shop and cooking instruction classes offered by Ruth and Skitch Henderson.

In former stables and dairy barns are displayed everything from oversize Mexican pottery planters in shapes of rams and hens to a sizable collection of cookbooks interspersed among cooking equipment and jars and bottles of the most wonderful jams, sauces and herbs. The Gallery features changing exhibitions of Connecticut artists and craftspersons.

Well-known cooking teachers give classes here. Many chefs from area restaurants do as well, and there are two-week seminars and interesting one-session courses – for example, "Decadent Do-Ahead Desserts," "Healthy Cooking for Busy People," "Two in a Tuscan Kitchen," "A Mediterranean Rim Picnic" and "My First Dinner Party" (ages 8 and up). In 1995, the miniature gingerbread houses made by instructor Sandy Daniels and students in the cooking school were used to decorate one of the Christmas trees at the White House.

The 200-acre Hunt Hill Farm, set among rolling hills and flower gardens where kittens tumble around and horses and cows are pastured nearby, is a destination in itself.

(203) 355-0300. Open daily, 10 to 6.

Seagull and sailboat are part of typical scene viewed from restaurant along Connecticut shore.

Southeastern Connecticut
Down the River and Along the Shore

For reasons not entirely evident, many of Connecticut's better restaurants have clustered through the years along the lower Connecticut River and the shore of Long Island Sound.

Perhaps it is the natural affinity of restaurants for water locations. Perhaps it is the reputation for the good life that accompanies people of affluence with demanding palates and high tastes. Perhaps it is the busy but low-key resort status of the shore, summer home to thousands of inland Connecticut and Massachusetts residents.

Some of Southern New England's top innkeepers and restaurateurs put the area on the dining map in the 1970s. Several fine French restaurants followed, and in recent years, more inns of distinction and restaurants have joined the scene.

"We've found this area full of people with discriminating tastes," says Bob Nelson, a New Jersey corporate dropout who has given new life to the old Bee and Thistle Inn in Old Lyme.

Except for Mystic, the Connecticut shore has been discovered relatively lately by most tourists.

The area this chapter covers has no large cities. Rather, it harbors quaint villages like Chester and Stonington, affluent enclaves like Essex and Old Lyme, and resort areas like Mystic and Old Saybrook. It also has the growing Foxwoods and Mohegan Sun resort casinos, two of the largest and most profitable in the world for the Indian tribes that own them.

Because this is our home territory, we cover our favorites in a broad sweep down the lower Connecticut River and along the shore of Long Island Sound.

Dining-room decor is country French at Restaurant du Village.

Dining

The Best of the Best

Restaurant du Village, 59 Main St., Chester.

Of all the Southern New England restaurants in which we've dined, we think this is the most like what you would find in a French village. Its blue wood facade – with specially grown ivy geraniums spilling out of window boxes and the bottom half of the large windows curtained in an almost sheer white fabric – is smack on the main street of tiny Chester, but one enters by walking up a brick path attractively bordered with potted geraniums to a side door.

Alsatian chef Michel Keller and his Culinary Institute-trained American wife Cynthia run their top-rated establishment very personally. A third-generation pastry chef, Michel spends his time in the kitchen and bakes the breads and desserts. Cynthia does the soups and some of the fish dishes, but is in the front of the house to welcome guests in the evening.

Through the small bar-lounge, decorated with plump piggies (the logo of the restaurant) with a few tables for overflow, you reach the small dining room. Along one wall, two sets of french doors open onto the brick walk for welcome breezes on warm nights. A sideboard between the doors contains the night's desserts and a large floral arrangement. A few lighted oil paintings adorn the stucco-type walls; a high shelf over the front windows displays antique plates.

The air of elegant simplicity is enhanced at the thirteen tables by white cloths and napkins, carafes of flowers, votive candles, open salt and pepper dishes, and blue sprigged service plates.

What may be the best French bread you will taste in this country is brought to the table with generous cocktails. Crunchy and chewy, made of Hecker's unbleached flour that gives it a darker color, the baguette is cut into thick chunks. Each diner is served an individual crock of sweet butter. If you get near the last piece of bread – and most do – the basket is whisked away and refilled, which could be detrimental to one's dietary health. On one of our visits it came back three times.

Of the six appetizers ($5.50 to $8.50), standouts are the cassoulet, a small copper casserole filled with sautéed shrimp in a light curry sauce; the croustade with grilled vegetables, and escargots with shiitake mushrooms in puff pastry. We also like the baked French goat cheese on herbed salad greens with garlic croutons. The soup changes daily, but often is a puree of vegetables or, on one summer night we dined, a cold cucumber and dill.

The ten or so entrées ($23 to $26) might include Rhode Island striped bass in parchment, steamed fillet of salmon wrapped in a leaf of savoy cabbage with salmon mousse, rabbit flamande (a specialty of Belgium), roast duckling with cranberry chutney, pan-seared veal cutlet with a flan of wild mushrooms obtained by a local purveyor from nearby woods, roast leg of herb-marinated lamb with French green kidney beans, and Cynthia's specialty, a stew of veal, lamb and pork with leeks and potatoes. These are accompanied by treats like dauphinoise potatoes with melted gruyère, julienned carrots, and yellow squash and zucchini with a sherry vinegar-shallot flavoring. The salad of exotic greens is tossed with a creamy mustard dressing that packs a wallop.

The well-chosen, mostly French wine list is priced from $18 to $95 and features vintages from Alsace.

Desserts change daily and are notable as well. At a recent visit, Michel was preparing an open fruit tart with blueberries and peaches in almond cream, a gratin of passionfruit, and paris-brest, in addition to his usual napoleons, soufflés glacé and crème brûlée.

(860) 526-5301. Dinner, Tuesday-Saturday 5:30 to 9, Sunday 5 to 9. Closed Tuesday in winter.

Steve's Centerbrook Cafe, 78 Main St., Centerbrook.

What a difference a change in concept can make. Master chef Steve Wilkinson decided it was time to lighten up the interior of Fine Bouche, his small French restaurant and patisserie that had been a culinary beacon in the area since 1979. Next we knew, Fine Bouche was out and Steve's Centerbrook Cafe was in. A big change? Yes, and no. As the owner put it, "we didn't want to throw out the baby with the bath water."

The interior, even lightened up, still resembles the old Fine Bouche. The menu, although more varied and appearing more affordable, retains some traditional specialties. And, a nice touch, fifteen quality wines are available for $15, although the full, 250-selection cellar especially strong in French Bordeaux retains the Wine Spectator award of excellence.,

Steve's is possibly the highest-style cafe around. Cheery with cream-colored walls and accents of light pastels, it seats 45 at well-spaced tables in three small rooms and an enclosed, lattice-trimmed wraparound porch. Works of local artists provide decoration. The white cloths are covered with butcher paper, a stash of bread sticks and a container of olive oil. Colorful Fiestaware is interspersed with the traditional Villeroy & Boch place settings.

Steve, who trained in London and San Francisco, now offers a with-it menu that spans the globe. Salads and pastas come in two sizes, the better for making a meal of one of each. Consider crab salad with avocado, tomatillo and belgian endive, followed by linguini with grilled salmon or wild mushroom and spinach ravioli – an exquisite light supper for about $12. Or graze through starters ($4.50 to $5.95) like a velvety scallop and saffron bisque, sourdough bruschetta bearing grilled shrimp and white beans, and a black bean crêpe with Thai duck, jícama, mango and fennel slaw.

Main courses are priced from $12.95 for crawfish and chicken étouffée to $17.95 for rack of lamb with mint pesto. Among the possibilities are seared tuna with ginger glaze, Moroccan lamb stew with couscous, grilled veal chop with rosemary jus and sautéed beef filet with grilled shiitake mushrooms, Szechuan peppercorns and brandy-cream sauce.

Desserts are superlative, particularly the almond-hazelnut dacquoise, a light but intense chocolate cake with chocolate chantilly, and the marjolaine, a heavenly combination of almond praline, hazelnut meringue, crème fraîche and bitter Belgian chocolate. To the roster of old favorites (crème brûlée and bananas foster) have been added a green tea ice cream and mango sundae with candied ginger, and Julia Child's classic strawberry tart, described on the menu as "the one from her first book thirty-something years ago."

That's Steve, mixing the trendy with the tried and true, keeping his superb restaurant up with the times. We only wish Sweet Sarah's, his patisserie and takeout shop in back, hadn't succumbed along the way.

(860) 767-1277. Dinner, Tuesday-Sunday from 5:30.

J.P. Daniels, Route 184, Old Mystic.

Off the beaten path – as are many of the Mystic area's treasures – is this high-ceilinged old dairy barn, handsomely restored, elegantly appointed and operating at a consistently high level since 1981. Tables on two floors are set with white cloths and fresh flowers. The subdued lighting is by oil lamps and lanterns on the rustic barnwood walls. A pianist or harpist entertains some evenings, the welcome is friendly and the atmosphere is quite enchanting.

The menu, formerly continental, has been broadened to include regional American and ethnic influences. Most dishes come in full and lighter portions, priced accordingly.

Appetizers ($4.95 to $5.95) run the gamut from chicken teriyaki and stuffed mushrooms to crab cakes rémoulade and grilled mussels. Four "pastabilities" are available in two sizes. Entrées ($12.95 to $18.95) include seafood casserole, chicken française, veal oscar, lamb tenderloin with chutney-sage sauce, twin tournedos and filet au poivre. A tempting newer concoction is called Mirlton Porro, a pear-shaped Southwestern vegetable with a squash-like flavor, filled with jumbo shrimp, lobster, scallops and andouille sausage in cajun spices and topped with béarnaise sauce. A specialty from the beginning is boneless duck stuffed with seasonal fruits and sauced with apricot brandy.

Desserts include rum crisp, chocolate mousse, peach melba and chocolate-raspberry torte. The wine list contains a description of all the selections.

(860) 572-9564. Dinner nightly, 5 to 9 or 9:30; Sunday brunch, 11 to 2.

Quiambaug House, 29 Old Stonington Road, Mystic.

"It was bound to happen," said the ads touting this newcomer transformed from Mystic's oldest restaurant. Jerry and Ainslie Turner, who led the Harborview in Stonington to culinary heights in the 1970s and 1980s, emerged unexpectedly in 1996 from early retirement. They gave the sprawl of a building that formerly housed

Farm wagon greets diners outside J.P. Daniels restaurant in restored dairy barn.

Sailor Ed's a crisp new country look in four dining venues: the Olde Porch, the Library, the Atlantic Grille and the Club Room lounge. White tablecloths with cranberry-colored napkins, cushioned windsor chairs and wood paneling are the rule. The Turners' collection of Quimper plates from France is displayed on shelves near the ceilings and in a hutch in the reception area, where two glass cabinets retained from the Harborview hold antique jewelry and Ainslie's cookbook, *Mystic Seaport's Seafood Secrets,* which is for sale.

The Turners, who try to visit Brittany every year to catch up on the latest in French cuisine, bill this as "déja-view at the Q." Early reviews were mixed. Old favorites like a robust tomato-saffron bouillabaisse, baked oysters Ainslie, coquilles St. Jacques parisienne and grilled swordfish niçoise were as good as ever. Some of the newer dishes and the service were faulted.

The dinner menu in the main Atlantic Grille ($16.95 to $22.95) ranges widely from bombay scallops over puff pastry and stuffed shrimp to roast duckling with plums, prime rib with horseradish sauce, veal saltimbocca and steak au poivre. Entrées come with green or caesar salad, but you might start with a stellar french onion soup gratin, carpaccio of smoked salmon and the specialty strudel bearing country sausage and wild mushrooms.

Dinner in the Club Room lounge hearkens back to the days of the wildly popular tavern at the Harborview. You'll find most of the dining-room appetizers, plus all kinds of entrée treats in the $8.95 range, from seafood pie and bouillabaisse to grilled chicken and spinach salad and london broil with whiskey sauce. The only really double-digit item here is filet mignon with roquefort sauce.

The dinner appetizers also are available for lunch, when the menu ($6.50 to $10.95) varies from eggs benedict to Guinness beer-battered fish and chips, Stonington clam and codfish cakes, grilled salmon and baked stuffed lobster.

(860) 572-8543. Lunch daily, 11:30 to 3; dinner, 5 to 10.

The Harborview, 60 Water St., Stonington.

Newly settled in Stonington, his wife persuaded restaurateur Viktor Baker to come out of semi-retirement in 1996 to take over the Harborview, which had gone downhill since the departure of founders Ainslie and George Turner. "This was more than a restaurant," said Maureen Baker. "It was a destination, an icon. We didn't want it falling into the wrong hands. It had to be done right and I thought he was perfect for it."

So Viktor, the restaurant concept designer who had transformed New York's 21 Club, Washington's Jockey Club, Dallas's Mansion on Turtle Creek and San Francisco's Carnelian Room, among others, and had presided over New York's Rainbow Room, accepted the challenge. The Bakers gutted the kitchen and created a new one, lightened up the decor of the main dining room, refinished the bar in the tavern, upgraded the Skipper's Dock restaurant beside the water and revamped all the menus.

The transformation reflects Viktor's "vision of what the Harborview should be." That's according to the man who had conceptualized many a nationally known restaurant, from decor to menu to staff, since leaving the Swiss Chalet, the South County restaurant he owned in the 1970s in Rhode Island. Here he offers three different places to eat, with menus to match.

The main dining room is casually elegant, now that its dark walnut walls have been whitened and the formal draperies removed from the back windows to showcase the harbor view. The large, well-spaced tables are dressed in white and robin's egg blue, with dark blue napkins and stemware, flickering oil lamps and stunning little round porcelain vases – each different – holding fresh flowers.

The only holdovers on the traditional Harborview dinner menu are coquilles St. Jacques and bouillabaisse, the latter containing a whole shelled lobster and pronounced by a visitor from Marseilles the best he'd ever had. The specialty duck comes in four versions, from alsatian to fig sauce, but with a difference: the roasted breast is from muscovy duck and the leg is a confit of moularde. The grilled swordfish is counterpointed for taste and color with a watercress sauce and the escalope of veal is sauced with lobster and pernod. This is continental fare at its most classic, priced from $17.50 for chicken caprice stuffed with ham and bananas to $25.95 for the grand bouillabaisse, not to mention the lobster thermidor and lobster savannah that are priced daily. Tuna wellington, châteaubriand bouquetière and rack of lamb are prepared for two, $42 to $56. The signature dessert is a rich, dense flourless chocolate torte, which Maureen likens to "Godiva on a plate" and "so good that it's available in all three restaurants."

The second dining venue is the **Bistro at the Bar,** where patrons can dine casually all day long amid wine barrels, old Life magazine covers on the walls and a mermaid figure overhead. Here you might order the signature perigourdine onion soup with tomatoes. the seafood club sandwich, filet mignon on a stick with pommes frites, the house-cured gravlax, fish-shaped pescalloti pasta stuffed with smoked salmon and leeks, or a special of grilled rare tuna with tamari, pickled ginger and wasabi. Prices range from $6.75 to $14.95. Strawberry or lemon flan is the dessert of choice here.

The most exciting restaurant – and locally most controversial, because of its heritage – is **Skipper's Dock,** a large and casual seasonal place behind the main restaurant with a jaunty deck and a couple of interior dining rooms out over the water. The Bakers think its wraparound harbor view makes it too special to be a glorified clam shack, which is how some locals remember it. Yes, you can get a

Refurbished dining room at The Harborview has windows onto the water.

lobster salad roll for $9.25 or fried clams with french fries and coleslaw for $14.95. But you also can get lobster prepared about twenty ways, from bisque to salad to baked stuffed to thermidor to flounder stuffed with lobster mousse. In their first two months, the Bakers served a dozen of their special meals for four featuring ten-pound lobsters with a gallon of draught beer and strawberries ($140 to $180, depending on market price). The steamed chix lobster on a tray with corn on the cob, fries and coleslaw may be as low as $9.95. The original shore dinner adding clam chowder, steamers, a whole lobster and hot apple pie goes for $32.50, which raised eyebrows locally. With live jazz on weekend evenings, dixieland on the deck on Sunday afternoons, fun frozen drinks, a children's menu and old-fashioned desserts like hot fudge butterscotch sundae and strawberry shortcake, this is designed to appeal to all ages and tastes.

The Sunday buffet brunch at the Harborview ($16.95, including champagne) is an ever-changing treat, from borscht to jonnycakes to poached eggs on artichoke bottoms to an over-size halibut poached before your eyes. Soft jazz plays, occasionally accompanied by Maureen, a professional singer and a suave hostess.

(860) 535-2720. Harborview, lunch 11:30 to 2:30, fall to spring; dinner, 5 to 10; bistro, 11:30 to 10; Skipper's Dock, 11:30 to 10, May-October. Closed Monday.

A Midsummer Night's Dream

The Golden Lamb Buttery, Hillandale Farm, Bush Hill Road (off Route 169), Brooklyn.

We fell in love with this rural restaurant twenty years ago and every time we go back we are smitten again. It's a Constable landscape, a working farm, a hayride, folk music and much more.

It's also the home of Bob and Jimmie (for Virginia) Booth, who set the stage for the most magical evening imaginable. Bob is the genial host who makes wonderful drinks (the manhattan is garnished with a fresh cherry because the Booths don't like to use preservatives) and oversees the dining rooms. Jimmie does most of the cooking with originality, energy and love.

The evening begins around 7 with cocktails in summer on a deck off the barn overlooking a farm pond or on a wagon drawn by a tractor over fields while you sit – with drink in hand – on bales of hay, listening to the fresh voice of Susan Smith Lamb, who accompanies herself on the guitar. Before you set off on this adventure, your gingham-clad (and sometimes pigtailed) waitress takes your order from the four or five entrées written on the blackboard.

Dinner ($60, complete) starts with a choice of about four hot or cold soups. We have never tasted one that wasn't wonderful. Using herbs and vegetables from the farm's gardens, Jimmie makes soups like cold lovage bisque, a green vegetable one using "every green vegetable you can name," raspberry puree, scotch barley, cold cucumber and an unusually good cabbage soup made with duck stock.

Almost always on the menu are duck (a crispy half, done with many different sauces), châteaubriand for one, grilled lamb and fish (perhaps salmon or swordfish), cooked over applewood on the farm's smoker. Lately, Jimmie has added the occasional pasta entrée. Salt is not used, but many herbs, and essences of lemons and limes, are. Crisp and thinly sliced onion bagels are the only starch.

What we always remember best are the vegetables – six to eight an evening brought around in large crocks and wooden bowls and served family style (yes, you can have seconds). They could be almost anything, but always there are marinated mushrooms and nearly always cold minted peas. Tomatoes with basil, braised celery and fennel, carrots with orange rind and raisins, a casserole of zucchini and summer squash with mornay sauce – they depend on the garden and the season.

Desserts like coffee mousse, raspberry cream sherbet, heavy butter cake with fresh berries, pies (made by neighborhood women) and a chocolate roll using Belgian chocolate, topped with chocolate sauce and fruit, are fitting endings.

During all this, you are seated in a dining room in the barn or in the attached building with a loft that once was a studio used by writers. The old wood of the walls and raftered ceilings glows with the patina of age, as do the bare dark wood tables in the flickering candlelight. The singer strolls from table to table taking song requests.

It's all so subtly theatrical, yet with a feeling of honest simplicity, that you feel part of a midsummer night's dream.

Lunch, with entrées in the $13 to $18 range, might be oyster stew, salmon quiche, seafood crêpes or the delicious Hillandale hash. It may not be as romantic as dinner, but you get to see the surroundings better.

Folks reserve a year in advance for the December madrigal dinners, when a group of renaissance singers wanders the dining rooms singing carols.

Although we have had more interesting entrées on our wanderings, we never have had such a satisfying total dining experience. It's not inexpensive, but what price can you put on pure enchantment?

(860) 774-4423. Lunch, Tuesday-Saturday noon to 2:30; dinner, Friday and Saturday, one seating from 7. Dinner reservations required far in advance. Closed January-May. No credit cards.

More Dining Choices

Fiddlers Seafood Restaurant, 4 Water St., Chester.
Paul McMahon of Old Lyme, who started in the business washing dishes at the old Black Swan when he was 16 and spent five years with the Chart House opera-

Owners Jimmie and Bob Booth relax at entrance to Golden Lamb Buttery.

tion, named this restaurant for the boat of his father, who was his backer. His two dining rooms seat 60 in a cheerful cafe atmosphere (blue and white checked cafe curtains, shell stenciling, cane and bentwood chairs, pictures of sailing ships on cream-colored walls, and tables with pedestals of old gears), all enhanced at night by white linens and flickering candlelight.

Paul serves interesting seafood creations, rarely changing the menu or the prices. Three or four kinds of fresh fish can be ordered pan-sautéed, poached or mesquite-grilled. At lunch, when these are in the $6 to $8 range, he also serves a cream-style crab soup with sherry, a lobster roll with steak fries or rice pilaf, and mussels in puff pastry with salad.

In the evening, entrées are $12.50 to $17.95 for the likes of oysters imperial, poached scallops with shiitake mushrooms over a bed of spinach, baked stuffed fillet of sole with hollandaise sauce, bouillabaisse, baked salmon in a sweet-potato nest and a few chicken and beef dishes. A lobster dish with peaches, peach brandy, shallots and mushrooms is a favorite. Garlic bread comes with aioli dip, and different julienned vegetables are served daily. The house salads (tossed or spinach) have a choice of honey-celery seed, creamy dill, blue cheese and vinaigrette dressings. Conch fritters and oysters rockefeller are among the appetizers ($4.95 to $7.95).

Chocolate-mousse terrine with lingonberries, lime mousse and chocolate-pecan ganache torte are featured desserts. The house wines are from California, and the other wines are very reasonable.

(860) 526-3210. Lunch, Tuesday-Saturday 11:30 to 2; dinner, 5:30 to 9 or 10, Sunday 4 to 10.

Timothy's, 181 Bank St., New London.

Chef-owner Timothy Grills quickly found a niche in New London for his nifty restaurant transformed from the space that formerly housed James' Gourmet Deli. Opening in the summer of 1996 after months of renovations, he had to abandon breakfast service because more than 1,000 people were coming through for lunch and dinner each week.

Timothy, a Johnson & Wales culinary graduate, trained in the Hartford area at Carbone's, Cavey's and the Simsbury 1820 House before venturing out on his own. He describes his fare as continental and American, although others might call it simply contemporary. For dinner ($12.95 to $19.95), specialties are sautéed breast and braised leg of duck served with framboise and fresh sage velouté, sautéed loin of pork with a bosc pear, and grilled leg of lamb with an apple-onion-mint chutney. Favorite starters are the lobster and mushroom crêpe with a madeira-chive cream sauce and the sirloin carpaccio accompanied by basil focaccia and an eggplant, tomato and fennel salad. White chocolate-raspberry ganache tart and chocolate mousse cake are signature desserts.

For lunch ($4.50 to $10.95), Timothy touts the shrimp and scallops over angel hair, the chicken and duck confit with fettuccine and the "focaccia vegwich."

The kitchen is partially on view at the far end of the high-ceilinged storefront dining room, handsome in mauve and gray-green. Tall glass-enclosed shelves along the sides display antiques and vases, with bins of wine stored on top. Black cushioned chairs flank well-spaced tables dressed in white linens.

(860) 437-0526. Lunch, Monday-Saturday 11:30 to 2:30; dinner, Monday-Saturday 5:30 to 9 or 10.

Restaurant Bravo Bravo, 20 East Main St., Mystic.

Well-known area chefs Robert Sader and Carol Kanabis produce contemporary Italian fare at this 50-seat restaurant on the main floor of the Whaler's Inn, with a sidewalk cafe off to the side.

For dinner, sirloin carpaccio, grilled shrimp wrapped in prosciutto with skewered artichokes, seafood sausage stuffed with lobster and scallops, and interesting salads (one pairs chilled roast lamb and grilled eggplant with mixed greens and radicchio) make good starters in the $6.95 to $8.95 range. Creative pastas are priced from $13.95 to $16.95, the latter for lobster ravioli or shrimp oregano with feta cheese and tomatoes over angel hair pasta. Entrees ($13.95 to $24.95) might include Maryland crab cakes topped with lobster-chive sauce, roast duck with peach and pink-peppercorn sauce, osso buco and rack of lamb served over duxelles and grilled tomato sauce. The lengthy dessert roster includes the obligatory tirami su as well as tartuffo, raisin-walnut bread pudding, ricotta cheesecake with grand marnier sauce and cognac-pumpkin cheesecake. The mainly Italian wine list is one of the area's more affordable.

The down sides are the service, sometimes aloof and rushed, and the atmosphere. Dining is in a spare, noisy and rather cheerless room at tables quite close together. Much more appealing is the canopy-covered terrace with white molded furniture. The outdoor **Cafe Bravo** menu features grilled pizzas (we like the one with pesto, sundried tomatoes and goat cheese for $7.95), pastas and entrées from $10.95 to $14.95.

(860) 536-3228. Lunch, 11:30 to 2:30, October-May; dinner, Tuesday-Sunday 5 to 9 or 10. Cafe, open May-October for lunch, 11:30 to 3; dinner, 5 to 9 or 10.

Water Street Cafe, 142 Water St., Stonington.

The dining fortunes in the tony borough of Stonington were elevated a notch by Walter Houlihan, former chef at the UN Plaza Hotel in New York. He and his wife Stephanie, who runs the front of the house, upscaled the small storefront space previously occupied by Kitchen Little and, with the acclaim of locals, took over the Water Street Market across the street in 1996.

The base of the intimate operation is the cafe's pint-size kitchen, where Walter prepares every dish on the contemporary American menu for up to 30 diners at a time. The handful of close-together tables and booths turns over two or three times a night.

Favorite starters include seared scallops and duck with shiitake mushrooms in a miso broth, escargot pot pie and pear salad with endive, walnuts and cheddar dressing. Main courses ($14.95 to $17.95) could be roasted salmon in a mushroom crust and arugula, coriander-roasted cod over vegetables and green curry oil, grilled hangar steak with a red wine and blue cheese sauce, and roasted rack of lamb with a cumin-tapenade oil. Desserts vary from warm coconut-walnut wafer cake to crème brûlée to poached pears with ginger ice cream.

Now Walter's fans can get some of his prepared foods, pot pies, breads and salads to take home from the Water Street Market. The blackboard lists wonderful sandwiches in the $4.25 to $5.75 range, and we found a loaf of his boule (peasant bread) to be exceptional.

(860) 535-2122. Dinner nightly except Tuesday, 5:30 to 9 or 10.

Budget Gourmet

Noah's, 113 Water St., Stonington.

Owners Dorothy and John Papp have a winning formula: good food, informal atmosphere and affordable prices. Their two storefront dining rooms, colorfully decorated with pastel tablecloths and fresh flowers beneath a pressed-tin ceiling, are usually packed with loyal regulars.

Regional or ethnic specialties are posted nightly to complement dinners on the order of broiled flounder, cod Portuguese, pork chops, pasta, and grilled breast of chicken, with everything priced under $12.25 except for filet mignon – and that only $14.25.

Don't be misled: the fare is interesting, from the house chicken liver pâté with sherry and pistachios to the Greek country or farmer's chop suey salads at lunch. A bowl of clam chowder with half a BLT and a bacon-gouda quiche with side salad made a fine lunch for two for about $10.

Save room for the scrumptious homemade desserts, perhaps chocolate-yogurt cake, bourbon bread pudding, or what one local gentleman volunteered was the best dessert he'd ever had: fresh strawberries with Italian cream made from cream cheese, eggs and kirsch.

Noah's is fully licensed, offering most wines in the teens.

(860) 535-3925. Breakfast, 7 to 11, Sunday to noon; lunch, 11:15 to 2:30; dinner, 6 to 9 or 9:30. Closed Monday.

Offbeat Gourmet

Abbott's Lobster in the Rough, 117 Pearl St., Noank.

Gourmet it's not, but it's the closest thing to a Down East lobster pound this side of Maine, and goes through 80 tons of lobster a summer. We've been Abbott's fans for years, drawn by the rocky setting where the Mystic River opens into Fishers

Island Sound, thus providing a parade of interesting craft to watch. And when our sons were little, they could keep occupied finding briny treasures on the rocks.

You can eat inside at Abbott's, but it's much more fun outdoors at the brightly painted picnic tables set on mashed-up clam shells. The menu is fairly limited and the wait for a lobster can be long – we bring along a cooler with drinks and snacks for sustenance.

A 1¼-pound lobster is $14.95, including coleslaw and potato chips, while a New England feast goes for $21.95. Ram Island oysters are served on the half shell. Clam chowder or steamed clams, shrimp in the rough, lobster or crab rolls, steamed mussels and clams are other offerings; the only non-seafood items are barbecued chicken and hot dogs. Desserts include apple crisp, New York cheesecake and strawberry shortcake.

Beside the restaurant operation are the large lobster tanks that youngsters like to look at and a retail store. Here you may purchase a couple of lobsters or cans of Abbott's clam chowder to take home.

In 1996, Abbott's opened **Costello's Clam Co.** just beyond in Noank Shipyard, an open-air place beneath a blue and white canopy right over the water. It's smaller, less crowded and less known. Although you can get a lobster dinner here for $9.95, it's best for its fried clams ($8.95) and fried scallops ($9.25). The aroma of fried seafood is pervasive, but the water on three sides compensates.

(860) 536-7719. Abbott's open daily, noon to 9, May through Labor Day; Friday-Sunday, noon to 7, through Columbus Day. Costello's open daily, noon to 9, Memorial Day to Labor Day. Both BYOB.

Kitchen Little, Route 27, Mystic.

People line up for breakfast on hottest summer and coldest winter days at this little gem beside the Mystic River. We waited our turn in the January chill for a dynamite breakfast of scrambled eggs with crabmeat and cream cheese ($5.45), served with raisin toast, and a spicy scrambled-egg dish with jalapeño cheese on grilled corned-beef hash ($5.85), accompanied by toasted dill-rye bread.

The coffee flows endlessly into the red mugs, the folks occupying the nine tables and seats at the counter are convivial, and you can eat on picnic tables beside the water in season. Florence Klewin's open kitchen certainly is little (she says the entire establishment measures nineteen feet square). But it doesn't prevent her from putting out some remarkable omelets and other breakfasts "like Momma didn't used to make" with a creativity and prices ($3.25 to $6.95) that put bigger restaurants to shame. She also serves more ordinary weekday lunches, and offers dinner Thursday-Saturday in summer.

(860) 536-2122. Breakfast and lunch, Monday-Friday 6:30 to 2, weekends 6:30 to 1. Also dinner in summer, Thursday-Saturday 6 to 9.

Dining and Lodging

Bee and Thistle Inn, 100 Lyme St., Old Lyme 06371.

When Bob and Penny Nelson decided to leave corporate life in northern New Jersey and buy a New England inn, little did they think of southern Connecticut or the Bee and Thistle. But on their rounds they took one look at this tranquil yellow house with its center entrance hall and graceful staircase, parlors on either side and three dining rooms, and said, "this is it."

That was in 1982. The Nelsons since have refurbished the inn's eleven guest rooms and public rooms, added a riverside cottage and have elevated the dining situation to approach perfection. They won ten awards, more than any other restaurant, in Connecticut magazine's annual readers' choice poll two years in a row.

Executive chef Francis Brooke-Smith, who trained at the Ritz-Carlton in London, delights in innovative touches and presentations, including garnishes of edible flowers and fresh herbs grown hydroponically year-round. His sous chef is the Nelsons' son Jeff, a CIA grad who trained at the 21 Club in New York and the Ritz in Boston.

Dinner entrées range from $19.95 for fillet of sole drizzled with shrimp oil, served with pickled shiitake mushrooms and diamonds of parslied gnocchi and garnished with a tomato confit, to $28.95 for rack of lamb with a black olive tapenade and roasted eggplant puree. Other tempters are grilled shrimp with a lobster, arugula and porcini mushroom risotto; roasted Idaho trout wrapped in bacon and served on caramelized, balsamic-glazed onions; pork loin served on a bourbon-apple coulis with homemade Boston brown bread topped with rosettes of sour cream, and sliced duck breast with a portobello mushroom and duck confit burrito.

Dining porch at Bee and Thistle Inn.

Meals might start with almond-encrusted goat cheese served warm on a bed of apples and celeriac, beef carpaccio with sundried tomato tapenade, or wild mushrooms with mozzarella on grilled bruschetta ($6.95 to $9.95). Apricot bread pudding with brandied caramel sauce, banana flan over mango puree, white chocolate mousse with black currant and cassis sauce, and fresh fruit sorbets are among the luscious desserts.

Bob Nelson, who studied wines at the Cornell University Hotel School, put together the wine list with an eye to price "so people can afford a good bottle."

A harpist plays on Saturday and a guitar-playing duo sings love songs on Friday in this "inn designed for people to get away from their stresses and to relate to each other," in the words of Penny Nelson.

Lunch overlooking the lawns on the enclosed side porches – one with loads of plants hanging from the ceiling and the other full of Penny's collection of baskets – is a delight. Choices ($8.95 to $13.95) range from a smoked turkey sandwich to twin lamb chops with a tomato-mint chutney. The grilled Thai chicken salad, the sausage bruschetta and sautéed crab cakes with a mango-apple-chutney mayonnaise were recent favorites.

A fairly extensive breakfast at modest extra cost may be enjoyed by guests in their rooms, on the cheery sun porches with their floral tablecloths or mats and ladderback chairs, or in one of the parlors beside a fire. The Bee and Thistle popover filled with scrambled eggs, bacon and cheese ($4.75) and the beef and bacon hash with eggs ($5.25) draw the public by reservation as well as overnighters. So do the finger sandwiches and scones served with preserves and whipped cream at English tea ($12.95) in the parlor from 3:30 to 5 on Monday, Wednesday and Thursday from November to April.

Sunday brunch ($12.95 to $15.95) features sticky buns and the chef's potatoes with such entrées as scallops in brioche, stuffed french toast, grilled smoked pork loin and a variety of omelets.

Games and books are on the two stairway landings leading to guest rooms on the second and third floors. Rooms vary from large with queensize canopy beds and a loveseat to small with double or two twin beds. All come with private baths and antique, country-style furnishings. The cottage offers a riverside deck off the bedroom wrapping around to the fireplaced reading room, a TV room and a kitchen; its rate includes continental breakfast.

(860) 434-1667 or (800) 622-4946. Fax (860) 434-3402. Lunch, daily except Tuesday 11:30 to 2; dinner, nightly except Tuesday from 6, Sunday from 5:30; Sunday brunch, 11 to 2. Doubles, $75 to $155, EP; cottage, $210.

Old Lyme Inn, 85 Lyme St., Old Lyme 06371.

In contrast to the antique charm of the Bee and Thistle across the street, the Old Lyme Inn is pristine and chic, quietly sedate in royal blue and white. Inside a beautifully restored 1850s mansion is a formal restaurant with inventive French cuisine and seating for more than 200, as well as thirteen guest rooms upstairs and in a newer wing.

The setting in the main dining room is elegant if a bit austere – very tall and formally draped windows, walls papered in a gold pattern and chairs upholstered in deep blue velvet at tables angled in perfect formation. A single rose in a crystal vase is on each large, white-linened table, and tapestries and oil paintings (appropriately, some by the famed Lyme Impressionists) in elaborate frames adorn the walls. Beyond are two more dining rooms, one with an intimate windowed alcove embracing a table for four.

Under the aegis of owner Diana Field Atwood, the inn's restaurant has been awarded top ratings three times by the New York Times and its desserts were featured in successive issues of Bon Appétit magazine. Chef Stuart London implements an ambitious dinner menu. Among main courses ($19.595 to $27.95) might be planked swordfish roasted with a lemongrass-basil butter, sautéed lobster meat and jumbo shrimp served over sweet corn pancakes, sweetbreads sautéed with artichoke hearts and prosciutto on grilled polenta, grilled duck breast with a grand marnier-ginger sauce and grilled filet mignon with a maytag blue cheese crust.

Appetizers ($7.50 to $10.95) include Irish smoked salmon, a shellfish and polenta terrine served over field greens, an asparagus and foie gras tart, native bluefin crab cake with sweet pepper relish and caper-tartar sauce, and pâté of Connecticut pheasant with apples and walnuts. The soup might be dilled carrot bisque with bay shrimp; the salad, duck confit with spicy pecans on a bed of field greens.

For dessert, try the award-winning chocolate truffle tart, pumpkin cheesecake with cranberries, or layered gingerbread with buttercream, peaches and raspberries. Homemade ice creams include caramel and eggnog. We can vouch for a chocolate truffle cake with mandarin-flavored pastry cream topped with a layer of sponge cake soaked in cointreau, and a fruit tart with an apricot glaze and kiwi and strawberries on top. Cafe Diana with chambord and chocolate liqueurs is a fitting finale.

The indexed wine list, honored by Wine Spectator, is unusual in range and scope.

Mirror reflects tables in perfect formation in Old Lyme Inn dining room.

It's particularly strong on Californias, but offers a page of vintage wines up to $200.

A light supper menu is available in the stylish bar-lounge.

Luncheon brings some of the dinner appetizers, plus salads like oriental chicken, a smoked salmon club sandwich, and such entrées ($7.95 to $9.95) as chicken fricassee, grilled pizza, sweetbreads and "wild American meatloaf," a blend of wild boar and buffalo, served with mushroom gravy. The Sunday brunch menu ($9.95 to $14.95) includes zucchini pancakes with smoked ham, sundried-tomato waffles, sole and crabmeat au gratin, cheese blintzes, and smoked salmon with eggs and onions.

The eight newer guest rooms in the north wing are decorated in plush Victorian style. Marblehead mints are perched atop the oversize pillows on the canopy and four-poster beds, comfortable sofas or chairs are grouped around marble-top tables, and gleaming white bathrooms are outfitted with herbal shampoos and Dickenson's Witch Hazel made in nearby Essex. The five smaller rooms in the older part of the inn are not as elegant. Homemade croissants and granola are served for continental breakfast in the Rose Room.

(860) 434-2600 or (800) 434-5352. Fax (860) 434-5352. Lunch, Monday-Saturday noon to 2; dinner, Monday-Saturday 6 to 9; Sunday, brunch 11 to 3, dinner 4 to 9. Doubles, $109 to $158.

Copper Beech Inn, 46 Main Street, Ivoryton 06442.

This imposing mansion, shaded by the oldest copper beech tree in Connecticut, is back on top as one of Connecticut's premier dining spots. Owners Eldon and Sally Senner, he formerly with the World Bank in Washington and she an interior designer, have upgraded the accommodations and restored the dining experience to that of its glory days of the 1970s.

The Senners offer four period guest rooms upstairs, as well as nine deluxe guest rooms in an old carriage house behind the inn. Each of the latter has a jacuzzi, and french doors onto an outdoor deck or balcony overlooking the gardens; second-floor rooms have cathedral ceilings. Mahogany queensize beds, TVs and telephones are the rule. The Senners have added their own antiques and 19th-century art to the inn, and show fine oriental porcelain for sale in a small second-floor gallery, open by appointment.

They also have added an elegant, plant-filled Victorian solarium in the front of the inn, replacing a rear greenhouse that was accessible only in summer. Guests find it a pleasant and quiet retreat in which to relax.

A continental breakfast buffet of fresh fruit, cereals, breads and two kinds of French pastries is set out in the clubby blue Cooper Beech Room, where tables are spaced well apart and the windows afford views of the majestic tree outside.

Dining of distinction is offered in several elegant rooms, including the redecorated main Georgian Room with a floral Victorian motif, where twisted napkins stand tall in the water glasses, looking from afar like candles. The paneled Comstock Room with a beamed ceiling retains the look of the billiards parlor that it once was. Between the two is a pretty garden porch with intricate wicker chairs at four romantic tables for two set amidst the plants.

This is a place to be pampered. Expect dinner to take up to two and one-half hours, and pick out a choice selection from the Wine Spectator award-winning cellar that gets better all the time.

The Senners credit the rise in the inn's dining fortunes to executive chef Robert Chiovoloni, a Culinary Institute graduate who holds a master's degree in English literature. He was executive sous-chef at the Montpelier Room of Washington's Madison Hotel, which they considered the city's best restaurant at the time. Here he seeks out the best ingredients, importing, for instance, snails and wild huckleberries from Washington state.

His fare is country French, light but highly sophisticated. Witness such appetizers as smoked salmon with a garnish of three caviars and crème fraîche, a gratin of artichoke bottoms and mushrooms served in a crisp potato shell, seared duck foie gras with a sauce of duck glaze, pear brandy and sautéed pear, and blinis with ossetra caviar. Pricey indulgences ($8.75 to $26.75), but worth it to connoisseurs.

Main courses ($22.75 to $26.75) include bouillabaisse, sautéed fillet of salmon with champagne-cream sauce, veal sweetbreads madeira, sautéed breast of pheasant, grilled filet mignon glazed with cabernet, and loin of venison sauced with port wine and crushed black peppercorns.

Refreshing endings ($6.25 to $7.25) are chocolate gâteau layered with raspberry mousse, tarte tatin, orange mousse in puff pastry with coulis of fresh berries, and strawberry and champagne sorbet served with minted lemon sauce. A plate of almond-studded tuiles may come with coffee. Linger over a liquered coffee or a glass of port and savor a meal worthy of a special occasion.

(860) 767-0330. Dinner, Tuesday-Saturday 5:30 to 8:30 or 9, Sunday 1 to 8; closed Tuesday in winter. Doubles, $105 to $170.

The Inn at Chester, 318 West Main St., Chester 06412.

Deborah Moore returned home in 1992 after touring the world as a second mate in the Merchant Marine to run the inn her father had just purchased. The inn, built in 1983 around the 1776 John B. Parmelee House on twelve rural areas west of

Twisted napkins look like candles in Georgian Room at Copper Beech Inn.

town, had been closed a few years because of financial problems. Deborah and her parents took six months to restore the place and redo the layout. They added a comfortable lobby and a gift shop where her mother sells the works of local artists on consignment, put in a skylit tavern on the site of the former patio and relaid the patio beyond, carpeted the dining room and reopened the downstairs game room with fireplace and billiards table.

Deborah found the 42 guest rooms in two wings of modern construction rather spartan, so gradually added wallpaper, artworks, accessories, more comfortable chairs, a few kingsize beds and such. Most rooms are outfitted with Eldred Wheeler reproduction furniture, and come with TVs and telephones. Deborah's mother delivers candy in a basket to the guest rooms.

A 30-foot granite fireplace soars into the rafters between the tavern, where light dinners are available, and **The Post and Beam** dining room, whose name describes its interior construction. The high-ceilinged room has barnwood walls, a field-stone fireplace, two wrought-iron chandeliers, candle sconces and a plant-filled conservatory. The setting is serene with white linens, white china and fresh flowers in bud vases.

Our dinner began with a complimentary spread of duck liver pâté that arrived with hot, crusty rolls, a perfect match. A hearty butternut-apple bisque hinted of curry and an appetizer of crabmeat flauta, a tortilla laden with crabmeat, exploded with flavors from the ancho-chile sauce and a garnish of coriander-lime aioli. Among other starters ($5.50 to $7.50) were seafood risotto, smoked salmon roulades, Thai shrimp with a black bean and pineapple salsa, and warm duck salad with crispy fried potatoes and raspberry-walnut dressing.

Huge green salads with mustardy vinaigrettes preceded our main dishes, veal sweetbreads simmered with madeira and exotic mushrooms, served with fettuccine and snap peas, and grilled filet of beef with portobello mushrooms and dauphinoise potatoes. A Penfolds shiraz for $23 was the perfect choice from a fairly extensive wine list ranging up to $130. Other entrées were priced from $18 for grilled herbed chicken breast to $26 for delmonico steak with gorgonzola sauce.

Plums with cinnamon and the inn's signature orange crème brûlée capped a memorable meal.

Many of the appetizers and salads turn up on the lunch and tavern menu, which offers a good range from a BLT with basil mayonnaise for $5.50 to $11 for broiled trout with tomato-saffron sauce on a bed of leeks. The Spanish omelet and smoked salmon benedict are favorites at brunch. Continental breakfast is complimentary for house guests.

Ever promoting, the inn was about to stage a whiskey dinner at our latest visit. The $60 meal paired a different rare bourbon or malt scotch with each of five courses, from wild mushroom strudel to mince tartlet. The tavern offers an annual series of "Culinary Cruise" dinners, visiting ports from Sweden to Greece, for a bargain $18 on Tuesday through Thursday weekly in winter.

Incidentally, the inn is billed for romance and has an award to show for it. Deborah should know. She became friends with a businessman who frequently stayed at the inn and they were married in 1993.

(860) 526-9541 or (800) 949-7829. Fax (860) 526-4387. Lunch, Monday-Saturday 11:30 to 2; dinner, Monday-Saturday 5:30 to 9; Sunday, brunch 11:30 to 2:30, dinner 4 to 8:30. Doubles, $98 to $150; suites, $175 and $205.

The Inn at Mystic, Route 1, Mystic 06355.

This is the crown jewel of the Mystic Motor Inn, the area's nicest motel and inn complex beside Pequotsepos Cove. Above the motor inn (which also boasts deluxe inn-style rooms in its East Wing) is an eight-acre hilltop estate with a white-pillared Colonial revival mansion and gatehouse offering sumptuous bedrooms – spacious, full of antiques, and with whirlpool-soaking tubs and spas in the bathrooms. It's said that Lauren Bacall and Humphrey Bogart spent their honeymoon here.

As a guest in one of the five rooms in the mansion, you may feel like a country squire soaking in your private spa, relaxing on a chintz-covered sofa by the fire in the drawing room with its 17th-century pin pine paneling, or rocking on the wicker-filled veranda overlooking manicured gardens, with Long Island Sound in the distance. Behind the inn, the four guest rooms with fireplaces and jacuzzis in the secluded Gatehouse, redone with Ralph Lauren sheets and coverlets, could have come straight out of England.

Sisters Jody Dyer and Nancy Gray, whose father started this as Mystic's first motor inn of size in 1963, revamped the twelve rooms in the motor inn's East Wing, all with Federal-style furniture, queensize canopy beds, wing chairs and fireplaces, plus balconies or patios with views of the water. Six rooms here have huge jacuzzis in the bathrooms with mirrors all around. The 38 rooms in the original two-story motor inn are handsomely furnished as well.

Although breakfast is no longer included in the rates, complimentary tea and pastries are served from 3:30 to 4:30 at the **Flood Tide,** the inn's glamorous restaurant, which serves some of the area's best meals.

The spacious two-level dining room in elegant Colonial decor has large windows onto Pequotsepos Cove. Tables are appointed with white linens, etched-glass lamps, hammered silverware and small vases holding a single rose each.

Executive chef Robert Tripp is known for his wine list and a popular Sunday brunch ($16.95). We certainly liked the $10.95 luncheon buffet, which contained

Chef cooks hearthside dinner at Randall's Ordinary.

everything from seviche, caviar and seafood salad through eggs benedict, beef stroganoff, seafood crêpes and fettuccine with lobster alfredo, to kiwi tarts and bread pudding. You also can order dishes like curried chicken salad and baked fillet of sole with lobster and béarnaise sauce, from $7.95 to $19.95 à la carte.

At night, start with the chef's special baked escargots with mushrooms and garlic in puff pastry, brie and leek soufflé, smoked salmon rosettes or a crêpe filled with lobster madeira. Herbed mushroom soup is a house specialty. Entrées are priced from $18.95 for rainbow trout in chardonnay sauce, filet of sole provençal, seafood vol-au-vent, supreme of chicken, roast duckling and apple-cherry pork chops to $28.95 for a veal chop with crimini mushrooms, roasted garlic and sundried tomatoes. Whole roast pheasant, rack of baby lamb, beef wellington and châteaubriand are carved tableside for two.

Bananas foster, strawberries romanoff, raspberry-kiwi parfait, blackberry cheese-cake and chocolate fondue are among the renowned desserts.

A smaller menu, featuring some of the house specialties as well as lighter fare, is offered in the **Crystal Swan Lounge** with its plush leather chairs, piano and a wine bar. An outdoor deck is popular in summer.

(860) 536-9604 or (800) 237-2415. Fax (860) 572-1635. Lunch, Monday-Saturday 11:30 to 2:30; dinner, 5:30 to 9:30 or 10; Sunday brunch, 11 to 2:30. Doubles, $115 to $230 in motor inn, $165 to $250 in inn and East Wing, $95 to $250 in Gatehouse.

Gourmet from Days Past

Randall's Ordinary, Route 2, Box 243, North Stonington 06359.

Here's a unique Colonial inn and restaurant, where you can hearken back to pre-Revolutionary War times, enjoying hearthside dinners and historic accommodations in a rural farmhouse dating to 1685, sequestered in the midst of 27 acres at the end of a dirt road. Or you can partake of the more modern comforts of newer guest rooms in a restored 1819 barn dismantled and moved to the property from Richmondville, N.Y.

Using antique iron pots and utensils and cooking in reflector ovens and an immense open hearth, the staff serves food from the Colonial era to patrons in a thoroughly authentic 18th-century setting. Up to 75 diners gather at 7 in a small taproom, where they pick up a drink along with popcorn, crackers, and cheese. They are then shown through the house, after which they watch the cooks in Colonial costumes preparing their meals on the open hearth.

Seating in beamed dining rooms is at old tables with hand-loomed placemats, Bennington black and white pottery, flatware with pistol-grip knives and three-tined forks, and such unusual accessories as a salt plate and a sugar scoop.

The $30 prix-fixe dinner offers a choice among four or five entrées – roast capon with wild rice stuffing, roast ribeye beef, roast pork loin, hearth-grilled salmon, and Nantucket scallops with scallions and butter when we were there. The meal includes soup (country onion or Shaker herb, perhaps), whole-wheat walnut or spider corn bread, a conserve of red cabbage and apples, squash pudding, and carrot cake, apple crisp or Indian pudding. Choose a house Napa Ridge chardonnay or côtes du rhone from the small wine list to complement your meal.

Lunch is à la carte. We know local innkeepers who come here once a month and consider it the best value in the area. Start perhaps with parsnip and apple soup or Brunswick stew with spider bread. Try a hearth-roasted chicken sandwich with maple mustard, beefsteak pudding or broiled lamb chops with red potatoes and cranberry conserve for $4.95 to $8.50.

The restaurant offers breakfast to the public, perhaps maple toast with fried apples and Shaker apple salad or jonnycakes. All are in the $4 range, except for the "Ordinary breakfast" bringing the works for $8.95.

Three guest rooms in the main house have working fireplaces and queensize four-poster beds with hand-loomed coverlets, as well as modern baths with whirlpool jets in the tubs. Twelve rooms and suites are located to the rear in the old-style English barn with open bays, to which a milking shed and a silo have been attached. The framing was left exposed, random pine floors are covered with scatter rugs, and rooms are furnished to the period, though they strike some as rather spartan. With modern baths, built-in sofas, phones and TVs, they are quite contemporary. Two have lofts with skylights and spiral staircases, and the new Silo Suite is enormous.

The establishment was acquired in 1996 by the Mashantucket Pequot Tribal Nation, owners of the nearby Foxwoods Casino. The tribe maintained the tradition, but planned eventually to add more rooms and dining space, according to manager Bill Foakes.

(860) 599-4540. Breakfast daily, 7 to 11; lunch, noon to 3; dinner, Sunday-Friday at 7; Saturday 5 and 7:30. Doubles, $75 to $115; suite, $195.

Lodging

Riverwind, 209 Main St., Deep River 06417.

Her contractor didn't blanch when Barbara Barlow said in 1987 that she wanted to build an addition 100 years older than her existing 1850 inn. The result is a skillful blend of old and new, embracing eight guest rooms with private baths and an equal number of common rooms that afford space for mingling or privacy. An unexpected but happy side result: the innkeeper married the contractor, and Barbara and Bob Bucknall are now Riverwind's joint innkeepers.

Antiques from Barbara's former shop, wooden and stuffed animals in all guises (especially pigs), folk art, hand-stenciling, and tasteful knickknacks and memorabilia are all around. Each bedroom has thick robes in colorful patterns, some matching the decor. Poland Spring water and candies are put out in each.

The Hearts and Flowers Room has flowers on the bedroom wallpaper, hearts on the bathroom wallpaper and a specially made, heart-filled, stained-glass window. Every room is charming, but the ultimate is the Champagne and Roses Room with a private balcony, a wonderfully decadent (according to Barbara) bathroom with a shower and a Japanese steeping tub, a bottle of champagne cooling on a table between two wing chairs, and a fishnet canopy bed too lacy and frilly for words.

Barbara grew up in Smithfield, Va., where her father is a hog farmer. Naturally, she serves slices of red, salty Smithfield ham for breakfast every morning at a table for twelve in the new dining room and at a smaller table in the adjacent room. She may offer coffee cake, Southern biscuits, fresh fruit in summer and hot curried fruit in winter, as well as homemade jams and preserves. Lately she has added more breakfast casseroles to her repertoire. One like a quiche incorporates swiss cheese, eggs, asparagus, mushrooms, cream sauce and french-fried onion rings.

Besides a delightful living room with fireplace, a library and a trophy room for games, guests enjoy a keeping room with a huge fireplace in which Barbara was cooking stews, chili and soups at one of our winter visits. Guests also make quite a to-do over the life-size mounted moose, a century-old antique sited smack dab in the center of the living room – staring head-on at the decanter of sherry, which is always at the ready in this hospitable B&B.

(860) 526-2014. Doubles, $95 to $165.

Hidden Meadow, 40 Blood St., Lyme 06371.

The Connecticut shore area gained this badly needed country house of a B&B when the family homestead gradually emptied as Karen Brossard's four daughters went off to college. It's a beauty of a home on four rural acres, dating to 1760. Subsequent additions (some by Broadway actor Henry Hull in the mid-1930s) produced a rambling, pale yellow Colonial Revival with circular driveway, Georgian entry, a number of stone terraces, iron railings and a reflecting pool.

The Brossards offer three guest rooms with private baths. Each is nicely outfitted with family furnishings and queensize or king/twin beds. Guests enjoy a living room with fireplace and original beehive oven, a library with TV and a fireplaced dining room with a table set for eight ("we sometimes have extra visitors for breakfast," explains Karen, an engaging hostess who likes a good party). In summer, breakfast is served on an unusual curved slate porch overlooking the reflecting pool. Beyond are a large swimming pool, a raspberry patch, stables and riding trails. Karen keeps two horses, and used to teach her pony club here three days a week. Now she teaches paddle tennis as the pro at Old Lyme Country Club.

Breakfast is an event. The fare might be baked eggs with brie, basil and heavy cream; orange-flavored french toast with brandy, or gingerbread pancakes with fruit sauce. Fruits, homemade muffins and zucchini bread accompany.

(860) 434-8360. Doubles, $90 to $125.

Steamboat Inn, 73 Steamboat Wharf, Mystic 06355.

This fairly new inn, transformed from a vacant restaurant along the Mystic River, offers ten luxurious guest rooms beside the water in the heart of downtown Mystic.

Named after ships built in Mystic, all have jacuzzis, telephones and televisions hidden in cupboards or armoires and six have fireplaced sitting areas facing the river. A local decorator outfitted them in lavish style: mounds of pillows and designer sheets on the queensize canopy or twin beds; loveseats or sofas with a plush armchair in front of the fireplaces. Mantels and cabinet work make these rooms look right at home.

Our favorites are the second-floor rooms at either end, brighter and more airy with bigger windows onto the water, a couple with half-cathedral ceilings. Rooms in the middle are darker in both decor and daylight. Four rooms on the ground floor are suite-size in proportion and come with double whirlpool tubs and wet bars, but suffer from being on view to the constant stream of passersby on the wharf. Each room is distinctively different and has its own merits; "one couple stayed here four times in the first month and worked their way around the inn, staying in different rooms," reported co-owner John McGee.

There's a common room with all the right magazines and glass tables for continental breakfast. The innkeeper puts out fruit compote, homemade muffins, cereal and granola each morning.

(860) 536-8300 or (800) 364-6100. Fax (860) 572-1250. Doubles, $175 to $195; suites, $175 to $275.

House of 1833, 72 North Stonington Road, Mystic 06355.

Built by banker Elias Brown in 1833, this pillared, Greek Revival mansion on three hillside acres must have been the most imposing house in Old Mystic. Or so it's depicted by an artist in a stunning mural that wraps around its curving staircase and shows the way the hamlet looked at the time.

Californians Carol and Matt Nolan spent two years touring 36 states to find the perfect place to run an inn. They purchased this substantial residence and undertook renovations to create a luxurious B&B. They gutted the bathrooms, which had been modernized, and say they redid them to the period, although which period might be debatable. They installed a Har-Tru tennis court next to the swimming pool, and produced an assistant innkeeper, bright-eyed infant son Alexander, a year after opening in 1994.

This is one gorgeous house, from the formal dining room that dwarfs a long breakfast table set for ten, to the five large guest bedrooms, all with queen beds, fireplaces and private baths, some of them quite spacious and unusual. The double parlor is a knockout: the front portion, outfitted in Greek Revival, opens into a Victorian section notable for a crystal chandelier, a grand piano and an antique pump organ. A heavy door opens off the front parlor into the Peach Room, the former library. Here's a guest room with a mahogany canopy bed draped in peach fabric, a plush settee with matching chair on an oriental rug, a private wicker porch facing the pool, and a bathroom with a walk-in shower through which one passes to get to the double whirlpool tub.

Upstairs are three more guest rooms with thick carpeting and fine fabrics. Although Carol oversaw most of the decorating, each picked one room to do themselves. Hers was the rear Verandah Room done in cream and celadon green with a light pine queen bed enclosed in wispy sheer curtains, a ladyslipper clawfoot tub

Greek Revival mansion is now elegant B&B known as House of 1833.

on a platform beside the fireplace, a bathroom with oversize shower, a loveseat and an odd little wicker balcony upon which the roof overhang blocks the view unless you're sitting down. Matt's choice was the secluded third-floor Cupola Room, masculine in plum and gold with a four-poster bed draped from the ceiling, a potbelly stove, a double whirlpool tub in the bathroom in one corner and a separate stall shower off by itself under the stairs. The stairs rise to a cupola, holding two seats from which to observe the sunset.

Chocolate-chip cookies and tea or lemonade greet guests upon arrival. At 9 the next morning, breakfast begins with Matt's decorative fresh fruit plates ("he gets very creative," says Carol). His artistry continues as he plays light contemporary music on the grand piano during the main course, which might be baked custard french toast, eggs florentine in puff pastry with honey-mustard sauce or a specialty quiche with eggs, cottage cheese and corn chips. Homemade muffins accompany.

(860) 536-6325 or (800) 367-1833. Doubles, $145 to $195.

Stonecroft, 515 Pumpkin Hill Road, Ledyard 06339.

His international travels with Chase Manhattan Bank heightened their interest in running an inn, and his love of sailing led them to the Mystic area. Her counseling background and interest in psychosynthesis as a way of life seemed attuned for innkeeping. Add their oldest son's training in hotel management and their youngest son's service as a chef.

The result is this soothing four-room B&B, soon to become a full-service inn with eight more guest rooms and a restaurant in a restored three-story barn.

Lynn and Joan Egy started in phases, first renovating the handsome yellow 1807 Georgian Colonial that had stood empty for five years. The four downstairs common rooms are beauties, from the Snuggery library that once was a borning room to a luxurious rear great room with nine-foot-wide fireplace to the fireplaced dining room in which breakfast is served by candlelight on Villeroy & Boch china. The country French furnishings throughout lend an elegant and comfortable, uncluttered look. To the rear of the great room is the Buttery, smallest of the guest rooms with a beamed ceiling, queen bed, full bath and its own terrace. The lumber here and elsewhere in the house dates to the 1700s.

A young artist-friend of the Egys painted the mural of a hot-air balloon scene along the front staircase to be "cheerful and uplifting, as in the inngoing experience," said Joan. The stairway leads to two front corner bedrooms, one with queen bed and one with king. All are equipped with top-of-the-line mattresses and bath amenities that include inflatable tub pillows and aromatherapy bath salts for relaxation. Up a steep rear stairway reached through an unusual cut-out door is the prized Stonecroft Room with kingsize four-poster bed, loveseat and 22-inch-wide chestnut floorboards ("the 24-inch boards were reserved for the king," Joan advised). The walls above the wainscoting bear the young artist's wraparound mural depicting a day in the life of Stonecroft about 1820. Look for the faces of the Beatles in the string quartet entertaining beside a stone wall and for the house ghost in the drawbridge.

Terrycloth robes, bath sheets rather than towels, Crabtree & Evelyn toiletries and soft music throughout the common areas help Joan provide a serene, therapeutic stay. Guests respond with their thoughts in words and sketches in the room diaries. The six-acre rural property, surrounded by 300 acres of Conservancy woodlands and stone walls, add to the tranquillity. Guests report deer and coyote sightings and lots of birds, Lynn says.

Breakfast is a four-course event, served in the dining room or on the tiered flagstone terrace beneath a venerable maple tree. Juice and Lynn's baked bananas, pineapples and mangos in a lemon-rum sauce might precede buttermilk waffles with strawberries and whipped cream, herbed scrambled eggs with turkey bacon or a cloud (so-called because it's four inches high) omelet layered with smoked salmon or cheese. The final course might be ginger scones or strawberry-rhubarb crisp.

The Egys host a wine and cheese mixer for weekend guests, and offer wine upon arrival.

(860) 572-0771. Doubles, $129 to $169.

Antiques & Accommodations, 32 Main St., North Stonington, Conn. 06359.

Ann and Thomas Gray, who are into cooking, almost enrolled in the Johnson & Wales culinary program but decided instead to open a B&B. Their 1861 yellow house with the gingerbread trim of its era became the focal point for a complex that includes three guest rooms, two cottage suites, an antiques shop in the barn, and extensive gardens.

Tom puts his cooking skills to the test with an outstanding English breakfast, served by candlelight at 8:30 or 9:30 in the formal dining room, on the flower-bedecked front porch or the stone patio in the garden. It always includes fresh fruit in an antique crystal bowl, perhaps melon with a yogurt, honey and mint sauce or hot plum-applesauce. Main courses could be eggs benedict, an egg soufflé with homemade salsa and basil, a stilton and aquavit omelet with dill sauce, an apple-rum puff garnished with strawberries and a signature sweet bread pudding laced with dried apricots and cream sherry. "Breakfast goes on for hours," says Ann, who was still serving at 11 the December weekday we first called in. These hospitable hosts also have been known to dispense wine late into the evening while everyone lingers on the patio.

Memories of traveling in England inspired the Grays to furnish their home in the Georgian manner with formal antique furniture and accessories. Six rooms come with private baths, and all have canopied beds, fresh flowers and decanters of sherry. Besides a parlor with TV, the main house offers a downstairs bedroom with a working fireplace and a stereo system. Upstairs are two bedrooms, one a bridal room filled with photographs of honeymooners who have stayed there.

Families and couples traveling together tend to book the suites in the 1820 Garden Cottage, a two-story affair beside landscaped gardens in back. Each floor contains a sitting room and a kitchen. The first-floor quarters offer three bedrooms and a bath. The second floor has two bedrooms (each with new gas fireplaces), two baths and a fireplace in the common room. Rooms here contain some remarkable stenciling, sponge-painted furniture, marbleized dressers and floral curtains, along with the antiques that characterize the rest of the establishment, although here most of them are early American and country. One bedroom is furnished by Whitmore of Middletown, and the contents are for sale. "You can sleep in the canopy bed and take it home," advises Ann.

Another draw here, besides the antiques and breakfasts, are the exotic gardens. They provide plenty of herbs and edible flowers with which to garnish the breakfasts, and hours of enjoyment for guests.

(860) 535-1736 or (800) 554-7829. Doubles, $169 to $189; cottage, $199.

Gourmet Treats

Wheatmarket at 4 Water St., Chester, is a well-stocked specialty-foods store where you can order a prepared picnic (the Lovers' includes orange-passionfruit sodas, bliss potato salad and chocolate kisses) or eat at one of the small tables in the front. Nineteen sandwiches ($3.19 to $4.99) include country pâté with sweet and rough mustard, turkey breast with cranberry conserve and cheddar, and roast beef with garlic and herb cheese. Also on the docket are salads, soups, stews, a handful of hot entrées (all under $5) and deep-dish pizzas (the chicken with artichoke and the eggplant with sundried tomatoes are especially popular). Owner Dennis Welch also does low-calorie dishes. A specialty is custard-filled cornbread (obviously not low-calorie). Browse among the racks for Belgian butter-almond cookies, Guiltless Gourmet dips, beluga caviar, saffron and such.

Pasta Unlimited at 159 Main St., Deep River, is where to get the freshest pasta imaginable. Michelle St. Marie's pasta machine is in the window, and nothing gets cut until a customer orders it. Available types include spinach, pumpkin, tomato, lemon-dill and a dynamite black-peppercorn pasta that we tried with Michelle's good clam sauce. At a recent visit, we took home pumpkin pasta and topped it with the raphael sauce (artichoke hearts, plum tomatoes and romano cheese) – oh, so good. The little shop also has cookware and gourmet items.

Fromage at 1400 Boston Post Road, Old Saybrook, is an upscale shop where Christine Chesanek purveys wonderful cheeses, fine foods and coffees. She even stocks six kinds of olives, like french black olives in sunflower-seed oil and roasted garlic. Aged chèvre, her own cheese spreads, Harney & Sons teas, pâtés, pastas and more are on the shelves. Christine even has an Italian machine that makes a good cup of latte for $2.

The original clam hash draws food lovers to **Pat's Kountry Kitchen** at 70 Mill Rock Road (Route 154 at th*e junction of Route 1), Old Saybrook. It's an utterly delicious blend of clams, onions and potatoes, topped with a fried egg and sensational for breakfast or lunch with coleslaw. The hash ($5.29), for which Pat Brink closely guards the recipe, resulted from an accident (her kids threw out the broth distilled from two bushels of quahogs destined for the day's chowder, and she improvised to use up the dried clams). Pat's serves good, old-fashioned country meals daily, from 7 a.m. to 9 p.m.

CIA grads and ex-restaurant chefs David Courant and Lissa Loucks team up at **Vanderbrooke Bakers and Caterers,** 65 Main St., Old Saybrook. They produce dynamite breads, pastries, salads, sandwiches and hot entrées, available at their retail shop or from their deli to eat in or take out. Among David's bread repertoire are country french, flanders (a Belgian white with oats), squaw, mustard-tarragon, sourdough, and gorgonzola and roasted red pepper, about eight changing varieties each day. The pastry case is full of delights. The deli also impresses with sandwiches (roast beef and brie or genoa salami, capicola and roasted peppers, in the $3.95 range), salads (Moroccan chicken, minty barley, ginger coleslaw in the $2.50 range), soups like shrimp and corn chowder and the day's entrées (flank steak stuffed with spinach and mozzarella, zucchini and corn fritters with red onion confit, sausage and tomato quiche, and crab cakes rémoulade).

We've seldom seen so many unusual flavors as at **Mystic Drawbridge Ice Cream Shoppe,** 2 West Main St., Mystic. Rod Desmarais and his wife Cheryl, a pastry chef, say they get their ideas from their travels. Among the 25 changing choices, you might find macadamia nut, kahlua-mocha fudge, praline-pecan, southern peach, spiked apple pie (with a touch of rum), ginger-chocolate chunk, pumpkin pie ("sorry, no crust") and the perennial favorite, Mystic mud. With less air overrun than usual, Mystic ice creams made at their Pumpkin Hill Creamery in Ledyard are creamier and richer than most. Shakes, sundaes, gourmet coffees and pastries are also served. Check out the mural on the wall: it's an endearing picture of Mystic, to which staff and customers keep adding local folks and landmarks.

A Choice Winery

Chamard Vineyards, 115 Cow Hill Road, Clinton.

The owner of this money-is-no-object winery is Bill Chaney, chairman and CEO of Tiffany & Co., so you know things are done with class. And classy all the way is Chamard, reached via an unremarkable residential street off Exit 63 of I-95. Overlooking a farm pond, the winery occupies a gray shingled house built in 1988 as "a New England château" near the front entrance to the 40-acre property that is half planted with vines. Wines are tasted with crackers and cheese in a richly furnished living room with vaulted ceiling, a fieldstone fireplace and the air of a deluxe hunting lodge. Although Larry McCulloch is the active winemaker, Bill and Carolyn Chaney remain involved on weekends, from planting and picking to leading tours and pouring wines. Eighty per cent of the 6,000-case annual output is white wines, primarily a premium chardonnay that sells here for $8.99. Bill Chaney acknowledges that his connections helped place his chardonnay in some of New York's finest restaurants, but merit keeps them there. Chamard's emerging chardonnay style is more European than Californian, and wine writers have ranked it among the best wines produced in this country.

(860) 664-0299 or (800) 371-1609. Tours and tastings, Wednesday-Saturday 11 to 4.

Commodore's Room at the Black Pearl restaurant looks onto the waterfront.

Newport, R.I.
In Pursuit of Pleasures

Few cities its size can match in quality or quantity the astonishing variety of restaurants of Newport, R.I.

Little wonder. Newport has been a symbol of high living since the Victorian era when America's affluent built summer "cottages" that now form the nation's most imposing collection of mansions in one place. Visitors from around the world have come to view the mansions as well as the restorations of some of America's oldest buildings. Sailing and tennis have given modern Newport a sporty face, too.

With all the attractions come the trappings. Restaurants, inns, B&Bs and shops are part of a tourist/building boom that has transformed Rhode Island's most visited city in recent years.

It was not until the early 1970s that Newport's restaurants became known for much more than fresh seafood, served to the masses on venerable waterfront wharves. An immensely popular establishment called The Black Pearl changed that. The first of the town's innovative restaurants, it blended elegant cuisine with more casual fare in a mix that triggered a trend.

Now Newport is home to notable small French restaurants, the nation's oldest continuously operating tavern, small eateries with pace-setting chefs, contemporary seafood houses, assorted ethnic spots and sidewalk cafes everywhere in a growing smorgasbord of fine and fast food. "The best of the lot here match the best restaurants in Boston," said the mâitre-d' at the Clarke Cooke House, whose owner also owns Locke-Ober in Boston.

Summers and weekends in Newport are pricey and crowded; dinner reservations a week in advance are the alternative to two-hour waits. It's best to visit mid-week or in the off-season.

The myriad pleasures of this small historic city will surprise you. So will the numbers of people pursuing them. On a sunny day, it may seem as if the whole world has come to Newport and its restaurants.

Dining

The Best of the Best

The Place, 28 Washington Square, Newport.

This wine bar and grill has Newport abuzz with its exciting cuisine. An adjunct to Yesterday's, a pubby downtown institution, it was opened by owners Maria and Richard Korn as a showcase for their longtime chef, Alex Daglis. Alex moved to a separate kitchen, hired a staff and devised a contemporary American menu with a European flair that, Richard says, "expands and challenges your tastes."

We'd happily order anything on the changing dinner menu. Everyone raves about the entrées, priced from $17.95 for grilled jerk-marinated pork loin with jalapeño salsa to $23.95 for grilled tenderloin stuffed with goat cheese. Pan-seared red snapper served on lobster and guava sauces with black and white angel-hair pasta, spicy Southwestern barbecued duck with napa cabbage and blue corn cakes, and pecan-crusted lamb loin garnished with sweet potato also entice.

But we never got beyond the appetizers ($6.25 to $8.50), which were so tantalizing that we shared and made a meal of five. The shrimp and corn tamales, terrific scallops with cranberries and ginger, the gratin of wild mushrooms, and raviolis of smoked chicken and goat cheese were warm-ups for a salad of smoked pheasant with poached pears and hazelnuts that was out of this world. Each was gorgeously presented on black octagonal plates. Strawberry margarita sorbet with fresh fruit and a warm apple crêpe with apple fries and apple sorbet were worthy endings to a fantastic meal.

To accompany, 33 wines are offered by the glass and 150 by the bottle. "Flights" offer a tasting of four wines for $13.50. New from Yesterday's adjacent Ale House come not flights but "schooners" featuring 36 microbrews. Four seven-ounce pilsener glasses for $6 arrive in an elaborate homemade wooden schooner.

All this is stylishly served at white-clothed tables on two levels of a long, narrow dining room with brass rails, oil lamps and sconces. A vaudeville curtain from a New Bedford theater, framed and back lit on one wall, dominates the decor.

(401) 847-0116. Dinner nightly, 5:30 to 10 or 11. Closed Monday and Tuesday, December-March.

The Black Pearl, Bannister's Wharf.

Since this rambling establishment opened in 1972 as the first of Newport's innovative restaurants, it's been one of our favorites, serving a staggering 1,500 meals a day in summer from what owner Tom Cullen calls "the world's smallest kitchen."

Outside under the Cinzano umbrellas, you can sit and watch the world go by as you enjoy what we think is Newport's best clam chowder – creamy, chock full of clams and laced with dill, served piping hot with a huge soda cracker ($2.75 a bowl, and seemingly better every time we order it). You also can get a Pearlburger

Framed vaudeville curtain is dominant decorative piece along wall at The Place.

with mint salad served in pita bread for $5.95, and a variety of sandwiches or stew of the day.

Inside, the tavern is informal, hectic, noisy and fun, offering much the same fare as the outdoor cafe plus a few heartier offerings (baked cod with pepper jack cheese, 21 Club chicken hash and veal picante, $13.50 to $23) that can serve as lunch or dinner. In fact, after a bowl of chowder, the crab benedict with french fries ($8.50) was almost too much to finish. You also can get several desserts – we remember a delectable brandy-cream cake – and espresso as strong as it should be, plus cappuccino Black Pearl, enhanced with courvoisier and kahlua.

The pride of the Pearl is the **Commodore Room,** pristinely pretty with white linens, dark walls, ladderback chairs and a view of the harbor through small-paned windows.

Chef Dan Knerr's dinner appetizers run from $6.75 for fried brie or charred peppers with sundried tomatoes to $9.50 for Scotch smoked salmon. Start, perhaps, with a shrimp, crab and lobster cocktail with three sauces, "black and blue" tuna with roasted pepper sauce or a salad of boston lettuce, radicchio, apples and walnuts with a creamy blue cheese dressing. Entrées are priced from $17.50 for pepper chicken breast to $26 for rack of lamb with roasted garlic and rosemary. Among the choices are salmon fillet with mustard-dill hollandaise, calves liver with bercy sauce, breast of pheasant with perigueux sauce and special, dry-aged T-bone steaks obtained from a New York butcher.

It's an ambitious menu, the more so considering the size of the kitchen. But the Black Pearl can expand or contract its service with the season and the crowds. While others have come and gone, it's been a pearl on the Newport scene for well over two decades.

(401) 846-5264. Tavern and outdoor cafe open daily from 11; dinner in Commodore Room, 6 to 11, jackets required. Closed six weeks in winter.

Restaurant Bouchard, 505 Thames St.

After training in France and sixteen years as executive chef at the famed Le Château in New York's Westchester County, Albert J. Bouchard III decided in

1995 it was time to be on his own. He, his wife Sarah and their three youngsters moved to Newport because of its water and yachting (they live on their yacht in the summer). They sought a small establishment where he could exercise "total artistic control," which turned out to be the former tea room at the Hammett House Inn.

The two-section, 43-seat dining room is a beauty in celadon and cream. Assorted chairs with upholstered celadon or mauve seats are at well-spaced tables dressed in cream-colored, floor-length cloths and topped with Wedgwood china, expensive stemware and tall oil lamps bearing small shades. Four shelves of demitasse cups and saucers, part of his father's collection, separate the front section from the back, and a small bar in the front room looks to be straight out of Provence.

The food is classic French with contemporary nuances in the style of Albert's former domain. It has received rave reviews and, combined with the elegant sense of comfort and flawless service, contributes to a memorable dining experience.

Entrées at our winter visit ran from $18.75 for sautéed cod oscar, embellished with crab and asparagus, to $24 for loin of wild boar with a spicy game sauce. Sole stuffed with lobster and mushroom duxelles, sweetbreads in tarragon sauce, duck breast with raspberry sauce and sliced saddle of lamb provençal testify to the small kitchen's range.

Typical starters ($6.25 to $9.75) are lobster vol-au-vent, sweet and sour confit of duck oriental, and shrimp, smoked chicken and haricots verts in rémoulade sauce. Warm pear salad with walnuts, blue cheese and greens was a mid-winter refresher.

Albert, with two talented assistants in the kitchen, prepares the crusty sourdough rolls as well as the desserts ($7.50 to $8.50), which range from a mocha phyllo napoleon to chocolate crêpes and grand marnier soufflés. Some of the wines, which date back to the 1960s, come from his personal cellar.

The Bouchards landscaped a rear brick patio for drinks and hors d'oeuvres in summer, and had an option to buy the five-room B&B operation upstairs.

(401) 846-0123. Dinner nightly except Tuesday, 6 to 9:30 or 10; Sunday brunch, 11 to 2.

Asterix & Obelix, 599 Lower Thames St.

With worldly talents, youthful bravado and Danish good looks, John Bach-Sorenson alighted in 1995 at age 33 in Newport – "it reminded me of home" – and looked for a restaurant site. The scion of a family of Copenhagen restaurateurs found it in a working auto-repair garage. Three whirlwind months of sweat equity later, he had transformed it into an airy, high-ceilinged and colorful space with a partly open rear kitchen, a remarkable hand-crafted bar along one side, and mismatched chairs at white-linened tables topped with white butcher paper, votive candles and vases of alstroemeria. Two front garage doors open to the street for a European sidewalk cafe atmosphere in summer.

John, partner Tracy Tarigo and an artist friend are responsible for the splashy effects and artworks. The artistry continues in the kitchen, where this 1986 World Culinary Olympics winner holds forth day and night, seven days a week in summer. Asked how he could maintain the pace, he enthused: "This is my hobby, my life."

He calls his fare Mediterranean-Asian. The dinner menu is priced from $14 for mussels in tomato broth over linguini to $25 for filet mignon à la milanaise (a mouthful of a menu description: tomato espagnole sauce, shredded ham, mushrooms and white truffle oil with roasted pasta). Possibilities range from chicken pot pie jardinière to grilled tuna with Thai noodles and Asian slaw or rack of lamb with a Lebanese couscous.

Albert and Sarah Bouchard in front of display of demitasse cups at Restaurant Bouchard.

Among appetizers ($8 to $10) at our latest visit were escargots en cocotte, Maryland crab cakes with rémoulade sauce, firecracker spring rolls with peanut dipping sauce, carpaccio of black angus beef with arugula, and a salad of arugula and celery root with portobello mushroom. Raspberry torte, key lime pie and chocolate mousse are favorite desserts.

Come here in summer for brunch (perhaps eggs copenhagen or potato galette with smoked salmon and served daily from 11 to 4 along with lunch), or afternoon cappuccino or espresso. An exotic and quite lengthy lunch menu is priced from $6 for a burger to $17 for grilled swordfish.

A rack of newspapers for reading and an energetic young staff contribute to a laid-back, brasserie atmosphere. The place is named for John's two favorite French comic-strip characters, known for fighting the bureaucracy, which John was doing in pursuing a liquor license. He finally received a beer and wine license on Labor Day weekend in 1996.

(401) 841-8833. Open daily, 11 a.m. to 11 p.m. or midnight. Closed Tuesday and Wednesday in winter.

The White Horse Tavern, corner of Marlborough and Farewell Streets.

Claiming to be the oldest operating tavern in the United States, established in 1673, the tavern was restored by the Newport Preservation Society and opened as a restaurant in 1957. It's also known for some of the best – albeit expensive – food in town.

The White Horse is a deep red Colonial building that imparts a palpable feeling of history. We find it most appealing for cozy, cold-weather dining, with its dark interior, wide-plank floors, beamed ceilings, huge fireplace and classical music. The dark rose and white draperies complement the handsome burgundy and off-white china and the winter arrangements of silk flowers and dried berries. Brass candlesticks with Colonial candles inside large clear hurricane chimneys are on each table.

Service by a tuxedo-clad staff is formal and even at lunch, prices start at $9 (for a grilled chicken or club sandwich) and top off at $17 for sautéed veal served over pasta with arugula, mushrooms and roasted red peppers. On a spring afternoon, we tried the day's soup, an interesting chilled mixture of yogurt, cucumber, dill and walnuts. Baked marinated montrachet with baked garlic puree and herbed croutons was a delicious appetizer. The fish of the day, halibut in a sauce with grapefruit pieces and a hint of brandy, was excellent. The chicken salad resting in a half avocado was decidedly bland.

Wines are, as you would imagine, expensive, but many are available by the glass. The old bar room in one corner of the building is atmospheric as can be.

Chef Brian Conners presents classic continental fare with trendy twists at night. Appetizers are $8 to $10 for the likes of a sauté of snails with fennel, wild mushrooms and hot cherry peppers in an Absolut pepper and tomato coulis; baked oysters with oven-dried tomatoes, grilled garlic sausage and horseradish crème fraîche, and peking raviolis stuffed with shrimp and pork and served on a star-anise and blood-orange reduction sauce. Entrées start at $23 for simple roasted chicken breast and rise rapidly to $33 for bouillabaisse. Menu staples are individual beef wellington and châteaubriand for two. Soy and ginger lend an oriental flavor to a sauté of shrimp and scallops; the mesquite-grilled veal tenderloin is rubbed with ancho chile and served with an applejack sauce.

You might like to finish with a triple silk torte on a bed of raspberry-melba sauce. It's not exactly Colonial fare or prices, but well-heeled folks who like good food and formal ambiance keep the White Horse busy most of the time.

(401) 849-3600. Lunch, daily except Tuesday noon to 3; dinner nightly, 6 to 10, jackets required; Sunday champagne brunch, noon to 3.

Pronto, 464 Thames St.

Some of the most innovative cooking in the city emanates from the partially open kitchen of this dark and cozy cocoon of Victorian romance. Owner Janne Osean's vintage decor is a melange of gilt mirrors, heavy dark draperies, potted palms, crystal chandeliers (a different one over almost every table), pressed-tin walls and ceiling, and oriental rugs on the floors. One innkeeper calls it the most romantic dining spot in the city, but we find the tables too close for comfort, let alone romance. A new upstairs room doubles the seating capacity with tables spaced a bit farther apart.

Soft jazz played as we lunched, fortunately nearly alone, here one winter weekday. The vegetable soup ($4.25) was hearty and the wild mushroom crostini ($5.75) quite tasty. Truly terrific was a special of chicken breast encrusted in pistachios and walnuts ($9.75), served on a bed of many greens with red and yellow pepper vinaigrette, the plate colorfully decorated with flecks of parsley and squiggles of vinaigrette. It was so good we asked the chef afterward how he prepared it. We also could understand how Newporters felt a favorite haunt, once perceived as

Decor is elegant Colonial at historic White Horse Tavern.

quite reasonable, had become more expensive. Bread was extra (50 cents for half a loaf). A masterful apple tart with praline ice cream (razor-thin apple slices flecked with cinnamon and fanned around the perimeter of a dinner-size plate) turned out to be $6 on the bill. Add a couple of glasses of the house Sicilian wine and our luncheon tab escalated to about $50 for two.

Yet we'd gladly go back (on an uncrowded night) for a dinner repertoire that yields some wonderful (and quite reasonable, $10.50 to $13.75) pastas, like the signature farfalle with shiitake mushrooms, kalamata olives, spinach, roasted red peppers, pinenuts and chèvre – all the currently "in" ingredients in one dish. The specials ($19.50 to $24.50) here are indeed special, perhaps pan-seared red snapper with a ginger-jasmine sauce, grilled ahi tuna with orzo pilaf and mango chutney, adobo barbecued duck breast with wild rice ravioli, and grilled angus ribeye steak with asparagus, smoky catsup, fried shallots and stuffed red bliss potatoes. Start with carpaccio of beef with arugula, shaved reggiano and white truffle oil or grilled lobster and sea scallops with a wilted spinach and endive salad. Finish with key lime pie or white and dark chocolate mousse. Be enticed by the specials, and happy to pay the piper.

(401) 847-5251. Breakfast daily in summer, 9 to 3; lunch rest of year, 11:30 to 4; dinner nightly, 5 to 10 or 11.

La Petite Auberge, 19 Charles St.

Dining on classic French cuisine in the historic Stephen Decatur House has been a fairly serious matter since chef-owner Roger Putier opened his small and charming restaurant in 1975. He has lightened up with a new courtyard/bistro menu, although traditionalists still like the rich French sauces and the air of romance..

The dark green house, warmed by roses climbing fence posts and trellises, is typical of many in old Newport, smack up against the sidewalk.

In two main-floor dining rooms, each with a handful of tables, the atmosphere is convivial and intimate – not for naught is this called petite. To the side and rear are a cozy bar with a sofa in front of a fireplace and a courtyard with five tables for outdoor dining. Up steep stairs are three more small dining rooms. Elegant lace tablecloths are layered over blue or gold linens, and the large menu is in French with English translations. The printed menu rarely changes, but is supplemented by many nightly specials.

The only description for the sauces is heavenly – from the escargots with cèpes, a house specialty (the heavily garlicked sauce fairly cries out to be sopped up with the crusty French bread) to our entrées of veal with morels and cream sauce and two tender pink lamb chops, also with cèpes and a rich brown sauce.

Appetizers and soups are $5.75 to $8.50 (for smoked salmon). They include a fish soup Marseilles style, mussels in a light cream sauce and duck pâté.

Entrées, including vegetables (crisp green beans and creamy sliced potatoes topped with cheese at our visit), are priced from $19 for frog's legs provençal to $25.75 for beef wellington with truffle sauce. Other choices are salmon in cream sauce with pink peppercorns, trout with hazelnuts, duck with raspberry sauce and four presentations of beef.

Service by black-suited women is efficient. Most dishes are finished at tableside, even the tossed salad with choice of dressings.

We ended with strawberries romanoff, one of the old favorites. The desserts are mostly classics like crêpes suzette, pear hélène and cherries jubilee. The excellent wine list is mainly French and reasonably priced.

The bistro menu, served on the trellised courtyard or in the charming rear bar, is short and to the point. Start perhaps with fish soup, crab cakes or a charcuterie assortment of pâtés and dry-cured sausage. Move on to swordfish with citrus-chile butter, sirloin strip steak, grilled quail or grilled lobster with fresh herbs ($10.95 to $15.95). Finish with chambord cheesecake or amaretto tartuffo.

(401) 849-6669. Dinner, Monday-Saturday 6 to 10 (courtyard to 11), Sunday 5 to 9.

The Clarke Cooke House, Bannister's Wharf.

Dining is on several levels and a breezy yet formal upper deck in this 1790-vintage Colonial house, another venerable Newport establishment. Two kitchens, offering different renditions of contemporary European fare, are under the aegis of executive chef Ted Gidley, who returned to the Cooke House in 1994 after several years at Pronto.

The most casual venue is the ground-level Candy Store cafe and espresso bar. Up a level on the other side is the Grille, a middle-of-the-road bistro offering lunch and dinner. Proceed up past the Midway Bar on the stairway landing to the winter Gilbert Stuart dining room, the semi-private Skybar and the glamorous summer Porch with a panoramic harbor view.

Casual fare is served at down-to-earth prices in the Candy Store. We can vouch for a lunch dish of eggs benedict, salad vinaigrette and great french fries ($7.25), and a thick and creamy cup of clam chowder – one of the best we've had lately – with a juicy hamburger on an onion roll ($5.95), again with those addictive french fries. The dinner menu is priced from $14.75 for sesame-grilled rare tuna fanned on mesclun salad to $21.50 for Mediterranean fish stew.

The food gets considerably more expensive, the service more polished and the atmosphere more haute in the Porch and Skybar. The dining area is formal in green and white, with high beamed ceiling, green high-back chairs and green banquettes awash with pillows. Hurricane chimneys enclose silver candlesticks, and fresh flowers and ornate silver top the white-linened tables. The doors open onto a canopied deck called the Porch, overlooking the harbor scene.

The upstairs menu has gone through contemporary French and northern Italian

Waterfront is on view from glamorous upper Porch at Clarke Cooke House.

phases lately before settling into what the chef calls modern European, incorporating elements of both. Among appetizers ($8.50 to $17.50) are a trio of seafood cakes, curried tartare of tuna, and terrine of duck foie gras with black mission fig compote. A salad of lobster, mango and avocado is dressed with coriander and lime.

Entrées run from $22 for steamed fillet of sole japonaise to $30 for sautéed lobster with pink peppercorn sauce. Others include peppered tuna steak, wood-grilled veal chop and rack of lamb persillade.

Among desserts are chocolate mascarpone terrine, a signature "snowball in hell" teaming chocolate roulade and vanilla ice cream, and Indian pudding à la mode – the last a fixture at Locke-Ober, the Boston institution also owned by proprietor David Ray.

The wine list ranks as the city's priciest, with many in the triple digits.

Decide before you leave if you wish to have an after-dinner drink in the Skybar, which the management treats as a private preserve. A foursome of our acquaintance was refused re-entry upon their return after spending $300 for dinner.

(401) 849-2900. Dinner nightly in season, 6 to 10 or 10:30, weekends in off-season. Candy Store and Grill, lunch daily, 11:30 to 5, weekends in winter; dinner nightly from 5, Wednesday-Sunday in winter.

More Dining Choices

The West Deck, 1 Waite's Wharf.

Modern bistro cuisine and a cozy grill room with a waterside deck are the hallmarks of this local haunt off the tourist path. Chef-owner James Mitchell, whose cooking we first encountered when he was at the Inn at Castle Hill in its heyday, took over a century-old structure that once served as a garage for an oil company. Here, in a small, garage-like space that's one-third cooking area, he seats 30 diners at tables dressed in pink and white and ten more at an L-shaped eating bar facing the open kitchen. A potbelly stove warms an enclosed sun porch for dining on a chilly day, and in summer the seating of choice is on the outside deck where there's a wood grill.

The dinner menu, printed nightly, is surprisingly extensive. At our latest

December visit, the sixteen entrées were priced from $14.50 for roasted half chicken with creamed leeks to $26.50 for venison baden-baden with brown game sauce, chestnuts and mushrooms. Almond-crusted mahi-mahi with Thai lobster curry sauce and coconut milk, grilled swordfish with Jamaican jerk sauce, and confit of duck with French lentils and rouen sauce indicate the range. Fourteen appetizers ($5.25 to $8) included a grilled seafood medley with roasted pepper and watercress sauces, duck pâté with a toasted baguette, and warm goat cheese salad. Among the rich desserts ($5) were a peach bread pudding with whiskey-caramel sauce, chocolate-praline torte with mocha sauce and maple crème brûlée. Most of the well-chosen wines, nicely priced in the teens and twenties, are available by the glass.

In season on the waterfront deck, the outdoor grill furnishes the bulk of the dishes on a simpler, all-day menu. Prices range from $6.25 for a fish sandwich or a burger with fries to $12.75 for teriyaki steak with fries. The mixed grill combines ribs, chicken and sausage with coleslaw and fries.

(401) 847-3610. Lunch in summer, noon to 2:30; dinner nightly in summer, 6 to 10, Wednesday-Saturday in off-season; Sunday brunch in winter, noon to 3.

Le Bistro, Bowen's Wharf.

The French provincial menu has been greatly expanded since Le Bistro moved from a small upstairs dining room on Thames Street to its two-story location (with a view of the harbor) on the wharf. Chef Kevin Wood, who served as sous chef for seven years under longtime chef-owner John Philcox, continues the tradition under auspices of James Beaulieu, also owner of the Wharf Pub & Restaurant below.

White and hunter linens, white china, bow chairs and a beamed ceiling set a mood of country elegance on the second floor. The convivial third-floor wine bar has been redecorated in shades of hunter green with French pencil sketches framed in gold on the walls. Honored by Wine Spectator, the wine list contains more than 140 labels, with many offered by the glass.

For lunch, from a menu on which everything sounds (and later looks) good, we've enjoyed a fine salade niçoise ($6.95) and a classic bouillabaisse ($9.95), which is worth going back for. Our latest visit with visitors from Europe produced a delicious sausage with warm potato salad, codfish cakes with curry sauce, a grilled pizza with scallops and wild mushrooms, and a warm duck salad with walnuts.

On a winter's night, the atmosphere is enchanting as you gaze from a window table onto the wharf, its historic buildings shining under street lights as passersby stroll from restaurant to restaurant. Hot oysters with golden caviar and a special pheasant pâté were tasty appetizers ($6.50 to $9.75). Entrées range from $14.95 for grilled chicken with lemon and garlic to $26.95 for rack of lamb with prosciutto and rosemary. We enjoyed the veal kidneys in port and mushroom sauce and a hefty plate of roast duck in a red cream sauce with endives.

A dessert tart of green grapes in puff pastry with whipped cream was a fine ending, as was Irish coffee. Creole bread pudding with bourbon sauce is always on the dessert menu, and you might find Ivory Coast cake, a rum-flavored chocolate cake with chocolate chantilly cream.

Le Bistro offers seasonal variations: wild game in the fall, a salute to great bistros in the winter and a culinary Tour de France in spring.

(401) 849-7778. Lunch daily, 11:30 to 5; dinner nightly, 5 to 11; Sunday brunch, 11:30 to 2:30.

Scales and Shells, 527 Thames St.

This perhaps epitomizes the Newport restaurant phenomenon. It was standing-room-only in its first week without so much as a word of advertising. Later, it expanded with a second-floor addition called **Upscales,** a smaller and quieter room open from May-September.

Plain and exotic seafood – simply prepared and presented in stylishly simple surroundings – is offered by retired sea captain Andy Ackerman. He and his staff cook up a storm in an open kitchen near the door, as fast as the seafood can be unloaded from the docks out back.

The delicious aromas almost overpowered as we read the blackboard menu with an immense range but nary a non-fish item in sight. Start with deep-fried calamari, grilled white clam pizza, Sicilian mussels or mesquite-grilled shrimp from the list of appetizers ($6.95 to $9.95). From this you could make a meal and, Andy says, many people do, ordering Chinese style. Monkfish, scallops, shrimp, swordfish, snapper, scrod – you name it, it comes in many variations as a main dish ($10.95 to $19.95), wood-grilled, broiled or tossed with pasta. Shrimp fra diavolo and clams fra diavolo are served right in their own steaming-hot pans. Entrées come with a choice of house salad, grilled vegetables, corn on the cob or french fries.

Tabasco, red pepper and parmesan cheese are on the tables, which are covered with black and white checked cloths. The floors are bare, and the decor is pretty much nil except for models of fish on the walls. You can pick and choose from the raw bar near the front entrance.

Italian gelatos (apricot and hazelnut are a couple) and tarts comprise the dessert selection. The short list of Italian and California wines is affordably priced.

(401) 846-3474. Dinner, Monday-Saturday 5 to 9 or 10, Sunday 4 to 9. No credit cards.

Cheeky Monkey Cafe, 14 Perry Mill Wharf.

The owners of Providence's acclaimed Gatehouse Restaurant branched out in 1996 with this small, two-level dining room, bar and an upstairs cigar lounge with a great view of the harbor.

The name refers to the British expression of endearment for a fun-loving, devilish person. Owner Henry Kates chose it to reflect a cheeky point of view on foods and spirits, and provided a dark and vaguely jungle-look decor of black wood tables and faux-leopard skins on the benches and wainscoting. Dining is on two levels, facing an open kitchen.

Executive chef Holly Dion works with Gatehouse chef Steven Marsella on creating contemporary cuisine with a Southern accent. The short dinner menu harbors such eclectic starters ($5 to $8.95) as a gumbo yaya of New England chicken, greens and andouille sausage, New Orleans-style barbecued shrimp with green onion popcorn rice, vegetable spring rolls with a tamari-ginger dipping sauce, and a smoked chicken quesadilla with goat cheese, creole tomato salsa and chipotle-avocado cream.

Main courses range from $12.95 for creole mustard beer-batter fish and chips to $25 for baked lobster with seafood and andouille sausage paella. Typical are grilled Atlantic salmon with tamarind glaze, grilled pork chop with a spicy banana sauce and grilled Colorado steak with "homemade monkey sauce."

Dessert could be bananas foster, raspberry tart with vanilla ice cream or chocolate suicide torte with peanut butter whipped cream.

Start with a drink in a separate bar across the hallway. Finish with an after-dinner

Restored YMCA building houses deluxe new Vanderbilt Hall hotel.

drink in the upstairs cigar lounge, with a parlor-like ambiance of sofas, overstuffed chairs, floor lamps and – what every parlor needs – a humidor cabinet. Sandwiches and the full menu are offered upstairs as well.

(401) 845-9494. Dinner, Wednesday-Sunday 6 to 9 or 10.

Dining and Lodging

Vanderbilt Hall, 41 Mary St., Box 840, Newport 02840.

This deluxe "mansion house hotel" was on schedule to open in May 1997 in a former YMCA building in the heart of Newport's Historic Hill district. Partners in the $10 million venture were a management team that opened the opulent Inn at Perry Cabin in Maryland and Keswick Hall in Virginia and Providence investor Arnold Chace, who was familiar with the property. Built in 1909 by Alfred Vanderbilt to be granted to the town for a YMCA in memory of his father, Cornelius, it had been unoccupied since 1975.

The red-brick hotel's 50 guest rooms, including 28 on the second and third floors of the restored hall and the rest in a new wing, are divided into five categories, from four "cozy house rooms" to a couple of 700-square-foot suites. Twenty-eight are "state rooms" that measure up to their name. Ten of the more unusual on the third floor are classified as "executive studies," with spiral staircases leading to skylit lofts with office equipment. All are appointed with period furnishings and rich wallpapers, fabrics and linens in the style we've experienced at Perry Cabin and Keswick. The king and queen bed canopies and treatments are distinctive here; a couple of rooms have kingsize beds in the center draped in fabric. Heated towel warmers and makeup mirrors are among the amenities.

The main floor is a ramble of rooms with fireplaces, polished hardwood floors and graceful arches leading to a bright and airy garden conservatory and an outdoor courtyard with terrace and herb garden. There are snug reading nooks, a carpeted music room, a board room and a morning room.

Executive chef is Scott Hoyland, who was opening chef at the Inn at Perry Cabin and lately was an award-winner at Baltimore's top dining room, Hampton's in the Harbor Court Hotel. Upscale international cuisine (the menus for which were evolving as this book went to press) was to be served in a wood-paneled dining room and in the greenhouse conservatory. The richly appointed main room with a fireplace is flanked by three smaller private rooms: a wine-tasting room with bottles in racks along the walls, a cigar room with humidors and a club-like "en famille" room for single diners to join a common table. Afternoon tea is served in the English tradition.

The hotel's fitness center and a billiards room are on the lower level near the Y's restored indoor pool.

Lewis Kiesler, general manager who was preparing for the hotel's opening, had hopes it would become a Relais & Châteaux property.

(401) 846-6200 or (888) 826-4255. Fax (401) 846-070l. Breakfast daily, 7:30 to 10; lunch, noon to 2:30; dinner, 6 to 9:30. Doubles, $195 to $395; suites, $395 to $650.

Castle Hill Inn & Resort, Ocean Drive, Newport 02840.

Originally called "a country inn by the sea," the old Inn at Castle Hill has a new name and a new life. The main-floor restaurant has been refurbished, a pair of chefs are providing what the manager calls "probably the most exciting food program on Aquidneck Island," and accommodations are being upgraded.

The locally owned Newport Harbor Corp. reassumed control of the oceanside Victorian mansion in 1995 and renewed the richly paneled lobby, the inner Castle Hill dining room, our favorite Sunset Room with expansive windows jutting out toward the water, and the smaller Agazzi and Newport dining rooms. Only the elegant, romantic bar – long a favorite hangout of the in crowd – remained untouched.

Into this opulent setting came executive chef Wayne Gibson, a Providence chef who trained with Madeleine Kamman in California and cooked with Lydia Shire at Biba in Boston, and pastry chef Nancy Starziano, who was chef and general manager at the South Shore Grill in Wakefield. Specialists in Northeastern regional cuisine with indigenous ingredients from Maine to the Chesapeake Bay, they quickly changed Castle Hill's image from that of a swinging, drinking spot back to fine dining.

The fare is contemporary to the max and worded in the Lydia Shire style: "a tangle of pappardelle, chives, truffle butter and reggianita" and a "demitasse of rich lobster broth, stir of seared scallops" among starters ($6 to $18); a "shallow chowder of big sea scallops and seared wolffish, leeks, crisp potatoes," "bound and grilled tail" of lobster, and "dark roasted leg of lamb, red-chile jelly, quick greens and spicy whipped wheats" among "mains" ($19 to $30). Dishes could be as basic as braised chicken breast with orzo or as exotic as seared rare foie gras with pecan sandies and peach jam, a little appetizer indulgence for $18. The cooking and presentation were said to be far more sophisticated than we had encountered here at earlier meals.

Sous chef Nancy, who trained at La Varenne in Paris and does the cooking at lunch, is known for incredible desserts ($6), among them a baked chocolate terrine with white chocolate grid and a pecan-walnut-pignoli tart. Her lunch offerings range from $7 for a grilled turkey baguette sandwich to $12 for provimi calves liver with vidalia onions and caraway-shiraz glaze. There's no more refined place for an oceanside lunch in Newport than the oval Sunset Room, redecorated with a billowing pale yellow canopy on the ceiling. This is also the place for Castle Hill's long-popular Sunday brunch. Afterward, some people spill out onto the lawn for drinks, jazz and an afternoon barbecue.

The new ownership team, led by veteran restaurateur Leonard C. Panaggio of the Mooring restaurant, started upgrading the accommodations in late 1996. First on the agenda were the six outlying Harbor House units, which were winterized and given kingsize beds, whirlpool baths, televisions, fireplaces and french doors onto private decks overlooking Narragansett Bay. Also refurbished was what Leonard considered the shabbiest of seven Victorian upstairs guest rooms(all with private baths) and a suite in the main inn.

Enhancement of the rest and the three small rooms sharing baths in the former servant quarters awaited completion of refurbishing in 1998 of the side Swiss-style Chalet, former laboratory of original owner Alexander Agassiz, the Harvard naturalist. Kingsize beds and private baths with whirlpool tubs were in the works for its main-floor suite and three upstairs bedrooms that had shared baths. No changes werc planned for the spartan little efficiency cottages beside the beach – calling them rustic is generous, Leonard conceded – that are rented by the week for $800 to $900. A continental breakfast is served to inn guests.

(401) 849-3800. Fax (401) 849-3838. Lunch, Tuesday-Saturday 11:30 to 3:30; dinner, Monday-Saturday 6 to 10; Sunday brunch, 11:30 to 3:30, afternoon barbecue with jazz on the lawn, 3 to 8. Doubles, $145 to $250; suites, $275 to $325.

Oceancliff, 63 Ridge Road, Newport 02840.

Occupying a key oceanfront ridge across Smuggler's Cove from the legendary Castle Hill Inn & Resort, Oceancliff was reborn in 1996 and vying with its more established neighbor to attract the moneyed crowd. Run for some time and with little success by a group of contractor-investors who also developed two time-share buildings on either side, the 1895 landmark Hutton estate was taken over by Thomas Roos, owner of Newport's Goat Island properties, who was pouring millions into its renovation as a country hotel.

The accommodations took priority here. Under the management of Jim Maher, formerly of the smaller Francis Malbone House Inn downtown, twelve rooms and suites on the hotel's second floor were handsomely redone with marble baths, king or queen sleigh beds with down comforters, TVs in armoires or on tables, plush seating areas, and oriental carpets on polished wood floors. Decor throughout is elegant but a bit monotonous in endless shades of gray and beige that Jim called sand colors. Rooms vary widely. One of four standard queensize rooms is rather tight, while a one-bedroom king suite with sitting room offers separate his and hers bathrooms, both marble and, except to the affluent city folk who we're told insist upon them, a bit of overkill. The head-on bay view from the porch of a junior suite is marred by an air-conditioning unit and the raised ceiling of the ballroom below, but the sought-after northwest corner junior suite compensates with a perfect view from the window and one of the establishment's four jacuzzi tubs (the rest have showers only). Most rooms have ornamental fireplaces, some bearing showy original tile work. The Gate House in front holds a main-floor suite as well as three upstairs bedrooms, two of them sharing a bath. The hotel closed in early 1997 to renovate seven more guest rooms with unobstructed bay views on the third floor.

Guests gather in a fireplaced library off the lobby full of plush sofas and chairs. Continental breakfast is served in a cozy breakfast room with a fireplace. For recreation, there are tennis courts and a massive, square indoor swimming pool enclosed in a waterfront room with retractable windows beneath the patio.

The crystal ballroom with windows onto the water is now a function room. What is billed as "classical casual dining" takes place in the smaller **Hutton Room** with white-clothed tables and a bar. The prime luncheon spot is the huge outdoor **Patio Bar & Grill** adjacent, with ringside seats above the water (those who want to be even closer can occupy the Adirondack chairs scattered about the back lawn).

Dinner fare starts with traditional soups and salads and seafood, from clams casino to oysters rockefeller, from the raw bar. Main courses ($16.95 to $18.95) include grilled teriyaki tuna steak with wasabi mayonnaise, sauté of shrimp scampi over penne pasta, cornmeal-crusted chicken breast with black bean sauce, and stuffed pan-seared beef tenderloin with roasted garlic sauce.

Sunday brunch is served buffet style for $17.95. It's followed by live entertainment on the patio and lawn from 1 to 5.

(401) 849-3311. Fax (401) 849-3927. Lunch daily, 11 to 6; dinner nightly, from 6; Sunday brunch, 10:30 to 2:30. Doubles, $165 to $350; suites, $395.

Lodging

Rooms in Newport are a glut on the market or scarce to come by, depending on the day and season. A deluxe room that goes for $300 a night on a summer weekend may be available for $100 or so on a winter weekday. Some of the largest and most advertised "inns" tend to be time-sharing condos on the water; a couple of innkeepers own several B&Bs. Breakfasts are usually continental and, in general, the owners are seldom to be seen. We focus here on some of the exceptions.

The Francis Malbone House, 392 Thames St., Newport 02840.

A former nursing home, converted into an imposing residence by a physician, was acquired in 1990 by five partners who turned it into one of Newport's more inviting inns. In 1996, they added a handsome rear wing around a rear courtyard, doubling its size and doing so with such exquisite taste and attention to detail that the first-time visitor would think it had been part of the inn all along.

They started in the original residence with eight attractive bedrooms and a suite, all with private baths and six with fireplaces. For space and privacy, we've always liked the sunken Counting House suite (formerly the physician's office) with its private entry, a queensize four-poster bed facing the TV, a sitting area with a sofabed and two chairs, and a two-part bathroom with shower and dressing room/vanity.

Although still the premium accommodation, the suite has competition from the nine new courtyard rooms in the rear, all with kingsize poster beds and jacuzzi tubs, writing desks, fireplaces and TVs hidden in recessed bookshelves. Bigger, more private and quiet because they're away from the street traffic, they encompass all the nuances that "we couldn't have in the original house and wanted here," in the words of innkeeper Will Dewey. A couple open onto private courtyards with wrought-iron furniture; the courtyard suite adds a wet bar and a sitting area. Oriental rugs, rich appointments, down comforters and duvet covers monogrammed in white are the rule.

Guests enjoy a couple of lovely, high-ceilinged front parlors, a library with TV and a small dining room that served as the kitchen when the house was built in 1760 for a shipping merchant. Check out the hidden servants' stairway leading to the attic beside the tiled fireplace and the old bread oven in the hearth.

A spectacular new dining room goes off a corridor walled with glass and Portuguese tiles leading to the courtyard wing. It's a beauty in pale yellow and gray with a domed ceiling, four round tables and two tall shelves displaying Will's collection of blue and white English china. Will, a culinary graduate of Johnson & Wales University in Providence, and his staff prepare a full breakfast. The fare includes fruits, breads, perhaps raspberry croissants or cinnamon-raisin strudels, and a main course ranging from eggs benedict to belgian waffles. Homemade cookies and beverages are offered in the afternoon.

(401) 846-0392 or (800) 846-0392. Fax (401) 848-5956. Doubles, $165 to $245; suites, $295 and $325.

Cliffside Inn, 2 Seaview Ave., Newport 02840.

Big bucks and great taste have been rendered unto this Victorian charmer. In a textbook example of how to transform a small and quirky place, owner Winthrop Baker has created one of the most elegant and comfortable B&Bs in the land. The summer villa, a short block from the ocean, was built in 1880 by a governor of Maryland. It later was owned by Newport artist Beatrice Turner, a fact that prompted its new owner to gather many of her paintings from hither and yon and mount a fascinating retrospective exhibit that commanded wide attention for the inn. The Cliffside now offers fifteen air-conditioned bedrooms and suites, the nine largest of which Win Baker considers the most upscale in Newport with their jacuzzi baths, fireplaces and sitting areas with TVs.

No room in the house has escaped his touch, be it the sumptuous Governor's Suite with its working fireplace visible

Breakfast table at Cliffside Inn.

from both the bedroom and the jacuzzi in the bathroom or the newly enlarged Garden Suite, a great summer space with a bay window off the front porch and a 28-foot-long "habitat bathroom" beneath, so-called "because you can live in it," what with a Victorian book nook at one end and french doors at the other opening onto a private courtyard. The inn's many floor-to-ceiling and bay windows bathe the rooms with light, blending rich Victoriana with an airy Laura Ashley freshness.

The newest accommodations are in the Seaview Cottage, a onetime ranch house at the foot of the property. It was transformed in 1996 into two suites, the Atlantic with a massive stone fireplace and half-vaulted ceiling and the Cliff, a two-room affair with full vaulted ceiling and a two-sided "see-through" fireplace visible from the kingsize plantation bed and the plush living room.

Although the suites are so self-sufficient one feels no need to leave, the Cliffside is a convivial place, thanks to a young and personable staff, a welcoming veranda, the hallway and staircase lined with fascinating Beatrice Turner paintings, and a large parlor, cheerfully decorated in shades of orange-coral and moss green with stunning faille draperies. Classical music or opera plays in the background as Victorian tea is presented with finger sandwiches and sweets in the afternoon.

A full breakfast is served here by innkeeper Stephan Nicolas, a Johnson & Wales hospitality graduate whose experienced demeanor belies his youth. The 25-year-old son of a French chef and cookbook author, he's a font of culinary knowledge and prepares memorable fare. Our meal began with fresh orange juice, two kinds of muffins and a remarkable (for winter) array of raspberries, blackberries and strawberries to lather upon homemade granola and yogurt. The main event was eggs benedict with a subtle hollandaise sauce. The calories were worked off with a jaunt along the oceanside Cliff Walk nearby.

(401) 847-1811 or (800) 845-1811. Fax (401) 848-5850. Doubles, $165 to $205; suites, $255 to $325.

Elm Tree Cottage, 336 Gibbs Ave., Newport 02840.

Here is one beautiful "cottage," situated in a quiet neighborhood a block from the sea. Large and comfortable rooms appointed in elegant country style and artist-innkeepers with outgoing personalities help make the place special. Priscilla and Tom Malone and their three young daughters acquired the mansion, built in 1882 and later owned by Mrs. Crawford Hill, the Pennsylvania Railroad heiress and member of Newport's 400. "Our entire house fit into this living room," Priscilla said, recalling their move from Long Island and how they furnished the huge home "from auctions and estate sales."

Furnish it they did, quite grandly yet unpretentiously. There's an 87-foot sweep from dining room to parlor, which ends at expansive windows overlooking Easton's Pond and First Beach. Chintz sofas and a grand piano welcome guests to a living room that could be pictured in a design magazine. To the side are a morning garden room great for lounging and a bar room furnished in wicker. Here the Malones put out munchies for guests to BYOB and sit at the great old bar with 1921 silver dollars embedded in its top and pictures of the former owner's Pekinese dogs reverse-painted on the mirror behind.

At three tables in the fireplaced dining room, the Malones serve extravagant breakfasts by candlelight: perhaps heart-shaped waffles, Portuguese sweet bread french toast or apple crêpes in the shape of calla lilies. "No bacon and eggs here," says Priscilla. "I try to treat guests the way I want to be pampered when I'm away from home." Our autumn breakfast started with juice and homemade oatmeal (the dish arrived on a saucer delightfully decorated with five varieties of dried leaves) and culminated in delicious pumpkin waffles. The day's calligraphed menu went home as a souvenir.

On the second floor are four large bedrooms and a master suite; all with private baths and four with fireplaces. The suite, all 23 by 37 feet of it, is pretty in salmon and seafoam green. It has a Louis XV kingsize bed with a crown canopy, two sitting areas (one in front of the fireplace) and a huge bath with a dressing table and Austrian crystal legs on the washstand. Country French and English linens and antiques dress this and the other four rooms, which pale only modestly in comparison. The newest room is the main-floor corner library-bedroom, lovely in wine and teal colors and outfitted in an equestrian theme with a TV. After more than a year of renovations and flat-out work in getting the place furnished, Priscilla has fulfilled her desire to "fluff up the rooms" with such touches as dried flowers, mounds of pillows, racks with old hats and individual stained-glass pieces reflecting the couple's artistry. At one visit, her eye for fluff produced a goat cart in the foyer, brought in for fall to showcase the harvest.

Priscilla's background in fine arts and woodworking and Tom's in interior design have stood them in good stead for the inn's refurbishing as well as for their thriving stained-glass business.

(401) 849-1610 or (888) 356-8733. Doubles, $175 to $325.

The Inn at Old Beach, 19 Old Beach Road, Newport 02840.

Look beyond the ornate Victorian facade, colorful in grayish beige, yellow and green, and you might see an old anchor embedded in the third-story turret of the home built as the Anchorage in 1879. It's one of the surprises that abound in this stellar B&B run very personally by Luke and Cyndi Murray.

They offer seven guest rooms with private baths. Cyndi says she likes "a lot of different styles." They are reflected in the English country decor in the rooms, named after flowers or plants and full of whimsical touches. In the Rose Room, a pencil-post canopy bed angles from the corner beneath a bamboo-beamed ceiling. Done up in black and pink, it has a fireplace and a handpainted dresser with hand-carved rose drawer pulls. Handpainted Victorian cottage furniture, a faux bookcase along one wall and an antique woodburning fireplace grace the Ivy Room. Check out the bishop-sleeve draperies with valances and the fireplace in the first-floor Wisteria Room, and the wicker loveseat and chair in the Forget-Me-Not Room. The newest rooms are two with separate entrances in a rear carriage house, part of which the Murrays converted into quarters for themselves and their young sons. These have TVs and a more contemporary air; the Sunflower, lovely in pale yellow and burgundy, contains a wicker queensize sleigh bed, a wicker loveseat and two chairs, and a sunflower motif, from the lamps on the nightstands to a hand-painted shelf. Cyndi decorates for the season, but the front hall's original stained-glass window representing the four seasons shines at all times.

Guests gather in a small front parlor or in a new and larger Victorian living room where two plush chairs and a couch face a glass cocktail table resting on four bunnies. Here are a pretty tiled fireplace, a rabbit fashioned from moss and a copper bar in the corner. Outside are a back porch and a brick patio overlooking a pleasant back yard with a gazebo and a fish pond. The Murrays serve continental breakfast at four tables in the dining room or on the porch. It usually involves juice, fruit and pastries like muffins, croissants and coffee cake. The Murrays also have put together a categorized collection of restaurant menus, drawing on Luke's experience as a restaurant consultant and beverage manager for the Black Pearl.

(401) 849-3479 or (888) 303-5033. Fax (401) 847-1236. Doubles, $135 to $165.

Rhode Island House, 77 Rhode Island Ave., Newport 02840.

Cooking instructor Michael Dupré makes this elegant B&B special for those with an interest in matters culinary. Trained at La Varenne in Paris, the former private chef for the Auchincloss family offers culinary weekends in winter and

Expansive living room is furnished with comfort in mind at Elm Tree Cottage.

serves breakfasts to remember in a dining room with Chinese Chippendale chairs at tables for four. The meal starts with a buffet on the sideboard: bowls of fresh fruit, whole-grain cereals, scones, pumpkin or lemon-poppyseed breads, and a "dessert" like banana-rum bread pudding or peach-cranberry crisp. These are preliminaries to the main event, perhaps eggs benedict with asparagus and tomato or popovers with basil-scrambled eggs, grilled tomato, asparagus and sausage. These treats originate in a great professional kitchen, where Michael caters and gives cooking lessons, including wintertime classes in which everyone participates and then sits down to eat. "I used to peek in the windows and say 'I want that kitchen,'" Michael said as he told how he acquired the property in 1993. The kitchen came with an 1882 Victorian estate that a previous owner had turned into a low-profile B&B.

As most of the restoration work had been done. Michael, an avid collector, had only to furnish the house. This he has done with taste and flair, in both common rooms and bedrooms. The great hall/foyer is remarkable for yellow faux-marble walls. Off one side is an airy sun room. In front is a cozy library and on the other side is an inviting living room with a remarkable set of elaborate arched windows.

Upstairs are five guest rooms with private baths and queensize beds, each with its own distinction. The bath in the small Mary Kay Room, for instance, occupies a sun porch and retains the original pink and gray fixtures. The antique headboard on the bed matches the chest of drawers in the creamy white and floral green front Garden Room. The Auchincloss Room is "dainty, lovely and nice – just like her," says Michael of Mrs. Auchincloss, who was his favorite grande dame. It has a fireplace and a full bath with an enormous jacuzzi, as does the rear Hunter Room, masculine in hunter green and complete with a private balcony overlooking the back yard. All the rooms have large windows and are bright and airy, unusual for Victorian houses of the period.

(401) 848-7787. Doubles, $150 to $225.

The Victorian Ladies, 63 Memorial Blvd., Newport 02840.
Helene and Donald O'Neill took fourteen months to gut and renovate these two

Victorian beauties, one behind the other, before opening their nine-room B&B, all with private baths and TV. The front building contains a small parlor with a crystal chandelier and crystal sconces on the mantel and an adjacent dining room where an enormous 1740 hutch-sideboard of English pine displays plates and country knickknacks. Here Helene serves a full breakfast buffet. The fare includes fruits, juices, sweet breads, croissants and an egg dish, perhaps a soufflé or a particular guest favorite, sausage ring stuffed with eggs.

Helene had never decorated before, but she has done a super job on her rooms, with a prevailing pink and blue color scheme and striking window treatments. One of the nicest is the room she calls the honeymoon suite in the main house, which has a queensize bed and sitting area. With puffy curtains, dhurrie rugs in pastel colors or rose carpeting, vials of dried flowers on the doors, potpourri, down comforters, eyelet ruffles, and thick pink and blue towels, all is fresh, pretty and feminine. Her favorite room, upstairs in the rear Carriage House, has pink walls, lace curtains and an antique white gown and straw hat hanging from hooks on the wall. Although the theme is Victorian, the look is light and uncluttered.

The newest rooms are two deluxe suites upstairs in the rear caretaker's cottage just behind the Carriage House. Both contain lavender carpeting with which Helene paired a pale yellow color scheme in one suite and red and dark green in the other. Both have telephones as well as the televisions common to all rooms.

Don, a contractor, built the gazebo and the courtyard, and his green thumb shows in a profusion of flowers.

(401) 849-9960. Doubles, $135 to $185.

Culpeper House, 30 Second St., Newport 02840.

Winter dinners prepared by house guests in a rare brick oven are among the attractions at this dark brown house built in 1771 in the historic Point section of Newport. Restoration developer Ann Wylie oversaw its refurbishment for her brother, who bought it as an investment. Now Ann, a former publicist for a San Francisco hotel, is running the B&B as a retirement project.

She loves to show off the myriad historic details of her home, which is a curious blend of old and new, furnished with her California possessions. Up a short but steep staircase are two guest rooms, comfortable with feather beds, down comforters and modern bathrooms.

A lot of living and camaraderie go on in the small downstairs living room and the larger library/dining room. The latter is Ann's pride and joy with its shelves of good books (particularly strong on mysteries, Newport history and cooking) and a basket of tiny flags representing the fifteen countries from which her worldly guests have come. Here is where she serves French wine and cheese in the afternoon and a three-course breakfast in the morning. The fare might be orange juice and a fresh fruit platter with yogurt, homemade blueberry cake or homemade bread with English jams and marmalades, and french toast with grand marnier and rum, Spanish shirred eggs, individual egg soufflé or hot porridge. "I've only begun to cook in this house," Ann said at our first visit as she was looking to expand her repertoire. It seems her guests would have none of that, insisting she serve the same treats they had had before.

She also lined up visiting chefs to cook dinner, but guests preferred to cook it themselves in the historic kitchen with its waist-high brick fireplace, open to the room, arched and very deep. Roasting or grilling at the rear of the fireplace imparts a smoky taste that she calls "dynamite good." So, on occasion, with input from

Ann, her guests cook up dinner and then everyone sits down together to partake. She adds, "This has evolved into a place where people feel at home, take over the entire house and we all have the best time."

(401) 846-4011. Doubles, $110 to $135.

Gourmet Treats

With everything from delis to food boutiques, the Newport area is a paradise for the palate of the wandering gourmet. Among the possibilities:

Newport Mansions. On most visitors' must-see lists, several hold special culinary appeal. The dining rooms in all are on display, and at the Marble House is a gold ballroom in which the owner once gave a ten-course dinner for 100 dogs in full party dress. At the fabulous Breakers, you get to see a number of kitchens and butler's pantries, an area larger than most houses. The dining room at Kingscote, an oft-overlooked Greek Revival cottage, is one of the nicest rooms in all the mansions – decorated with Tiffany glass tiles and stained-glass panels of dahlias.

The Market on the Boulevard, 43 Memorial Blvd., is a large, upscale grocery store with a market cafe and espresso bar, a bakery, deli and "gourmet to go." And what wonderful things do go – in our case, a dish of oriental beef with a vegetable medley for supper at home, plus a ginger-pear tart and lemon-raspberry roulade for dessert. There are wonderful breads, choice meats, exotic produce, fresh pastas – you name it, Newport's beautiful (and ordinary) people come here to buy it. From salads to pastries to sandwiches (the last delightfully named for behind-the-scenes workers at the mansions), all the makings for a gourmet picnic, lunch or dinner are here.

Anthony's Seafood, Waite's Wharf, is a good fish market with a few deli items and specialty foods. Everything from codfish to oysters is available. It supplies the seafood for the 200-seat **Shore Dinner Hall** next door, a vast enclosed lobster pound with garage-size doors opening onto the harbor and colorful banners hanging from the ceiling. This is the kind of casual family waterfront place Newport needed. It offers lobsters in many guises, as well as three versions of clam chowder ($2.75), fish and chips ($6.95), steamers, fried dinners, pastas, burgers and even honey-mustard chicken. A full lobster boil, including lobster, steamers, mussels, corn, potatoes, sausage and chowder, is $21.95. Sit at picnic tables and have yourself a feast without breaking the bank. Wine and beer are served. Open daily 11 to 10 or 11, April-October.

For casual dining, **Cappuccino's** at 92 William St. is a nice little breakfast and lunch cafe in the uptown Bellevue Avenue area. The salads are great, the chicken-onion-bacon quiche was hearty and we drooled over the white-chocolate and straw-berry bars. **Ocean Breeze Cafe** at 580 Thames St. stocks gourmet coffees and teas, baked goods and an array of sandwiches and salads. **The Wharf Pub & Restaurant** on Bowen's Wharf offers build-your-own sandwiches and 36 microbrews, best taken on an outdoor deck. Nearby, the aromas drifting through the door may draw you into the **Cookie Jar** for chocolate-chip, gingersnap or oatmeal-raisin cookies.

Coffee and espresso are the rage in this seaport town, as elsewhere. A new **Starbucks** occupies a prime corner at Thames & Church, beside the Trinity Church green. Farther along Lower Thames are the excellent **Steaming Bean Espresso**

Cafe, where old magazines displayed in the windows draw browsers inside for pastries, sandwiches and desserts; **Jeanine's Beans & Gizmo's,** where if you get past the coffee and tea bar in front you'll find "a kitchen cottage" of specialty foods and kitchenware, and **Espressibles of Newport,** which advertises collectibles, gifts and antiques but seems to be mainly coffee.

Fragrant dried flowers hang from the ceiling and jars of loose teas, herbs and teapots line the shelves at **Tea & Herb Essence,** 476 Thames St. Proprietor Laureen Grenus offers everything from passionfruit to hibiscus heaven teas to herbal remedies and health-care products, handmade soaps, gifts and more. Some of the herbs and flowers come from her gardens out front. Lower Thames harbors not one but two gourmet pet stores, **Salty Paws** ("gifts for cats and dogs and the people who love them") and **The Gourmet Dog,** with a fire hydrant at the entrance and a "dog bakery" dispensing all-natural premium dog biscuits.

A most colorful kitchen shop is **Runcible Spoon** (the title taken from "The Owl and the Pussycat") at 180 Bellevue Ave. Amid the garlic salsa and the lobster platters, we were taken with a line of Portuguese pottery with tiny vegetables like radishes and scallions depicted thereon.

Another good shop is **Kitchen Pot Pourri** at 42 West Main Road, Middletown, a house full of kitchen gadgets and accessories, baking items, pots and pans, placemats, cookbooks and the like. Nearby, the fledgling **Newport Vineyards & Winery** at 909 East Main Road (Route 138) harvested its first grapes in 1996 under the ownership of John Nunes. Its new port wine is one of the few ports released along the East Coast. The winery is open for tours and tastings daily, 10 to 5, Sunday noon to 5. Also of interest in Middletown is **Coddington Brewing Co.,** Newport County's first brew pub and restaurant, open daily from 11:30 at 210 Coddington Hwy.

A Gourmet Side Trip

Take a side trip down Route 77 along the East Bay. In Tiverton, stop at **Past and Presence** at 2573 Main Road, where Judy Galway stocks tea sets, linens and "Angel Duds" made from old chenille bedspreads in her gift shop. Adjacent is her **Here & Now Tea Room** with a wall-size mural of an English garden, a water view and a deck for lunch or English cream tea (by reservation at 4).

In the quaint hamlet of Tiverton Four Corners is **Provender,** a specialty-foods store and upscale sandwich shop, where you can obtain lunch to eat in or take out. Farther along are **Walker's Farm Stand,** where the folks from suave Little Compton shop for produce and preserves, and **Olga's Cup & Saucer,** a small place next door, where you can stop for coffee, biscotti or pizzas.

Nearby at 162 West Main Road in Little Compton is **Sakonnet Vineyards,** the largest and oldest continuously producing winery in New England. Owners Earl and Susan Samson are known for some of the East's better wines, among them an estate chardonnay and a pinot noir, both retailing in the $12.50 range. You can sample their offerings in a large tasting room with oriental rugs on the floors, daily 10 to 6. The winery hosts numerous special events of culinary interest, including a Master Chef Series.

Water scene is on view from table for two at **The Regatta at Falmouth.**

Cape Cod
New Capers on the Old Cape

The time was not all that long ago when dining on Cape Cod meant, for many, the three C's: Chillingsworth, the Christopher Ryder House and clam shacks.

When you thought of places to stay, you hoped to luck into a friend's summer house or you rented a cottage, preferably somewhere near the water. The few inns tended to be large and posh and were far outnumbered by all those funny-looking motels with glassed-in swimming pools near Hyannis.

Well, Chillingsworth is still there, better than ever. The Christopher Ryder House has been converted into condominiums, and the clam shacks are overshadowed by a burst of serious restaurants.

There are more summer houses, cottages, posh inns and funny-looking motels than ever, of course. But there's also a new breed of country inns – not full-service like their predecessors, but more than bed-and-breakfast houses.

In spring, the season starts gearing up, yet crowds and prices are less than at summer's height. Then comes the July and August crush, and the high season ends abruptly after Labor Day.

Knowledgeable visitors have long preferred the Cape in the off-season. They avoid the tourist trappings of Hyannis, whose restaurants this chapter purposely omits. For the Cape is a place for escape, for relative solitude, for respite in a sandy, seaside setting unsurpassed in New England.

Note: Although the Cape's season is lengthening every year and more places remain open year-round, the owners' plans may change. Restaurant hours vary widely. Reservations are required in advance for peak periods. Minimum stays for lodging are not unusual. Such caveats are overcome by planning, flexibility and/or luck.

People who haven't been to the Cape lately – or who haven't ventured far from the beach if they have – might be surprised by the "new" Cape that has emerged and co-exists with the old.

Dining

The Best of the Best

Chillingsworth, Route 6A, Brewster.

The revitalized dowager of Cape Cod restaurants offers what some reviewers call the best serious resort-area dining in New England. For two years in a row it outranked all 500 Boston restaurants in the Zagat survey. Recently, it won a Distinguished Restaurants of North America award, along with the Chanticleer on Nantucket and three Boston restaurants, and was featured on the Great Chefs of the East television series.

For most, this is a special destination – so special, in fact, that we stopped by to reserve a table six weeks in advance for a mid-October Saturday. As it turned out, we didn't get the specific time nor the table we had picked out, but that was our only complaint from a memorable dinner that lasted past midnight.

The restored 1689 house is named for Chillingsworth Foster, son of its builder. Its quaint and unassuming Cape Cod exterior gives little clue to the treasures inside – room after room full of priceless furnishings, antiques and museum pieces. The large Terrace Room in which we ended up dining is not, to our mind, as intimate or as special as one of the smaller rooms like the Empire, where we had booked, or the table for four in an alcove off the living room, which one innkeeper of our acquaintance thinks is the most exquisite around.

A hurricane oil lamp, Limoges china and a vase of flowers graced our heavily linened table. A harpist was playing in the background as the waiter asked if we had questions about the menu, which is typewritten daily. The meal consists of seven courses at a fixed price of $43.50 to $57.50, depending upon choice of entrée. Although locally considered pricey, Chillingsworth offers better value than do its peers elsewhere – far better in that you get seven exotic courses. And the bistro menu is a relative steal.

We chose a French vouvray ($23.50) to accompany our appetizers, grilled duck and pepper quesadilla with coriander and tomatillo salsa and a feuilleté of oysters with spinach and lemon-butter sauce with roe. A dozen appetizers were offered, from a jumbo ravioli of salmon, smoked salmon, mascarpone and spinach with lobster butter and basil to carpaccio of veal tenderloin with truffle oil, grilled olive bread and shaved parmesan.

The cream of mussel soup that followed was superb, as was the consommé of mushrooms. A second helping of the night's squash bread – after all, we weren't seated until 9:30 – was followed by a salad of four baby leaf lettuces, arugula, radicchio and sorrel, enriched with a crouton of warm chèvre and dressed with a zesty vinaigrette. A grapefruit sorbet with a sprig of mint, served in a crystal sherry glass, cleared the palate.

All that was literally prelude to the main event – stunning entrées, beautifully presented. The breast of duck was garnished with citrus rind and fanned out in slices around the plate, interspersed with kiwi and papaya slices. A side plate contained julienned carrots and a spinach soufflé with nutmeg and wild rice. Our

Chef-owner Robert (Nitzi) Rabin outside Chillingsworth.

other entrée was an equally imaginative treatment of lamb with veal kidneys, grilled with herbs from Chillingsworth's garden. With these we had a 1982 Rodney Strong cabernet ($27), the least expensive California vintage on a choice wine list priced well into the hundreds.

Others among the night's ten entrées might be rare grilled tuna loin with wasabi butter sauce, sweetbreads and foie gras with asparagus and sweetbread and veal raviolis, and loin of elk with fig and sundried cranberry sauce.

Desserts are anything but an anti-climax. One of us chose a raspberry tulipe, an intriguing presentation atop a speckled-striped pattern of napoleon. The other enjoyed a hazelnut dacquoise with coffee butter cream. Before these came the "amusements" – a plate of gingerbread men, rolled cookies around citrus and macaroons. The finale was a serving of chocolate truffles, intense to the ultimate.

Chef-owner Robert (Nitzi) Rabin made the rounds of diners as they lingered over coffee. He and wife Pat, whose youthful appearances belie their fortyish years, work fourteen-hour days overseeing the expanding operation they purchased in 1975 following the death of the previous owner. Both had worked summers at Chillingsworth, he advancing from busboy to captain to manager and managing to pick up an MBA at the Tuck School at Dartmouth. The Rabins travel every spring to France or California to continue to enhance their highly creative American version of new French cuisine.

Lunch and dinner are available in a contemporary bistro and greenhouse lounge area with skylights, walls of glass and plants. The lunch menu embraces some of the dinner items as well as other creative fare at more affordable prices (appetizers, $5.75 to $6.75; entrées, $8 to $11.50). A broader bistro menu at night offers exotic appetizers in the $7.25 to $9 range and main courses from $9.50 for grilled baby chicken with field salad and warm mushroom vinaigrette to $21.50 for grilled veal chop with garlic-mashed potatoes and red onion marmalade. This is the place for those who find that the main Chillingsworth dining room serves more food than they can eat, or who don't like precise seatings at perhaps awkward hours.

Beyond the lounge, the **Le Bistro** gift shop offers many Chillingsworth specialties for sale. Nitzi calls it "a nice catering business without the delivery problems." The shop was crowded on a summer Sunday with tourists seeking to get a taste of Chillingsworth without paying full price. Frankly, we'd go all-out and splurge – the experience is worth the tab.

Upstairs, the Rabins offer three elegant guest rooms and suites for overnight stays. Rates are $95 to $135, B&B.

(508) 896-3640 or (800) 430-3640. Lunch in summer, Wednesday-Sunday 11:30 to 2:30; dinner by reservation, Tuesday-Sunday, seatings at 6 and 9; weekends only in spring and fall. Closed after Thanksgiving to Memorial Day.

The Regatta, Scranton Avenue, Falmouth.

One of the Cape's best waterfront locations, a jaunty pink and white decor, inventive food and a smashing wine list – it's little wonder that Upper Cape folks rate this long-established restaurant right up there with Chillingsworth and keep it consistently crowded and lively. And to offer New England specialties in an historic setting, owners Wendy and Brantz Bryan took on a year-round venture, the Regatta at Cotuit (see below), which some consider the best restaurant on Cape Cod.

The original Regatta takes its name, no doubt, from its location in a gray- shingled building with black and white awnings and a profusion of pink geraniums and purple impatiens beside Falmouth's inner harbor. The structure was totally rebuilt in 1992 after suffering severe damage during Hurricane Bob. Most of the 100 seats in the main dining room take advantage of the view.

Pink cloths, dusky rose napkins fanned in the water glasses, pink bows on the pillars and pink banquettes around the perimeter set the color scheme. Chairs and plates are white. Waitresses are outfitted in pink and waiters in black vests and bow ties. As the hurricane lamps are lit at dusk, the setting is colorful, to say the least.

Wendy Bryan is in charge of the wine list, which has many available by the glass since no hard liquor is served. The unusual selection, mainly French with a nod to California, is priced from the high teens to $250.

Appetizers ($6.50 to $9.50) are oriented toward the sea: grilled tiger shrimp with a sauce of three mustards and roasted corn chutney, pan-seared soft-shell crab with basil beurre blanc and grilled native calamari with ginger-wasabi sauce. We gobbled up a rich chilled lobster and sole terrine, served with a saffron sauce garnished with truffles, and loved the broiled Wellfleet oysters with black American caviar.

A complimentary sorbet follows the appetizer course. Our dinner could have ended happily there, but the entrées were equal to the task. The seafood fettuccine contained more shrimp, scallops, lobster and artichoke hearts than it did spinach pasta, and the seared Norwegian salmon came with oysters and a leek and chardonnay sauce. Vegetables, served on clear glass side plates, were two kinds of squash, piquant red cabbage and new potatoes.

Other entrées are priced from $20 for broiled citrus-cured salmon with lemon-lime butter sauce to $26.50 for the signature loin of lamb in puff pastry with cabernet sauce. On our latest visit we sampled a palette of two fish, each with its own sauce (yellowfin tuna with pinot noir sauce and roasted shallots, and swordfish with caramelized-lemon and white-butter sauce), and the grilled breast of pheasant.

Gallery dining room at Abbicci features hand-drawn maps of Italy on walls.

Desserts ($4.50 to $7.50) are inventive as well: among them, a towering Nantucket oatmeal spice cake with rum-caramel sauce, strawberry napoleon with a mascarpone anglaise, and a selection of homemade ice creams and sorbets. Best bet is a tasting trilogy of three favorites ($9). Ours brought a chocolate truffle cake, almond torte with framboise sauce and hand-dipped chocolate strawberries. With dessert comes coffee in delicate cups.

The nautical flags fluttering outside in the breeze are a wonderful sight, matched by the colorful trousers of Brantz Bryan, who explains that he wears them "to make people laugh and feel at ease." He and Wendy were the first high-end restaurateurs on our travels to anticipate the economic slowdown, holding the line on prices and even reducing them at the low end following the 1987 stock-market crash. Since rebuilding following the hurricane, they have added three-course early dinners for $19.97, available before 6 p.m., as well as a lighter menu with entrées priced at $14.95 and $15.95. Perhaps such flexibility is why the Bryans have been so successful at the Regatta for nearly 30 years.

(508) 548-5400. Dinner nightly, 4:30 to 10, Memorial Day to mid-September.

Abbicci, 43 Main St. (Route 6A), Yarmouth Port.

Veteran Cape restaurateur Marietta Hickey took over the beloved Cranberry Moose in 1989, returning to the town where she had founded La Cipollina down the street. But, she said, the Moose never really prospered in its New American realm. She longed to restore Italian fare but did not want to compete with La Cipollina. The opportunity arose in 1992 when La Cipollina was sold to become a Japanese restaurant. The Cranberry Moose closed for redecoration and a reconfiguration of the kitchen. The restaurant reopened with a new name, a new look and a new menu. And a new lease on life.

"Business is up bigtime," says Marietta, "even though the average check has dropped." No longer merely a special-occasion place, Abbicci offers a variety of dining options. Locals crowd into the 75 seats in four dining areas for food that consistently ranks among the Cape's best.

The kitchen executes an ambitious menu created by Marietta, who oversees the front of the house. A dozen entrées are priced from $14.95 for calves liver veneziana to $27.50 for grilled veal chop with mushrooms. Options include grilled fillet of salmon with scallion cream and port wine demi-glace, seafood stew, braised rabbit, osso buco and pistachio-crusted rack of lamb with a red wine and shallot demi-glace. Fresh asparagus, haricots verts or sautéed spinach come with.

The antipasti and pastas ($14.95 to $19.95) are first-rate, especially the lobster and scallop ravioli. Desserts are to die for, especially the mascarpone with crisp phyllo and fresh berries, the lemon mousse topped with blueberries, and the apricot dacquoise. Finish with the seductive Abbicci cappuccino, a heavily liqueured concoction that may just finish you off. The extensive wine list is heavily Italian, well chosen in a broad price range.

We returned lately for a lunch that got off to a shaky start with too-loud jazz playing in the background and niggardly glasses of white wine for $4. Things improved with crumbly, piping-hot rolls and our main choices: a kicky steak sandwich with arugula, gorgonzola and grain mustard served open faced on grilled country bread ($9.95) and an assertive linguini and shellfish ($9.50), with all kinds of vegetables from squash and peppers to tomatoes and asparagus. Warm raisin gingerbread with lemon mousse and applejack brandy sauce was a memorable dessert.

The decor is spare, with splashes of yellow and blue amid the prevailing white walls, white tablecloths and an array of cactus plants. The subdued maps of Italy on the walls were hand-drawn by Marietta's son, a San Francisco architect who oversaw Abbicci's redesign.

(508) 362-3501. Lunch daily, 11:30 to 2:30; dinner nightly, 5 to 9 or 10; Sunday buffet brunch, 11:30 to 2:30.

The Red Pheasant Inn, 905 Main St. (Route 6A), Dennis.

The exterior is strictly old New England – a rambling, red, 200-year-old saltbox house and barn. Inside is a reception area-living room (used for wine tastings), a couple of dining rooms and an enclosed porch, a mix of bentwood chairs and white linens, barnwood and walls with painted flowers, hanging plants and flickering oil lamps. It's a very comfortable place with tables well spaced, background music at the right level and the service deft and unobtrusive.

The food is on the cutting edge, with inspired touches of regional New England cuisine. The creative hand in the kitchen belongs to chef Bill Atwood Jr., son of the founder, who left the stove to manage the front of the house with Bill's wife Denise. The Atwoods have been involved in the Red Pheasant since 1977.

Bill, elected to the Master Chefs of America, says his efforts have evolved over the years into a Cape Cod cuisine with "a truly local flavor." He smokes his own bluefish and cod cakes, mixes local cod and calamari in new presentations, makes smoked-venison sausage and stuffs quails with duck sausage.

For starters ($5 to $10), we were impressed with a caesar salad as good as we can make at home and the fried goat-cheese raviolis, an incredibly smooth-tasting presentation on a lovely tomato coulis, with asparagus spears and frizzles of leek radiating out. Other choices might include carpaccio of venison, grilled shrimp with a spicy onion and roast red pepper confit, and rillettes of salmon with its roe on field greens.

Among main courses ($15 to $24) were cedar-planked salmon with chive beurre blanc, pan-roasted sesame sea bass, tuna niçoise, grilled veal chop with portobello mushrooms, and native bouillabaisse in a tomato-saffron broth, served in custom-designed bowls from the nearby Scargo Pottery. Our choices could not have been better: roast boneless Long Island duckling served with a rhubarb, dried cherry and caramelized-ginger sauce, and grilled pavé of beef with fried oysters, wrapped in leeks with bordelaise sauce. Side plates carried different assortments of grilled and roasted vegetables, including sliced potatoes, zucchini, yellow squash and green tomatoes, as well as some barely cooked green beans. Our only disapppointment was an over-battered, tough asparagus spring roll that came with the duck.

We were too full to sample the desserts, which for a warm summer night seemed rather heavy. Typical choices are sacher torte and linzertorte, Mom Atwood's rich and creamy cheesecake and profiteroles.

The distinguished wine list, priced starting in the high teens, has been cited by Wine Spectator.

(508) 385-2133. Dinner nightly, 5 to 8:30 or 9. Reduced schedule in winter.

The Bramble Inn & Restaurant, Route 6A, Box 807, Brewster 01631.

White linens, stunning floral china in the Victoria pattern from Czechoslovakia, candles in hurricane lamps and assorted flowers in vases grace the five small dining

rooms seating a total of 60 at this inn renowned for its restaurant. Ruth and Cliff Manchester, who got their start at his parents' Old Manse Inn nearby, have continued the tradition launched by former owners Karen Etsell and Elaine Brennan, who wrote the book on "How to Open a Country Inn" and soon afterward sold to pursue their artistic and antiquing interests.

The Manchesters' chief interest is the restaurant, and they have shed some of their inn rooms lately. Ruth is an inventive cook, whose four-course, prix-fixe dinners ($43 to $52, depending on choice of entrée) draw a devoted following and rave press reviews. Her soups are triumphs: perhaps chilled cherry with port and crème fraîche, four-

Front dining room at Bramble Inn.

onion soup with brie croutons or a lettuce and scallion bisque. Other starters might be seafood seviche, grilled oysters in prosciutto, an artistic smoked seafood palette "with painter's spatter sauce," and grilled venison sausage on a warm lentil salad. We were impressed with a unique dish, New England seafood chili: cod, clams and tuna in a spicy tomato sauce with black beans, jack cheese and sour cream.

The seven main-course choices could include grilled fillet of Atlantic salmon, seafood stew, filet mignon with roquefort cream and, a novel twist on surf and turf, parchment-roasted chicken breast with a grilled chicken lobster, served with lobster and champagne sauce. A signature dish – assorted seafood curry – combines lobster, cod, scallops and shrimp in a light curry sauce with banana, coconut, almonds and chutney.

Among desserts are white-chocolate coeur à la crème (a recipe requested by Bon Appétit magazine), dense chocolate terrine, bourbon pecan tart and a treat called lemon damask, a toasted coconut butter pastry filled with silky lemon mousse and berry chambord consommé.

The small, paneled Hunt Room houses a service bar. The limited but serviceable wine list offers good values.

Upstairs in the main 1861 house are three guest rooms with sloping floors, furnished in a comfortable country style. Five more rooms are in the 1849 House, a Greek Revival structure two doors away. All have private baths. Guests enjoy a full breakfast on the cheery dining porch of the main inn.

In 1996, Ruth's daughter, Suzanne Plum, who had worked with her mother for two years in the kitchen at the Bramble Inn, returned to the family's early beginnings when she and her husband purchased the nine-room Old Manse Inn from her grandparents. They planned to operate the restaurant as **Plum's Cafe.** Meanwhile, daughter Elise Cox continued the family tradition, joining her mother in the Bramble Inn kitchen.

(508) 896-7644. Dinner nightly by reservation, 6 to 9, Wednesday-Sunday in spring and fall. Closed January to May. Doubles, $95 to $125.

The Regatta of Cotuit, 4631 Falmouth Road (Route 28), Cotuit.

This elegant restaurant in a handsome 1790 Federal-style house has been lovingly run for ten years by Wendy and Brantz Bryan of the Regatta in Falmouth. "You couldn't have two more extremes," admitted Wendy. While the Falmouth restaurant features seafood and is summery, New Yorkish and on the waterfront, the Cotuit venture serves up regional dishes and Americana on a year-round basis. It has a full bar and a broad new tavern menu.

Seven dining rooms, one with only two tables, are beautifully appointed in shades of pink and green, with authentic print wallpapers, needlepoint rugs and furnishings of the period. Tables are set with pink and white Limoges china, crystal glassware and fine silver.

Chef Heather Allen has helped the Regatta earn a reputation for fine dining every bit as stellar as that of Chillingsworth, which is more widely known.

Entrées are priced from $17.95 for roasted Chatham cod with pan-seared rock shrimp to $26 for grilled ribeye steak with maitre-d'hôtel butter. Among the possibilities are seared sesame-crusted swordfish steak with a scallop and shrimp farci, broiled apple-smoked salmon with lemon-tarragon vinaigrette, roasted Long Island duck with madeira port glaze and seared filet mignon with a stilton and rosemary crust. Specials could range from soft-shell crabs to seared tenderloin of buffalo or elk.

Among starters ($6.50 to $9) are grilled tiger shrimp in a crispy wonton cup with sweet and sour sauce, sautéed crab cakes with basil aioli, and grilled portobello mushrooms with herbed chèvre. The brandied lobster bisque with a confetti of lobster and fresh chervil also merits attention. Desserts are similar to those of the Regatta at Falmouth, including house-made ice creams and sorbets and a trilogy of three favorites ($9). The chocolate seduction on a lovely patterned raspberry sauce and the crème brûlée garnished with red and gold raspberries and blackberries are among the best we've tasted.

Wendy and Brantz Bryan outside Regatta of Cotuit.

The Regatta's lighter fare menu is perfect for grazing. It modifies some of the regular appetizers, salads and entrées, at prices from $5 to $16.50. Most are under $10.

The wine list, which emphasizes good reds, is priced from the high teens.

(508) 428-5715. Dinner nightly, from 5, 4:30 to 8:30 in winter.

More Good Dining

Inaho Japanese Restaurant, 157 Route 6A, Yarmouth Port.

The little white house that long harbored La Cipollina restaurant is the home of a Japanese restaurant that relocated from Hyannis. Ugi Wantanabe, who had worked as a sushi chef in New York and Newport, and his Portuguese-American wife Alda live upstairs, in the European fashion, and travel every other day to Boston for fresh fish and provisions.

A long sushi bar where singles can be comfortable faces one wall of the rear dining room; three Japanese-looking booths flank the other. The far end is all windows gazing onto a courtyard garden, where spotlights focus on a few Japanese plantings (the Japanese garden in front seemed to be thriving better at our visit). There are two front dining rooms as well. The bare wood tables topped only with chopsticks and napkins hint that here you'll find the real thing.

An order of gyoza dumplings staved off hunger as we nursed a bottle of Chalk Hill sauvignon blanc from a small but well chosen wine list. One of us sampled the nine-piece sushi plate for $15; the sushi was fresh and delicious. The other was pleased with the bento box ($16) yielding salad, a skewer of chicken teriyaki, tempura and a California roll. Sashimi, teriyaki, tempura and katsu items completed the menu, priced from $12 to $17. Also available are shabu shabu and sushi special dinners, $36 to $39 for two. Desserts included a frozen chocolate cake as thick as fudge, served with vanilla ice cream, and a poached pear on ice cream with ginger sauce. But we could not be dissuaded from our favorite ginger ice cream, rendered here to perfection.

(508) 362-5522. Dinner nightly except Monday, from 5.

Aardvark, 134 Route 6A, Yarmouth Port.

Upon opening in late 1995, this homey little restaurant in a gingerbread house became so popular that a policeman had to direct traffic in and out of the parking lot. The two owners started it as a coffee shop but soon evolved into cooking what chef Joshua Blakely called "North American cuisine with seasonal ingredients." Along with countless flavors of coffees and teas, espressos and lattes, there's full bar service with a couple of special drinks featured every day, taken in four small dining rooms and a porch.

Cotton bandannas depicting perhaps elephants or zucchini are under the glass-topped tables. Interesting local art adorns the walls, and lush desserts beckon from glass cases. Otherwise, decor is rather plain, with bare floors and windows.

At lunch, sandwiches like the Javaport (mixing hummus, tabbouleh, sunflower seeds, sprouts, carrots and greens) and roast turkey with cranberry-orange chutney are in the $4 to $5 range. The long list of specials might include a terrific grilled chicken caesar roll-up or a tantalizing lemon-pepper penne tossed with mushrooms, sundried tomatoes, pinenuts and basil ($4.95 to $6.95). We thought the assertive gazpacho and the grilled chicken bulgur salad, brimming with tomatoes, olives, goat cheese and green beans, were sensational. And when a sort of cobbler/pie of strawberries, rhubarb and apples appeared on the countertop fresh from the oven, one of us couldn't resist a wedge ($3).

The dinner menu changes weekly. We'd gladly have made an entire meal of a couple of appetizers ($4.25 to $6) like roasted potato and garlic frittata with smoked gouda, grilled tomato and asparagus, and blackened cajun-spiced salmon with eggplant and roasted sweet pepper risotto. But then we'd miss such entrées ($12 to $16) as pan-roasted free-range chicken breast, white bean and grilled corn salsa with feta polenta, or grilled spicy jumbo shrimp skewers over saffron risotto with basil aioli.

Aardvark seems to have overcome the shortcomings of various predecessors that have failed at this location. Everyone obviously likes a welcoming place where one can stop in for coffee and dessert, take out some cookies or have an interesting meal.

(508) 362-9866. Breakfast, Monday-Saturday 7 to 10:30, Sunday 9 to 2; lunch, 11:30 to 3; dinner, Wednesday-Saturday 6 to 9.

The Brewster Fish House Restaurant, 2208 Route 6A, Brewster.

David and Vernon Smith took over what had been a retail fish market and converted it into one of the Cape's best seafood restaurants. For years it was so low-key that, despite countless trips through the area, we were unaware of its existence until a knowing innkeeper tipped us off. Good thing, for we found a simple but stylish little cafe where the young brothers, both self-taught chefs, man the kitchen and produce a satisfying array of treats incorporating the freshest fish available. And now, for some it's their favorite restaurant along the length of Route 6A.

Small and personal, this is a pure place – nothing like the take-a-number-and-hope-for-the-best of the ubiquitous fried-fish ilk. There's no meat on the menu, although one of the three nightly specials involves a beef, lamb or poultry dish. Otherwise it's all seafood, from $12 for fish and chips to $21 for steamed lobster with a shellfish garnish. In between are treats like grilled Atlantic salmon with spinach and prosciutto, broiled halibut with a plum-tomato and herb sauce, baked pollock under a horseradish crust with a grilled corn and red-onion salad, and walnut-crusted catfish sautéed with marsala wine. The mixed grill combines swordfish, shrimp, scallops and andouille sausage with an oriental dipping sauce. Specials at our latest visit were poached salmon with raspberry sauce and poached leeks, and grilled tuna over bok choy with sesame-soy sauce. Three pastas can be ordered as appetizers or main courses.

All the appetizers save one – fried artichokes with a garlic and ginger ketchup – involve seafood. Dill-and-brandy-cured salmon, crab cake with a mixed fruit and bell-pepper marmalade, and fried calamari with a tomato and red-pepper aioli are favorites. Or you can start with chowder, lobster bisque or billi-bi.

The day's three desserts could be crème brûlée, flourless chocolate torte with raspberry sauce and roasted hazelnut cheesecake. The wine list is as well chosen as the rest of the menu, and many wines are available by the glass.

Dining is at white-clothed tables topped with glass, pinkish napkins, candles and fresh flowers. Classical music or soft jazz plays in the background.

(508) 896-7867. Lunch daily, 11:30 to 3; dinner, 5 to 9:30 or 10; closed Monday in off-season. Open April-November.

The Arbor, Route 28 at Route 6A, Orleans.

Our kind of food – meaning assertive and out of the ordinary – is served in this old sea captain's house with an attached barn. The several dining rooms (one on a porch with slanting floor, one in a paneled room with a fireplace, one in a quiet back room with four tables for two) are unusual, to say the least. Decor is sort of early-to-late attic; the owners scour flea markets, especially Brimfield, and have they got a collection! From old toys to 1,000 early cans, the stuff covers every possible surface. Even the tablecloths are flowered cotton like those our grand-mothers used to have in the kitchen – each is different and has to be ironed on a mangle. It's funky but charming, and the food is highly regarded.

With the extensive menu came a tray decorated with grapes and bearing three small glasses of the wines of the night, so you could taste before you chose – a nice idea that, we regretted to learn, has been discontinued. We ordered a glass of the chardonnay ($3) and liked it enough that we ordered a bottle. The wine cellar is extensive with a special list of rare bottles priced in the hundreds of dollars. A complimentary tray of pickled peppers and crudités with a dip as well as large buttermilk biscuits sustained us until we could dig into the appetizer, a hot seafood platter ($9.95 for two). Two each of clams casino, oysters rockefeller, crab-stuffed mushrooms and stuffed mussels were delicious. A good caesar salad and a house salad of romaine with crushed pineapple and shredded carrots with a honey-fennel dressing preceded the entrées.

The choice embraces a staggering 41 items, from five pastas and five veal dishes to five cajun-style offerings and three of "the Arbor's best" – two preparations of lobster and one of pasta, each bearing a name (including lobster Kendall for the late co-owner Kendall Bowers). The prices are $13.95 to $18.95, and you wonder how they can do it so cheaply, as well as how they can succeed so handsomely with so extensive a repertoire.

One of us had bouillabaisse, which came in a huge crock – it was crammed with so much seafood she could eat only about a quarter of it, and was given a doggy bag (make that a plastic Stop & Shop container) to take home. The other had oysters and scallops Stephen in a cream sauce on pasta and loved it. A shared dessert of a meringue shell filled with coffee ice cream and praline sauce was heavenly.

Don't be put off by the exterior of the Arbor and its grotto-like **Binnacle Tavern,** all covered with buoys. Inside is some mighty interesting food.

(508) 255-4847. Dinner nightly, 5 to 10, weekends only in off-season. Closed January to Valentine's Day.

Christian's, 443 Main St., Chatham.

Chef Christian Schultz's family endeavor has grown from something of a summer lark into a year-round venture with the popular Upstairs at Christian's, a classic English bar and lounge, and an outdoor deck for drinks and light eating.

The fare, long ranked among the Cape's best, has been downscaled lately. The Schultzes found seats in the two more formal downstairs dining areas going begging while lines were waiting to get into the casual, reasonably priced upstairs. Now basically one menu serves all, and it follows the cutesy cinema theme of the upstairs, with every item named for a movie. The garlicky shrimp with fettuccine and parmesan that we remember from earlier days is now called, inexplicably, "Divorce Italian Style," and the medallions of veal sautéed with shrimp, garlic, lemon and white wine, a memorable presentation at the time, is "Two for the Road."

Christian hasn't lost his cooking touch, however. Among entrées ($9.50 to $16.50) he might present grilled lamb loins with two sauces, pair his grilled swordfish with an anchovy, tuna and garlic sauce, and season his pork tenderloin with Jamaican jerk. You can order basic (roasted chicken over buttermilk biscuits with homemade gravy and mashed potatoes) or exotic (lobster, shrimp and scallops tossed with scallions, garlic, artichoke hearts, mushrooms and sundried tomatoes over penne).

Clams casino, cod cakes on a red pepper mayonnaise, and fiery crab and corn fritters are among the appetizers. Caesar salads can be topped with chicken, shrimp, scallops or poached salmon to make a light meal. Desserts have been scaled down from the trio of mousses and a grand-marnier torte topped with a chocolate shell filled with grand marnier that we recall fondly from meals past.

The settings remain the same. Oriental rugs dot the floors and woven cloths cover the tables in two non-smoking dining rooms, one of them an enclosed porch, on the main floor. The atmosphere in Upstairs at Christians is like dining in a library, what with African mahogany paneling, shelves full of books, a handsome homemade curved oak bar, and a distinctive mix of eaves and niches with tables, chairs and a few loveseats. In addition to the downstairs menu, you can order pizzas and burgers. The food remains creative at times, although we must say our latest lunch on the canopied upstairs deck was on the pedestrian side.

(508) 945-3362. Lunch upstairs in summer, 11:30 to 3; dinner nightly, 5 to 10, upstairs and down. Downstairs closed Columbus Day to May. Upstairs open fewer days in winter.

The Impudent Oyster, 115 Chatham Bars Ave., Chatham.

With a name like the Impudent Oyster, how could this small restaurant miss? An avid local following jams together at small, glass-covered tables under a skylit cathedral ceiling, beneath plants in straw baskets balancing overhead on the beams.

The changing international menu, based on local seafood, blends regional, French, Mexican, Chinese and Italian cuisines, among others.

Dining porch at Christian's in Chatham.

We couldn't resist starting with the drunken mussels, shelled and served in an intense marinade of tamari, fresh ginger, Szechuan peppercorns and sake. The Mexican chicken, chile and lime soup, spicy and full of interesting flavors, was one of the best we've tasted. Other unusual starters ($5.95 to $7.95) could be curried mussel stew, oysters sardinia, shrimp simmered in garlic with red chiles, swordfish and avocado seviche, and Caribbean plantains served with a fresh mango and papaya salsa.

Entrées run from $14.95 to $23.95 (for a house specialty, bouillabaisse). Grilled yellowfin tuna in soy sauce and cumin, celestial oysters poached in champagne and mixed seafood fra diavolo over fettuccine are some of chef-owner Peter Barnard's changing offerings. Local seafood is highlighted. Many of the preparations have been simplified lately, but you might find a pasta with grilled duck, chicken saltimbocca, Szechuan beef sauté and a mesclun salad garnished with grilled shrimp, tuna and chicken. At one visit we liked the feta and fennel scrod (a Greek dish touched with ouzo) and the swordfish broiled with orange and pepper butter. A plate of several ice creams made with fresh fruits was a cooling dessert.

Creativity extends to the wine list, which, like the food, is reasonably priced (some in the mid-teens, with a few up to $50), and to the lunch menu with a changing array of salads, sandwiches and entrées. Some of this is the exciting kind of food of which we never tire, although we might prefer to have it in more tranquil and less crowded surroundings.

(508) 945-3545. Lunch daily, 11:30 to 3; dinner, 5:30 to 10.

Campari's, 352 Main St., Chatham.

Talented chef Bob Chiappetta cooks in an open kitchen in this pleasant Italian bistro in the Dolphin inn and motel. By day it's the Bittersweet Cafe, serving breakfast. At night it turns dark and intimate as diners partake at tables covered with black-checked cloths and candles in chianti bottles amid hanging plants, two working fireplaces and a couple of prominently displayed aquariums. Italian opera music plays in the background. Cocktails are served in summer at Alfresco's, an appealing screened porch in front.

The kitchen, open to the dining room and imparting tantalizing odors throughout, resembles the household kitchen it once was. It provides inspiration and recreates childhood memories for Bob, who recalls watching with interest the preparation of family meals in various regions of Italy. His short menu reflects such ethnic specialties ($17 to $25) as changing raviolis, broiled swordfish siciliana served with capellini, chicken tuscano, veal pepperonata and scampi luciano, the last a mix of tiger prawns and lobster meat served with wine-simmered mussels on a bed of capellini. Soup and salad come with. Crab cakes parmigiana, baked artichokes with prosciutto and three cheeses, grilled crostini and risottos are possible starters ($4 to $8). Bob's wife Lisa prepares the desserts, perhaps chocolate chip and almond cannolis or zabaglione cream with fresh fruit. She also oversees the short Italian wine list.

As if they weren't busy enough with breakfast and dinner, the couple also operate **Carmine's,** a cappuccino and pizza place with Italian pastries, desserts and gelatos in the Galleria at 595 Main St., Chatham.

(508) 945-9123. Breakfast daily, 8 to 1; dinner nightly except Monday, 6 to 9; off-season, Wednesday-Saturday 6 to 9.

The Cape Sea Grille, 31 Sea St., Harwich Port.

A few tables on the sun porch in this former sea captain's house offer a view of the ocean down the street. The scene inside the pale yellow and green main dining room is handsome as well with white linens and lalique-style lamps atop nicely spaced tables. It's a serene setting for some highly regarded food offered by chef-owner Jim Poitras and his fiancée, Beth Bryde.

Both working in the kitchen (they met while cooking in Miami), the couple have changed the emphasis from country French to new American since they took over the old Cafe Elizabeth in 1994. They offer a dozen straightforward entrées nightly from $13.95 to $22.75. Pastas could be grilled shrimp and penne carbonara with sugar snap peas, and angel hair with clams, roasted garlic and cilantro pesto. Seafood choices include crispy sole piccata with lemon and tomatoes, roasted salmon glazed with creole mustard, seafood paella over toasted pasta, and a mixed grill of swordfish, lobster, salmon and barbecued shrimp. Meat-eaters can opt for crisp roasted duck, Mediterranean-style chicken stuffed with sundried tomatoes and goat cheese, or grilled tenderloin with roquefort butter and toasted pecans.

Seared tuna marinated with ginger and orange over field greens is a favorite starter, as are the shrimp and vegetable tempura, Wellfleet oysters with a ginger-shallot mignonette, and roasted corn and cod chowder. Desserts ($4.50) include twin brûlées (one vanilla, one espresso), lime pie with banana whipped cream, and warm apple tart with cinnamon sauce and vanilla bean ice cream.

On busy nights, the rear garden room that used to be a country lounge is opened for overflow. It's a delightful space with a remarkable, full-length mural of a Cape Cod scene on the far wall.

(508) 432-4745. Dinner nightly from 5; closed Tuesday in spring and fall. Closed November-March.

Chapaquoit Grill, 410 West Falmouth Hwy. (Route 28A), West Falmouth.

People wait up to two hours on busy nights for one of the 95 seats in this trendy but affordable grill. A no-reservations policy means the tables turn up to four times a night, says chef Carl Bonnert. The throngs don't seem to mind, although local gourmands say they would prefer less of a wait and less of a rush once they're seated.

But the owners of the Chappy, as it's called, are on to something hot: Wood-fired pizzas from a huge brick oven that occupies an open room off the entry, "big-flavored" appetizers and entrées, specials that are really special and a good wine list with nearly every choice priced under $20.

Unassuming on the outside, the place is much bigger than it looks (and encompasses a basic cafe alongside for daytime coffee, pastries, sandwiches and pizzas). The main building has a bar and waiting area and a large rear dining room with a vaguely tropical theme: splashy patterned cloths on the widely spaced tables, colorful sea prints on the salmon-colored walls and the odd fish silhouette hanging from a trellis screening the two-story-high ceiling. The printed menu offers appetizers like littleneck clams steamed Portuguese style, deep-fried calamari, caesar salad and the chef's antipasti. Entrées range from $5.50 for linguini marinara or bolognese to $12.95 for shrimp creole. Specialty pizzas are available in small ($5.50 to $7.50) and large ($9.95 to $12.95) sizes,. They include margherita, shrimp diavolo, southwestern and the chef's favorite – grilled chicken with broccoli, mushrooms and provolone.

The specials board generates the most excitement. Consider a few of one night's selections ($10.95 to $15.95): snapper marinated in tequila and ginger and served with coconut mango relish, cumin-rubbed swordfish with roasted jalapeño butter, roasted coffee-encrusted pork tenderloin with raspberry and hoisin sauce, and chargrilled sirloin marinated in tequila and cilantro with a chipotle demi-glace.

Desserts follow suit: a classic tirami su, mango cheesecake with macadamia-nut crust, exotic gelatos and sorbets made by a person down the road.

"We keep things changing so people will come back," says Carl. That they certainly do.

(508) 540-7794. Dinner nightly, 5 to 10, pizzas weekends until 11. Cafe, Monday-Saturday 8 to 5.

Offbeat Gourmet

Stir Crazy, 626 MacArthur Blvd., Pocasset.

A couple of the Cape's leading restaurateurs tipped us off to this endearing little place dispensing Cambodian and Vietnamese "gourmet cuisine." It's a real find, they said. It's also hard to find, identified by a computer store and Village Realty along Route 28 three miles south of the Bourne Bridge. People heading to and from Falmouth and the islands consider it a rewarding stop.

Tantalizing aromas wafted from the semi-open kitchen as we debated whether to pause for a late lunch. "That's the best choice you ever made," the waitress of the old school advised when we finally sat down. "The food is fabulous."

The place fulfills the dream of Bopha Samms, who lost sixteen members of her family in Cambodia before she and four siblings fled to the United States. After working in a variety of Cape restaurants, she opened her own in 1989 in Buzzard's Bay. People came, especially for the stir-fries that inspired the name, and in 1993 she moved to this "bigger place, closer to home."

The bigger place holds 24 seats, and a lively young son had just gotten off the school bus as Bopha returned to the kitchen to cook for customers who arrived as lunch was ending. We were impressed with the luncheon special of shrimp khemara ($6.25). It arrived in a plain white bowl, a mound of hot rice hidden beneath a salad topped with six jumbo shrimp and a scallion and peanut sauce. Who would have guessed that rice and iceberg lettuce alone, dressed with a zesty sauce, could taste so good? The shrimp were simply the extra fillip, and we could understand why the khemaras with chicken or tofu are staples on the menu.

We also knew why folks gobble up the dinner stir-fries and such Cambodian specialties ($7.95 to $10.95) as sirloin tips over watercress, marinated steak with vegetables and rice, spicy curry with chicken or shrimp and the house egg rolls. The marinades and dressings turn the ordinary into something quite exotic. Finish with palm fruit pudding, longan (tropical fruit) or key lime pie. Beer and wine are available.

(508) 564-6464. Lunch, Friday 11:30 to 2:30; dinner, Tuesday-Sunday 4 to 9 or 10.

Dining and Lodging

High Brewster, 964 Satucket Road, Brewster 01631.

Only a discreet sign in front of the large brown Colonial house on a hill with beautifully landscaped grounds gives a clue that this is more than someone's private home. And for 25 years, it was indeed the home of William Arbuckle and Walter Hyde, two gentlemen in the old-fashioned sense of the word, who – with little fanfare, no advertising and much acclaim from those in the know – welcomed guests to their home for dinner four nights a week.

After the death of his partner, Walter ran the restaurant for a couple of seasons until he sold it in 1987 to pursue his painting and decorating interests. It was purchased first by absentee owners, who upgraded the guest rooms, installed a professional kitchen, extended the meal hours and hired good chefs and managers. In 1995, it was acquired by Timothy and Catherine Mundy from Pennsylvania, who switched careers to be in residence at what they bill as "a classic country inn celebrating American cuisine."

The dining experience in the shingled house overlooking Lower Mill Pond remains the essence of Cape Cod, much as it was when we first ate here. Chef Kevin Jamieson's fare straddles both contemporary and classic lines, as in his treatment of the duck entrée: grilled breast with corn sticks and cranberry vinaigrette, served either as a salad atop baby field greens or traditionally with summer vegetables and potatoes. The four-course dinner is prix-fixe, $32 to $42, depending on choice of entrée ($52 in the case of lobster). At a recent visit, you could start with spicy grilled shrimp and scallops with mint and melon salsa, seared ahi tuna on spicy greens with wasabi-tomato vinegar or pan-seared quail with roasted corn and black bean relish. Following a salad of mixed field greens with citrus vinaigrette, the eight main-course choices included grilled swordfish drizzled with shiitake butter, grilled game hen with scallion-curry sauce and roasted rack of lamb with watercress demi-glace. Dessert could be fresh berry tart, crème caramel, chocolate cheesecake or chocolate mousse.

Traditionally, High Brewster lacked a liquor license but allowed patrons to bring their own. Now it serves beer and wine, inside in the cozy lounge or outside in summer on a small terrace overlooking the scenic pond. The wine choices are mostly $30 and up, although High Brewster's private-label chardonnay and cabernet are good bets at $24.

Outdoor terace at High Brewster looks toward Lower Mill Pond.

The 18th-century Cape Cod house, its age wearing well, contains three cozy, low-ceilinged dining rooms seating a total of 75. Tables are of deeply polished dark wood, and those in the keeping room are set with crisp off-white linens and Blue Willow tableware. Dark beams, wide paneling and barn boards are displayed to advantage by candlelight and track lights, as are the oil paintings and antiques all around.

Upstairs are two refurbished guest rooms with private baths, sloping ceilings and a lived-in, historic feel. Outside are an efficiency cottage for two as well as two fireplaced houses sleeping up to four adults, rented by the night or week. A substantial continental breakfast is included in the rates.

(508) 896-3636 or (800) 203-2634. Dinner nightly by reservation, 5:30 to 9, Memorial Day to Columbus Day; Wednesday-Sunday in off-season. Closed January-March. Doubles, $90 and $110; cottage and houses, $150 to $210.

Wequassett Inn, Pleasant Bay, Chatham 02633.

Cape Cod has perhaps no more majestic water view amid more elegant surroundings than from the restored, 18th-century "square top" sea captain's mansion that houses this venerable inn's dining room.

Floor-to-ceiling windows on three sides is all the decor necessary in the expansive main dining room that looks quite summery with rose-cushioned chairs, linens from France and oil lamps. A new, two-tiered garden deck off the lounge is a treat for lunch or cocktails overlooking Pleasant Bay.

Fresh seafood and continental cuisine are the themes of longtime chef Frank McMullen, a Culinary Institute of America graduate who came here from Pier 66 in Fort Lauderdale. Our dinner began with a special terrine, one part scallop and the other part salmon, garnished with grapefruit and a tangy sauce, and escargots with pinenuts in puff pastry.

Among entrées ($18.25 to $22.75, except $32.50 for grilled lobster with steamed clams), we liked the grilled lamb loin marinated in garlic-rosemary mustard and the twin beef tenderloins with smoked cheddar sauce, both accessorized with crisp snow peas, carrots, cauliflower and roast potatoes. Other options were grilled swordfish with avocado cilantro and corn salsa, seafood linguini, Norwegian salmon dusted with star anise and baked on a cedar plank, and veal chop with port-scented sundried cranberries.

Desserts included cranberry mousse in an almond tuile with a red and white sauce underneath looking as lacy as a doily, and a frozen chambord mousse in a parfait glass. With all the candles lit and reflecting in the windows, it was a romantic atmosphere in which to linger over cappuccino and cordials.

We had only to amble off to our room, one of several in duplex cottages right by the bay, with a deck almost over the water. The 104 handsomely furnished rooms with all the amenities are in eighteen Cape-style cottages, motel buildings and condo-type facilities. They range from water-view suites to tennis villas with cathedral ceilings and private balconies overlooking the woods and courts.

(508) 432-5400 or (800) 225-7125. Fax (508) 432-1915. Lunch daily, 11:30 to 2; dinner, 6 to 10. Doubles, $255 to $360, suites $495, EP. Open May-October.

The Bradford Inn and Motel, 26 Cross St., Chatham 02633.

An exceptionally attractive motel-inn, this growing establishment with its cheery exterior of yellow awnings and fine gardens is well situated in a residential section just off Chatham's Main Street.

Always upgrading, innkeepers William and Audrey Gray added four deluxe rooms with fireplaces, canopy beds and TVs hidden in armoires in the Jonathan Gray House, which they built to look old and named Jonathan, Bill Gray explained, "because the name sounds old." They added the Lion's Den, a lounge for reading and games, and opened a two-bedroom cottage as the Captain's Hideaway. The adjacent Mulberry Inn is a deluxe B&B with two guest rooms, a suite and fireplaced parlor (doubles, $139 to $179). Their latest creation is the Azubah Atwood Inn at 177 Cross St., a circa 1789 sea captain's home that's the innkeepers' residence, with three queensize rooms with TVs and private baths for $135.

Five large rooms are in the Bradford House in front, which we found cozy with a fireplace on a fall evening, while four are in the Carriage House near the pool. Eleven more are in the L-shaped motel building in back. All are individually decorated and have private baths, television and phones.

A complimentary breakfast is served in the 1860 Captain Elijah Smith House, which serves as the office. Breakfast, also available to the public, includes choice of eggs (from omelets to eggs benedict), french toast and wonderful pancakes like cranberry or apple with cinnamon sugar and sour cream. Belgian waffles with bananas and pecans in brandy and brown sugar, made from scratch, are a highlight of the Sunday brunch.

Guests linger over coffee on the garden patio beside the small pool, savoring the extravagant roses and watching the birds feed.

With the opening of **Champlain's,** the Grays added two more dining areas to the original poolside breakfast room. The full-service restaurant is homespun with Hitchcock chairs, white woven mats over mulberry cloths, captain's chairs, a fireplace and a couple of saltwater aquariums that "everyone likes to watch," says Audrey. The Grays' son, Robert, is chef for the dining venture named for explorer Samuel de Champlain, who sailed into Chatham's Stage Harbor in 1606.

His extensive dinner menu is priced from $19.95 for fire-roasted breast of chicken or baked Chatham scrod to $24.95 for rack of lamb. Grilled salmon, lobster crumb pie, scallops barbados, chargrilled breast of duck and filet mignon are other possibilities. Meals include breads, salad, sorbet, starch and vegetables. Dessert could be a meringue glacé or a tart apple-cranberry pie with french vanilla ice cream.

(508) 945-1030 or (800) 562-4667. Fax (508) 945-9652. Breakfast, 8 to 11; dinner nightly in season, 5:30 to 9:30. Doubles, $139 to $249.

Wedgewood Inn at Yarmouth Port occupies restored 1812 house.

Lodging

Wedgewood Inn, 83 Main St. (Route 6A), Yarmouth Port 02675.

Built in 1812, this distinguished white house with black shutters was restored from top to bottom in 1983. The result was one of the first in the new breed of Cape Cod B&Bs offering superior lodging.

All six air-conditioned guest rooms are spacious with private baths and sitting areas. A third-floor room affords a view of Cape Cod Bay. The two main-floor rooms have screened porches and one has a separate sitting room. Four rooms hold working fireplaces and pencil-post beds. All are comfortably and artfully furnished with quilts, wing chairs, oriental rugs on wide-board floors and spiffy period wallpapers, mostly in shades of Wedgwood blue, pink and white. A charming rear room with a double and single bed is done in Laura Ashley style. Fresh flowers and fruit are in each room, and a tea tray with munchies is offered about 4 p.m.

The cream-colored dining room is particularly attractive, with windsor chairs at tables for two set with china patterned with swallows (from the Country Diary of an Edwardian Lady) and sunlight streaming through a plant-filled bow window.

Four kinds of pastries, cold cereals, fresh fruit and yogurt are set out on the sideboard for breakfast. Guests have a choice of scrambled eggs, french toast or belgian waffles.

Innkeepers Gerrie and Milton Graham (she a former teacher and he a retired FBI agent who played pro football with the Ottawa Rough Riders and the old Boston Patriots) have added Williamsburg gardens and a walk leading to a new entry and common room with oriental rugs, a small TV and a Colonial air. Lately, they built a gazebo in the perennial gardens, and were adding three large and luxurious suites, each with kingsize bed, TV, fireplace, soaking tub and balcony or patio, in a rear barn.

(508) 362-5157. Doubles, $125 to $165; suites, $175.

Cobb's Cove, Powder Hill Road, Barnstable Village 02630.

Down a country lane off Route 6A, this house was built to look old in 1974 by engineer Henry Chester, whose wife Evelyn is innkeeper.

You can tell they have a sense of humor when you see the Scargo Pottery bird feeder in the back garden. It's a replica of St. Basil's in the Kremlin and the birds (including "Cardinal Richelieu") really flock to it.

In the dining room/library is a piano surrounded by a fascinating collection of books of all kinds, many of the coffee-table variety. Behind it is the Keeping Room with its Count Rumford fireplace, unusually shallow and designed to send out much heat, and beyond that is the sunny terrace where guests keep an eye on the many feathered visitors.

Six unusually large guest rooms are on two floors. The honeymoon suites on the third floor afford spectacular views of Barnstable Harbor and Cape Cod Bay, each with two chairs in front of a huge window from which to enjoy it. Windows dip to the floors in all the rooms. Most walls are of barnsiding for a pleasantly rustic look, the floors are tiled and the closets huge. King or queensize beds, loveseats or wing chairs, antiques, pottery, vases of pampas grass, baskets of pine cones, terrycloth robes, magazines and bowls of nuts make each room special. Bathrooms are modern and sometimes divided; each tub has a whirlpool, and Pears soap and bath oil are provided.

Guests are served wine in the afternoon and a full breakfast, sometimes peach crêpes with mint, fish cakes with scrambled eggs or french toast made with raisin-nut bread.

Outspoken Henry, in his other guise as Henri-Jean, serves dinners by request to groups of six to eight or more. The gala five-course meal with wine ($50 a head) could include Portuguese soup, asparagus vinaigrette, a whole bass garnished with herbs from the garden, salad and a fruit tart or crème caramel with espresso or sambuca-laced coffee.

"We try to get a full table," says Evelyn. "The fun is having our guests sitting down together." Knowing the Chesters, it would be a lively dinner party indeed. *(508) 362-9356. Doubles, $169 to $189.*

Ashley Manor, 3660 Olde Kings Highway, Box 856, Barnstable 02630.

One of the more gracious houses on the north shore is a serene and elegant B&B with notable breakfasts prepared by innkeeper Don Bain, a dropout from the New York corporate scene.

In summer, breakfast is served on a delightful brick terrace in back of the house, with a fountain garden, a tennis court and spacious lawns beyond. In other seasons, guests breakfast by the fire on Chippendale chairs in the dining room, the original 1699 part of the house, with candles lit in crystal candelabra. It's a fairly elaborate affair – "almost like an early brunch," says Don – accompanied by the house coffee with "our own spices." We enjoyed watching the birds flit in and out of a remarkable Scargo cathedral birdhouse as we feasted on fresh orange juice, a stuffed baked apple, the best raspberry muffins we've ever tasted (Don even packed a couple to go), his delicious and not too sweet homemade granola and, the crowning glory, stuffed crêpes with farmer's cheese, strawberry sauce and sour cream. Other main courses include omelets that guests say are the world's best (light, soft and fluffy, with changing fillings), quiche and a french-toast sandwich with cream cheese, nuts and currants.

Both a keeping room and a well-furnished living room with a grand piano and three navy blue sofas contain fireplaces; the massive one in the living room has a

beehive oven. Decanters of wine, sherry and port are set out for guests. Five bedrooms are in the main house; a cottage out back comes with a small kitchenette. The spacious master bedroom in which we stayed on the main floor has a floor that is painted, stained and turpentined, giving it an elegant sheen; the same treatment is in the living room as well. By the fireplace in the master bedroom is a secret stairway to the second floor.

Upstairs are four bedrooms with private baths, three with working fireplaces and one with an outdoor balcony. All are welcoming, but we especially like the one with a kingsize canopy bed, a beautiful breakfront, two pumpkin-colored velvet wing chairs beside the fireplace, and deep

Outdoor breakfast at Ashley Manor.

blue wallpaper and bedspread. Interestingly furnished in antiques, all rooms have flowers, magazines, bedside candies, coffee and tea service, and wine glasses tied with white ribbons. Some rooms sport colorful Nantucket spackled floors.

The personable innkeeper serves fruit and nuts in the afternoon, and sometimes mingles with guests over wine and cheese.

(508) 362-8044. Doubles, $115 to $175.

Fox Glen Manor, 4011 Main St. (Route 6A), Cummaquid 02637.

Head down a dirt road past a horse pasture to this stately yellow Georgian Colonial manor house, reached via an exotic front courtyard that imparts a European air. Step inside and you're in the elegant home of retired antiques dealer Doug Kelly. Look out back, across the pool toward the pond, and you may be in nirvana. Doug and his brother built the mansion to hold their furnishings and fulfill their avocations, Doug to run a B&B and his brother to raise Morgan horses.

The house is part of five acres away from the highway and backing up to Flax Pond. It's an unexpected world of gardens, apple trees, horses and water. Common areas include three elegant living rooms, a little B&B kitchen where Doug whips up breakfast to serve at a table for ten in the dining room, and a rear terrace facing a swimming pool.

There's plenty of room for privacy and to spread out, as a couple of famous young Kennedys and their guests did in the two-bedroom upstairs suite in a new wing of the house. The retreat offers a living room with crown and dentil moldings, bedrooms with a poster queen and a canopied king, a modern bath and lots of oriental rugs atop ultra-thick carpeting. A private deck overlooks the apple orchard. The deck below, beneath the billowing tree branches, yields a view of the pond for occupants of a one-bedroom suite with a four-poster queen and a wet bar at the end of the living room. Other guest rooms are upstairs at the other end of the main house. The largest has a kingsize four-poster bed, wing chairs in front of the fireplace, more thick carpeting and sliding doors onto a big wicker porch overlooking pool and yard. The full bath includes a bidet. Two smaller rooms across the hall share a bath.

Breakfast is basically continental, since town regulations do not allow B&Bs to use an open stove. Doug gets around that in his little pantry/kitchen by serving belgian waffles from a portable waffle iron.

Best of all, considering the luxury and the country-house surroundings, are the rates.
(508) 362-4657. Fax (508) 362-3382. Doubles, $99 to $140. Closed November-April.

The Brewster Farmhouse Inn, 716 Main St. (Route 6A), Brewster 01631.

In an area where antiquity is cherished, it's refreshing to come across a country-modern B&B with a more contemporary feeling. Behind its prim and proper 1850 exterior is a smashingly remodeled and decorated California-type interior with a central cathedral ceiling. The airy main room has a dining area with a table for ten, where gourmet breakfasts are served, and a gathering room with comfortable sofas and chairs facing a fireplace. Oriental rugs accent the Mexican tile floors. Through sliding glass doors onto an enormous deck (where breakfast is taken in warm weather), one can see the large pool and hot tub. At the side are prolific flower and vegetable gardens.

Sophistication extends to the inn's creative brochure, which contains watercolors faithful to the facilities and colors of each room. The five guest air-conditioned rooms (three with private bath and two that share and can be rented individually or as a suite) are nothing short of gorgeous. One, up its own staircase, is a real hideaway with a hand-carved, queensize acorn bed and the two arm chairs that are the norm in all rooms. We fell for the main-floor garden room with a canopied, kingsize rice-carved bed, a comforter matching the valances and curtains, and its own private deck near the pool. Amenities include terrycloth robès, hair dryers, toiletries, sherry and chocolates at nightly turndown. Remote-control TVs are available in each room.

The breakfasts served by new innkeepers Carol and Gary Connors are a treat. At our visit, fresh melons and plums and a variety of breads and croissants preceded the main course, individual spinach quiches with sundried tomatoes. Pecan waffles, blueberry buttermilk pancakes and Portuguese sweet bread french toast were on the docket for later in the week. Gary, an amateur pastry chef who won an award for the best chocolate dessert in a contest in his native Delaware, prepares pastries for afternoon tea. They include chocolate torte, cheesecake and brownies.
(508) 896-3910 or (800) 892-3910. Fax (508) 896-4232. Doubles, $110 to $175; suite, $220.

The Captain Freeman Inn, 15 Breakwater Road, Brewster 02631.

The innkeeper teaches cooking classes at this twelve-room inn in an 1860s sea captain's home, grandly reborn in 1992 into a place of great comfort and warmth. Carol and Tom Edmonson, both formerly in computer marketing, reopened the inn following a total renovation. Trained by her grandmother, a professional chef, Carol conducts cooking schools on winter weekends. Participants take part in a hands-on Saturday afternoon class in which they prepare a four-course dinner to be served that evening. Her 1997 series featured the cuisines of Tuscany and the Mediterranean region. Some of the recipes are detailed in her new *The Captain Freeman Inn Cookbook.*

Guests share the bounty of her expertise at breakfast, the menu for which is placed in the rooms each day. At our visit it started with a variety of fresh juices, ginger-poached pears and exquisite little blueberry muffins served with crumbly

Conservatory sitting area at Nauset House Inn.

strawberry and orange/grand-marnier butters. Homemade oatmeal and cranberry granola accompanied. The main event was a prosciutto and cheddar quiche; other days could see eggs Brewster with a cranberry compote, prosciutto and tabasco-hollandaise sauce; cinnamon french toast with homemade blueberry-rum syrup, or homemade granola pancakes with dried cranberries and currants. Tom furnishes the herbs, wild berries and fruits from his gardens and trees on the two-acre property.

Guest rooms come in three configurations. The Orleans, with shiny, patterned inlaid parquet floors and a high, hand-carved ceiling medallion from Italy, is typical of the six mid-range rooms with private baths. It has a lace-canopy queensize bed, a reading area with a loveseat and a wing chair, and five tiny straw hats on the wall of a bathroom outfitted with Whitemor & Keach toiletries. Most deluxe are three air-conditioned suites at the rear, each with its own whirlpool spa on an enclosed balcony, a sitting area with fireplace, reading lamps with three-way bulbs, cable TV/VCR, telephone, mini-refrigerator, queensize canopy bed and full bath. Carol, who did the decorating, is partial to floral patterns, roman shades on the windows, lace swag curtains and straw hats. Three more rooms on the third floor share a hall bath and are available May-October only.

The common areas are comfortable as well, from the Victorian parlor to the fireplaced dining room to the wraparound veranda outfitted in wicker and wrought iron. Guests enjoy a swimming pool, woodland trails and a Victorian specimen garden along a hillside in back. They report the results of their dining ventures in a guest diary beside a basket full of menus. Afternoon refreshments might be iced tea or hot mulled cider with almond biscotti and a basket of fruit.

(508) 896-7481 or (800) 843-4664. Fax (508) 896-5618. Doubles, $95 to $135; suites, $205.

The Nauset House Inn, 143 Beach Road, Box 774, East Orleans 02643.

Here's a B&B with exceptional personality and character, reflecting the tastes and energies of its owners, Diane and Al Johnson, now joined by their daughter and son-in-law, Cindy and John Vessella.

Well-known for her stained-glass objects, artistic Diane has refurbished the inn with many of her works, and has painted artistic touches here and there. She and Cindy stenciled most of the sweet bedrooms where quilts, crewel work and afghans abound. Named for native wildflowers, eight of the fourteen rooms in the main inn and a couple of cottages have private bathrooms with showers. Diane painted a trompe-l'oeil cabinet on the wall of the Sea Oats Room to make it appear bigger. She painted a curtain for the bathroom window of the pale yellow Rosebud, which comes with a queen bed, rattan loveseat and two chairs plus a rear balcony enhanced by flowers in window boxes. The biggest room, the Beach Plum, has a kingsize bed and sofa with a crazy quilt on the wall. The most coveted accommodation is Outermost Cottage, where the bed is situated beneath a stained-glass window.

Breakfast ($5 extra per person, $3 for continental) is served in the beamed, brick-floored dining room with its huge open hearth, looking for all the world like a British pub. Guests have so enjoyed Diane's unusual treats (hardy sausage pie, potato casserole, strawberry frosty) that she has published the recipes in a small cookbook. We can attest to her veggie frittatas and raspberry pancakes.

The dining room separates the plush and comfortable living room, where guests congregate around the fire and play board games, from the fabulous Victorian glass conservatory, filled with wicker furniture and plants centered by a weeping cherry tree. Rhododendron and clematis were in bloom at one visit; at another, grapes from the vines garnished the breakfast plates. Folks hang out in the spacious conservatory in the off-season and feel is if they've been transported to a tropical island.

Every afternoon around 5:30, Diane sets out hors d'oeuvres like guacamole, an olive-nut spread, or a cream-cheese and chutney spread with crackers to accompany complimentary wine and cranberry juice. Guests debate the spirited reviews of their predecessors in a guest book called "Where Did You Eat and How Did You Like It?"

The inn is so comfy and the grounds so pretty that you might not want to leave, but Nauset Beach is nearby. Don't miss the shop out back where Diane sells her stained glass, painted furniture, picture frames, little boxes and other handicrafts.

(508) 255-2195. Doubles, $65 to $115. Closed November-March.

The Whalewalk Inn, 220 Bridge Road, Eastham 02642.

It's easy for a New England inn to get indigenous food for the evening meal, says innkeeper/cook Richard Smith, but breakfast is another matter. That's why he occasionally incorporates seafood into the morning feast, as in a dynamite crustless crab quiche. And why he adds cranberries to the Cape Cod pancakes. And bakes pumpkin and squash breads. And serves strawberry shortcake or apple crêpes à la mode as "a dessert surprise" to start his guests' day.

The culinary treats continue with hot mulled cider or tea and cookies at mid-afternoon and with assorted hors d'oeuvres during the BYOB cocktail hour that Dick and his wife Carolyn host nightly.

The food at this suave, welcoming refuge in a quiet residential area is Dick's bailiwick. The decor is his wife's. She has outfitted their twelve bedrooms and five suites with English country antiques and family heirlooms. "Sophisticated country charm" was her goal. She achieved it with a light and airy style that's more often associated with California than New England. There are no bed canopies or knickknack clutter. Expect plump chairs and down comforters, interesting art, fresh flowers, dhurrie rugs and whimsical accents – a floral wallpaper border in place of a chair rail here, a lush potted geranium in a bathroom window there. All

Breakfast treats include "dessert surprise" at The Whalewalk Inn in Eastham.

rooms have private baths, and suites include kitchen facilities, from tiny to full. Six come with fireplaces and several with private balconies or patios. Most in demand are a deluxe room with kingsize four-poster off the patio, the studio suite in the secluded Salt Box cottage, and ample suites in the attached barn or the outlying Guest House. In Carolyn's favorite Ivy Room you can "lie in bed and feel you're in the treetops," thanks to a lineup of windows onto the greenery. Her decorative scheme here incorporates ivy, from bed linens to the Kleenex box in the skylit bathroom.

New for 1997 was an addition off the Guest House, with four more guest rooms on the first floor and two larger accommodations with sitting areas upstairs.

Accommodations vary widely in size, but guests have plenty of space to spread out. There are a handsome living room, a cozy den with windows onto a large and colorful courtyard terrace (a festive setting for breakfast in summer), a sun porch where breakfast is served at a long antique table for ten in the off-season and a butler's pantry with a guest bar. The three-and-one-half-acre property is laced with gardens and pleasant outdoor sitting areas.

The place emits a palpable air of warmth, comfort and verve. So you are not surprised to learn that both Smiths had successful careers in advertising in New York and Boston before taking over an 1830 homestead-turned-inn in 1990 and elevating it into one of Cape Cod's finest.

(508) 255-0617. Fax (508) 240-0017. Doubles, $105 to $135; suites, $160 to $190. Closed December-March except certain holiday weekends.

The Captain's House Inn of Chatham, 371 Old Harbor Road, Chatham 02633.

"We liked Chatham and particularly this inn," says Jan McMaster, innkeeper with her husband David, a former California computer company CEO. They took over a going concern from the founding innkeepers who transformed the 1839 house built by Captain Harding. The McMasters as well as repeat guests were wowed by the improvements and expansion that had turned this into one of the first AAA four-diamond country inns in New England.

Set on two acres of green lawns and shrubbery in a residential section, the Captain's House is dignified and quiet. All sixteen guest rooms and three suites have private baths, French toiletries, pretty sheets, thick towels and comfortable chairs for reading. Many have canopy beds, and some offer fireplaces and jacuzzis. Five deluxe rooms, a couple with beamed and peaked ceilings, have been fashioned from a rear carriage house. Another coveted room is in the 1930 Captain's Cottage, where the sumptuous suite looks like an English library with dark wood paneling, a fireplace, plush sofa, wing chair, oriental rug and canopied four-poster king bed.

Ready for opening in 1997 were three top-of-the-line accommodations with whirlpool tubs in the Stables, a new building behind the cottage. The upstairs suite has fireplaces in both living rooom and bedroom, a kingsize bed and a full-length balcony.

Jan McMaster, faithful to her British background, serves a true English tea in the afternoons. She also has enlarged the breakfast offerings to include things like quiche, frittata and hot apple crunch along with the usual breads and fruits, and offers continental breakfast in bedrooms as a service to guests. Homemade cookies accompany nightly turndown. The McMasters added classical music, planned to enlarge the sunny dining porch, where linens and flowers adorn individual tables, and set out to make the gardens a focal point of the inn. "And that lawn was made for croquet," says Dave. The McMasters are continuing their predecessors' tradition of staffing their inn with English students from the University of Bournemouth, which happens to be Jan's hometown. They also continue to own their Fleur de Lys Inn and pub at Dorchester-on-Thames near Oxford.

(508) 945-0127 or (800) 315-0728. Fax (508) 945-0866. Doubles, $135 to $275; suites, $200 to $300.

The Inn at Fernbrook, 481 Main St., Centerville 02632.

Grounds landscaped by Fredrick Law Olmsted, a mansion where Cardinal Spellman entertained the cream of the crop, and breakfasts to savor – that's The Inn at Fernbrook, converted to an inn in 1987 by Brian Gallo and Sal DiFlorio. Add the fact that Sal is a professional massage therapist and has his practice at the inn and, well, you can expect a relaxing time.

Breakfast is "the best part," says Brian, who serves fruit courses of gingered rhubarb with egg cream, orange sections with sambuca and baked apples with rum. Maybe he'll bring out eggs benedict with homefries, dutch babies with marmalade and powdered sugar, brandied french toast, oatmeal pancakes or eggs goldenrod, which is creamed eggs with chipped beef. Irish sodabread or raisin-buttermilk scones might accompany, and the coffee is hazelnut.

Situated on gorgeous grounds (enjoy the heart-shaped Sweetheart Rose Garden and the little fish pond filled with Japanese koi), the Queen Anne Victorian offers five rooms and suites and a cathedral-ceilinged garden cottage. The ground-floor Spellman Suite was a chapel when the Cardinal used the mansion, willed to the Diocese of New York by the previous owner, Dr. Herbert Kalmus, inventor of technicolor. It has a fireplace in the corner, a pyramid ceiling, a canopy bed, stained-glass windows and its own entrance. The Kalmus Suite done in shades of blue is

Side porch overlooks Olmsted-designed grounds at Inn at Fernbrook.

on two levels, and the homey Marston Room affords a good view of the rose garden. On the third floor is the large Olmsted Suite, with two bedrooms, a living room with fireplace, walls of bookcases and a rooftop deck overlooking the duck ponds. Cream sherry awaits in each room.

Check out the collection of French porcelain bottles depicting soldiers of Napoleon in the Victorian parlor with its fine antiques, polished wood floors and oriental carpets. Then take your afternoon tea or lemonade to a wicker rocker on the side porch. Pretend you're Gloria Swanson (who was entertained here along with many other early Hollywood luminaries) and living the high life. For a while, it's possible.

(508) 775-4334. Doubles, $130 to $150; Olmsted Suite, $200.

The Simmons Homestead Inn, 288 Scudder Ave., Hyannis Port 02647.

"I can't abide empty spaces," says Bill Putman, who has filled every available space, and then some, at this winner of a B&B. Built by a sea captain, the restored country estate was acquired in 1988 by Bill, then recently widowed, and turned into a B&B of great personality.

Part of the personality comes from Bill, an outgoing, marketing type who proudly displays his varied collections throughout the house. But most comes from the inn and its furnishings. Start with the 32-foot-long living room, comfortable as can be and now a jungle of hanging plants as "the only empty spaces left are on the ceiling." The room is notable for all the brass birds on the mantel and inanimate wildlife everywhere, a remarkable tapestry of animals done by his late wife, and large parrots from Pavo Real. Parrots are a theme repeated in many rooms. For instance, they are on the chandeliers in the 20-by-40-foot dining room, which has a fantastic collection of mugs depicting different fruits to coordinate with the fruit du jour china. Here guests gather at two tables for a full breakfast with perhaps cheese omelets or blueberry pancakes. Bill does the cooking – "I learned quickly," says he, although he did defer once to a skeptical guest, Dinah Shore. He serves complimentary wine in the early evening on the breezy porches in summer and in front of the roaring fireplace in winter, and invites guests to sample single-malt scotches a couple of nights a week.

Along with a lively house-party atmosphere ("the place is simply fun," Bill says in a letter to prospective guests), it is the two-bedroom suite and ten guest rooms with private baths that are most unusual. Room 3, the elephant room, has a working fireplace and a queensize four-poster with a fishnet canopy. Its theme is elephants, and they are everywhere – inside the shutters, on the windows, on the mantel. Room 6 is the rabbit room, with a kingsize bed and bunnies all around. Room 7, Bill's concession to country decor, has a cherry four-poster bed and a country goose theme. It also serves as a transition to Room 8, which is simply wild: beneath the cathedral ceiling is a loft that's a jungle of plants and animals, including a purple rhinoceros. Animals are appliqueed all over the walls, the queensize bed is purple and the floor is painted green, and somehow it all works. Traditionalists might prefer the new rooms in the old servants' quarters. Room 10, the largest and brightest, has its own little patio bedecked with spirea. It's outfitted in white wicker with a kingsize bed and blue summery prints. Families go for a new two-bedroom suite in the barn annex.

Bill, a former race-car driver, displays the hoods of his race car and Paul Newman's on the upstairs landing and racing photos in a long upstairs hallway. There's also a bulletin board with letters from guests, sheets of personalized ideas and directions for what to do around the Cape, and a map with pins showing where guests have come from. Not to mention several plants adorned with tiny white lights. Or a new billiards room in the barn annex. "I wanted to create a place where you feel at home," Bill says. Although it's not like any home we know, we'd be quite at home as guests.

(508) 778-4999 or (800) 637-1649. Fax (508) 790-1342. Doubles, $125 to $170; family suite, $240.

Mostly Hall, 27 Main St., Falmouth 02540.

In the heart of Falmouth's historic district, this 1849 house with the wraparound veranda looks as if it came right out of New Orleans. As a matter of fact, it was built by a sea captain as a wedding present for his bride from New Orleans, and is named for its extra-large hall. Innkeepers Caroline and Jim Lloyd say it got its name from a young child who entered the home and blurted, "Why, Mama, it's mostly hall!"

Off that hall with a thirteen-foot-high ceiling are two guest rooms and a long living room with striped velvet sofas, oriental rugs, Victorian furnishings and a dining table at one end. Four more guest rooms go off the second-floor hall. All six refurbished corner guest rooms have private baths, queensize canopy four-posters and two comfortable chairs for reading. They're outfitted with floral wallpapers, oriental rugs, ceiling fans and a mix of antiques and traditional furnishings.

An enclosed widow's walk with peach-colored walls, two comfortable arm chairs and a TV/VCR is a great retreat, from which you can see the garden gazebo out back. Adirondack chairs are scattered around the deep back yard, a secluded and quiet refuge seemingly far from the heart of town.

Outdoor deck wraps around pool at The Inn at West Falmouth.

The hospitable Lloyds serve lemonade or tea in the handsome living room or on the veranda, which are also the sites for a sumptuous full breakfast in the morning. Caroline might whip up cheese blintzes, muffins with warm blueberry sauce, eggs-benedict soufflé, puffy fruit pancakes or stuffed french toast. She says she goes several weeks before repeating a recipe – twenty of which are included in her cookbook, *Mostly Hall Breakfast at 9,* now in its third printing after selling 2,000 copies. Ever the accommodating hostess, she will pack breakfasts to go for guests daytripping to Martha's Vineyard or Nantucket.

(508) 548-3786 or (800) 682-0565. Doubles, $125. Closed January to mid-February.

The Inn at West Falmouth, Box 1208, West Falmouth 02574.

The outside is a typical large, shingled turn-of-the-century summer mansion nestled in cedar trees on Telegraph Hill off Blacksmith Shop Road, bordered with lush impatiens and yielding a distant view of Buzzards Bay. The inside is a stunner, one of the more smashingly decorated and luxurious B&Bs we have encountered.

Opened in 1986 by a young Connecticut man who likened it to a small European hotel and catered to weddings and groups, it was sold in 1996 to Karen and Steve Calvacca of Florida. She had summered all her life in New England and they wanted a better quality of life and a year-round house on the Cape. Disappointed by what they had been shown, they came across the inn and decided to buy it for their house. "This is my little nirvana and now my vocation," says Karen, whose husband commutes to and from his law practice in Orlando. They and their 11-year-old son took over the third floor, reducing the number of guest rooms from nine to six, and added a welcome presence to a place that had seemed aloof in recent years.

It already had a lot going for it – fabulous bedrooms (four with fireplaces and three with balconies), a clay tennis court, a small heated swimming pool enclosed by a wooden deck with smart lounging chairs, another large deck for gazing at the bay, a conservatory, a screened porch furnished in wicker, a wonderful living room filled with the latest books and sofas and nooks for reading, and a breakfast room with a pale peach tropical decor, a faux-marble floor and a sideboard in the center bearing a small collection of sea shells. Add arrangements of flowers from the extensive English gardens, guest passes to one of the area's nicest beaches and a friendly owner who will "give guests their space or hold their hand," and you have a nearly perfect place in which to get away from it all.

Walk up the grand staircase to the guest rooms on the second floor, past a landing with topiary trees and plump pillows on the window seat. The spacious bedrooms are done in continental, English and Oriental antiques and pretty pastel colors. Each offers a marble bathroom with a jacuzzi tub. Comfortable sitting areas include chaise lounges and good reading lamps. Some beds are draped with a colorful rainbow fabric, some have embroidered covers and about six eyelet-edged pillows, the floors are covered with gorgeous Moroccan area rugs – it's all too sophisticated for words.

Karen serves a continental breakfast of juices, fresh fruit, cereal, pastries and muffins at tables for two set with white linens and Villeroy & Boch china in the attractive breakfast room. A decanter of sherry is set out in the afternoon.

The Inn at West Falmouth does not even have a sign to direct you to it (get directions from the innkeeper, who wants to keep things quiet and peaceful for her guests). It's great for a getaway in every sense of the word.

(508) 540-7696 or (800) 397-7696. Doubles, $175 to $300.

Gourmet Treats

The Cape is full of kitchen and specialty-food shops, along with every other type of shop imaginable. Among our favorites:

The **Green Briar Jam Kitchen,** 6 Discovery Road, East Sandwich. The first stop on the Cape might be this charmingly low-key place, where four paid cooks and many volunteers employ turn-of-the-century methods, to produce jams, continuing a tradition begun in 1903. You get to see the old wood stove that founder Ida Putnam started with, as well as probably the oldest solar-cooking operation in the country – the hot-house windows in which ingenious racks slide in and out to make the prized sun-cooked strawberries with vodka, as well as blueberries with kirsch. Of course, you get to watch – and smell – some of the 20,000 bottles of jams, chutneys and relishes as they are lovingly prepared for sale in the gift shop. You also see Thornton Burgess's framed, handwritten description of the Jam Kitchen in 1939: "It is a wonderful thing to sweeten the world which is in a jam and needs preserving." Adjacent to the kitchen is the Green Briar Nature Center, including the Old Briar Patch conservation area, home of Brer Rabbit and his animal friends. Kitchen open Monday-Saturday 10 to 4, Sunday 1 to 4; winter hours vary. Shop open Monday-Friday 9 to 4, year-round.

Madden & Co., at 16 Jarves St. in the center of historic Sandwich, purveys unexpected gourmet treats among its antiques and "gatherings for the country home." Owner Parke Madden offers choice specialty foods and cookbooks, including those by his niece, Sarah Leah Chase of Nantucket.

Oven-ready prepared foods are the forte of **Mill Way Fish & Lobster Market** at 275 Millway beside Barnstable Harbor. Chef Ralph Binder, a Culinary Institute grad who worked at Chillingsworth, makes everything himself, according to season. "People are looking for prepared foods, even fish," says Ralph. He obliges with takeout treats like seafood sausage (composed of crawfish, shrimp and scallops), salmon manicotti, codfish cakes, lobster pie, bouillabaisse and finnan haddie. A meal in itself is the seafood Tuscan bread, which he likens to a deep-pan pizza with shrimp, pesto, spinach, sundried tomatoes and parmesan cheese. You can get anything from a clam roll to a calamari salad to an oyster platter, to eat outside at picnic tables or to go.

The **Lemon Tree Village** complex along Route 6A in Brewster is worth a visit. The Lemon Tree Pottery is full of interesting pottery and other crafts. **The Cook Shop** is a kaleidoscope of kitchen things, table linens, baskets and glassware. **Cafe Alfresco,** with tables inside and out, is a great place for an interesting meal or to get something to take out. Marcia Clark and her son, Dale, who used to own the Tower House Restaurant in Brewster, offer excellent food at refreshing prices. We enjoyed a smoked salmon sandwich with avocado and sprouts ($5.95) and a lobster club with pancetta and the works for $9.95. A raspberry square made for a tasty dessert. Pick up a homemade pastry from the deli case, or order a dinner special from the blackboard. All priced unbelievably at $5.95 at our visit, they included swordfish Mediterranean on linguini, spaghettini with spicy scallops, linguini with bitter greens and pancetta, and a shrimp, bacon and spinach ragoût. No wonder the place does a land-office business at all hours. Open daily, 9 to 8:30 in summer, shorter hours in winter.

The open-air showroom of **Scargo Stoneware Pottery** is quite a sight off Dr. Lord's Road South in Dennis. Harry Holl and his family have been producing the stunning stoneware for decorative and kitchen purposes since 1952. Harry, whose majestic bird feeders grace the back yards of some of our favorite B&Bs in the area, has been turning his hand to painting lately. His four daughters and a son-in-law continue at the potter's kiln.

The Chocolate Sparrow at the Seatoller Shops in North Eastham is where dietitian Marjorie Sparrow produces her luscious chocolates, chocolate-covered cranberry cordials, English toffee crunch, assorted nut barks and more. Its offshoot is **Hot Chocolate Sparrow,** the quintessential coffee and dessert bar along Route 6A at Lowell Square, Orleans. We stopped at the espresso bar here for fat-free cranberry muffins and a latte and watched touring families devouring the candies and terrific ice-cream concoctions, among them a raspberry-sorbet lime rickey and a frozen espresso shake.

Fancy's Farm Stand, 199 Main St., East Orleans, is the Cape's ultimate produce stand. It also purveys potpourris and wreaths (we coveted a huge one with all kinds of geese for $100), fancy cheeses and local jellies, baked goods and soups. You can make up a meal to go with, perhaps, kale and corn chowder, the offerings from an extensive salad bar, and a pastry or piece of pie.

Chatham Cookware, 524 Main St., Chatham, offers all kinds of kitchen items and colorful pottery as well as fine foods to eat in or to go. Proprietor Vera Lynne Champlin no longer gives cooking demonstrations in her open kitchen based on the one at La Varenne, but she and her staff certainly put out some delectable sandwiches, soups, salads, quiches and desserts. There are a few tables in a little pink room at the rear and on a side courtyard.

Founded by Art and Meredith Fancy of Fancy's Farm Stand, the **Cornfield Market** complex at 1297 Main St. in West Chatham is a haven for gourmets. **The**

Pampered Palate is an excellent deli and gourmet foods shop. Owner Virginia Sharpe, who honed her cooking knowledge in Paris, offers all sorts of nifty foods to go, from pumpkin-pecan muffins to cranberry-glazed stuffed game hens. Fireworks coleslaw and fiesta corn are among the salads; cheese tortellini with sundried-tomato pesto is one of the pastas. Pick up a Queen Anne sandwich (avocado, smoked turkey and fresh tomato salsa on a whole-wheat baguette, $4.95) and a slice of orange yogurt cake for a super picnic. Supplement this fare with impeccable produce from the large Fancy's farm market, the all-natural baked goods and sweets at **Cookies and Creams** or the extensive selection at **Chatham Fish and Lobster** next door and you have the makings for a great party.

Located upstairs at the Cornfield, **Chatham Winery** offers tastings of its unusual fruit and flower-based wines, such as cranberry mead, red currant and belle of Georgia peach, an award-winning dessert wine. Their popular Midnight Blue, a $9 blend of red grapes and blueberries in a cobalt blue bottle, won a silver medal in an international wine competition in Toronto. The Chatham blush comes in a bottle shaped like a lobster. Owners Glenn and Susan Smith-Elion price their 30 wines in the $7 to $10 range.

The Casual Gourmet, a catering service in the Bell Tower Mall at 1600 Falmouth Road, Centerville, has a large deli section dispensing salads, sandwiches, baked goods and prepared foods. Try the egg, bacon and cheddar calzone ($1.75) for breakfast or a hefty tarragon chicken salad sandwich ($4.25) for lunch.

In Falmouth, the understated **Bean & Cod** at 95 Palmer Ave. is a paradise of specialty foods and gourmet items, from cookbooks to napkins to dishes. The selection of crackers, cheeses, vinegars, pâtés, preserves and candies is exceptional, and surprises unfold on shelf after shelf. The blackboard might list prepared foods and breads, from crab cakes and lobster ravioli to dessert squares.

Our favorite shop for browsing at the Cape is **Tree's Place,** Route 6A at 28, Orleans. An art gallery, a tilery (the largest selection of designer tiles in the country, they say) and a gift shop occupy several rooms filled with such diverse items as Russian lacquer boxes, jewelry, Swiss musical paper weights, Hadley stoneware, Salt Marsh Pottery, carved birds – even tartan ties. We love the biscuit baskets of glazed stoneware made by Eucalyptus Pottery in California. You can choose any of the tiles to be framed for use as a trivet. One of us could spend hours mooching around here, but the other always says that it's time to be moving on.

Gourmet Chips

Do you think, as we do, that Cape Cod potato chips are absolutely the best? Then stop in Hyannis at their place of origin, **The Cape Cod Potato Chip Co.,** Breed's Hill Road, in an industrial park area off Route 132. There's an informative, self-guided tour of the plant, which evolved from Steve and Lynn Bernard's storefront kitchen that started in 1980 producing 200 bags of Cape Cod Potato Chips a day. Still hand-cooking their chips in kettles one batch at a time, they produce 80,000 bags a day and go through 48 million pounds of potatoes a year. This is big business, and we were surprised by the number of people touring on a summer weekday. You can pick up samples as well as buy more in the gift shop at tour's end. Tours, Monday-Friday 10 to 4.

Table at Straight Wharf Restaurant overlooks Nantucket harbor.

Nantucket

The Ultimate Indulgence for Gourmets

For an off-shore island with a year-round population of 6,000 (augmented by up to 40,000 high-livers and free-spenders in the summer), Nantucket has an uncommon concentration of uncommonly good restaurants.

Ever since French chef Jean-Charles Berruet took over the rose-covered Chanticleer Inn in the hamlet of Siasconset in 1969, knowledgeable diners have been flocking to Nantucket in droves. Other restaurateurs and culinary businesses have followed.

"I don't know of another resort area that can beat Nantucket for good restaurants per square mile," says Neal Grennan, chef-owner of Le Languedoc.

Given its small size and island remoteness, "it's amazing," adds Chick Walsh, owner of the highly acclaimed 21 Federal, who started as maître-d' at the old Opera House restaurant in 1970 when it was about the only game in town. "When I arrived here, we couldn't have had a restaurant like this. We used to have difficulty flying in Haagen-Dazs ice cream. Now, fancy food products are at our doorstep, and we make ice cream ourselves. Twenty-five years ago, the local population wouldn't have supported this restaurant, and now they do. The whole food awareness has changed."

Indeed it has. The island now has a dozen superior restaurants, another dozen good ones, and countless more of the ordinary variety.

At one of our visits, two cookbooks by Nantucket chefs had just been published and another was in the works. And the 21 Federal restaurant had opened a "branch" in Washington, D.C., putting its culinary mark on the mainland.

What other seaside resort dines so fashionably late? Many restaurants don't open for dinner until 6:30 or 7 – the 4:30 early-bird specials of Cape Cod don't play here. Dining is an event and a pricey one, given local chefs' preoccupation with fresh and exotic ingredients, their island location and a captive, affluent audience.

We have friends who vacation at Nantucket for a month every summer, eating out almost every night, and relishing every minute as the ultimate gustatory experience. Book a room, reserve the ferry or an airplane seat, bring your wallet and indulge in the gourmet splendors of Nantucket yourself.

Dining

The Best of the Best

The Chanticleer Inn, 40 New St., Siasconset.

Lunch in the rose garden is a local tradition, as is an after-dinner drink in the old Chantey Bar, lately rechristened the Grill Room. But the four-course dinners and the extraordinary wine cellar are what draw the knowing from hither and yon to the world-class restaurant built by Jean-Charles Berruet since he took over in 1969.

Prix-fixe dinners are $65 "and worth every penny," all kinds of fans had told us. The setting, the service and the food are nearly perfect, which is exactly the way Jean-Charles wants it.

You are greeted at the door and directed to your table: in the sought-after, formal main-floor dining room with a fireplace at the end and a greenhouse on one side (rather brightly illuminated, we thought – the better to see and be seen, perhaps?), or in the convivial, informal grill (a bit too bistro-ish, we felt, considering the tab), or in the upstairs dining room to which we were assigned, serene in gray and white and dim enough to be just right.

The complex French menu and the endless wine list are so staggering that both first-timers and knowing regulars put themselves in the hands of a solicitous, knowledgeable staff to help with their selections. Also available is an à la carte menu, equally complex and astonishingly pricey (most appetizers $25, entrées $29 to $38 and desserts $18).

We, like most, chose the prix-fixe route. A tiny cheese gougère was served with drinks, "compliments of the chef." For starters, one of us had Nantucket oysters served in a warm mussel broth topped with American sturgeon caviar (a small portion, but ever so delicious). The other had lobster and sole sausage poached with a puree of sweet red peppers (ever so presented, but super).

From a choice of six entrées (all of which we gladly would have sampled), we decided on the Nantucket-raised pheasant, stuffed with mushrooms, herbs and ricotta, and the roasted tenderloin of lamb served with a venison sauce. A triangle of potato pancake, spinach and ratatouille niçoise accompanied. The salad of greens with two kinds of cheeses that followed was unwieldy to eat because the leaves were too large.

For dessert, the assortment of sorbets was a pretty plate of small scoops interspersed with fresh fruit on a raspberry sauce. Creole-style lime meringue pie was an ethereal second choice. Over demitasses of decaf and espresso, we savored an experience that ranks with the ultimate in fine dining.

Not that it's for everyone. Without background music, the atmosphere is hushed until the room fills up. The tastes are complex and the portions small. Riffling

Chef Jean-Charles Berruet takes break outside Chantecleer Inn.

through the thousand selections on the wine list – winner since 1987 of Wine Spectator's Grand Award as one of the world's best– is so mind-boggling that you're apt to ask the waiter to make the choice for you, and ours chose on the high side.

And yet, young and old alike go back time after time, such is the spell of the Chanticleer and the output of the energetic owner and his kitchen staff of eleven. Jean-Charles proudly showed us his expansive facility, including a big walk-in cooler in back. "You can tell how good a kitchen is by the condition of its cooler," said he. His was organized and spotless.

If you can't get in for dinner (tables are booked far in advance), splurge for lunch in the garden, beneath trellised canopies of roses and surrounded by impeccably manicured hedges. Entrées are $18 to $25, and you might try lobster en croûte with arborio risotto, a mousse of eel and salmon rolled in a crêpe, or scrambled eggs put back in the shell and topped with sevruga caviar, garnished with a puree of potatoes with olive oil.

If you can't get here for a meal, pick up some of the delicacies at **Chanticleer to Go,** the in-town gourmet shop run by the chef's daughter, Nathalie. Or look through Jean-Charles's beautiful cookbook, *Here's to Nantucket: Recipes for the Good Life and Great Food.* This could be the slogan for all Nantucket. And Jean-Charles certainly knows the recipes.

(508) 257-6231. Lunch, noon to 2 in summer; dinner, 6:30 to 9:30. Closed Wednesday. Open late May to early December. Reservations and jackets required.

21 Federal, 21 Federal St., Nantucket.

If Chanticleer is the venerable old-timer, 21 Federal is the acclaimed newcomer. It did so well that only two years after opening in 1985 it added a second establishment in Washington, D.C. Executive chef Bob Kinkead was dispatched to the D.C. operation, called 21 Federal as well, which consistently won high ratings until it closed in 1993 and reopened to rave reviews as Kinkead's in a new Foggy Bottom location.

Owner-manager Chick Walsh runs a tight ship here on the island. Known for its new American grill cuisine, 21 Federal presents a limited menu, but one that's compelling and not in the vanguard of Nantucket's high prices. There are six intimate dining rooms – some with their white-linened tables rather close together – on two floors of museum-quality, Federal period decor. In summer, lunch is served on a nifty outdoor courtyard ringed with impatiens, where the whine linens on the tables are topped by herbs in clay pots and classical music wafts across the scene.

Our courtyard lunch arrived on large wicker trays. The pheasant and wild rice soup of the day ($6) was sublime, as was the linguini salad with shrimp and pinenuts ($10.50). The five-salad sampler ($9.50) was less interesting, the chicken with green salsa and oriental noodles outshining the ratatouille and the eggplant, which were a bit too much of the same thing. Calvados ice cream and an intense pineapple-mint sorbet served with wonderful small coconut or lemon squares topped off a flavorful meal.

Chef Russell Jaehnig changes the short dinner menu weekly. For openers ($7 to $14), you might start with corn and seafood chowder with fried leeks, salmon tartare with cucumber salad, lobster and warm spinach salad with chardonnay hollandaise, or the signature parma ham with tomatoes, mozzarella and pesto vinaigrette.

Entrées ($19 to $29) could be sautéed arctic char with lentils and baby fennel, rare yellowfin tuna with clams and white bean ragoût, charred leg of lamb with roasted eggplant and, from the grill, aged sirloin steak or veal loin chop with potato gratin. Dessert ($6 to $6.50) might be a blueberry/montrachet tart with whipped cream, chocolate-hazelnut torte with raspberries or homemade sorbet with fresh berries. The fare changes with the seasons, but always appeals and asserts.

(508) 228-2121. Lunch daily, 11:30 to 2:30; dinner, 6 to 10. Closed Sunday in off-season. Open April to mid-December.

The Second Story, 1 South Beach St., Nantucket.
Still more assertive fare – a couple of fans allow as how some think it's outrageous – is doled out by chef-proprietor David Toole in his second-floor walkup across from the harbor. The space, done up in Nantucket pink and green, is illuminated entirely by candles in enormous hurricane chimneys.

The setting could not be more romantic and the menu, which changes nightly, is the kind on which everything appeals, influenced by regional cuisines from around the world, including Thai, Vietnamese, French and Italian. Starters ($8 to $14) might be grilled shrimp and cucumber soup with coriander, smoked duck mousse with goat cheese bruschetta and black currant-mustard vinaigrette, rice noodles tossed with crab and peanuts in a Thai cilantro vinaigrette and Korean pork, pear and pinenut salad with kimchi and spicy chile-garlic dressing.

Entrées ($19 to $27) include Tanzanian seafood stew, halibut with a Thai basil-lemon crust, grilled duck breast with a smoked jalapeño sauce, and sirloin steak with crumbled maytag blue cheese and a peppered mushroom sauce.

We can vouch for the hot country pâté (a huge slab of goose, duck, chicken and sausage), served piping hot and bathed in a creamy green-peppercorn sauce; the scallops au gratin with tomato, avocado, garlic and cream, and the Thai shrimp with black bean and coriander sauce, so spicy that it left the mouth smoldering long into the night.

Our amaretto soufflé turned out neither hot nor cold, but more like a mousse

Setting is elegant in dining rooms at 21 Federal.

with a hint of amaretto. Other desserts ($7) were grand marnier crème caramel, pumpkin-ginger spice cake with vanilla ice cream and spiced wine sauce, and an Asian napoleon (layers of fried wontons with a citrus pastry cream, fruit and a ginger-raspberry sauce).

At our latest visit, the Second Story had squeezed in a bar area to offer a cafe menu of soups, salads and light entrées in the $10 to $14 range.

(508) 228-3471. Dinner nightly, Tuesday-Sunday from 6. Open April-December.

Le Languedoc, 24 Broad St., Nantucket.

After a brief stint with a hired chef, longtime chef-owner Neal Grennan is back in the kitchen, where he can keep better rein on what he admits are Nantucket's steep prices and where he produced one of our best meals in Nantucket a few years back.

An autumn dinner began with an appetizer of smoked Nantucket pheasant with cranberry relish, very good and very colorful with red cabbage and slices of apples and oranges on a bed of lettuce. For entrées ($19.75 to $35), one of us tried the noisettes of lamb with artichokes in a rosemary sauce and the other enjoyed sautéed sweetbreads and lobster in puff pastry. Nicely presented on piping-hot white oval plates, they were accompanied by snow peas, broccoli, pureed turnips, yellow peppers, sweet potatoes and peach slices. We ended with a dense chocolate-hazelnut torte spiked with grand marnier.

Recently, we liked the sound of cream of crab soup, an escargots bundle with roasted garlic and gorgonzola, and a "short stack" of foie gras, potato brioche and duck rillette, followed by cedar-planked salmon with lobster mashed potatoes, grilled rare tuna with seaweed salad and honey-crusted rack of lamb with garlic bread pudding.

The dessert list included banana-butterscotch meringue tart with caramel drizzle, vanilla crème brûlée and three-chocolate terrine with praline chantilly.

These treats are served in four small upstairs dining rooms amid peach walls and white trim, windows covered with peach draperies and valances, and changing art from a local gallery. Windsor chairs are at well-spaced tables topped by candles in hurricane lamps and vases, each containing a salmon-hued rose.

The downstairs has a small pub-like dining room with checkered cloths. Off the side entrance is a canopied terrace for summer lunches. Everyone loves the cafe menu, from which you can dine very well for $8.75 to $18.50, the latter for a grilled open-faced lobster reuben with frizzled leeks. The warm duck hash with poached egg, asparagus and gaufrette potatoes makes a super lunch.

(508) 228-2552. Lunch in summer, Tuesday-Saturday noon to 2; dinner nightly, 6 to 9:30. Open mid-April through December.

The Boarding House, 12 Federal St., Nantucket.

When it opened in 1973, the Boarding House was the summer's success story and provided our first great meal on Nantucket. It since has moved around the corner to considerably larger quarters, and several owners (and chefs) have come and gone. It's better than ever lately, having been taken over by Seth and Angela Raynor, he a former sous chef at 21 Federal and both having worked at the Chanticleer.

A beauty it is, its cathedral-ceilinged Victorian lounge with small faux-marble tables on a flagstone floor opening into a sunken dining room. The latter is striking as can be in rich cream and pink, with a curved banquette at the far end in front of a mural of Vernazzia, a culinary destination featured in Gourmet magazine the month after the mural went up. The Raynors own the originals but sell lithographs of the exclusive Nantucket series "Streets of Paris," which hang on the walls. Villeroy & Boch china of the Florida pattern graces the nicely spaced tables, which allow for one of Nantucket's more pleasant dining situations.

Equal to the lovely setting is the cooking of Seth, who said he was "honored but amazed" to be chosen one of 30 chefs to appear on the "Great Chefs of the East" public television series only nine months after opening his restaurant in 1992. We certainly liked our latest dinner here: mellow sautéed crab cakes with scallion crème fraîche, and grilled quail with crisp fried onion rings and baby mixed greens, among starters from $6.50 to $12, and pan-roasted salmon with Thai curried cream and crispy rice noodles, and a spicy Asian seafood stew with lobster, shrimp and scallops, among entrées from $23 to $30 Accompanying was a powerful Caymus sauvignon blanc from a well-chosen wine selection with less than the normal Nantucket price markup and an award of excellence from Wine Spectator. Coffee ice cream with chocolate sauce and a dense chocolate-kahlua terrine were worthy endings.

Other starters include a carpaccio of sirloin with bruschetta and fried onion rings, and sautéed codfish cakes enlivened with a spicy crème fraîche. Signature main dishes are grilled rare yellowfin tuna with wasabi aioli, bok choy and soy ginger glaze, and grilled veal chop with thyme jus and spiced tempura onion rings.

The dinner menu also includes a short, changing category labeled bistro fare ($7.50 to $11). It might offer a bento box, smoked salmon with Asian sticky rice, lacquered shrimp with Thai pesto noodles, an Asian noodle sampler and risotto of the evening.

The outdoor terrace is appealing for a bistro lunch and drinks. We've also found it a felicitous setting for an after-dinner liqueur while watching the late-night parade pass by.

(508) 228-9622. Lunch daily in summer, noon to 2; dinner nightly, 6 to 10. Closed Monday-Wednesday in winter.

Archways and mural evoke Mediterranean feeling at Boarding House.

American Seasons, 80 Centre St., Nantucket.

This innovative establishment is a find for those who want distinguished, ever-changing regional cuisine at affordable prices. New owners made Michael Getter, formerly of 21 Federal, a partner and chef. They also retained the concept and decor of their predecessors.

The 50-seat dining room is notable for high-backed banquettes serving as room dividers and polyurethaned tables whose tops are game boards. A local artist painted the table tops as well as a stunning wall mural of a vine-covered Willamette Valley hillside in Oregon. A couple of dim wall sconces and candlelight provide illumination.

Chef Michael says he has "cranked up the menu a notch" in terms of sophistication. Typical entrées ($19 to $24.50) are seared rare yellowfin tuna with green peppercorn sauce, roasted halibut with grilled shiitakes in a red wine fish reduction, grilled herb-rubbed quail with creamy goat cheese polenta, and breast of duck with root vegetable risotto and fried celeriac.

As our meal unfolded, we discovered why people had said that the presentations were so striking and that every plate was different. It turned out it wasn't the plates (most are white) but the decorative garnishes on the rims that made them look different.

Interestingly, the menu is categorized by four regions – Pacific Coast, Wild West, New England and Down South – each with two or three appetizers and entrées. You're supposed to mix and match, pairing, say, a Florida rock shrimp gumbo with andouille sausage, okra and biscuits ($7) with a lobster and corn enchilada in a blue cornmeal crêpe ($12). Those and a lentil salad with goat cheese, frisée and grilled leeks ($10) made a memorable meal. Or you could start with salmon tartare with buckwheat blinis and cucumber salad and move on to a main course of leg of lamb with flageolet beans, a roasted eggplant and tomato compote and sautéed chard.

We shared a dessert of raspberry-mango shortcake with raspberry coulis, presented artistically with fresh fruit on a square plate decorated with squiggles of chocolate and crème anglaise. Other choices ($7) included spiced pear and toasted black walnut cake with vanilla ice cream, banana bread pudding with Vermont maple anglaise, and baked caramel apple with toasted coconut and cinnamon ice cream. Dessert chef George Bozko, who's been wowing patrons from the beginning, appeared on the "Great Chefs of the East" television series with the former owner.

The all-American wine list has been honored by Wine Spectator.

(508) 228-7111. Dinner nightly, 6 to 10, April to mid-December.

Moona, 122 Pleasant St., Nantucket.

Just what the doctor ordered for Nantucket's surfeit of pricey restaurants is this casual new grill, where the food sparkles and the prices make you think the island might have a middle class, after all. Located on the outskirts of town and upstaging many in-town restaurants, it's run by chef Everett Reid, who founded American Seasons with his brother in 1988. Everett and his wife Linda decided in 1995 it was time to move on. Here, in what was described as a former roadhouse, a designer covered the walls with black burlap, shellacked the windows and added copper-topped tables for the look of an 18th-century home. With candles lit and light jazz playing, it's a dark and casual spot for an innovative dinner at affordable prices. And, unusual for Nantucket, most of the menu is available for takeout – a boon for those who want an interesting picnic supper for the beach.

A Culinary Institute of America graduate who had worked in Boston, New York and at the Summer House in Siasconset, Everett shares the cooking duties with Frenchman Jean Dion, who joined him from the old Beach Plum Cafe. They were featured on the PBS series "Great Chefs of the East" and were invited to prepare a James Beard Foundation dinner in New York.

Moona is the name of a tract of land designated on old Nantucket maps as part of South Pasture. The menu headings – divided into four categories as they had been at American Seasons – denote areas known for fishing, farming, hunting and grazing. The categorization is generally logical, although one wonders why the peppered rare tuna with gingered black bean sauce and wasabi mayo is listed under "The Woods" and why the risotto of roast rabbit, wild mushrooms and lobster with fried eggplant chips falls under "Head of the Harbor."

Not to quibble. This is gutsy cooking, without nouvelle conceits. One of us happily made a dinner of three first courses in the $5.75 to $9 range: a bowl of smooth, chilled tomato and leek soup with herb brioche croutons and goat cheese, with sprinkles of parsley on the accompanying plate. This was followed by lamb and goat cheese "poverty" hash with a poached egg and spicy ketchup, the plate decorated with stripes of red pepper puree interspersed with specks of green herbs. Then came an interesting salad of wild greens, smoked cheddar and crabmeat, decorated with carrots, green onions, celery and more. The other diner had wild mushroom and tomato pasta with garlic, olive oil and clams ($16). Two long strips of chives were crossed on top of the pasta, which entered the annals as one of the most powerful-tasting ever. A side dish of crisp carrots, zucchini, beets, summer squash, turnips and a section of corn on the cob accompanied.

Desserts ($5.95) ranged from a sweet potato pancake with candied pecans and butterscotch ice cream to a banana split with coconut ice cream, roasted macadamia nuts and rum-chocolate sauce.

All but three entrées were priced in the teens, grilled leg of venison being one of

Local artist painted mural and table tops at American Seasons.

the exceptions at $23.50. Other possibilities ran the gamut from a warm open-face tongue sandwich ($12.50) to confit of duck with ginger-blackberry sauce and grilled salmon with an Indian succotash of corn, lobster and black beans.

Beers from microbreweries are featured, and the dessert menu lists American dessert wines, single-malt scotches and single-barrel bourbons.

(508) 325-4306. Dinner nightly, 5 to 9 or 10.

Straight Wharf Restaurant, Straight Wharf, Nantucket.

Chef Marian Morash of television and cookbook fame put this summery restaurant on the culinary map. She left in 1987 to finish a seafood cookbook, but the menu style and the spiffy decor remained the same. The level of food has been raised lately by new partner Steve Cavagnaro, chef-owner of the much-acclaimed Cavey's restaurant in Manchester, Conn., who cooks here summer nights. His wife Kate, who runs the front of the house, has warmed the welcome as well. They spend the season in Nantucket, but return to their Connecticut base the rest of the year.

The interior is a pristine palette of shiny floors and soaring, shingled walls topped by billowing banners and hung with striking paintings by an island artist.

We wish that the June night we first dined here had been warm enough to eat outside on the canopied, rib-lit deck beside the water, and that the acclaimed vegetables were more exciting than plainly cooked broccoli and carrots. But the complimentary smoked bluefish pâté with drinks, the grilled salmon with tarragon-mustard sauce and the lobster crêpes were first-rate, the peach bavarian laden with raspberry sauce was outstanding and, a nice touch, the elaborately written bill came with two chocolate shells.

Our latest September visit was warm enough to relax on the deck as we waited for the 7:10 ferry back to the mainland. We expected only to stave off hunger, but ultimately made a meal of the smoked bluefish pâté with focaccia melba toasts, the basket of breads to dip into a pool of olive oil made tart by the addition of raspberry vinegar, a rich lobster bisque heavily laced with sherry, and an appetizer of seared beef carpaccio with shards of parmigiano reggiano, white truffle oil and mesclun. The new Hy-Line catamaran arrived so quickly we had to forego the dessert trio of sorbets and rush off to catch the ferry with only the cookies that came with. It was enough that we couldn't even think of a snack back in Hyannis.

Other favorites among appetizers ($9 to $18) are sauté of wild mushrooms in a potato basket with watercress broth and Wellfleet diver scallops with cranberry bean and sea urchin sauce. Main dishes run from $28 for sautéed salmon with red wine-onion broth to $33 for rack of lamb with a garlic crust and spiced lentils. The dessert specialty is warm Valrhona chocolate tart with orange cardamom gelato, but we'd return for the missed trio of plum-banana, lemon-thyme and mango-pineapple sorbets.

The grill menu, served from 7 to 10, is very popular (there's apt to be a long wait to get in, the bar is noisy and crowds spill outside onto the terrace). It yields some of the same appetizers and desserts as those in the dining room plus five entrées at half the price. The latter might include a warm shellfish, bean and pasta salad; mixed seafood grill with couscous, and skirt steak with ratatouille.

(508) 228-4499. Dinner by reservation, nightly except Monday 6 to 10. Open mid-June to late September. Bar open to mid-October; no reservations.

The Club Car, 1 Main St., Nantucket.

Creative chef Michael Shannon is a local institution at this sumptuous establishment entered through a red train car used as a lounge (open from 11 o'clock and lately the scene of sandwich or salad lunches, $3.50 to $6) and a lively piano bar. The lounge represents a bit of history: it is the last remaining club car from the old Nantucket Railroad Co., which operated from here out to 'Sconset. Beyond the lounge is an expansive dining room of white-over-red-linened tables topped by enormous wine globes, upholstered cane-back chairs, an array of large artworks and a colorful shelf of copper pans.

The continental menu has traditionally ranked as the town's priciest. Appetizers start at $8 for sautéed calves brains with tomato concassé or broiled sesame eel and go to $24 for fresh New York State duck foie gras ($75 for beluga caviar and vodka). Roasted quail with truffle polenta, cold Nantucket lobster with asparagus flan and "squid in the style of Bangkok" are among the possibilities.

Typical entrées ($26 to $36) include shrimp scampi dijonnaise, Norwegian salmon steak with roasted red beet sauce, veal sweetbreads with belgian endive, rare breast of muscovy duck chartreuse and grilled sirloin au poivre.

Finish with one of a dozen desserts, perhaps fresh berries with devonshire cream, crème brûlée or chocolate-mousse cake with creme anglaise.

The seafood salad ($5.95) is a big hit on the short lunch menu. Also popular are the food and wine-tasting dinners scheduled throughout the fall.

(508) 228-1101. Lunch daily, 11 to 3, dinner nightly, 6 to 10. Open Memorial Day to December.

Cioppino's, 20 Broad St., Nantucket.

This house in the heart of the town's restaurant district has been home to many an eatery. Its latest incarnation by Tracy and Susan Root (he the former maître-d' at Chanticleer and she a bartender at the Summer House) raised the hopes of fans that it might endure. And endure it has, the Roots proving to be hands-on restaurateurs in a town where that's not always the case. "We're working this ourselves, staying open year-round, and it's paying off," said Tracy.

Dining is in a couple of small rooms on the main floor, pretty in white, black and mauve. Upstairs are larger rooms, one with a skylit peaked ceiling and a stunning mural of what looks to be a Monet's Garden by a Nantucket artist. In season you can dine at umbrellaed tables on the side and rear patio, a lovely setting.

At a September lunch, the special fried oysters with béarnaise sauce ($9) was a nouvelle presentation with rice, broccoli, strained zucchini and swirled yellow squash. Also excellent was the caribbean shrimp and asparagus salad ($9.50). Good sourdough rolls came first; a mellow key lime pie was the finale. The folks at the next table were exclaiming over the soup and half a sandwich ($7.50 for conch chowder and roast beef with boursin) and the shrimp, tomato and mozzarella pizzetta ($10.50). On our way out, we paused to look at the wine labels inlaid in the bar, representing a few of the owner's collection of 12,000 labels.

At dinner, a three-course prix-fixe menu ($34) changes every two weeks. Three choices are offered for each course. We would gladly have sampled the yellowfin tuna sashimi, the grilled Atlantic salmon with salsa fresca and the blueberry crumb pie offered at our latest visit. There's also an à-la-carte menu, priced from $18.50 for roasted chicken with lemon and fresh herbs to $29.50 for rack of lamb provençal. The namesake San Francisco cioppino is served over linguini.

Start with sautéed scallops niçoise or a fricassee of wild mushrooms in puff pastry. Finish with warm pecan pie with bourbon ice cream or the chocolate-kahlua fantasy cake.

Tracy has developed the wine cellar to the point where it recently won the Wine Spectator award of excellence.

(508) 228-4622. Lunch daily, 11:30 to 2:30; dinner nightly from 5:30; Sunday brunch.

Company of the Cauldron, 7 India St., Nantucket.

The former quarters of the Boarding House is now Steve McCluskey's intimate little restaurant. The night's prix-fixe, no-choice menu is posted outside the door about 9 a.m. and patrons make reservations for the nightly seatings and take what's served, which is reputed to be excellent.

Behind a wrought-iron shelf divider laden with flowers at the entry are a number of small tables rather close together, colorful with a mix of orange and purple floral cloths on old wood tables. Copper pots, cauldrons and ship's models hang from the stucco walls, and it's all very close, dark and romantic.

A typical dinner ($44) brings a smoked salmon cake with roasted red and yellow pepper sauce and chive crème fraîche, shrimp scampi with grilled medallions of veal, roasted asparagus, wild rice and summer succotash, and a plum-nectarine crumb tart. Another could be white gazpacho with lobster meat, individual beef wellington with wild mushroom duxelles, roasted potatoes and grilled green beans, and chocolate-pecan pie with vanilla ice cream. The small but select wine list is rationally priced.

(508) 228-4016. Dinner nightly, seatings at 7 and 9 in summer, one seating at 7 in fall. Open Memorial Day to Columbus Day.

West Creek Cafe, 11 West Creek Road, Nantucket.

Our favorite little Beach Plum Cafe gave way in 1995 to this creative establishment owned by Patricia Tyler, whom we first knew at the Second Story. Taking over from chef Jean Dion, who moved around the corner to Moona, she reconfigured the layout and eliminated the former bakery. Now there are three small rooms, each sponge painted in shades of yellow, burnt orange or gray, with the tablecloths in each room color-coordinated with the walls and a mix of sprightly pillowed banquettes and old-fashioned cane chairs.

Chef Dan Ferrare presents a short but innovative menu in the New American style. Likely entrées are pan-seared red snapper atop a basmati pilaf, pan-seared salmon with caramelized onion vinaigrette, sweet chile-glazed pork chop with bourbon sauce and oven-roasted tenderloin with red wine sauce. Chèvre mashed potatoes accompany the salmon dish while the pork chop comes with creamy collards and jalapeño corn cakes.

For starters ($6 to $10), how about Nantucket oysters on the half shell with champagne mignonette, sautéed soft-shell crabs with chive sauce or duck confit and apple walnut salads with truffle vinaigrette? Desserts are the owner's prerogative. She might make crème brûlée, rum torte, a pecan tart or profiteroles.

A couple of Nantucket Vineyard wines are available on the well chosen list priced from $18 to $48.

(508) 228-4943. Dinner nightly except Tuesday, 6 to 9:30, to 9 in off-season.

India House, 37 India St., Nantucket.

The Sunday garden brunches are legendary, but this 1803 house with two small, candlelit dining rooms is praised for dinner fare as well.

The basic menu remains the same year after year. You might start with a lobster-artichoke crêpe, Key West conch fritters, wild-mushroom strudel or a trio of seafood cakes with three sauces – sundried tomato, basil-lime-caper and whole-grain mustard. Entrées are priced from $15 for wild Russian boar ribs with grilled-pineapple barbecue sauce to $28 for tournedos of beef singapore with ginger and sake. Planked swordfish with cashew-pecan glaze and lime beurre blanc, and lamb tenderloin with dijon and red rose mint sauce are house specialties. Dessert could be a sweet-potato/pecan pie, autumn harvest cake or raspberry soufflé.

The Sunday brunch ($9.95) involves seven choices from eggs benedict to grilled tenderloin of pork with bourbon apples and herbed scrambled eggs.

The daily breakfasts here are not to be overlooked. The prix-fixe menu yields fresh orange juice, homemade fruit breads and muffins, and a choice of eggs benedict, fruit pancakes, Mexican omelet or a fruit boboli breakfast pizza.

On warm nights when the old house can get steamy, many patrons prefer the outdoor garden cafe.

(508) 228-9043. Breakfast, Monday-Saturday 8:30 to 10:30; dinner nightly, 6:30 to 9:30; Sunday brunch, 9 to 1. Open April-December.

The Woodbox, 29 Fair St., Nantucket.

Nantucket's oldest inn (1709) provides atmospheric meals in three of the town's oldest dining rooms bearing the patina of age. Pine-paneled walls, low beamed ceilings and brass candlesticks are the norm; the rear room fashioned from the original kitchen adds an open hearth. White quilted mats, candles in hurricane chimneys and a fresh rose grace every table. Little wonder the Woodbox was voted "most romantic" for dining on the island.

Chef Joseph Keller lately has spiced up his traditional menu. The formerly classic shrimp cocktail might come with a spicy Asian vegetable salad and a lemon-garlic vinaigrette. Grilled squid could be marinated in ginger, garlic and chipotle chiles and paired with napa cabbage. The angus filet carpaccio could come with red pepper tapenade and smoked scallion aioli on crostini. For the main course ($16.50 to $23.50), you might choose seared sea scallops with salsify and roasted corn and basil sauce, pan-roasted salmon with a lemon-port sauce, or black angus sirloin with yukon gold potatoes and vidalia onions. Traditionalists still can opt for the rack of lamb provençal or, the house specialty, individual beef wellingtons. A garden salad and hot popovers come with. Dessert could be crème brûlée, bananas foster or fruit crumb cake.

(508) 228-0587. Dinner, Tuesday-Sunday, seatings at 6:30 and 9, Thursday-Saturday in off-season. Open Memorial Day to January.

Casual Dining Choices

Even the most determined Nantucket gourmet may tire of fancy, high-priced meals. Luckily, the island has other possibilities, among them:

Black-Eyed Susan's, 10 India St., Nantucket.

Some of the talk about dining in Nantucket lately has focused on Black Eyed Susan's, a small storefront run by partners Susan Handy and chef Jeff Worster, both with long backgrounds in local restaurants, the most recent being the Summer House. The space was formerly a breakfast bar, said Susan, and "all we had to do was clean it up." They still serve breakfast, probably a bit more fancy than before, with the likes of sourdough french toast with orange Jack Daniels butter and pecans and a spicy Thai curry scramble with broccoli and new potatoes (both $6.50). Most dishes come with a choice of hash browns or blackeyed peas, and you can add garlic, cilantro and/or salsa to your omelet for 25 cents each.

From his open kitchen behind the counter, Jeff, a chef-taught chef with experience in Los Angeles, where he got many of his creative ideas, offers such pasta dishes for dinner as wild-mushroom ravioli on carrot-ginger puree with organic greens and romano cheese ($16, or $9 for a half order). Grilled halibut served on saffron orzo, venetian whitefish and parmesan polenta with eggplant and onion compote, and Moroccan lamb stew on minted couscous are a few of the intriguing dishes (all $16 to $19.50) on his fall dinner menu. We liked the sound of lemon-parsnip soup with peppered grilled tomato. Lighter eaters could order a huge hearts of romaine salad with caesar dressing (a whole head of romaine, says Susan) for $8. There's one dessert a night, perhaps a cobbler or bread pudding.

There's a social, European cafe atmosphere, and singles love to eat at the long bar. Summer diners face waits of more than an hour; says Susan; "you put your name in and then go off and have a cocktail somewhere." She added that the idea was to be here for the local population more than for the tourists, but the word got out.

In 1996, the partners opened a casual restaurant called **Patio J,** behind the mini-golf course out near the airport at 12 Nobadeer Farm Road. Most of the fare is Mexican and Latin-American, and it's available for takeout.

No phone. Breakfast daily, 6:30 to 1 or 2; dinner, 6 to 10. No credit cards. BYOB. Closed six weeks in winter.

The Cafe on Old South Wharf, 14 Old South Wharf, Nantucket.

Formerly the Morning Glory Cafe, this is where everyone who is anyone seems to gather for breakfast to exchange gossip about the night before. They sit at tables on the wharf and wake up with good strong coffee and the famous Morning Glory muffins, made from carrots, raisins, nuts, apples and coconut – everything but the kitchen sink, according to the former owner. She sold in 1996 to the local group that bought American Seasons as well. Here they installed a former chef from 21 Federal, Carl Keller.

Inside, Carl works in an open kitchen beside a small cafe with striking trompe-l'oeil paintings on the walls, recently redone by an artist neighbor. More substantial breakfast fare ($5.95 to $7.95) includes Cuban spiced smoky chicken hash with coddled eggs, cardamom-spiced Portuguese sweet bread french toast, eggs benedict, and a grilled tortilla bearing scrambled eggs and peppers, black beans, salsa and sour cream.

The lunch menu ($6 to $11.50) offers caesar salad with chicken or garlic shrimp and another salad of smoked salmon, watercress and arugula. Sandwiches include a smoked turkey club and grilled rare tuna with scallion, pepper and ginger relish. You also can order quahog chowder and a lobster and crab spring roll. Beer and wines by the bottle, glass or carafe are available.

(508) 228-2212. Breakfast and lunch, daily except Tuesday, 7 to 3.

'Sconset Cafe, Post Office Square, Siasconset.

The founder of the Morning Glory Cafe, Pam McKinstry, moved on to the 'Sconset Cafe before giving it up to lead treks to Africa. Now she leases it to Rolf and Sue Nelson, who continue to pack in habitués at eight tables for three meals a day amid a casual green and white decor, track lighting and arty accents. We enjoyed a delicious lunch of croque monsieur ($8.50) and boboli, a pizza-like creation with pesto and artichoke hearts ($8). Finishing touches were homemade rum-walnut ice cream with chocolate sauce and a slice of frozen key lime pie, both heavenly.

Dinner dishes ($18 to $26) could be Thai seafood pasta, salmon with Mediterranean sauce, confit of duck or lamb dijon. Start with filetto carpaccio, crab cakes rémoulade, pot stickers or the cafe ravioli with artichokes and cheese. Save room for desserts like fresh peach pie, bête noir and bread pudding flavored with grand marnier. Some of the recipes are detailed in the cafe's three cookbooks.

(508) 257-4008. Lunch daily, 11:30 to 2:30; dinner, 6 to 9:30. Open mid-May to early October. BYOB. No credit cards.

Changes of Pace

Espresso Cafe, 40 Main St., Nantucket.

The foods of the local caterer, Fast Forward, have moved into this snazzy location with a mod interior in black and white and an appealing, two-level rear garden patio that's an oasis away from the hustle and bustle, with ivy twining all over the stucco walls. We know people who go here just for the desserts, perhaps lemon-almond pound cake or one of the gigantic cookies with cappuccino or the best cup of coffee in town. Scones, bagels and Mexican eggs are among the breakfast items. At lunch, we were impressed by a garden burger with Mexican sage cheese and salsa ($6.95) and a grilled spinach and mozzarella sandwich with garlic and roasted red peppers ($5.25), both served with zesty cafe potatoes. Another time, a big chocolate-chip cookie and a mocha cappuccino ($2.40) made a nice mid-afternoon break. Light entrées supplement the lunch items in the evening.

(508) 228-6930. Open daily in season, 7:30 a.m. to 10 or 11 p.m.; off-season, 7:30 to 5:30.

Off Centre Cafe, 29 Centre St., Nantucket.

Another of Nantucket's ubiquitous cafes, this small place offers creative breakfasts in the $5 to $7 range – perhaps nectarine pancakes, huevos rancheros with black beans, breakfast burritos or caramelized-banana popovers. The kitchen and the counter are bigger than the six-table cafe, which is augmented by a sidewalk cafe in the summer. The cafe branches out with elegant little dinners at night. You might find shrimp and artichoke hearts over angel-hair pasta or grilled lamb chops with red currant demi-glace.

(508) 228-8470. Breakfast daily, 8 to 1; dinner, Thursday-Monday from 6. Breakfast and lunch only in off-season. No credit cards.

Claudette's on the Porch, Post Office Square, Siasconset.

Casual fare is served up on the front deck by John Pearl. He learned to cook from his mother, Claudette, who started in 1967 and built this thriving little establishment from scratch. Ice-cream-parlor chairs and small round tables are the setting for muffins, lemonade, iced tea, soups like homemade turkey, and sandwiches (meat loaf, veggie, ham and cheese, $5.75). A box lunch ($6.75) yields a sandwich, veggie sticks and a brownie or Claudette's famous lemon cake, the recipe for which was published in Gourmet magazine.

(508) 257-6622. Open daily 9 to 4, May to mid-October.

Ethnic Choices

Chin's, 126 Chin's Way, Nantucket.

Ensconced in a house across from the Finast market south of town is this pleasant restaurant owned by Chin Manasmontri, a Chinese native from Thailand, who has been cooking and catering on the island since 1972. This is the real thing for the island's only Chinese and Thai foods (entrées, $10.50 to $18, the latter for seafood steamed with wine sauce and ginger in a clay pot). They're served in a Chinese decor that's surprisingly glamorous, save for the glass tops over the linens and the coffee cups and upside-down water tumblers at each setting.

(508) 228-0200. Lunch daily except Wednesday, 11:30 to 2; dinner nightly, 5 to 9:30.

Sushi by Yoshi, 2 East Chestnut St., Nantucket. (508) 228-1801.

This is the latest takeout endeavor associated with the folks at 21 Federal. Actually, they lease the space to Tokyo-born Yoshi Mabuchi, whom we remember from the halcyon days of Hatsune in New Haven. Here he seats up to eighteen people at three tables and a small sushi bar, and offers his sensational sushi to go.

Besides more kinds of sushi than you probably thought existed in so small a place, Yoshi offers other Japanese appetizers and entrées at moderate prices, here or to go. By reservation, he offers a seven-course Japanese dinner at 9 o'clock.

Open daily, 11:30 to 10:30. Closed Tuesday and Wednesday in off-season and mid-December to April.

Natural Gourmet

Something Natural, 50 Cliff Road, Nantucket.
Gourmet magazine requested the recipes for the carrot cake and the herb bread made at this rustic cottage at the edge of town. There are old school desks on the deck and picnic tables on the grounds for enjoying one of the nineteen sandwiches ($4.50 to $6.95 whole, $2.50 to $4.30 for a half), available on the wonderful whole wheat, oatmeal, rye, pumpernickel, herb, six-grain and Portuguese breads baked here and served at many a restaurant in town. We found half a sandwich of smoked turkey with tomato and swiss cheese plenty for a late lunch. You also can get salads, Nantucket Nectars and, for breakfast, muffins and raisin rolls. Owner Matt Fee recently branched out with the **Nantucket Bagel Company,** offering breakfast and lunch year-round, across town at 5 West Creek Road.
(508) 228-0504. Open daily 8 to 6 in summer, shorter hours in off-season. Open May-October.

Dining and Lodging

The Wauwinet, Box 2580, Wauwinet Road, Nantucket 02554.
Gloriously situated on a strip of land between Nantucket Bay and the Atlantic, the Wauwinet House had seen better days before it was acquired by Stephen and Jill Karp of Weston, Mass., island vacationers who restored the place to the tune of many millions of dollars for a grand reopening in 1988.
The original building in a rural section of parkland was gutted to make a dining room with french doors and windows taking advantage of the view, a common sitting room with a fireplace, and 24 air-conditioned rooms with private baths, antique pine armoires, and iron or wicker headboards. Five cottages (containing eleven more rooms and suites) were added across the road.
Our bayview bedroom – as opposed to deluxe or suite – was not large but was nicely located on a third-floor corner facing the harbor so that we were able to watch spectacular sunsets at night. Fresh and pretty, it had a queensize bed, upholstered armchairs and a painted armoire topped with a wooden swan and two hat boxes (one of the inn's decorating signatures). The modern bathroom contained a multitude of thick white towels and a basket of Crabtree & Evelyn amenities. During turndown service, the towels were replenished and mints placed by the bed.
All the rooms we saw had different, striking stenciled borders (some turning up in the most ingenious places), interesting artworks and sculptures, ceiling fans, and such fillips as clouds painted on the ceiling. TVs and VCRs are hidden in armoires and trunks.
Outside are chairs lined up strategically on the back lawn and a beachside platform where guests may play "beach chess" with lifesize pieces. You can swim from a dock in the bay, or walk a couple of minutes through the dunes in front of the hotel to the most gorgeous, endless and unoccupied strand we've seen along the Atlantic coast. A 21-foot runabout will transport guests to town or to a remote beach for the day. You can play tennis or rent a sailboat, all complimentary.
A full breakfast is included in the room rate. Guests order from a menu spanning a spectrum from strawberry and rhubarb pancakes to egg-white omelets with spa cheese and fresh vegetables.
General manager Russell Cleveland (earlier of Williamsburg Inn and Salishan

Toppers is luxurious dining room at the Wauwinet.

Lodge renown) ensures that everything is first-rate as far as lodging goes. The restaurant and its wine cellar are overseen by his wife Debbie, food and beverage manager, who was pleased as punch that Wine Spectator had just announced it as a grand award winner, one of six new ones worldwide, in 1996.

Toppers, named for the owners' dog, is a refined summery setting for some of the island's best food. Two elegant, side-by-side rooms harbor masses of flowers and well-spaced tables with upholstered chairs in blue and white. The outdoor terrace overlooking lawn and bay is favored for lunch and drinks.

Executive chef Peter Wallace's dinner menu, printed daily, is priced from $29 for a seven-vegetable napoleon to $39 for pan-seared sea scallops with lobster risotto.

Among appetizers ($16 to $21, except $40 for ossetra caviar), we savored the lobster and crab cakes with smoked corn and a super mustard sauce, and grilled quail on a toasted brioche.

Stellar seafood dishes include local tuna sashimi with pickled vegetables and condiments, and grilled striped bass with creamy polenta. We enjoyed the grilled rack and leg of lamb with a tomato-eggplant timbale and peppered veal chop with cognac-mustard cream. Both were accompanied by baby vegetables (tiny pattypan squash and sliced carrots about as big as a fingernail) and a wedge of potatoes.

Desserts like molten chocolate cake with a trio of ice creams and a classic crème brûlée are worthy endings.

The lunch menu is a tasting selection of tapas. It's designed so you can sample several items and the portions are purposely small. Most choose four for $19.75. Three for $16.50 make a light lunch, according to the menu, and five for $23.50 represent an "active" lunch.

A special treat for visitors in town is a cruise to the Wauwinet for lunch or dinner. *(508) 228-0145 or (800) 426-8718. Fax (508) 228-7135. Lunch daily, noon to 2; dinner nightly, 6 to 9:30, jackets requested; Sunday brunch, 10:30 to 2. Doubles, $290 to $590; suites, $490 to $1,000. Three-night minimum on summer weekends. Open April through Christmas Stroll.*

The Summer House, 17 Ocean Ave., Box 313, Siasconset 02564.

A more romantic setting for dining could scarcely be imagined than the front veranda of this low-slung, Southern-style house or its summery interior dining room. It's a mix of white chairs (many with billowing blue-cushioned backs) and painted floors, good 'Sconset oils and watercolors on the whitewashed walls, and fresh flowers and plants everywhere.

We chose one of the handful of tables on the veranda yielding a view of the moon rising over the ocean that we could hear lapping at the foot of the bluff across the road. The setting remained etched in our memory longer than our dinner, which was more ordinary than the tab would have suggested. But the new manager advises the dining situation has improved under chefs Ruth and Timothy Pitts, she formerly the chef at DeMarco in town.

You're paying for the setting as well as the food, of course. Appetizers ($8 to $13) might be sautéed lobster cake with cucumber, chive and crème fraîche, or prosciutto with roasted portobello mushrooms, fontina and sundried tomatoes. Main courses ($26 to $32) include grilled arctic char with citrus vinaigrette, pan-roasted halibut with lobster and potato hash, roast loin of rabbit with porcini risotto and grilled venison chop with apple-cognac sauce.

A brandy tart with dollops of whipped cream, blueberries and slices of kiwi proved a memorable choice from a dessert selection that included crème brûlée, key lime pie on a raspberry coulis, chocolate sin cake with crème anglaise, and pecan tart with bourbon ice cream and fresh berries. The extensive wine list, priced from $28 to $160, concludes with a page of cigars.

Our meal was enlivened by the piano stylings of Sal Gioe, an island institution who was playing in the white rattan-filled lounge and whose 87-year-old fingers still fly across the keyboard of a new grand piano. We were content to toddle off to our room in one of eight Bermuda-like cottages strung in a horseshoe pattern around a garden between restaurant and sea.

Beneath a canopy of trees and ivy with bridal veil spilling over the roofs, the charming, rose-covered cottages have been redecorated with antiques, eyelet-embroidered pillows and lace-edged duvets on the beds, lace curtains, and painted floors and chests. An art student hand-painted floral borders along the tops of the walls for the finishing touch. Interesting roof lines, stained glass, leaded windows, and little nooks and crannies contribute to the charm. Modern amenities include telephones and renovated bathrooms, each with a marble jacuzzi.

Jimmy Cagney cherished the privacy of the cottage-suite named in his honor. Although each has its own or a shared small terrace, we felt on display reading on ours as arriving diners passed at cocktail hour. There are no real sitting areas, public or private, inside the cottages or main building.

An elaborate continental breakfast buffet – juices, fresh fruit, granola, bran cereal and baked goods – is offered in the morning on the sun-drenched veranda, where you can savor the sun rising over the open expanse of azure-blue ocean.

Lunch is available on a landscaped bluestone terrace beside the pool, sequestered halfway down the bluff in the dunes, a long stone's throw from the beach. Everything's pricey ($6 to $17), but there's a good selection and the eight-ounce burger is advertised as the best on the island. Look at it this way: lunch patrons get to use the pool (others are charged $15), and the view is free.

(508) 257-9976. Lunch at poolside, daily noon to 3:30; dinner, 6:30 to 10, bar menu to 10:30. Doubles, $350 to $400; suites, $385 to $500. Open May-October.

Summery dining room at Summer House in Siasconset.

Cliffside Beach Club, Jefferson Avenue, Box 449, Nantucket 02554.

The Cliffside Beach Club, situated for more than 70 years on the marvelous open beach on the north shore, has been owned since 1954 by the Currie family, whose offspring now run a deluxe small inn/hotel and an oceanfront restaurant.

Club members coveted the same umbrella and assortment of chairs and used to wait years to reserve one of the more prestigious spots on the west beach, according to general manager Robert F. Currie. Now guests don't have to wait – they simply walk out of their rooms onto the beach. Some of the old bathhouses have been converted into fourteen contemporary bedrooms with cathedral ceilings and modern baths. All the beds, doors, tables, vanities and even the pegs for the beach towels were fashioned by Nantucket craftsmen. Angled wainscoting serves as the headboards for the built-in queensize beds. Prints by local artists and oriental rugs on the dark green carpets set off the old wood walls. Wicker furniture, antique wooden toys and black leather couches are among the appointments.

Nine air-conditioned beachfront studio apartments, each with a private deck and the phones and TVs characteristic of all the rooms, were added in 1987. Two suites were added in 1990, and a new exercise room is said to be one of the busiest spots in town. Plans were in the works in 1996 for four two-story suites on the west side of the property.

A continental breakfast is served in the club's spectacular high-ceilinged lobby that Monique Currie decorated in South of France style. It has quilts on the ceiling and is full of smart wicker furniture and potted flowers, so prolific and splashy that tending them has "become my full-time job," says Monique.

Lunch and dinner are available to guests and the public at **The Galley at Cliffside Beach,** situated between the club and the studio apartments, with an L-shaped, canopied deck facing the ocean. Here you sit on blue wicker chairs at tables with floral cloths, backing up to planters filled with petunias and geraniums with hanging pink paper globes overhead. It's enchanting by day or night.

We thoroughly enjoyed a couple of the best bloody marys ever (spicy and generous, as they ought to be for $5) before a lunch of salade niçoise and chicken salad Hawaiian ($11 and $12). Service is by waiters who spend their winters working at a club in Palm Beach, which helps explain the level of professionalism here.

A jazz pianist plays at night, when the place conveys a clubby air. The dinner menu is priced from $21 for drunken mussels with grilled garlic bread to $32 for a whole lobster stew in saffron broth with mussels, roasted tomatoes and tagliatelle. Among the choices are grilled tuna with Asian stir-fry, Szechwan-seared Atlantic salmon on Thai curry sauce, grilled breast of duck with pomegranate glaze and pistachio-crusted rack of lamb. Start with beer-battered calamari with pepper aioli, lobster cake with avocado and roasted corn relish, or spinach salad with warm goat cheese and seared portobello mushrooms. Finish with homemade cognac ice cream, French blueberry-peach pie or chocolate-soufflé cake.

Owner Jane Currie Silva's sons David, who used to be sous chef, and Geoffrey, the maître-d, oversee the front of the house. Many of the Galley's paintings and the menu cover are by Belgian artist Lucien van Vyve, the first chef at the old Opera House here, whom Jane considers her mentor.

(508) 228-0618. Lunch daily, noon to 2; dinner nightly, 6 to 10, mid-June to mid-September; Thursday-Monday until Columbus Day. Doubles, $270 to $425; suites, $525 to $695; lodging, late May to mid-October.

Ships Inn, 13 Fair St., Nantucket 02554.

Built in 1831 by whaling captain Obed Starbuck, this was nicely restored by chef-owner Mark Gottwald and his wife Ellie. It now claims some of Nantucket's most comfortable accommodations as well as a highly regarded restaurant.

The ten guest rooms with private baths, named after ships that Starbuck commanded, contain many of original furnishings. They have been refurbished with new wallpapers and tiled baths and come with interesting window treatments, down comforters, Neutrogena toiletries and mini-refrigerators in cabinets beneath the TV sets. Most have reading chairs and half have desks. All but two tiny single rooms are more spacious than most bedrooms in Nantucket inns.

Guests enjoy afternoon tea with coffeecake and cookies. Innkeeper Meghan Moore sets out a continental-plus breakfast of fruit, cereal, scones and muffins.

Dinners here have received considerable attention since the Gottwalds took over. Chef Mark, who trained at Le Cirque in New York and at Spago in Los Angeles, oversees the cooking duties with a sizable kitchen staff. He calls the style California-French. Among entrées ($18 to $24), you might find crispy salmon with cabernet sauce and niçoise vegetables, stuffed prawns with lobster-tamarind sauce and roasted beet and garlic raviolis, roast duck with foie gras and plum wine, and steak au poivre with braised endive and haricots verts. Or consider a pasta ($15 to $18.50), perhaps lamb lasagna with spinach and goat cheese or medallions of lobster on homemade fettuccine. Start with chilled tomato-ginger soup with avocado, fried calamari with ponzu sauce or chive scrambled eggs with sevruga caviar. Finish with chocolate voodoo cake or passionfruit crème brûlée studded with fresh cherries. A well-chosen but pricey wine list starts in the twenties.

The dining room is attractive with apricot walls over white wainscoting, exposed beams, a white fireplace in the center of the room, candles in the many-paned windows, and white-linened tables dressed with candles and fresh flowers. There also are tables for eating in the adjacent Dory Bar.

Canopied outdoor deck offers seaside dining at The Galley on Cliffside Beach.

The Gottwalds winter with their young children in Vero Beach, Fla., where they opened Ellie's, a new American restaurant on the waterfront, in 1994. They and their staff go back and forth between Vero Beach and Nantucket.

(508) 228-0040. Dinner, nightly except Tuesday, 5:30 to 9:15. Doubles, $125 to $150. Open April-November.

Lodging

Westmoor Inn, Cliff Road, Nantucket 02554.

The secluded hilltop location at the edge of town is one of the drawing cards at this substantial inn, with fourteen guest rooms on the second and third floors, all with private baths and some quite spacious by Nantucket standards. Other draws are the continental breakfasts in the cheery solarium dining room, the nightly wine and hors d'oeuvres offered in the elegant living room, the small library/TV room dressed in wicker, and the inviting rear patio and gardens.

Guest rooms and a suite vary in size (some are quite small), but all are lavishly furnished with a mix of modern and antique furnishings and have telephones. Most contain king or queen beds and one suite has a jacuzzi. We liked Room 206 with a kingsize bed and a fireplace. The bathroom in its neighbor is as big as the bedroom, but surprisingly, most have showers only rather than tubs (a pattern repeated at many local B&Bs). Abundant toiletries are in each bathroom.

Innkeeper Nancy Walsh attends the wine and cheese party, which runs from 6 to 7 and "becomes a real gathering," she says. Also special is the breakfast, beautifully served on tables with white cloths and decorative overlays in the skylit solarium, where three walls of windows afford a panoramic view. It's apt to include fresh fruit, wild blueberries, cereals, yogurt and an elaborate spread of croissants, muffins, breads and scones, and two kinds of fruit muffins.

"This house is unique here because of its grand open public rooms and its grand scale," says Nancy.

(508) 228-0877. Doubles, $115 to $255. Open mid-April through December.

Centerboard Guest House, 8 Chester St., Box 456, Nantucket 02554.

A Victorian guest house of quiet country elegance is how its brochure describes it. That doesn't entirely do justice to this appealing B&B, which is a cut above the rest in town. Each of the seven air-conditioned guest rooms has private bath, color TV, phone and mini-refrigerator, and is furnished with panache by owner Marcia Wasserman, a Long Island artist and interior designer.

We lucked into the main-floor suite, with a library-style living room in dark woods and hunter green, a bedroom with a queensize canopy feather bed, and a glamorous bathroom in deep green marble, with a jacuzzi in one section, a large marble-tiled shower in another, and the sink and toilet in still another. The suite had two TVs, plush masculine furnishings, and no fewer than six bouquets of fresh and dried flowers scattered here and there.

The upstairs rooms are romantic, if not quite so glamorous. All with queens or two double beds, they show decorative flair, with lacy pillows and the odd mural on the wall. Refrigerators with soft drinks, baskets of Gilbert & Soames toiletries, a bowl of toffee and a welcoming basket of apples and cheeses are in the rooms. A studio apartment in the basement has built-in double beds and a small kitchen.

A resident innkeeper puts out a bountiful continental breakfast buffet: bowls of fresh fruit salad, cereals, granola, cranberry and coconut muffins, and Portuguese bread for toasting. This can be taken in the dining room, on the front porch or at the window seat in the living room.

(508) 228-9696. Doubles, $165; suites, $285.

Cliff Lodge, 9 Cliff Road, Nantucket 02554.

Eleven guest rooms, designed for comfort and decorated with flair, are offered at this 1771 sea captain's house in a residential neighborhood overlooking town and harbor. John and Debby Bennett bought the establishment in 1996 and immediately enhanced the gardens, a talent he learned from his father, a professional landscaper. A Nantucket native, he met his wife-to-be at the local hospital, where both were employed.

Bedrooms here are notable for spatter-painted floors, Laura Ashley wallpapers, frilly bedding, fresh flowers and antiques. Many boast kingsize beds and fireplaces, and all have private baths, telephones and TVs nicely built into the walls or concealed in armoires.

Few B&Bs have so many neat places to sit and relax, inside or out. There are five sitting rooms on three floors, a rooftop deck with a view of the harbor, reading porches and a couple of brick patios beside the lovely gardens.

Debby serves a buffet breakfast in one of the sitting rooms, or guests can adjourn to the patio, where she matches the tablecloths with the flowers that are in bloom. Fresh fruit, cereal, muffins and Portuguese toasting bread are typical fare. She offers hot or iced tea and snacks in the afternoon.

(508) 228-9480. Doubles, $125 to $165.

Union Street Inn, 7 Union St., Nantucket 02554.

A hotel manager from Connecticut and his wife, Ken and Deborah Withrow,

Greenhouse breakfast room at Westmoor Inn offers view across town.

took over this newish inn in 1995 and gave it the professional, in-residence care it needed. The restored 1770 house, converted from a guest house into a luxury B&B by previous owners, offers twelve spacious bedrooms with private baths, antique furnishings and cable TV. Six have working fireplaces. Many have canopy or four-poster beds, and scatter rugs dot the original wide-plank pine floors.

Because of its location (and zoning), the Union Street can offer more than Nantucket's highly regulated continental breakfasts. The Withrows serve things like scrambled eggs and bacon, blueberry pancakes, french toast and, every fourth day, eggs benedict. These are in addition to a cold buffet that includes a fresh fruit platter, cereals and muffins. The repast is taken in a large dining room or at three handsome garden tables on the side patio beneath an ivy-covered hillside.

"Debbie cooks and I'm the bus boy," says Ken, who had been manager of the Hyatt UN Plaza Hotel in New York and the Ambassador East Hotel in Chicago. They wanted their own business and a family life for their young son, and found both here.

(508) 228-9222 or (800) 225-5116. Doubles, $140 to $195; suite, $230.

The Sherburne Inn, 10 Gay St., Nantucket 02554.

Built in 1835 as headquarters for the Atlantic Silk Company, this house in a residential area has been a lodging establishment since 1872. When Pennsylvanians Dale Hamilton III and Susan Gasparich purchased The House at 10 Gay in 1993, they changed its name and continued upgrading it into a first-class B&B.

The pair offer eight guest rooms, now all with private baths. Two have king beds and six are queensize. Four are on the main floor and four on the second; a beautiful staircase connects the two. Interestingly, there's a fireplaced parlor with television on each floor. The bedrooms, bright and cheery, are decorated to the Federal period. They contain canopy and poster beds, oriental rugs and fine artworks. We liked No. 8 upstairs in the rear with a king bed, clawfoot tub with shower and a private balcony overlooking the side and rear yards. Another room holds a small library and a mini-refrigerator.

Susan bakes blueberry or rhubarb muffins to supplement the natural breads, bagels and English muffins served for continental breakfast. Fresh fruit and juice accompany. The meal is taken in the main-floor parlor, on a deck on one side of the house or in the yard surrounded by gardens and a privet hedge on the other side. Tea and cookies or wine and cheese may be served in the afternoon.
(508) 228-4425. Doubles, $125 to $160.

Cobblestone Inn, 5 Ash St., Nantucket 02554.
Wooden lighthouses line the stairs at this B&B, lovingly tended by Robin Hammer-Yankow, a past Chamber of Commerce president and civic booster, and her husband Keith, a local attorney. Their 1725 house beside a cobblestoned street offers five guest rooms, all with private baths and queen canopy beds and nicely furnished with period pieces. Painted Colonial windows and beams, oriental rugs and swag curtains that match the canopies are some of the decorative touches. History shows up in the wide-plank floors, narrow closets and tilted doorways.

Given its in-town location and the cobblestoned street, we were surprised to find our second-floor room so utterly quiet, until the church bells tolled at 7 a.m. We were ready to arise anyway to prepare for Robin's continental breakfast, served family style at a long table in the dining area behind the living room. Fresh fruit, orange juice, homemade granola, cereals and melt-in-the-mouth pumpkin and zucchini breads were the fare.

Guests spread out in a living room with TV, a sun porch with wicker furniture, and a brick patio overlooking the garden. Cold beverages and treats like fresh brownies are put out in the afternoons.
(508) 228-1987. Doubles, $125 to $160.

Martin House Inn, 61 Centre St., Box 743, Nantucket 02554.
Hard work and T.L.C. by owners Ceci and Channing Moore have upgraded this 1803 mariner's home, a guest house since the 1920s and heretofore rather short of creature comforts. No more. The Moores, who lived previously in Hong Kong and Wilmington, Del., have taken to it with heart and soul.

Exceptionally pretty are the large open front foyer and the long front parlor and dining area, with sponged royal blue walls and lovely oriental rugs. The dining-room table is set for eight, although some prefer to eat on a tray at one of the wicker chairs on the side veranda. An expanded continental breakfast of two fresh fruits, cereal, granola, Nantucket breads and homemade muffins is the fare.

The Moores offer thirteen guest rooms, nine with private baths and most with queensize beds. We saw a couple of spacious rooms with canopy beds, fireplaces, cherry dressers and either a loveseat or two plush club chairs. Four rooms on the third floor share baths. One room with two double beds can accommodate four people, and two single rooms are offered at $55 a night.
(508) 228-0678. Doubles, $90 to $160.

Anchor Inn, 66 Centre St., Nantucket 02554.
Charles and Ann Balas, who used to own the Nantucket Fine Chocolates store, are the hands-on innkeepers at this venerable B&B and feel their in-residence position helps set the inn apart. Built by a whaling ship captain, this was the home in the 1950s of the Gilbreths of "Cheaper by the Dozen" fame, who wrote of their experience in the book *Innside Nantucket*.

Eleven guest rooms, named after whaling ships, have private baths, queen or twin beds, and period furnishings amid the original random-width floorboards and antique paneling. Guests help themselves to continental breakfast on an enclosed side porch with cafe curtains. Charles's homemade muffins are served to the accompaniment of classical music.

The Balases, who by nature and avocation know all the food goings-on around the island, share their insights with guests in the front parlor.

(508) 228-0072. Doubles, $115 to $160.

Gourmet Treats

Rarely have we seen a small place so chock full of gourmet shops, specialty-food takeouts, caterers and other services pertaining to matters culinary.

At **Chanticleer to Go,** 15 South Beach St., Nathalie Berruet manages her family's gourmet takeout shop. Most of the food is different from that at the renowned Chanticleer ("we cater more to the tourists here," Nathalie explains). But the foods "reflect the Chanticleer flair," as in coq au vin, osso buco and beef bourguignonne, which are made at the kitchen in 'Sconset. She also sells some of the same wines and her pastry chef here sends some of his desserts to the restaurant. You'll find basic sandwiches in the $5 range, some not-so-basic salads, soups, wonderful appetizers, rotisserie chicken and duck, and pastries galore. Open Monday-Saturday 10 to 8, Sunday noon to 6. Closed November to April.

Many cheeses, gazpacho, Thai noodle and curried couscous salads, muffulettas, apple-peach muffins and sandwiches in the $5 to $6 range are available from **Provisions,** behind the bandstand on Straight Wharf. Also part of the food complex here are **Stars,** a seasonal ice cream and frozen yogurt shop with a porch where you can sit right by the water, and the **Straight Wharf Fish Store,** where soft-shell crab and swordfish steak sandwiches were going for $8.25 and fish fillet sandwiches for $7.25 last we knew. The store carries some specialty foods along with fresh fish.

For our money, the best homemade ice creams and yogurts in town are served at **The Juice Bar,** a pastry and ice cream shop at 12 Broad St. across from the Whaling Museum. We enjoyed an oversize cup of different fruit sorbets after one dessert-less dinner. Frozen yogurt with a choice of more than 25 toppings and island-baked pastries are available at **Yogurt Plus,** a sit-down place that formerly was a restaurant at 6 Oak St.

Satisfy your sweet tooth at **Sweet Inspirations** at 26 Centre St. You can indulge in handmade chocolates, pecan and caramel tuckernucks, award-winning cranberry truffles, chocolate-almond buttercrunch, and an exclusive line of Nantucket fruit preserves and chutneys. A recent favorite is cranberry bark, available in dark, milk or white chocolate, each studded with bright red dried cranberries. The confections are made here daily the old-fashioned way, smoothed and cut by hand.

The Complete Kitchen at 25 Centre St. offers Nantucket jams, jellies and ketchup made just for the store, caviars, crème fraîche and California tortas with fresh basil, garlic and pinenuts or smoked salmon, mustard and dill. All those items the beautiful people need for their cocktail parties are here, as are a good selection of cookbooks and cookware. Around the corner is the **Nantucket Gourmet,** with more specialty foods and a lot of high-tech kettles, toasters and such as well as a practical oyster opener for $13.95. **Zazou** at 50 Main St. features MacKenzie-Childs pottery among its gifts and home accessories.

If you're interested in pepper grinders, check out the Peppergun, invented and made on the island. Ads headlining it as "Nantucket Native" tout the fast-grinding one-hander as the world's most efficient peppermill. It's on sale at local stores.

The Lion's Paw at the foot of Main Street carries wonderful handpainted pottery, including great fish plates. We think it's the nicest of several gift shops of interest to gourmets.

Majolica at 1 Old North Wharf specializes in handpainted, one-of-a-kind pieces of the imported Italian pottery and ceramics. The colorful store displays teapots, trays, vases, salad bowls, demitasse cups and the trademark rooster pitchers in several sizes. You can even buy a set of handpainted animal plates from Tuscany.

Only in Nantucket would you not be surprised to find **Cold Noses,** a small gourmet shop for cats and dogs near Straight Wharf. As well as gourmet natural dog cookies, you'll find "doggie duds," cat beds, pearls pour le pouch and perfect purrls for cats, and even cologne from Paris for Fluffy or Spot.

Although its wines don't seem to turn up in many local restaurants, **Nantucket Vineyard** produces 3,500 cases a year. Vintners Dean and Melissa Long started as an offshoot of Bartlett's Ocean View Farm out Hummock Pond Road, where everybody on the island seems to go for fresh produce (if they don't get to the morning selection at the sidewalk stand at Main and Federal streets in town). The Longs grow five varieties of vinifera grapes, but import most from Long Island and Washington. On sale at the winery at the side of their home at 3 Bartlett Farm Road are their latest bottlings of chardonnay, riesling and merlot. Tastings are offered daily, 11 to 6.

They're Juice Guys

Nantucket Nectars, juices that seem to be showing up everywhere, got their start in Nantucket. Tom First and Tom Scott, fresh out of Brown University in 1988, started Allserve, a floating convenience store, to serve boats in Nantucket Harbor. During the off-season, they recreated for island friends the taste of a peach nectar that Tom First had enjoyed in Spain. They began making it in blenders and selling it in cups off the stern of the Allserve boat in 1990.

Starting with three flavors, the pair known as "Tom and Tom – we're juice guys" expanded to the point where, seven years later, they were the fastest-growing New Age beverage company in the country. These beverages that the locals contend are a bigger and better phenomenon than Snaffle and Celestial Seasonings are now headquartered in Boston and produced in five plants around the country. Thirty varieties of all-natural fruit juices are sold through their own distribution network in 30 states.

They come with distinctive purple caps and colorful labels that depict fond memories of days spent in the Allserve General Store behind the Hy-Line terminal at 44 Straight Wharf. Most varieties cost 99 cents a bottle here, more around town and on the mainland. The bottle caps contain nuggets of Nantucket lore, and it's the in thing locally to rate mention on a cap.

Boston skyline as viewed from the Rotunda at Boston Harbor Hotel.

Boston and Cambridge
Baked Beans to New Cuisine

If Los Angeles is our last culinary frontier, as one food magazine has suggested, Boston is our first. This city situated not far from where the Pilgrims landed has had more than 350 years to refine and redefine itself, to become civilized in cuisine as well as in culture.

No American city has given its name to, nor been associated with, more indigenous foods. Boston baked beans, Boston scrod, Boston lettuce, Indian pudding, Boston brown bread and Parker House rolls got their start here. The nation's first French restaurant dates back to 1793 in Boston. The Parker House opened in 1854 as New England's first leading hotel and dining room. The famed Durgin-Park can safely proclaim it was "established before you were born." Locke-Ober still serves lobster savannah in the same manner it did when one of us first had it there as a teenager more decades ago than she cares to remember. Julia Child launched her national reputation in Boston and still calls Cambridge home.

Boston's food scene has perhaps changed more in the last fifteen years than in its first 350, however. Some of the staples remain, but the new regional cuisine is everywhere – reigning a tad preciously in some of the East's great restaurants (most of them creatures of the 1980s and '90s), simply evolving or being accommodated in more traditional places. Boston was among the first to take to bistro cooking, even before its restaurants started the trend toward downscaling as the economy softened in the early 1990s. And Boston restaurants were among the first to upscale again as the recession eased.

Boston is at the heart of an emerging New England cuisine, with chefs seeking out the best regional ingredients and developing original recipes. Some are on the cutting edge, and several have been ranked by national magazines among the country's best. Lydia Shire, who led the revolution in Boston food circles while at the acclaimed Seasons, returned to Boston to open her own restaurant after a brief stint in southern California, where she said she could not find as good local provisioners. Several of the city's hotels are in the forefront of the city's growing culinary reputation, and the chefs they import tend to stay to open their own restaurants.

The leading chefs in America's largest small town consider themselves a family, it seems. They've reached the bigtime here, and have little inclination to move on. Which makes Boston an exciting destination for those seeking adventure in food and wine.

Dining

The Best of the Best

L'Espalier, 30 Gloucester St., Boston.

The first – and, many think, still the best – of Boston's great restaurants, L'Espalier offers cuisine, setting and style for a special occasion. It makes such demands upon your palate that we cannot imagine dining here every week, as some habitués are known to do. Not to mention the fact that the money we spent for a birthday dinner for two could have fed a couple of hundred souls at a soup kitchen we know of.

L'Espalier opened in 1978 under the auspices of Tunisian-born French chef Moncef Meddeb, who sold it a decade later to his sous chef, Frank McClelland. Frank and his wife Catherine, who live upstairs with their young children, devote full-time-plus to the effort. "We're putting lots of energy into upgrading every aspect of the cuisine, service and decor so that we have something very special here," says Frank, whose youth and unassuming demeanor belie his stature as one of the nation's top 25 chefs in the nation in Food & Wine magazine's estimation.

Despite a tough economy, the McClellands.have taken the high-end market and made it virtually their own. L'Espalier is the only major Boston restaurant left that has a totally prix-fixe menu. It charges $62 for three courses or $78 for the dégustation menu, for which the chef makes the choices, taking two first courses, a fish course, a main course and a selection of desserts from the regular menu. Since we wanted to taste as much as possible, we put ourselves in the chef's hands.

You might start with a cappuccino of chanterelles and white truffles, a vegetarian broth with a foamy topping of essence of mushrooms and truffles steamed in the manner of cappuccino, enhanced with Wellfleet oysters baked with cider and cracked white-pepper glaze. That could be followed by roasted New York foie gras with quince tatin and pomegranate savory sauce. Next, how about glazed Maine lobster in curry and carrot juice with lobster and avocado mousse and a watercress-tarragon sauce? A sorbet of blood orange and fruit coulis with star anise prepares the palate suavely for the main event, perhaps roast rack and loin of lamb on fava beans with artichoke and vidalia onion soufflé, grilled tomato and fresh oregano. Then follows a selection of cheeses and desserts, perhaps coconut mille-feuille with passionfruit mousse and mango, an apricot, honey and poppyseed torte with white-chocolate crème anglaise and raspberries, and a trio of intense rhubarb-ginger, pineapple and honeydew sorbets with berries and fruit coulis.

The menu descriptions belie the complexity of flavors and tastes. Frank cooks in an intellectual style, working daily in a test kitchen on taste and composition so that the diner senses the essence of the food. Perfection is his goal (he received the

Frank and Catherine McClelland pause for dessert at L'Espalier.

new Boston Globe food critic's first four-star review). He also has a passion for vegetables. Indeed, his was the first mainsteam restaurant we encountered to offer a dégustation vegetarian menu, $68 for seven remarkable courses plus dessert.

No matter what you choose, whether the roast stuffed rabbit loin with kale and vegetables or the grilled rack of venison mole with morel risotto, asparagus spring roll and chervil puree, you can be assured of the ultimate in flavors.

The lamb, rabbit, produce – most grown organically – come from L'Espalier's own purveyors. Frank personally buys the selections for the thirteen-page wine list, especially strong on Bordeaux and wines from Alsace and Rhône, well aged in three cellars. Although he has twelve professional cooks in the kitchen, he works a station and personally oversees every dish that goes out. You also can be assured that he's on the scene – when he goes to France for his annual busman's holiday to study with three-star chefs, he closes the restaurant.

His renovated Back Bay townhouse has a supremely elegant atmosphere in which to sample this changing blend of classic French and nouvelle cuisine. After buzzing a doorbell to gain entry, diners proceed to the second floor, which has two high-ceilinged dining rooms in shades of taupe and cream, or to the third floor, where the dining-room walls are a warm lacquered and stenciled terra cotta and the kitchen is next door. There are marble fireplaces, carved moldings, beautiful flower arrangements in niches, pin spotlights on tables set with damask linens and fresh flowers, and comfortable and luxurious lacquered chairs with curved arms.

From the complimentary fennel and leek mousse wrapped with smoked salmon and topped with ossetra caviar that might accompany cocktails to the petit fours that gild the bill, diners here relish a rare culinary treat.

(617) 262-3023. Dinner by reservation, Monday-Saturday 6 to 10.

Salamander, 1 Athenaeum St., Cambridge.

"Bursts of flavors" is how chef-owner Stan Frankenthaler describes the fiery, fusion-style grill cuisine at his top-rated restaurant named for the elusive animal associated in mythology with fire. His patrons certainly agree.

Taking over quarters formerly occupied by Michela's restaurant on the lobby level of the historic Carter Ink Building, Stan opened up the substantial dining space to show off the pillars and dressed it in earth tones of mustard yellow, rust and gray. Tables, seating 125 and spaced comfortably apart, are covered with white linens for dinner.

From the wood-fired grills, rotisseries and tandoor ovens in an open display kitchen come explosive tributes to the Middle East and southeast Asia. Expect tantalizing main dishes ($19 to $35) like lightly fried lobster with chiles, lemongrass and Thai basil, red snapper wrapped in banana leaves and roasted with a stir-fry of rock shrimp, oysters and littleneck clams, and tea-scented rotisserie chicken on a cucumber puree with soft flour dumplings and Asian greens. Each is a feast for the eye as well as for the tastebuds.

Prepare your palate with such heady starters ($7 to $14.50) as a sizzling rice noodle pancake filled with sweet tamarind shrimp, fried oysters on creamed spinach with queso manchego and serrano ham, or seared foie gras over a salt-roasted organic heirloom potato with creamy roasted cipollini (Italian onions).

Refresh with a dessert ($7) like the signature sweet banana-stuffed wontons with rum-caramel ice cream and macadamia brittle, crispy pastry treats layered with cinnamon couscous custard and a spiced quince compote, or warm apple coupe served with a crispy apple dumpling and concord grape sorbet.

The wine list, starting in the mid-twenties, is as exotic as the fare. There's also quite a selection of after-dinner wines, beers, ports, single-malt scotches and bond bourbons.

By day, Salamander operates a **Food Shop** dispensing a changing menu of exotic salads and sandwiches. The food is great for takeout or for eating in the adjoining lobby's soaring indoor atrium, which becomes Salamander's lounge at night. We joined the lineup for lunch, each picking out a couple of salads doled out generously for $4.50 a half pound. Tuscan white beans and braised eggplant, yellow mein noodles with julienned vegetables in a Thai crab paste, sweet and sour fried tofu, and coleslaw in a sweet mustard vinaigrette were each distinct bursts of flavors. A mellow raspberry cheesecake square was a refreshing ending. And we couldn't believe the price – $10.70, for a dynamite lunch for two. Little wonder that many computer techies in surrounding office buildings lunch here several times a week.

Stan, who trained with famed local chef Jasper White and at the Hotel Meridien and Hamersley's Bistro before opening his own place in 1994, has a great thing going. In late 1996, he expanded part of the Salamander concept to downtown Boston's Theater District. The 50-seat **Red Herring** wine and tapas bar at 1 Columbus Ave. offers small plates of Salamander flavors weekdays from 11 to 11, Saturday 4 to 11. The adjacent **Beehive** sells Salamander provisions, wines and takeout foods.

(617) 225-2121. Dinner, Monday-Saturday 6 to 10:30. Food Shop, weekdays 7 to 5:30.

Display kitchen at right opens onto spacious dining room at Salamander.

Hamersley's Bistro, 553 Tremont St., Boston.

Anticipating the trend to downscaled food and prices, this bistro was an instant hit when it opened in the South End. Then it moved to much larger quarters nearby, upscaling the food and prices along the way. It's a friendly, with-it, 120-seat place run very personally by two redheads, Gordon Hamersley, once apprentice to Wolfgang Puck at Ma Maison in Los Angeles and then executive sous chef to Lydia Shire at Seasons, and his English-born wife Fiona, former New England director of the American Institute of Wine and Food. He and his assistants wear red baseball caps in the open kitchen along the side of the long dining room (the ceiling at his former place was too low for a white toque, he explained). The bobbing baseball caps came to symbolize a refreshing lack of pretense.

In typical bistro style, large squares of white paper are clipped over the table-cloths, the silverware is rolled inside white napkins, bottles of S. Pellegrino water serve as centerpieces, track lights provide illumination and the noise level is high enough that you can't really overhear the couple at the next table. Fiona presides at the bar, which is now part of a cafe that offers the same menu.

"We serve high-quality food stripped down to the basics," Gordon says. "Rustic, peasant food" is what he calls it. We call it gutsy.

Our dinner began with a memorable grilled mushroom and garlic "sandwich" on country bread, not really a sandwich but two toasted bread slices flanking an abundance of mushrooms and watercress ($9.50), and a tasty but messy whole braised artichoke stuffed with olives and mint ($9).

Among main courses ($20 to $32), we loved the duckling with turnips, endive and apple slices – an enormous portion, including an entire leg and crisp slices of breast grilled and blackened at the edges like a good sirloin steak – and a Moroccan lamb stew with couscous and harissa that everybody raves about. The roast chicken with garlic, lemon and parsley is said to be a standout. Other possibilities range from sautéed gray sole with mussels, stuffed kohlrabi and vermouth to brandied filet au poivre with chanterelles. A four-course vegetarian dégustation menu offers four courses for $36.50.

Given the comfort level of most of the menu, we were surprised by the unfamiliar and somewhat confusing wine list ($19 to $69). The Hamersleys seek out the unique among wines from around the world and there was scarcely a vintner we recognized. Symbols distinguish the type of grape for the uninitiated.

Desserts, which originally seemed rather mundane for the $7 price tag, have been elevated lately. Typical are chocolate crème caramel with chocolate swirls, crème fraîche ice cream with cinnamon walnut cookies, and a trio of apple, concord grape and raspberry sorbets. The souffléd lemon custard is a menu fixture.

(617) 423-2700. Dinner nightly, 6 to 10 or 10:30, Sunday to 9:30.

Biba, 272 Boylston St., Boston.

Lydia Shire, who established Seasons at the Bostonian Hotel as an early culinary landmark before launching the Four Seasons Hotel in Beverly Hills, returned in 1989 to open a restaurant of her own. And it's one like no other, which is not surprising to those who know Lydia.

The two-story emporium in the tony Heritage on the Garden shopping/residential complex seats 50 in a main-floor bar serving tapas and such, and 150 in a wildly colorful dining room up a curving staircase. The bar features a Winston Churchill-style smoking couch, a mural of chubby, well-fed people, a lineup of photos taken by Lydia on her various travels, and framed shopping bags from the late Biba, her favorite London store.

The Biba Food Hall upstairs is notable for a glassed-in wine cellar along the staircase, an open space with a tandoori oven, pale yellow walls, ceilings with patterns taken from Albanian carpets, warm woods and white-clothed tables covered with butcher paper and placed rather close together.

Lydia refutes those who classify her decor as Southwest; "if anything, it's Mediterranean in feeling," she counters. Her menu defies classification as well. Instead of appetizers and entrées it's categorized according to fish, meat, starch, legumina, offal and sweets. Full of surprises, it's hard to follow (and figure) but delightfully quirky, as in – we quote – mondongo...uncommon tripe soup with plantain and avocado, arugula salad with very special walnuts, bollito mixto of parsley and pignoli stuffed pigs feet, chuck, shank and tongue with salsa verde, and unusual salad of chestnut whipped potato in crisp potato shell, dark garden greens and grilled bacon...with or without. Without what, you might wonder. But you get the idea.

At a springtime lunch, we devoured the yummy onion, tandoori and French breads that preceded our entrées: chickpea and potato rolled in thin pasta with Moroccan tenderloin of lamb ($14) and citrus salmon with crackling skin and parsley cakes ($16.50). Artfully presented on rectangular white plates, each was an explosion of tastes. A $16 bottle of Hogue fumé blanc from the Yakima Valley accompanied from an unusual, fairly priced wine list starting at $18 for a Canadian vidal. We finished a memorable meal with a terrific warm tarte tatin with cinnamon ice cream ($7) and a cassis and champagne sorbet with linzer cookies ($8).

Dinnertime brings the ultimate grazing menu, as Lydia breaks all the rules regarding appetizers, entrées and such. Under fish, you might order a warm rare tuna with risotto of marrow and fresh white truffle ($13) or grilled two-pound lobster with scotch whiskey butter ($39). Ditto for meat: handcut steak tartare on toasted soured potato bread served with chilled oysters on the half shell ($16) or grilled Catalonian lamb chops with quince aioli ($32). Legumina items vary from a stew of chanterelle and matsutaki mushrooms to steaming polenta in a bowl of spinach soup with soft egg and shaved white truffle from Alba, Italy ($14).

Chef Lydia Shire at Biba.   Chef Todd English at Olives.

While food reviewers swoon and restaurateurs of our acquaintance think this is the most exciting eating in New England, mere mortals are not universally charmed. Some think it's awful for a restaurant to present a menu with four items listed as "offal." Others complain of a high decibel level and slow service. But we found that the dining experience fully measured up to its high advance billing.

And success spawned another Shire venture, **Pignoli,** an upscale Italian restaurant around the corner at 79 Park Plaza, 338-7500 – same restaurant designer, same Lydia theme, with sidewalk seating in summer and the **LMNOP Bakery** for Biba breads, delectable desserts and takeout lunch. The lunch and dinner menus bear Lydia's touch, but the execution is left to chef Daniele Baliani, whose Italian-French background comes through strong and clear.

(617) 426-7878. Lunch, Monday-Friday 11:30 to 2:30 (Saturday in bar only); dinner nightly, 5:30 to 10 or 11; Sunday brunch, 11:30 to 3.

Olives, 10 City Square, Charlestown.
Celebrated chef Todd English and his staff build three wood fires a day in the open kitchen of his much-loved restaurant at the foot of America's oldest main street, just across the Charles River from Boston. One fire is in the brick oven, a second is in the grill he designed himself and the third is for a rotisserie – all the better for his roasts and grills fired by such New England hardwoods as apple, oak and ash. And all the better for his stand-in-line clientele who appreciate robust cooking and spirited surroundings.

Olives has come a long way since it opened in 1989 in small quarters up the street. Todd and wife Olivia, both Culinary Institute of America grads, kept the original space and rechristened it **Figs,** a cafe/pizzeria, now with a Beacon Hill offshoot at 42 Charles St. The new Olives is far more upscale in price and setting, and takes no reservations. Lines start forming at 4:30 and the place is filled many nights by 6.

Once inside the high-ceilinged space with walls of brick and tall windows on two sides, you'll find a mix of plush and rustic. Upholstered banquettes and booths are situated side-by-side with bentwood chairs at bare wood tables. Lights in the form of stars hang over the bar, which is separated from the dining room by a divider with arched windows. Most of the color comes from the crowd and the activity in the huge open kitchen at the rear.

Diners munch on marinated olives and crusty focaccia as they watch Todd and a large crew whip up starters ($6.95 to $14.95) like tuna tartare served over an asparagus salad with fried oysters dressed with sesame and tahini, a portobello tart with roasted garlic custard, and a warm truffled lobster salad. Homemade pastas come in two sizes and in such unusual combinations as shrimp agnolotti on a roasted asparagus hash and spaghettini with fried, soft-shell and Venetian crab sauce.

The chef, known for the bold and robust flavors of Italy where he did most of his training, has mellowed a bit from the time when he said "I couldn't see myself doing all that nouvelle, prissy stuff. It just wasn't lusty and full-bodied enough."

Now many of his entrées ($19.95 to $24.95), still hearty and abundant in portion, have been prissied up. Brick-oven-roasted halibut is served over a potato-leek roesti cake in a clam and cabbage stew with chanterelles and truffle glaze. The wood-grilled turkey chop is served over a risotto of turkey-thigh bolognese with a salad of watercress, goat cheese and cherry-glazed country ham. The spit-roasted ribeye of pork rests on a "pot roast" of black beans with chorizo, creamy honeyed semolina polenta and mustard-almond romesco.

Desserts are a high point: perhaps pumpkin-brioche pudding with pumpkin anglaise and poached cranberries, tirami su crêpe soufflé with rum-raisin sauce and espresso glaze, or fried banana ravioli with banana flan gâteau.

This is not leisurely or intimate dining (the lights are bright and the music loud to discourage lingering). But there's no denying the food, which is the rage in Boston and the wave of the future.

(617) 242-1999. Dinner, Tuesday-Saturday 5:30 to 10:15.

Ambrosia on Huntington, 116 Huntington Ave., Boston.

Its considerable hype touts this ground-floor space in the corner of an office high-rise as a French Provincial living room, with high-tech overtones and wriggling metal work decoration. "A little bit like SoHo meets French Riviera," in the words of chef-owner Anthony Ambrose.

To the more casual eye, it's a soaring, two-story space with floor-to-ceiling windows onto the Prudential Center and the sumptuous look of a big-city hotel dining room. Which is not surprising, given the owner's background as the first American chef de cuisine at Julien at the Hotel Meridien and his stint as executive chef at Seasons at the Bostonian Hotel.

Here he's been freed of hotel dining constraints. His provincial French fare with Asian twists mixes outrageous combinations of ingredients and architectural presentations to a degree perhaps unrivaled in New England.

Where else could the signature appetizer be a martini of lobster sashimi, curled inside a papery seaweed leaf with stoli anise and cellophane noodles and presented in a martini glass? Or a favorite main dish be a "smoked pig chop" painted with Chinese five-spice glaze and served with Japanese rice cakes bearing skewers flying flags of homemade potato chips?

The fare and the presentations are theatrical, even flamboyant. For "exotic appetizers" ($9 to $15), Tony Ambrose sautés foie gras in coconut oil with fava beans, mango and sweet garlic sauce. He pairs native ostrich with a simple potato,

Architectural space brings architectural food presentations at Ambrosia on Huntington.

and offers salmon sushi maki style with coconut wasabi and sweet and sour shaved eggplant. His "simple salads" might combine smoked salmon with English cucumbers, celery and fennel, or chanterelles with parmesan-flavored parsnips and carrot-coriander vinaigrette.

The curtain rises on main dishes ($17 to $29) like garlic and ginger shrimp on Japanese noodles, St. Peter fish steamed in bamboo and tingling with fourteen Asian spices, and grilled rack and saddle of lamb in an Indonesian sauce. The wood-roasted sirloin is served with garlic, galanga and honey over foie gras sauce.

The French pastry chef's desserts ($7.50), the most constructed in Boston, must be seen to be believed. The dacquoise is layered with ganache and white chocolate mousse in orange sauce. A tarte tatin yields caramelized apples perched on a circle of crust propped above a little cookie circle, all sprinkled with caramel straws. A cookie sail and chocolate rudder turn the dense warm chocolate pudding cake with scoops of white chocolate ice cream into a boat from Candy Land.

The desserts and breads are prepared in a chartreuse-colored pastry oven that's a focal point of the comfortable, 90-seat dining room. Waiters holding trays aloft parade down a nearly perpendicular staircase from the glass-enclosed kitchen visible on the second level, ceremoniously unveiling each presentation on fine Limoges china. The show is theatrical, so settle in for a bravura performance.

(617) 247-2400. Lunch, Monday-Friday 11:30 to 2:30; dinner, Monday-Saturday 5 to 10 or 11.

Maison Robert, 45 School St., Boston.

As up-to-date as having its own Web site and as traditional as its dover sole meunière, this bastion of French cuisine celebrated its 25th anniversary in 1996 with a new chef and something of a new look. Jacky Robert, who helped his uncle open Boston's then most glamorous restaurant in 1971, returned after twenty years in San Francisco, where he was chef at Ernie's before opening the four-star Amelio's. Meanwhile, chef-proprietor Lucien Robert from Normandy and his wife

Ann, the hostess of Norwegian descent, had evolved their restaurant with the times, particularly since their daughter Andrée joined the operation in the early 1990s. "We've hung around long enough that French is back," noted Andrée, whose kitchen weathered the era when Italian cuisine dominated and now, with Jacky at the helm, is in the vanguard of French restaurants in the Northeast.

Always formal and to some a tad forbidding, this sizable operation on two floors of Boston's old City Hall has been lightened up in decor and cuisine lately.

The Empire-style Bonhomme Richard dining room with its lofty molded ceiling, three majestic crystal chandeliers, twenty-foot-high velvet draperies and warm peach-colored walls with rich butternut paneling is elegant and expensive. Ben's Cafe downstairs is less so. New silverware and Villeroy & Boch china dress its tables, the walls are hung with a revolving art show and the curtains have been removed to open the window wells to art of another sort: stunning displays of tulips in spring, geraniums and herbs in summer, mums and pumpkins in the fall, and evergreens in the winter.

The menus in both venues reflect the culinary flair and Asian accents of Jacky, who oversees both kitchens, with assistance downstairs from Andrée.

The upstairs dinner menu, still printed in French but with oversize English translations, bears little resemblance to the haute cuisine with classic sauces that prevailed when one of us dined regally here 25 years ago as the guest of an entertaining businessman.

Typical appetizers ($8 to $15) are lobster baked in a salmon mousse with passionfruit butter, crab soup with a dim sum dumpling full of shrimp, a chestnut soufflé served with a small stew of turkey and white wine, and clams and Virginia ham "baked in a large bone." Entrées ($22 to $32) could be salmon baked in parchment paper soaring like a sail above the plate and bearing pears and mango-walnut dressing, ostrich marinated in pomegranate juice and roasted with a potato basket, and smoked venison steak sautéed with a licorice and pepper sauce. Desserts ($8 to $12) run from traditional soufflés and flambéed crêpes to upside-down apple tart with cinnamon sabayon and homemade sorbets in a giant cookie shell.

The fare is more earthy and bistro-like in Ben's Cafe, where lunch and dinner are served. Fifteen dinner entrées are priced from $12 for calves liver with bacon and onions to $28 for grilled filet mignon with béarnaise sauce. A couple of appealing prix-fixe menus offer three courses each for $18 or $25. Many of the night-time items are available on an expanded lunch menu.

Lately, Maison Robert has been offering monthly Scandinavian dinners, wife Ann's counterpart to Lucien's traditional monthly French table, at which up to 75 people show up to speak French and enjoy a thoroughly French meal. Ever evolving and not afraid to change with the times, theirs is a restaurant with tradition and soul.

(617) 227-3370. Lunch, Monday-Friday 11:30 to 2:30; dinner, Monday-Saturday 6 to 10 or 10:30.

Upstairs at the Pudding, 10 Holyoke St., Cambridge.

A hallway wall in Harvard's famed Hasty Pudding Club building is lined with the portraits of five club members who have been elected to the White House. You pass the portraits as you climb two flights and 37 steps to this northern Italian restaurant with a small rooftop garden terrace that's been voted the best site for al fresco dining in Boston.

Jacky and Andrée Robert toast the future at the new Maison Robert.

Owners Mary-Catherine Deibel and Deborah Hughes have created a real charmer in the Pudding's venerable refectory, its beamed cathedral ceiling hung with brass chandeliers and its soaring green walls decorated with posters from Pudding shows long gone. Heavy wood chairs flank widely spaced tables set with pink linens, gleaming crystal and silver. If the weather suits, we'd opt for one of the tables on the adjoining terrace, amid herbs, flowering topiaries, and prolific flowers and greenery cascading down the sides of a trellis, with tiny white lights twinkling beneath the cross beams. Day or night, it's one of the most exotic spots for dining in the area.

Chef Michael Leviton changes the extensive menu nightly. The meal begins with a freebie, perhaps a plate of marinated kalamata olives and a marinated artichoke heart amidst a sunburst of roasted red peppers and anchovy filets. Expect first courses ($7 to $14) like roasted sweet red pepper soup, grilled portobello mushroom with shaved fennel and arugula salad, and rustic pizza with cob-smoked bacon, clams, asiago cheese and scallions.

Entrées run from $23 for pan-roasted chicken breast with roasted garlic jus to $28 for seared beef tenderloin with port-balsamic sauce. Autumn choices include roasted cod with truffle-herb vinaigrette and grilled veal chop with cider-maple jus. The plate overflows with interesting accompaniments, artfully arranged: maybe chèvre mashed potatoes, sweet potato puree or potato and bean ragoût, with young asparagus, baby carrots, braised leeks and salsify.

Among desserts ($7 to $8) are charlotte au chocolate, white chocolate chestnut mousse in a praline basket, and pumpkin cheesecake with biscotti crust and almond tuille.

The Pudding also offers a tasting menu for $42, consisting of one choice from each category as well as salad, which, if you ordered it all à la carte, could set you back $59.

An abbreviated version of the dinner menu is available for lunch ($10 to $17).

The special "rapido lunch" – usually soup and a sandwich "served within five minutes" – puts $9 to good use.

(617) 864-1933. Lunch, Monday-Friday 11:30 to 2:30; dinner nightly from 6; Sunday brunch, 11:30 to 2.

More Dining Choices

Lala Rokh, 97 Mt. Vernon St., Boston.

Home-style Persian cuisine is offered up by Azita Bina-Seibel and her brother Babak Bina at the only eastern Mediterranean restaurant of its kind in New England. The pair also own **Azita,** a small Tuscan charmer at 560 Tremont St. in the South End, where we had a memorable lunch a few years back. Now Azita oversees both places but does the cooking here. She says she's more at home with the food of her native Azerbaijan, which she considers every bit as sophisticated as that of Tuscany.

Ensconced in the former quarters of our late favorite Another Season, the two cozy dining rooms in a Beacon Hill townhouse have been redone country style in mustard yellow and burgundy. The family's notable collection of early Persian memorabilia – framed photographs, antique maps and calligraphy dating to the ninth century – adorn the walls. Classical Persian music plays in the background.

It's a subdued setting for food that is anything but subdued. Although unfamiliar in terminology and combinations of ingredients, it's aromatic, heavily spiced and ever-so-good. The wait staff can steer you to a succession of mix-and-match appetizers, entrées and side dishes that make for novel taste sensations. The breadth of the offerings defies description. Eggplant, a staple of the cuisine, appears in several appetizers ($4 to $7), one of the best being kashk-e-bademjan, a warm dip of roasted eggplant, caramelized onions and goat's milk yogurt, to stand alone or be spread on the complimentary sesame-topped bread.

Main courses ($12 to $16) are categorized by cooking style and yield flavorful combinations mainly of chicken, beef, lamb and veal with basmati rice. Diners are encouraged to complement them with mazze (side dishes) and torshi (pickled chutneys and relishes). Particularly tempting are abgusht (lamb shank in spiced broth with string beans, chick peas, okra and eggplant) and joojeh (a kabob of grilled chicken breast marinated in saffron, lemon and onions and served with saffron-perfumed basmati). A short, wide-ranging wine list is priced from the mid teens to $35.

Desserts ($4.50) are as exotic as the rest of the fare. You might try ranghinak, squares of layered dates stuffed with walnuts and dusted with pistachio, or Persian ice cream scented with saffron and rose water and studded with chunks of frozen cream.

Lala Rokh (pronounced la-la-roke) is the name of a fictional Persian princess seduced by a storytelling suitor in the epic poem of the same name by 19th-century Irish poet Thomas Moore (a slightly faded copy of the work is displayed near the entrance). The spell of the food and the ambiance here will likely seduce you, too.

(617) 720-5511. Dinner nightly, 5:30 to 10.

Cafe Louis, 234 Berkeley St., Boston.

As precious as the clothing and staff in the ultra-suave men's clothing store called Louis is this tiny cafe at the back. It was instantly in with the in-shopping crowd as a daytime eatery, but not truly up to the Louis cachet. So the owners

Rooftop terrace at Upstairs at the Pudding is an exotic place for dining.

redesigned the space, hired a talented young chef, deleted breakfast in favor of dinner, and became a dining sensation.

The walls are mustard yellow, the trim burnt red and teal, the floor tiled and the tall windows draped in bronze curtains. The marble tables are covered with linens at night to soothe a fashionable clientele that loves being squeezed into 46 seats in a space that's intimate, to say the least.

Chef Michael Schlow, who worked with restaurateur Pino Luongo in New York City, prepares sophisticated, contemporary fare whose depth belies the apparent simplicity of the menu. Given the menu's range and price, the chef's six-course tasting menu for $59 (plus $29 with appropriate wines) represents good value for those who want to sample a number of treats.

Typical dinner entrées range from $19 for garlic and herb rubbed chicken breast to $33 for New Zealand loin of venison with beet jus and truffled polenta. The seared sea scallops might be paired with a puree of potato and shiitake, chanterelle and button mushrooms; the grilled swordfish with smoked bacon, creamed lentils and caramelized onions.

First courses start at $8 for the traditional fish soup of Provence, and the rest run from $11 for a wild mushroom and potato torte to $16 for seared foie gras. Among desserts ($7 to $11) are a banana ice-cream sandwich and a honey-vanilla poached pear with roquefort mousse, sauternes sorbet and quince compote. Except for a few whites in the twenties, the choice little wine list borders on the prohibitive.

Many of the night's first courses also are on the lunch menu, as first courses at similar prices. Main courses ($10 to $18) range from grilled vegetable panini and Asian salmon salad to crunchy rare tuna and shrimp and beet risotto. The steak sandwich here is elevated to new heights: seared filet mignon with fig and black truffle jam.

(617) 266-4680. Lunch, Monday-Saturday 11:30 to 3; coffee and dessert, 3 to 5; dinner, 5:30 to 10 or 11.

Galleria Italiana, 177 Tremont St., Boston.

Unlike its showy compatriots, this hot new downtown restaurant puts more emphasis on food than decor. It has to, for it's a tiny hole-in-the-wall in a rundown block and, upon venturing in past the deli case, we had to ask where the restaurant was. "That's it," responded one of the female co-owners in an Italian accent, pointing to a drab space between deli and kitchen holding close-together tables seating about 50. The rough-block walls are accented with colorful art and black and white photos, and wine bottles are lined up on a wraparound shelf beneath the ceiling. White tablecloths dress up the place at night.

The deli counter is popular for self-serve breakfasts and lunches to go, but it's at night that the place shines. Chef Barbara Lynch was voted Boston's best new chef in 1996. She and a sommelier regarded as Boston's best joined the all-female team from the showy Rocco's, now closed. Here they pair a broad, all-Italian wine list with gutsy Tuscan dinner fare.

Consider main courses ($19 to $22) like potato-wrapped salmon over potato and baccalà puree, Tuscan-style chicken "under a brick" with mashed potatoes and onion sauce, and braised lamb shank with shell bean ragú. Or pastas ($16.50) like handcut lasagna al forno with tiny veal meatballs, riccioli with creamy gorgonzola sauce and diced pears, and whipped ricotta and goat cheese pillows with roasted tomatoes.

Start with spicy sausage-stuffed quail over roasted apple polenta or grilled octopus and calamari over a crispy potato cake, or a salad of baby romaine with duck prosciutto and roasted pears ($8.50 to $9.25). Finish with an almond-crusted quince soufflé with spiced quince sauce or a walnut crespelle pouch bearing spiced apples, sweet mascarpone walnut crème anglaise and cinnamon gelato.

(617) 423-2092. Breakfast and lunch, Monday-Friday 7 to 4:30; dinner, Wednesday-Saturday 5:30 to 10.

East Coast Grill, 1271 Cambridge St., Cambridge.

"Grills just want to have fun" is the motto on the menu and the T-shirts of the staff at this former Inman Square luncheonette that's hot, hot, hot. The hottest dish in New England is said to be an appetizer called sausage from hell ($7.50), tossed with cornbread and grilled pineapple and lime-guava vinaigrette and fired by the house-bottled Inner Beauty Real Hot Sauce – the label cautions: "This is not a toy. This is serious." So serious that the second time we bought a bottle we dropped down a degree to "mild." The mustard-colored liquid fire derives its wallop from scotch bonnet chiles, which make jalapeños taste like tofu in comparison. Those with less incendiary tastes can start with buttermilk fried oysters on a bed of arugula or grilled chicken livers with a seared green salad.

Chef-owner Chris Schlesinger, grandson of the late Harvard historian Arthur Schlesinger, is co-author of *The Thrill of the Grill* and other cookbooks. He bases his changing menu on equatorial cuisine – food from hot places. "The closer you get to the equator," says he, who has traveled there frequently, "the more spicy and intense the flavors are." He offers three kinds of barbecue from his native South: North Carolina shredded pork flavored with vinegar and hot peppers ($12.50); succulent Memphis pork spare ribs, and Texas beef brisket with sweet barbecue sauce (both $13.50). The uninitiated can try a sampler of all three ($14.50).

Since he sold the Blue Room to concentrate on his original grill, Chris has enlarged and gentrified its space, menu and wine list. The lengthy specials board at our

Busy in kitchen at left is chef-owner Chris Schlesinger of East Coast Grill.

latest visit offered such entrées ($14.50 to $21.50) as grilled mackerel with pomegranate vinaigrette, grilled pepper-crusted tuna with pickled ginger and wasabi, pan-seared crispy skate on local greens with persimmon barbecue sauce and a steamed Asian basket of shrimp, salmon, scallops and littlenecks with jasmine rice, watercress, and lime-chile and peanut-ginger sauces. The extensive list of sides varies from pickle mix to fried plantains to seared collard greens and "damn good" fries. Cool off with a dessert like pumpkin bread pudding, guava caramel custard or apple-pear-cranberry cobbler. The choice wine list is priced mainly in the twenties and thirties, and numerous boutique beers are available. The "mixology staff" at the bar offers unusual concoctions to fire or cool one's thirst.

More space for eating and a slightly less hectic atmosphere have resulted from the grill's move into Chris's former Jake and Earl's Dixie Barbecue on one side and expansion into a former Haitian restaurant on the other. The three side-by-side rooms remain a funky melange of geometric shapes in earthy colors on the walls, splashes of neon, a marble-topped bar with diner stools, and a side wall of stainless steel that reflects the flames from the open-pit barbecue. The galvanized hanging lights were fashioned by a local artist from ice-cube trays, forks, graters and other kitchen utensils.

(617) 491-6568. Dinner nightly, 5:30 to 10 or 10:30.

Icarus, 3 Appleton St., Boston.

A statue of the mythological Icarus, poised for flight, looms above tree branches lit with tiny white lights high on the rear wall of this chic restaurant. It oversees a sunken, split-level room full of rich dark wood and a mix of booths and round mission oak tables. The tables are left bare except for dusky pink napkins folded sideways between fluted silverware. Recessed aqua lighting outlines the perimeter of the ceiling.

It's an altogether pleasant backdrop for the fare of longtime chef Chris Douglass, whose low public profile masks his standing as one of the best in town. His menu is brief but the equal of any in the city. Expect entrées ($19.50 to $29.50) like brook trout topped with crab and chanterelle-herb sauce, paella with saffron and handmade chorizo, seared duck breast and confit with quince preserves, and grilled veal chop with porcini sauce and white-bean puree.

Appetizers ($5 to $14) are unusual: seared foie gras over endive and apple salsa, grilled shrimp with mango and jalapeño sorbet, oven-roasted crab cake with curry and cucumbers, and dark and spicy turkey mole over a chile tortilla quesadilla.

Save room for dessert, perhaps wildflower honey mousse with figs and peppered blackberry coulis, white chocolate bread pudding with walnut-praline sauce and white chocolate ice cream, or vanilla bean crème brûlée with assorted meringue cookies.

The "square meal" offers four exotic courses for $38, prix-fixe. The green plate special ($18) might be mushroom cannelloni filled with swiss chard and goat cheese and sauced with roasted yellow tomatoes and lima beans.

Many of the dinner starters turn up on the menu for Sunday brunch, which is popular with South End neighbors.

(617) 426-1790. Dinner, Monday-Friday 6 to 10 or 11, Saturday 5:30 to 11; Sunday, brunch 11 to 3, dinner 5:30 to 10.

The Cafe Budapest, 90 Exeter St., Boston.

The late Edith Ban, a Hungarian who came to Boston after the 1956 uprising and who was the grande dame of Boston restaurateurs, had a reputation for imperiousness, one no doubt enhanced by her commanding presence always garbed completely in white. So we were stunned after staggering through a January blizzard for a 1 p.m. lunch reservation to learn that Mrs. Ban had decreed that the first patrons of the day were to be her guests, and that we were they.

Many are the times since that we and friends have dined in regal splendor in our favorite oak-paneled dining room, all red and white with old Hungarian flasks, walking sticks, wine jugs and decorative plates on the walls. The tradition has been maintained by Mrs. Ban's sister, Dr. Hedda Rev-Kury, who practices medicine by day and restaurateuring at night.

Our first memorable lunch began with a hearty peasant soup topped with fried noodles and exquisite chicken paprikas crêpes. It continued with gypsy baron rice pilaf and the authentic beef goulash that an Austrian friend who manages a fine hotel thinks is the best anywhere. The finale was a sensational Hungarian strudel, accompanied by fragrant Viennese coffee, made from beans ground fresh hourly and served in glass cups.

Meals here are fit for royalty, and the setting is so old-world romantic that you'd almost expect to see Zsa Zsa Gabor dallying with an admirer in one of the intimate alcoves off the lounge (actually, she has dined here, on chicken paprika, we're told). At night, when things get busy and up to 500 meals may be served, the Hungarian menu carries French accents. For appetizers, you can get the great chicken paprikas crêpe ($7), or you can try Hungarian goose liver with truffles ($12) or caviar à la russe ($12.50).

Most of the 26 entrées ($19.50 to $33) are Middle European. Sweetbreads à la hongroise under glass, veal gulyas and wiener schnitzel vie for attention with broiled lemon sole and châteaubriand with mimosa salad. Each comes with different vegetables and salads. One night, three in our party declared spectacular the veal served with rice, string beans and carrots tied in a bundle, and a special salad of grapes and endive arranged like a star. Most of the unusual desserts like a champagne torte or crêpes with farm cheese and raisins are in the $5.50 range.

If you have any romance in your soul, you'll love Cafe Budapest – particularly the small pink dining room with pink chairs off the lounge, almost too pretty for words, and the Empire-style lounge where, ensconced in gilt and brocade chairs, you can have dessert crêpes flambéed tableside while a pianist and a violinist entertain nearby.

(617) 734-3388. Lunch, Monday-Saturday noon to 3; dinner, 5 to 10:30 or 11:30, Sunday 1 to 10:30.

Jae's Cafe & Grill, 1281 Cambridge St., Cambridge.

One look and we were smitten. How could you not like a place where three long tropical fish tanks divide the bar from the dining room, the white brick walls are handpainted in multi-color abstracts by the owner, and three chefs man the 40-item sushi bar? This is the contemporary and expanded outpost of the original Jae's at 520 Columbus Ave. in Boston's South End. Here, Korean-born Jae Chung has added grills to his Korean-Japanese-Thai offerings.

Artistry in the kitchen seems to come naturally to Jae, who studied fine arts in college. It turns up in all kinds of decorative (and tasty) morsels, from Jae's tidbits (an appetizer sampler for $11.95) to his ginger custard, dark-chocolate mousse and lemon framboise for dessert. In between are all kinds of noodle, pad thai, vegetable, fried rice and curry dishes, pleasantly priced from $7.50 to $12.95. Upon the waitress's recommendation, we lunched on the Party Boat 1, $34.95 for two, a feast of impeccably fresh sushi that arrived in a wooden boat and was almost more than two could finish. A glass of house wine accompanied from an exceptionally appealing – and affordable – American wine list priced mainly in the teens. We would have liked to have tried any of Jae's designer rolls, his hosomaki in seaweed rolls, the spicy squid Korean style, the basil Wellfleet clams with mixed vegetables or noodles, the grilled shrimp scampi, the tuna or salmon tartare, the dumplings with curry sauce – in fact, almost everything on the menu. That, however, would take a number of return visits, something the locals are better able than we to do. They take seriously the restaurant's slogan: "Eat at Jae's...and live forever."

(617) 497-8380. Lunch, Monday-Saturday 11:30 to 4; dinner nightly, 5 to 10:30; late-night sushi, 10:30 to 1; Sunday brunch, 10 to 3.

The Elephant Walk, 900 Beacon St., Boston.

Miniature elephants parade around the moldings above the arched main dining room of this sleek and inviting French-Cambodian restaurant, comfortably housed in an old brick bank building. Ficus and palm trees lend a vaguely oriental look to the expansive main dining room and front sun porch, where blue cushioned chairs are at tables covered by white cloths and alstroemeria afloat in brandy snifters. This is the newer and bigger offshoot of the original founded in 1991 in Somerville by an American, four Cambodians and a Frenchman. The former, Robert Perry, is joined by his mother-in-law as executive chef, his wife Nadsa (the chef here) and his son-in-law Gerard Lopez (the chef in Somerville), whose wife is manager here.

The menu, divided into French and Cambodian sections, lists most dishes in French with English translations. Even the French dishes (entrées $14.50 to $18.95) have oriental accents, as in "noisette d'agneau grillée au riz parfumée à la citronelle" – wood-grilled New Zealand lamb loin sliced over lemongrass-scented jasmine rice, crunchy Chinese broccoli and grilled eggplant, garnished with a flash-fried julienne of carrot and leek. Whew! You might start with a salade l'eurasienne, shredded chicken with mung bean sheets, julienned cucumber, scallions and portobello mushrooms over mesclun greens.

Many of the Cambodian dishes, from $5.95 for soups to $13.95 for the most expensive main dish, are seasoned with tuk trey, a marinade of fish sauce, vinegar, lime juice, sugar and garlic. We like the sound of crevettes kep-sur-mer, black tiger shrimp in a sauce of tamarind, lemongrass, cilantro, kaffir lime leaves and coconut milk with bok choy, button mushrooms and snow peas. The menu also lists two dishes of "challenging flavors," one of which is called amok, a spicy flan of crabmeat and catfish with coconut milk and complex seasonings, steamed in a banana leaf cup.

At lunchtime, soups, salads and entrées are mostly in the $3 to $8 range.

(617) 247-1500. Lunch, Monday-Saturday 11:30 to 2:30; dinner nightly, 5 to 10 or 11, Saturday and Sunday from 4:30.

Brew Moon Restaurant & Microbrewery, 115 Stuart St., Boston.

Creative contemporary cuisine and hand-crafted beer in beautiful surroundings. That's the concept behind this restaurant and microbrewery launched in 1994 in the heart of Boston's Theater District. There quickly followed three offshoots in the Boston area, with seven more planned across the East by 1999.

Brewmaster Tony Vieira, formerly of Anheuser-Busch, produces five beers ranging from a golden ale "for the budding beer connoisseur" to a full-bodied stout brewed with eight different malts and roasted barley. The lunar sampler offers a selection of four for $5.

Executive chef Donald Chapelle's light, healthful food in the California style helped Brew Moon earn a ranking as one of the year's best restaurants in 1996, as determined by Bon Appétit magazine. It cited his crostini, sandwiches and salads, plus more substantial offerings like beer-battered flounder, spiced swordfish, and molasses and cumin-charred pork tenderloin, the last served with potato hash, garlic sausage and grilled vegetables. The day's eight entrées are priced from $9.75 to $17.75 (for charred pepper-crusted sirloin with roquefort butter).

Nurse your beer with snacks like sesame-seared tuna with somen salad or pan-seared salmon-lobster cakes. Chase it with a cappuccino ice-cream sandwich, sourdough bread pudding or a "wicked" chocolate sampler. There's even a root-beer float.

All this is served up in a surprisingly large, contemporary setting of wood sculptures and glass panels with a vaguely lunar-like motif.

(617) 523-6467. Open daily from 11:30.

Legal with a Difference

Legal Sea Foods, 35 Columbus Ave., Boston.

No mention of Boston dining would be complete without a reference to this local institution, now with a new twist. Jasper White closed his temple of contemporary New England cookery of the same name in 1995 to spend more time with his young family. He resurfaced in 1996 as executive chef of Legal Sea Foods, the Berkowitz family's popular retail market and restaurant chain with roots back to 1904.

With three markets, a mail-order business and thirteen restaurants, including one far from its New England base in McLean, Va., the enterprise sought a name chef to oversee the move into a new century. To the Legal's extensive traditional menu (dinner entrées, $11.95 to $23.95), Jasper gradually added homemade seafood sausages and baked halibut with crab imperial, and upgraded the Portuguese fisherman's stew. His clam fritters and a crab and avocado quesadilla showed up as specials on the lunch menu. Otherwise, the extensive seafood-oriented menus range widely from steamed lobster to grilled arctic char to Shandong Chinese specials, but more changes were anticipated.

The original seafood market and restaurant was in Cambridge's Inman Square. Since its demise, the flagship is considered to be this vast operation on the ground floor of the Boston Park Plaza hotel.

(617) 426-4444. Lunch, Monday-Friday 11 to 1:30; dinner, 4:30 to 10 or 11, Saturday noon to 11, Sunday noon to 10.

Gourmet's Digest

Parish Cafe, 361 Boylston St., Boston.
Sandwiches created by some of the area's best-known chefs – many of them mentioned in this chapter – are featured at this funky establishment opened by the owners of the Rattlesnake Bar & Grill across the street.

The nearly two dozen choices are priced from $7.95 to $10.25 (for Biba's steak and blue – grilled tenderloin on Lydia Shire's homemade blue cheese bread with roquefort butter). The Schlesinger is warmed banana bread topped with melted monterey jack, smokehouse ham and mango chutney. The Ambrosian spreads chilled leg of lamb with Asian mayo on Tuscan wheat bread. Parish's own chefs have added appetizers, salads and entrées like fishcakes, BLT pasta and grilled half duck in the $8.95 to $13.95 range.

There's an impressive list of wines and ales to go with. The prominent bar plays a major role, and a rear mural portraying laid-back diners on an outdoor patio sets the theme. Given their pedigrees, most of the sandwiches are first-rate.

(617)247-4777. Open daily, 11:30 to 1 a.m., Sunday from noon.

Hotel Dining

Aujourd'hui, Four Seasons Hotel, 200 Boylston St., Boston.
A window table at Aujourd'hui is a prospect on the finer things in Boston life, among them a view of the swan boats plying the pond of the Public Garden and the cooking of world-class chefs.

The second-floor restaurant's setting is serene: floral-fabric banquettes, rich oak paneling, Royal Doulton china atop white damask cloths and floor-length skirts, nicely spaced tables, and a solicitous staff in subdued outfits that match the colors of the 110-seat room.

At lunch, we loved the subtle tomato and fennel soup with toasted focaccia and the smoked duck pieces encased in tiny herbed rice pancakes with a sesame-flavored dipping sauce. Entrées ($17 to $22.50) were a tasty grilled pork tenderloin with plum-pepper marmalade and potato pancakes and a special of medallions of wild boar with pearl onions and madeira, accompanied by tiny beans, baby carrots and small roasted potatoes. The fruit tart that we'd admired in the enticing pastry display near the entry was perfection, filled with oversize blackberries, blueberries and strawberries in a pastry cream with a shortbread-like crust. The sorbet lover among us freaked out on the day's trio – pear, mixed berry and mango.

Dinner begins, compliments of the chef, with a freebie like salmon mousse with black-pepper vodka and crème fraîche. First courses run from $12.50 for grilled vegetable strudel with watercress sauce to $16.50 for foie gras with sauerkraut and sweet corn. We found both the Thai spring roll with duck confit and the pappardelle with braised rabbit, chanterelles and barolo wine extraordinary.

Our main dishes ($34 to $42) were a burst of flavors: grilled lamb chops with ginger-lime sauce, salsify and white eggplant, and roast ribeye of veal with port wine, onions and sage. The mascarpone and espresso cheesecake, the warm mango tart and the grand marnier nougat soufflé came highly recommended, but we settled on a trio of delicious frozen parfaits. A tray of candies accompanied the bill.

The regular menu is supplemented by specials, including a number of marked selections containing reduced levels of calories, cholesterol, sodium and fat. A five-course tasting menu is offered for $78, with vegetarian substitutes for $52.

The wine list, one of Boston's best, includes a full page of wines by the glass and two pages of domestic chardonnays. We found a couple of good sauvignon blancs and a pinot noir in the high twenties.

The Four Seasons offers Viennese dessert buffets (a dozen fabulous concoctions, of which you may choose two for $11.50 or four for $22 – the idea is to share) on weekends from 9 to midnight in its airy **Bristol Lounge,** where tea is served by the fireplace daily from 3 to 4:30. An elegant Sunday breakfast buffet for $29 is considered one of the best in the city. Speaking of breakfast, among the options is a Japanese breakfast, from grilled salmon and nori to miso soup, for $18.50.

(617) 338-4400. Lunch, Monday-Friday 11:30 to 2:30; dinner nightly, 6 to 10:30 or 11; Sunday brunch, 10 to 2.

Julien, Hotel Meridien, 250 Franklin St., Boston.

The setting is historic: the former Members Court of the stately Federal Reserve Building built in 1922, across from the site of Boston's first French restaurant, opened in 1793 by French-émigré Jean-Baptiste Julien. But its spirit is highly contemporary. French chef Dominique Rizzo, a protégé of Sylvain Portay of Le Cirque in New York, trained with Michelin chefs in France.

Some of Boston's most distinguished food is served in this palatial room with towering gilded ceiling, five crystal chandeliers and lattice work on the walls with lights behind. Mushroom velour banquettes or Queen Anne wing chairs flank tables set with heavy silverware, monogrammed china, tiny shaded brass lamps and Peruvian lilies.

Dinner begins with a complimentary hors d'oeuvre – a small vegetable quiche at our visit. If you're not up to an appetizer ($15 to $19 for the likes of terrine of foie gras or warm shrimp and spinach salad with a tomato compote), splurge on one of the masterful soups ($9), perhaps lobster velouté with julienned celery or chilled gazpacho with vegetable pearls.

The terminology is deceptively understated for what one veteran reviewer called "a dazzling new menu that's comparable to the best you'll find anywhere. Julien has never been better." For $27 to $32, you might find sautéed salmon provençal, black sea bass with pesto sauce, roasted squab with celeriac puree and cabbage

Window tables at Aujourd'hui overlook Boston Public Garden.

flan, and filet mignon with bone marrow sauce. We'll never forget our lobster ravioli, the lobster reconstructed from its head and tail, the body made from ravioli filled with lobster mousse, the legs and feelers represented by green beans and asparagus or snow peas, and the whole topped with tomatoes and truffles – presentation personified.

Desserts from the menu and a pastry cart ($8.50 to $10) include apricot tarte tatin molded into the shape of an apple, resting on a pool of champagne sabayon sauce and flanked by pistachio ice cream. We tried a delicious almond ice-cream cookie and two mille-feuilles, pastries layered with whipped cream and peaches in one case and strawberries and raspberries in the other. The bill was sweetened with a plate of homemade candies and cookies.

Although offering impressive French wines that helped win Wine Spectator's Best of Award of Excellence, the sommelier also recommends a number of Californias.

The formal atmosphere and service are lightened somewhat by piano music in the adjacent Julien bar, the bank's former counting room, where two original N.C. Wyeth murals embellish the walls.

(617) 451-1900. Lunch, Monday-Friday noon to 2; dinner nightly, 6 to 10 or 10:30.

Rialto, One Bennett St., Cambridge.

The old Rarities, the high-style dining room at the Charles Hotel, proved a tad too rare. It succumbed with little notice to await the opening of Rialto, a happening accompanied by great fanfare. And why not? The owner-principals are Michela Larson and Jody Adams, whose fare we had sampled at Michela's in the former Carter Ink building before they vacated the space (now Salamander) and moved into the thick of things in Harvard Square.

Chef Jody, nominated for a James Beard Foundation award for her Italian cuisine at Michela's, broadened her culinary reach here to include southern France and Spain. Her artfully presented dishes won a rare four-star rating from the Boston Globe and acclaim in the national press. The romantic ambiance is likened to that of a soigné living room, with comfortable sofa-like booths and dressy floor lamps.

The menu is refreshingly concise and straightforward. For starters ($7 to $16), consider a goat cheese terrine layered with hazelnuts and black mission figs, warm curried lentil and chick pea salad with shiitake and butternut squash fritters, and lobster and salt cod casserole layered with potatoes and salsify. Typical main courses ($21 to $29) include grilled salmon with dried cranberries and pinenuts, grilled quail stuffed with fig and shallot jam with blood orange sauce, and seared venison on a vermicelli-pinenut cake with spinach and fruit compote.

Desserts ($7 to $10) are a high point of the meal. They're novel and refreshing, from warm banana rum cake with cardamom ice cream and banana sorbet to a tropical fruit terrine of grilled pineapple, blood oranges and passion fruit.

After dinner, tarry for a drink outside Rialto in the romantic Quiet Bar, all loveseats and plush chairs, or go on to the Regattabar, which is known for top jazz. Celebrating the culinary bounty of New England, the Charles Hotel's warm and inviting **Henrietta's Table** combines a little farm stand in front with breakfast, lunch and dinner prepared in an open kitchen.

(617) 661-5050. Dinner nightly, 5:30 to 10 or 11.

Rowes Wharf Restaurant, Boston Harbor Hotel, 70 Rowes Wharf, Boston.
Since 1990, the Boston Harbor Hotel has garnered national attention for its annual Boston Wine Festival, fifteen weeks of wine tastings, dinners, seminars and other events involving many of the world's leading winemakers. A principal reason is the distinguished food offered by executive chef Daniel Bruce in the hotel's harborfront dining room.

Boston's longest-lasting celebrity hotel chef, Dan is an innovator in New England cuisine and a promoter of healthier dining (he spearheaded the first "Food and Wine for Life" conference at the hotel in 1996). His menus change daily, although red flannel hash (a Boston mainstay of beef, beets and potatoes) is offered for breakfast year-round.

He forages for the fungi that turn up in a signature appetizer of wild mushrooms over stone-ground cornmeal polenta, another staple on the menu. Other starters at dinner ($11.50 to $14) could be maple-smoked Atlantic salmon with potato cake and caviar, foie gras and butternut squash risotto, and charred venison carpaccio with artichokes and wild mushrooms. Typical entrées ($24 to $31) are grilled swordfish with carrot-ginger butter, fricassee of lobster and chorizo, juniper-roasted Vermont pheasant and herb-crusted rack of lamb.

A three-course "preview menu" might offer the mushroom appetizer, fennel-rubbed Atlantic halibut with periwinkle sauce and warm vanilla cake with plum compote for $40. A four-course gourmet menu ($50) adds different choices and a salad.

For a winter lunch, we began with the caramelized sweet onion soup with New Hampshire cheese croustade and the crab, salmon and cod cakes with celery root rémoulade. A salad of grilled sea scallops over baby spinach, red onions and hickory-smoked bacon ($12) and the grilled duck breast with braised red cabbage and currants ($16.50) made fine main dishes. A chocolate-chestnut dacquoise and an assortment of raspberry, strawberry and blackberry sorbets were grand endings.

The setting is masculine and clubby with dark mahogany walls, recessed lighting in the ceiling, and a deep blue decor from chairs to vases to carpeting. About 250 people can be seated in a variety of rooms, all with at least a glimpse of the water. A seasonal outdoor cafe serves lunch and dinner overlooking the harbor. The $42 Sunday brunch is considered one of the city's best.

(617) 439-3995. Lunch, 11:30 to 2:30; dinner, 5:30 to 11; Sunday brunch, 10:30 to 2.

Seasons, Regal Bostonian Hotel, 4 Faneuil Hall Marketplace, Boston.

This is the culinary heart of the Bostonian Hotel, its curved, windowed dining room on the fourth floor looking out over Quincy Market. Part of the ceiling is stainless steel and part glass, and an odd-shaped drapery affair moves back and forth electrically, depending on sunshine and temperatures.

Generally well-spaced tables seat 125 on several tiers to take full advantage of the view. Silver-rimmed service plates, heavy cutlery and a pristine freesia in a bud vase on each table add to the feeling of warm, contemporary elegance. Service is by an army of fresh-faced, tuxedoed waiters.

The food has been ranked among Boston's best since noted chef Jasper White helped open Seasons in the mid-1980s. Locally high-profile successors including Lydia Shire, Gordon Hamersley, Jody Adams, Tony Ambrose and Bill Poirier maintained the concept and a menu that changes with the seasons. Chef Peter McCarthy, who joined Seasons as a line cook after graduation from the Culinary Institute of America, worked his way up the ranks in six years. An advocate of cooking light, he uses almost no butter or cream.

At our stay, an appetizer of smoked fish – red sturgeon with scallops and salmon in a horseradish-champagne vinaigrette, with a side presentation of cucumbers, watercress and capers – was superb, as was the smooth lobster and sweet-corn chowder. Other starters ($9 to $13.75) could be Maine crab and potato spring rolls with melon chutney, ragoût of clams and smoked bacon, and a crock of baked cranberry beans with duck confit and fried onions.

Main courses ($22 to $38) include lobster and corn risotto with Nova Scotia chanterelles, maple-glazed Vermont pheasant with purple potato waffles, and herb-roasted loin of venison. We liked the signature roast duckling with ginger and scallions, surrounded by Chinese vegetables, and grilled red snapper with thin jonnycakes and mustard greens.

A sensational array of sorbets – papaya, pear, apple and raspberry – was most refreshing. The sweet potato cheesecake, Bostonian cream pie, and sekel pear and camembert tart also tempted. Cappuccino and decaf coffee were served in silver pots. The bill arrived with chocolate truffles and a macadamia-nut pastry on a doily.

The choice all-American wine list is enormous, with no fewer than 50 California cabernet sauvignons priced from $27 to $150.

(617) 523-4119. Lunch, Monday-Friday 11:30 to 2; dinner nightly, 6 to 10:30.

Lodging

Hotel Le Meridien, 250 Franklin St., Boston 02110.

Known for its gastronomic flair (its chefs offer periodic cooking classes for guests), Le Meridien is run in European splendor by Air France. It occupies the 1922 Federal Reserve Bank building, a National Historic Landmark, reincarnated 60 years and $40 million later into an elegant hotel.

Rather hard to find in the heart of the Financial District, it has 326 recently renovated guest rooms on nine floors, with more than 150 variations from two-story loft suites to rooms on the three top floors with sloping windows and mansard roofs. Contemporary sofas, artworks (striking caricatures by local artist Ken Maryanski), live plants and minibars are in each room. Beds are made up in the French style (an extra sheet on top of the blanket), and maids provide turndown service at night with mints and a written weather forecast. A French news sheet is distributed to the rooms, and French cable television is available in the evening. The large bathrooms contain scales, telephones and baskets of assorted amenities. The third-floor health club has a glassed-in pool with skylights.

The Meridien offers a chocolate lover's weekend package from September through May. It features the ultimate chocolate bar, an all-you-can-eat buffet of light and dark chocolate desserts, served Saturdays from 1 to 3 for $15.50 in the **Cafe Fleuri,** the hotel's airy brasserie. Chocolate raspberry mousse cake, chocolate croissant pudding and orange chocolate tart, each identified by a handwritten label, are among the 25 creations. On a typical afternoon, pastry chef Gina Cosentino goes through more than 40 pounds of chocolate. A nine-station Sunday brunch ($39), voted Boston's best, is served in the cafe's soaring interior courtyard atrium.

(617) 451-1900 or (800) 543-4300. Fax (617) 423-2844. Doubles, $285 to $335; suites, $450 to $1,300.

Boston Harbor Hotel, 70 Rowes Wharf, Boston 02110.

A more sumptuous hotel could scarcely be imagined. The floors are marble, the sides of the elevators are brocade, and the walls of the public spaces are hung with fine art and antique nautical prints. Redwood furniture surrounds the 60-foot lap pool and a large lounge at the rear of the main floor has huge sofas in plums, golds and teal blues for relaxing as you enjoy live piano music and absorb the view of boats and airplanes around the harbor.

Luxury and care extend to the 230 rooms and suites on Floors 8 through 16 (the lower floors are offices). Our oversize room had lovely reproduction antiques, a sofa and an upholstered chair with good reading lamps in a sitting area, a kingsize bed and an enormous bathroom full of amenities from fine soaps to terrycloth robes and a hair dryer. Breakfronts concealed the TV and a minibar, atop which were three kinds of glasses – highball, lowball and wine. Luggage racks, removable hangers, soundproof windows that open and enormous towels are other assets.

Afternoon tea and drinks are served in a handsome Harborview Lounge on the main floor, and private parties and special events take place in the two-story Rotunda, a copper-domed observatory with views of harbor and city. Guests enjoy the health club and spa, which besides a lap pool has steam rooms and saunas, a hydrotherapy tub and an exercise room with all the latest equipment.

Rowes Wharf is "elaborate, dramatic, even operatic," gushed the Boston Globe's architectural critic shortly after its 1987 opening. It is "an expression of the new wealth of Boston." Stay here, indulge, and you'll surely feel part of it.

(617) 439-7000 or (800) 752-7077. Fax (617) 330-9450. Doubles, $270 to $415; suites, $340 to $1,300.

Four Seasons Hotel, 200 Boylston St., Boston 02116.

From the hotel's eighth-floor health spa that has Caribbean-style patio furniture around a swimming pool and a jacuzzi, you can look out over the Boston Public

Garden and, at night, the lights of Boston. "Very romantic while relaxing in the jacuzzi," our informant advised.

It's also very serene and comfortable, this grand hotel with 288 guest rooms and suites reflecting the understated style of a traditional Beacon Hill guest bedroom. All rooms have Henredon cherry furniture, writing tables, TV in an armoire, a minibar, three telephones, hair dryers, windows that open, terrycloth robes and such, and the 64 Four Seasons mini-suites add alcove seating areas. Executive suites with a living room contain two TVs and stereos with CD players, although we never found ours hidden in a cabinet and pulled the other out from the bedroom. That was the only glitch in an experience that lived up to its AAA five-diamond rating.

The luxurious health spa has treadmills with TVs and VCRs, and spin-dry machines for wet swimsuits. Public rooms are quietly decorated with antiques and fine art. A five-foot crystal chandelier lights the grand stairway to the second-floor Aujourd'hui restaurant.

(617) 338-4400 or (800) 332-3442. Fax (617) 426-7199. Doubles, $335 to $455; suites, $495 to $2,950.

The Ritz-Carlton, 15 Arlington St., Boston 02117.

The Ritz is not just a hotel. It's an institution – *the* place where proper Bostonians put up visitors or go themselves for lunch in the cafe, tea in the lounge, or drinks and dinner in the Ritz Bar and the Dining Room. Even with all the new hotel competition in which the Ritz risked becoming passé, it remains Boston's bastion of Brahmin elegance.

The elevator operators wear white gloves – yes, there still are elevator operators, to say nothing of white gloves – as they take guests up to the 280 rooms, perhaps one of the 42 fireplaced suites billed for romance. Could romance be why the Ritz perpetuates its tradition of nightly dancing in the lounge and weekly Thursday tea dances in the French and Adam Room? And why the Ritz presents "a weekend of social savvy" for budding socialites aged 8 to 12?

Yes, romance and the Ritz are legendary: Rodgers and Hammerstein wrote many of their musical favorites here, and in the 1930s and '40s, more romantic Broadway musicals were worked on at the Ritz than at any other location in the country.

The martinis in the Ritz Bar are legendary, as is English tea while a harpist plays in the Victorian parlor-salon (full tea, $16.50; light tea, $12.50). The Dining Room fare has been rejuvenated lately to embrace the trendy as well as the tried and true. The dinner menu is priced from $29 for rack and leg of rabbit with green lentil cream and cabbage to $41 for dover sole meunière. Chef Didier Rosa offers a nightly dégustation table for up to fourteen guests, $85 each for four courses and wines.

French provincial furnishings, imported fabrics, distinctive artworks, windows that open onto a view of the Public Garden and all the amenities of a four-diamond hotel are here, even if a few think they've seen better days.

(617) 536-5700 or (800) 241-3333. Fax (617) 536-1335. Doubles, $245 to $385; suites, $325 to $495.

The Inn at Harvard, 1201 Massachusetts Ave., Cambridge 02138.

Add innkeeping to Harvard University's script of accomplishments. The university has opened a fine hotel with the atmosphere of a private club, cloistered at the edge of Harvard Square. Enter the arched, four-story palazzo that blends nicely with the buildings of Georgian red brick with white trim indigenous to the Harvard campus. Ahead lies a stunning four-story skilt atrium that imparts the feeling of an Italian courtyard. Rich cherrywood balconies and mullioned windows accent the sponged terra-cotta walls, hiding from public view the 113 guest rooms on all sides. Shelves of books and colorful murals line the main floor. Sofas, wingback and Queen Anne-style chairs are grouped for conversation in this soaring lobby to end all lobbies. And lo! Tables along one side are set with white linens and china for dinner. You're home – away from home.

Architect Graham Gund, a Harvard alum, met the challenge of creating the warm atmosphere of an inn living room in what could have been a stark hotel lobby. The atrium is a true gathering spot, both because it is so inviting and because seating is at a premium in some of the guest rooms, at least those we saw. The bedrooms, all pleasantly decorated in sand tones, come with queensize or two double beds, armoires holding TVs and modern bathrooms with pedestal sinks. Some offer outdoor balconies. There are amenities aplenty: terry robes, turndown service, chocolates on the pillows, Dickens & Hawthorne toiletries and complimentary newspapers. Each room contains an original print from the 17th or 18th century, on loan from Harvard's Fogg Art Museum, which also is responsible for the prints of Harvard personages and scenes lining corridors and public spaces.

Breakfast is offered in the lobby. Many guests opt for the European buffet ($11.95), an elaborate spread including cheeses, meats, granolas, fruits and pastries. A full menu is available as well. The library side of the lobby is the setting for candlelight dining at tables spaced among the books near an oversize baroque statue of Bacchus, which oversees all. The chef prepares a short menu for inn guests. The seven entrées ($18 to $23) might include sautéed salmon served on a warm fennel, lobster and leek salad, and grilled veal chop with smoked tomato and onion ragoût. Lighter fare also is available, and there's a concise but well-chosen wine list. Inn guests also enjoy dining privileges at the Harvard Faculty Club next door.

(617) 491-2222 or (800) 222-8733. Fax (617) 492-4896. Doubles, $159 to $239.

Regal Bostonian Hotel, 4 Faneuil Hall Marketplace, Boston 02109.

Its location next to Quincy Market could lead you to think this is good for families, but the recently renamed Bostonian (it became a Regal International hotel in 1996) is quiet, deluxe and, above all, grown-up. Although the 153 rooms on three floors are rather small, they are beautifully decorated and equipped, and the bathrooms with deep tiled tubs, French soaps and huge towels are a delight. In most rooms, french doors open onto tiny balconies with wrought-iron railings and planters filled with flowers. The television set is tucked discreetly into the armoire. There are two telephones (one in the bathroom), two AM/FM radios (one in the bathroom). You get the picture.

Since its 1982 opening, the Bostonian has been acclaimed for its European style, its small residential lobby with a corner fireplace around which are comfortable wing chairs, its spacious Atrium Lounge where you can sink into upholstered chairs and sofas to order a fine wine by the glass, espresso or a light lunch, and especially for Seasons, its rooftop restaurant.

Eleven suites come with fireplaces and some have oval tubs and jacuzzis. The

Atrium at Inn at Harvard imparts feeling of Italian courtyard.

hotel is basically in two wings – one called the contemporary, especially attractive to business travelers, and one in the 19th-century Harkness wing.

(617) 523-3600 or (800) 343-0922. Fax (617) 523-2454. Doubles, $245 to $355; suites, $450 to $655.

The Charles Hotel, One Bennett Street, Cambridge 02138.

Iced mineral water, Godiva chocolates and honor bars (supposedly the best in the area) are attributes of this small independent hotel, opened in 1986 at Harvard Square. An international feeling prevails, from the European door handles to the Euro-chic atmosphere of Rialto, the fine-dining restaurant.

The entire hotel, including 296 guest rooms and suites on ten floors, has a noticeably low-key, intimate feeling. Rooms are of different shapes, sizes and decor. All possess down quilts, three telephones (bedside, bathroom and armoire), two TVs (black and white in the bathroom), terrycloth robes, bathroom scales and nightly turndown service. Adaptations of Early American Shaker pieces such as armoires, four-poster beds and apothecary chests are combined with antique and contemporary accessories. The hotel recently became the first in America to install Bose wave radios in every room.

The expanded health and fitness center includes an indoor lap pool, whirlpool, steam room and three floors of exercise rooms. The day spa offers beauty treatments and massages.

The 50 original works of art commissioned for the Charles are said to represent the largest such acquisition program by an American hotel. Especially stunning are the antique New England quilts hung along the hotel's main oak staircase, a theme repeated in the quilts at the entrance to each guest-room floor.

(617) 864-1200 or (800) 882-1818. Fax (617) 864-5715. Doubles, $275 to $295. Suites, $389 to $1,500.

Bed and Breakfasts

A Cambridge House, 2218 Massachusetts Ave., Cambridge 02140.

Now mostly outfitted with private baths, this B&B headquartered in an elegantly restored 1892 wooden house, set back a bit from Mass. Ave. but right in the thick of things, seems to have it all. The public rooms and bedrooms are lavishly decorated, breakfast is a feast, hot and cold hors d'oeuvres are served with cold beverages in the evening, rooms have TVs, telephones and clock radios (some have fireplaces), and classical music plays.

We especially liked the Isaac McLean room, with its canopied queensize bed and chaise lounge beside a working fireplace. Since it was the original master bedroom, it has a particularly spiffy bath with a bidet, a shower up a few stairs and theatrical lighting. Innkeeper Ellen Riley offers eleven rooms in the main house, with five more in a carriage house out back. All are named for such local historic personages as Margaret Fuller and Alexander Agassiz, whose lives are detailed briefly in the appropriate room.

Drifts of pillows are on the beds, some of them brass, some rice-carved four-posters. The side patio, with candles and white lights lit at night, is a pleasant retreat.

Breakfast in the formal dining room might include fresh orange juice, a fruit course like baked pears in vanilla yogurt with raspberries, buttermilk belgian waffles or chocolate waffles. The Sunday breakfast might be a frittata with asparagus and roasted red peppers, Italian fried dough, and fennel sausage made to order by a North End market.

(617) 491-6300 or (800) 232-9989. Fax (617) 868-2848. Doubles, $129 to $250.

Newbury Guest House, 261 Newbury St., Boston 02116.

Nicely situated in the heart of the Back Bay neighborhood, this 1882 townhouse and two adjacent houses have been restored to provide 32 guest rooms that represent good value. Rooms at the top of the four-story walkups are a bit of a hike (there's no elevator). All have private baths, queensize beds, Victorian furniture, TVs and telephones.

Armenian owner Nubar Hagopian is usually on hand to orient guests and to help serve a continental breakfast (fresh fruits, cereal, bagels and muffins). The meal is taken in a new downstairs breakfast room or out front on a sunken brick patio, where guests can glimpse the passing Newbury Street parade.

(617) 437-7666. Fax (617) 262-4243. Doubles, $95 to $125.

Gourmet Treats

Faneuil Hall Marketplace, the East's busiest tourist destination after Disney World, is a festival arena for foodies, from the great **Crate & Barrel** store to the approximately twenty restaurants and thirty snackeries, salad bars and food stalls in Quincy Market. As you stroll through, pick up a wild berry bagel from **Finagle a Bagel,** a non-alcoholic banana daiquiri from the **Monkey Bar,** a spanakopita from **Mykonos Fair,** sweet and sour chicken from **Ming Tree,** or mussels with garlic butter from **Boston & Maine Fish Co.** There probably aren't any foods you can think of that you can't find here, and prices are gentle. **Boston Cooks** purveys a selection of cookbooks and cooking accessories. The restaurants, though frequented by tourists, are nothing to write home about, with the possible exceptions of historic **Durgin-Park** and the trendy Tex-Mex **Zuma.**

Under the market's north canopy is **Le Saucier,** where Lisa Lamme stocks, at latest count, more than 700 sauces from 37 countries. There are many items to taste; we tried a potent potion called Mad Dog Inferno made in Boston, and eyed a couple more called Dare Double Dare Sauce and Mike's Kissed by Fire salsa. The first hot sauce store in the country ("we started a trend," Lisa says), the place also offers mustards, oils and vinegars, condiments, hot lollipops, New England products and gift baskets.

One of the better places in the waterfront area to pick up lunch or a snack is **Rudi's Cafe Bistro** at 30 Rowes Wharf, near the Boston Harbor Hotel. Billed as a boulangerie, pâtisserie and croissanterie, Rebecca Thomas's upscale spot offers delectable salads, prepared foods and colorful pastries in a curved display case, along with gourmet foods and books. You can eat in a pleasant dining area at the side or take out to the waterfront.

Across town are the fashionable stores at **Copley Plaza** and the grandly redone **Shops at Prudential Center.** The shops at tony **Heritage on the Garden** include Villeroy & Boch and Waterford-Wedgwood.

The 100 block of increasingly fashionable Newbury Street holds special interest for food lovers. An artist from MacKenzie-Childs Ltd. in New York's Finger Lakes region was painting a table in the front window during a special exhibition when we visited **LaRuche** at 168 Newbury, notable for unique place settings and decorative accessories. **Kitchen Arts** at 161 is full of neat gadgets, including a good little hand-held knife sharpener ($8.95) that went home in our shopping bag. Vermont's **Simon Pearce** glass has a branch at 115 Newbury, next door to **Pierre Deux.** Next to the Armani designer store at 214 Newbury St., the showy **Emporio Armani Express** offers designer Italian fare for lunch and dinner.

The old Coffee Connection (at 165 Newbury St. and countless other locations around town) has been absorbed by **Starbucks,** which helps account for the latter's omnipresence across Boston. (Starbucks has a new cross-town competitor: **Seattle's Best Coffee** occupies a prime corner location at Marketplace Center, opposite the east end of Faneuil Hall Marketplace, inside which Starbucks is ensconced.) More coffee is available, along with tea, chocolates and Italian sodas, on a little sunken patio in front of **Espresso Royale Caffe,** 286 Newbury. Adjacent is **Emack & Bolio's,** one of a small local chain offering ice cream, yogurt and a juice bar; the day's special at our visit was a "thick as a brick oreo frappe" for $3.40. Just up the street at 302 Newbury is the new **Nantucket Ice Cream Co.**

A "best office takeout" award helps account for the throngs at **Caffe Gianni,** 500 Boylston St. Besides the predictable espresso bar is a lineup of deli stations, from salads (the North African chicken looked great) to sandwiches ($4.50), an express salad and sandwich bar, and at one end a pizza station.

The finest in pots and pans, plus some cookbooks, are featured at **Seasonings,** a good cookware and accessory store at 65 Beacon St., near Charles Street.

Monadnock Region
A Step Back in Time

"The Quiet Corner," the Monadnock area is called. Also "the Currier and Ives Section." Both with good reason.

Many of the trappings of contemporary civilization have passed this region by. So have many tourists. The restaurant scene here seems to be in a continual state of flux, and we've had to stretch the region's borders a bit to find enough good places to eat. But exciting things have been happening lately in terms of food, particularly in Peterborough, the region's biggest community (population 5,000), and the college town of Keene to the west.

Otherwise, during our explorations through the heart of the region, we noticed only two motels worthy of the name, nary a fast-food outlet, and only a single shopping plaza, that on the outskirts of Peterborough.

Instead there are picture-book villages with Colonial houses, churches and perhaps a general store, antiques shops but rarely a boutique or gift shop, the occasional inn or restaurant, countless streams, lakes and hills, and Mount Monadnock, the ubiquitous, 3,165-foot mountain that is supposedly the world's most climbed. It seems fitting that the area's most popular tourist attraction is the Cathedral of the Pines, an outdoor shrine on a garden-bedecked knoll of pines east of Rindge; the sounds of the carillon are soothing and the view of Grand Monadnock inspiring.

It's a distinct pleasure to stray off the beaten path to encounter a place like the old mill town of Harrisville, which is striking for its red brick structures. They stand quite in contrast to the white frame buildings elsewhere in the region and perhaps epitomized in nearby Dublin, New England's highest village and home of Yankee magazine. In Harrisville, the brick buildings surrounding the duck pond lend an air of old England.

The Quiet Corner is ripe for such rural discoveries. You can find tranquil, postcard New England settings around almost every turn. And like the rest of Monadnock, many of the restaurants and inns are rustic and low-key, capitalizing on the fact they have changed little over the years. Nor have their prices.

They invite you to relive the old days.

Dining

The Boilerhouse at Noone Falls, Route 202 South, Peterborough.

A heron catching fish at the foot of Noone Falls just beyond our window table caused a good bit of diversion for people eating here. "He comes every day," advised our waitress – which was just as well, for we welcomed a distraction to make up for a mediocre meal. Lunch, since discontinued, may have been an aberration, for the Boilerhouse traditionally has been known for some of the best food in southwestern New Hampshire.

The setting and the scenery couldn't be nicer – an expansive, second-level dining room with white-brick and maroon walls, white-linened tables and black lacquered chairs facing huge windows onto the waterfall.

Votive candles cast neat shadows at night, when diners feast on interesting fare as well as the lovely setting. Chef Dave McCarty offers one of the region's more

Window table looks onto water at The Boilerhouse at Noone Falls.

innovative menus. Entrées ($13.95 to $18.95) could be fillet of Atlantic salmon poached in sherry and topped with chanterelles and lump crab, chicken sautéed with lingonberry and port wine sauce, grilled duck with brandied cherry sauce, roast pork tenderloin forestière and pepper-charred filet mignon. House specialties are loin of New Zealand venison with black currants and sundried cranberry sauce, and pan-seared rack of lamb with a honey vinaigrette on a bed of sautéed spinach.

New Orleans-style crab cakes, house-cured gravlax, a ragoût of shrimp and artichokes, and sherry-battered lobster tail with ginger and tamari sauce are favorite appetizers ($5.95 to $6.95). Or start with the signature gratinée of three-onion soup (vidalia, spanish and bermuda with emmanthal cheese). Save room for one of the desserts ($2.50 to $3.95), which are more creative than most in the area. They include the chef's homemade ice creams (perhaps fresh peach with almonds or bittersweet-chocolate with kahlua), strawberries romanoff, wild-berry napoleon with blackberry coulis and white chocolate crème brûlée with fresh fruit. We remember fondly the chef's special dessert of minted pineapple and grapes in peach schnapps from our otherwise forgotten lunch.

Honored by Wine Spectator, the wine list is far better than New Hampshire's average and priced accordingly. And, an endearing touch, the names of all the staff, from the chef to servers and busboys, are listed on the menu.

Outside the entrance in the Boilerhouse arcade is the recently expanded **Café at Noone Falls,** a cafeteria-style cafe offering informal breakfast, lunch and dinner, to eat at little tables or to go.

(603) 924-9486. Dinner, Tuesday-Saturday 5:30 to 9, Sunday 5 to 8; Sunday brunch, noon to 3, October-May.

Latacarta Restaurant, 6 School St., Peterborough.

Inspired cookery and a decided New Age feel emanate from this restaurant, owned by Japanese master chef Hiroshi Hayashi, in the old Gem Theater. He moved to Peterborough from Newbury Street in Boston where, he says, "I never had to serve meat, but I do here." Offering what he calls an "epicurean collage," he is a student of cosmic philosophy (explained on the back of the menu) and gives seminars in natural-foods cooking at his home.

Latacarta is a simple but stylish place, with bentwood chairs, salmon-colored walls on which are some sensational Japanese prints, track lighting, sheer and swagged curtains and many plants. A gorgeous kimono made by Hayashi's wife is spotlit in a niche.

A lunchtime taste of the two soups of the day, cream of butternut squash and a chunky fish chowder, made us wish we could stay for dinner. We returned another time for a lunch of black bean soup, the Latacarta grilled tofu sandwich ($8.95) served on sourdough bread with fried potatoes, and the special of linguini with vegetables provençal ($8), served with a salad – all in more than generous portions. The delicious and piping-hot pear crunch with ice cream ($3.50) was enough for two to share.

Specials augment the regular evening fare ($12.95 to $15.95), but you'll likely find wild mushroom udon, a tofu skillet with vegetables and Japanese dumplings, grilled swordfish with a sherry wine sauce, teppanyaki chicken and a colorful vegetarian dinner. The last, $12.95 at our visit, produced a zucchini boat filled with mushrooms, tomatoes, eggplant and cheddar cheese, vegetables in phyllo, green beans and roasted almonds with olive oil, plus soup and salad. Appetizers vary from gyoza to hummus served with pita bread. Spring rolls, smoked seafood and shrimp tempura with sweet potato and carrot fritters were recent offerings. A large salad is topped with tofu, which the chef calls "sage's protein." Using little salt and sugar, he and his staff turn out desserts like mocha custard, apple pandowdy, banana supreme and strawberry mousse.

A typical dish at an elaborate Sunday brunch is linguini with smoked salmon, snow peas, broccoli, zucchini and mushrooms with a fresh dill sauce.

A light menu is served most of the day in the adjacent bar/cafe. Nibble on enchiladas, Bavarian country chicken or fish and chips ($8.95 to $9.95), while you listen to the New Age music or, on some nights, live music. The short wine list is more sophisticated than you might expect.

"There's a lot going on here," the hostess informed. A series of "Food for Thought" luncheon lectures was on at our latest visit, and workshops and lectures are scheduled upstairs in The Meeting Place. The Peterborough Community Film Society presents classic movies in the theater portion of the building behind the restaurant.

(603) 924-6878. Lunch, Tuesday-Friday 11 to 2; dinner, Tuesday-Saturday 5 to 8:30 or 9, Sunday 5 to 8. Cafe open daily except Monday for cocktails and light meals, 11:30 to 9.

Mangos & Manners, 39 Central Square, Keene.

The area's most contemporary fare and most urbane setting are offered at this trendy newcomer across from the state courthouse on Winter Street in downtown Keene. Young Aram Haroutunian, son of a longtime physician at Mount Snow ski area in Vermont, opened in 1995 at age 26 after deciding work toward a law degree from Boston University was not for him and that cooking was.

Apprenticeships at restaurants in Florida, Newport and Boston gave him good training, and his wife Robin helped produce a good-looking venue in a long and narrow storefront that bears little resemblance to its heritage as a Sears, Roebuck catalog store. Philodendron spills down the sponged-green side wall from pots in the high windows. The other side wall is yellow and encloses a small service bar. Ropes of chile peppers frame the open kitchen at the rear. Tables are dressed with beige linens, bottles of olive oil and votive candles in stained-glass containers.

Clad in colorful chef's pants (flowers one day, chile peppers the next and wild mushrooms another), Aram and sous chef Antonio Quintillio handle the cooking chores from their open stage. They call their cuisine "eclectic contemporary," with an emphasis on Indonesia, the Pacific Rim, the Southwest and the Mediterranean. They paint their plates with purees and garnishes and stack the contents architectural style.

"It's all pretty wild for this area," Arum concedes, but their first year brought good reviews locally ("what a surprise to experience such delectable fine dining right here in Keene, N.H.," gushed one columnist) and interest from outside the area via the Great Chefs television series and Saveur magazine.

The menu changes monthly and reads like those of the metropolitan big boys it emulates (at rich-for-the-area prices). We wanted to try every single dish. Among starters ($6.95 to $8.50) is a remarkable presentation called a Greek pinwheel pie: a puff pastry standing tall with grilled eggplant, zucchini and feta cheese and surrounded by roasted garlic, radish strips, carrots, sprouts and who-knows-

Aram Haroutunian at Mangos & Manners.

what-all. Grilled smoked quail with serrano chile-mango sauce, sautéed crab and goat cheese empanadas and a crispy Asian lobster spring roll with pineapple-jícama salad were other choices.

The ten main dishes are priced from $14.95 for the chef's vegetarian sampler to $23.50 for herb-crusted rack of lamb served with rosemary-roasted red bliss potatoes, pumpkin-pecan pancakes and apple-mint relish. Seafood cannellonis, Marseilles bouillabaisse, oven-roasted ginger duckling and pecan-crusted pork tenderloin are among the possibilities. The wine list is well chosen, and priced from the mid-teens.

Desserts ($5.50) follow suit, from raspberry-apple bread pudding served warm with a rich caramel sauce and peach coulis to pumpkin-walnut pie and crème brûlée. The chef's sampler brings a choice of any three for $10.50.

The choice of name was random, Aram says. "Mango has a light tropical theme and manners connotes civility and refinement. It's a duality reflected in our decor and food. We want people to have fun. That's what we're all about." One hopes their idea of fun will keep playing in Monadnock.

(603) 357-1041. Lunch, Tuesday-Friday 11:30 to 2; dinner, Monday-Saturday 5:30 to 8:30 or 9.

Martinos, 276 West St., Keene.

"Rome all you like without leaving Keene," says the business card of this wildly popular restaurant that started as Martinos Spaghetti House.

Chef-owner Donna Sears, following some of her grandmother's recipes, cooks creatively with a penchant for garlic and oregano. The short menu changes daily and is posted on a couple of hard-to-read blackboards on either side of the small, jam-packed and dimly lit dining room. You'd best determine your choices from the blackboard posted in the rear waiting area, where an assortment of magazines and complimentary hot spiced cider and pretzels keep would-be diners contented. Fortunately, reservations are advised (and honored), but walk-ins may slip into an open slot. "There's one table available for 45 minutes," the hostess advised the Friday night we stopped by to find the place otherwise filled at 5:45.

Spaghetti is featured, but here you can order it with sausage, fresh vegetables or rosemary chicken ($6.95 to $9.95) from one night's selections. The offerings were typical: starters of creamy lobster bisque, baked stuffed focaccia and tuna crostini; the "spaghetti and..." section, and five other main dishes, priced from $8.95 for homemade manicotti or lasagna to $14.95 for shrimp and shiitake mushrooms in pesto cream sauce over linguini. The other options were crabmeat manicotti and a suave scallops and saffron risotto, both $11.95. Portions are huge, and nearly everyone leaves with a foil-wrapped doggie bag shaped like a swan.

Sliced Italian bread and garlic-oregano butter are served as you are seated. Main dishes come with an interesting mixed salad, and the creamy gorgonzola dressing is wonderful. Desserts could be apple crumb tart à la mode, cappuccino silk pie and tirami su.

The place is dark and intimate and nicely outfitted in a simple country look (note the changing displays of healthful foods on the glass shelves in the front window). It's convivial and welcoming, and much admired for great food at bargain prices.

(603) 357-0859. Lunch, Monday-Friday 11:30 to 1:30; dinner nightly, 5 to 9. No credit cards.

Del Rossi's Trattoria, Route 137 at Route 101, Dublin.

The aroma of garlic wafts through this pretty Colonial house – the setting for some fine Italian fare, cooked up by chef David Del Rossi, co-owner with his wife Elaina. The two Jaffrey natives also run a music store, which accounts for the fact they feature live music (mostly bluegrass and folk with name entertainers) on Saturday nights on a stage in a corner of the main dining room.

With its wide-plank floors and post and beam construction, the dining room is plain and comfortable with sturdy captain's chairs at the tables, some left bare and some with beige linens and burgundy napkins. There are a couple of smaller rooms (away from the entertainment) plus a sun porch with a stained-glass window, where we enjoyed lunch.

For dinner, you might begin with crostini with calamari or polenta topped with a tomato and basil (from the chef's garden) sauce and melted gorgonzola, and go on to a pasta ($7.95 to $12.95) – all made in house by this talented chef who recreates dishes he tasted as a child with his grandparents from Abruzzi. Among the favorites are gnocchi bolognese, four-cheese ravioli, and fettuccine with shiitake mushrooms.

Entrées ($10.95 to $16.95) include seafood fra diavolo, shrimp scampi, scallops broiled in a wine sauce topped with bread crumbs and grated romano, pork scaloppine with prosciutto and cheese, chicken piccata and steak cacciatore. Loaves of homemade Italian bread, vegetable of the day and a side of pasta accompany. The lengthy wine list is well chosen and reasonably priced, and beers are a bargain.

"Once you try my Sicilian cake, you want it again and again," says David. The homemade pound cake has ricotta cheese and chocolate filling between its layers and couldn't be more lush. Another favorite is Roman cheese pie, an old recipe featuring ricotta with a marsala wine crust on a bed of honey with grapes.

The menu for lunch, recently served seasonally on a somewhat iffy basis, changes every day; there are always two salads, a frittata, a quiche and a pasta. Our quiche of smoked oysters and cheese with a generous salad and a PLT version of a BLT (prosciutto, lettuce, and tomato on grilled garlic bread) were super.

The Del Rossis relocated their music store from Jaffrey to the second floor above the restaurant in 1997. They thought the move would help both businesses, and might prompt the resumption of regular lunch service.

(603) 563-7195. Dinner, Tuesday-Saturday 5 to 9, Sunday 4 to 8.

Carolyn's Bistro, 5 Depot Square, Peterborough.

Carolyn Bonner is in the kitchen, but her efforts are also visible on the walls. For the cook is also an artist, and her watercolors are on display for all to enjoy. She and husband Ted renovated an old furniture warehouse and "found the Nubanusit River out back at the last minute," Ted said. They inserted a couple of large windows in the whitewashed cinder-block walls to access the view and illuminated the river at night. "It was the best thing we ever did," said Ted, who was in the computer business and "came in for a few weeks to help out with the opening" and stayed. Their regular customers think the best thing was having Carolyn share her cooking talents.

From her semi-open kitchen comes an array of treats, most of them light and with an emphasis on seafood, pastas and stir-fries. The dinner menu ($13 to $17.50) offers sole amandine, shrimp and scallops fra diavolo, chicken stir-fry, southwest chicken and shrimp with pineapple-mango salsa, grilled pork tenderloin marinated in homemade barbecue sauce, veal piccata and sirloin steak with choice of sauces. The signature bistro chicken is sautéed with artichoke hearts, sundried tomatoes, black olives, roasted garlic and white wine. Homemade bread and salad come with.

Coquilles St. Jacques, grilled shrimp with stir-fried vegetables and the house antipasto are favored appetizers ($5 to $7.50). Dessert could be apple crisp or blueberry pie.

Dining is on two levels, the higher rear level looking onto the stream and the front section screened by cafe curtains from the parking area. The cafe is simple yet elegant with tablecloths, track lighting and candles at night.

(603) 924-2002. Lunch, Monday-Saturday 11:30 to 2; dinner, Monday-Saturday 5 to 9.

Lilly's On the Pond, Route 202, Rindge.

The core of "the Old Forge," the last remaining of seven mills in Rindge, dates back to 1790 when it was a sawmill. Previously known as the Old Forge restaurant, the historic site took on a new life in 1994.

Two women who had managed area restaurants, Suanne Yglesias and Helen Kendall, and their husbands transformed the once dark and dingy establishment. They painted the interior white with dark trim for a Tudor tavern look, hung quilts on the walls, scattered oriental rugs on the floors, enclosed a porch overlooking the mill pond and installed a wood stove on the site of the original forge in the pub. The large main dining room is properly historic looking with captain's chairs at bare wood tables, wagon-wheel chandeliers overhead and wide-plank floors beneath. The porch offers the best view of the water wheel and ducks on the mill pond.

The owners keep their large place busy with an extensive menu that encourages grazing as well as full-course meals. Chef Tim Hills is known for his pork spare ribs with a spicy Jamaican jerk sauce that comes in three degrees of heat: "wimpy, hot or industrial." Those with less incendiary tastes can opt for grilled salmon fillet with artichokes and béarnaise sauce, seafood niçoise, tequila-lime or kiwi-apple chutney chicken, pork tenderloin in a creamy dijon sauce, wiener schnitzel or blackened sirloin or steak au poivre, among entrées priced from $8.95 to $14.95.

The all-day menu also offers eight kinds of burgers, snacky appetizers like nachos and potato layers ("better than skins," according to the menu) and countless sandwiches, from philly cheese steak and reubens to veggie stir-fry pitas, all in the $4 to $6 range. There's also a full page of specials for lunch and dinner. No one goes hungry here, nor will the bill break the bank.

Lilly's chocolate-topped peanut-butter cheesecake won first prize in a chocolate jubilee locally. The raspberry pie and grand-marnier chocolate mousse also are highly rated.

(603) 899-3322. Lunch, Tuesday-Saturday 11:30 to 5; dinner, 5 to 9 or 10; Sunday, brunch 10 to 3, dinner noon to 8. Closed Monday.

Twelve Pine, 11 School St., Peterborough.

Although not a restaurant as such, this gourmet takeout spot is the "in" place for area food-lovers. Daniel Thibeault, who worked his way through art school in Boston in the employ of hotel restaurants, and his wife Joan started a catering business at their home (from whose address was derived the name). Success prompted a small downtown takeout operation, which moved in 1996 into an old grain warehouse at Depot Square.

Unexpectedly large and stylish, the barn of a place is a perfect showcase for the specialty foods, bakery, produce, cafe and deli items offered by the couple. This destination for gourmands even has a juice and espresso bar.

Old farm carts and wagons display the season's bounty in a fresh and airy, market-type setting with beamed ceiling, shiny floors and mustard yellow walls. There's cafe seating at a handful of tables inside or outside on the side train platform. About half the space is given over to cafeteria-style counters and display cases full of delectable-looking treats. White chocolate mousse cakes, raspberry-strawberry shortcakes and hazelnut-cappuccino cheesecakes are lined up in one case next to another full of salads, phyllo rolls, polenta triangles and pesto ovals.

You can pick up the makings for lunch or a picnic or get an entrée for dinner, to eat here or to go (there's no table service or liquor). The changing blackboard

Old farm cart displays season's bounty at Twelve Pine market and cafe.

choices are legion. How about one of the soups (perhaps Russian peasant, gazpacho or tomato and cheddar), with a ham and potato tart or a crabmeat quiche? Or one of about a dozen enticing salads? We made a picnic of three – linguini with chicken and pesto, antipasto with shrimp and a red cabbage slaw with capers and almonds – and a couple of peanut-butter chocolate-chip cookies, and trundled off to partake on the side porch. Moussaka, chicken rosemary, stuffed cornish game hens and baked salmon with rice are some of the heartier entrées in the $4 to $7 range. Burritos and gourmet pizzas are popular.

(603) 924-6140. Open Monday-Friday 8 to 7, Saturday and Sunday 8 to 3.

Dining and Lodging

Chesterfield Inn, Route 9, West Chesterfield 03466.

Young corporate dropouts Phil and Judy Heuber from Connecticut stayed in 80-odd country inns before deciding to purchase the two-year-old Chesterfield Inn in 1987, proclaiming the guest rooms here "the finest we'd seen." That, it turns out, was just the beginning. They added four more luxury rooms, a beautiful new dining room and plush common areas to create what they call "a luxurious country hotel" that justifies an AAA four-diamond rating.

The thirteen spacious guest rooms are stunning with cathedral ceilings, exposed beams and barn boards. Each has a comfortable sitting area, three-way reading lamps, a full bath (two with jacuzzis) beyond a separate dressing area, period antiques and quilts. All have kingsize or two double beds.

The Heubers have stocked mini-refrigerators in the rooms with a variety of beverages and have outfitted the bathrooms with Gilchrist & Soames toiletries. All rooms have televisions and telephones, all different and some cleverly tucked away in boxes. "These are really elegant and beautiful rooms," says Judy, "but we want them to be comfortable and livable."

The latter was a prime consideration when the Heubers added a new structure to the side with four spacious bedrooms in the same style. These come with corner fireplaces and private brick patios overlooking the gardens – "great places to sit and watch the sunset," says Judy.

Elegant porch dining at Chesterfield Inn.

The latest addition, to the rear off the entry lobby, produced a stylish living room, a commercial kitchen and a dining room with windows on three sides and a dining porch overlooking a patio. Now 50 people can dine by candlelight at tables set with crisp white over pink linens, Dudson floral china, big wine globes and crystal water glasses.

Chef Carl Warner, who has been with the Heubers from the beginning, changes the short dinner menu seasonally. A complimentary starter like smoked salmon pâté is on the table as guests are seated. Appetizers ($7 to $9) might be lobster and corn chowder, crab cakes with rémoulade sauce, prunes stuffed with foie gras or grilled vegetables with aioli. Entrées ($18 to $22) could be grilled swordfish with orange vinaigrette, pork kabobs with a sauce of chiles and sesame seeds, beef tenderloin stuffed with herb cheese or a Brazilian mixed grill for two of flank steak, pork tenderloin and sausage.

For dessert, try Carl's fresh berry trifle, flourless chocolate cake with custard sauce, pumpkin cheesecake or walnut pie. The wine list is a well-chosen mix of American and French, with some not-often-seen Californias among the selections priced from $16 to $50.

The Heubers cook a hearty breakfast for overnight guests. The main course might be french toast soaked in triple sec, blueberry pancakes, a fancy omelet or featherbed eggs (similar to a cheese strata). Corn fritters, potato pancakes, hash browns, granola and homemade muffins might accompany.

(603) 256-3211 or (800) 365-5515. Fax (603) 256-6131. Dinner nightly, 5:30 to 9. Doubles, $115 to $160; suites, $155 to $170.

The Hancock Inn, 33 Main St., Hancock 03449.

New Hampshire's oldest operating inn (1789) doesn't look that old because of the later addition of a mansard roof. Its elegant, pillared facade enhances the main street of the picturesque hamlet of Hancock. It also doesn't feel that old, thanks to the redecorating and upgrading done by new owners Linda and Joe Johnston, formerly of the New England Inn at Intervale, N.H. They have lavished much time and money in redoing the inn, from top to bottom, to create in Linda's words, "a genuine inn experience for our guests."

They started with the tavern, "because we strongly believe that an inn should be an inn – with a common room." Here is a welcoming place where folks gather not only to imbibe but to play checkers and other board games or to simply read in the corner. Remarkable Linda painted a Rufus Porter-style mural around the walls of the tavern. It bears an uncanny resemblance to the artist's trademark murals that adorn the upstairs Rufus Porter bedroom and those at other hostelries in the area.

The Johnstons also put new emphasis on the inn's dining. They have gussied up all three dining areas, sponging the walls of the main room a Colonial red color, nicely trimmed in grayish-blue, which with a blazing hearth is a favorite in winter. The tables are elegantly set with cream-colored linens, modern glass oil lamps, oversize pewter cutlery and napkins stashed in wine glasses. In summer, we prefer the more casual, beamed dining room in the rear, with barnwoods walls and windows onto the lawns. Here is where house guests also enjoy a breakfast buffet of homemade granola, scones, juices, fruits and a cooked-to-order dish, perhaps banana-pecan pancakes with sausage or a sausage and egg casserole.

The dinner fare has been upgraded as well since we supped here a few years back. Instead of vegetable juice, cellophane-wrapped crackers with crocks of Wispride and tossed salads of iceberg lettuce, now you might start with a lobster tart, Nantucket seafood chowder or a salad of wild greens with a goat-cheese timbale ($4.50 to $8.25). The ten or so entrées are priced from $14 for homemade turkey pie to $22.50 for black angus steak with caramelized onion and red wine sauce. Although the fare has contemporary overtones, the house specialty (brought here from the New England Inn) remains Shaker cranberry pot roast – "which outsells anything else on the menu, two to one," says Linda.

Desserts also mix the traditional with the trendy. Indian pudding à la mode and bread pudding with caramel sauce vie for attention with chocolate-chestnut tart, three-chocolate terrine and a crème brûlée napoleon with hazelnuts.

Most of the inn's eleven guest rooms are done in handsome period furniture. The Johnstons have added telephones, air-conditioning, queensize or twin beds, bath toiletries and cassettes with tapes for music. The rooms look far more comfortable than when we stayed here a decade ago. We'll never forget being awakened on the hour all night by the Paul Revere bell in the nearby church steeple – "gently lulling you to sleep" was how the inn's brochure put it. Now the rooms have TVs enclosed in what Linda calls TV cozies, quilted covers that mask their presence. A small sign cautions: "Do not remove unless you wish to return to the 20th Century."

(603) 525-3318 or (800) 525-1789. Fax (603) 525-9301. Dinner nightly, 6 to 9, Sunday 5 to 8. Doubles, $98 to $138.

Colby Hill Inn, The Oaks, Box 778, Henniker 03242.

Vastly upgraded lately in terms of food, hospitality and decor, this sixteen-room inn with a good dining room was a working farm until 1959 and the old barn is still attached to the inn. You go through it to get to the secluded swimming pool, with views of hills and meadows and a pond that is used for ice-skating.

Built about 1800, this is a cheery, cozy inn with two sitting rooms, one with a flickering fireplace and the other with games, television and rear windows looking onto gardens and a new gazebo. Business transplants from Maryland, Ellie and John Day and their daughter Laurel, took over the inn in 1990 and have infused it with enthusiasm and good taste. They redecorated six rooms in the rear carriage house and ten rooms in the main inn with antiques. All have private baths and telephones, and four of the most prized in the main house have working fireplaces. One with an ornate brass kingsize bed is especially appealing in Waverly fabrics.

Pots of coffee and tea and a cookie jar full of the best crunchy oatmeal-raisin cookies are at the ready for guests in the entry to the dining room. A full country breakfast is served in the morning. A couple of large, friendly dogs are very much in evidence in the common rooms.

The newly air-conditioned dining room has become increasingly known for good food under the aegis of CIA-trained chef Michael Mack, who has been with the Days since they took over. The dozen or so dinner entrées ($15.95 to $25.95) include a signature breast of chicken stuffed with lobster, leeks and boursin; grilled salmon with lemon-dill beurre blanc, horseradish-crusted baked salmon with leek and wine sauce, and rack of Australian lamb with a lamb demi-glace.

The starters are more limited but no less enticing, among them lobster bisque, scallops and bacon en croûte, pan-fried lobster cake and mushroom crêpe with sherried cream sauce. Ellie Day prepares the scrumptious desserts, always a cheesecake (pecan-pumpkin-praline at our autumn visit) and perhaps amaretto crème caramel, pecan-carrot cake, blueberry-cream pie and cream puff swans with raspberry puree. The short but good wine list is priced in the teens and twenties.

All this is served in a couple of serene dining rooms. One is a wainscoted tavern room and the other a stenciled room with big windows onto the back gardens. Twining grapevines above the windows are strung with tiny white lights all year. Cream-colored linens, pink napkins, candles in hurricane lamps and oriental runners contribute to the country elegance.

(603) 428-3281 or (800) 531-0330. Dinner nightly, 5:30 to 8:30, Sunday 4:30 to 7:30. Doubles, $85 to $165.

The Birchwood Inn, Route 45, Temple 03084.

Judy and Bill Wolfe, originally from New Jersey, have been operating this red brick inn, built around 1800 and now listed on the National Register, since 1980. They have earned wide acclaim for their bargain-priced dinners, served to the public as well as inn guests, and one area booster thinks they serve the best meals in the region.

The small dining room, its walls covered by Rufus Porter murals, is candlelit. The blackboard menu usually lists three entrées that could be seafood chautauqua (a medley of shrimp, scallops and lobster in herbed butter sauce over rice), roast duckling with grand marnier sauce and tournedos of beef béarnaise. Meals start with relishes like cottage cheese with horseradish and curried kidney beans and a choice of two homemade breads from Judy's repertoire of 100. Then comes juice or soups, among them minestrone, French onion, black bean, she-crab and lobster bisque (offered only on Saturdays). Dessert could be an apple-raspberry cobbler, tortes, cheesecake, cream cheese-pecan pie and ice cream with a homemade sauce, perhaps rum-maple.

The four-course meal costs $16.95 to $19.95, depending on choice of entrée. "We do everything ourselves – that's how we can keep these prices," Bill explained.

Upstairs are six small guest rooms with private baths. Each is charmingly decorated around family collection themes: a seashore room, music room, editorial office (with an ancient typewriter and wallpaper of front pages) and the like. A newer bedroom on the ground floor, where a large shop used to be, has TV, private bath and a brightly-colored quilt, with old produce signs on the walls. Room rates include a full country breakfast, which also draws the locals (as you might expect, considering its $3.95 price).

Twining grapevines are strung with tiny white lights in Colby Hill Inn dining room.

A quaint piano with sheet music is ensconced in the country parlor, and in front is a small shop and game room.

(603) 878-3285. Breakfast, Tuesday-Sunday, 7:30 to 9:30; dinner, Tuesday-Saturday 5 to 8:30. BYOB. Doubles, $60 to $70. No credit cards.

The Inn at Crotched Mountain, Mountain Road off Route 47, Francestown 03043.

This rambling red brick inn, with a renovated red and white barn attached, is at the 1,300-foot level with the former Crotched Mountain ski area almost at the front door, so the air is sparkling and the view, 40 miles across the Piscataquog Valley, is grand.

Owners Rose and John Perry are both schooled in the restaurant business and their dining room is highly regarded in the area. Lately they have curtailed its operations to weekends only, leaving house guests somewhat high and dry – and hungry – at other times, now that several nearby restaurants have closed.

The aromas emanating from the kitchen indicate a culinary master at work. Chef Rose's nightly specials strike us as more interesting than the regular menu. Treats like lobster strudel, grilled tuna with cucumber dressing, babi ritja (an Indonesian dish with pork and ginger) and pot stickers supplement the regular entrées of shrimp scampi, cranberry pot roast, chicken teriyaki, calves liver with onion and bacon, and filet mignon béarnaise. Entrée prices ($13.95 to $18.95) include cellophane-noodle or apple-curry soup, salad with one of the inn's home-made dressings, homemade breads and vegetables grown on the premises. A sur-charge brings appetizers like herring in wine, shrimp cocktail or smoked mussels.

Guests eat in two dining rooms or at a couple of tables set up in the huge living room, which has lovely oriental rugs and a fireplace at either end. A display case shows off jars of the Perrys' homemade goodies, including jams, tarragon vinegar and celery seed dressing, which are for sale. The inn has eight other working fireplaces, four of them in the guest rooms (of which there are thirteen, eight with private baths). Both a continental and full breakfast are included in the rates.

Two clay tennis courts and a large swimming pool taking full advantage of the view give guests a choice of activities. This is a place where you can really feel secluded and almost on top of the world.

(603) 588-6840. Dinner, Friday-Saturday 6 to 8:30. Doubles, $140 to $180, MAP on weekends; $60 to $100, B&B on weekdays. Closed April and November. No credit cards.

Fitzwilliam Inn, Route 119, Fitzwilliam 03447.

Dating to 1796, this venerable establishment has been re-energized by the McMahon family, who took over in 1996 and undertook modest cosmetic enhancements. It remains an inn of the old school – and looks it, from its charming bar and dining room to the 25 upstairs guest rooms, fourteen with private baths. All kinds of stenciling, cows on the shower curtains and wreaths of dried flowers brighten what many would consider an old-fashioned, spartan feeling to the bedrooms. The larger rooms with two double beds are twice the size of the standards, which are just big enough to hold one double bed.

The main floor is a ramble of rooms, including a front library with an old English rebus over the fireplace. It's a seemingly nonsensical inscription that guests delight in trying to figure out (one of the inn's postcards gives the answer). Local crafts are sold in a small gift shop in the reception area. There's a swimming pool in back.

The heart of the operation is the restaurant, which for years has been enormously popular with traditionalists. Wagon-wheel chandeliers, hanging baskets, stenciling and a dark beamed ceiling mark the spacious, 65-seat dining area with its bare floors and wood tables. CIA-trained chef-owner Mark McMahon, who cooked at the Ritz-Carlton and managed country clubs in the Boston area, has made the fare more consistent but knew the Fitzwilliam's traditional format "works, so why change it?" His sister Lois manages the front of the house.

The dinner menu arrives on a paddle board listing fifteen entrées from $8.25 to $16.95 (add $4 for a complete dinner, including appetizer, salad, dessert and beverage). The choice includes things like Boston scrod, chicken florentine, lobster newburg and veal oscar. People return year after year for the black diamond steak marinated in soy and herbs and the roast duck stuffed with scalloped apples and served on a bed of brown sauce.

Desserts run to crème de menthe parfait and Indian pudding. Those in the know opt for the Fitzwilliam nutty pie and the toasted coconut-almond cream pie.

Scallops mornay and mixed seafood Sicilian are featured on the lunch menu ($4.95 to $7.95 à la carte, add $3 for soup or juice, dessert and beverage). The breakfast menu offers a range ($3.95 to $6.95) from buckwheat pancakes and french toast to eggs benedict and corned-beef hash with a poached egg.

(603) 585-9000. Fax (603) 585-3495. Breakfast daily, 8 to 9:30, weekends from 7; lunch, noon to 2; dinner, 5:30 to 9. Doubles, $45 to $60.

Lodging

Amos A. Parker House, Route 119, Fitzwilliam 03447.

A travel agent in Chicago, Freda Houpt had been nearly everywhere in the world except India and New England when she first visited her son in Boston. After that visit, she went home, sold her house the next day and wound up in Fitzwilliam, where she runs one of the region's most appealing B&Bs.

A Renaissance woman if ever there was one, energetic Freda does everything at the four-room B&B herself. She still finds time to develop and tend the incredible gardens with more than 1,500 perennials in back, dabble in sculpture and host workshops on drying flowers. And, on a rare busman's holiday, she traveled around Russia staying at B&Bs.

Her 1780 house, backing up to fields and forests at the western edge of town, is a beauty. The main floor harbors a cozy "great room" (her words) with comfortable furniture, wood stove, barnwood walls, shelves of books and old crockery, and dried flowers hanging from the beams. There also are a charming fireplaced dining room painted a striking burnt orange, a kitchen in which guests tend to congregate, and a TV room with sliding doors to a rear deck overlooking the gardens and a pond "with 22 frogs and seven goldfish," Freda specifies.

The main floor also contains a suite with a private entrance. It has a large bedroom with queensize bed, a sitting area with a sofabed and a fireplace, a small kitchen and stenciling all around. Upstairs are two front guest rooms with fireplaces and private baths (one a two-room affair with a w.c. and sink in one and the smallest shower ever in the other). Two back rooms form a suite with sitting room and a full bath with a bidet. Two Winchendon women were responsible for a couple of stunning trompe-l'oeil wall murals: a floral trellis behind the bed in the suite, and a vase of flowers over the fireplace mantel in a front room. Oriental rugs warm the wide-plank floors and lace-edged pillows and comforters cover the beds. Fresh flowers, colorful towels and terrycloth robes in every room are among caring touches. As guests arrive, a silver tray on the dining-room table awaits with hot or cold drinks, fruit, cheese, crackers and cookies.

Breakfast is quite a feast, starting with cold fruit under a glass dome garnished with flowers in the summer and hot fruit like apricot and blueberry compote in long-stemmed Waterford glasses in the fall. The main course might be a "pullapart," a huge puffy pancake done in an iron skillet and sprinkled with lemon and powdered sugar, or an apple soufflé pancake with sour cream. Spinach soufflé crêpes with mushroom sauce are garnished with vegetables like snow peas or squash with walnuts and cranberries. Another favorite is a dish of rice and dried fruits topped with maple syrup, accompanied by a medley of breakfast meats. Freda loves to experiment, so who knows what yummy dishes you will find at the breakfast table.

She planned to open a perennial garden nursery behind her home in 1997, and was to be listed on National Garden Conservancy tours of private gardens for public viewing.

(603) 585-6540. Doubles, $80; suites, $90.

Hannah Davis House, 186 Depot Road (Route 119), Fitzwilliam 03447.

This elegant, 1820 Federal house was restored into a B&B in 1990 and now offers three rooms and three suites, all with private baths. Kaye and Mike Terpstra, who "always traveled on our stomachs," expect their guests to do the same, so extravagant breakfasts and afternoon refreshments are a priority.

The heart of the house is an enormous, open country kitchen made cozy by prolific plants (including one hanging from a butcher scale). Guests breakfast here at a large table beside the fireplace. Afternoon treats, from popcorn to chocolate chip cookies, are served in a common room or on the rear deck overlooking colorful gardens and a pond occupied by a resident beaver. Another common room holds a piano and stereo system.

Upstairs are three guest rooms with private baths. All the beds are angled into the corners and the large bathrooms have clawfoot tubs and pedestal sinks. Kaye's collection of quilts, teddy bears and an old nightdress and cap decorate the rooms. A high chair in the hall contains the necessities a guest might forget, including a hair dryer, a steam iron and a wine pull.

Two large and airy guest suites out over the garage and carriage barn have private entrances. One is called Popovers because its deck and elevated walkway to the breakfast area "pops over" the back yard and bog. It has nice oak furniture, an angled antique cannonball queen bed, a sofa and another bed tucked into a corner. Mount Monadnock is on view from the window of the bathroom, which, Kaye quips, has the best seat in the house. The lofty bedroom in the Loft Suite opens onto a sitting room below with a queensize sofabed, walk-in closet and a bathroom with clawfoot tub and separate, glass-enclosed shower. A new main-floor suite has two fireplaces, a kingsize bed, a sofabed in the sitting room and a private porch.

The hearty breakfast one day we visited included juice, homemade granola and applesauce, cinnamon-raisin bread and banana bread with fresh ginger, pears poached in syrup and ginger, and french toast stuffed with ham and cheese topped with a dijon sauce. Nasturtiums and snow peas garnish the main courses, which could be scrambled eggs with green beans, ratatouille-stuffed crêpes or a sandwich of stuffed french toast with peaches and cream cheese. An occasional treat is stuffed french toast with seafood and cream cheese.

(603) 585-3344. Doubles, $60 to $75; suites $95.

The Benjamin Prescott Inn, Route 124 East, Jaffrey 03452.

This handsome pale yellow 1820s Greek Revival house in a rural setting east of town was the first of Monadnock's upscale B&Bs. Since 1988 it's been run by Barry and Janice Miller, he with 26 years in the hotel business – half of them at Henry Ford's Dearborn Inn in Michigan.

The Snyders have added their own hallmarks and upgraded the nine guest rooms, all with private baths and ranging from standard size to a suite that can sleep eight. Rooms are stenciled and furnished with antiques, handsome quilts, items from the owners' seemingly myriad collections and interesting touches like handpainted antique irons used as door stops. The John Adams Attic Suite on the third floor is a delight with a living room/wet bar and a balcony overlooking the rural back yard, plus another room with a kingsize bed. Both rooms have unusual sleeping alcoves that Barry calls "closet beds" – a Scottish practice using the eaves to cram in extra sleeping space.

A full country breakfast is served at a large table in the dining room or at smaller tables in the common sitting room with a fireplace and TV. Juices and three of Janice's fruit breads precede the main course, perhaps scotch eggs, eggs benedict or Prescott rarebit, or a bread dish like cinnamon-sourdough french toast shaped in a fan of maple leaves, multi-grain waffles with raspberry butter, or dutch apple pancakes made with granny smith apples. Check out Barry's collection of sands from across the world, stocked in test tubes and displayed on three shelves in the common room. And don't miss the inn's mailbox across the street, an intricate replica of the house itself.

(603) 532-6637. Doubles, $75; suite $130.

Apple Gate Bed & Breakfast, 199 Upland Farm Road (Route 123), Peterborough 03458.

Tiny electric candles glow year-round in the windows of this handsome 1832 Colonial surrounded by prolific gardens, trees and apple orchards. The wraparound veranda with its dark green Adirondack chairs is a perfect spot for taking in the rural surroundings.

Apples are the theme inside, done in exquisite taste by Dianne and Ken Legenhausen, formerly of Long Island, where she was a music teacher and he a police officer. Colorful stenciling leads guests up the front staircase to three of the four fresh-looking guest rooms, all with private baths. We like best the buttery yellow Cortland corner room with a queensize bed, hooked rugs on the wide pine floors and basket of Woods of Windsor amenities in the bathroom. The small McIntosh room with a clawfoot tub in the bath is barely big enough for a three-quarter bed.

Particularly attractive are the main-floor common rooms, including a fireplaced parlor opening into a library, where a stuffed bear is perched on the bench at the piano. A full breakfast is served by candlelight at a table set for six or eight beside the fireplace in the beamed dining room. Specialties are oven-baked apple pancakes and various kinds of omelets.

(603) 924-6543. Doubles, $65 to $75.

Gourmet Treats

Peterborough is the center of the area's culinary, cultural and shopping attractions.

The **Sharon Arts Center** on Route 123 south of town has a super shop with items from the League of New Hampshire Craftsmen and exhibits in the Kilian Gallery. In summer and fall, the **Saltbox Cafe** in a classroom building opens for lunch, served Friday-Monday 11:30 to 2.

The North Gallery at Tewksbury's, Route 123, is a favorite shop of many, representing more than 500 American craftsmen and carrying everything from cards to toys to paintings to collectibles and a small section of specialty foods and jams, not to mention all the crafts, on three floors of a newly reconstructed, post and beam barn. Other good gift shops with specialty foods and dishware as sidelines include **The Field Mouse, The Winged Pig, At Wit's End** and **Ginger and Pickles.**

Maggie's Farm Natural Foods at 14 Main St. is a large and good natural-foods store with healthful cookbooks, vinegars, sundried tomatoes, salsas and such, plus organic produce, wines and coffee. Next door is **Cook's Complements,** a nice kitchen shop. Proprietor Janet Quinn stocks all the proper equipment from gadgets to coffee makers to pretty placemats.

Aesop's Tables at 12 Depot Square is a coffee bar and tea room with a difference. For one thing, it's in a corner of the Toad-Stool Bookstore, and is a comfy refuge of mismatched tables and chairs with a hand-me-down sofa along one side. For another, it dispenses pastries, sandwiches and desserts to go with. Owner Janice Hurley offers soups and sandwiches in the $4 range (cajun meatloaf and chicken burrito, at our recent visit) along with pastries and sweets.

For a taste of rural New England, **Parker's Maple Barn,** Brookline Road, Mason, is a favorite stop of many for breakfast – for pancakes, of course – and breakfast is served all day, until dinner service starts at 4:30. Besides old-fashioned home cooking in a 19th-century barn, there's a country store with gifts and maple items produced on site. Open daily from 7 or 8 a.m., March-December.

Garden Gourmet

Rosaly's Farm Stand, Route 123, Peterborough.

Some of the salads at local restaurants bear the name Rosaly, as in "Rosaly's Garden" at Latacarta. They contain fresh organic baby greens, tomatoes, cucumbers and whatever and come from the certified organic gardens of Rosaly S. Bass just southeast of Peterborough .

The farm stand, the retail adjunct to the 23-year-old **Rosaly's Garden** enterprise, is a fascinating stop for people interested in exotic produce and flowers. It also offers cookies, scones and the odd prepared foods and vinegars, among them hot pepper. We bought some yukon gold potatoes, lavender peppers and pattypan squash and admired the pick-your-own flower and herb gardens, a well-marked showplace of prolific blooms and color.

Open daily in season, 10 to 6.

Herbal Gourmet

Pickity Place, Nutting Hill Road, Mason.

Usually it's "over the river and through the woods" to Grandmother's house, but in this case it's up, up, and up a mountain on some bumpy dirt roads and, if you didn't see the odd small sign tacked to a tree, you would swear you were on a wild goose chase.

It's worth the jolts, for eventually you come to a 1786 house and barn embracing a restaurant, herb shop, museum, garden shop, greenhouse and, in the Little Red Riding Hood Room (because Elizabeth O. Jones used the house to illustrate her version of the book), you guessed it, a big bad wolf in a nightcap, lying in grandmother's canopied bed.

The shop smells marvelous, with its wares of herbal teas, potpourris, pomanders, soaps, dried apple wreaths and even a dill pillow (which apparently will help soothe a baby to sleep). We picked up a tea drinker's gift box ($12.95 – four teas, bamboo strainer, honey and honey dipper) for a tea-loving grandpa.

And, shades of our local, much-loved Caprilands in Coventry, Conn., Pickity Place offers herbal luncheons, five courses for about $15. You're encouraged to bring your own wine (not too much, or you'll never negotiate down the mountain). In a room where bunches of herbs hang on the walls and a huge swag of bay leaves is over the mantel, you will be served foods appropriate to the season (and often in honor of the ancient farming festivals of Europe). The October menu, for instance, might have creamy spinach dip, tomato-barley soup, eight-grain bread, herbed pasta salad, a choice of beef crêpes with horseradish sauce or vegetable stroganoff, spinach mornay and pumpkin squares.

(603) 878-1151. Seatings at 11:30, 12:45 or 2, daily except major holidays year-round. Reservations required.

Summer Suite at Inn at Harbor Head yields view toward ocean from Cape Porpoise.

Southern Maine
Sophistication by the Sea

It wasn't so long ago that proper Bostonians thought fine dining ended at Portsmouth and the New Hampshire-Maine state line.

The Southern Maine coast was known for lobster shacks and seafood roadhouses, and about the only restaurants of note were the Whistling Oyster in Ogunquit and the Roma Cafe in Portland.

How times have changed. The restoration of the historic Old Port Exchange area in Portland has spawned a proliferation of restaurants, both fine and casual, in Maine's largest city. And the sophistication of summer resort areas like Ogunquit and Kennebunkport has attracted new restaurants and inns.

Many of the better establishments simply did not exist twenty years ago. A restaurant supplier said that in one boom year in the late 1980s, twelve major restaurants had popped up along the Maine coast since the previous summer. The boom continues, with more opening in the mid-90s, when other locales barely held to the status quo.

Now a center of culinary interest – from intimate restaurants serving contemporary American cuisine to casual spots, gourmet shops, delis and inventive vegetarian eateries – Portland offers more quality and variety in dining than most cities its size.

The other centers of culinary interest are in York-Ogunquit and Kennebunkport, two of the more luxurious summer colonies along the coast. Ogunquit's famed Whistling Oyster has closed, but worthy successors remain. And George Bush and his summer neighbors in Kennebunkport no longer have to go to Ogunquit for a fine meal – they have plenty of good restaurants of their own.

Dining

The Best of the Best

Arrows, Berwick Road, Ogunquit.

Two young chefs who apprenticed with Jeremiah Tower at Stars in San Francisco came east in 1988 to take over this off-again, on-again restaurant that had great potential. Clark Frasier and Mark Gaier quickly fulfilled that potential and more. With great attention to detail, they have painstakingly crafted a chic and uniquely personal destination restaurant that offers the most exciting – and probably the most expensive – food in Maine.

Their setting is hard to beat: a 1765 Colonial farmhouse that imparts a vision of pastoral paradise just west of the Maine Turnpike. Through leaded panes reminiscent of the Mission style, patrons in the spacious rear dining room look out onto fabulous gardens. On the entry table, flowers and branches of berries rise to the ceiling from a bowl flanked by produce spilling out of baskets. The dark wood ceiling, wide-plank floors, handsome service plates, crisp white linens, fresh flowers, and new cherry and walnut chairs with upholstered seats are as pretty as a picture.

The affable owners' insistence on purity and perfection goes to extremes. Their full-time staff of 28 includes two gardeners on the property. One, Robin Barnard, tends a showplace acre of vegetables and herbs, presenting a detailed list of what exotica is available each day to the chef. Raised beds and cold-frame covers allow her to produce lettuces for salads from April to Thanksgiving. The owners recently replaced every piece of glassware with fine crystal, the better for connoisseurs to enjoy the most extensive wine cellar in Maine, which includes twenty by the glass, many by the half bottle and an impressive selection of Bordeaux from the 1960s.

Surrounded by trees, fields and flowers (spotlit from above and below at night), up to 70 diners feast on the view of jaunty blackeyed susans and a sea of zinnias as well as some of Maine's most sophisticated fare. Formally clad waiters in black and white take orders without making notes, quite a feat since the New American menu with Pacific Rim overtones changes nightly.

For starters ($9.95 to $13.95), how about the nightly Arrows bento box. a tiered, wooden Asian lunch box filled one night with Glidden Point oysters, beef brochettes and crab wontons, and the next night with paper-wrapped chicken, crispy catfish with carrot and papaya salad and a vegetable spring roll? A roulade of foie gras might be teamed with poached pears and a vidalia onion confit. We liked the tea-smoked quail with a garlic-ginger vinaigrette and red-chile mayonnaise (the description cannot do justice to its complexity) and one of the evening's three salads, a trio of Japanese delicacies: zucchini with soy, carrot with sweet peanut dressing and mushroom with green onion. Each was a visual as well as a gustatory work of art, as was each dish to come.

Among the six entrée choices ($28.95 to $31.95), you might find sautéed pepper-coated bluefin tuna with a corn and sugar snap pea ragoût or grilled Atlantic salmon with haricots verts and a potato and braised leek gratin. The tea-smoked duck breast and ginger confit duck leg with garlic greens, jasmine rice and a scallion and Chinese black bean sauce was a masterpiece. The only dish we weren't wild about was the grilled tenderloin of beef, which we thought had too intense a smoky taste. The accompaniment of fire-roasted red onion, grilled radicchio, green and

Clark Frasier and Mark Gaier with Robin Barnard and bounty from garden at Arrows.

yellow beans, tarragon mayonnaise and the best thread-thin crispy french fries ever more than compensated.

A dessert of pineapple, peach-plum and mango sorbets, each atop a meringue and each with its own distinctive sauce, was a triumph. But we'd return anytime for any of pastry chef Lucia Velasco Evans's offerings, say the frozen pistachio mousse with pistachio coulis and coconut shortbread or the orange cream tartlet with warm plum compote and hazelnut crème chantilly, each $7.50 but worth every pretty penny.

At meal's end, chef-owners Clark and Mark table-hop and chat about food with their customers. Clark, who studied cooking in China, hails from California. Mark trained with Madeleine Kamman and was executive chef at the late Whistling Oyster in Perkins Cove. They take turns in the kitchen and the front of the house, so each can keep tabs on what's going on. And they take advantage of their winter break to travel, research food ideas and rejuvenate. "Instead of burning ourselves out," says Clark, "we come back re-energized and ready to go again. This is our tenth season and we're still excited." So are their fans.

(207) 646-7175. Dinner nightly except Monday, 6 to 10, fewer nights in off-season. Open late April through Thanksgiving.

Cape Neddick Inn and Gallery, 1233 U.S. Route 1 at Route 1A, Cape Neddick.

Combine an artistic setting and an innovative menu and you have one of the most interesting restaurants in southern Maine. Pamela Wallis and Glenn Gobeille recreated their original restaurant that burned to the ground in May 1985 and reopened by that Thanksgiving.

The dining room on two levels has windsor chairs at nicely spaced tables covered with beige cloths, a remarkable variety of old china for service plates, glass candlesticks, rose napkins and cobalt blue water glasses. Vases of flowers, potted palms, fancy screens, and paintings and sculptures illuminated by track lights make you feel as if you're dining in a gallery, which you are (the artworks are for sale). A more casual dining area in a smaller room with a bar is perfect for enjoying the new "light side" menu, but both menus are available in either room and are designed for devotees of mix and match.

The menus executed by longtime chef Burton Richardson change every six weeks. The nightly specials of fish, veal tenderloin, tournedos and pasta vary, the preparation not decided until that afternoon.

The night's soups might be lamb broth with roasted vegetables or seafood and corn chowder with a southwestern accent. Appetizers ($6.50 to $8) at a recent visit included foie gras pâté, green curried shrimp wontons on sweet and sour plum-cranberry sauce, chilled smoked salmon with chèvre and an extraordinary macadamia-lobster tart served on mushroom duxelles. The house salad ($4) is bathed in fresh basil-caesar or cucumber-dill dressings.

Entrées run from $19 for grilled Jamaican jerk chicken breast with curried cauliflower rice and a mango "shake" to $27 for individual beef wellington. We passed up one of the night's specials of swordfish grilled with ginger and gin for a fantastic fettuccine with lobster, shrimp, scallops, scallions, peas and artichokes, and a Korean-style lamb kabob on rice with sesame sauce and a spicy vegetable relish. Served on large oval plates, these came with glazed parsnips, broccoli and yellow beans. Those with lighter appetites or pocketbooks could opt for such "light side" choices ($13 to $14) as salade niçoise, warm duck breast with toasted sesame-orange-ginger dressing over angel-hair pasta, and barbecued flank steak with black bean relish, avocado and sour cream.

"Save room for one of Varel's desserts," the menu correctly advises. Sous chef Varel McGuire's creations include a dynamite peach pie, lemon tart with apricot glaze, kahlua cheesecake with hot fudge sauce, plum crumble with ginger-custard sauce, what Pamela touts as "a state-of-the-art dacquoise," chocolate-cognac ice cream and strawberry-wine sorbet. The wine list is appealing and fairly priced.

(207) 363-2899. Dinner nightly in summer, from 6, Wednesday-Sunday in winter; Sunday brunch, noon to 3, mid-October to May.

98 Provence, 104 Shore Road, Ogunquit.

Team a local restaurateur and his French-Canadian wife with her talented brother as chef. The result is this winner, a true place seemingly transplanted from the countryside of France to the Ogunquit hubbub. Johanna Gignach had run a small French restaurant in Old Montreal during the Olympics before being wooed to Ogunquit to marry Paul Haseltine, known to everyone at Barnacle Billy's Etc. restaurant as "Hez." It seems her brother, Pierre Gignach, was too young then to be a chef, but after training at Chez la Mère Michel, one of our favorite Montreal restaurants, and working in Winnipeg, he was ready. The Haseltines fashioned a country-pretty dining room and living room/lounge from the old 98 Shore Road breakfast eatery, added a new kitchen and bar, and awaited the arrival of Pierre with his visa.

Chef and visa arrived in the nick of time for the 1996 summer season. They started serving breakfast, "which was the best advertising for us," said Johanna, and soon opened for dinner. Breakfast is a treat, what with asparagus and bacon omelet, eggs florentine and belgian waffles in the $1.95 to $5.75 range. But it is dinner for which Pierre had prepared.

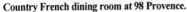

Country French dining room at 98 Provence.   **Prize-winning table setting at Seascapes.**

He excels with the classic dishes of Provence, perhaps fillet of salmon with basil oil and porcini mushrooms or grilled lamb chops served with a flageolet and chard red wine sauce. You can order inexpensively, goat cheese ravioli with mussels marnière for $12.95, or splurge on venison medallions with sour cherry sauce for $23.95.

But don't miss one of the starters, perhaps snails in puff pastry with a creamy leek and mustard sauce, grilled scallops on a red pepper coulis, shrimp and vegetable fritters with saffron aioli or beef carpaccio served with marinated fennel and fresh gouda. And don't skip dessert, prepared in the French style. Savor fruit napoleon, profiteroles, strawberry bavarois or poached pear with homemade sorbet.

The dining room with its cafe curtains, barnwood walls decked out with plates, and its colorful mismatched tablecloths and service plates will charm you into thinking you're in the South of France. The food will convince you.

(207) 646-9898. Breakfast, 7 to 11; dinner, 5:30 to 9:30. Closed Tuesday and December-March.

Seascapes, On the Pier, Cape Porpoise, Kennebunkport.

The smashing table settings at this elegant seaside restaurant won a national tabletop competition sponsored by Restaurant Hospitality magazine as "the prettiest tables in America." No wonder. The plates and candle holders are of handpainted Italian pottery in heavenly colors, the napkins are ringed with fishes, and the unusual wine glasses are fluted. Angela and Arthur LeBlanc, then owners of the Kennebunk Inn, found them on their travels and knew they were perfect for their new restaurant, with its sea of windows onto the waterscape. The colorful table – pictured on the cover of our book, *The Restaurants of New England* – is the match for the view of boats in quaint Cape Porpoise Harbor.

Chef Martin Carlton from California enjoys a reputation for pan-Asian and Mediterranean fare that gets better and better. Excellent dark wheat rolls get dinner here off to a good start. For appetizers ($7.50 to $8.95), we've enjoyed a stellar seafood chowder, the marinated portobello napoleon with roasted peppers, zucchini, smoked mozzarella and shaved peppered fennel, and the fabulous Maine lobster and crab egg roll with a seasoned seaweed pickled ginger salad, almost a meal in itself. Also almost a meal is the novel Seascapes caesar salad like none we've seen – chiffoned lettuce wrapped in a grilled flour tortilla and served sliced with prosciutto, reggio parmegiano and chives. A sorbet precedes the entrées ($17.95 to $27.50). At one dinner they were a classic Mediterranean bouillabaisse with rouille and a breast of chicken coated with pistachio nuts and stuffed with scallops; at another, a rich lobster tequila over linguini, a garlicky shrimp Christina with feta, cilantro and tomatoes, and grilled salmon with a sesame-soy-sherry marinade and a trio of julienned vegetables. Lately, as chef Martin moves into the vertical style, the rack of lamb arrives looking like flying buttresses. And he pairs lobster with pheasant, an unusual combination of delicacies, served with a mushroom corn salad and wild rice ginger pancake.

We're usually too full after the main courses to order dessert, but you might succumb to an ethereal strawberry torte, blueberry cheesecake, chocolate decadence or polenta pound cake with berry sauce. The select, primarily California wine list is reasonably priced and merits annual Wine Spectator awards.

Ever-improving, the LeBlancs have added a fireplace to the dining room and a piano bar in the reception area. For 1997, they were planning to open a hidden side terrace with a little pond and fountain for lunchtime dining beside the water.

On the adjacent pier, they operate **The Lively Lobster,** a seafood shanty. In the walkout basement beneath Seascapes is the casual **Porpoise Pub,** serving light fare from 2 p.m. to closing..

(207) 967-8500. Lunch daily, noon to 3, late June to late October; dinner nightly, 5:30 to 9 or 10, Wednesday-Sunday in May and June. Closed November to mid-April.

Grissini Trattoria & Panificio, 27 Western Ave., Kennebunkport.

If you think the folks at Kennebunkport's White Barn Inn know how to do things right, wait until you see their new Italian bistro. "We know our inn guests don't want to eat every meal at the White Barn," said co-owner Laurie Cameron, "and we were sending them to a lot of more casual restaurants around town. So we thought we might as well offer them another choice that was our own."

When the old Cafe Topher became available in 1996, Laurie and her husband Laurie Bongiorno bought it, undertaking a big-bucks renovation right down to the studs. They opened it up into a perfectly stunning space, with vaulted beamed ceilings three stories high and a tall fieldstone fireplace, looking straight out of the Adirondacks, that fits right in. Sponged pale yellow walls, large tables for four spaced well apart, comfortable lacquered wicker armchairs, white tablecloths covered with paper, rather bright pinpoint lighting, and fancy bottles and sculptures backlit in the windows add up to a thoroughly sophisticated feeling, not exactly what one expects in a rural seaside town. The talented chef, Barbara Porta, and much of the kitchen staff is direct from Italy. The waiters are young, handsome, Italian and ever-so-discreetly flirtatious. And what charming accents!

Opera was playing in the background as a plate of tasty little crostini, some with pesto and black olives and some with gorgonzola cheese and tomato, arrived to start our dinner. We liked the bread, prepared in the in-house bakery and served in slabs unexpectedly plunked – in most un-White Barn-like fashion – smack onto the table, with the server pouring an exorbitant amount of olive oil into a bowl for dipping. Everything else came on enormous white plates, except for the wine (in beautiful stemmed glasses) and the ice water (in pilsener glasses).

Fieldstone fireplace and beamed ceiling contribute to Adirondack lodge look at Grissini.

The exciting, oversize menu is made for grazing. Among antipasti in the $3.95 to $6.95 range, we loved the wood-grilled local venison sausage on a warm caramelized onion salad and the house-cured Maine salmon carpaccio with olive oil, herbs and lemon juice and topped with pasta salad. Pastas come in small and large sizes, as do pizzas. We were tempted by the "porto livorno" pizza with scallops, mussels, calamari, tomato and mozzarella, but finally chose the barbarucci with duck sausage, goat cheese and pesto.

Secondi ($10.95 to $13.95) are dishes like osso buco, wood-oven roasted half duck on a bed of baked tomato and eggplant, and – you know there has to be a lobster dish here somewhere – pan-seared lobster tail with olive oil, smashed potato and herbs. We split the wood-grilled leg of lamb steak with Tuscan white beans, pancetta, garlic and rosemary. The steak was a bit tough but had great flavor. The "insalata mista della casa" was a nice mixture of field greens, kalamata olives, tomato, gorgonzola and pinenuts for $4.50. Accompanying the meal was a fine reserve chianti for $18 from an affordable, all-Italian wine list.

A sampler plate of tirami su, a chocolate delicacy and strawberries in balsamic vinegar with mascarpone cheese ended a memorable dinner.

The turnaway crowds spill on warm nights onto a tiered outdoor courtyard that looks rather like a grotto. It was easy to understand why one local innkeeper who knows her food had dined at Grissini eleven times the first two months it was open. Eating well here could easily become a habit.

(207) 967-2211. Lunch daily, 11:30 to 2:30; dinner, from 5:30.

Salt Marsh Tavern, 46 Western Ave. (Route 9), Kennebunkport.

If the makeover of the old Hennessy's restaurant reminds people of the old White Barn, that's the way its new owner planned it. Jack Nahil recreated the White Barn restaurant he used to know, before its elevation into the rarefied realm of Relais & Châteaux. The focal point here, as in days gone by, is a piano bar in the center beneath a soaring barn ceiling.

After selling the White Barn he'd run since 1973, Jack ventured to Florida but "didn't like the market" and returned to Kennebunkport for another restaurant challenge. "There's a lot of déjà-vu here," he acknowledged. "Barns speak to me, I guess."

This barn speaks with oriental scatter rugs on the wide plank floors, the owner's oil paintings on the barnwood walls, farm implements and wood carvings on the lofts, and large rear windows onto gardens and a salt marsh stretching toward Kennebunk Beach. Tables dressed with white over forest green cloths and brass candlesticks are spaced throughout the open main floor and the upstairs loft.

The exterior speaks with a showy array of exotic gardens, lovingly tended by Jack and a gardener as "art – an extension of my painting." Diners find the beauty "an extension of the dining experience," Jack says.

The food, under chef Rich Lemoine, blends the classic and the creative with equal flair. Among main courses ($17.95 to $25.95), the grilled salmon fillet might be served with a charred tomato vinaigrette and fried parsley, the grilled swordfish with a ginger butter and vidalia onion compote and toasted almond basmati rice, the roast duckling with a raspberry-rhubarb glaze and gingered whipped potatoes, and the rack of lamb with a mint demi-glace and warm tabbouleh. Even the "simply broiled fresh haddock" comes with a pecan crumb topping and mango lobster salsa.

Among starters, roasted chicken and green chile soup with cilantro cream is a counterpoint to the traditional lobster, scallop and shrimp bisque, lately enlivened with Thai spices. Baked oysters come with a wild mushroom duxelles and double smoked bacon, and the escargots in herb-crusted red bliss potatoes served on wilted greens. The carpaccio of house-smoked sirloin centers an antipasto of roasted peppers, garlic confit, kalamata olives and mozzarella.

Desserts here are described on the menu with a bit of overkill: oven-roasted Elegant Lady peaches with homemade cinnamon ice cream and brandied peach puree, say, or Callebaut bittersweet chocolate torte with kahlua crème anglaise, warm chocolate sauce and a pillow of whipped cream. Even the classic crème brûlée comes "with a torched crust."

A pianist entertains nightly.

(207) 967-4500. Dinner, Tuesday-Sunday 6 to 9 or 10. Closed January and February.

Back Bay Grill, 65 Portland St., Portland.

A twenty-foot-long mural along one wall attests that this grill isn't in Back Bay Boston. Done by local artist Ed Manning Jr., it is a fanciful rendering of restaurant scenes and characters that are very much the Back Bay Grill. It's also so life-like that it makes the intimate room seem bigger, according to owner Joel Freund, who commissioned it in 1993.

The mural is a focal point of this highly regarded and urbane establishment, with its high ceilings, track lighting, antique mirrors, modern upholstered chairs (obtained from an office furniture company) and mahogany tables rather close together. Roses and candles are atop the tables.

Author Stephen King's daughter runs stylish Tabitha Jean's Restaurant.

The chef changes the handsomely printed menu monthly. Entrées ($16.95 to $21.95) might be sautéed pecan-crusted salmon on sweet-potato sauce, grilled Maine brook trout on a lentil dal with red pepper coulis, Jamaican rubbed pork loin with jícama slaw, and grilled sirloin with chianti sauce and poached shallots. These could be accompanied by haricots verts, julienned carrots, corn with sugar snap peas and grilled red potatoes.

Start perhaps with chilled cantaloupe soup in summer; black bean and pancetta soup in winter. Peeky-toe crab cakes, house-smoked arctic char with rémoulade sauce, and lobster ravioli with scallions and ginger-orange beurre blanc might be among appetizers in the $5.95 to $9.95 range. Typical desserts ($5.95) are an acclaimed crème brûlée, chocolate banana mousse, and pecan bourbon tart with caramel ice cream.

The 100-bottle wine list, which changes every week or two, is fairly priced from $15 to $195. Many wines are available by the glass.

(207) 772-8833. Dinner, Monday-Saturday 5:30 to 9:30 or 10, also Sunday 5 to 9 in July and August.

Tabitha Jean's Restaurant, 94 Free St., Portland.

Innovative American and vegetarian cuisine, a top wine list and sophisticated decor are the hallmarks of this promising newcomer, opened in 1995 by the daughter of Maine author Stephen King. Naomi King named it for her mother, Tabitha, and the mother of her former partner. It took a couple of chefs and a major rehab to get the onetime pancake house the way she wanted it.

We were impressed with both service and food at a summer lunch, chosen from a diverse menu upon which every item appealed. One of us wanted to order the special bluefin tuna burger, served on a fresh bulkie roll with cucumber-yogurt sauce, but it had already sold out. We substituted an assertive crab cake ($6.95), small but nicely presented with an exceptional jalapeño-peach relish. The other chose the oaxaca quesadilla ($6.95), two good size tortillas bearing monterey jack cheese, tomatoes, onions, roasted corn and grilled chicken with a chunky tomato, avocado and watercress salsa, presented on a plate dotted with puree of red peppers. Good sourdough bread accompanied, and a glass of "today's memorable wine," a Handley-Anderson gewürtztraminer for $4, indeed proved memorable. For dessert, tirami su made with Maine blueberries rather than the usual chocolate (and soaked with Bartlett blueberry wine) was delicious right down to the sponged blueberry sauce the chef had painted onto the plate.

The lunch treats gave an indication of what's in store at dinner. Chef Christopher Eaton's menu changes nightly. Expect a dozen entrée choices ($10.95 to $19.95), perhaps grilled farm-raised salmon crusted with almonds and topped with a ruby peach crush, grilled maki shark with an opal basil-pesto compound butter, saffron-roasted chicken breast over Tuscan crostini, and grilled filet mignon with a sour cream-horseradish sauce. Choices include at least five intriguing vegetarian items, among them grilled vegetable paella, sautéed ginger spring vegetables and hot Thai basil leaves with baby bok choy and seared tofu in a spicy vegetarian chili sauce over sushi rice.

Starters here aren't quite as diverse as the main dishes. Butternut squash soup with toasted walnuts, caesar salad, grilled vegetable napoleon, mussels with drawn butter and Tuscan crostini, and smoked mozzarella and roasted red pepper ravioli were the choices at our visit. Save room for dessert, perhaps chocolate mousse cake, cappuccino cheesecake or that great blueberry tirami su.

No longer looking like a pancake house, the two smallish dining rooms and a bar at the side are sleek and elegant with mod black tables and chairs and a vaguely oriental look. White linens dress the tables at night.

(207) 780-8966. Lunch, Monday-Friday 11:30 to 3; dinner nightly, from 5.

Fore Street, 288 Fore St., Portland.

Two of Maine's best-known restaurateurs, Sam Hayward and Dana Street, joined to open this hot-ticket establishment in 1996. The menu is as understated as the name, but rest assured, there's more here than meets the eye.

Start with the exterior, an unlikely looking, garage-like brick low-rise beyond the edge of the Old Port. You'd more likely guess it was still the tank-storage warehouse it was built as during World War II. Inside is a soaring space with brick walls, tall windows, and assorted booths and tables on two levels, all overlooking a large and busy open kitchen. At least a dozen cooks are evident around the applewood-fired grill, rotisserie and oven at the edge of the room. There's a small, intimate cocktail lounge with waiting area in front.

"Refined peasant food" is how Sam Hayward describes the fare. The founder of 22 Lincoln in Brunswick and former executive chef at the Harraseeket Inn in Freeport, he left for a simpler operation, one that he could call at least partly his own. The emphasis, as at his former venues, is on Maine ingredients and produce. The exotica and complexities of his past performances are understated here, as they always have been at his partner's Street & Co. seafood restaurant.

The menu, printed nightly, offers about a dozen main courses priced from $13.95 to $19.95. They're categorized as roasted (turnspit-roasted pork loin, wood-oven roasted Maine lobster or whole Maine brook trout). Or grilled (swordfish, duckling breast or venison steak). Or braised (seafood misto, penne and polenta with wild mushroom ragoût). That's it – no highfalutin language, just grilled calamari with cannellini beans and grilled vegetables, or grilled duckling breast with pancetta and roasted shallots. The place was so popular we couldn't get a reservation on a midsummer Thursday night, but fellow inn guests who did snag a table, both high-living Californians, were mighty impressed with the food and style.

We'll try again, if only for the desserts: roasted banana mousse, wood-baked plum and almond tart, a trio of mango, blackberry and peach sorbets, or lemon sherbet with black granita in an almond tuile. The wine list is short but select and affordable, and reflects Sam's previous award-winners.

(207) 775-2717. Dinner nightly, from 5:30.

Fore Street reflects warehouse heritage.

Street and Co., 33 Wharf St., Portland.

Pure, pure, pure is the feeling of the small "eating establishment" run by Dana Street in the Old Port Exchange. You enter past an open grill and kitchen and face a blackboard menu, both good indicators. Ahead is a small room with bare pegged floors and 40 seats, where strands of herbs and garlic hang on a brick wall. Lately, Dana acquired an adjacent space that gave him twenty more seats as well as a wine bar that doubles as a waiting area. Outside are twenty more seats along Wharf Street for summer dining. The tables might turn four times on a busy night.

The freshest of seafood and a purist philosophy draw a steady clientele. The night we visited, the blackboard listed six varieties of fish that could be grilled, blackened or broiled for $14.95 to $17.95. Mussels marinara, clams or shrimp with garlic were offered over linguini. Other possibilities were scallops with pernod and cream, sole française and lobster fra diavolo, $34.95 for two. That was it. Sometimes there's pasta alfredo, the only non-seafood item. Meals come with French bread, tossed salad with a balsamic vinaigrette and fresh vegetables (asparagus, zucchini and red bell peppers at our visit) sautéed in butter and white wine.

Equally straightforward are such appetizers as mussels, steamers and crab sauté. Most of the wines are priced in the teens and twenties..

(207) 775-0887. Dinner nightly, 5:30 to 10 or 11.

Cafe Always, 47 Middle St., Portland.

This mod, new-wave-style cafe with white tablecloths, different-colored utensils, black chairs and multi-colored walls with ivy trailing from the cherub wall sconces has been packing in appreciative diners since it opened in 1985. The founders, chef Cheryl Lewis and partner Norine Kotts, tired of the pace and started a catering business and food shop, selling in 1996 to Maureen Terry, one of their cooks. She and co-chef Tracy Burke sought to maintain the tradition "with a lighter touch."

The assertive tastes that lingered in our memories had been tempered in a recent menu. Among entrées ($18 to $20), the salmon was pan roasted with a mango salsa, the chicken grilled with a duo of red and yellow bell pepper sauces, and the sirloin steak grilled with a roasted shallot demi-glace. The most unusual choice may have been the steamed tofu spring rolls served with Asian slaw and Thai dipping sauce.

Newlywed Maureen's husband is a lobster fisherman, and she'd just returned from her first fishing expedition having trapped her limit for dinner that night. Lobster was turning up in a Thai-style entrée simmered in coconut-curry sauce, in a salad with soy-peanut sauce on a bed of greens, and in risotto cakes with goat cheese. Other starters were a wild rice and duck nori roll with sesame dipping sauce, asparagus strudel with gruyère, and fig salad with caramelized nuts and goat cheese.

Desserts include a lemon pudding cake with strawberry sauce, chocolate-espresso terrine with chocolate-mint anglaise and blueberry-plum upside-down cake. Homemade strawberry-wine sorbet and ginger-wasabi ice cream were reminiscent of flavorful desserts at earlier visits.

In the new owner's effort to lighten up the fare, a special winter spa menu offers four courses for $30.

(207) 774-9399. Dinner, Tuesday-Sunday from 5.

Zephyr Grill, 653 Congress St., Portland.

In almost a matter of months, peripatetic Portland restaurateur Jim Ladue closed his long-running Alberta's Cafe, turned up at Bella Bella and finally opened Zephyr Grill with a partner in 1996. Zephyr is in an odd-looking downtown storefront, with walls sponged in tangerine above green wainscoting, custom-designed mod tables randomly painted by a local artist, and rather weird orange shaded lamps hanging from the ceiling. Local foodies did not know quite what to make of the place (one said the appetizers were great, the entrées not; another indicated vice-versa). Nor could they fathom the unusual hostess/waiter station – an open counter with four seats facing the diners – at the far end of the dining room.

From their odd perch, the co-owner and a couple of waitresses kept watch on us (which we found most disconcerting) and the other patrons the night we were here. As was the case at Alberta's, the food is a mix of inspiration and value. One of us grazed through soups and starters. The chilled tomato and lemongrass soup garnished with cilantro and scotch bonnet pepper-marinated shrimp ($3.95) was a sure winner, laden with more shrimp than one would expect from a garnish. Also good was a salad of mesclun greens and assorted vegetables with roasted garlic, a huge portion for $2.95. Not so successful was the intriguing crisp-fried Cuban-style sandwich of lobster, smoky bacon, marinated tomato and blended cheeses with shaved lettuce and banana-chipotle catsup ($6.95), which was fried *so* crisply that it was difficult to chew. Among main courses ($9.95 to $15.95), we liked the succulent grilled salmon with watercress salad (more like a garnish), teamed with roasted potatoes. Other possibilities ranged from vegetarian dishes (one with stir-fried sugar snap peas, tofu and mushrooms with peanuts on rice) to hardwood-smoked cornish hen with grilled crepinette of rabbit, pork, sage and juniper; grilled lamb loin, and Korean-style barbecued sirloin with kimchi stir-fried vegetables and roasted potatoes.

With choices like these, the dessert repertoire seemed almost ordinary: chocolate cheesecake, lemon mousse with berries and stirred custard. We will put in a good word for the exotic and reasonably priced wine list, all available by the bottle or the glass. A bottle of South African chardonnay was a mere $12.75.

(207) 828-4033. Dinner, Wednesday-Sunday 5 to 10.

More Dining Choices

Hurricane, Oarweed Lane, Perkins Cove, Ogunquit.

This trendy spot has been upgraded by Brooks and Luanne MacDonald, he the working chef who has elevated its already high reputation. "Our view will blow you away – our menu will bring you back" is its slogan, a realistic claim based on our meal there and the crowds waiting to be seated for lunch at 2 o'clock on a September weekday. Although recent reviews have been mixed, there's said to be a three-day waiting list for dinner reservations in midsummer.

Every table has a view in two small summery rooms beside the ocean. Most desirable is the enclosed but breezy porch. The all-day menu is divided into soups and salads, small plates, and lunch and dinner entrées. You could make a good lunch or supper of lobster gazpacho ("so hot it's cool") or lobster chowder ($6.95, the house specialty), a five-onion soup with gorgonzola crust (which a friend found surprisingly flavorless), the house salad of field greens with roasted shallots and pistachios, the deviled lobster cakes with cilantro salsa, the salmon tartare with lemongrass citronette or the pan-seared foie gras with pear relish. More substantial are the interesting lunch entrées ($6.95 to $13.95), among them cobb salad, firecracker shrimp and tabbouleh salad, grilled chicken with black beans and rice, Thai steak salad with soba noodles, open-faced swordfish sandwich, and caesar salad with swordfish or lobster.

For dinner ($14.95 to $25.95), consider pan-roasted sea scallops with coconut couscous and red curry oil, baked salmon and brie baklava, lobster cioppino, chargrilled tournedos of beef with crabmeat and béarnaise sauce, and grilled veal chop with parmesan crust and morel-wine sauce. Hearth-baked sourdough bread, house salad, potato and vegetable come with.

Among desserts are banana cream pie, fresh fruit tart, crème brûlée and mile-high cheesecake.

(207) 646-6348. Lunch daily, 11:30 to 4; dinner, 5:30 to 10:30.

Ida Reds, Route 1 South, Ogunquit.

Situated beside the Ogunquit Playhouse, this little house deceives. It's rustic and quite unremarkable on the outside. Inside is an art-deco showplace with an arched ceiling, green and yellow walls, tiered wood dividers holding upside-down lamps and a copper espresso bar.

Named for a rare variety of apple, it was opened with fanfare in 1995 by Joel Freund, owner of the acclaimed Back Bay Grill in Portland. Closing unexpectedly after its first summer, it reopened in 1996 with a new partner, Steve Einstein, owner of the former Einstein's Deli Restaurant in downtown Ogunquit, who had left to administer the local Chamber of Commerce. He longed to get back in the restaurant business and here was the opportunity.

Ida Reds is actually two restaurants, fine dining upstairs with inventive renditions of traditional New England specialties, and casual dining downstairs in the American Cafe, a plainer-than-plain space with a copper bar and windows onto a little river. Lobster is featured, in the rough downstairs and upstairs in four presentations (from raviolis to roasted twin lobster tails with cognac butter sauce to stuffed in a pistachio-crusted chicken breast with a roasted red pepper coulis). There's even a lobster gazpacho with crème fraîche and lime zest, and a crispy lobster spring roll for starters.

Upstairs dining room at Ida Reds is an art-deco showplace.

The upstairs dinner menu ranges widely, priced from $14.95 for fettuccine primavera with vegetables in an oriental ginger-cream sauce to $20.95 for grilled New York sirloin with wild mushrooms and roquefort butter. The grilled pork chop might be served with red wine-fig sauce and crumbled goat cheese, and the pan-seared tuna with cracked peppercorns, smoked tomato sauce and chilled asparagus spears.

Desserts include seasonal fruit sorbet, orange cake with white chocolate and grand marnier ganache, and a phyllo purse filled with spiked baked apple and walnuts with crème anglaise.

(207) 646-0289. Dinner nightly, 5 to 10; cafe, 5 to midnight. Closed January to mid-February.

Cape Arundel Inn, Ocean Avenue, Kennebunkport 04046.

A Portland caterer of our acquaintance thinks the Cape Arundel has the best breakfasts this side of home, and we think the setting couldn't be nicer. The simple dining room with lots of windows has nothing to detract from the view of the sparkling ocean outside, with a bird's-eye peek at George Bush's Walker Point compound. We're partial to the fried codfish cakes served with baked beans and broiled tomato ($6.25), a standard on the menu, and at one visit enjoyed an omelet generously strewn with wild mushrooms.

If breakfast here is a great way to start the day, dinner is the way to end it. Try for a window table and watch wispy clouds turn to mauve and violet as the sun sets, followed perhaps by a full golden moon rising over the darkened ocean. Chef Ron Bogart is back in the kitchen and satisfying diners' palates after a brief hiatus during which the food had slipped.

An excellent warm pheasant salad on radicchio with Thai dressing and wild mushroom crostini got our dinners off to a good start. The highlights were sweetbreads with a tart grapefruit sauce and rack of lamb with pear and mint chutney, accompanied by rice pilaf, crisp ratatouille, and julienned carrots and turnips. Other entrées ($17.25 to $26.95) include pan-roasted salmon fillet served on stir-fried vegetables and topped with wasabi butter, broiled swordfish with a papaya and macadamia nut butter, sautéed duck with risotto confit cake and sundried cherry sauce, and roasted veal chop with wild mushrooms and madeira.

Flourless chocolate torte, macadamia key lime pie and berry cobbler could be among the offerings on the changing dessert tray.

The inn also offers seven guest rooms with private baths and ocean views, as well as a wing with seven motel rooms with private balconies.

(207) 967-2125. Breakfast daily, 8 to 10:30, Sunday to 11; dinner, Monday-Saturday 5:30 to 8:30. Doubles, $130 to $155. Closed November to late May.

Madd Apple Cafe, 23 Forest Ave., Portland.

An American bistro with a Southern accent is offered by Martha and James Williamson in a pleasant space beside the Portland Performing Arts Center. The accent comes from Jim's background in the South; hence all the barbecue items from secret family recipes and the fresh catfish, crawfish, boudin blanc, cornbread and sweet-potato pie. They're served up in two small rooms containing half a dozen tables each, crisp white linens, walls painted in tangerine, lemon and frosted beet colors, and interesting murals and art.

Having discontinued lunch service, at least temporarily, the Williamsons were offering an interesting dinner menu of appetizers, light fare and main courses, a perfect mix for the regulars who come in before or after performances at the arts center. You could sup on a Carolina pulled pork barbecue sandwich, a smoked Atlantic salmon sandwich, vegetable boudin or creole salad ($5.95 to $7.95). Or combine it with an appetizer ($4.95 to $7.95), perhaps a pan-fried shrimp cake with rémoulade sauce, escargots bourguignonne or frog's legs creolaise. Or opt for an entrée ($13.95 to $18.95), maybe trout anglaise, barbecued pork tenderloin, ground lamb patties with a minted demi-glace or steak New Orleans, sautéed with mushrooms and scallions and served with a brandy-worcestershire sauce.

Key lime pie, profiteroles and sweet-potato pie are signature desserts. We loved the classic bananas foster ($4.95), a huge portion that even two of us could not finish, accompanied by a glass of port and cafe au lait. They're the real thing, as is everything in this beguiling little refuge.

In New Orleans style, background jazz is played on the sound system. Before turning to cooking, Jim, a jazz guitarist and composer, taught at Berklee School of Music in Boston. After ten years, he and Martha find themselves the "veterans" among Portland's small, chef-owned restaurants.

(207) 774-9698. Dinner, Tuesday-Saturday from 5:30.

Walter's Cafe, 15 Exchange St., Portland.

Noisy and intimate, this "now" kind of place has been packed to the rafters since it was opened by Walter Loeman and Mark Loring in 1990. It doesn't advertise and doesn't have to, its spirited food at pleasant prices producing lengthy lineups at peak periods.

We faced a twenty-minute wait for a weekday lunch in July, but were glad we waited. A BOLT ($6.75) – bacon, lettuce, tomato and red onion sandwich with sweet cajun mayonnaise – arrived in a pita, served with a pickle and "gnarly" fries. The "chilling pasta salad" ($7.75) yielded a zesty plateful tossed with chicken, avocado and red peppers.

From our table alongside a brick wall in the long and narrow, high-ceilinged room we could see the cooks splashing liberal amounts of wine into the dishes they were preparing in the open kitchen. Green plants backlit on a shelf above the kitchen area provided accents amid the prevailing brick. Glass covered the black vinyl tablecloths.

Dinner entrées ($12.95 to $17.95) have been known to be categorized by "flippin' pans" and "thrill of the grill." One possibility is "crazy chicken" with prosciutto, sweet peas, red wine and cream over capellini. Others are Thai spice-rubbed shrimp with lobster nori rolls, grilled mustard-crusted salmon over watercress and cucumber salad, and grilled Moroccan lamb tenderloin over veggie couscous salad.

Irish cream cheesecake, orange mousse with wild blueberries, and varied chocolate creations typify the dessert list. Lots of nice wines are priced in the teens and twenties.

Success has spawned offshoots. To accommodate their overflow, the partners opened **Perfetto,** a trendy Italian bistro almost across the street, and the casual **Joe's Boathouse** at Spring Point Marina in South Portland. Lately, Mark took over operation of Walter's and Joe's, while Walter concentrated on Perfetto's. He also planned to open a new Mexican restaurant in 1997 on Fore Street in a section called Gorham's Corner between downtown and the West End.

(207) 871-9258. Lunch, Monday-Saturday 11 to 3; dinner nightly, 5 to 10.

Healthful Gourmet

Frankie & Johnny's, 1594 Route 1 North, Cape Neddick.

It isn't much to look at, this gourmet natural-foods restaurant in a manufactured home beside the highway, painted with colorful triangles and sporting a Haagen-Dazs sign in front. But stop, venture in and have a healthful meal, either inside in a whimsical dining room, outside at a couple of picnic tables or to go.

Personable Frank Rostad handles the front of the house while partner John Shaw, formerly with the late Laura Tanner House restaurant in Ogunquit, cooks in a state-of-the-art kitchen. Everything is made from scratch and almost all of it on site, say these purists (it took them fourteen months to find an all-natural cone to serve with their Haagen-Dazs ice cream). They even squeeze juices at their juice bar.

John produces "gourmet food that's good for you." The soups could be vegetarian or vegan (dairy-free). Seven remarkable "entrée salads" ($8.75 to $11.75) are served on dinner plates. They range from tabbouleh and hummus to grilled chicken on assorted greens to blackened salmon and shrimp salad with cheeses and grilled veggies. Under spaetzles ($13.75) you'll find chicken, shrimp, seafood diablo, vegetable harvest and, most recently, broccoli alfredo ("there is a little Italian in all of us," the menu notes). Favorites among entrées ($10.75 to $12.75) are poached or blackened Atlantic salmon, and blackened chicken served over sweet and sour cabbage with potatoes and feta cheese.

The pair are best known for their trademarked crustolis ($10.50), ten-inch-round French bread crusts made from unbleached flour and not unlike pizzas. For dinner, we ordered one with shrimp, pesto and goat cheese and another with capers, olives, red onions and feta cheese, split a house salad and had more than enough left over for lunch the next day. Dinner is by candlelight and the food is serious, but it's dispensed in a relaxed and playful environment. Decor in the pine-paneled room is nil except for a few abstract oils by Frank's sister at one end and a handful of rocks and perhaps a miniature dinosaur on each table. "It's hard to take yourself seriously with rocks and a little dinosaur in front of you," says Frank, whose aim is for customers to have a good time.

It's also hard to imagine that reservations are advised, but this place is very popular. So popular that they've discontinued lunch to concentrate on dinner. How many other natural-foods restaurants can say the same?

(207) 363-1909. Dinner from 5, nightly in summer, Thursday-Sunday in spring and fall. Closed Dec. 21 through March. BYOB. No credit cards.

Pepperclub, 78 Middle St., Portland.

"World cuisine" is the theme of this hip organic-vegetarian-seafood establishment, part of the Middle Street "Restaurant Row." It's the creation of Jaap Helder, a Danish-born chef-artist who owned the late, great Vinyard restaurant nearby. He re-emerged here with his paintings and a partner, former art editor Eddie Fitzpatrick, to produce something of a showplace of culinary design. Fresh flowers on the tables, a crazy paint job with many colors on the walls, and a bar made of old Jamaican steel drums, painted and cut in half, create a vivid setting.

The food is colorful as well. The blackboard menu lists such starters as curried corn chowder, brie with casaba and cantaloupe, Caribbean shrimp cakes, vegetarian samosas with beet chutney, hummus salad, Armenian stuffed flatbread and Moroccan vegetable stew. Main dishes range from $6.95 for a pepper burger to $10.95 for linguini with scallops and pesto or fillet of salmon with braised fennel. Other possibilities could be Mongolian cashew chicken, North African stuffed peppers, chicken and leek pie, Tunisian couscous, mahi-mahi with ginger and cilantro, Greek lamb with minted green beans, pinto bean flautas with salsa fresca, and anaheim pepper and cheese enchiladas.

Among desserts are orange chiffon cake, bourbon-pecan pie and mocha-butternut crunch.

(207) 772-0531. Dinner nightly, 5 to 9 or 10. No credit cards.

Dining and Lodging

White Barn Inn, Beach Street, Box 560C, Kennebunkport 04046.

Long known for its restaurant, the White Barn has been vastly upgraded in terms of accommodations as well. Such has been the infusion of money and T.L.C. by the hands-on Australian owner, personable Laurie Bongiorno, and his wife Laurie Cameron, that the inn was quickly accepted into the prestigious Relais & Châteaux, the world-wide association of deluxe owner-operated hotels. In 1993, its restaurant was the first to be accorded five stars for all three categories of food, service and atmosphere from the Maine Sunday Telegram. In 1994, the restaurant became the AAA's first five-diamond dining establishment in all New England. And yes, it's really that good.

Dinner is served in a three-story barn attached to the inn, where you can look out through soaring plate-glass windows onto an incredible backdrop that changes with the seasons – lush impatiens in summer, assorted mums in fall, and spruce trees dressed with velvet bows and tiny white lights for Christmas. Up to 120 diners can be seated at tables spaced blessedly well apart in the main barn and in an adjoining barn. They're filled with understated antiques and oil paintings dating to the 18th century, and the loft holds quite a collection of wildlife wood carvings. The tables are set with silver, Schottsweizel crystal and Villeroy & Boch china, white linens and white tapers in crystal candlesticks. At one of our visits, a Russian pianist, here on a scholarship, played seemingly by ear in the entry near the gleaming copper-topped bar.

The food is in the vanguard of contemporary American regional cuisine. Dinner is prix-fixe ($56 in four courses), with about eight choices for most courses. The complex menu changes weekly. It's executed by a kitchen staff of sixteen and served with precision by a young wait staff who meet with chef Jonathan Cartwright beforehand for 45 minutes each night. Guests at each table are served simultaneously, one waiter per plate.

Our latest dinner began with a glass of Perrier-Jouët extra brut (complimentary for house guests) and the chef's "welcome amenity," an herbed goat-cheese rosette, an onion tart and a tapenade of eggplant and kalamata olives. Interesting olive bread and plain white and poppyseed rolls followed. We'd gladly have tried any of the appetizers, but settled on a lobster spring roll with daikon radish, savoy cabbage and hot and sweet glaze, and the seared Hudson Valley foie gras on an apple and celeriac tart with a calvados sauce. Both were sensational.

Champagne sorbet in a pool of Piper Heidsieck extra-dry cleared the palate with a flourish for the main courses, of which a recent entry – "roasted rack of lamb and medallions of Kennebunk venison with caramelized potato timbale and two textures of peaches" – might be considered typical. One of us settled for a duo of Maine rabbit, a grilled loin with roasted rosemary and pommery mustard and a braised leg in cabernet sauvignon, accompanied by wild mushrooms and pesto-accented risotto. The other chose pan-seared tenderloin of beef topped with a horseradish gratin and port-glazed shallots on a pool of potato and Vermont cheddar cheese, with a side of asparagus. A bottle of Firestone cabernet accompanied from an excellent wine list starting at $22 and especially strong on American chardonnays and cabernets.

Dessert was anything but anti-climactic: a classic coeur à la crème with tropical fruits and sugared shortbread and a trio of pear, raspberry and mango sorbets, served artistically on a black plate with colored swirls matching the sorbets. A tray of petits fours came with the bill. After an after-dinner brandy in the inn's living room, the little raisin cookies we found on the bed back in our room were somewhat superfluous.

The 24 guest rooms in the main inn and outbuildings vary considerably, as their range in prices indicates. The seven fireplaced suites in the refurbished Carriage House are the height of luxury. Each has a library-style sitting area, chintz-covered furniture, plush carpeting, wood-burning fireplace, dressing room, spacious bathroom with a marble jacuzzi, Queen Anne kingsize four-poster bed, secretary desk and a television set hidden in the armoire. We felt quite pampered in the Green Room here, thanks to a personal note of welcome from the innkeeper, fresh fruit, Poland Spring water, terry robes and Gilchrist & Soames toiletries. Four large renovated rooms in the Gatehouse also claim fireplaces and jacuzzis, as well as cathedral ceilings, queensize sleigh beds and sitting areas with wing chairs. The renovated cottage overlooks an elegant new swimming pool. The thirteen rooms upstairs in the inn, although nicely furnished and cheerfully decorated with

Floral backdrop in window changes with seasons in glamorous dining room at White Barn Inn.

whimsical handpainted furniture and trompe-l'oeil accents, could not possibly be as spacious or sumptuous.

A lavish continental breakfast is served in the elegant Colonial dining room. Fresh orange juice and slices of cut-up fruits are brought to your table by a tuxedoed waiter. You help yourself to assorted cereals, yogurts and an array of muffins and pastries the likes of which we've seldom seen before – including a sensational strawberry-bran muffin with a top the size of a grapefruit and a cool crème d'amandes with a sliced peach inside.

(207) 967-2321. Fax (207) 967-1100. Dinner nightly, 6 to 9:30. Closed Monday and Tuesday in February and March. Jackets requested. Doubles, $140 to $170; Gatehouse rooms, $205; suites, $320.

The Inn by the Sea, 40 Bowery Beach Road, Cape Elizabeth 04107.

Nearly $7 million went into this luxury resort that opened in 1987 on the site of the former Crescent Beach Inn. And it looks it, from the marble-tiled lobby and the fourteen Audubon hand-colored engravings gracing the inn's walls to the luxury suites with two TVs (the one in the sitting room hidden in the armoire) and no fewer than three telephones. There's an ocean view from every patio and balcony.

Handsomely done in Maine shingle style, the angled complex consists of 25 one-bedroom suites in the main building and eighteen condo-style one- or two-bedroom suites in four attached cottages. The loft suites on the second floor are most in demand, each with a kitchenette, a large living room opening onto a private balcony, and a loft bedroom and an enormous bathroom/dressing area upstairs. We liked our first stay in a garden suite facing the lawn and ocean on the first floor, its living room – with reproduction Chippendale furnishings and a blue chintz sofa – with sliding doors allowing us to walk right outside onto a patio. Its small bedroom with a four-poster bed was quite adequate, even though the windows opened onto the parking lot. Next time we reveled in the extra space of a loft suite, which offered a better water view from its balcony.

New owner Maureen McQuade, a Maine native who had managed large properties, lucked into buying this inn in foreclosure. A hands-on innkeeper, she's very much at home here and her enthusiasm shows. The friendly young staff is dressed in khakis, the formal croquet tournaments are no more and families are in evidence, at least in summer, as the inn presents a more welcoming face.

You can swim in a pleasant pool or saunter down a boardwalk to a private entrance to the beach at Crescent Beach State Park. The tea garden with rose bushes and fish swimming in a fountain pool is a quiet retreat.

Breakfast and dinner are served in the Audubon Room, a harmonious space striking in white, with comfortable chairs and an enclosed porch around two sides. Tables are topped with white linens, lovely English bone china and fresh flowers. The dinner fare has been elevated by chef Mark Boucher. Choices are priced from $13.95 for seared chicken with artichokes and yellow sundried tomatoes to $21.95 for filet mignon with potatoes galette. An ample section of the dinner menu is devoted to light fare and pastas in two sizes, the easier to mix and match. We hear the rack of lamb is to die for, but were quite content with a couple of salads (spinach with grilled portobello mushrooms and caramelized walnuts, and fanned breast of duck on baby spinach and arugula) and main dishes of grilled medallions of jerk-spiced pork on a papaya and sundried cherry relish and shrimp szechwan, tossed with broccoli rabe, snow peas and a zesty orange-ginger sauce on cellophane noodles.

Breakfast prices have been reduced under the new regime, making breakfast here one of the better values around. You can order a cheese and chive omelet for $3.95, grand marnier french toast for $4.95 and eggs benedict with lobster for $10.95. Portions are abundant, and the lady at the next table exclaimed that her pancakes and blueberries were the biggest she ever saw.

They do things up big here. Even the bill comes on an oversize computer printout. *(207) 799-3134 or (800) 888-4287. Fax (207) 799-4779. Breakfast, 7 to 11; lunch, noon to 2; dinner, 5:30 to 9:30. Doubles, $180 to $250; cottage suites, $330 to $410.*

Lodging

Wooden Goose Inn, Route 1, Box 195, Cape Neddick 03902.

Here is the stuff of which design-magazine editors' dreams are made. A parlor displays a magnificent collection of 23 crystal candelabra on a square glass table and an equal number of silver candlesticks on another. Bedrooms sport fabric pillow shams matching the window treatments. One has a custom-designed corner headboard to make more room for a queensize bed, and a carpeted bathroom with a freestanding clawfoot tub and two rocking chairs. The gorgeous, glass-enclosed dining room overlooking an English garden contains wrought-iron tables set with white linen, Lenox china and Waterford crystal. Every room is decorated to the nth degree.

That this seven-bedroom B&B is such an extravagance of eclectic furnishings and decor should come as no surprise. Jerry Rippetoe was a decorator in New York and New Jersey before he and Anthony Sienicki acquired the ramshackle home in 1984. "It took ten painters seven days just to scrape the house," Jerry recalls. "It was horrendous." Nonetheless, they opened within two weeks with four guest rooms, and have been going strong ever since. Lately the pair bought 750 yards of fabric to redo three bedrooms and learned to use a sewing machine when they found it would cost $11,000 to have done what they wanted. Their do-it-yourself window treatments, billowing canopies and coordinated pillows – most in their favorite colors of hunter greens and burgundies – are incredible. Tony also builds the remarkable decorative birdhouses that are scattered about the house and are for sale.

Each air-conditioned room has a queensize bed, private bath and a sitting area, and offers the ultimate in good taste and comfort. The house has been turned cocoon-like to the inside since it's right up against Route 1. "We're trying to create a romantic mood," says Jerry. Those who venture forth from their rooms can enjoy the two parlors or the airy dining porch. Beyond are lush gardens (the nasturtiums at one visit were so profuse as to be unbelievable), in the midst of which is a trickling pool bordered by rocks, with wrought-iron chairs scattered about.

"People always bring us geese as gifts," says Jerry. "We incorporate them into the inn" – and the results are ingenious.

Afternoon tea is taken in the dining room or in the gardens. Eleven varieties are offered, as are such changing treats as a green bean and walnut pâté, chocolate ganache with macadamia crust and caramel sauce, a tart of granny smith apples and lemon, chocolate sheba with crème anglaise and other fancy desserts prepared by Tony.

Breakfasts are as luscious as they are varied. One day, it started with fresh orange juice, date bread, cinnamon muffins and strawberries romanoff, culminating in eggs oscar accompanied by steamed broccoli and homefries. The next day, peach and cherry soup was the fruit course; the entrée, potato pancakes topped with poached eggs and hollandaise sauce, with sausage and sautéed peppers and onions. Recent breakfasts are beginning to sound more like dinner: lobster quiche, poached fillet of sole stuffed with Maine shrimp and topped with dill hollandaise, pan-roasted salmon with choron sauce, crab cakes with dijon mustard sauce, chicken breast with peaches and zucchini and sour-cream sauce, and baked swordfish with mustard topping, curried potatoes and vegetables. The special roulade – a soufflé with ham, mustard, shallots, and parmesan cheese – is rolled, baked, topped with gruyère, then broiled and sliced. It looks like a jelly roll and "is heaven," says Jerry.

So into food are this hard-working pair that they now offer weekday dinner packages in the off-season and on July weekends. They even close their inn to the public in July, opening only by invitation for weekend guests who book three nights, two dinners, two continental breakfasts and a full breakfast, $375 for two. The same package also has proven successful Monday-Wednesday in the off-season. A typical dinner includes five-onion soup, salad with dijon vinaigrette, chicken breast with shiitake mushroom sauce, oven-roasted rosemary and thyme potatoes, panfried asparagus, and a choice of desserts, perhaps butter-pecan cheesecake or

coeur à la crème with raspberry sauce. BYOB and join the party as these caring hosts ply you with culinary treats.
(207) 363-5673. Doubles, $125. Closed to public in July.

Hartwell House, 118 Shore Road, Box 393, Ogunquit 03907.
The British flag flies alongside the American in front of this sophisticated B&B on the main road between the center of Ogunquit and Perkins Cove. Owners Jim and Tricia Hartwell have an English background, which explains their extensive use of English antiques in the thirteen guest rooms and three suites, all with modern baths, and the lush lawns and sculpted gardens out back, which provide the profusion of flowers inside.

The enclosed front porch is a lovely space with arched windows, colorful French chintz on the loungers and wicker chairs, and an array of plants and flowers. Here is where guests gather for an afternoon pick-me-up of iced tea, poured from a glass pitcher topped with strawberries and orange slices on a silver tray. Everything except the wood floor in the stunning living room is white. The formal dining room has one long table, willowware china and a silver service on the sideboard. Hooked rugs dot the wide-board floors. Guests gather here or on the enclosed porch for a full breakfast of fresh fruit and a hot dish, perhaps stuffed crêpes, frittatas, baked chicken in puff pastry or belgian waffles. Chef-innkeeper William Moringo and his wife Anne also serve intimate, seven-course dinners for eight on Saturday nights in the winter as part of a weekend package.

Some of the nine rooms in the main house have private balconies looking over the rear yard. Across the street in a new addition to the house where the innkeepers reside are seven more luxurious rooms, including three suites. Trisha's favorite is the James Monroe Suite, a two-level affair all in white.
(207) 646-7210 or (800) 235-8883. Fax (207) 646-6032. Doubles, $120 to $145; suites, $165 to $185. Closed first two weeks in January.

The Inn at Harbor Head, 41 Pier Road, R.R.2, Box 1180, Kennebunkport 04046.
Chocolate french toast for breakfast? Yes – it's from the repertoire of Joan Sutter who, with husband David, runs one of the more special B&Bs in Maine. Honeymooners are smitten with it, and it's easy to see why. The Sutters' picturesque shingled home is on a rocky knoll right above Cape Porpoise harbor, and it is lovely to swim from their float or to loll in a hammock or a comfy garden chair and watch the lobster boats go by. There are a pleasant living room and a large library, where two chairs face the window for a good look at the harbor.

Breakfasts are served at 9 o'clock at a long table in the dining room amidst gorgeous flower arrangements, soothing New Age music and lots of fine china, crystal and silver. The fruit course might be poached pears with grand marnier custard sauce, broiled bananas or melon balls with a ginger, lime and honey sauce. With luck, you'll be there when Joan serves her homemade roast-beef hash with poached eggs and salsa, or creamed chicken and mushrooms on sourdough rounds. Puff pastry with eggs, feta cheese and spinach or dutch babies with peaches and melba sauce are other goodies. And the chocolate french toast is topped with raspberries and served with crisp bacon. "I want everything to look pretty," says Joan, an artist who has also painted wonderful murals throughout the house. And pretty her dishes are, garnished with nasturtium blossoms and the like.

Five bedrooms with private baths are decorated to the ultimate. The Greenery, where we stayed, has a little sitting area and a kingsize bed covered in white with tons of lacy pillows. The barnwood walls are painted a deep green, and Joan's mural of fir trees by the shore highlights the side of the peaked ceiling. The luxurious bathroom has a step-up jacuzzi. The entrance to the Garden Room is paved with stones, which with exotic plants give it an oriental feeling. French doors open onto a private deck. The Summer Suite upstairs, with the best view of the harbor from its new balcony, is painted with clouds drifting across the ceiling and comes with a kingsize bed, gas fireplace and a huge bathroom with skylight, bidet and jacuzzi. The murals of Cape Porpoise are exquisite in the fireplaced Harbor Suite, which also has a new balcony.

Rooms are outfitted with thick towels, terrycloth robes, hair dryers, irons and boards, books and magazines, good reading lights, clock radios, a decanter of sherry and fresh flowers from Joan's backyard cutting garden. The Sutters put out wine and cheese and crackers in the afternoon. When you are out for dinner, they turn down your bed and leave Godiva chocolates on a silver tray. Some guests stay for two weeks, the Sutters say, and we can understand why.

(207) 967-5564. Fax (207) 967-1294. Doubles, $180 to $215; suites, $240 and $275.

Bufflehead Cove Inn, Gornitz Lane, Box 499, Kennebunkport 04046.

Past a lily pond at the end of a long dirt road is this hidden treasure: a gray shingled, Dutch Colonial manse right beside a scenic bend of the Kennebunk River. Owners Harriet and Jim Gott have turned their family home since 1973 into a stunning, six-room B&B – the kind of waterfront home we've always dreamed of.

The public rooms and the setting are special here. A wide porch faces the tidal river and downtown Kennbunkport in the distance; there are porches along the side and a huge wraparound deck in back. A large and comfy living room contains window seats with views of the water, and the dining room, which is shaped like the back of a ship, has a dark beamed ceiling, paneling, stenciling and a carpet painted on the floor. There are a dock with boats and five acres of tranquility with which to surround oneself.

All bedrooms are bright and cheerful, but the Balcony Room is perhaps the most appealing of those in the main house. It has a wicker-filled balcony overlooking the river, a sitting area with window seats, a queensize brass bed, a gas fireplace and dramatic decor with splashes of black, including the striking glossy stenciling – green leaves on a black band. In the small Teal Room, the bathroom is stenciled like the bedroom with ribbons and bouquets of flowers. The walls and ceilings are handpainted with vines in the Cove Suite, two rooms with lots of wicker, a gas fireplace and a private bath. The Garden Studio in back has its own entrance and patio, a wicker sitting area, a hand-crafted queensize bed and grapevine stenciling that echoes the real vines outside the entry.

The crowning glory is the secluded Hideaway, fashioned from the Gotts' former quarters in the adjacent cottage. Mostly windows, it holds a kingsize bed, a tiled fireplace open to both the bedroom and the living room, rattan chairs, and an enormous bathroom with a double jacuzzi surrounded by a tiled border of fish. Pears seem to be a decorative theme, showing up on the fireplace tiles and at the base of a huge twig wreath over the mantel. Outside is a private deck where early-morning coffee was provided and we would gladly have spent the day, if we hadn't been working.

Breakfast on the inn's front porch brought fresh orange juice and an elaborate dish of melon bearing mixed fruit and homemade pineapple sorbet. The main event was a delicious zucchini crescent pie, teamed with an English muffin topped with cheddar, tomato and bacon, and roasted potatoes with onions and salsa. Lobster quiche, soufflés, asparagus strata, green-apple stuffed french toast, waffles and popovers are other specialties. Jim often cooks breakfast when he's not out on his rounds as a lobster fisherman.

Wine and cheese are served in the afternoon, and there are decanters of sherry plus bottles of sparkling water in each room.

(207) 967-3879 or 967-5151. Doubles, $95 to $210.

The Captain Lord Mansion, Pleasant Street, Box 800, Kennebunkport 04046.

Rick Litchfield and his wife Bev Davis bought this inn, which they consider "probably the finest example of Federal architecture on the coast of Maine, if not the country," in 1978. It was then a home for elderly women; five stayed on for the next two years while the couple went to work and totally restored the place, putting in private baths for each of the sixteen bedrooms.

Two chocolates are placed every evening in the bedrooms, which are elegantly furnished in antiques, most with four-poster or canopied beds. Eleven have working fireplaces. The corner rooms in this square, cupola-topped yellow mansion are especially spacious and airy. All have period wallpaper and nice touches like sewing kits, Poland Spring water, and a tray with wine glasses and a corkscrew.

Guests gather beneath crystal chandeliers in the richly furnished parlor for herbal tea or Swedish glögg, or beside the fire in the Gathering Room.

Ever on the move, the Littlefields opened an annex called Phoebe's Fantasy with four guest rooms, all with king or queen beds and fireplaces. Guests here take breakfast at a seven-foot harvest table in a gathering room with chintz sofa, fireplace and television.

In 1997, the inn's main-floor Merchant Room was expanded into a deluxe suite with king canopy bed, fireplace, double jacuzzi and a hydro-massage shower.

Breakfast for guests in the inn is served family-style in the big, cheery kitchen. The fare includes a main course like apple-cinnamon pancakes, cheese strata or quiche as well as soft-boiled eggs, french vanilla yogurt, nutri-grain cereals and all kinds of muffins and breads.

(207) 967-3141 or (800) 522-3141. Fax (207) 967-3172. Doubles, $155 to $249; suite, $349.

Pomegranate Inn, 49 Neal St., Portland 04102.

Isabel Smiles and her late husband Alan picked Portland as the small city in which to launch a B&B when they decided to move from Connecticut. They "turned the conventional idea of a bed and breakfast on its side and created a funky, relaxed and stylish inner-city space," in the words of the Portland Press-Telegram. They also made heads turn in local art circles, not to mention those of their B&B colleagues.

Called the "queen of the B&Bs" by no less than the New York Times, the Pomegranate is an art lover's paradise – part museum, part gallery, part antiques collection and part inn. The last attribute gives the unlikely-looking, 1884 Italianate Victorian with Colonial Revival facade in Portland's residential West End its raison d'être. It's filled with antiques (Isabel was in the decorating and antiques business in Greenwich) and contemporary art collected by the couple.

Bedrooms at Pomegranate Inn in Portland are a kaleidoscope of design.

The seven bedrooms on the second and third floors, all with modern tiled baths, televisions and telephones, are a kaleidoscope of design. Each is unique, mixing antique rugs, colorful fabrics, antique and contemporary furnishings, charming eccentricities and prized artworks. Even the bed configuration is mixed: five rooms come with queensize beds, another with kingsize and one has twins. Four have gas fireplaces. A deluxe, two-room suite has been added upstairs in the renovated carriage house across the terrace from the main inn. We happily splurged for the downstairs room in the carriage house with two plush chairs and a puffy duvet on the bed, a marble bathroom and walls painted with riotous flowers. It opened onto a secret courtyard, so quiet and secluded it was hard to imagine we were in the midst of a city.

Walls in ours and seven other guest rooms were handpainted by Portland artist Heidi Gerquest Harbert and are themselves works of art. Most striking is one on a robin's-egg-blue wall with a swirl design taken from a pattern on a Japanese kimono. Paisley, birds and flowers are painted in other rooms, and the hallways are sponged a golden color. Isabel's daughter, Amy Russack, painted faux finishes on moldings, fireplace mantels and columns. The downstairs parlors are almost a gallery of marble columns, Greek statuary, contemporary artworks and, near the long handpainted Italianate dining table, three huge papier-maché vegetables, each perched atop a small clay pot on a shelf in the front window.

Breakfast is served between 8 and 9:30 at the aforementioned communal table, or at a couple of small tables for those who prefer. Poached eggs with capers, creamy quiches and pancakes with sautéed pears turn the meal into another show of artistry. Our tasty waffles with bananas and raspberries were preceded by a dish of dainty nectarines with tiny blueberries and vanilla yogurt and a glass of mystery juice, whose contents no one could fathom. "Just orange and cranberry," Isabel said breezily. "I should tell everybody it's pomegranate juice."

(207) 772-1006 or (800) 356-0408. Doubles, $125 to $155.

The Danforth, 163 Danforth St., Portland 04102.

Energetic young owner Barbara Hathaway from Connecticut never dreamed she'd be running a full-service inn, let alone a landmark 1821 brick Georgian mansion that used to be the rectory for the Archdiocese of Portland. She opened in 1994 with two rooms, finished the ninth and last guest room a year later, was remodeling the dining room and adding a third-floor solarium at our visit, and was about to launch dinner service seven nights a week.

So much is going on here that the guest rooms might be considered an after-thought. Not so. The nine accommodations (one a two-bedroom suite) on the second and third floors are spacious, light and airy with tall windows and thick off-white carpeting. They're outfitted with updated baths, queensize beds bearing pillow-top mattresses, remote-control television, telephones, loveseats or wing chairs, antique armoires, writing desks with dataport terminals and all the accouterments of the good B&B life. Indian shutters cover the windows, Baccarat crystal knobs open the doors and all the tiled fireplaces are working and wood-burning.

On one side of the main floor is a double parlor, a portion of which was being restored as a dining room, with a sun porch alongside. Across the wide entry hall are a function room and a garden solarium about to become a game room and eventually a gift shop. To the rear is a cozy den with a wet bar in an old vault and one of the mansion's thirteen fireplaces. The day's newspapers are set out here with morning coffee. Late afternoon brings cookies and lemonade or tea and, in cool weather, hot soups with rustic breads.

Downstairs is the original billiards room, paneled and looking much as it did a century ago. Way upstairs on the rooftop is the widow's walk, occasionally used for sunrise breakfasts. It gives wraparound views of downtown Portland and the waterfront, plus a quite unexpected vista to the west of countless brick chimneys – a remarkable scene "straight out of England," says Barbara.

There's more. A vacant third-floor room was being converted into a skylit garden "solarium" because the owner believes guests on every floor should enjoy a common area. Occupants of the six second-floor rooms have a parlor opening onto a new deck overlooking the colorful side garden.

The day's breakfast fare is posted on a menu at the reception desk: perhaps baked apple, bacon and scrambled eggs in puff pastry one day; blueberry buckle, sausage and french toast the next.

Optional dinner service for house guests is available nightly from 7 to 9, in the refinished dining room or al fresco on the garden patio beside. Barbara and an assistant chef prepare a prix-fixe menu with a choice of two main courses. A typical night might feature braided salmon and flounder fillet with portobello cream sauce over pasta or black pepper-crusted pork tenderloin with roasted peppers. With appetizer, salad and dessert, the tab is in the $25 range. "I love to cook," says Barbara. Her talent showed in a local fund-raiser when she won the People's Choice award for best dessert with a mouthful called "white chocolate ganache caramel swirl macadamia nut cheesecake."

As we paused to take everything in atop the widow's walk following a whirl-wind tour, Barbara acknowledged she "saw the building, fell in love with it and turning it into an inn was the only way for me to have it." Her guests are lucky to share it.

(207) 879-8755 or (800) 991-6557. Fax (207) 879-8754. Doubles, $95 to $140; suite, $160.

Gourmet Treats

Along with its restaurants, the restored Old Port Exchange area of Portland is the center of shops appealing to those interested in food. The owners of **The Whip and Spoon,** a fascinating store for serious cooks at 161 Commercial St., say "if it's worth using in the kitchen, we have it." From fifteen-cent lobster picks to expensive food processors, you can find everything including magazines for cooks, a great collection of cookbooks and local products like herbs and spices from Ram Island Farm in Cape Elizabeth. All kinds of supplies are available for beer-makers, too. This store is one you could spend hours in, browsing and buying.

Modeled after a European coffee bar, the **Portland Coffee Roasting Co.** at 111 Commercial St. draws locals as well as tourists for a coffee fix or the "eggspresso" breakfast (scrambled eggs, bagel and coffee, $3.25). Small sandwiches, pastries like sticky buns and almond crescents and delicious Samantha juices (made in nearby Scarborough – we loved the strawberry-orange) are also on the board. Tall windows reveal the passing scene as you sip cappuccino or cafe au lait at modern little tables beneath a high pressed-tin ceiling. Owner Gerrie Brooke now offers a traditional cream tea, with scones and double devon cream. As we nursed a latte and caffe mocha outdoors on a ledge with a view of the waterfront and the sounds of the seagulls, we could picture ourselves back in Seattle, the latte capital of the world.

La Galette, 25 Pearl St., is a French patisserie newly opened by Renee and Alain Pabor, he from Southern France. Alain starts baking at 3 a.m. and she is in charge of the artful decorating and glazing. The aromas almost make you swoon. We drooled over the napoleons, apple custard and lemon tarts, and the tomato-dill quiche, but came away with just a couple of loaves of their wonderful breads to take home. Partake, perhaps, of a croissant made from scratch or a croque monsieur and a fancy coffee at one of the little tables here.

With plump red radishes on its sign, **The Portland Greengrocer** on Commercial Street is the place to pick up incredible breads like peach foccacia from Black Crow Bakery in Litchfield, imported beers, wines, oils and vinegars. The deli looks fantastic and the produce section pristine, with such fancy items as imported Italian onions.

Go into the **Port Bake House** at 265 Commercial St. to get one of the magnificent cheesecake brownies, a frangipane tart, a white-chocolate mousse cake or a honey macaroon. The thirteen breads include Irish oatmeal, peasant rye and nine-grain sesame. The soups, salads and sandwiches – from veggie hummus to croque monsieur, $4.25 to $4.75 – here are scrumptious.

Our favorite **Food Works,** which started in the current Port Bake House quarters, turned up most recently in a corner storefront with a handful of tables at 47 India St. Owners Robert and Pamela Hastings offer all kinds of goodies, from a deli full of salads (broccoli with bacon and raisins; smoked turkey and corn) to veggie rollups to sandwiches to gourmet lunch boxes to good-looking, vacuum-sealed dinner entrées to heat up in the microwave at home. We picked up a chicken and sweet-potato pie, and a pasta with wild mushrooms to bring home for dinner that night, after sampling a glass of their delightful and refreshing homemade lemon-ginger-honey fizz.

Della's Catessen, lately relocated into the thick of things at 92 Exchange St., is a fun place where Della Parker, who once was a sous chef at Cafe Always, sells soups like carrot-ginger, haddock chowder and gazpacho, bacon corn muffins, chicken pot pie, cheese burritos, Peruvian pâté, salads and quiches. Sandwiches are in the $2.95 to $4.95 range. Top off your lunch with a chocolate fudge grand slam brownie. Beers and wines, herbs, oils, vinegars, gift baskets and exotic jars of pickled fiddleheads, cajun ketchup and rhubarb chutney are displayed around the cheery yellow and red room, with framed old Life covers on the walls and several tables.

In 1997, chef Cheryl Lewis and Norine Kotts, who made Cafe Always what it was, were opening a health-food and specialty-food store and small cafe called **Aurora** at 62 Pine St. in the West End.

The Barking Squirrel - Cafe in the Park, set in the middle of Deering Oaks Park, is a great place to have a summer lunch under Poland Spring umbrellas on the terrace while watching the paddle boats navigate the nearby pond. We had the most delicious Mediterranean rollup sandwiches, with herbed white bean spread, feta cheese, mixed greens, oil-cured olives and red onions on lavash bread ($3.75). A lobster roll with handcut french fries was a mere $6.95, and those fries sure did look good, as did the burgers and the Thai salad. Plans for Sunday brunch, a big outdoor barbecue pit and winter dinners (maybe after skating on the pond?) by the huge stone fireplace inside were in the works.

Berry Gourmet

If you love raspberries as much as we do, don't miss **Whistling Wings Farm** at 427 West St., Biddeford. Don and Julie Harper started with a card table and umbrella in their driveway; now people come from across the world, among them George and Barbara Bush, "our down-the-road neighbors." Julie gets up at 1 in the morning to do the day's baking, producing 30 to 40 dozen muffins, 50 to 100 turnovers, 30 to 40 loaves of bread and an equal number of pies. "Many days there's nothing left by 1:30," says Don, who oversees the growing retail and mail-order business. He says their toppings, syrups and raspberry vinegars are totally different from others on the market – the last is like raspberry with a touch of vinegar, not the other way around. "The secret is in the berries and our cooking methods." Get a turnover or a dish of homemade raspberry ice cream and take it to a picnic table beside a little pond, where ducks and geese make their presence known. Open daily, 7 to 6.

Kennebunkport and South

In Kennebunkport, **Keys to the Kitchen** out Port Road (Route 35) in the Lower Village is well worth a visit. Owners Dodie Phillips and Daisy Arnold have an unusual flair for displays, both on the main floor and upstairs on a balcony around an open atrium. The cookbook area is distinctive, there's a wine and cheese section in back, and upstairs we found some pretty and summery placemats that now grace our patio table at home.

The place in Kennebunkport to pick up the makings for a picnic is **Bailey's,** a deli/market/coffee bar at Port and Western Avenues. We were impressed by the produce, the wine selection and the array of sandwiches available on subs or croissants, nicely priced from $2.70 to $4.25. You can make your own salad from the salad bar ($2.89 a pound). Out of town in Cape Porpoise, the market of choice is **Bradbury Brothers,** with the usual, plus essentials for summer residents like bread from When Pigs Fly in York, Greek olive pesto, Rose's lime juice and local jams.

The way proprietor John Audley figures it, there are ten trillion possible combinations in his food at **Pizzoodles,** at the Shipyard off Western Avenue in the Lower Village. Patrons choose the toppings for his wood-fired, brick-oven gourmet pizzas, perhaps caramelized onion, chèvre, sundried tomatoes, spam (yes, spam), wild mushrooms and more (he even offered a gator pizza one holiday weekend). He makes his pastas the Italian way, offers a variety of sauces, pasta salads, panini (Italian sandwiches – the toppings chosen from the pizza selections and spread on foccacia, $4.25 to $4.75), coffees, bagels and pastries. There are tables inside or out upon which to enjoy, and you can BYOB. Open daily, 11 to 9 or 10.

The high-end, dark beers are particularly good, we're told, at the **Kennebunkport Brewing Co.** at the Shipyard, facing the river in the Lower Village. You can tour the main-floor brewery and sample the beers upstairs at its **Federal Jack's Brew Pub,** where lunch and dinner are available daily at sturdy wood communal tables in a big room beside the water.

Cherie's Sweet Treats & Other Eats at 7 High St., Kennebunk, was jammed at our noontime visit with folks picking up moderately priced lunches. Most took out, as we did, but there are a few stools at a counter for those who wish. "That Sandwich" is a perennial favorite: the mixture of artichoke hearts, red pepper, red onion, pesto and olives was delicious. But we also could have gone for the seafood quiche, the peanut-ginger or lentil-mint salads, the jambalaya or one of the six soups of the day. And we wouldn't have minded at all having a slice of fresh strawberry pie.

A huge grapevine moose was at the entrance to **Marlow's,** 39 Main St., Kennebunk, a gift shop stocked with "swell stuff and terrific things," itemized literally from A to Z. There's a section for specialty foods, local mustards and jams, as well as cookbooks.

A couple of places are worth noting in Ogunquit. **Cafe Amoré** at 37 Shore Road is just the ticket for those into exotic coffees and food more creative (and healthful) than fried clams. Go for the blackboard specials: interesting salads and sandwiches in the $4 range, good bagels and desserts like peach pie. For provisions, head for **Perkins & Perkins,** purveyors of fine foods, wines and gifts along Route 1 north.

Gourmet Success

Stonewall Kitchen Company Store, 469 U.S. Route 1, York, Me.

The jams and condiments that are turning up in specialty-food stores across the nation are sold here in a small, upscale retail setting in the front of the production facility, which was fashioned from an old grocery store in York Corner.

Jonathan King and Jim Stott, who met as waiters in leading restaurants in Portsmouth, N.H., started selling homemade jams and vinegars at the Portsmouth farmers' market in 1991 for extra spending money. One customer bought out their entire inventory for her store, and therein began, by happenstance, a phenomenon that quickly projected them into Dean & DeLuca, Williams-Sonoma and 3,000 stores nationwide. Now with 45 products and $7 million in annual sales, they are the talk of the gourmet food industry. In 1996 they became the first company ever to win the Outstanding Product Line award at the International Fancy Food and Confection Show in Philadelphia two years in a row. Their ginger-peach tea jam – a concoction of peach chunks, tea leaves and ginger – was named the outstanding new product in 1996.

"We love to create new products," says Jonathan, who loves to cook and first gave his jams to his family as Christmas presents. "Some people think in words or in pictures, but I think in terms of tastes." Those tastes have led to 45 different jams, oils, vinegars and mustards, which sell here for $5 to $13 and appeal to the high-end market.

(800) 207-5267. Open daily, 10 to 5 or 6.

Lobster Spots

Two Lights Lobster Shack, Two Lights Road, Cape Elizabeth.

Near Two Lights State Park and almost in the shadow of the two lighthouses south of Portland, this is located on a bluff overlooking nothing but rocks and open ocean. You can eat inside, but we prefer sipping a drink outside at a picnic table (BYOB) as we await our order. This is a great place to bring youngsters because they can clamber around on the rocks while waiting for dinner and because the Lobster Shack offers hamburgers, fried chicken and clam cakes as well as boiled lobsters, chowder and steamers. A lobster dinner was $11.95 at our last visit.

(207) 799-1677. Open daily from 11 to 8, mid-May to mid-October, to 8:30 in July and August.

Nunan's Lobster Hut, Route 9, Cape Porpoise.

The decor is rustic, to put it mildly, and kind of schlocky with paraphernalia like you wouldn't believe (a friend who waitressed here some 40 years ago has her picture on the wall, along with all the others through the years). But people from common folk to movie stars start lining up before Hoppy Nunan, daughter-in-law of the late founder, Captain Nunan, opens the doors at 5 o'clock. Lobsters trapped by her son Richard are cooked to order; some think they are the best in Maine. Steaks, steamed clams, lobster stew, salads and sensational homemade pies are among the offerings. Beer and wine are available.

(207) 967-4362. Open daily in season, 5 to 10.

The Lively Lobster, On the Pier, Cape Porpoise.

If you like your lobster in an informal outdoor setting, head right to the pier at Cape Porpoise. This is the former site of Tilly's Shanty, taken over by Angela and Arthur LeBlanc of the adjacent Seascapes restaurant. Here they feature steamed lobsters, lobster rolls, fried seafood and what Arthur touts as the best onion rings "made from scratch." You place your order and sit at a battered picnic table inside or out beside the water.

Open daily in season, 7 a.m. to sunset.

The most atmospheric place for lobster in this area, we're told, is the **Chauncey Creek Lobster Pound** off Route 103 in Kittery Point. It's open from 5 until the bugs force them to close. We missed the sign, coming and going, and never did find it.

Everyone likes to eat lobster beside the ocean, as here at Two Lights in Cape Elizabeth.

Mid-Coast Maine
Where the Real Maine Starts

The sandy beaches of Southern Maine yield to Maine's more typical rockbound coast north of Portland. There are those who say that this is where the real Maine starts.

The coastline becomes more jagged, its fingers protruding like tentacles toward the sea between inlets, rivers and bays. Poke down remote byways to Bailey Island, Popham Beach, Westport, Christmas Cove and Pemaquid Point. You'll find life quieter here and the distances between points long and roundabout. One look at the map as you eye the shore across the inlet and you'll understand why the natives say "you can't get theah from heah" – except by boat.

Here also are two of Maine's leading tourist destinations – crowded Boothbay Harbor, a commercial fishing village surrounded by a choice and remote shoreline beyond and on either side, and upscale Camden, where the mountains meet the sea and the windjammer fleet sets sail from the colorful harbor.

These two resort areas have long been favored by visitors, whose arrival has produced the inevitable influx of souvenir shops and golden arches nearby. But the Mid-coast's increasing gentrification also has attracted new and better restaurants, inns and B&Bs, and – a surprise at our latest visit – a little landmark called Lighthouse Espresso, "serving Downeast coffee," a beacon amid the tickytack of Route 1 above Rockland.

Side by side with touristy Boothbay and Camden are postcard fishing hamlets like Ocean Point and Port Clyde. The busy towns of Brunswick, Bath and Rockland co-exist with salt-washed villages like Rockport and South Harpswell.

Before you head Down East, tarry along Maine's mid-coast.

Dining

The Best of the Best

The Robinhood Free Meetinghouse, Robinhood Road, off Route 127, Robinhood.

Yes, this place with the odd name really was a church until 1989. In 1996, it was transformed into a restaurant-cum-gallery by chef-owner Michael Gagné, who moved up the road after putting the Osprey restaurant at Robinhood Marine Center on the culinary map.

Well known in the area for his catering and cooking classes, he oversees an ambitious, contemporary fusion menu that has gone beyond its original New American base to embrace continental and oriental cuisines (some dishes are marked "very peppery" and "spicy hot"). He and his staff make their own breads, pastas, sausages and ice creams. From their new dream of a kitchen, they turn out about three dozen entrées a night, not to mention two soups, ten salads, twelve appetizers, six pastas and a staggering seventeen desserts. Skeptics call it overkill, but they recognize Michael as one of Maine's best chefs.

In leaving the nearby Osprey, Michael gave up a waterfront location for a better arena in which to show his stuff. The lower floor of the meeting house bears a clean, stark New England look. It's pristine in white and cream, with oriental runners on the wide-board floors and Shaker-style chairs at tables clad in white. Arty sculptures dress a window ledge, and the upstairs meeting house has been turned into a gallery.

Michael invites customers to "mix and match appetizers, pastas and salads to make up a meal that fits your appetite." The smoked seafood sampler served with a baguette and horseradish-mustard mousseline ($9) is sensational, as are the corn-fried oysters with fresh salsa and chipotle cream. The grilled sausage sampler is a meal in itself, with two six-inch sausages (one garlic, one Sicilian) and a sliced baguette. A tart cherry-lemon sorbet cleared the palate for our entrées ($18 to $22). We found the gutsy scallops niçoise in puff pastry with saffron rice and the grilled chicken with sundried tomatoes over fettuccine both so ample as to require doggy bags, since we wanted to save room for the trio of ice creams – ginger, raspberry swirl and childhood orange. The signature "obsession in three chocolates" – white, dark and milk, all flavored with different liqueurs ($6.50) – is as good as it gets. No wonder the Maine Sunday Telegram reviewer awarded the ultimate five stars in his 1996 review.

Quite a selection of wines is available by the glass ($4 to $6). The wine list is priced mostly in the teens and twenties, with less than the usual markup. The dessert list offers a flight of six ports for $12.95, as if anyone could manage.

Michael was considering opening for lunch in summer, starting in 1997.

(207) 371-2188. Dinner nightly, 5:30 to 9, fewer nights in off-season.

Jessica's, 2 South Main St. (Route 73), Rockland.

A loyal following from miles around is drawn to chef-owner Hans Bucher 's European bistro in a pleasant Victorian house south of town. The front veranda has a barber's chair and deck chairs scattered about for pre-dinner drinks, which are also available upstairs in a spiffy parlor. Three small main-floor rooms seat 40 diners at bare wood tables set with cloth mats, fresh flowers and small candles.

Chef-owner Michael Gagné in dining room of The Robinhood Free Meetinghouse.

The early bundnerfleisch and raclettes from Hans's Swiss background have evolved into more intricate treats like lobster ravioli, an appetizer served in a sauce of sherry, garlic, coriander and tarragon – so good that one innkeeper of our acquaintance said she would gladly make it her dinner. Other worthy starters are crostini topped with eggplant, roasted peppers and fontina cheese and Corsican bruschetta with crabmeat. The focaccia bears plum tomatoes and basil or eggplant, goat cheese and black olives.

Among main courses ($12.50 to $16.50), we've heard nothing but raves for the lamb provençal and the tournedos, the latter served amid a cluster of artichokes, onions, mushrooms and potatoes. Also memorable are a classic bouillabaisse, veal Zurich and paysanne pork stew, a robust potpourri of pork, bratwurst, bacon and vegetables served with garlicky mashed potatoes. One section of the menu details eight pasta and risotto dishes, from seafood basque ladled atop homemade pasta to sweetbreads lyonnaise with a light risotto.

Desserts include a smooth crème brûlée, a rich chocolate truffle cake topped with white chocolate mousse, a walnut torte and grand marnier parfait.

(207) 596-0770. Dinner nightly except Tuesday, 5:30 to 9.

Cafe Miranda, 15 Oak St., Rockland.

The beige and green colors of the exterior are repeated inside this surprisingly trendy cafe at the edge of downtown Rockland. Opened in 1993 by chef Kerry Altiero and his wife, Evelyn Donnelly, a craftswoman by day, the cafe quickly drew throngs from throughout the meat-and-haddock Rockland area for its laid-back atmosphere and the gutsy cooking emanating from the wood-fired brick oven in the open kitchen.

At our first visit, patrons were extolling the carrot-ginger soup served with herbed flatbread, the bruschetta with grilled chicken, artichoke spread and greens, and the mushroom pizza with three cheeses and red onions. The ambitious menu denotes small plates and "big, bigger, biggest" plates, ranging from appetizers for one to dinner for one or appetizers for two, at prices from $5.50 to $13.50. Kerry cooks almost everything in the brick oven, going through a cord of wood a month.

His offerings range widely, from pasta with sundried tomatoes, ricotta and artichoke hearts to ziti bolognaise with pork, veal and wine cream sauce. Lest Cafe Miranda be categorized as Italian, Kerry injects Thai and North African influences, as in a pork dish with gorgonzola, polenta and three chiles with avocado salsa or grilled salmon with mandarin oranges, cilantro and roasted peppers and served with couscous. Expect innovations like chargrilled pork and shrimp cakes with peanuts and stir-fried veggies in a coconut-peanut sauce, stir-fried salmon strips tossed with Thai chiles, lime, mint and greens, and chicken cubano with yellow rice and black bean salad. Consider the grilled chicken with roasted peppers and basil on saffron risotto, the lamb korma, the sliced duck breast with ginger-plum sauce and Chinese noodles, or the flank steak with sautéed peppers, mushrooms, garlic, gorgonzola and black pepper pasta. There are a number of vegetarian items, too.

We would gladly make a meal of appetizers like shrimp tossed with avocado-corn salsa on roasted romano grits, lamb and lentils with feta and greens or the mussels steamed in saffron cream.

Evelyn's talents are evident in the desserts, perhaps zabaglione with fresh fruit, trifle with chocolate sauce and blackberries, frozen lemon mousse pie, walnut crostada or ice cream with homemade Italian cookies.

Rainbow-colored cloth napkins and candles grace the blond wood tables. Single diners enjoy gathering at one of the three counters – two smack in the middle of the room and one facing Kerry in the kitchen. There's a select and varied, reasonably priced wine list.

(207) 594-2034. Dinner, Tuesday-Sunday 5:30 to 8:30 or 9.

More Dining Choices

Kristina's, 160 Centre St., Bath.

From a tiny bakery with a few tables and a display case full of sticky buns, Kristina's has evolved into a full-service restaurant and lounge. You can still get sticky buns and other good things to take out from the display cases at the entrance, but now there are two dining rooms, a front dining deck with a tree growing through it and, upstairs, **Harry's Bar,** an attractive room that is all blond wood and deck chairs, with windows onto the outdoors. Jazz groups play here at night.

For breakfast we like to feast on such treats as a Mexican omelet, strawberry waffles or a seafood quiche ($3.50 to $6.95). Soups, quiches, salads (smoked trout or crabmeat in avocado), sandwiches and burgers make up the lunch menu.

At dinner start with one of the changing seafood bisques, clams steamed in Bass ale, cornmeal and basil crêpes with ratatouille and chèvre, or grilled lamb sausage in zinfandel sauce with pistachios. Entrées ($11.95 to $19.95) include grilled salmon steak au poivre with lime vinaigrette, sautéed lobster and avocado over scallion fettuccine, Caribbean pepper pot (seafood in coconut milk and scotch bonnet pepper broth with sweet potatoes and coconut jonnycakes), grilled lamb chops with roasted-eggplant puree on minted tabbouleh and Jamaican mixed grill on coconut-basmati rice. You know you're in creative culinary hands when Kristina's teams the Maine fish staple haddock with crabmeat and serves it in a brandied mushroom sauce. Desserts from the bakery case taste as wonderful as they look.

For weekend brunch, try the Swiss panfkuchen (a pancake filled with berries), Kristina's french toast made with cinnamon swirl bread, huevos rancheros or four kinds of benedicts, including crabmeat.

(207) 442-8577. Breakfast daily, 8 to 11; lunch, 11:30 to 2:30; dinner, 5 to 9. Harry's Bar, with light menu, open weekdays to 10, weekends to midnight.

Ristorante Black Orchid, 5 By-Way, Boothbay Harbor.

Rather New Yorkish in a seaside kind of way is this intimate Italian trattoria run by chef-owner Steven DiCicco, a Culinary Institute of America grad. The unpretentious interior is done up in black and white, with pink stenciling on the walls, beams strewn with odd-looking grapevines and baskets of hanging fuschias. The upstairs cafe and raw bar overlook the downtown harbor scene.

The highly rated food includes fourteen pasta dishes with salad, from $9.95 for rigatoni with meat sauce to $20.95 for the signature fettuccine alfredo with lobster and mushrooms. Lobster also appears alla diavolo and teamed with sundried tomatoes over linguini. Seven poultry and five veal dishes head the list of entrées ($13.95 to $22.95). Look for things like salmon with mushrooms and cream, shrimp diavolo, pork tenderloin with raisins and pinenuts, petite filets diavolo and veal scaloppine with prosciutto and mushrooms.

Desserts include amaretto bread pudding and chocolate-chambord torte.

(207) 633-6650. Dinner nightly except Tuesday, 5:30 to 10; raw bar from 5. Closed mid-October to mid-May.

Harbor View Tavern, 1 Water St., Thomaston.

Want good food with a water view? Try this hard-to-find, funky eatery with a darkened dining room/tavern that's too atmospheric for words and, beyond, an enclosed porch and a new deck overlooking the water. It's a favorite with locals, and probably only locals could find it down an unmarked roadway near the town landing.

Would-be diners line up outside at peak periods. Inside the entry, an upside-down perambulator is on the ceiling. Ahead, every conceivable inch of wall space is covered with old license plates, photos, books, signs, masks and such, and musical instruments hang from the ceiling. But there's much up-to-date in this old boat-building facility, from the day's USA Today sports page posted in the men's room to the artful presentations of the lunches we were served. The chicken and basil pasta salad ($7.95) was garnished with sliced strawberries, oranges and watermelon; ditto for crab cristo ($6.95) that came with french fries and coleslaw. Two candies arrived with the bill.

Votive candles in little pewter dishes flicker on the tables set with mismatched cloths and colorful napkins at night. The menu lists appetizers, light fare and entrées ($12.95 to $15.95) like baked stuffed haddock, scallops au gratin, chicken imperial and sirloin steak St. Jacques, smothered with scallops and mushroom-cream sauce. We're told the place is famous for its brownie à la mode, grapenut parfait, "strawberry fields forever" cake and apple crisp.

(207) 354-8173. Lunch daily, 11:30 to 4; dinner, 5 to 10. Shorter hours in winter.

The Craignair Inn, Clark Island Road, Clark Island, Spruce Head 04859.

Some of Maine's more eclectic fare is served in this out-of-the-way, seaside establishment that began life as a boarding house for workers from the nearby quarries. Converted to an inn in 1940, it has a cheery parlor-library, a mix of guest rooms with shared and private baths, an old-fashioned kitchen dominated by an antique cast-iron stove and a summery dining room where patrons can feast on unusual food while overlooking the water.

"We try to be different," concedes Terry Smith, owner for twenty years. "That's the only way to get people down here." She travels far and wide in the off-season, finding "all these wonderful dishes to try." Regulars say they can tell Terry's itinerary from the resulting menu.

Dinner choices ($12.95 to $16.50) might yield Hong Kong hot shrimp over noodles, Tahitian stuffed prawns served on a bed of sprouts, Jamaican rum-roasted pork negril with cucumber-papaya salsa and the Indian vegetarian dish matar panir, along with more traditional fare. The latter includes baked stuffed haddock, monkfish medallions sautéed with tomato-lemon coulis, veal oscar, chicken roulade and bouillabaisse, a house specialty.

The appetizer list ranges from shrimp cocktail and herring in sour cream to mozzarella cakes and crostini. Desserts could be chocolate crème brûlée, strawberry-rhubarb or peach pie, apple crisp and mocha mousse.

The homey dining room is refreshing in peach and blue, the colors picked up from lovely oriental rugs covering the floors. Prolific ferns hang in the windows and an amazing collection of blue plates and pottery decorates high shelves around the room.

Upstairs are simply furnished bedrooms sharing three baths on each floor. The Vestry Annex contains five bedrooms, all with private baths.

(207) 594-7644. Dinner, Monday-Saturday 6 to 9. Open mid-May to mid-October.

The Waterfront Restaurant, Harborside Square off Bay View Street, Camden.

Rebuilt following a damaging 1995 fire, this popular restaurant is notable for its large outdoor deck shaded by a striking white canopy resembling a boat's sails, right beside the windjammers on picturesque Camden Harbor, and for its affordable, international menu. Purists say the location surpasses the food, though we've been satisfied each time we've eaten here.

At lunch, the most costly entrées are fried clams and crab cakes (both in the $10.95 range, including salad or gazpacho and french fries). Seven delectable salads in glass bowls are dressed with outstanding dressings, among them sweet-and-sour bacon, lemon-parmesan, dijon vinaigrette and blue cheese.

At night, when the luncheon salads are still available, the menu turns more eclectic. Among appetizers are calamari and shrimp, mussels marinière, baked brie and soups, perhaps chilled raspberry accented with grand marnier. The superlative smoked seafood sampler was our choice for sharing. Entrées are priced from $14.95 to $18.95, except $23.50 for lobster and mussels sauté. We've enjoyed the Maine crab cakes with creamy mustard sauce, an assertive linguini with salmon and sundried tomatoes, shrimp with oriental black beans over angel-hair pasta and a special of swordfish grilled over applewood with rosemary, which was juicy and succulent. Grilled chicken with quinoa polenta and sirloin steak are the only meat offerings. Mint chocolate chip pie with hot fudge sauce and whipped cream proved to be the ultimate dessert at one visit; the next time we passed on the heavy offerings and walked up the street to Camden Cone for some raspberry frozen yogurt.

All sorts of shellfish and light fare from hamburgers to lobster rolls are available at the oyster bar and outdoor grill, open from 2:30 until closing.

Billowing canopy shades dining deck at Waterfront Restaurant in Camden.

The Waterfront is understandably a busy, convivial spot on a sunny summer day. Its owners run an offshoot, The Cannery, at Lower Falls Landing in Yarmouth. *(207) 236-3747. Lunch daily, 11:30 to 2:30; dinner, 5 to 10.*

Frogwater Cafe, 31 Elm St., Camden.

Healthful and innovative fare at kindly prices is offered by Erin and Joseph Zdanowicz, young New England Culinary Institute graduates who moved across the country from Tacoma, Wash., to open this homey little storefront cafe in 1995. The name was inspired by a favorite street on Bainbridge Island in Puget Sound, and some of the primarily domestic wines come from Washington and Oregon.

Food with a flair is featured in simple surroundings. Joseph's menu ranges widely, from $8 for garlic ziti or vegetable pasta to $15 for herb and dijon-crusted lamb chops or grilled tenderloin stuffed with blue cheese, caramelized onions and sundried tomatoes. In between are braised haddock, warm orzo salad, crab cakes, mussels florentine, wild mushroom ravioli and more. Start with some of the luscious looking onion rings or grilled flatbread. Finish with Erin's peach bread pudding with butterscotch sauce, chocolate-hazelnut layer cake or berry crisp with vanilla ice cream.

The fare sounds simple, but takes on complex tastes, as we found at lunch (since discontinued, when the couple decided after two years to concentrate on dinner). We enjoyed a hearty bacon-leek-potato soup, an open-faced grilled baguette with feta cheese, tomato, cucumber, black olives and sundried tomato pesto, and a "BLT and Then Some Club" sandwich adding onions, cucumber and cheddar cheese on Texas toast. Sides of nippy macaroni and vegetable salads came with each, and the meal indicated the style that this couple added to the Camden dining scene. The locals return the favor by packing the place at night.

There's a belted galloway cow at the door (this used to be Galloway's, a family restaurant), and the walls bear hand-painted windows for art.

(207) 236-8998. Dinner, Tuesday-Sunday 5 to 9.

Chez Michel, Route 1, Lincolnville Beach.

This country French restaurant was opened in 1990 by Michel and Joan Hetuin, he a former chef at the Helm restaurant in Rockport. The main floor is a simple room crowded with formica tables and pink-painted wood chairs with green upholstered seats. The seats of choice are upstairs in a cheery new dining room that offers a head-on view of the water, or at the four tables on a screened balcony off the side.

For a quick lunch, we enjoyed an avocado-tomato-cheddar melt ($4.95) and a fried clam roll ($6.95), plus Joan's fantastic raspberry pie with a cream-cheese base and an extra-good shortbread crust ($2.50), so good that regulars call to reserve a slice before it runs out.

A subsequent dinner began with great french bread, two slabs of rabbit pâté resting with cornichons on oodles of lettuce, and house salads dressed with creamy Italian and pepper-parmesan. A special of salmon béarnaise arrived on a bed of spinach. The only disappointment was the bouillabaisse, more like a spicy cioppino with haddock substituting for most of the usual shellfish. Other dinner entrées ($10.95 to $14.95) include vegetarian couscous, scallops provençal, mussels marinière, grilled chicken béarnaise, beef bourguignonne, lamb kabob and steak au poivre. Although we'd opt for the French specialties, we know others who think there's no better place for lobster or even a crab roll with homemade potato chips and a bowl of Maine chowder. Save room for the superlative desserts, including strawberry torte, caramel custard, chocolate mousse and especially that raspberry pie. The short, mainly French wine list is priced in the teens.

(207) 789-5600. Lunch and dinner daily except Monday, 11:30 to 9. Closed December-March.

Gourmet with a Wallop

Dos Amigos, 144 Bayside Road, Northport.

Pink stucco with aqua trim, the exterior of this unlikely-looking Mexican cantina alongside Route 1 deceives. It appears small, but inside is a colorful space with quite a collection of sombreros on the walls and seating for 125. The food is authentic and packs a wallop as well.

Chips and excellent salsa laced with cilantro get meals off to a good start, along with, perhaps, a zinger of a "cadillac" margarita incorporating cointreau and grand marnier. For a summer lunch, the chorizo and corn chowder was excellent, and the fire-roasted chicken fajita salad ($6.95) assertive. So was the open-faced steak fajita sandwich ($5.95), accompanied by spicy island fries. Our mouths were left tingling long after lunch, even after sharing the margarita cheesecake for dessert.

The interesting menu covers all the usual bases and then some: aztec chicken, smoked duck pasta, scallops acapulco, spicy crab cakes with smoky chipotle cream sauce and roasted red chile pork over rice, nicely priced from $8.95 to $12.95. All dishes are considered mild to mildly spicy, but can be made hotter and spicier on request. Ask for the red-hot firecracker salsa if you like really hot. The jalapeño corn fritters, the crab empanadas, and the smoked duck and jalapeño jack flautas are recommended starters. The kahlua mousse and chambord torte are refreshing endings.

Don and Tarijita Warner have themselves a winner of a place.

(207) 338-5775. Lunch daily, 11 to 3; dinner to 9. Closed January and February.

Budget Gourmet

Mama & Leenie's, 27 Elm St., Camden.

A small cafe with a cheery atmosphere, this opens at 7 for breakfast (blintzes with fruit and sour cream are in the $4 to $5 range, as are waffles with fruit), and continues with lunch and supper.

Mama does such dishes as Mama's special peasant soup with beef, kielbasa and vegetables. Her daughter Leenie, an artist, bakes goodies like fresh raspberry or Maine blueberry pies with whipped cream and New England pumpkin-pecan pie. For lunch, try the pasta-primavera salad with Leenie's garlic, olive oil and raspberry vinegar dressing or the green garden salad "of whatever looked good at the market – you'll have to trust us."

Bring your own wine for dinner, when you might find Indonesian marinated chicken on a skewer or a bowl of chili with homemade bread. Leenie is a master baker, as evidenced by the apricot strudel with coconut and walnuts, the double-chocolate-fudge brownies with orange zest and the pineapple upside-down cake. The fresh berry pies with real whipped cream are masterpieces. Peanut-butter granola cookies, sugar cookies with a creamy filling or butter shortbreads are good with a cup of Green Mountain coffee, perhaps on the shady side patio with its yellow tables. Check out Leenie's artwork on the walls and the display of greeting cards she designed.

(207) 236-6300. Open daily, 7 a.m. to 11 p.m., Sunday to 8 p.m.; fewer hours in off-season. BYOB.

Dining and Lodging

Harraseeket Inn, 162 Main St., Freeport 04032.

In Freeport, where the supply of rooms can hardly keep up with the onslaught of shoppers, sisters Nancy Gray and Jody Dyer of Connecticut's Inn at Mystic got their foot in the door in 1984 with an elegant, five-room B&B. A few years and many millions of dollars later, a handsome, three-story white building connecting smaller existing structures houses a fine 85-seat restaurant, an informal tavern and 80 posh guest rooms and suites.

The original 1850 Greek Revival farmhouse is now overshadowed by a large 1989 building and a planned 1997 wing linking the two. Standard rooms contain two double beds or one queensize with blue and white fabric half-canopies, a single wing chair, and baskets of Lord & Mayfair amenities on the pedestal sinks in the bathrooms. Our large third-floor room offered a kingsize bed with a partial-canopy headboard and botanical prints, a sofa and wing chair beneath a palladian window, a working fireplace, a wet bar and a small refrigerator, TV hidden in an armoire, and an enormous bath with a jacuzzi. Turndown service produced chocolates at night.

The 1997 wing was designed to hold 30 more rooms, a mix of luxury units with fireplaces and jacuzzis and others with two double beds for traveling families. Also planned were a heated indoor lap pool in a garden solarium and a relocated tavern, enlarged to handle increased numbers of casual diners who had been turned away in the old quarters.

Fine artworks, fresh flowers and many of Nancy Gray's personal antiques are

Buffet table is ready for lunch at Harraseeket Inn.

evident throughout. Afternoon tea with quite a spread of pastries and sandwiches is served in a large and sumptuous drawing room notable for mahogany paneling. The attractive Broad Arrow Tavern is outfitted with old snowshoes, paddles, fly rods and a moosehead. "It's my life in review," says Nancy, recalling her upbringing in a Maine sporting camp. The extensive tavern menu features hot-rock cooking, as well as grills from a new wood-fired oven.

The stylish Maine Dining Room, divided into three sections, is pretty as a picture. Substantial black windsor chairs and a few banquettes flank tables set formally with white linens, heavy silver, silver service plates and pink stemware.

Chef Chris Toole features products from area farmers and growers, all of whom are nicely credited on a page at the back of the menu. The highly rated dinner fare is priced from $13 for a couple of vegetarian dishes to $26 for saddle of venison with saffron risotto and ratatouille. Recent choices included Atlantic salmon with potato risotto and asparagus, lazy lobster with a sweet corn coulis and corn soufflé, pan-seared quail and duck with roasted potatoes and beets, and grilled lamb sirloin with red lentils, eggplant and oregano. Fettuccine with grilled portobello mushrooms, châteaubriand and rack of lamb are prepared tableside for two.

Starters could be sherried lobster stew, smoked salmon with a lemon-vodka sorbet and golden whitefish caviar, foie gras with a raspberry coulis and toasted brioche, and roasted goat cheese with spicy greens and garlic croutons. Finish with a flourish: rum-flamed Jamaican bananas, chocolate overdose flamed with grand marnier, or one of the exotic homemade ice creams and sorbets. The wine list has been honored by Wine Spectator.

A full breakfast buffet, from fresh fruit and biscuits to scrambled eggs and french toast, is included in the rates. The buffet lunch at $10.95 is exceeded in bounty only by the Sunday brunch ($15.95, with music by a classical guitarist).

(207) 865-9377 or (800) 342-6423. Fax (207) 865-1684. Lunch, daily 11:30 to 2:30; dinner, 6 to 9 or 9:30. Doubles, $145 to $220; suites, $235.

Log Cabin Lodging & Fine Food, Route 24, Box 41, Bailey Island 04003. This started as a restaurant in a log cabin, but you'd never know it following its 1996 upgrade. Downsizing their popular restaurant to add lodging, Sue and Neal Favreau offer six comfortable accommodations, each with its own deck upon which to savor the water views. We liked the looks of the bright and airy York Room with queen bed, TV and telephone, kitchenette, jacuzzi tub and separate shower. The Mount Washington suite atop a former garage comes with a full kitchen, separate kingsize bedroom, two TVs, stereo and a deck with a private hot tub, from which you can see New England's tallest peak 90 miles away on a clear day. All the summery lounge chairs on the decks and in the rooms are display models for the line Sue carries in her gift shop. Guests enjoy a complimentary breakfast of eggs or french toast with meats and home fries.

Dinner is served in a cozy, lodge-like room with a moosehead above the fireplace, in an intimate front bar and on enclosed porches with water views. Sue, who has been in the restaurant business since she was 13 and originally ran the late Rock Ovens nearby, oversees the kitchen. Her baker, Sue Bear, has been with her for 22 years, and her grown sons have recently gotten into the act.

The changing menu ranges widely, from $12.95 for orange chicken and rice to $19.95 for black angus filet mignon. Seafood is featured, including three versions of haddock, shrimp scampi over capellini, scallops fried or honey glazed, and grilled salmon provençal. A complete shore dinner, served in courses, goes for $26.95. Start with the seafood sampler: gulf shrimp, scallops in bacon, lobster, seafood dip and crackers. Finish with one of the delectable desserts, perhaps strawberry-rhubarb pie, peach pie with crumb topping, sugar-free blueberry crisp or cheesecake with strawberries.

While the menu sounds basic, this is honest cooking done with a deft hand. As a feature spread in Down East magazine put it, "there is nothing easy about making food this simple taste this good."

(207) 833-5546. Fax (207) 833-7858. Lunch daily, 11:30 to 2; dinner, 5 to 8 or 9. Doubles, $99 to $109; suite, $150. Closed November to mid-March.

Lawnmeer Inn and Restaurant, Route 27, Box 505, West Boothbay Harbor 04575.

Virtually every table has a water view in the long, pine-paneled dining room of this Southport Island restaurant. Redone in burgundy and white with green napkins that match the carpet, it's dramatic by day and romantic by candlelight at night.

Chef Bill Edgerton supplements the regular menu with a page of daily specials – things like garlicky linguini tossed with smoked salmon and peas alfredo, $4.95 as an appetizer, and a trio of fish (swordfish with pesto, tuna with soy and garlic, and sole with crabmeat and tomato, $16.95 as an entrée), both of which proved exceptional. When one of us chose the fish trio over the lobster Johnny Walker but wanted to sample the sauce, the chef obliged with a taste on the side.

We also can vouch for the shrimp in parchment with julienned vegetables, new potatoes and crisp yellow squash and zucchini, and the poached salmon with dill-hollandaise sauce, among entrées priced from $11.95 to $20.95.

Vermont maple crème brûlée, blueberry bread pudding with crème anglaise, grand marnier mousse and key lime pie are among the delightful desserts.

Owners Lee and Jim Metzger have renovated thirteen inn rooms and suites, all with private baths. Twenty more modern rooms are in two motel buildings on either side of the inn, and there's a charming cottage for two with a kingsize bed and a sun deck at the water's edge. Lee, who is constantly upgrading, has recovered the beds in the motel buildings in lovely fabrics. She did the stunning, free-flowing stenciling that graces many of the rooms and bathrooms as well as the diverse wreaths in each room. Breakfast is extra, but the roast-beef hash topped with two poached eggs and the tomato and herb omelet with whole-wheat toast are worth the $4.95 tab.

(207) 633-2544 or (800) 633-7645. Dinner nightly, 6 to 9; Sunday brunch, 8 to 11. Doubles, $60 to $110, EP; suites and cottage, $120 to $150, EP. Open mid-May to mid-October.

The Newcastle Inn, River Road, Newcastle 04553.

Rebecca and Howard Levitan arrived from Boston in 1995 to maintain the dining tradition launched here by Chris and Ted Sprague. The new owners have enhanced some of the accommodations, common areas and grounds at this fifteen-room inn and restaurant beside the Damariscotta River as well.

The Levitans opened the rear dining room onto a deck overlooking the broad lawns and lupine gardens sloping toward river's edge. Breakfast and cocktails may be served out here. They installed a small pub area with bright red walls and green chair rail off the rear parlor, redid the front living room with a more traditional look and hung a picture of lupines ("our logo") over the sofa, and outfitted a cheery side sun porch with wicker furniture and a wood stove.

More improvements were made to the guest accommodations upstairs. Two small rear bedrooms with a bath in between became the inn's premier suite. It has a kingsize bed, corner fireplace, sitting area and a jacuzzi for two. A room in which we once stayed became a second suite with sitting area, fireplace and jacuzzi. A fireplace and king bed were added to a third room and more changes were in the works. "We have lots of ideas," Rebecca advised. All rooms in the Federal-style Colonial house and annex have private baths and are furnished with a mix of antiques and New England crafts. Canopy beds, hand stenciling, floral wallpapers and wreaths on the doors are among their attributes.

The dining situation was put in the hands of Robert Teague, who had tired of running his Secret Garden restaurant in Camden. Here he and wife Sally concentrate their talents in the kitchen, he as chef and she as baker. The contemporary continental menu offerings are expanded and dinner seatings are staggered throughout the evening in two country-charming dining rooms. Candlelit tables are covered with quilt-look squares over white cloths. Complimentary hors d'oeuvres are offered when the full-service pub opens at 5:30.

Dinner is prix-fixe, available two ways: $30 for appetizer or soup, salad and entrée, or $37.50 for five courses (appetizer and soup plus dessert). Up to six choices are offered for each course. At our visit, appetizers included homemade ravioli stuffed with chicken, spinach and cheese, mussels in saffron cream, crab cakes with rémoulade sauce, and baked Pemaquid oysters sauced with basil and pesto. Among entrées were shrimp à la grecque, lobster bouillabaisse, duckling au cassis and filet mignon with crushed pepper-cognac sauce. Sally's desserts were a rich lemon tart, kahlua-chocolate fudge cake and creamy strawberry cheesecake.

Overnight guests enjoy a full breakfast of juice, fruit, pastry and a hot entrée. The last might be eggs benedict, cheese and vegetable strata or an acclaimed Santa Fe french toast made with crushed corn flakes. The fruit course becomes extra

Fresh raspberries and blueberries are breakfast treat at The Belmont.

hearty in winter: perhaps hot baked bananas (like bananas foster), poached pear or apple-cranberry crisp.

The Newcastle Inn is a stylish but relaxed place where guests like to read and contemplate the river from hammocks or Adirondack chairs on the lawn, watch the many birds in the feeder off the deck and enjoy the gardens that change with the seasons. The Levitans were adding more gardens and beautifying the adjacent property that had been a town fire pond.

(207) 563-5685 or (800) 832-8669. Fax (207) 563-6877. Dinner by reservation, Tuesday-Sunday 5:30 to 7:30; Thursday-Sunday in winter. Doubles, $95 to $175.

The Belmont, 6 Belmont Ave., Camden 04843.

An 1886 Victorian house on a residential side street, Camden's oldest inn was charmingly restored into a small and intimate, full-service village inn with six guest rooms and a dining room of distinction. Chef-owner Jerry Clare and partner John Mancarella upgraded the rooms and changed the pioneering nouvelle cuisine from French to American. The Belmont and its chef appeared in the Discovery Channel/PBS Great Chefs of the East series, the only Maine restaurant so honored.

The upstairs guest rooms, all now with private baths, are cheerfully decorated with floral wallpapers and a mix of traditional and new. Their light, sunny quality is in keeping with the yellow exterior. The two third-floor rooms we once occupied with our sons have been converted into one extra-large room. A suite has a separate sitting room. Fresh towels are supplied with turndown service at night.

Wicker rockers on the side porch invite dalliance with a cocktail from the small bar off the parlor. A comfortable parlor with a nifty window seat and small built-in benches beside the fireplace leads into the main dining room. It's serene and lovely with well-spaced tables dressed in white linens, floral china and tall flowers sprouting from clear glass vases. The adjacent sun porch that we like best contains a handful of pristine white tables and chairs.

Chef Clare's menu changes often. Some of it is inspired, as in an appetizer of grilled oysters in pancetta with two sauces (a triumph, as it should have been for $8.50) and a white gazpacho with delicious homemade croutons. Stir-fried mussels with black beans, ginger and lemongrass; grilled prawns with an eggplant timbale and a warm oriental duck salad are other starters.

We enjoyed grilled chicken with toasted polenta and a tri-pepper compote – accompanied by julienned carrots, creamed spinach and new potatoes – and a special of poached salmon with a citrus sauce, very good but a smallish portion. The half-dozen or so entrées are priced from $15 for spinach and ricotta torta with a tomato-basil coulis to $26 for an exotic lobster pad thai.

The sour-cream/blueberry cheesecake was sensational. Other desserts were a warm plum tart, chocolate dacquoise, kahlua-espresso ice cream and a trio of sorbets. The wine list is distinguished and priced accordingly, though there are plenty of affordable choices.

For continental breakfast, we loved the fresh raspberries and blueberries with cream and the flaky hot croissants with berry preserves, accompanied by a pot of strong, fragrant coffee.

(207) 236-8053 or (800) 238-8053. Dinner nightly except Monday, 6 to 9:30. Two-night minimum stay, including two breakfasts and one dinner: Doubles, $260 to $320; suite, $360. Single-night stay with dinner, spacing permitting, $165 to $195, suite $215. Open May-November.

The Youngtown Inn & Restaurant, Route 52 and Youngtown Road, Lincolnville 04849.

The restaurant here, which we enjoyed so much when it opened in the mid-1980s, reopened in 1992 after being abandoned for five years. The dining rooms are exceptionally pretty, the setting is rural and the food is French-inspired and getting better all the time, according to local consensus. It's run by Manuel Mercier, a chef who trained in Cannes, and his wife Mary Ann, a former Wall Street bond trader whom he met on a cruise ship. They live on the premises in the French style with their young family.

Two pristine dining rooms and a sun porch seat 60 at well-spaced tables covered with white linens, oil lamps and fresh flowers. Floral stenciling and oriental rugs add color.

Manuel says the cooking is "strictly traditional French, using American products." The short menu lists ten entrées ($12 to $19), of which the salmon fillet with potato crust, the grilled duck with madeira sauce and the rack of lamb with rosemary are house favorites. Contemporary accents show up in the grilled Atlantic swordfish with mango salsa and the grilled cornish hen with spiced tomato jam. Starters ($5 to $7) include a stellar lobster ravioli with fennel sauce and the local Ducktrap smoked salmon with smoked fish mousse. Dessert brings a crème brûlée that one reviewer said was the best he ever tasted, classic soufflés, cappuccino mousse cake and homemade sorbets in a meringue shell.

Four upstairs guest rooms have private baths and three have balconies. Two rooms with an adjoining bath, one with a queen bed and the other with twins, form a family suite. Each is decorated simply but attractively in country French style with colorful comforters and hand stenciling. A small second-floor common room with TV opens onto a deck with umbrella-covered tables above the front porte cochere.

A full breakfast, from homemade croissants to omelets or french toast stuffed with apples and walnuts, is served to overnight guests.

(207) 763-4290. Dinner nightly, 5:30 to 9; closed Monday in off-season. Doubles, $80 to $99.

Lodging

181 Main Street Bed & Breakfast, 181 Main St., Freeport 04032.

One of the more engaging of the B&Bs popping up around busy Freeport is this 1840 Greek Revival cape, opened in 1986 by Ed Hasset and David Cates in a residential area of substantial homes, many of which are being converted to guest houses. They offer seven upstairs guest rooms with private baths and queensize beds, nicely furnished but rather small, as rooms in some historic homes are apt to be. They compensate with extra common space – twin front parlors, one like a library with TV and the other containing quite a collection of ceramic animals in a sideboard and a long coffee table made of glass atop an old ship's rope bed.

Two dining rooms dressed with calico tablecloths and Hitchcock chairs are the settings for breakfasts to remember. When we were there, the feast began with a choice of juices and zucchini muffins. A fruit platter bearing slices of three kinds of melon, kiwi, pineapple, strawberries and cherries followed the main dish, cheese strata with English muffins and bacon. The day before produced apple-walnut coffee cake and belgian waffles with baked apple and sausage.

A real bonus here is a secluded rear swimming pool, surrounded by flowers, blessedly removed from the hubbub of the Freeport shops a couple of blocks away. *(207) 865-1226 or (800) 235-9750. Doubles, $85 to $100.*

Five Gables Inn, Murray Hill Road, Box 335, East Boothbay 04544.

Perched on a hillside overlooking Linekin Bay, this five-gabled establishment dates back more than 125 years and was the last remaining summer hotel in the area. It was love at first sight for peripatetic Mike and De Kennedy, who had just concluded a "mid-life break" in which they crewed on a yacht in French Polynesia and backpacked for six months from Bali to Nepal.

Previous owners had renovated the old Forest House into their dream B&B by the water. The Kennedys had only to add their personal touches and experiences, which they have in abundance. Mike, a graduate of the Culinary Institute of America when it was in New Haven, has worked his way around much of the world. He and De moved to Maine from Atlanta, where he renovated old homes, performed in TV commercials and gave historic tours. De, an artist, comes from an old southern family and prepped for innkeeping by organizing house parties at her family's ante-bellum retreat in the Georgia hills.

Here they entertain guests in fifteen rooms on three floors, all with a water view. All have modern baths and queensize beds (one kingsize), and five have working fireplaces. Lace curtains and quilts color-coordinated to De's artistic accents and the pictures on the walls enhance the decor, all of which is light, airy and new. De hand-crocheted the afghans that grace many of the rooms.

Mike puts his cooking background to the test at multi-course breakfasts, served in a spacious common room appointed with wing chairs and bouquets of fresh flowers. His repertoire lasts for two weeks, a daily procession of, say, zucchini-walnut pancakes, quiche lorraine, blueberry french toast or basil-tomato frittata. Potatoes anna, fried tomatoes, blueberry crisp and pear in puff pastry might accompany, along with fresh-ground Columbian coffee.

De offers afternoon tea in the English manner, served with chocolate-chip cookies and poppyseed or banana bread and taken on the wraparound veranda, where a hammock and abundant sitting areas take in the view of the bay. Port, sherries and madeiras are put out on the sideboard in the evening.

(207) 633-4551 or (800) 451-5048. Doubles, $90 to $160. Open mid-May through October.

Norumbega, 61 High St., Camden 04843.

Ensconced in one of the finest "castles" along the Maine coast is this elegant B&B with great style and a combination lock on the front door to deter curious passersby.

The cobblestone and slate-roofed mansion, built in 1886 for the inventor of the duplex system of telegraphy, was for a few years the summer home of journalist Hodding Carter. The hillside property was acquired in 1987 by Murray Keatinge, a Californian who summers in Camden.

Inside are endlessly fascinating public rooms (the woodwork alone is priceless), nine large bedrooms and three suites, all with private baths, sitting areas and telephones and some with TVs. The ones in back have breathtaking views of Penobscot Bay. Most have fireplaces and canopy beds, all of them kingsize. The ultimate is the penthouse suite, a bit of a climb up a spiral staircase from the third floor. It offers a kingsize bed, a regal bath with pillows around a circular ebony tub big enough for two, a wet bar, a sitting room in pink and green, and a see-through, three-sided fireplace, plus a little porch with deck chairs and a fabulous water view.

Guests have the run of the parlors and a small library, an intimate retreat for two beside a fireplace on the landing of the ornate staircase, as well as flower-laden rear porches and balconies on all three floors overlooking expansive lawns and the bay.

Soup, cookies, mineral water and soft drinks are offered in the afternoon, and wine and hors d'oeuvres in the early evening – enough food that some guests pass up going out to dinner. But breakfast is the day's highlight. Served at a long table in the formal dining room or at a round glass table beside the telescope in the conservatory, it is a feast of juices and fruits, all kinds of breads and muffins, and, when we stayed, the best french toast ever, topped with a dollop of sherbet and sliced oranges. Eggs florentine or benedict, vegetable omelets, crêpes with an almond filling and peach topping, and ginger-apple pancakes are other favorites.

Amazingly, Norumbega is not a whit pretentious, thanks partly to Murray's ebullient personality. He commutes back and forth to California to run his businesses there, but spends most of the summer and fall here helping his staff. Although proud of "what we've accomplished in nine years" (Glamour magazine called it one of America's top 25 inns), Murray says he believes in "keeping it informal. Guests appreciate the homey, country atmosphere." They often go into the kitchen and help the cook; in return, the refrigerator always contains bread pudding to which guests may help themselves.

(207) 236-4646. Fax (207) 236-0824. Doubles, $195 to $325; suites, $310 to $450.

Windward House, 6 High St., Camden 04843.

Bountiful breakfasts and beautiful gardens await guests at this cool blue 1854 Greek Revival, a stylish B&B being upgraded by new owners Tim and Sandy La Plante from Ontario. The food background of the couple, who owned food stores in Ottawa, shows. They prepare exotic breakfasts, serve afternoon tea with cookies and dessert squares, offer complimentary port and sherry, and put chocolate mint truffles in every room.

Breakfast is served in formal dining room at Norumbega.

Upstairs are five guest rooms, each with queensize bed and private bath, and a suite with sitting room and a new clawfoot tub in the enlarged bathroom. The most choice accommodations are more recent, and reflect the La Plantes' determination to attract the winter trade. In the rear Garden Room, a favorite of honeymooners, light pours through a skylit cathedral ceiling to reveal a pink and green space with a Maine maple cannonball bed and a Vermont Castings stove. The La Plantes consider the newest Carriage Room their signature: a ground-floor space in the front carriage section of an old barn with pine-board floors, two wing chairs in front of the gas stove and a queen canopy bed with Ralph Lauren sheets and duvet. The oversize bathroom has a clawfoot soaking tub and a corner shower.

Breakfast is served at individual tables in the elegant dining room where abundant plants, a gleaming silver service, lace curtains and a blue patterned rug catch the eye. Sandy does the baking and Tim the entrées. We were mighty impressed with a bowl of fresh strawberries and blueberries in cream, the raspberry-cream cheese coffee cake and the peaches-and-cream french toast with bacon. Orange-yogurt pancakes, ham and cheese strata, frittatas and eggs olé with homemade salsa are other treats.

Guests gather in a nicely furnished parlor where the fireplace seems to be ablaze morning and night, a library where tea and coffee are available all day, a cozy new game room stocked with puzzles and board games, and a rear deck, where Tim likes to serve breakfast on nice days. The deck looks onto a long back yard and an English garden, a showplace of annuals, perennials and herbs, carefully planned and tended for color all season long.

(207) 236-9656. Fax (207) 230-0433. Doubles, $100 to $170.

A Little Dream, 66 High St., Camden 04843.

Piles of thank-you notes on the table at the entry, books of love letters and poems, an abundance of lace and a welcoming lemonade, served in a tall glass

Windward House is decked out in Christmas finery.

with a sprig of mint plus blueberries and strawberries, signify that this charming place is special. It's a little dream for Joanne Fontana and her husband, Billy, a sculptor and handyman-remodeler. From the looks of all the dolls and teddybears, the Fontanas must have brought their entire inventory with them when they sold their toy stores in New York City and Boston. Joanne has decorated and accessorized their turreted Victorian house with great flair.

She pampers guests in a parlor furnished in wicker and chintz, an elaborate dining room beside a conservatory and a side porch. Three spacious bedrooms in the house are decorated to the hilt with Victorian clothing, lace, ribbons and at least eight pillows on each bed. All have private baths, as do two more in a rear carriage house with wet bars and small refrigerators. Always perfecting, Joanne was planning to redo the carriage house in 1997 as a replica in miniature of the main house.

Breakfasts, served on lace-clothed tables topped with floral mats and heavy silver, are gala here. Guests choose from a fancy menu placed in their rooms the night before The choice might involve lemon-ricotta soufflé pancakes with fresh raspberry sauce, banana-pecan waffles with maple country sausage, or three kinds of omelets: smoked salmon, apple-cheddar and ham-swiss. The coffee is breakfast blend or chocolate-raspberry or hazelnut. There's also a choice among four teas. Orange or cranberry juice, fresh fruit and muffin of the day come with.

(207) 236-8742. Doubles, $100 to $140.

The Inn at Sunrise Point, Box 1344, Camden 04843.

This is the inn of inn reviewer Jerry Levitin's dreams. The California travel writer, who took over Norman Simpson's *Country Inns & Back Roads* guidebooks and ruffled the feathers of a few longtime innkeepers along the way, opened his own B&B in 1992 on four forested acres at the foot of a dirt road leading from Route 1 to Penobscot Bay in Lincolnville.

"I built what I'd like to stay at," says Jerry with characteristic candor. The result is mixed —contemporary and Californian in style, but small and pricey for some New England tastes. Jerry offers three rooms in the main house plus four cottages. The Winslow Homer Cottage that we occupied right beside the water featured a kingsize bed, a fireplace and an enormous bathroom with a jacuzzi for two and a separate shower. It was luxurious indeed, but there was nowhere to stash luggage other than in the bathroom, and the waterfront deck was so narrow as to be useless (the front porch of the main house compensated). Though small, the three upstairs rooms have fireplaces and music systems, queensize beds, swivel upholstered or wicker chairs in front of the window, built-in desks and armoires holding TVs and VCRs. The two newest cottages possess queensize beds and the other inn amenities, and one has a kitchenette. All have been upgraded with paintings, deck chairs and accessories to "make the rooms more warm and homey," in the words of an innkeeper.

Jerry or his innkeeper greet arriving guests in the main inn with tea, coffee, wine and hot and cold appetizers, which are substantial enough that some forego dinner. The main floor offers a wonderful living/dining room that's mostly windows onto Penobscot Bay, an English hunting-style library with a fireplace and a small conservatory for tête-à-tête breakfasts. We feasted here on fruit, pecan coffeecake, a terrific frittata with basil, bay shrimp and jack cheese, potatoes dusted with cayenne, crisp bacon and hazelnut coffee.

Upon departure, we found a card under our windshield: "Our porter has cleaned your windscreen to allow you to get a clear picture of our Penobscot Bay."

(207) 236-7716 or (800) 435-6278. Fax (207) 236-0820. Doubles, $160 to $205; cottages, $250 and $325. Open mid-May through October.

Gourmet Treats

The treats in this area begin at **Clayton's,** 106 Main St., Yarmouth, a must stop right off Route 1. Starting as a gourmet market affiliated with Treat's in Wiscasset (see below), Martha and David Clayton made good use of their space in the old Masonic Hall, adding a coffee bar in the center and a cafe for lunch on the stage. The latter serves good sandwiches, salads and vegetarian items in the $5 range from 11 to 6 in summer. We still think of Clayton's for all its copper pots, cheeses, specialty foods, baked goods and even a canoe stocked with bargain wines.

In Freeport, home of outlets to serve almost every interest, a large **Ben & Jerry's Ice Cream** stand is set up right beside L.L. Bean. All the flavors of one of Vermont's best-known exporters are available. A small cone at $2.25 and a large cone at $3.45 are not exactly outlet prices, however.

And you thought **L.L. Bean Co.** was just for great sportswear and equipment. This ever-changing and expanding emporium has a gourmet food shop with Maine-made and New England mail-order products, including its own line of raspberry jams, bittersweet fudge sauce, maple syrup and the like. From saltwater taffy and dandelion greens to Bean's-blend coffee beans, this place has it – or will soon.

If you tire of the Freeport outlet scene, head for South Freeport Harbor wharf and the **Harraseeket Lunch & Lobster Co.** This is what coastal Maine is supposed to look like, a lobster pound by a working dock. While it used to be little known, at our last visit there was no place to park and the lineup stretched a long way from the outside service window, where we like to pick up our food and then eat at a picnic table on the dock (there's a small dining room as well). The owners are noted for their basket dinners, priced from $4.75 for clam cakes to $11.25 for fried clams. Other favorites are a fishwich, clamburger royale and lobster roll ($9.95). Lobsters can be packed for travel.

Two worthy seasonal places are found on the peninsula from Brunswick out to

Bailey Island. Located next to the rare cribstone bridge onto Bailey Island, **Orr's Island Chowder & Coffee Co.** is known for its all-natural seafood chowder, a thick and ultra creamy brew of haddock, scallops, clams and shrimp for $3.50 a bowl. Penny Michaud also offers lobster rolls ($6.50), vegetarian soups, pies and homemade muffins daily from 11 to 6. The last go well with the Caravali coffees from Seattle. Across the bridge, **The Blueberry Pancake** in what passes for downtown Bailey Island is a "breakfast restaurant" owned by Aleesa Baker Coffin, who is busy with lunch and dinner at her Great Impasta restaurant in Brunswick. We stopped in for a dynamite salsa and sausage omelet ($4.95) and a fancy crêpe stuffed with ricotta, eggs, artichoke hearts and scallions, served with home fries, quite a plateful for $5.95. Breakfast daily, 7:30 to 11, weekends to noon.

Native produce, specialty foods, wine, candies, pâtés, smoked salmon and croissants abound at **Weatherbird,** a gourmet food store and gift shop in a sprawl of a building off Main Street in downtown Damariscotta. There are a few tables out front upon which to partake.

You'll find at least 42 flavors at **Round Top Ice Cream,** Business Route 1, Damariscotta. This is the original home of the ice cream favored by restaurants throughout the region, an unpretentious little spot on the farm where it began in 1924. The choices range from cappuccino to watermelon, from ginger to raspberry. Cones come in three sizes, priced from about $1 to $2. You also can get a banana split for about $3.50.

"Color is our passion," say Chris and Richard Hilton of **Edgecomb Potters,** Route 27, Edgecomb. And colorful is their extraordinary glazed porcelain in various hues, shown inside and out at this must-stop place on the road into Boothbay Harbor (there are also branches in Boothbay and Freeport). They have all kinds of pottery for kitchen and dining room, from garlic cellars and pâté dishes to snack trays and soup tureens, as well as decorative accessories.

Specialty foods, cookware, kitchen gadgets and fine pottery are among the wares at the rambling **Village Store,** part of the suave House of Logan enterprise in Boothbay Harbor.

Toward Rockland, the **School House Farm** produce stand, a few miles west of Thomaston on Route 1, displays baskets of fresh vegetables, local cheeses and eggs, jams and jellies, homemade breads, muffins and blueberry pies, as well as the lovely watercolors of flowers and local landscapes by owner Debbie Beckwith, whose gallery may be visited next door.

Let the Treats Begin

In Wiscasset, English cheeses from a Covent Garden firm are one of the strengths of **Treats,** a special store on a prime corner of Main Street. Owner Paul Mrozinski offered a taste of cashel blue and we had to buy some, it was so buttery and delicious. We also had to buy one of the "bodacious breads" that are made in Waldeboro, a crusty olive loaf (one of the others was rosemary and hazelnut). Paul describes the flavors of his cheeses much the way he distinguishes among his fine wines. Across the street at the Marston House, Paul and his wife Sharon rent two B&B rooms with private baths in the carriage house behind their home, which is also an antiques shop. The $75 tab gets you a queensize bed, fireplace and a hearty breakfast.

In Rockland, the **Wine-O-Mat** at 27 Oak St. stocks 450 labels, European beers, cheeses and accessories. Owner Peg Laurita also offers upscale coffees, pastries and a deli case with prepared foods to go.

The Brown Bag at 606 Main St., Rockland, is everyone's favorite casual spot for breakfast, lunch, supper or a snack. The owners, four sisters, started with a bakery and deli in the middle and expanded into a restaurant on one side and a gourmet food shop on the other. The extensive menu lists healthful selections at prices from yesteryear. Stop here for an oversize blueberry muffin (85 cents), a lentilburger on a whole-wheat roll, a crab and cheddar melt, a loaf of basil bread or a slice of apple-raspberry pie ($1.95).

A striking, plum-colored building with lavender trim houses **Miss Plum's Parlour** along Route 1 in Rockport. It's famous for its ice creams and yogurts, served at a takeout window and available in changing flavors from red raspberry chip to toffee bar crunch. Sundaes, frappes, root-beer floats, lime rickeys, banana splits and more may be taken to lavender-colored picnic tables at the side. Owners Elaine and Bill Pellechia added a stylish little restaurant and a clever menu for inside dining. Come for a heart-healthy breakfast, a midday plum dog (frankfurter with chili, cheese, onion, salsa and sour cream, $4.75) or a crabmeat cobb salad, fried clams, or meatloaf and gravy for a light dinner anytime.

In Camden, Maine beers and ales are the rage at **Sea Dog Brewing Co.,** which emerged no-expense-spared in 1993 in one of the former Knox Mill buildings at 43 Mechanic St. Tours of the downstairs brewery are given daily at 11 and 4 in summer and there's a brewtique for bar ware and apparel. Most visitors gravitate to the fancy tavern – a mix of booths, beams, oriental runners and stone walls that's too atmospheric for words. The splashy waterfall outside the soaring windows adds to the effect. The brewery's Penobscot Maine lager, Windjammer Maine ale and Owl's Head light are featured, along with a variety of snacks and sandwiches ($4.95 to $8.95). More substantial fare is available at night.

For casual seafood, head for **Lobster Stu's** on Sharp's Wharf in Camden. The food is higher quality than at some of the better-known restaurants nearby, and you can enjoy it at picnic tables on the dock where windjammers come and go. Stu Brady's lobster rolls and lobster stu are each $9.95; his lobster dinners, $9.95 to $12.95.

Our favorite shop among many in Camden is **Lily, Lupine & Fern,** lately relocated to larger quarters at 37-39 Bay View St. Its traditional flowers are augmented with cheeses, gourmet foods and a huge selection of wines and microbrewery beers. At our visit, owners Gary and Bunni Anderson were about to add a wine and espresso cafe.

Lobster by the Shore

One of the all-time great places to eat lobster has to be the secluded **Waterman's Beach Lobster,** Waterman's Beach Road, off Route 73 near Spruce Head in South Thomaston. Place your order for a lobster roll, lobster stew or a one-pound lobster dinner (all $7.95), or splurge on the lobster-clam combo with sides of coleslaw and corn ($13.95). Take it to one of the picnic tables on an open deck right beside the water and enjoy. No buildings are in sight to mar the view. Owner Ann Cousens also bakes great blueberry, rhubarb and pecan pies. Open daily in summer, 11 to 7. BYOB.

Down East Maine
Lobster, Plus

We know, we know.

You're going Down East on vacation and you can't wait to clamp your teeth around a shiny red lobster. In fact, you can hardly think of anything else. Oh, maybe some fried clams or a bucket of steamers, but lobster is what you're really after.

So you'll stand in line to get into some dive for the $8.95 lobster special. You'll suck out the feelers and wrestle with the claws of your one-and-one-quarter-pound (if you're lucky) crustacean. You'll end up with about three ounces of lobster meat, debris all over your clothes and hands that reek for two days.

And you'll probably gush, "That was the *best* lobster I've ever had!"

Well, friends, we're here to tell you that there is life after lobster in Maine. A lot of fine, creative cooking is going on in the Pine Tree State, and in the last decade a number of excellent restaurants have emerged Down East along the coast, many of them with young and innovative chefs.

Also available are a number of suave inns and bed-and-breakfast places, which are giving visitors an alternative to the traditional cabins, campgrounds and motels that abound along the coast.

And, sign of the times, the coffee craze has come to Maine. On our latest trip we were surprised by the Coffee Express Drive-Thru at the Maine Coast Mall in Ellsworth.

In this final chapter, we meander our way along the coast, peninsulas and islands, hitting the high spots from East Penobscot Bay and Deer Isle to Bar Harbor, Acadia National Park and the Schoodic Peninsula – the epitome of Down East Maine.

Dining

The Best of the Best

Firepond, Main Street, Blue Hill.

Of all the restaurants we know, Firepond lingers in the memory as one of the most romantic – that is, if you can snag a table downstairs on the screened porch, beside a trickling stream. Chef-owner Craig Rodenhiser, who bought the place in 1994 after serving as assistant chef for a couple of years, has undertaken a major renovation and expansion of the former mill complex. He opened two new dining rooms on the main floor, one of them in a former gourmet shop, where shelves full of antique books line the walls and oriental carpets dot the original wood floors. French doors look onto a new outdoor dining terrace facing Main Street.

Even with all the changes, we're still partial to that great porch, a fixture for dinner almost every summer as far back as we can recall. The setting is enchanting, with water rippling down the stream into the tidal pool below and spotlights highlighting the shining rocks.

Drinks here are generous, and we enjoyed ours with a selection of pâtés ($8.95) that included pork, chicken liver and vegetable, garnished by cornichons – plenty for two, along with crusty French bread. Other of Craig's starters include an assortment of salads, vegetable caviars and pickled vegetables he calls a vegetarian

Porch at Firepond provides enchanting dinner setting beside trickling stream.

zakuska, raviolis stuffed with smoked salmon and gruyère cheese, brandied escargots in puff pastry, caesar salad prepared tableside and soup du jour, perhaps gazpacho or brandy-mushroom.

Among main courses ($15.95 to $21.95), you'll likely find things like scallops with leeks, medallions of veal with sundried tomatoes, grilled pork chops with an apple-rosemary demi- glace, roast Long Island duckling with raspberry-chambord sauce, and varying treatments of the lamb specialty, perhaps sliced with wild mushrooms in a rich brandy sauce or a New Zealand rack marinated in burgundy wine. At recent visits we've enjoyed a fabulous fettuccine with crabmeat and pinenuts, a zesty chicken with walnuts in plum sauce and ginger, and halibut espagnole, topped with mussels and a saffron beurre blanc.

Desserts could be a terrific chocolate truffle dacquoise, lemon-raspberry cheesecake, raspberry decadence, and Bailey's chocolate mousse. We've found the ginger ice cream to be a refreshing finish after the hearty main dishes, and the Jamaican coffee with Irish whiskey and tia maria a fitting flourish to a meal of intense flavors in a magical setting.

(207) 374-9970. Dinner nightly, 5 to 9:30, fewer nights after Columbus Day. Closed January to early May.

Jonathan's, Main Street, Blue Hill.

Innovative cuisine, an award-winning wine list and then a cookbook. These are the claims to fame of Jonathan Chase, owner of this informal restaurant now well into its second decade. The cookbook, *Saltwater Seasonings,* written in collaboration with his sister, Sarah Leah Chase, the Nantucket caterer and cookbook author, was much in evidence in kitchen stores across Maine after receiving accolades from Down East magazine as "quite possibly Maine's best regional cookbook in fifty years."

The book incorporates some of the menus that have made Jonathan's a culinary star. Take, for example, some of his recent additions to an already interesting menu: an appetizer of baja fish taco with fresh tomato salsa and minted yogurt, and entrées of lobster "fried over cold" with buttermilk biscuits and braised lamb shank simmered with Bass ale, bourbon and maple barbecue sauce.

For starters, we've enjoyed his crostini with roasted elephant garlic and chèvre, served with ripe tomatoes, and a remarkable salad of smoked mussels with goat cheese and pinenuts. Also good are the soups, a choice of cold minted pea or hot cauliflower and blue cheese at one visit. Among entrées ($15.95 to $19.95), Arizona skirt steak came with a dynamite salsa of tomatoes, chile peppers, garlic and tequila, while the rabbit braised with smoked bacon, sundried tomatoes, rosemary and garlic was served with carrots and red-skin potatoes. Risotto "via veneto" combining shellfish with imported cheeses and a pasta dish blending sautéed mahogany clams and hot Italian sausage with kale, tomatoes and onions reflected the owner's tour of Tuscany.

Cantaloupe sorbet with macaroons and frangelico cheesecake are among the sweet endings. Honored by Wine Spectator, the wine list is exceptional and pleasantly priced – when did you last enjoy a Firestone merlot for under $20?

Dining is in the restaurant's original front section, done up in nautical blue with captain's chairs, skylights and alcove windows filled with plants, or in an expansive rear addition with bar and dining area. Its bow windows, pitched ceilings and well-spaced tables provide an airy contrast to the front's dark and intimate quarters.

(207) 374-5226. Dinner nightly, 5 to 9. Closed Monday and Tuesday in winter.

George's, 7 Stephens Lane, Bar Harbor.

This hard-to-find restaurant in a little southern-style house behind the First National Bank has long offered some of the most creative food on Mount Desert Island. Run with a Greek accent by retired local high-school history teacher George Demas, it's a summery place, lately gone glamorous. George is still in the kitchen, never taking a night off, we're told.

The table appointments are stylish and the track lights are draped with white cloths in the piano bar, to which we were assigned at our latest visit. The menu is unusual in that all appetizers are $8; all grazers, $12, and all entrées $23. You can graze or order a prix-fixe meal (appetizer, main course and dessert) for $32. The award-winning wine list is also unusual, in that entries are categorized under full-bodied, medium and light. Precious few are priced in the teens and low twenties.

Four cheese crisps were served as we sat down for our most recent dinner, and then we waited and waited – at least an hour and a half – until our entrées arrived. An appetizer of salmon quesadilla (great tastes, served on an unusual plate with a fish head and tail on either side) and a salad dressed with George's special vinaigrette and feta helped stave off hunger. The wait was worth it for a special of elk medallions; not so for a lamb dish that was overdone, or for a paltry medley of strawberry, pear and orange-passionfruit sorbets. The waiter even mixed up our wine order and charged us for an appetizer we never ordered. Ours must have been an off night, since the local consensus was that George's had never been better.

At an earlier dinner, hot crusty French bread and the best Greek salads ever preceded the entrées: distinctive smoked scallops on fettuccine and a special of shrimp on a fresh tomato sauce with feta cheese, rice pilaf and New Zealand spinach with orange juice and orange zest.

The appetizers remain assertive (perhaps kasseri cheese broiled with garlic, baked phyllo shells with lamb and tzatziki, seared tuna loin with pickled ginger and wasabi), and the "grazers" rich (seared foie gras with fruit glaze, eggplant cockle with orange salsa and sour cream). Desserts are usually first-rate, from chilled champagne sabayon with figs to fresh peach crème brûlée and, one night, an irresistible fresh blueberry and peach meringue.

(207) 288-4505. Dinner nightly, 5:30 to 11. Open mid-June through October.

The Porcupine Grill, 123 Cottage St., Bar Harbor.

Owner Tom Marinke's antiques business provided the furnishings and impetus for this trendy grill. It takes its name from the nearby Porcupine Islands and has given George's competition for top honors in town.

"Everything is real," says Tom, showing the assorted antique oak drop-leaf tables and Chippendale chairs, the rugs on the honey-colored wood floors, the Villeroy & Boch china, and different fresh flowers scattered about the dining areas on two floors. Also, "everything's homemade with Maine ingredients where possible."

Antique bulls-eye glass dividers and period sconces help create a cafe atmosphere in the main-floor bar area, where many like to sip champagne cocktails pairing French sparkling and Maine raspberry wines or Porcupine punch (rum and fruit juices) before snacking on New England cheddar and black-bean fritters with a creamy garlic and herb dipping sauce, salmon cakes with minted cucumber vinaigrette and pickled ginger, or a terrine of shiitake mushrooms, crabmeat and cheese with a roasted tomato and sherry sauce, the mushrooms grown by Tom.

We prefer the quieter upstairs, where on a busy night we lucked into a private dining room for two. Our appetizers, smoked salmon and jonnycakes with caviar and sour cream and a signature caesar salad topped with fried shrimp ($7.95), lived up to advance billing. Among entrées ($16.95 to $19.95), we were smitten with the grilled chicken with ginger-peach chutney and the sautéed shrimp and peas in a light garlic-cream sauce over fresh egg noodles. Other possibilities might be grilled Maine salmon with a Caribbean marinade and mango and papaya salsa, a lightly smoked roasted duck breast served over a warm wild rice and walnut salad, pork tenderloin with plum chutney, and grilled porterhouse steak with smoked shiitake mushrooms.

A $17 McDowell fumé blanc accompanied our meal, chosen from a well-selected, rather expensive wine list augmented by "celebration wines." Desserts included a wonderful pear and rhubarb crisp with homemade ice cream, cantaloupe sorbet, white chocolate cheesecake with blueberry sauce and coconut-strawberry shortcake.

(207) 288-3884. Dinner nightly from 6, June-October; off-season, Friday-Sunday from 6.

The Burning Tree, Route 3, Otter Creek.

Everybody's list of culinary havens includes this simple restaurant in a rural setting south of Bar Harbor. There are tables on the long front porch, one section of which is a waiting area. Beyond are two small dining rooms, cheerfully outfitted in pinks and blues, their linened tables topped with tall, blue-edged water glasses. Local art and colorful paintings adorn the walls.

Such is the summer-cottage setting for what chef-owners Allison Martin and Elmer Beal Jr. call "gourmet seafood" with a vegetarian sideline. The only meat dishes are a couple of versions of chicken: smoked with a marjoram and spinach pesto, and sautéed with basil and balsamic cream. But it's seafood that most customers are after – basic like baked cod with black bean sauce and lofty as in grilled swordfish with watercress-lime sauce. Vegetarians relish such treats as swiss chard, potato and artichoke pie and pan-fried polenta with pigeon peas, hominy, ceci beans, sweet peppers and a tomato-ginger sauce. Prices are down to earth: $4.50 to $6.50 for most appetizers, $12.50 to $17.50 for entrées.

Our party was impressed with starters of mussels with mustard sauce, grilled scallops and an excellent vegetarian sushi. The cioppino for $13 was so highly rated that two of us ordered it. The others chose baked monkfish with clams and artichokes on saffron orzo and the cajun crab and lobster au gratin, a fixture on the blackboard menu. The garden out back provides vegetables and herbs, and the owners use organically grown produce whenever possible. Entrées come with fresh vegetables (carrots and snow peas, at our visit) and a choice of garlicky potatoes or three-grain rice salad in a lemon vinaigrette.

Desserts are to groan over: perhaps nectarine mousse cake, Ukranian poppyseed cake, chocolate-orange cheesecake or fresh strawberry pie. A good wine list, chosen with as much care as the menu, is priced mostly in the teens.

(207) 288-9331. Dinner nightly except Tuesday, 5 to 10. Open June to mid-October.

Redfield's, Main Street, Northeast Harbor.

The sign on the door is apt to say "Thank You – Full" at this, the hottest dining ticket on Mount Desert Island. Scott and Maureen Redfield's trendy restaurant, located next to family's Redfield Artisans showroom and beneath their personal quarters, would be quite at home on Nantucket, although the prices and lack of pretensions are refreshingly Down East.

Decor in two small dining rooms is simple yet sophisticated. Tiny lamps hanging from long cords over most tables illuminate some large, summery, impressionist-style paintings and make the rooms rather too bright for our tastes. But they do highlight the food, which is worth the spotlight. We staved off hunger with a basket of Maureen's fabulous foccacia topped with tomatoes and goat cheese, exquisite house salads and a shared appetizer of venison carpaccio as we nursed the house La Veille Ferme wine. Lemon sorbet in a lotus dish prepared the palate for the main dishes: sliced breast of duck with fresh chutney and marinated loin of lamb with goat cheese and black olives, both superb. Strawberry sorbet and a chocolate-almond mint tart ended a memorable meal.

Scott, who used to cook at Cranberry Lodge of Asticou, changes his menus frequently. Sesame-seared tuna with wasabi scented coconut-ginger compote, grilled swordfish with gingered tomato-tamari sauce, and roast quail with westphalian ham and mushroom stuffing were on the docket for $17.95 to $22.95 at our latest visit. Starters included chicken, lime and coconut soup; house-smoked mussels with corn pudding and tomato mint compote, and stilton soufflé with shiitake, portobello and crimini mushrooms. Among desserts were almond frangipane with blueberry-ginger sauce and a chocolate genoise and almond mousse torte.

(207) 276-5283. Dinner, Monday-Saturday 6:30 to 8:30; weekends only in off-season.

The Bistro at Seal Harbor, Route 3, Seal Harbor.

They have only eight tables and a kitchen not much bigger than that in a studio apartment, and they grow their own herbs in wine casks on the back porch. Such is the homespun endeavor of Donna Fulton and Terri Clements, who teamed up in

Tiny hanging lamps illuminate meals and artworks at Redfield's.

1993 to open a bistro in the heart of old-money Seal Harbor. Formerly at the late, lamented Fin Back in Bar Harbor, they offer a short and understated menu (somewhat pricey for the area) in a charming setting.

The storefront room is pristine with tables topped with white napkins, votive candles, fresh flowers and white china. Behind is a small service bar and afore-mentioned kitchen, snug with ten-burner stove. Donna handles the cooking chores, preparing half a dozen main courses ($16 to $21) like grilled salmon with pasta in garlic-basil cream, roasted swordfish with white beans and preserved lemon, sautéed pork tenderloin with prune sauce and spice-rubbed loin lamb chops. The Bistro salad comes with feta, apples and spiced pecans. Other appetizers range from polenta with marinara, gorgonzola and basil to smoked salmon with ginger-scallion pancake. Soup might be lobster with jalapeño peppers and corn. Desserts include crème brûlée, seasonal tarts and pies, plus intense ice creams (coffee-almond-praline or ginger) and orange-buttermilk sorbet served with biscotti. A well-chosen, all-domestic wine list is priced mostly in the twenties.

This is obviously a pure place, where the owners make everything from scratch. They even pick their own berries for the blueberry pie and grate their own vanilla beans for the extract . A local blacksmith crafted the striking wine-glass rack that hangs over the copper bar. Donna and Terri made the interesting table pottery during their winter off-season in Arizona.

(207) 276-3299. Dinner, Tuesday-Sunday from 6. Open Memorial Day to October.

More Dining Choices

The Landing, Steamboat Wharf Road, South Brooksville.

The schooners and windjammers sailing into the harbor provide a colorful back-drop for the food of new Swiss owners and their young chef. Kurt and Verena

Stoll took over in 1996 the second-story waterfront restaurant, which has had a succession of operators over the years. They installed former area resident Forrest Lyman, a New England Culinary Institute grad, as chef and were undertaking renovations for 1997. The setting is lovely, given the water views and two serene, candlelit dining rooms. On the walls, paintings by Joy Biddle, whose gallery lies below, are a joy to look at.

The dinner menu changes daily. The best value is the nightly pre-fixe dinner ($26). One Saturday it brought a sampling of both soups (tomato-basil and potato-leek with roasted garlic and sage), mixed grill of stuffed quail, chorizo and foccacia, a mesclun salad with fresh herbs, plank-roasted salmon with wilted spinach, crispy leeks and dried cranberry salsa, and a summer fruit gratin.

Or you can order à la carte. Appetizers ($4.25 to $5.50) could be crab cake with roasted corn, baby greens and saffron aioli or pistachio-crusted chèvre with mixed greens and roasted peppers. Main courses ($14.25 to $21) range from pan-roasted breast of chicken with a wild rice pancake to rack of Australian lamb with garlic mashed potatoes, tobacco onions and red pepper coulis or grilled veal chop with fried polenta, red-chile crème fraîche and blackberry jus. The dessert pastries change daily as well.

There's a pleasant bar and cocktail lounge at one side of the restaurant. Below is the seasonal **Buck's Harbor Cafe,** also run by the Stolls, offering lunch and snacks taken at picnic tables overlooking the idyllic harbor.

(207) 326-8483. Dinner, Tuesday-Sunday from 5. Open Memorial Day to Oct. 20.

Jordan Pond House, Park Loop Road, Acadia National Park.

Tea on the lawn is a Bar Harbor tradition at this landmark with an incomparable setting in the national park. Green lawns sloping down to Jordan Pond and the Bubbles mountains in the background are the backdrop for a steady stream of visitors who start arriving at 2:30 for tea (two popovers with butter and strawberry preserves, $5.50) and, more recently, cappuccino or espresso and popovers ($6.50).

The dinner menu is fairly standard, with the predictable Maine salmon, baked haddock, prime rib, surf and turf, and steamed lobster in the $11 to $18 range. If you're hungry, start with a smoked seafood sampler ($6.75). Flickering candles, flowers and the sunset over pond and mountains create an unforgettable setting.

For lunch, we like to sit outside on the "porch," which is more like a covered terrace. The last time we enjoyed a fine seafood pasta and a curried chicken salad, garnished with red grapes and orange slices, and shared a popover – good but a bit steep at $2.25, given that it was hollow. There's a full bar, and the large gift shop (one of several Acadia Shops on the island) is fun to browse in.

(207) 276-3316. Lunch, 11:30 to 2:30; tea on the lawn, 2:30 to 5:30; dinner, 5:30 to 8 or 9. Open mid-May to mid-October.

Ocean Wood Gallery & Restaurant, Birch Harbor.

Sitting on the porch of this summery restaurant, overlooking colorful gardens bordering a lovely cove, is to us the epitome of the Maine summer experience. A couple of miles from Winter Harbor on the Schoodic Peninsula, the charming little house doubles as a gallery for the intricate baskets and carvings of the natives of La Palma, a village in the Panamian rain forest, which owner Jim Brunton came to know when he was in the Peace Corps. The small carvings are made from the cocabola nut. All the profits from sales go to the craftspeople.

Diners on porch at Ocean Wood Gallery feast on view of flowers and water as well as good food.

The restaurant section on a wraparound porch is simple, with white tables, chairs and linens, fresh flowers in vases and huge windows so one can savor the view. We thought the panacea soup (garlic and ginger broth with mushrooms, carrots and chicken) sounded good, but decided instead on the curried chicken salad that incorporated candied ginger and cashews and was delicious (although someone had used rather a heavy hand with the curry powder) and the roast beef sandwich on foccacia. The latter came with vidalia onions and horseradish cream sauce, and was a huge affair. Both dishes were served with a choice of garden or potato salad and chunks of watermelon. A glass of Bartlett coastal white wine and a tart lemon mousse with two ginger shortbread cookies added up to a perfect lunch for a summer afternoon. Lobster stew, lobster or crabmeat salad and a chicken, bacon and brie sandwich are other possibilities, all in the $5.50 to $9.50 range.

On the evening menu you'll find the same salads and soups, plus smoked salmon and mussels for appetizers, and entrées ($9.50 to $17.50) like finnan haddie pie, lobster alfredo, rack of lamb, pesto pasta and pork tenderloin with bourbon-laced sweet potatoes. Bread pudding with butter-rum-raisin sauce and the bull mousse (deep chocolate with kahlua, Jack Daniels and a mystery ingredient – guess it and you get another one) make worthy endings.

(207) 963-2653. Lunch daily, 10:30 to 5:30; dinner 5:30 to 9. Open late June to early September.

Ethnic Gourmet

Jean-Paul's Bistro, Main Street, Blue Hill.

Gaelic charm has come to Blue Hill in the form of this delightful bistro opened by Jean-Paul Lecomte, taking full advantage of its view onto Blue Hill Bay. In his classic white Maine home with green shutters, the former waiter at some prestigious New York City restaurants, including the 21 Club, offers lunch and tea as well as a new pastry kitchen producing delectable treats for takeout. Jean-Paul takes care of the front of the house and several relatives, among them his mother, father, brother and sister-in-law, help out.

You can come in at 11 a.m. for a cup of cappuccino and a chocolate croissant. For lunch, the menu might yield a salade niçoise, couscous salade provençal, a New Orleans muffuletta sandwich, a sausage tart, a French farmer's plate of charcuterie and cheeses, and pumpkin tortellini with pesto, crème fraîche and toasted pinenuts. We thoroughly enjoyed the croque monsieur with a side salad of mixed baby greens and the grilled chicken caesar salad, layered rather than tossed and served with a baguette. The side terrace with its custom-made square wooden tables topped with canvas

Jean-Paul Lecomte on terrace at bistro.

umbrellas proved such a salubrious setting that we lingered over a luscious strawberry tart and a slice of midnight chocolate cake that Jean-Paul insisted we taste, calling it a French-Japanese cake – inexplicable, but very good. Other desserts from the patisserie might be blueberry and peach bread pudding, chocolate truffle terrine and the specialty lemon-blueberry madeleines. Lunch prices are in the $3.95 to $7.50 range.

From 4 to 5, relax with tea and a pastry on one of the side-by-side Adirondack chairs for two scattered around the back lawn that slopes toward Blue Hill Harbor. Enjoy, as you really can't from any other establishment in town, the pristine view.

Inside, the dining room has cathedral ceilings, local art, white tablecloths, and blue and white spattered Bennington pottery for a simple and fresh yet sophisticated look. And it has big windows for enjoying that view. Wines and beers are available.

Jean-Paul has toyed with offering prix-fixe dinners cooked on his outside rotisserie, but at our latest visit still had not found the time.

(207) 374-5852. Coffee, lunch and tea, daily except Sunday 11 to 5, July-October.

XYZ Restaurant & Gallery, Shore Road, Manset.

The letters stand for Xalapa, Yucatan and Zacatecas, and the food represents the Mexican interior and coastal Maine. Owner Janet Strong had the West Side Gallery here for a year before opening this enterprise in 1994 with chef Robert Hoyt, who's traveled in Mexico for years and describes himself as "a nut for the food there for a long, long time."

We could easily become nuts for his food, too, after a summer dinner. Everything here is, as Robert says, "real," from the smoked jalapeño and tomatillo sauces served with the opening tortillas to the fine tequila he offered with dessert as a chaser. Busy hostess Janet recommended we try her partner's sampler plate ($11 each): two chiles rellenos and a chicken dish with mashed potato and pickled cucumber. Now smitten, we'll opt next time perhaps for the Mexican beef tongue, the pork loin tatemado, the tiger shrimp with guajillo and poblano chiles or the tenderloin zacatecas, among entrée choices priced from ($10 to $15).

Part of the main floor of the Dockside Motel, the L-shaped dining room is colorful in white, red and green, the colors of the Mexican flag. The front windows look out onto Somes Sound across the road.

(207) 244-5221. Dinner nightly except Tuesday in summer, 5:30 to 9:30. Seasonal.

Offbeat Gourmet

Keenan's, Route 102A, Bass Harbor.

From the outside, this little place where Route 102A meets Flat Iron Road at "the Triangle" looks like a seafood shack, what with lobster traps perched on the roof and steaming pots of water out front. Step inside and be surprised: it's bigger than you think and pleasantly rustic with driftwood paneling and a roll of paper towels on each table.

This is a seafood shanty with high culinary aspirations. From the galley-size kitchen come remarkable treats that draw locals-in-the-know: lobsters, of course, but also barbecued back ribs marinated in a mysterious red sauce known only to contain tomatoes and vinegar, crab cakes and seafood gumbo. Chef Frank Keenan, of French-Canadian descent, and his wife Liz call their blend of Cajun and Down East cooking "Acadian cuisine," much like that you find around the bayous of southwestern Louisiana.

Among dinner entrées ($6.95 to $12.95), consider the much-acclaimed crab cakes, the shrimp étouffée or the blackened swordfish. There are also appetizers like fried clams and sandwiches in the $3.95 to $8.95 range.

(207) 244-3403. Dinner nightly in summer, from 4:30; fewer days in off-season.

Lobster Pounds

Okay, okay, we can hear some of you thinking.

"Roast quail with westphalian ham, for heaven's sake," you sneer. "Garlic and ginger broth, what kind of garbage is that? Snap peas, schnapp peas. We want *lobster.*"

We confess. Once each Maine trip we want lobster, too. But not a one-pound weakling. What we do is go to a lobster pound, order steamers and maybe onion rings and a couple of two-pound lobsters. We sit at picnic tables beside the water and watch the boats, and we pig out, just like everyone else.

In this area, our favorites:

Union River Lobster Pot, South Street, Ellsworth.

Ellsworth got its first waterfront restaurant when Brian and Jane Langley opened this sprightly place at the back of a former seafood market. The Langleys had put the Oak Point Lobster Pound in Trenton on the culinary map for ten years. Here they continue the tradition, boiling lobsters outside and serving inside at windows yielding a glimpse of the river. The lobster roll has all the meat from a whole lobster for $10.95; lobster stew is $14.50 and a whole shore dinner is $19.95. Brian's stews and chowders are renowned, as are the blueberry pie and chocolate mousse pie. Although it's a simple place, the menu is fairly extensive and Brian teaches cooking in Ellsworth, so he knows what he's doing. How often have you seen strawberry-amaretto torte on the menu at a lobster pound?

(207) 667-5077. Lunch and dinner daily, 11 to 9, mid-June to mid-October.

Thurston's Lobster Pound, Steamboat Wharf Road, Bernard.

From the jaunty upstairs deck here you can look below and see where the lobstermen keep their traps. This is a real working lobster wharf. And if you couldn't tell from all the pickup trucks parked along the road, one taste of the lobster will convince you. You can get a lobster roll for $6.95 or a lobster dinner for $6.75 to $7.75 a pound, plus $3.75 for the extras. Steamers, mussels, chili, hamburgers and more are available at this true place opened in 1993 by Michael Radcliffe, great-grandson of Thurston's founder, and his wife Libby. A local couple, whose license plate said "Pies," was delivering the apple and rhubarb pies for the day the first time we stopped by. Pick out one of the twelve square tables for four on the covered deck and dig in. The new wine list ranges from white zinfandel to pouilly fuissé.

(207) 244-7600. Open daily, 11 to 8:30, Memorial Day through September.

Head of the Harbor, Route 102, Southwest Harbor.

You place your order for lobster and other goodies at the outdoor steamer and grill and a waitress will deliver to the citronella-lit picnic tables on the expansive deck looking down toward Somes Sound or a screened porch adjacent. At one visit, we enjoyed a sunset dinner of stuffed shrimp with potato salad, and sautéed scallops with french fries and three-bean salad (both $12.95), washed down with a Napa Ridge chardonnay for $11.95 and followed by fresh raspberry pie. The lobster here is $8.95 a pound; add $2 for a complete dinner.

(207) 244-3508. Open daily in season, noon to 10.

Fisherman's Landing, 35 West St., Bar Harbor.

We've been going to this lobster pound on the working pier, the only one beside the water in town, since the '70s. From inside a cramped shack come succulent lobsters; you dine at picnic tables on the wharf, inside an enclosed pavilion or on an upstairs deck, sip wine or beer obtained from the adjacent bar, and watch all the harbor activities. For visitors, it's the essence of Down East Maine, all wrapped up in one convenient package. The lobster here is $7.25 to $8.25 a pound. The french fries are especially good, and hamburgers and other items are available.

(207) 288-4632. Open daily in summer, from 11:30.

Dining and Lodging

Castine Inn, Main Street, Box 41, Castine 04421.

A pleasant wraparound porch with polka-dot-covered seats and a profusion of flowers welcomes guests to the Castine Inn, built in 1898 and operated continuously since. The interior is a virtual art gallery, from artist Margaret Hodesh's stunning murals in the dining room to her mother's paintings and quilts enhancing the walls of the third-floor hallway.

Margaret and her husband Mark have redone the inn's front parlor and spiffed up twenty guest rooms and suites in which personal and artistic touches abound. All with private baths and queensize or twin beds, the bedrooms open hotel-style off long, wide corridors on the second and third floors. Decor is simple yet stylish.

Tea on the lawn, a Bar Harbor tradition, is served at the Jordan Pond House.

A fairly new addition is the sunny side deck with a view of Mark's elaborate gardens. Another change at this ever-upgrading inn is a new outdoor entry to the cozy, convivial pub.

Margaret's murals grace the walls, pillars and even a new service area in the pleasant dining room, which is the setting for creative cuisine. Although Mark is in the kitchen, he defers to his chefs, who have "taken us to new heights. I'm a cook; they're the chef." Their offerings are as varied as crab cakes with mustard sauce ($4.50 as an appetizer, $14 as an entrée), billi-bi, salmon ravioli, lentil salad with goat cheese, chicken and garlic stew, braised rabbit with mushrooms and cream, sweetbreads with green peppercorn sauce, pork loin with braised red cabbage, and steak and mushroom pie. The lobster curry, in which a one-and-one-half-pounder is deshelled and reassembled with peach chutney, shredded coconut and basmati rice, is a house specialty. So are the veal stew with green olives and the chocolate soufflé cake and chocolate pudding. The price of the entrée ($13 to $19) includes biscuits, potato or rice and vegetable. One night when we were there, broiled Stonington scallops with tomato-basil butter were on the menu, the scallops having been collected that day by a Stonington fisherman whose wife was a waitress at the inn.

Cocktails may be taken on the side deck. Later in the evening, desserts and nightcaps are served in the living room or on the front porch. Mark specially opened the dark and cozy pub, tucked away in a corner, to serve us an after-dinner brandy at one visit. This is an inn that's nothing if not accommodating.

Complimentary breakfast includes a choice of corned-beef hash, pancakes, sausages and fresh muffins.

The *Castine Inn Cookbook* (on sale at the front desk for $12.95) combines Mark's favorite recipes with his wife's illustrations and a history of this historic town.

(207) 326-4365. Fax (207) 326-4570. Dinner nightly, 5:30 to 8:30; Thursday-Saturday at 6, late October to Dec. 21. Doubles, $75 to $125. Two-night minimum in summer. Open May to late December.

Pilgrim's Inn, Deer Isle 04627.

An aura of history and an aroma of fine food emanate from this impressive, dark red 1793 house run with great taste and flair by Jean and Dud Hendrick. With a harbor in front and a mill pond in back, inviting common rooms and thirteen guest rooms (plus two new efficiency suites in a house next door), it's a quiet place that beckons guests to stay for extended periods.

Jean and her longtime chef, Terry Foster, are known for creative cooking. They favor local ingredients and do their grilling on an enormous barbecue on a rear deck. Following cocktails at 6 in the downstairs common room or outside on the deck (where guests nibble on abundant hors d'oeuvres like bluefish pâté and mingle with Jean and Dud, who fixes a neat raspberry daiquiri upon request), a single-entrée, prix-fixe dinner ($29.50 for the public) is served at 7 o'clock. You

Pilgrim's Inn is in handsome 1793 house.

move into the charming dining room in a former goat barn, with farm utensils and quilts on the walls, hand-hewn beams, mismatched chairs, tables with fresh flowers and ten outside doors that open to let in the breeze. Depending on the night, you might be served a trio of seafood cakes garnished with condiments, an applewood mixed grill of pork, gulf shrimp and duck confit, pepper-crusted tenderloin of beef with local shiitake mushrooms or roasted farm-raised chicken, often accompanied by a dynamite risotto and delectable vegetables.

Never will we forget a Sunday dinner of salad with goat cheese, homemade peasant bread, a heavenly paella topped with nasturtiums (such a pretty dish that it should have been photographed for Gourmet magazine) and a sensational raspberry-chocolate pie on a shortbread crust. Terry varies his menu annually and according to whim, but whatever is served, you can expect it to be a treat.

Homemade granola, scones, fresh melon and omelets are typical breakfast fare.

The handsome guest rooms, ten with private baths, are decorated in sprightly Laura Ashley style. Most in demand are the larger rooms at the back. Two bedrooms on the newly renovated third floor have private baths featuring vanities topped with Deer Isle granite. Oriental rugs and quilts lend color to the prevailing simplicity. The main-floor library has an exceptional collection of books; another parlor is a showroom for local artists. The Hendricks have added appropriate art to every guest room. It's typical of the TLC that they lavish on the inn as well as their guests.

Recently, they transformed a rear shed into **The Rugosa Rose,** a stylish craft and gift shop. In 1997, they bought the adjacent property to double the size of their grounds and were converting its vintage house into two housekeeping suites that were "proving to be real sweethearts," Jean advised. Each has a living room with cable TV, cast-iron stove, queen bed, full bath and efficiency kitchen, plus a deck overlooking the water.

(207) 348-6615. Dinner by reservation, nightly at 7. Doubles, $150 to $175, MAP; efficiency suites, $205. Open mid-May to mid-October. No credit cards.

Goose Cove Lodge, Deer Isle, Box 40, Sunset 04683.

Some of the most inspired meals in Maine are served at this food-oriented, family-style lodge on 70 acres along the remote shores of Deer Isle. The only problem (?) is that you may have to stay for a week in season to partake or manage to slip in for dinner as a transient via a one-and-one-half-mile-long dirt road through the evergreens, starting in the middle of nowhere and terminating at the open ocean at the End of Beyond.

Joanne Parisi, a former Massachusetts caterer and now innkeeper with her husband Dom, hired Douglas Albertson as the lodge's chef. They present healthful, contemporary American fare for up to 80 lodge guests and outside diners by reservation. Sturdy, shiny pine tables are set communally for four to eight in a handsome dining room wrapping around the ocean end of the main lodge, which gained a new outside deck in 1997.

The innovative, prix-fixe menu changes with every meal, and a special vegetarian appetizer and entrée are offered nightly. Guests gather at 6 o'clock for cocktails and complimentary hors d'oeuvres in the bar. A typical dinner ($30 for the public) might start with black bean soup with cornbread croutons and cilantro-lime cream. The main course could be grilled butterflied leg of lamb with roasted shallot juice, garlic mashed potatoes and butternut squash puree, followed by a salad of mixed field greens wrapped with prosciutto in a sunflower seed vinaigrette. Cardamom crème brûlée with a tuile could be the finale.

Breakfast ($9 for the public) is quite a feast, too. One Sunday's fare included fresh pineapple, bananas and nutmeg flamed in spiced rum, homemade granola with yogurt, an assortment of fresh breads, buttermilk pancakes with spiced plum topping and a choice of eggs or omelets prepared any style, served with pan-seared red bliss potatoes and grilled ham.

The Friday night lobster feast on the new lodge deck or at the beach is a highlight of the week for the long-termers, who tend to be repeat guests year after year. Counselors entertain and supervise children during the adult dinner hour. String quartets, folk singers, a lobster fisherman or a local writer may entertain after dinner.

Accommodations are booked MAP by the week (Saturday to Saturday) in summer, B&B or MAP in the off-season. The Parisis offer "simple, rustic and comfortable lodging" in twelve rooms and suites upstairs in the main lodge or in the nearby East and North annexes. Most in demand are the new upstairs Lookout Suite, in essence a complete two-bedroom apartment, and the seven secluded cottages and four duplex cottages, each with ocean view, sun deck, kitchenette or refrigerator and fireplace. Planned for opening in 1997 were two new houses, each with a beamed living room with a queen bed in an alcove, two bedrooms with twin beds, and country French doors onto front decks, sleeping up to six.

The lodge property – marked by five trails, sandy beaches and tree-lined shores – is a paradise for nature lovers. At low tide, you can walk across a sand bar to Barred Island, a nature conservancy full of birds and wildlife.

(207) 348-2508 or (800) 728-1963. Fax (207) 348-2624. Dinner by reservation, nightly at 7. Doubles, $164 to $260 MAP; off-season, $90 to $170 B&B. Open mid-May to mid-October.

Blue Hill Inn, Union Street, Box 403, Blue Hill 04614.

Dating to 1840, this small village inn offers twelve overnight rooms and a dining room of distinction since affable owners Mary and Don Hartley took over innkeeping duties and upgraded the kitchen.

The energetic Hartleys have enhanced the guest rooms, all with private baths and three with fireplaces, some with sitting areas converted from small bedrooms. Our rear bedroom – occupied the previous night by Peter of Peter, Paul and Mary fame following the trio's concert at the Blue Hill Fair Grounds – was comfortable with a kingsize bed, two blue velvet wing chairs, colorful bed linens, plump towels and windows on three sides to circulate cool air, which was welcome after a heat wave. The others we saw also are nicely furnished with 19th-century antiques and traditional pieces reflecting what Mary calls "a homey Down East style." Home-made chocolates come with nightly turndown service. For 1997, the Hartleys were adding an efficiency suite next door with a cathedral-ceilinged living room, fireplace, bedroom and kitchen.

It is dining for which the inn lately is best known. The Hartleys serve hors d'oeuvres (perhaps smoked mackerel or local goat cheese) with cocktails at 6 in the large parlor or outside on the side lawn. A leisurely, multi-course dinner ($30 for the public) begins at 7. Dining is by candlelight at white-linened tables in an enclosed sun porch-style room where classical music plays in the background.

Chef André Strong, an American whose mother came from France, changes the handwritten menu nightly. Braised shiitake mushrooms with saffron risotto was the appetizer at our dinner, which was artistically presented and exceptionally tasty throughout. A blueberry-campari ice cleansed the palate for the main course, a choice of ethereal paupiettes of trout with salmon mousseline and mint or tender noisettes of lamb with cob-smoked bacon, garlic and chèvre. A salad of local greens preceded the dessert, a remarkable frozen nougat with spiced orange rum – so good that we requested the recipe and quickly realized we could never accomplish the feat at home.

Breakfast here is no slouch, either. Ours started with the usual juices, a plate of cut-up fresh fruit and a wedge of apple-custard pie that one of us thought was dessert. The main course involved a choice of eggs scrambled with chives in puff pastry, an omelet with chèvre or brie and Canadian bacon, waffles with strawberry topping or blueberry pancakes. Excellent french-roast coffee accompanied a repast fit for royalty.

The inn has excelled at wine dinners in the off-season, attracting an equal number of locals and out-of-town returnees.

Besides the main living room in blue and white with a fireplace, guests enjoy a sunny library-game room with comfortable chairs for lounging. Outside is a lovely perennial garden with lawn furniture, a gazebo and, at our visit, a profusion of huge yellow lilies.

(207) 374-2844 or (800) 826-7415. Dinner by reservation, nightly at 7, June-October; weekends in off-season. Doubles, $165 to $185, MAP; suite, $210. Closed December to mid-May.

Lindenwood Inn, 118 Clark Point Road, Box 1328, Southwest Harbor 04679.

"I always wanted an inn with a restaurant – to appeal to all five senses." So explains Jim King, innkeeper-turned traveler-turned decorator-turned hotelier. And now he has it all.

The former owner of the nearby Kingsleigh Inn returned from traveling around the world in 1993 to take over the old Lindenwood B&B, which had fallen on lean

Lindenwood Inn offers fine dining as well as wide variety of accommodations.

times. He quickly imbued the main house with his eclectic decorating touch, setting palm trees on the wraparound porch, splashing vivid colors on the walls and spattering collections of shells and stones in the nine bedrooms. "We don't have New England decor here," he asserts, "and people love it." Next he redid waterfront cottages and converted an adjacent apartment house into six efficiency units he called the Lindenwood Annex. Full breakfasts, perhaps herbed omelets or french toast with homemade blueberry sauce, were served in the main dining room furnished in what Jim called "tropical primitive."

All of this, it turns out, were mere preliminaries to what emerged unexpectedly in 1996 – a full-service, small hotel open year-round. Suddenly the breakfast room had evolved into a dynamite restaurant. Outdoors at the side and screened by a trellis from the street was a flagstone terrace with a heated gunite pool and a separate spa topped by a sculptured mask spraying a stream of water. The redone penthouse suite, complete with curved sofa and gas fireplace, opened onto an enormous rooftop deck holding almost as enormous an oversize spa. Across the street, another house was being converted into yet another annex with six guest rooms with private baths. An addition was in the planning stage for the main inn's living room and dining room, and the pool-side cottage in which we were quite happily ensconced with cable TV in the cathedral-ceilinged living room, efficiency kitchen and queensize bedroom was about to be rehabbed for greater space and comfort.

Now with 23 rooms and suites and a restaurant, Jim has what he wanted – a small hotel. Chef Bill Morrison joined the Lindenwood's 30-seat restaurant by way of Aspen and Boston. He offered a short, changing menu ($16 to $22) that was every bit as eclectic as the rest of the inn. Organic foods and vegetarian dishes were among the wholesome fare. For dinner in the small bar room, a basket of breads with pesto sauce and butter in mini-crocks arrived at a table flanked by sleek European-style chairs and dressed with exotic flowers, a silver elephant and an oil lamp bearing a shade atop a wrought-iron twig. A South African chardonnay accompanied what proved to be a superb meal: for one, a pair of appetizers ($7 and $9) – crab, avocado and cilantro Japanese mako sushi rolls and Thai mussels steamed in sake with basil, cilantro, ginger and hot pepper; for the other, a spinach salad with roasted portobello mushrooms and parmesan ($7) and a main course of crab and cod cakes with saffron rémoulade ($16). Homemade bourbon ice cream with chocolate biscotti and a strawberry tart with mascarpone were refreshing counterpoints to such assertive tastes.

In the morning, seated in another of the three small dining rooms, we helped ourselves to fresh fruit and raspberry-banana muffins from the buffet and were served a main dish of fruit crêpes. We vowed to return the next year to see what whirlwind Jim and his staff were up to.

(207) 244-5335 or (800) 307-5335. Dinner by reservation, Tuesday-Saturday 6 to 9:30 in season, weekends through Christmas. Doubles, $85 to $135; suites, $115 to $225.

Le Domaine, Route 1, Box 496, Hancock 04640.

Here is a perfect getaway for gourmets: a country auberge with a handful of elegant upstairs guest rooms, some with private decks overlooking the gardens, and a main-floor restaurant and lounge purveying classic French cuisine and fine wines.

The red frame building semi-hidden behind huge evergreens seems as if it were lifted from provincial France and plunked down in rural Hancock, which is even down east from down east Bar Harbor. Inside is an extraordinarily appealing place in which to stay and dine.

Founded in 1945 by a Frenchwoman, Marianne Purslow-Dumas, Le Domaine is run now with equal competence by her daughter, Nicole Purslow, a graduate of the Cordon Bleu School and an advocate of country-French haute cuisine.

Beyond a delightful wicker sitting area where French magazines are piled upon tables is the long and narrow, L-shaped dining room, dominated at the far end by a huge stone fireplace framed by copper cooking utensils. Walls (red above, green below and separated by dark wood beams) are decorated with maps of France and pictures of folks in provincial costumes. A porch room in back, its tables covered with gaily colored cloths from Provence, takes full advantage of the sylvan view.

The menu changes frequently and features local produce from nearby gardens and herbs that grow by the kitchen door. Six or seven entrées in the $17.75 to $23 range are offered each night. They could include veal with wild mushrooms, steak au poivre, and poussin roasted with madeira and cream. We'd return any time for the sensational sweetbreads with lemon and capers, the grilled salmon with fennel, lamb chops dusted with rosemary, and a house specialty, rabbit with prunes marinated in brandy. Zucchini, snap peas and gnocchi might accompany.

The French bread is toasted in chunks and the rolls are marvelous. For starters ($5.50 to $7.50) on various occasions, we've tried malpeque oysters with a shallot-sherry vinegar dipping sauce, coquilles St. Jacques in a heavenly wine sauce, smoked trout and a salad of impeccable greens, including baby spinach, tossed with goat cheese and walnuts.

The cheesecake on raspberry sauce is ethereal, as is the frozen coffee mousse. Another visit produced a raspberry tart and frozen raspberry mousse with a meringue, plus perfect french-roast coffee. The wine list (mostly French, of course) is expensive, but some bargains are to be found.

Relaxing after dinner on wicker chairs in the sitting room with snifters of heady eau de vie, we almost didn't care about the cost ($7 each). We toddled upstairs to

Wicker sitting area and curved bar lead into dining room at Le Domaine.

our overnight home in the king-bedded Tarragon Room, one of seven attractive, country-fresh guest rooms named after herbs.

All with private baths, they're exceptionally outfitted in chintz. The amenities you'd expect are here, including antiques, clock radios, books, French magazines, bedside reading lamps, French soaps and bath oils (and a night light in the shape of a shell), plus complimentary Perrier water. Behind a studied simplicity are many artistic touches. On our rear deck, for instance, a spotlight shone on a tree growing through it and a piece of driftwood was placed perfectly on the stairs.

The next morning, we admired a circular garden surrounded by large rocks in back, looking casual but probably taking hours to plot. A number of trails had been cleared through a forest of pine trees on 85 acres. We took a long walk to a pond, picking blueberries for sustenance along the way.

A breakfast tray was delivered to our deck, bearing bowls of peaches and raspberries, granola, crème fraîche, hot milk in a jug, homemade blueberry preserves, three of the flakiest croissants ever and a pot of fragrant coffee, all on floral china with linen napkins. Sheer enchantment!

(207) 422-3395 or (800) 544-8498. Fax (207) 422-2316. Dinner nightly, 6 to 9 (closed to public on Sunday). Doubles, $200, MAP. Open May-October.

Asticou Inn, Route 3, Northeast Harbor 04662.

A bastion of elegance since 1883, this historic resort hotel is grandly situated on a hillside at the head of Northeast Harbor.

From window tables in the spacious, pillared dining room, you get a view of the harbor goings-on from on high. The room is restful with handpainted murals of trees and flowers on the deep yellow walls, small oriental rugs and lovely floral china.

The elaborate dinner menu, offered to the public as well as guests, is priced from $17.95 for citrus chicken to $32.95 for lobster grand marnier served over puff pastry or rack of lamb with a minted glace di viande.

We lunched on the outdoor terrace high above the sparkling harbor, choosing the buffet over the grilled sandwiches (both $12). The buffet included a choice of chicken-vegetable soup or a most refreshing chilled lime-yogurt soup, cold meats and many salads, beverage and choice of five or six desserts. The Sunday brunch ($16.50) is a panoply of treats, from eggs benedict and crêpes cooked to order to poached salmon, pastas and desserts.

Upstairs via a carpeted staircase or an ancient elevator are 50 simple guest rooms of varying configurations. Seventeen more rooms are available in guest houses and the striking, circular Topsider cottages (each with deck, full-length windows, attractive parlors and kitchenettes).

The traditional Thursday buffet dinner-dances were discontinued in 1996 in favor of live entertainment by a pianist or harpist at dinner nightly and more special events throughout the week. Lately, the Asticou has extended its season and dropped its MAP requirement for "country view rooms" (EP, $150 to $180).

(207) 276-3344 or (800) 248-3344. Lunch daily, noon to 2:30; dinner, 6 to 9:30, jackets required. Doubles, $250 to $297, MAP; suites, $269 to $356, MAP. Asticou open May 10 to Oct. 15; cottages year-round.

Lodging

Eggemoggin Reach Bed & Breakfast, The Herrick Road, RR 1, Box 33A, Brooksville 04617.

Surrounded by 70 forested acres at the end of a long driveway, this prize of a waterside B&B is situated along a particularly picturesque section of water known as Eggemoggin Reach.

The convivial B&B reflects the transformation of a summer/retirement home for Susie and Mike Canon, who built it in 1989 and decided they were hardly ready for retirement. When energetic Susie found she "couldn't sit still," they had the house winterized, outfitted it with comfortable furnishings and oriental rugs, and opened in 1993 with three suites upstairs and a duplex cottage, all facing the water. The Wheelhouse Suite spreads across the entire third floor with bath, king bedroom and a large living room with a sofabed, chairs, a desk and two twin beds tucked beneath the eaves.

Our idea of a night in paradise is a stay in one of the rustic-looking but ever-so-plush duplex cottage units facing Deadman's Cove. Paneled in pickled pine, it has a cathedral ceiling, king bed, an efficiency kitchen and a sitting area with sofabed and franklin stove. The screened porch overlooking the water was perfect for enjoying a takeout lobster dinner by candlelight (the Canons sometimes prepare lobster bakes by the shore for groups of eight guests or more).

The cottages were our idea of paradise, that is, until 1997 when the Canons completed their nearby Bay Lodge, a newly built Maine-style farmhouse with six large efficiency suites on three levels. Patterned after the cottage units but larger, each offers a king bed, sitting area with sofabed, kitchenette and a substantial screened porch facing Deadman's Cove head-on.

The Canons also rent a neighbor's carriage house as Tuckaway, with a huge great room, rear bedroom, Stickley mission-style furnishings, fully equipped kitchen and water-view decks up and down.

In the morning, breakfast for all is served on the full-length porch across the front of the main house. Five of Susie's recipes – more than from any other Maine lodging establishment – were included in 1996 in Yankee magazine's *New England Innkeepers' Cookbook.* Over the course of a repast that included juice, a fresh fruit plate, cereal, granola, a zesty frittata and coffeecake, we knew why. And as we watched the resident osprey and cormorants and looked for the seals that cavort in Deadman's Cove, we thought, this is the life.

(207) 359-5073 or (800) 625-8866. Fax (207) 359-5074. Cottages, $140; suites, $150; Tuckaway, $165. Open mid-May to mid-October.

John Peters Inn, Peters Point, Box 916, Blue Hill 04614.

Surrounded on two sides by water and 25 acres, this B&B is in an 1810 white-pillared and red-brick house that looks rather like a Southern plantation. Although close to Blue Hill, it's off by itself on its own idyllic hilltop peninsula. It also offers some of the nicest guest rooms and some of the most gourmet breakfasts around.

Energetic Barbara and Rick Seeger acquired the house in 1986, rebuilt the kitchen, added a dining porch, moved all the guest rooms upstairs and have a real winner of a place. To the original eight rooms they added six more in a rear carriage house.

All have private baths, most have king or queensize beds, half have fireplaces and some of those in the carriage house come with private decks. They are handsomely furnished, even the newer ones in back. There, you could have a room with queensize brass bed and a loveseat looking onto a private deck, or a larger room that's almost a studio apartment with queen bed, fireplace, kitchen with a dishwasher and dining table, and private deck.

We enjoyed our stay in the main house in the Blue Hill Room, which has a kingsize bed, working fireplace, lovely carpets, a wet bar and refrigerator, and a large rooftop deck looking up at Blue Hill. The deck is so pleasant that many guests bring dinner in and eat right there; "almost everyone who stays in this room eats a lobster dinner here at least once," says Barbara.

Extra touches include fresh fruit and flowers in the rooms, a small swimming pool, and a canoe and a couple of sailboats. Musicians from the nearby Kneisel Hall School of Music like to gather around the grand piano in the living room.

The Seegers and their staff put out a remarkable spread for breakfast, served on the enclosed side porch amid delicate blue and white floral china, heavy silver, etched water glasses and classical music. One repast started with fresh orange juice, local blueberries and cream, and grilled blueberry and corn muffins. Then came a choice of nine entrées, from eggs any style to blueberry waffles, cheese eggs and a crabmeat/monterey-jack omelet. One of us liked the poached eggs with slender asparagus on whole-wheat toast, garnished with crisp bacon and edible flowers. The other ordered the lobster and artichoke omelet with hollandaise sauce. Garnished with lobster claws, it was so colorful that it cried out for a photo. It also was so good that he ordered it two mornings in a row. The waitress acknowledged that her father supplies the lobster and her mother the crabmeat. Now that's down-home, with class.

(207) 374-2116. Doubles, $95 to $150.

Waterside deck at Inn at Canoe Point has sweeping view of Frenchman Bay.

Pentagoet Inn, Main Street, Box 4, Castine 04421.

All is serene and sophisticated in this century-old inn run since 1985 by Lindsey and Virginia Miller from Arkansas.

He a physician and she a nurse, they refurbished in seafoam shades the main-floor parlors. One is a well-outfitted library and the other offers a nifty window seat looking toward the harbor. The pristine dining room has an addition looking out over terraced gardens. The main inn holds eleven guest rooms, all with private baths and antique furnishings. We thought the bathroom off our kingsize turret room – with color-coordinated wallpapers, curtains and patterned rug and a basket of towels in shades of pink – a work of art. Perhaps the nicest rooms are the six behind the inn in the 200-year-old Perkins House.

For ten years, the Millers laid claim to gourmet fame by requiring MAP meal plans and hosting a nightly cocktail hour for guests as "an integral part of the inn experience." In 1996, they discontinued the acclaimed prix-fixe dinners, explaining "the market won't bear that any more. People want choices, we've discovered."

Now functioning as a B&B, they offer afternoon refreshments and spirits from a full liquor license. They focus on their breakfast, a buffet spread available from 7:30 to 9:30. Between 8 and 9, guests may order from an array of cooked items: perhaps sourdough blueberry pancakes, french toast and brunchy egg dishes, among them the delectable eggs Pentagoet with spinach, tomatoes and marchand du vin sauce.

The meal is taken in the main dining room, where the rose-colored walls are a backdrop for polished wood floors and well-spaced tables draped in linens, or in a rear dining area beside a small deck with gardens beyond.

(207) 326-8616 or (800) 845-1701. Fax (207) 326-9382. Doubles, $95 to $125. Open Memorial Day to mid-October.

The Inn at Canoe Point, Route 3, Box 216-B, Bar Harbor 04609.

Here is one of Mount Desert Island's few small B&Bs right on the ocean, and it is a stunner of a place. Nancy and Tom Cervelli, formerly of the Kingsleigh Inn in Southwest Harbor, acquired a going concern in 1996 from founder-turned-realtor Don Johnson, who similarly had started with a B&B in Southwest Harbor. Blessed with the best waterfront location imaginable and a smashing deck that takes full advantage, the inn was in the enviable position of accepting bookings a year in advance. When the Cervellis took over in May, the inn already was "basically full for the 1996 season."

Formerly a private residence, the stucco house with Tudor trim is set well back and below Route 3 in an acre and a half of woods flanking Frenchman Bay. Five of the six guest rooms with private baths enjoy water views. We're partial to the front Master Suite with fireplace and deck and the side Garden Room, which has three walls of glass and its own door onto the garden and sea. The third-floor Garret Suite comes with wicker chairs, a neat captain's chest and a kingsize bed from which you can look out at an endless expanse of water. All are discreetly decorated in exquisite taste and muted colors so as not to detract from the view.

Guests enjoy a handsome living room, which has an elegant grouping of seats around the fireplace, and the waterfront Ocean Room with a huge curved sectional, fireplace and stereo. The latter room is where breakfast is served at tables for four topped with candlesticks – when the weather isn't suitable for eating on the spacious deck at water's edge.

Breakfast might be eggs benedict, omelets or french toast, plus a choice of juices and a fruit course. Decanters of port or sherry are in all the guest rooms, and Nancy serves tea, cookies, cheese and crackers on pleasant afternoons on the deck.

The Cervellis had only to fine-tune, adding a fireplace in the Anchor Room and remodeling the baths in the Garret and Portside during their first season. "We'll upgrade one room at a time," said Nancy.

(207) 288-9511. Doubles, $135 to $245.

The Inn at Bay Ledge, 1385 Sand Point Rd., Bar Harbor 04609.

Reindeer fashioned from vines stand sentry at the entrance to this clifftop retreat overlooking Frenchman Bay. They reflect the "upscale country ambiance" that Jack and Jeani Ochtera, former owners of the Holbrook House in town, have imparted since our first stay.

King or queen canopied and four-poster beds plump with feather mattresses and pillows, Ralph Lauren towels and linens, and colorful quilts with matching window treatments are the rule in the seven guest rooms with private baths, two with jacuzzis. All have picture windows affording splendid water vistas. Balconies were added to three upstairs rooms in 1996. A paneled upstairs sitting room harbors a hidden TV/VCR amidst a decorative scheme of old family fishing gear, handcarved birds and Jeani's handmade samplers.

Rolling lawns and gardens lead to a sheer cliff, where a steep staircase descends 80 feet to the stony beach and a cave along the bay. An expansive, tiered deck stretches along the front of the inn; here are umbrellaed tables and twig chairs where you may read and relax at this truly relaxing place. A small swimming pool and whirlpool are on a lower level of the deck, and tall pine trees all around make the salt air even more refreshing.

The inn's first floor contains a sauna and steam shower, as well as a breakfast room where Jeani offers fresh fruit, cereal, granola, breads and muffins and perhaps three-cheese and bacon quiche, blueberry buckle or cheese strata. We took ours out to the deck and watched cheeky chipmunks race around, vying for crumbs. Typical of the pampering touches are going-away boxes of Bay Ledge candies given to guests upon departure.

The inn also offers three cottages, one with kingsize bed and fieldstone fireplace, hidden in the trees across the road.

(207) 288-4204. Fax 288-5573. Doubles, $150 to $250 in inn; cottages, $130 to $150. Two-night minimum in season. Closed November-April.

Ullikana Bed & Breakfast, 16 The Field, Bar Harbor 04609.

Hospitable owner-innkeepers, creative breakfasts, a quiet in-town location near the water and a guest book full of grateful raves. These are among the attributes of this summery but substantial, Tudor-style cottage built in 1885, tucked away in the trees between the Bar Harbor Inn and "the field," a meadow of wildflowers. Transplanted New Yorkers Roy Kasindorf and his Quebec City-born wife, Hélène Harton, bought it in 1991 from a woman who had turned it into a B&B at the age of 86. They retained many of the furnishings, adding some of their own as well as artworks from artist-friends in New York.

Ten bedrooms with private baths hold lots of chintz, wicker and antiques; some come with balconies, fireplaces or both. One dubbed Audrey's Room (for Roy's daughter) on the third floor contains two antique beds joined together as a kingsize and a clawfoot tub with its original fixtures, from which the bather can look out the low window onto Frenchman Bay. We were happily ensconced in the second-floor Room 5, a majestic space outfitted in country French provincial fabrics with king bed, two wing chairs in front of the fireplace and a water-view balcony.

The main floor harbors a wicker-furnished parlor with lots to look at, from collections (including two intricate puppets beside the fireplace) to reading materials. It's the site for a convivial wine and cheese hour in the late afternoon. Beyond a dining room with shelves full of colorful Italian breakfast china is the kitchen from which Hélène produces the dishes that make breakfasts here such an event. In summer, they're served outside at tables for two or four on a pleasant terrace with glimpses of the water. Roy is the waiter and raconteur, doling out – in our case – cantaloupe with mint sauce, superior cinnamon-raisin muffins with orange glaze, and puff pancakes yielding blueberries and raspberries. Your feast might start with Hélène's grilled fruit brochettes bearing peaches, strawberries and kiwi with a ricotta-cheese sauce, followed by an Italian omelet with homemade tomato sauce and mozzarella cheese or crêpes with frozen yogurt or a rum-cream sauce. All this is served on matching dishes and placemats – a rainbow of pastels, as cheery as the setting.

(207) 288-9552. Doubles, $110 to $190. Closed November-April.

Breakwater 1904, 45 Hancock St., Bar Harbor 04609.

Fresh flowers abound and taped classical music fills the air as you enter one of Bar Harbor's more majestic seaside mansions, a 1904 English Tudor rescued from dereliction in 1992 by Bonnie and Tom Sawyer of Bangor.

The public spaces of this showplace, built by John Kane, the great-grandson of John Jacob Astor, are impressive. A fire was blazing in the central fireplace of the "great living hall" on the cool summer day we first visited. A large portrait of the owners gazes down on two plush sofas in front, a 1918 Steinway grand piano beyond and guests as they descend the six-foot-wide cherry staircase past six chairs on the minstrel's landing, where musicians once entertained the Kanes. A side parlor, done up in burgundies and greens, harbors a multi-cushioned window seat from which to view Bald Porcupine Island through one of the mansion's countless leaded-glass windows. A custom-made billiards table is the focal point of the library. An oval oak table, especially made for the dining room, is flanked by twenty tapestry-covered chairs. Guests may use the butler's pantry, a space bigger than most kitchens. They also enjoy a huge piazza with granite walls and herringbone-brick floors, awash with chintz and wicker and overlooking the end of the town's Shore Path above Frenchman Bay.

Most of the six guest rooms, all with gas fireplaces and private baths, are in keeping with the scale, except for the small Abigail's Chamber, the former maid's room in the third-floor front corner, with a bathroom big enough for a shower only. Touches of whimsy like a rocking horse and teddybear in a crib mark the third-floor Nursery, side-by-side with the Nanny's Room. Ambassador Jay's Room holds a leather sofa, chair and deck. There are a clawfoot tub and a pull-chain toilet in the bath of the prized Mrs. Kane's Room; its more than 600 square feet of space features two settees, a tapestry spread on the tester bed matching the tapestry on an overstuffed sofa and chair, and a cheery decor in pinks and creams. Mr. Kane's Room, masculine in burgundy and blue, has a stuffed sofa and polo mallets on the wall. Mrs. Alsop's Room on the oceanfront is rich in rose and blue. It contains a kingsize mansion bed and two cushioned benches beside the fireplace. The decor was overseen by Bonnie Sawyer, who furnished it as a showcase for Drexel-Heritage furniture and County Inns magazine.

Resident innkeeper Margaret Eden serves breakfast in the formal dining room. The main course might be vegetable omelet, blueberry-stuffed french toast or lemon pancakes with raspberry sauce. Afternoon tea is served by the fireplace in the great hall. The Breakwater has a full liquor license, and complimentary hors d'oeuvres are put out in the late afternoon.

(207) 288-2313 or (800) 238-6309. Fax (207) 288-2377. Doubles, $195 to $335. Open mid-April to mid-November.

The Tides, 119 West St., Bar Harbor 04609.

Listed on the National Register, this classic 1887 Greek Revival mansion faces Frenchman Bay head-on. A sensational wraparound veranda is full of upholstered wicker furniture that's all-matching to the max. Complete with its own fireplace, the veranda encloses a dining room with what must be a twenty-foot-long banquette along the window, plus a formal living room and entry foyer.

Joe and Judy Losquadro, formerly of the nearby Graycote Inn, acquired the establishment in 1996 from Tom and Bonnie Sawyer of Bangor. They offer lodging most of the year in three two-room suites. Ours, the master bedroom, was the epitome of comfort, from the kingsize bed, coordinated Laura Ashley prints and gas fireplace to the wing chairs and TV in the living room and a luxurious bathroom with clawfoot tub and tiled shower. Every room in the ocean suite has a water view, even the bathroom; other attributes are a tiny balcony and a living room with fireplace. The captain's suite on the third floor is similar, but lacks a fireplace.

Breakfast in the dining room yields fresh fruit, baked goods and a main dish, perhaps quiche, breakfast casserole or French-Canadian buckwheat pancakes. Tea is available in the afternoon – on the veranda in summer or in front of the living-room fireplace in cool weather. The one-and-a-half-acre property, with lovely rolling green lawns and old lilac trees and Japanese maples, has 156 feet of bay frontage. You couldn't ask for a nicer place to unwind.

(207) 288-4968. Doubles, $215 to $255.

Stonethrow Cottage, 67 Mount Desert St., Bar Harbor 04609.

Bar Harbor natives Peggy and Ed Douglas bought this charming cottage with dormers and turret in 1991 from a friend of her grandmother and took four years to restore it into the beauty it is today. There's a curved window seat in the corner turret of the living room. A lovely rear porch, furnished in wicker, looks onto a long and shady back yard so secluded you don't realize you're in the heart of town – just a stone's throw away.

The Douglases offer seven guest rooms, all with queen beds, private baths and whirlpool tubs. The showy bathrooms are each uniquely tiled and their washbasins handpainted in different motifs. The fixtures are gold, even the whirlpool jets, and the towel bars are made of brass. Goose down pillows and comforters and colorful florals enhance the bedrooms, which are outfitted with antiques, chintz and lace.

Guests rave about Peggy's spinach quiche with scallions and red peppers, a favorite main dish at breakfast served at two tables for six in the fireplaced dining room. The ebullient innkeepers offer wine and cheese in the afternoon.

(207) 288-3668 or (800) 769-3668. Doubles, $135; turret suite, $175.

The Kingsleigh Inn, 100 Main St., Box 1426, Southwest Harbor 04679.

An unusual pebbledash stucco-stone exterior with a great wraparound porch full of wicker and colorful pillows houses one of the area's more inviting B&Bs.

Ken and Cyd Collins from Newburyport, Mass., who took over in 1996, added their own antiques and artworks to the eight bedrooms, some with harbor views and all with private baths. One has a new balcony with chairs overlooking the water. The Turret Suite on the third floor offers television and a great view from a telescope placed between two cozy wicker chairs; the bedroom comes with a kingsize bed and fireplace. The other rooms are lavishly furnished with queensize beds, Waverly wall coverings and fabrics, plush carpeting, lace curtains, country accents and woven baskets filled with thick towels. Afternoon tea and homemade cookies are served on the porch or in cool weather by the fireplace.

Breakfast by candlelight is taken at tables for two in a dining room with polished wood floors, dark green tablecloths, and pink and green china. The repertoire includes eggs florentine, waffles with different fruits and lemon french toast with blueberry drizzle.

(207) 244-5302. Fax (207) 244-0349. Doubles, $90 to $125; turret suite, $175.

The Black Duck on Corea Harbor, Crowley Island Road, Box 39, Corea 04624.

This century-old fisherman's house, converted into a B&B in 1990, sprawls across a harborfront property with a variety of intriguing public spaces, eclectic decor and a small menagerie of pets that includes a Vietnam potbellied pig named Dolly Bacon. Barry Canner and Robert Travers, a realtor, share the property with guests in four bedrooms and two cottages.

Theirs is a much-lived-in (and loved) house, from the cozy den off the entry with not one but two fireplaces to the enormous living room with fireplace, a carved Indian in one corner, a dramatic screen in another, assorted carved birds and quite a toy collection in a glass case. A front deck offers sitting areas on either side of the entry for viewing the harbor goings-on across the street. And a trail meanders through a portion of the twelve-acre property to a cove in back.

Upstairs are three bedrooms, one in front with a queensize metal sleigh bed topped by a bright floral coverlet, sitting area and large private bath. Two with

Fine kitchenware is on display in **Rowantrees Pottery showroom.**

queen or twin beds share a bath and may be rented as a suite. Our favorite is a cute side room off the main floor with private entrance and deck, good reading lights over the double and twin bed and a private bath. Across the street are two waterfront cottages, one a studio rented by the night.

A dark and historic looking dining room is the setting for healthful, low-fat breakfasts. Barry says his repertoire doesn't repeat for ten days. The meal might be melon drizzled with blueberry-raspberry sauce, carrot-raisin muffins and a main dish like baked orange french toast with orange glaze and walnuts, eggs Black Duck (like benedict but with horseradish sauce) or eggs frittata made with egg beaters.

(207) 963-2689. Doubles, $60 to $80; two-room suite, $125; studio cottage, $90.

Gourmet Treats

Potteries and crafts places abound in the vicinity of Blue Hill and Deer Isle. Foremost is **Rowantrees Pottery,** 9 Union St., Blue Hill, where Sheila Varnum and her associates continue the tradition launched in 1934 by Adelaide Pearson through her friend, Mahatma Gandhi. Named for the mountain ash tree above the green gate in front of the rambling house and barn, Rowantrees is especially known for its jam jar with a flat white lid covered with blueberries, as well as for unique glazes. **Rackliffe Pottery** on Route 172 also makes all kinds of handsome and useful kitchenware.

Local farmers, food producers and artisans gather at the **Blue Hill Farmer's Market** at the Blue Hill Fairgrounds Saturday mornings in July and August to sell everything from fresh produce and goat cheese to handmade gifts and patterned sweaters. It's a fun event for local color and foods.

The **Blue Hill Tea & Tobacco Shop**, in an aromatic modern shed attached to a home on Main Street, carries an abundance of teas, coffees and fine wines as well as rare tobaccos. Partners David Witter and William Petry also have related gift selections and do an extensive mail-order business.

Nervous Nellie's Jams and Jellies, Sunshine Road, Deer Isle, makes the products you see all over Maine the old-fashioned way. Founded by Peter Beerits, the business puts up 30,000 jars each year in the little house with a big kitchen. So many people were stopping in that Peter decided to serve refreshments as well. His **Mountainville Cafe** offers morning coffee and afternoon tea with homemade breads and pastries. Included is a frozen drink called a Batido, a refreshing but caloric mix of cream cheese, freezer jam and crushed ice cubes. Besides all the wonderful jams (we especially like the wild Maine blueberry-ginger conserve and the hot tomato jelly), Peter's quirky sculptures outside make this kitchen and cafe worth a visit. We were intrigued by a sculpture of a lobsterman with huge red wooden claws for arms. Jelly kitchen is open most weekdays; cafe is open Monday-Saturday, noon to 4.

Maine stoneware pottery, cobalt blue songeware plates, hand-painted stoneware from Silesia and unusual candlesticks for the dinner table are among the design items of interest to cooks and hostesses at **Harbor Farm**, a store and showroom in an 1850 schoolhouse along the causeway on Little Deer Isle. It features unique, made-to-order home and kitchen accessories, from tinware and tiles to an apple peeler and a maker of toasted sandwiches with sealed edges.

When a realtor said that what Blue Hill needed was a good deli, Paula Briggs and Stacey Mann obliged. **The Red Bag Deli** on Water Street offers pâtés, sandwiches, salads, changing dinner items and desserts to eat in or to go. We enjoyed the zesty gazpacho, the curried chicken and nutted brown rice salads, one of the hefty sandwiches ($3.50 to $5.50) made on breads from Little Notch Bakery, and the kahlua-brownie cake. Everything leaves in shiny, bright red bags.

Rooster Brother, 18 West Main St., Ellsworth, is an exceptional store for cooks, serious and otherwise. Occupying a large Victorian building, it has a specialty food and wine shop downstairs and a wide variety of cookbooks and assorted kitchen equipment upstairs. More than 60 cheeses and an expanded wine selection known for good values are available. Lately, owners Pamela and George Elias have been concentrating on coffee roasting and an expanding bakery, in which the store produces its own French bread. We came away with four types of dried chile peppers we have trouble finding in the Northeast as well as a cookbook called *Hotter Than Hell.*

Little Notch Bakery, based in The Shops at Hinckley Great Harbor Marina in Southwest Harbor, is a great bakery producing more than 4,500 loaves of bread weekly for avid customers, including some of Down East Maine's finest inns and restaurants. Specialties include Italian breads, focaccia, olive rolls and onion rolls. In 1996, young owners Art and Kate Jacobs opened the year-round **Little Notch Cafe** and retail outlet at 340 Main St. in the center of town. Art said the bittersweet belgian chocolate brownie he urged us to sample tasted like fudge, and it sure did. Had it been lunch time, we'd have gone for the grilled flank steak sandwich with roasted peppers and onions on a French baguette for $5.95.

Little Notch Bakery products and Seal Cove goat cheese are hot numbers at **Sawyer's Market**, the Southwest Harbor grocery with all the right stuff, including a rear deli case of fantastic-looking salads, marinated cooked salmon and other gourmet items prepared exclusively for Sawyer's. You could fashion yourself a delightful picnic here or at the brand new Sawyers gourmet store selling wines, cheeses, pâtés and such just across Main Street.

Jumpin' Java Espresso Cafe Bar, Main Street, is an espresso bar with a bakery.

Ex-Californians Tom and Donna Wogan purvey croissants, cinnamon buns, baguettes, bagels and brownies to go with their cafe au lait and latte, among a host of coffees and beverages at their year-round storefront. There are a few stools and tables at which to partake.

In Northeast Harbor, **A Way of Life Specialties Market** adds prime meats, pastries, breads and wines to the predictable array of natural foods and organic produce, including organic herbs. Besides wines, **Beal's Wine Cellar** displays the most unusual and colorful (and expensive) hand-painted champagne glasses, Asticou Inn preserves and fine caviars.

Special places of interest in Bar Harbor are **Chaudier Cookware Factory Store** at 23 Cottage St., owned and operated by the Prince Edward Island maker of professional stainless-steel kitchen tools, pots and pans that last forever, and the **Pine Island Co.** In a little mall at Cottage and Main, Pine Island claims the largest selection of Maine specialty foods in the state. Owner Bambi Mohr makes the exotic Porcupine Island Sauces, including a dynamite tropical pepper and honey dijon roasting grill sauce, all natural and without preservatives.

The grocery store in Bar Harbor is the **J.H. Butterfield Co.,** a fixture since 1887 at 152 Main St. Catering to the upper crust, it has a fine supply of gourmet foods, chocolates, picnic items and luscious fruits, and there are good sandwiches to go for picnics. Never have we seen so many varieties of Walker shortbreads and biscuits. There's also an extensive selection of beers and wines, including those from the nearby Bartlett Winery.

Worth a stop on the Schoodic Peninsula is the **Chickadee Creek Stillroom** on Route 186 in West Gouldsboro. An array of herbs and everlastings is charmingly displayed in a ramble of rustic little rooms. More than 250 varieties of herbs, spices and seasonings are sold by the ounce. Jeanie and Fred Cook grow some 40 varieties of herbs. They offer something called "Maine Woods, a walk through the pines and firs," for $3 a scoop, along with closet spices and bath herbs. They also sell garlic bread ($3 a loaf) and a six-ounce log of herbed goat's cheese for $5. Jeanie will cut fresh herbs while you wait, $1 a bunch.

Award-Winning Fruit Wines

A winery in far Down East Maine? Yes, the **Bartlett Maine Estate Winery** off Route 1 in Gouldsboro, east of Hancock, is in the forefront in producing premium fruit wines.

Finding conditions unsuitable for grapes, winemakers Robert and Kathe Bartlett substituted local apples, pears, raspberries and blueberries, and pioneered in making fine wines that have won best-of-show awards in the East (including, in 1989, the most medals of any winery in the New England Wine Competition and a total of 53 medals in nine years). They employ grape wine techniques in the production of 16,000 gallons annually, and the wines are aged in French oak.

The Bartletts consider their apple and pear Coastal White perfect for a picnic along the shore, and we're partial to the nouveau blueberry, fit for the finest of gourmet dinners. Prices range from $6.95 to $12.95 for blueberry French oak reserve.

Winery tours, Tuesday-Saturday 10 to 5, Sunday noon to 5, June to mid-October.

Index

Also by Wood Pond Press

Weekending in New England. The best-selling travel guide by Betsy Wittemann and Nancy Woodworth details all you need to know about 24 of New England's most interesting vacation spots: more than 1,000 things to do, sights to see and places to stay, eat and shop year-round. First published in 1980; fully updated and expanded in 1997. 448 pages of facts and fun. $16.95.

Waterside Escapes: Great Getaways by Lake, River and Sea. The expanded book by Betsy Wittemann and Nancy Woodworth relates the best lodging, dining, attractions and activities in 36 great waterside vacation areas in the Northeast, from the Chesapeake Bay to Cape Breton Island, from the Thousand Islands to Martha's Vineyard. Everything you need to know for a day trip, a weekend, or a week near the water is told the way you want to know it. Published in 1987; fully revised in 1996. 474 pages to discover and enjoy. $15.95.

Inn Spots & Special Places in New England. Much more than an inn guide, this book by Nancy and Richard Woodworth tells you the choicest places to go, stay, eat, and enjoy throughout the region. Focusing on 32 special areas, it details the best inns, restaurants, sights to see, and things to do. Published in 1986. Fully updated in 1995. 488 pages of timely ideas. $16.95.

Inn Spots & Special Places/New York and Mid-Atlantic. The second volume in the series, this book by Nancy and Richard Woodworth guides you to the best places to eat and stay in 32 of the Mid-Atlantic's choicest areas, from New York to Virginia. Published in 1992. Fully updated in 1995. 504 pages of great ideas. $16.95.

The Restaurants of New England. This book by Nancy and Richard Woodworth is the most comprehensive guide ever to restaurants throughout New England. The authors detail menu offerings, atmosphere, hours and prices for more than 1,000 restaurants. Ratings designate several hundred for exceptional food, atmosphere, and/ or value. Published in 1990; fully revised and updated in second edition in 1994. 490 pages of savory information. $14.95.

The Fireside Guide to New England Inns and Restaurants. This book by Betsy and Ross Wittemann details romantic places to stay and dine by the warmth of a crackling fire. The off-season companion to Waterside Escapes, it tells which inns to go to for in-room fireplaces and which restaurants to seek out for tables beside the hearth. Published in 1995. 282 pages of warm information. $14.95.

The Originals in Their Fields

These books may be ordered from bookstores or direct from the publisher, pre-paid, plus $2.00 handling for each book. Connecticut residents add sales tax.

Wood Pond Press
365 Ridgewood Road
West Hartford, Conn. 06107
Tel: (860) 521-0389
Fax: (860) 313-0185
E-Mail: woodpond@pop.ntplx.net
Web Site: http://www.ntplx.net/~woodpond/